LEARNING RESOURCES CENTER
MONTGOMERY COUNTY COMMUNITY COLLEGE
BLUE BELL, PENNSYLVANIA

The End of Austria-Hungary

The End of
Austria-Hungary

LEO VALIANI

ALFRED A. KNOPF
New York
1973

Library of Congress Cataloging in Publication Data

Valiani, Leo, 1909–The end of Austria-Hungary.

Translation of La dissoluzione dell'Austria-Ungheria.
Includes bibliographical references.
1. Austria—Politics and government—1867–1918.
2. Nationalism—Austria.   3. Karl I, Emperor of
Austria, 1887–1922.   I. Title.
DB92.V313   1973   943.6'04   72–4840
ISBN 0–394–46641–1

46296

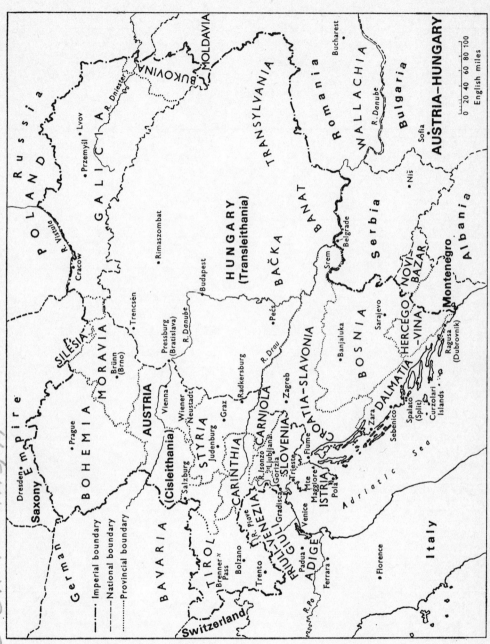

German Empire

Saxony

Dresden

POLAND

Russia

R. Vistula

Cracow

GALICIA

Przemyśl • Lvov

R. Dniester

BUKOVINA

MOLDAVIA

TRANSYLVANIA

Romania

Bucharest

WALLACHIA

R. Danube

Bulgaria

Sofia

AUSTRIA–HUNGARY

0 20 40 60 80 100
English miles

Niš

Belgrade

Serbia

Srem

BANAT

BAČKA

HUNGARY
(Transleithania)

Budapest

R. Danube

Pécs •

Rimaszombat •

SILESIA

MORAVIA

Brünn
(Brno) •

Prague •

BOHEMIA

Trencsén •

Pressburg
(Bratislava)

AUSTRIA

Vienna •

Wiener
Neustadt

Salzburg •

Judenburg

Graz •

STYRIA

CARINTHIA

Radkersburg •

R. Drau

CROATIA-SLAVONIA

Zagreb •

CARNIOLA

Ljubljana •

SLOVENIA

Gorizia

Trieste •

R. Isonzo

FRIULI

VENEZIA

Gradisca

Bavaria

TIROL

Brenner ×
Pass

Bolzano •

Trento •

R. Piave

ADIGE

Padua •

Venice •

Mte
Maggiore

ISTRIA

Pola •

Fiume •

Adriatic Sea

Italy

Florence •

Ferrara •

R. Po

Switzerland

BOSNIA

Banjaluka •

Sarajevo •

HERCEGO-
VINA

DALMATIA

Zara •

Sebenico •

Spalato
(Split) •

Curzolari
Islands

Ragusa
(Dubrovnik) •

NOVI
BAZAR

Montenegro

Albania

—·— Imperial boundary
——— National boundary
········· Provincial boundary

AUSTRIA
(Cisleithania)

To the memory of Gaetano Salvemini

Contents

Key to Abbreviations

A.C.S.	Archivio Centrale dello Stato, Rome
A.S.M.E.	Archivio Storico del Ministero degli Esteri, Rome
A.D.M.A.E.	Archives Diplomatiques du Ministère des Affaires étrangères, Paris
H.H.St.A.	Haus-, Hof- und Staatsarchiv, Vienna
P.A.A.A.	Politisches Archiv des Auswärtigen Amtes, Bonn
P.R.O.	Public Record Office, London

Preface

The Italian edition of this book was published in 1966. For the English edition I have added two appendixes (Appendix I and Appendix III) on new diplomatic documents, particularly German, British and French, which have been published or have been made free for consultation since then. It may be argued that I should have devoted more space to the economic causes of Austria-Hungary's break up. But though these have been thoroughly investigated in the well-known work by Gusztáv Gratz and Richard Schüller (though it is in need of revision now), we do not yet have an exhaustive analysis of the economic trends prevailing in the immediate pre-war years in the various parts of the Habsburg monarchy. Most Austrian and some Hungarian scholars hold that up to 1914 the Austro-Hungarian economy was vigorous and healthy, set to make further progress such as to justify the survival of the empire, while Czecho-slovak, Yugoslav, Romanian and several Hungarian authors take an opposite view. Possibly, a more complete application of modern methods of quantitative economic history is still required in order to reach definite conclusions. Anyhow, a few very gifted Hungarian historians (László Katus, Iván Berend, György Ránki, Péter Hanák) have drawn quite recently some 'provisonal conclusions'. They acknowledge that 'the connection between Austria and Hungary was on both sides much more a stimulating than a retarding factor in economic growth' and that this was true not only for the more developed, but also, although to a lesser extent, for the underdeveloped regions of the Habsburg monarchy.

This means that the main reasons for the disruption of Austria-Hungary were not economic. The problems which required more urgently basic choices arose as a result of demography and democracy.

The Habsburg empire had always been a multinational state. After 1867 it had two ruling nations, the Austro-Germans and the Magyars. They made up only a minority of its population. According to the census of 1910, Austria-Hungary had about 51·4 million inhabitants. Roughly 12 million of them were Germans (by language) and 10·1 million Magyars. With the then unavoidable progress of democratic ideas, and the growth of the national (as well as of political and social) consciousness of the middle classes and of the toiling masses of all nationalities, the supremacy of the Austro-German and Magyar minorities could not have been upheld for long, even without defeat

[xi]

in war. The alternative was between some sort of agreement on federation between the different nations of the Habsburg monarchy and its disruption, with the birth, on its ruins, of independent national states.

The Austro-Hungarian government declared war in 1914 in order to solve, by military victory, at least one of its most difficult problems, the Southern Slav problem. Retrospectively, it is quite clear that even the victory of the Central Powers could not have solved this problem by military means alone. The Southern Slavs were there to stay. The defeat of Serbia would not have decreased the number of Austria-Hungary's Slavonic subjects. The dilemma would still have been a kind of Southern Slav state inside the Habsburg monarchy or an increasingly rebellious frame of mind in its Southern Slav lands, and in Serbia. The same can be said (of course in different degrees) for the Czech provinces and for those other regions of Austria-Hungary which were inhabited, in the majority, by non-German or non-Magyar nationalities. Only the regions with Austro-German or Magyar majorities would have been safe.

The defeat of Austria-Hungary stimulated the various nationalisms. The course of war shows that its victory would have stimulated them too. The defeated Germans and Magyars did not become less nationalistic. They become more exasperated and therefore more intensely nationalistic. But the victorious Romanians, Serbs, Italians and Czechs were also nationalistic. If victorious, the Magyars, for instance, would not have accepted unchanged the continuation of the 1867 settlement, which already before 1914 they considered as not satisfactory for themselves.

It is possible to affirm that a federalistic reorganization of the Habsburg monarchy, at least after 1914, never had much chance against the explosive character of the different, antagonistic nationalisms of its peoples. Even before that its chances were slim. Still, the problem of federalism was there until the last year of the war as I have tried to show in this book. Before the war, it was dependent upon the succession to the throne. During the war it was interwoven with the search for a compromise peace. This is not to say that Francis Ferdinand or Charles I seriously wanted federalism. It just happened that the problem of federalism was interwoven with any important change in Austria-Hungary. Francis Ferdinand disappeared before the test came. Charles I failed because he did not dare to accept, before it was too late, this unavoidable connection. His failure was, of course, the expression of his personal feebleness, but also of the refusal of the ruling nations and classes to face unpleasant realities.

Also it seemed to me that, because of the language barrier, the part played by Hungary in the break up of the Habsburg monarchy was not sufficiently known either in Italy or in most other western countries. In this work I have therefore devoted a great deal of space to developments in Hungary and in Croatia-Slavonia, which belonged to it until 1918.

Finally, using still largely unpublished Italian documentary sources, I have tried to throw light on the policy pursued by Italy towards Austria-Hungary in general and in particular towards those of its nationalities (the Croats and the Slovenes) that are Italy's neighbours on its eastern frontiers.

LEO VALIANI

Milan
February 1971

I

Centrifugal National Movements, 1905–1914

The memoirs of H. Wickham Steed, D. Lloyd George, Poincaré, T. G. Masaryk, E. Beneš, Luigi Albertini, and other works published between the world wars, to which I shall continually refer in the course of this volume, gave the first picture of the struggle that developed during the First World War, both on the allied side and in the Habsburg empire, between those who believed that Austria-Hungary should be preserved and those who believed that it should be broken up. Some of them also contain an apologia for the triumph of the latter in 1918 as a result of the imposition of what, in Italy in particular, came to be known as the nationality principle; the right of the nationalities which under the Austro-Hungarian monarchy had been in a position of inferiority in relation to the dominant position of the Germans and Magyars to dissociate themselves from it and establish themselves as independent states at the cost of the dismemberment of the empire that had held them together.[1]

In the past few years these works have been superseded by numerous publications by authors who, in addition to the documents transferred to the Prague archives after 1918 which were used by Beneš and Opočensky, and the Tsarist archives made public by the Soviet government, have also had access to American documents (partly published in the *Papers relating to the Foreign Relations of the United States*), as well as German, Austrian, Yugoslav, Polish and Hungarian documents. The British and to a lesser extent the French records are now accessible. The present author has also been able to consult a variety of public and private papers, both in Italy and in other countries, as will be indicated when they are referred to in the course of this book.[2]

Before the Imperial and Royal Austro-Hungarian government declared war on Serbia on July 28, 1914, few had thought of a possible break up of the Danubian monarchy.[3] True, its decline and fall had been prophesied by Giuseppe Mazzini and by Lajos Kossuth, who, though in 1848, as leader of the patriotic and constitutional Hungarian movement, he still acknowledged the legitimacy of the ties that bound his country to the House of Habsburg, a year later proclaimed the independence of Hungary and the dethronement of the Austrian dynasty. In exile, though more flexible than Mazzini in his search for allies, Kossuth remained inflexible in his refusal to compromise with the restored Habsburg dynasty even after the failure of all attempts to restore Hungarian independence.

In 1867, however, when, in spite of the exiled Kossuth's admonitions, the *Ausgleich*, or Settlement, between Francis Joseph and the leaders of the Hungarian Diet was arrived at and constitutional liberties were restored, the terms obtained and the monarch's coronation in Budapest roused such a wave of dynastic enthusiasm throughout Hungary as to make impossible any attempt even platonically to revive the proclamation of the dethronement of 1849. Even the party of Kossuth's own supporters did not dare revive the revolutionary programme of 1849, but fell back on demanding the full enactment of the constitutional laws which the Crown had had to sanction in 1848 but which had been amended in accordance with the royal will under the Settlement of 1867. Nineteen years before, the Magyars, somewhat straining the interpretation of those laws had been able to consider themselves tied to Cisleithania, or the western part of the monarchy, only by being subject to the same dynasty and to the obligation to joint defence of the hereditary territories; in 1867 they agreed to sharing with Austria not only a common army and a common foreign policy, but also common finances.[4] Kossuth himself never took part in this retreat from the principles of 1849 to those of 1848, but he agreed to his followers' adopting them as a tactical necessity, besides issuing profuse instructions on ways and means of agitating in the country for a separate army and financial and customs autonomy. Making these their supreme objectives implied acceptance of the personal dynastic union with Austria, even if it was out of necessity rather than conviction (apart from the fact that if they had claimed complete Hungarian independence there would have been no point in demanding autonomy only in defence and in finance and customs matters). But on the basis of this retreat, the so-called Party of Independence and of 1848 did not dispute the right of the House of Austria to St Stephen's Crown until October 1918.[5]

Apart from a handful of little-known agitators with still less following, no republican separatist movement existed in Hungary. The only Hungarian party that could be called revolutionary in a country governed by the nobility (the gentry), was the Social Democratic Party, with its workers' trade-union base. The Hungarian Social Democrats shared the position of the Party of Independence and of 1848 on constitutional questions, but they would have been satisfied

[2]

if the dynasty introduced universal suffrage in Hungary, as had happened in Austria.

The much stronger and better organized Austrian Social Democratic Workers' Party had done their best, by means of large demonstrations and strikes, to secure the passing of the bill granting universal suffrage, which, after the events of 1905 in Hungary and the Russian Revolution of that year, Francis Joseph was the first to accept. The elections of 1907 multiplied the representatives of Austrian Social Democracy in the parliament, the Reichsrat, by six. This secured them eighty-seven seats and transformed them into a party whose loyalty to the state was henceforth indisputable.

At the 1907 elections, the first to take place under universal suffrage, the Austrian government had encouraged voters in Bohemia and Moravia to vote for the Social Democrats (German or Czech, depending on the constituency) against the Czech National Socialists.[6] In the following years the Czech Social Democrats, who, with the advent of universal suffrage, became the strongest party in Bohemia and Moravia in votes (though not in parliamentary seats), broke away from the Austrian Social Democratic parliamentary party in the Reichsrat and set themselves up as a group of their own, forcing Social Democrats of other nationalities, beginning with the German Austrians and the Poles, to follow suit. The split, which reflected the secession of the Czech trade unions from the trade-union federation in Vienna, was certainly an indication of a sharpening of national susceptibilities, but did not change the attitude of the Czech Social Democratic leaders to the state. Like their comrades of other nationalities, they continued in the face of nationalist arguments to maintain the necessity of the preservation of an empire that assured the economic unity of vast complementary territories.

Being afraid, as Democratic Socialists, of war in general and of the menace of Tsarist Russia in particular, they were equally concerned with the likely political consequences of a collapse of Austria-Hungary. One of the most thoughtful leaders of Czech Social Democracy, Bohumir Šmeral, in a great speech held at the last pre-war Congress of his party, held in December 1913, put the question in dramatic and even prophetic terms. Should the Habsburg empire not survive a coming international crisis, the result could be—he warned his comrades—a new thirty years war, of which Bohemia might be the chief victim again. But, in order to survive, Austria-Hungary, in Šmeral's opinion, had to reform its constitution, before it was too late and transform the existing dualistic system, giving too great privileges to the Austro-Germans and the Magyars, in a democratic federation of all its peoples.[7] Like his Austro-Marxist

[3]

comrades in Vienna, Šmeral conceived this federation on the basis not of the historical regions (many of them, beginning with Bohemia, had large ethnically mixed territories), but of self-governing national groups, giving each nationality, on a local level, its full cultural and administrative autonomy, whereas the empire as a whole would continue to form an economic unity.

The economic unity which Austria-Hungary secured was advantageous to the working classes and, in this instance, was specially advantageous to the industrially most advanced territories, those inhabited by the Czechs. According to the 1910 census, 56·5 per cent of the working population of Austria-Hungary was still engaged in agriculture, cattle-breeding or forestry. In the Austrian provinces properly so called the figure was 42·3 per cent, while in Bohemia it was only 38·1 per cent. Industrialization was taking place rather rapidly in the monarchy as a whole, though at an unequal rate in different areas, and the principal beneficiaries were the great industrial centres situated primarily in Bohemia and Moravia.

A republican movement existed only in part of Austria's Italian provinces. It was very weak in the Trentino where loyalty to the dynasty had historical roots. In Trieste the Italian socialists were considered to be no less legalitarian than their Austrian comrades, from whom they diverged only in August 1914 when they rejected solidarity with the Central Powers more out of internationalism than for ethnical reasons. Republicanism in Trieste was confined to the Mazzinians. Republican irredentism, though it differed in ideology and institutional and social aims from nationalist irredentism, aimed merely at the reunification with Italy of the provinces of Trent, Trieste and Pola. The movement refrained from harbouring vaster plans for revolutionizing Danubian Europe such as Mazzini and Kossuth had once indulged in, not because its more radical militants, among whom Garibaldian traditions still survived, wanted none of them, but because the situation put them out of court. Incidentally, *L'Emancipazione*, the weekly newspaper of the Trieste republicans, was forced to cease publication in 1912, not so much as a result of police persecution as because it ran out of funds. Nationalist irredentism was far more substantial, though the circulation of its organ, *L'Independente*, barely exceeded 1,000, in comparison with the 100,000 of *Il Piccolo*, which reflected the views of the Trieste National Liberal Party. These were strongly Italian in feeling, but took account of the fact that the governing class in Italy could not repudiate the Triple Alliance by which Italy was tied to Austria-Hungary.[8] Thus the National Liberal deputies in the Reichsrat had to restrict themselves to fighting for such things as the establishment of an Italian university in Trieste. In practice it was the Slovene nationalists rather than the Austrians with whom the Italian nationalists in Trieste came into conflict.

The followers of what might be called the Bakuninist doctrine— that Austria-Hungary must be destroyed in the interests of the revolution in general as much as of the Slav peoples in particular— were far more violent but hardly much more numerous.[9] The anarchistic type of revolutionary socialism which from 1870 to 1885 had had some support in a number of towns in Austria, Bohemia and Hungary had vanished from the scene a considerable time earlier. But the Belgrade regicide of 1903, the Russian Revolution of 1905, the Young Turk revolt in 1908, the annexation of Bosnia-Hercegovina, the revolutionary ferment in Macedonia and the Balkan wars of 1912–13 were accompanied by a wave of nationalism among the Southern Slavs and revived the memory of the libertarianism that underlay the terrorist struggle against the Tsarist régime, of which there was a recrudescence during those same years. Of the indirect inspirers of the plot leading to the Sarajevo assassination, Gačinović, who, writing in the Belgrade *Pijemont* about the suicide of the young perpetrator of the first political assassination attempt in Bosnia (in 1910) recalled Orsini and the heroes of the Narodnaja Volja, had associated with Russian socialists during his years of exile in Vienna and Lausanne. Of those actually involved in the Sarajevo assassination, Čabrinović, who had been a militant member of Serbian anarchist groups and claimed at his trial that he was a libertarian socialist, and Princip, who described himself as a radical nationalist, were eager readers of Bakunin, Kropotkin and Stepniak.[10] This, far from keeping them away from the bellicose nationalism of the so-called Black Hand, the Serbian organization that supplied their weapons, made them value it the more highly, inasmuch as it put the means for terrorist action into their hands. The fact is that the great mass of students, particularly in Bosnia-Hercegovina, but also in Croatia, Dalmatia and Slovenia, and in Bohemia, where so many Serbo-Croat students went, was growing more radical and that nationalism was gaining an increasing hold on them with the result that the most revolutionary were, or seemed to be, those determined to act with the greatest decisiveness and ruthlessness.

There seems to be no doubt that, unlike the young, naïve and *exalté* Bosnian assassins, the leaders of the Black Hand, believing it to be the duty of Serbia to fight for the independence and unity of all the Southern Slavs, counted not on revolution but on Tsarist Russia, with whose military authorities they maintained close contacts.[11] The same applied to those Czechs and Slovaks who, in the

[5]

post-1848 tradition of the Slovak patriot Ludovit Štur (revived by the pan-Slavist Russian Danilevsky in the period of ideological preparation for the war of 1877, which had roused such great hopes, shortly disappointed, in Russian 'society' no less than among the Slavs of Danubian and Balkan Europe), also based their hopes of national independence on Russian intervention.[12] Sazonov, the Russian Foreign Minister, like Izvolsky, his predecessor and now ambassador in Paris, had some contacts with the so-called neo-Slav movement, which quickly spread when Russia turned to Europe after the liquidation of her war with Japan, and included many who were in favour of separating Austria-Hungary from Germany and for establishing closer relations between it and the Tsarist empire, as well as advocates for the detachment of the Orthodox Slavs (Serbians, Ruthenians) from the Habsburg monarchy. But when Scheiner, the head of the big Sokol gymnastic organization, who was one of the chief Czech delegates to the Slav congress in St Petersburg in May 1914, called on him, Sazonov very frankly advised him not to count on Russia. True, she was the ally of Serbia, but she was not well-informed about Bohemian affairs and had no direct interest in Bohemia, whose religion differed from her own, and above all she had no intention of risking a war for which she was unprepared.[13]

Austria-Hungary made repeated attempts to clip Serbia's wings, as for instance during the customs war that followed its ban, imposed in the short-sighted and selfish interests of Hungarian landowners, on Serbian pig imports, and which forced Serbia to turn elsewhere for export outlets; the Vienna military authorities periodically made plans for sending a 'punitive expedition' against its troublesome neighbour. But in spite of that the Belgrade government had no intention of risking a war that would be far more hazardous than any Balkan war, for the sake of liberating the Slavs of the Habsburg empire. That is shown both by the efforts made by Pašić between 1912 and 1914 to find a *modus vivendi* with the Vienna government and by his hostility to the leaders of the Black Hand, who wanted a policy of bold and unlimited nationalist expansionism, careless of the risks involved, and who accused him of opportunism, corruption and the renunciation of all vaster horizons out of a desire to perpetuate his power. During the war, at a time when the possibility of a separate peace could not be excluded, Pašić caused the leaders of the Black Hand to be tried for plotting against the Serbian Regent (a charge of which they were innocent), and they were shot at Salonica in 1917.[14]

In spite of the violent conflict between Germans and Czechs that paralysed the Bohemian Diet and the Reichsrat itself, and in spite of

[6]

the emergency régime imposed in Croatia in 1912–13, the Slav political parties in the Habsburg monarchy, with very few exceptions, remained aloof from the revolutionary trends that made headway between 1910 and 1914 among the more restless section of working-class and student youth from Prague to Zagreb and Sarajevo.[15] Among the political personalities who, at any rate to a certain extent, favoured these trends, the importance of Supilo is fully recognized by present-day Yugoslav historians. Another who must be included in the number is the deputy V. Klofáč, the future Defence Minister of the Czechoslovak Republic, who was the head of the Czech National Socialist Party, which was founded in 1898 by a minority nationalist group in the working-class movement. In the 1911 general election, thanks to the violence of its anti-German and anti-militarist agitation, this party increased its representation in the Reichsrat from nine seats to seventeen and lost no time in trying to exploit the advantages to be derived from its increased parliamentary strength. At all events, it is clear from Russian and Austrian documents that Klofáč personally engaged in serious plotting with a view to bringing about a disruption of Austria-Hungary in the event of its being involved in a war.[16] At the beginning of 1914 the small Czech Progressive Party also aimed at achieving the complete independence of Bohemia, but it carried little parliamentary weight.

The most authoritative personalities in Bohemia and its most respected representatives in the Reichsrat were Thomas Masaryk and Karel Kramář. The former, in spite of his slender electoral base, was the most formidable democratic opponent of the Imperial governments; the latter was the leader of a strong party which was the most influential of those supporting the governments (just because it did not invariably do so). Masaryk and Kramář also publicly maintained the most important contacts with Serbia and Russia. The learned Professor Masaryk enjoyed high prestige among both Russian and Yugoslav intellectuals. Kramář, who was as able an industrialist as he was a politician—his wife was a wealthy Russian landowner—enjoyed similar prestige in economic circles. Unlike Klofáč and Masaryk, who opposed the annexation of Bosnia-Hercegovina, Kramář accepted it, subject to its being a step towards the federal reorganization of Austria-Hungary. As, with the addition of the Bosnians, Slavs would form the majority of the population, it followed, in his opinion, that the Habsburg empire should detach itself from Germany and reach a *rapprochement* with Russia and Serbia.[17]

In 1913–14 the Austrian threats to make war on Serbia and the arbitrary closing of the Bohemian Diet, on which the Vienna

[7]

government thought it could unload responsibility for the bank-ruptcy of the Bohemian public finances, caused Masaryk and Kramář, who until recently, in spite of many disappointments, had continued firmly to believe in the Habsburg empire as an agent of European civilization and economic progress in the Danubian region, to begin despairing of its ability to adapt itself to the national reawakening of the Slav peoples living in its territories and to the south of them. Nevertheless, as leaders of political parties whose ultimate aims—Bohemia's historical right to self-government in the case of Kramář's 'Young Czechs', democratic ethnical federalism in the case of Masaryk's 'Realist' Popular Party—were not incompatible with the existence of the empire of which Bohemia had formed a part for four centuries, they continued to act constitutionally. This of course did not exclude use of the weapon of parliamentary obstructionism, first resorted to systematically by the German nationalists. The latter had succeeded in preventing Czech from being put on a footing of complete equality with German as the official language of the public administration in Bohemia and Moravia when the last government favourable to the Slavs, that of Count Badeni, had tried to introduce it in 1897. The government had been unable to enforce it for one thing because, when it tried to govern with decree laws, one of which prolonged for a year the lapsed financial agree-ments with Austria, the Hungarian parliament, delighted at the opportunity of obstructing a Slavophile government, rejected it as unconstitutional. After this demonstration of the efficacy of obstruc-tionism it was enthusiastically taken up by Klofáč and his colleagues in the Czech National Socialist Party. Masaryk, however, preferred the democratic mobilization of public opinion, while Kramář aimed at the inclusion of Czech political leaders in the Vienna govern-ment. In any case, they had no thought of subversive action, as they themselves admitted after Austria-Hungary had come to an end. They merely could see no way out of the paralysis that over-came political life when the Stürgkh government, which disliked the parliamentary system and was under strong pressure from Austro-German nationalism, reacted to the insistence of the Czech deputies on the obligatory use of their language 'internally' in the Bohemian administration (it was already in use 'externally', that is to say, in contacts with the public), and to the consequent obstructionism of the German deputies in the Bohemian Diet, by first suspending it, and then, in March 1914, suspending the Reichsrat. On July 4, 1914, Kramář proclaimed Czech loyalty to the Habsburg empire in a public speech, though some months previously, in view of the aggravation of Austro-Serbian tension and at the request of the

Russian journalist Svatkovsky, he had devised a plan for a kingdom of Bohemia under a Tsarist Grand Duke, and a federation of all the Slav peoples, from the Poles to the Serbians and the Bulgarians, under the aegis of Russia in the event of a European war won by the latter. Svatkovsky submitted this plan to Sazonov, the Russian Foreign Minister, in the middle of July. But, as Kramář later explained, only the outbreak of war between Russia and Austria-Hungary made him decide to cross the Rubicon.[18]

It was of course natural for the leaders of the political parties of the Slav and the Romanian nationalities, with few exceptions, to be legalitarian: the state in which they lived was a great military power and the administration, in Austria if not in Hungary, was honest and impartial and economic and social, and on the whole also political and cultural, conditions were relatively tolerable, at all events much better than in Russia or Romania. Indeed, for the bourgeois classes (as well as the old aristocracies, of course) conditions, except in years of cyclical economic crisis, could be described as good. The rural masses who formed the majority of the population, although their lowest layers lived at a level of chronic poverty slightly alleviated by transatlantic emigration and the demand for labour in towns where industrialization was taking place, were, except on the more rebellious Hungarian plain, sincerely attached to the symbols of the Habsburg monarchy. Moreover, it could now be a question of only a few years, if not months, before the octogenarian Francis Joseph was succeeded by Francis Ferdinand, from whom many Slavs and Romanians, who were well represented among his confidants, had some reason to expect great political innovations.

Francis Ferdinand was a prince of absolutist inclinations, but he had certain intellectual gifts and undoubted moral earnestness. One of his projects—though because of his impatient, suspicious, almost hysterical temperament, his commitment to it, and the methods by which he proposed to bring it about, often changed—was to consolidate the structure of the state and the authority and popularity of the Crown, on which he saw clearly that the fate of the dynasty depended, by abolishing, if not the dominance of the German Austrians, which he wished to maintain for military reasons, though he wanted to diminish it in the civil administration, certainly the far more burdensome sway of the Magyars over the Slav and Romanian nationalities which in 1848–49 had saved the dynasty in armed combat with the Hungarian revolution. Baron Margutti, Francis Joseph's aide-de-camp, was told by Francis Ferdinand in 1895 and—with a remarkable consistency in view of the changes that took place in the intervening years—again in 1913, that the introduction of the dual

[9]

system in 1867 had been disastrous and that, when he ascended the throne, he intended to re-establish strong central government: this objective, he believed, could be attained only by the simultaneous granting of far-reaching administrative autonomy to all the nationalities of the monarchy.[19] In a letter of February 1, 1913, to Berchtold, the Foreign Minister, in which he gave his reasons for not wanting war with Serbia, the Archduke said that 'irredentism in our country ... will cease immediately if our Slavs are given a comfortable, fair and good life' instead of being trampled on (as they were being trampled on by the Hungarians). It must have been this which caused Berchtold, in a character sketch of Francis Ferdinand written ten years after his death, to say that, if he had succeeded to the throne, he would have tried to replace the dual system by a supranational federation.[20] Francis Ferdinand was also influenced by his ardent though repressed desire to assure adequate rank for his sons—perhaps, for instance, in the role of viceroy in a kingdom of Hungary reduced to needing the royal goodwill, or in a Croatia separated from the Hungary to which it had been subject only since 1868, or in other states belonging historically to the Austrian Crown which might be restored to autonomy. He wanted this if possible for his sons, already born, who were excluded from the imperial succession because of his morganatic marriage, but in any case he wanted it for those who might be born after his coronation. Hungarian law, to which the concept of morganatic marriage was unknown, would have permitted his consort to be queen in Budapest even if she could not become empress in Vienna; it would have been sufficient for the Hungarian parliament to amend the resolution of 1900 in which it took note of the Archduke's renunciation of his wife's and their children's rights.[21] Moreover, Francis Ferdinand would not have had to pay the Hungarians too high a price; they would have been happy to meet him on this point, since to ensure that his consort, who was a Bohemian countess in her own right, was treated as royalty in Bohemia, he needed only to have an extra coronation ceremony in Prague, as Francis Joseph himself would have had in 1871 if he had not been prevented by the combined opposition of the German Austrian parties and the Hungarian government, which did not want the triple monarchy that would have resulted. Also, since time immemorial, the Croats had been wanting the Emperor to be crowned in Zagreb as King of Croatia.

As long as the aged Emperor was alive he had been bitterly opposed to Francis Ferdinand's morganatic marriage and had insisted on and obtained the complete exclusion of his consort and her children from all the privileges of their rank. Francis Ferdinand had no interest in

[10]

taking anyone into his confidence on the problems of his wife and children. His confidants, who were recruited among politicians who based their actions on their relations with him, nursed however plans either transforming the existing dual system into a system of trialism (in which case Croatia, with the possible addition of Dalmatia and Bosnia-Hercegovina, would again have become an autonomous kingdom, with a constitutional position similar to that of Hungary), or for a federal reorganization of the whole empire, involving a revival of the historical states belonging to the Crown in the Austrian territories and, in the event of irreconcilable conflict with the Magyars, in the Hungarian territories as well; or for dividing the whole empire into ethnically homogeneous units with local autonomy for each nationality.[22] Whichever plan was adopted would be accompanied by a reinforcement of the central executive power, which would retain or reassume responsibility for all the high political and military matters which Francis Ferdinand intended to be reserved for the Crown in any event, not only in Austria, where they had never substantially ceased to be its responsibility, though some encroachments had taken place at its expense, but also in Hungary, where, since 1867, government had become parliamentary in the true sense of the word. This was manifested in the ever-increasing difficulties experienced in inducing the Hungarian parliament to agree to the bigger army and the increased military expenditure that the international situation required. The Magyar nationalist parties tried to make this conditional on the extension of Hungarian emblems in the dual monarchy's common army.

Hence the heir to the throne was well aware that whichever course he chose, his first task, if he was to reinforce the imperial power, must be to diminish the privileged position that the dual system of 1867 had given the Magyar ruling class, which had succeeded in eliminating all interference in its own internal policy, including its policy towards the non-Magyar population of the territories of St Stephen's Crown (slightly less than half of it if Croatia was excluded, but slightly more than half if it was included). At the same time, by declaring the dual system to be sacrosanct Hungary had acquired a right of veto on any change of system in the Austrian territories, in which Germans constituted barely 36 per cent of the population. This meant that the dominant position of the latter (like that of the Magyars in Hungary) could be maintained only by artificial means, which were bound sooner or later to alienate from the dynasty even those sections of the Slav and Romanian populations which had been loyal to it for centuries.

It should be added that the German nationalists in Austria, who were only a minority though a very noisy one, the majority being either loyal Catholics or Social Democrats, looked much more to Berlin than to Vienna; their open pan-Germanism represented yet another threat to the equilibrium on which the fortunes of the Habsburgs depended. Thus, while on the one hand the Germans owed the survival of their dominant position in Austria to Hungarian attachment to the privileges they enjoyed under the dual system, on the other, pan-Germanism forced the Magyars to make insistent demands for economic and military autonomy to secure themselves against the threat of a vaster German hegemony which would have aimed at subjugating them too.

Francis Joseph had agreed to resort to equal and universal suffrage in Austria (and, if the Magyar oligarchy had not succeeded in preventing him legally, would have done the same in Hungary, where events had first suggested to him the idea of making supranational use of the popular vote) because, according to the calculations of his advisers, the result would be to weaken the nationalists and strengthen the parties which, like the clerical parties, had modernized themselves in order to resist the advance of socialism, and were on the whole more interested in social questions than in those of national supremacy, besides being more loyal to the dynasty. The reform of the franchise indeed strengthened the Christian Social, Agrarian and Social Democratic parties (and reconciled these last to the institution of the monarchy) among both the German Austrians and the Slavs. But it did not diminish the clash of nationalities because, as the Trieste socialist Angelo Vivante noted, the nationalist parties that stood for the restlessness of the petty bourgeoisie gained ground at the expense of the old parties that represented the feudal aristocracy or the liberal bourgeoisie. On the other hand, the fact that the German parties as a whole were seen to be in a definite minority in a Chamber elected by universal suffrage, obviously no longer representing any nationality other than their own, necessarily increased the awareness of the Slavs. They saw that, in spite of their superior numbers, they were being cheated of participation in the administrative, financial, customs and commercial decisions which, unlike the military and diplomatic matters which the Crown reserved for itself, had long since been abandoned by the latter in Austria to the Vienna bureaucracy and in Hungary to the parliament. In view of the restricted suffrage in the latter country and the non-secrecy of the ballot, this meant that in practice decisions were monopolized by the dominant Magyar classes. At the meetings of the delegations for the joint affairs of the Vienna and Budapest parliaments, the Hungarian, or Transleithanian, delegation, consisting exclusively of representatives

[12]

of the Magyar oligarchy whose parties shared a common nationalism, generally presented a united front; the Cisleithanian delegation, particularly after the extension of the franchise, consisted of representatives of parties of conflicting nationalities and social classes who were in no position to form a common *bloc* against the Hungarians, and in some instances (e.g. the German nationalists, who felt they enjoyed the protection of the Vienna bureaucracy) had no interest in doing so.[23]

As universal suffrage in Austria alone did not result in assuaging national conflicts, a search for other remedies became necessary. The task of deciding on a course of action that best corresponded with the interests of the dynasty and of imposing it against the resistance that any attempt to solve the problem would necessarily provoke—since it was manifestly impossible to hope to give equal satisfaction to all nationalities and all classes—naturally devolved upon the Heir Apparent. For the problem of universal suffrage and the conflict with the Magyars had exhausted the aged Emperor's last energies, and he no longer had the mental alertness necessary to face the problems of a reorganization of the state.

A number of political personalities were drawn into the Heir Apparent's orbit thanks to his former Hungarian tutor Bishop J. Lányi and, above all, to his aide-de-camp and the head of his military chancery from 1906 to 1911, Major Brosch, a man of great political intelligence who continued to influence him even after he left his office. These personalities came to form part of what was known as the Belvedere 'workshop', named after the Archduke's residence, which was established by Brosch and kept up by his successor Colonel Bardolff. The Austrian Christian Social Party, led by Karl Lueger, the celebrated burgomaster of Vienna, whose hostility to the Magyar governing class, whom he accused of pro-Jewish liberalism, was very welcome to the Archduke, was in a strong position at the Belvedere, followed by representatives of the non-Magyar opposition to the Hungarian hegemony, whether parliamentarians, members of the ecclesiastical hierarchy or spokesmen for public opinion. It was because of this that the Archduke wanted to obtain a bishopric in a Hungarian town inhabited by Romanians for Lányi. Among the political figures thus associated with the Belvedere were the Slovaks M. Hodža and C. Stodola, the Croats J. Frank and S. Zagorac, the Transylvanian Romanians A. Vajda-Voevod, J. Maniu, Miron Cristea (for whom Francis Ferdinand secured a see in spite of Hungarian opposition), and A. Popovici (who lived as a refugee in Vienna after being sentenced to imprisonment in Hungary in 1894 as a result of making a vigorous protest against the treatment of his Transylvanian co-

[13]

nationals), as well as the Slovene Catholics J. Šuštersić and A. Korošeć.[24] Lueger supported the Heir Apparent's move in this direction. Although the Christian Social Party had no sympathy with those Austrian nationalities (namely the Czechs and, above all, the Serbs) who were not loyal sons of the Catholic Church, it was opposed to pan-Germanism and publicly criticized the repression of all the nationalities in Hungary. If we are to believe Vajda-Voevod, the initiative in making contact with the Belvedere came from him and Popovici, for they saw it as offering the best hope of rescuing the Transylvanian Romanians from Magyar oppression. The step seems to have been approved by King Carol of Romania, who was a close friend of Francis Ferdinand's, and also by the Bucharest government, which was still allied to Vienna. Hodža, who had the best political brain among the Slovaks, had been motivated by similar considerations. Both Vajda-Voevod and Hodža no doubt also believed that they were laying the foundations of their own political career— they obviously could not foresee that Francis Ferdinand would never mount the throne. However that may be, the Heir Apparent had deeply-felt reasons for choosing such men to work with. Whatever plans for reorganizing the empire he ultimately put into effect were bound to be bitterly opposed by the Magyar oligarchy, which, for nationalist and class reasons, was the force which had the greatest interest in preventing any reinforcement of the dynasty's powers or the weight of the predominantly peasant subject nationalities.

The Archduke had always detested the Magyar aristocracy, if only because of the struggles for Hungarian independence they had conducted in the past, and was heartily detested by them in return, and he was determined to use against them the weapon of universal suffrage, whose introduction into Austria he had opposed in 1905–6. Secret and universal suffrage in Hungary might result in not much less than half the seats in the Budapest parliament going to the Slav, Romanian and German parties (the last were opposed to enforced Magyarization and had connections with the Heir Apparent through their representatives, of whom the best known was E. Steinacker), and at any rate some Magyar workers would not vote for the dominant oligarchy. In these circumstances the Crown would again become the arbiter of Hungarian politics, which it had ceased to be since 1867; it would at the same time earn the gratitude of the Slavs and Romanians and thereby acquire the strength necessary to give new vitality to the empire, among other things in relation to the Balkan nations, which were either slipping away from its influence or, like Serbia, were already defying it. The Habsburg empire was no less interested than that of the Romanovs in a conservative, antirevolutionary settlement of the dissensions that split central, east and south-east Europe, and Francis Ferdinand proposed to reconcile the Habsburgs with the Romanovs without weakening the alliance that bound Austria-Hungary to Germany.[25]

Those who favoured reform and who wanted the ball to start rolling (i.e. the most responsible Slav and Romanian politicians in Austria-Hungary—those who were also in closest contact with the Belvedere), were less sceptical about the practicability of such projects than we are today. Francis Ferdinand, despite his violent antipathy to Serbia (and also incidentally, to Italy), declared himself in favour of the maintenance of peace, both in 1909 and in 1913. Consequently, the most rational attitude for the Slav and Romanian politicians in his inner circle was to wait and see. Francis Ferdinand's succession to the throne seemed imminent. In a memorandum addressed to him on December 25, 1911, Hodža and Maniu themselves gave him the advice that he should proceed in stages. The revival of the Habsburg empire as a great power capable of holding its own with the other European great powers, presupposed its reorganization they said. Militarily and economically, greater unification was required, but politically it must become a federation to assure itself of the support of its numerous nationalities. The dual system and the Magyar aristocracy in control of Hungary stood in the way of this. The best way of circumventing these obstacles would be to suspend the Hungarian constitution, but for this a *coup d'état* would be required which could succeed only with the support of all the other large nations of the monarchy, the unity of which was the essential condition for immediate and complete victory over the Magyars. If this should not be feasible at the time of the succession to the throne, it would be necessary to postpone until later the more ambitious project to federalize the whole empire. This would begin with the appointment of a Hungarian government devoted to the Crown and including representatives of the non-Magyar nationalities, which would introduce the secret and universal suffrage by which that government, in view of the ethnic composition of the kingdom of Hungary, would be able to perpetuate itself in the service of the reforming monarch.[26]

With the Archduke's assassination and the war that followed, things inevitably took a different course. We have mentioned Klofáč and Supilo, the two political agitators who already aspired to the total independence of their nations. Klofáč was arrested immediately after the declaration of war on a charge of having secret contacts with the Serbian military authorities.[27] On the day after the Austro-Hungarian ultimatum to Serbia, Supilo, who was living in

Fiume (nowadays Rijeka) took the precaution of going to Venice, and so escaped arrest by the military authorities, unlike many politically suspect Serbs in Bosnia-Hercegovina and southern Hungary and many of his Croatian and Dalmatian compatriots, including the Dalmatian deputies to the Reichsrat J. Smodlaka, A. Tresić Pavičić, P. Čingrija and the Serbian deputies to the Zagreb Diet S. Budisavljević, B. Medaković and S. Pribičević. (These last, however, were immediately released due to the intervention of the Hungarian Prime Minister, Count Tisza, who insisted on their parliamentary immunity being respected.)

Masaryk, as he relates in his memoirs, crossed the Rubicon only after he had confirmation of the spontaneous desertion of Czech troops to the Russians or Serbs—such incidents cannot have been numerous, but they were premonitory of more important things to come. Supilo preceded him in working, both in Italy and in the Entente countries, for the independence of the Slav nationalities and the dismemberment of Austria-Hungary.

Frano Supilo, the son of a bricklayer, was expelled from school at Ragusa (Dubrovnik) at the age of fourteen for taking part in an anti-Austrian students' demonstration. In 1902 he went to Turin to call on the historian Guglielmo Ferrero, whose writings he admired, and he became a close friend of Ferrero and his wife, Gina Lombroso, a woman of great culture and intelligence. He was one of the first Croat politicians of the twentieth century to overcome the historical and religious barriers that divided his people from the Serbs and he wanted them to merge in a greater Yugoslavia based on the democratic and anti-clerical model of the Italian Risorgimento.[28]

Count Lujo Voinovich, the former tutor of Prince Alexander of Serbia and the secretary of Nicholas of Montenegro, who was later to become known as the historian of Dalmatia, described Supilo to the distinguished Italian historian Gaetano Salvemini as follows in a letter of April 19, 1916:

> Up to 1905 he belonged to the party of the Right and as such pursued Austrian policies. In that year he became editor of the Croat newspaper *Novi List* at Fiume and was converted to the cause of Serbo-Croat understanding, of which he became a vigorous advocate. He took part in the Declaration of Fiume *against* the Austrian government. After Kossuth's betrayal (the pact with Vienna and the disappointment of Croatian hopes), he left the coalition, which he regarded as too submissive, and conducted anti-Magyar politics on his own account (at the famous Friedjung trial, the notorious Baron Chlumecky accused him of having taken

money from the Austrian government at Ragusa, but was unable to produce any evidence). The war surprised him abroad. His Serbo-Croat patriotism is beyond doubt. I do not share some of his ideas, and his is an *envahissant* personality, with monopolistic tendencies because he is very ambitious, but I believe him to be genuinely devoted to the Serbian cause.[29]

At this point it is worth observing that Voinovich, as is shown by the end of his letter, automatically identified the Yugoslav cause with that of the Serbian, in whose service he was, and that his disagreement with Supilo turned on the fact that the latter demanded from the Serbian majority that guarantees of democracy and of respect for the autonomy of all its people should be incorporated in the future Southern Slav state.[30] But that is a matter to which we shall return.

Supilo's independent political activity in fact began in 1900 and not in 1905, as Voinovich believed, and it indeed coincided with his abandonment of the traditional policy of the Right Party in Croatia, which was anti-Hungarian because of national and economic conflicts and anti-Serb because of religious difference and historical rivalry (it was this that made it more favourably inclined towards Austria). He wrote to Gina Lombroso from Fiume on February 2, 1904:

> The Balkans are in ferment—people feel the inferiority of their position, but are not yet clear about the course to follow. Different points of view are discussed, different trends often clash and thwart the single universal aim of freedom from the foreign yoke. We have begun with the 'lowest'—but purest—levels of the people. No day passes without big meetings taking place throughout Croatia. A place is arranged and people pour in from everywhere. I have attended meetings of 10,000 people who have walked from places more than twenty or twenty-five miles away. . . . You wrote that Guglielmo was going to write some articles for *Novi List*. I have no need to tell you how gladly they will be received, you can imagine it for yourself. If you like, we could print them in Italian, or I should make an accurate translation, and I should use all my diligence to ensure that they emerged impeccably Croatian in both language and meaning. Only yesterday we reported from the Russian newspapers how pleased they are at the *rapprochement* between Italians and Croats.[31]

The *rapprochement* between Italians and Croats at Fiume was not consolidated, however. On February 24, 1905, Supilo informed Gina Lombroso that dissension on municipal, electoral, educational and other matters was once more drawing Italians and Croats apart.[32]

[17]

An opportunity for a reconciliation between Croats and Serbs on the one hand and Croats and Magyars on the other appeared on the horizon, however, when Count Khuen-Héderváry, who was noted for his expertise in the art of corruption—as Ban of Croatia he had for twenty years relied on the support of the Serbian minority against the Croat majority—became Prime Minister of Hungary in June 1903 and had to resign at the end of the year when a case of corruption came to light in which one of his friends, the governor of Fiume, was involved.

At the beginning of 1903, in order not to have to repudiate Khuen, on whose devotion to the dynasty he could rely, Francis Joseph had refused to receive a delegation of Croat deputies from Istria and Dalmatia, i.e. provinces directly dependent on Vienna, who wished to denounce the oppressive police régime to which Croatia was subjected by the Ban. Later in the same year he categorically and finally rejected the demand that Magyar should be the language of command in units of the Austro-Hungarian army recruited in Hungary. The Party of Independence and of 1848, which was in conflict with the Crown on this question, and backed its demand for the military use of Magyar by continual parliamentary obstruction of the military estimates and of votes to raise additional levies, considered it expedient to back the protests against the violations of the freedom of assembly and of the press in Croatia which Khuen's successor in the office of Ban, T. Pejacevič, was most reluctant to renounce.[33] This gesture opened up new horizons to those Croats who were most impatient at the lack of political liberty in their country.

As the preferential treatment of the Serbs in Croatia came to an end with the so-called Khuen era, the decline of which chanced to coincide with the displacement in Belgrade of the pro-Habsburg Obrenović dynasty by the more nationalist House of Karageorgević, which Vienna immediately regarded with suspicion, the way was paved for a reconciliation between the two Yugoslav ethnic groups. Supilo, who, as a good anti-clerical, did not allow himself to be influenced by religious differences between Catholic Croats and Orthodox Serbs, Russians, etc., became one of its most enthusiastic advocates. The interest that all the Slav peoples took in the Russo-Japanese war seemed to bring grist to the same mill. On April 26, 1904, Supilo wrote to Gina Lombroso, again from Fiume:

You will laugh, but if you could see the passion with which news of our brothers is awaited. If you could see how our people, in spite of their poverty, raise money for the Russian wounded. What grief, what tears (I do not exaggerate), at the defeat of

Petropavlosk. It's no good, we are all one, it is blood that speaks. In the face of the great spectacle of war everything takes second place. Absolutism, religion, parties—all these things are nothing but dirty washing to be dealt with at home, but the Slav world is united and harmonious. Agitation in the Balkans has disappeared as if by magic. Serbia, Bulgaria, Macedonia are quiet. There is no desire to disturb Big brother, the Russian . . .

In Supilo's opinion the Catholic Church was ranged against the fraternization of the Slav peoples.

So much so that all the Croatian bishops, together with the high aristocracy, are now founding a big clerical newspaper at Zagreb to combat the new spirit introduced by *Novi List*. And this is perfectly natural. If Austria wishes to advance in the Balkans, it seeks the support of papal Rome by conducting a religious policy (the 'conversion' of Mohammedans and the Orthodox) which the Vatican favours. In turn the Vatican has its most powerful ally in Vienna.[34]

For these reasons Supilo regretted that a section of French and Italian public opinion still regarded Russia with mistrust; his view, reiterated several times in his letters to the Ferrero couple, was that the advance of pan-Germanism should be resisted by a Slav-Latin alliance. This gained him the sympathies of H. Wickham Steed, the correspondent of *The Times* in Austria-Hungary, in circumstances that Steed has described.

In 1915 the anti-clerical Supilo was to learn to his cost that the Tsarist government was far more bound to clericalism than was the Austrian government. Russian clericalism was of course Orthodox, which caused it to mistrust the Croats because they were Catholic, while Austria, though it supported the Catholic Church and sought its backing, did not practise religious discrimination. But the idea of a new solidarity among the Slavs, and of an eventual alliance between them and the Latin nations against the German menace, was indeed written into the nature of things.

It was also true that community of religion was no longer sufficient to persuade the Catholic Croats that the Apostolic Monarchy in Vienna would one day free them from their political and economic subjection to Hungary. It seemed more sensible to rely on the biggest oppositional and apparently democratic force in Hungary itself, namely the Party of Independence and of 1848, in the hope that, once it had succeeded in its aim of gaining complete autonomy for the kingdom of Hungary in the fields (financial, customs and military)

B [19]

where it did not possess it, it would reward its allies by granting Croatia the self-government which Kossuth (who had been the spokesman of Magyar supremacy up to 1849) came to advocate in exile, not without being influenced in the matter by Mazzini. The historical Croat claim for reunification with Dalmatia, from which Croatia had been separated by the transfer of the former to Austrian administration while Croatia had been returned to that of Hungary, was backed by the Magyar independence movement, in whose eyes such a reunification would be a restoration of the rights of St Stephen's Crown, to which both territories had belonged in the Middle Ages. But it was above all the success of the Party of Independence and of 1848 and its allies in the Hungarian general election of January 1905, and the consequent clash with Francis Joseph, that caused Supilo and his friends to believe that Hungary was about to return to the path of 1848, and that this time the Croats must take advantage of it to achieve their own emancipation instead of once more acting as the dynasty's gendarmes.

Francis Joseph declined to entrust the government of Hungary to the 'national coalition' that the 1848 party, which drew its support from the gentry and the petty bourgeoisie, particularly in the Protestant provinces, as well as from university students, had formed with the various patriotic parties of the landed aristocracy. The royal refusal was based on the fact that the coalition seemed still to adhere to the military claims (that the language of command of units raised in Hungary should be Hungarian and that their flag and emblems should also be Hungarian) for which they had stood in opposition. The preceding Liberal government had been loyal to the terms of the union with Austria and had become unpopular for that reason, and it had been corrupted by an excessively long period in office; the Hungarian aristocracy had opportunely dissociated itself from it when it saw that this was essential if it were to maintain its centuries-old patriotic prestige in a country that since the end of the nineteenth century had been agitated by nationalist fervour of a typically Hungarian romantic type, which attached greater importance to symbols than to things, but basically did not differ from the nationalism affecting other European countries, particularly those bordering on Austria-Hungary. The monarch was naturally upset by this aristocratic volte-face; one of his major concerns had always been to avoid anything that might weaken the unity of command of his army, into which the Hungarians wished to introduce the dualist principle, though the proportion of recruits whose mother-tongue was Hungarian did not exceed one-fifth of the total, or one-half of the units, actually raised in Hungary. He therefore appointed an extra-parliamentary government led by a veteran general of Hungarian stock, Géza Fejérváry. This was vigorously opposed by the great majority of Magyars, from the aristocracy to the minor clerical nobility, from intellectuals to peasants. Resisters went so far as refusing to recognize the legality of orders given by the government to the civil service, and physical violence was done to those few officials who tried to carry them out. The situation grew incandescent and seemed to be approaching the point of rupture. As Supilo did not fail to note, fuel was added to the flames by popular revolutionary movements in Russia in the course of the year. At the end of February 1905, he wrote to Gina Ferrero that they stimulated hopes of liberty, though they simultaneously raised other problems that might, in his opinion, break up alliances at birth.[35]

We have already described in Supilo's own words his energetic campaign among the Croatian masses, whom it was easier to approach from Fiume, an enclave that enjoyed the relatively large amount of press freedom and freedom of assembly that prevailed in Hungary, than it would have been from anywhere in Croatia, where such liberties were exceedingly restricted. The decisive political impulse came from his native Dalmatia, which enjoyed the political liberties that existed in Austria. At a meeting on April 26–27, 1905, at Spalato (Split), presided over by Pero Čingrija, the mayor of Ragusa (Dubrovnik), and Ante Trumbić, the mayor of Split, the Dalmatian 'Right' Party, to which Trumbić himself belonged, and the Dalmatian Democratic Party founded by J. Smodlaka, the future deputy for the city, adopted a resolution declaring that the Croats regarded themselves as forming a single nation by blood, language and brotherhood with the Serbs, from whom they would henceforth no longer allow themselves to be divided in Dalmatia or Croatia.[36] This was followed by a meeting at Ragusa on August 24, attended by all the Croatian deputies to the Dalmatian, Croatian and Istrian Diets except those committed to the Ban, and the case put by Trumbić and Supilo, who were in agreement, prevailed over the anti-Serbian and anti-Magyar position of Dr Frank, the leader of the 'pure' Right Party, who walked out.[37]

The same deputies met again at Fiume on October 2–4, 1905, and on the last day passed a resolution drafted by Trumbić addressed to the Hungarians. It declared that they understood the Hungarian struggle for independence, 'since every nation has the right to determine its own way of life and destiny in liberty and independence'. The Croatian patriots offered the Hungarians, to whom they acknowledged that they were linked by history, geography and political circumstances, an agreement of reciprocal solidarity in the struggle

[21]

for liberty and the restoration of the constitutional guarantees of both nations, which implied on the part of the Hungarians the restoration of Croat rights and acknowledgement of the 'autonomous existence and political, cultural, financial and economic progress of the Croat nation'. The Croats also called for the reunification of Dalmatia and Croatia, the introduction of all the modern democratic freedoms, freedom of the press, freedom of assembly and free elections, the extension of the franchise (which in Croatia was restricted to a mere 2 per cent of the population as compared with 6 per cent in Hungary, where the Magyar industrial and agricultural proletariat and the vast, backward peasant masses of the non-Magyar nationalities still had no vote). They also asked for the independence of the judiciary, and for officials to be held liable for all violations of the law.[38]

Pero Čingrija, the chairman of the Fiume meetings, and Supilo, their organizer, immediately communicated the text of the resolution to Ferenc Kossuth, the leader of the Hungarian Party of Independence and of 1848, the son of the great patriot who had died in exile. On October 6, Kossuth promptly replied with a telegram of greeting to the Croats, welcoming the rebirth of Hungarian-Croat collaboration.[39]

The Serbian deputies to the Croatian and Dalmatian diets met at Zara (Zadar) on October 16 and 17 and endorsed the Fiume resolutions, including the demand for the reunification of Dalmatia and Croatia, thus accepting the Croat offer of fraternity, though they emphasized that this must be on a basis of equality. They were of course aware of the conditions in which the Serbian population of southern Hungary lived, and were more mistrustful of the Magyar independence movement than the Croats were. Their resolution consequently added that they expected that 'the parties of the Hungarian coalition for their part would put their own relations with the non-Magyar nationalities in Hungary on a just basis, guaranteeing the latter national and cultural life and progress.'[40] This stipulation was amply justified by the discriminatory treatment meted out by the Hungarian authorities to the languages, schools and representatives of the non-Magyar nationalities under the illusory belief that they would succeed in culturally assimilating, i.e. Magyarizing, them. The 1868 law that granted the nationalities the right to use their own languages in their dealings with the authorities and to have their own schools had been put through by the last genuinely liberal statesmen of the old Hungary, Deák and Eötvös, but because of the chauvinism of their own nationality and in particular that of their own social class, the gentry, they never succeeded in having it applied, and it remained a dead letter.[41]

On November 14, the principal Croat and Serbian parties in Croatia held a meeting at Zara and jointly approved the previous resolutions. Similar meetings of the Croat parties were held at Zagreb. A Serbo-Croat coalition was formed on the lines of the Hungarian national coalition, and it issued its manifesto on December 11, 1905, reiterating the demands of the Fiume resolution and proclaiming that the Serbs and Croats were a single people.[42]

The Croat 'Right' Party supplied the chairman in the person of its leader Grga Tuškan, but the backbone of the coalition was the new Popular Progressive Party established by Dr Lorković, who had been one of the leaders of the student movement at Zagreb at the time of the anti-government demonstrations in 1895–97, with the addition of J. Smodlaka's Democratic Party, organized on the basis of the principles of democratic liberalism, secularism and national unity with the Serbs. These last were represented in the coalition by Svetozar Pribčievič's Serbian Independent Party, the Radical Party, and the Serbian Progressive Party. Those not included in it on the Croat side, apart from the supporters of the government, were Dr Frank's 'pure' Right Party, which continued to look to Vienna, and the Peasant Party, founded a year previously by Stjepan Radić. The small Croat Social Democratic Party joined the coalition, but left it soon.

The democratic and progressive principles and the ideal of Slav cultural unity extending beyond geographical and religious boundaries which animated the most advanced members of the Serbo-Croat coalition were identical with those propounded by Masaryk either from his professorial chair or later in the Reichsrat. Many Southern Slav intellectuals had been his pupils at Prague University. He was a Slovak on his father's side and, because of his personal knowledge of the oppression to which the Slovaks in northern Hungary were subjected, he did not share the confidence placed in the Hungarian national coalition. The same scepticism with regard to the Magyars caused a number of deputies who represented the Istrian and Dalmatian Croats in the Reichsrat to withhold approval of the Fiume resolution passed by the respective diets.[43] The disagreement had no immediate repercussions because the Reichsrat in Vienna had no competence in Croatian matters, which were dealt with by the Zagreb Diet and the parliament in Budapest.

Thanks to the sacrifice of its demands for military autonomy, the Hungarian national coalition did not have to wait long before coming into power in Hungary. General Fejérváry's extra-parliamentary government succeeded in taming the opposition of the Magyar 'historical classes', thanks to the energy of his Minister of the Interior,

[23]

Kristóffy. The government first adjourned parliament, which was unanimously hostile to it, and then, in February 1906, dissolved it, in order not to have to respect the parliamentary immunity of the deputies of the 1848 party who were inciting the country to violence against the 'unlawful' administration; it stopped state financial payments to the Committees (the organs of provincial self-government, heavily over-staffed by members of the least prosperous section of the gentry), which had refused to recognize its authority; and announced its intention of extending the franchise to large numbers of peasants and workers of Magyar, Slav, Romanian and other stock, at the same time introducing secrecy of the ballot. As a Liberal deputy years before, Kristóffy had distinguished himself from his 'gentry' colleagues by the attention he paid to agrarian social problems and those of the non-Magyar nationalities, and now, significantly enough, he announced the electoral reform he had planned for both dynastic reasons and reasons of social progress when he received a delegation of Social Democratic leaders on July 27, 1905. The Hungarian Social Democratic Party, though its strength was based on the mass membership of the trade unions—it now had more than 70,000 paying members, more than half of them in the capital, and was rapidly growing—had no chance under the existing system of securing even a single parliamentary seat. Its leader, E. Garami, a self-taught worker of great political sagacity, whose guiding principles were realism and moderation, had assumed the responsibility of negotiating with the government, which the forty-eightist opposition denounced as unconstitutional.[44] In the middle of September, the Minister of the Interior did nothing to prevent the Social Democrats from organizing a twenty-four-hour general strike in Budapest in furtherance of the demand for universal suffrage. The strike went off without a hitch, and perhaps 100,000 persons took part in the procession that marched past the parliament building. In December 1905, Kristóffy published his electoral reform plan, which proposed to make the ballot secret and to give the vote to all able to read and write, thus nearly trebling the size of the electorate.[45]

The seriousness of the proposed reform was shown by the fact that a few weeks previously Francis Joseph had caused the Vienna government to introduce in the Reichsrat a bill giving the vote to all male citizens who had reached the age of twenty-four. This granted equal and universal suffrage in the Austrian territories, in which a quite high proportion of the population had had the vote since 1897, though until the passing of the Bill in 1906 the inequality in the value of votes (depending on occupational 'category') in relation to the number of seats had hampered development towards a democratic electoral system in Austria too.[46] The Emperor approved Kristóffy's idea, which was shared by Lueger, the leader of the Austrian Christian Social Party, of using the extension of the suffrage in the interests of the dynasty as a means of taming the most dangerous nationalisms, which were, or at the time seemed to be, those which had the backing of local oligarchies. Kristóffy did not, however, succeed in gaining the personal confidence of the monarch, who regarded him as excessively inclined to radical politico-social experimentation. He failed to persuade Francis Joseph to grant him the full powers necessary to impose his electoral reforms by decree, but in December 1905 he did not hesitate to authorize the setting up of a social democratic federation of agricultural workers, which all preceding governments had refused.[47] It recruited more than 100,000 members within a year, thus demonstrating its potential strength. But the Hungarian magnates had no desire for any such demonstration, and in 1907 the federation fell victim to the police repression which the oligarchy ordered after its return to power. The double threat of the extension of the secret ballot to the working masses, including the non-Magyar working masses, and of government tolerance of their political and trade-union organization not only in the towns—but also in the countryside, where the agricultural proletariat, which was truly oppressed and exploited, impatiently awaited the opportunity of securing more humane living conditions for themselves by means of organized strikes—was sufficient to cause the Hungarian national coalition to appreciate the necessity of coming to terms again with the monarch from whom General Fejérváry and his Ministers derived their authority.

In April 1906 Francis Joseph entrusted the government to the Hungarian national coalition having assured himself, in a series of conversations with eager intermediaries, its readiness to compromise. Firstly, he made sure that the opposition aristocrats, Count Apponyi, Count Andrássy and Count Zichy had no intention of following the road to independence on which their predecessors had inadvertently gone astray fifty-eight years before. (Count Apponyi had recently joined the 1848 party but had come from a line that in the past had been outstandingly loyal to the dynasty. Count Andrássy was the son of an 1848-49 revolutionary, the celebrated Austro-Hungarian Foreign Minister at the time of the Congress of Berlin; he had left the Liberal Party to form the so-called Constitutional Party. Count Zichy was leader of the Catholic Popular Party and was now a member of the coalition.) Secondly, he learnt that Ferenc Kossuth had no desire to follow in his father's footsteps. To facilitate matters the Hungarian coalition had announced that it would carry out constitutionally, by parliamentary means, the extension of the franchise that General Fejérváry's government had planned, but would have had to introduce any such extension by extra-parliamentary means of doubtful constitutionality in view of the lack of all support for it among the existing restricted electorate. Francis Joseph, who remembered the formidable resistance with which his absolutism had met in Hungary between 1850 and 1865, was the first to shrink now from acts of such doubtful legality. Universal suffrage had in fact figured in the programme launched by the venerable Lajos Kossuth in exile. As the Party of Independence and of 1848 was numerically far the strongest in the national coalition, its acceptance of the commitment to electoral reform on the scale that it undertook would be no less than that proposed by Kristóffy, disarmed the mistrustfulness of many people.[48]

The task of forming the coalition government was given to Wekerle, a former Liberal Prime Minister who had joined the new Constitutional Party, a man of great experience and ability but an inveterate cynic. Count Andrássy, a very learned doctrinaire who was less incisive as a man of action, went to the Ministry of Internal Affairs. Count Apponyi, the major spokesman of Magyar nationalism, became Minister of Education. The portfolio of Trade and Communication went to Ferenc Kossuth, who was a skilled parliamentarian but was much less democratic than the tradition represented by his name, and was much too ambitious to compromise his position by any reforms that were more than nominal and symbolic. A secret agreement between the sovereign and the leaders of the coalition stipulated that the latter would shelve their military demands and that in 1907 Hungary would renew the financial and customs union by which it had been bound to Austria since 1867—under the Settlement of that year the union was renewable every ten years. For its part, the Party of Independence and of 1848 intended that, when the franchise had been extended, as Francis Joseph had shown he wanted it to be, the subsequently elected parliament should be free, at least in financial and economic matters, which were subject to periodically renewable 'settlements', to raise the question of the modification of the existing situation again. Of the secret renunciations and mental reservations that accompanied this deal, the Hungarian electorate at first knew nothing. At the elections in May 1906 it gave a big majority to the 1848 party.

The commitments that Francis Joseph persuaded the coalition to accept were not, on paper, incompatible with Hungary's historical situation. If the extension of the franchise had been carried out at that time with the consent of the Magyar governing class (instead of in defiance of it, as the Archduke Francis Ferdinand desired), the latter would have been able, at the price of modern concessions, to come to an understanding with the by no means revolutionary bourgeois parties of the non-Magyar nationalities; even in combination the non-Magyars would have remained in a minority in view of the exclusion from the vote under the previous government's reform proposals of illiterates, who were especially numerous among those nationalities. An understanding of this kind, if reached in good time, might have assured historical Hungary of the lasting loyalty at any rate of those nationalities which, like the Slovaks, were not represented outside the borders of Austria-Hungary. The Croats wanted autonomy within the framework of loyalty to St Stephen's Crown, as the Fiume resolution showed. The demand for the introduction of Magyar as the second language of command in the joint army of the dual monarchy was purely a matter of prestige; if it had not been shelved, it would have turned against the Magyars, as the Czech, Polish, Croat and other peoples would have been entitled to demand the same for their languages, and this would have fatally undermined the unity and efficiency of the army, of which Hungary herself, as a beneficiary of the dual system, which enabled her to exercise a certain amount of influence on the monarchy's foreign policy and protected her against irredentist movements originating in Romania and Serbia, might well have need. Instead of worrying about military emblems and conventions (in Hungary proper, incidentally, the flag and language of local units had been Magyar since 1867), the Hungarians would have been better advised to try to increase their influence on the general trend of the monarchy's foreign policy when the latter began to cause concern, as it did in 1908.

The question of Hungary's possible abandonment of her customs union with Austria and of her setting herself up as an autonomous customs area had become more topical with the establishment of modern industry in Budapest, the future growth of which would have been more rapid with tariffs to protect it against the competition of the much more advanced industry of Austria and Bohemia.

Recent calculations by László Katus evaluate the average annual growth-rates of gross domestic material product from 1860/70 to 1913 at 2·4 per cent in Hungary (4·2 per cent in industry alone), compared with 2·3 per cent in Austria (3·9 per cent in industry alone). The corresponding growth-rate in the United Kingdom is evaluated at 2·2 per cent (2·1 per cent in industry alone). Under the customs union with Austria, Hungarian industry did also far better than was claimed by Magyar nationalists. However, industry accounted

[27]

in 1913 for 30 per cent only of the gross domestic material product of Hungary, 56 per cent of it still going to agriculture. In Austria the percentage of agriculture was only 35, that of industry 45 of the gross domestic material product. Of course, Austria-Hungary was still far from being an affluent country. The gross domestic material product per inhabitant amounted to less than 450 crowns in Austria and less than 350 crowns in Hungary. It did not reach half the equivalent figure for the United Kingdom.

Ending the customs union would certainly have damaged Hungarian agricultural exports. The Austrian territories, less fertile and with many more industrial cities, provided a secure and very convenient market for Hungary's big corn surpluses.

Nevertheless, feeling of the forty-eightist type was so strong among the Magyar gentry and petty bourgeoisie that formed the majority of the privileged electorate that, in spite of the latifundia they possessed, most of the aristocrats who engaged professionally in politics either did not dare oppose it or actually embraced it, at any rate nominally.[49] Incidentally, even the Hungarian Social Democratic Party, which under the restricted voting system had no parliamentary prospects and therefore no election problems, had in 1903 come out in favour of customs autonomy, which to the working masses seemed to hold out the hope of a more prosperous future. The Liberal Party, which was associated with financial and commercial interests whose leaders realized the damage that would result from a weakening of the links with the much stronger Vienna capital market and with those agrarian interests which did not allow themselves to be seduced by nationalist phraseology, had defended the economic union with Austria during the thirty-five years of its rule. But in the 1906 elections it disappeared completely.

The first grave mistake made by the Hungarian national coalition was in its relations with Croatia. A consequence of its election victory was that rapid strides were made by the Serbo-Croat coalition, which in 1906 won twenty-eight of the eighty-eight seats in the Croatian Diet; Dr Frank's 'pure' Right Party won twenty-three, and thirty-seven went to the supporters of older parties. In view of the impossibility of forming a majority, another election was held in 1907, which gave the Serbo-Croat coalition forty seats. In February 1908 yet another election gave it fifty-seven seats, an absolute majority.[50] But a few months earlier the good relations between it and the government coalition in Hungary had been shattered.

Ferenc Kossuth, the Minister of Trade and Communications, having had to swallow the bitter pill of agreeing to renew the customs and financial union with Austria for another ten years, chose what

[28]

seemed to him to be easier ground on which to show that he was not a weak man. The Hungarian Social Democrats made capital by attacking the Party of Independence and of 1848 for lack of courage and sincerity in putting off till Doomsday the fulfilment of its promises to extend the suffrage and aid industrial advance by establishing the country's customs autonomy. In 1904 a spontaneous general strike for higher wages by the Hungarian railway workers had been crushed with difficulty by the government of the time, led by Count Tisza, who had had to resort to military measures, and after that Social Democratic trade-unionism had made notable advances among this large category of public service workers. Kossuth decided that the time had come to put a stop to this spread of socialist ideas, which were a direct threat to his own party's popular base, by issuing new regulations governing employment on the state railways. These were drawn up by his Under-Secretary of State, Baron Szterényi, and in practice put railway workers on a par with public officials. This gave them certain small advantages, but deprived them of the weapon of the strike, under penalty of losing their employment.[51] The Hungarian state railway organization owned and managed the Croatian railways, and the new regulations imposed on Croatian railway workers a knowledge of Hungarian, though previously, like other state employees in Croatia, they had had the right to use their own language only. Under the new regulations, those who failed to learn Hungarian within a certain period would be considered as having lost their jobs. This was a piece of linguistic nationalism in the tradition of that proclaimed by Kossuth senior in 1840 or thereabouts, when, however, Croatia had been exempted. In 1907, however, the idea was manifestly absurd. Derisory though the amount of autonomy left to Croatia after its return in 1868 to the kingdom of Hungary was, it was hard to see why railwaymen should be singled out to learn Hungarian when other Croatian officials were not. Meanwhile, Apponyi, the Education Minister, was strengthening state control of Slav and Romanian private religious schools in Hungary with a view to ensuring that Hungarian would be taught in them. The Budapest government endorsed also the new railway regulations as fitting into the general line of their nationalistic policy.

These attempts to impose Magyarization led to violent opposition from the nationalities concerned. The government imposed severe penalties on those guilty of 'agitation' against the Magyar character of the state, and among those sentenced to prison in consequence were several members of parliament, of whom the best known was the Slovak Agrarian deputy Hodža. This repressive policy led to an unexpected tragedy. On October 27, 1907, to prevent a new church

[29]

in the Slovak village of Csernova from being consecrated by the parish priest, A. Hlinka, the future founder of the Slovak Catholic and autonomist Popular Party, on whom a sentence of two years' imprisonment for anti-Magyar agitation was pending, the gendarmerie fired on a crowd of parishioners gathered outside the church to prevent the ceremony from taking place in Hlinka's absence. Fifteen peasants were killed.[52] This crime was denounced to western public opinion by R. W. Seton-Watson, the British publicist and student of the history of the nationalities of central and south-eastern Europe, who was in Hungary at the time, and by the celebrated poet Björnson.

Under Supilo's leadership, the Croatian members of the Budapest parliament (to which the Zagreb Diet had the right to send a delegation when matters concerning Croatia arose) resorted to obstructionism against the bill incorporating the new railway regulations. Francis Joseph certainly had no sympathy for obstructionists in general, but even he thought they were justified in this instance, and the Ban of Croatia resigned in protest. Underlying this language quarrel there was also a clash of economic interests. The Budapest government, fearing Croatian and Bosnian competition in agricultural products on the Austrian market, had always obstructed development of the railway system in Croatia (as well as in Dalmatia and Bosnia, whose sole communications with the western territories of the empire were through Croatia), and in particular they blocked the building of a direct railway line between Vienna and Zagreb, Sarajevo, and Spalato. Emphasizing the outward signs of the Hungarian national character of the Croatian railway system formed part of this restrictionist policy.

In 1868 Croatia had been deprived by the Settlement with Hungary of that year of control over its agricultural, industrial and commercial affairs, responsibility for which was transferred to Budapest, and, in the view of Supilo and his friends, their alliance with the Party of Independence and of 1848 should now have assured them of the restoration of that control. But, far from seeing their hopes realized, the Serbo-Croat coalition, in spite of its absolute majority in the Diet, was now rebuffed by the Hungarian government formed by its former allies, to which the Ban, the chief executive in Croatia, was directly responsible.

Disillusionment with the Magyars might now have caused the majority of the Croats to revert to the pro-Habsburg attitude for which Dr Frank, the leader of the 'pure' Right Party, fought more vigorously than ever in his campaign against the Serbo-Croat coalition, gaining himself some support of the new Ban, Baron

[30]

Rauch, in the process. But an event of international importance that closely concerned all Southern Slavs set them against Vienna.

On October 5, 1908, Francis Joseph, at the proposal of the Foreign Minister, Baron Aehrenthal, signed a decree annexing Bosnia-Hercegovina to Austria-Hungary. The annexation itself was proclaimed forty-eight hours later. Those primarily affected were the Serbs, who formed the greater part of the population of the annexed provinces. Bosnia-Hercegovina had been militarily occupied and regularly administered by Austria-Hungary since 1878, though it remained nominally under the sovereignty of the Sultan. But the Young Turk revolution, with the introduction of constitutionalism into the Ottoman empire, might have led to revolutionary ferment in Bosnia. Muslims might have wanted to be represented in the parliament of Istanbul, while in the event of the introduction of an elected assembly in Bosnia, in all likelihood there would have been a majority for a Serbo-Croat coalition similar to that in the Zagreb Diet. Aehrenthal wished to avoid these problems but, in view of the prospect that the partition of European Turkey would set the Bulgarians against the Serbs, he was even more influenced by a desire to increase Austria-Hungary's prestige as a great power at the expense of the kingdom of Serbia, to which the necessity of recognizing the annexation to the Habsburg empire of almost another million of its co-nationals and co-religionists was certainly a grave humiliation.

Since the beginning of 1907, Aehrenthal and his colleague Baron Musulin had foreseen that the revolutionary ferment in Macedonia would make impossible the maintenance of the *status quo* in the Balkans. They believed that the inevitable decline of Turkish power would encourage the Yugoslav independence movement, and that to prevent its growth, Austria-Hungary must stabilize its position in Bosnia-Hercegovina. Their first intention was to annex it to Hungary, restoring Dalmatia to the latter at the same time, thus uniting the greater part of the Habsburg empire's Yugoslav provinces under Hungarian control. This, they believed, would persuade all the Magyars, including the forty-eightists, of their interest in the solidarity of Austro-Hungarian military power and economic indivisibility.[53] As appears from his still-unpublished diary, Count Burian, the Minister responsible for the joint finances of the empire, who was a good Hungarian though a loyal servant of Francis Joseph, had come to the same conclusion in May 1907 and had submitted it to Francis Joseph and to Aehrenthal.[54] Burian, who knew that he was disliked by Francis Ferdinand—the Austrian clerical newspapers close to the Belvedere periodically attacked the policy favouring Hungarian economic interests which he pursued at the joint Finance Ministry

[31]

(which was responsible for the administration of Bosnia-Hercegovina) —feared that the Archduke would one day use the Bosnian issue as a lever with which to create a third Habsburg kingdom consisting of the Yugoslav provinces, at the expense of the position that Hungary enjoyed under the dual system. His concern was shared by Wekerle, the Hungarian Prime Minister. Burian also hoped that the annexation of Bosnia-Hercegovina to Hungary, in the southern provinces of which there was a sizeable Serbian minority, would enable the Hungarians to govern Bosnia-Hercegovina with the aid of the Serbs, who could if necessary be divided from the Croats by some political manoeuvre, as had been done in the past. However, General Conrad, the Chief of the General Staff, though he favoured the absorption of Bosnia-Hercegovina, and was in fact the first to propose it at the Crown Council of December 1, 1907, wanted it to be annexed to Croatia-Slavonia, a plan that tacitly assumed the subsequent detachment of the latter from Hungary as a nucleus of a tripartite reorganization of the Habsburg empire. Aehrenthal decided to postpone the issue. As time went on, wishing to displease neither Francis Ferdinand, who had favoured his appointment to the Foreign Ministry, nor the Hungarians, whose opposition had been fatal to his predecessor, he decided on a judgement of Solomon, namely to annex Bosnia-Hercegovina to Austria-Hungary as a whole. Burian accepted this idea, which blocked General Conrad's proposal. He urged that the annexation should take place as quickly as possible, and secured Francis Joseph's consent in audiences on April 4 and 8, 1908. Aehrenthal still wished to temporize, however, but the victory of the Young Turks in July 1908, persuaded him that the time for action had come.[55] He interpreted his conversation with Izvolsky at Buchlau on September 16 as virtual Russian acquiescence in the proposed Austro-Hungarian move, since Russia was attracted by the opportunity of raising against Turkey the question of the Straits. At all events, behind Aehrenthal's attitude in the matter lay his knowledge of Russian military unpreparedness after the defeat and revolution of 1905.[56] If the longer-term effect of Aehrenthal's action was to make insuperable the breach between Vienna and Berlin on the one hand and St Petersburg on the other, as well as that between Vienna and Belgrade, its gravest immediate impact on the Habsburg monarchy derived from Bosnia-Hercegovina's being annexed to Austria-Hungary as a whole instead of either to Hungary or to Croatia-Slavonia. Instead of satisfying either the Hungarians and Hungarian Serbs or the Croats, it dissatisfied them all, and both in Croatia and in Bosnia, Serbo-Croat solidarity was reinforced. Russia took the news of the annexation very much amiss, but in March 1909, in response to

[32]

German pressure, she was forced to advise the Belgrade government to submit and recognize the *fait accompli*, failing which Austria-Hungary threatened to invade its small but recalcitrant neighbour. Nevertheless, Serbia did not emerge too badly from the Bosnian crisis, which gained her the sympathy, not only of the Serbs, but also of a great many Croats in the Austro-Hungarian empire. The fact that at the time of the annexation the Serbo-Croat coalition in Zagreb was in acute conflict with Hungary helped to rouse sympathy with Belgrade among the Croats.

In the Hungarian government, both Count Andrássy and Count Apponyi opposed the annexation because they foresaw that it would merely aggravate the problem of Austria-Hungary's undigested Southern Slavs.[57] Francis Joseph therefore summoned Count Andrássy to an audience and asked him not to make difficulties. The Party of Independence and of 1848, which had opposed the occupation of Bosnia-Hercegovina in 1878, could not oppose the annexation now, as one of the first to support the project was F. Kossuth, who believed the territory would be annexed to Hungary, to which it had belonged for some time before the Turkish invasions.[58] Thus Budapest was in agreement with Vienna in taking repressive measures against Southern Slav citizens of the monarchy who might be considered likely to side with Serbia in the event of war with the latter. Between October 1908 and January 1909, the Ban of Croatia, acting on higher instructions, had fifty-eight Croatian Serbs arrested and charged with high treason, among them two brothers of Svetozar Pribičević, a leader of the Serbo-Croat coalition in the Diet. At the trial that began at Zagreb in March 1909 and lasted for five months, thirty-one of the accused were sentenced to terms of from five to twelve years' imprisonment for subversive conspiracy, allegedly in conjunction with pan-Serbian organizations in Belgrade, aimed at the establishment of a state headed by the Karagjorgjević dynasty and including all the territories inhabited by Serbs.[59] As Professor Masaryk, who attended the trial and denounced its illegality in the Reichsrat, was able to show, the charge was not supported by juridically clear evidence and the proceedings created the impression that the court accepted fabricated evidence.[60] The sentences themselves implicitly confirmed the weakness of the prosecution case, as high treason required the death penalty, or at least life imprisonment. In fact, two years later the sentences were quashed on appeal and the prisoners were released, which was equivalent to an admission of the political nature of the prosecution, which had been begun at a time when war with Serbia had seemed likely.

None of the leaders of the Serbo-Croat coalition who were

covered by parliamentary immunity, was among the Zagreb accused, but, having set out on the path of repression, the Austro-Hungarian authorities had an interest in pursuing it to the point of morally decapitating the Yugoslav opposition. On March 25, 1909, when tension with Serbia was at its height and it seemed as if the Belgrade government would not yield and the Austro-Hungarian army was preparing to put itself on a war footing, the *Neue Freie Presse,* the most important Vienna newspaper, published an article by Professor H. Friedjung, Austria's most distinguished historian, accusing the Zagreb coalition, and Supilo in particular, allegedly on the basis of solid documents, of active connivance in a Serbian plot against the security of Austria-Hungary. Other articles in the *Neue Freie Presse* and in the Vienna Christian Social newspaper said that the leaders of the Zagreb coalition had taken Serbian money as a reward for their plotting.[61]

Supilo, personally and jointly with his colleagues Svetozar Pribičević and Lukinić, whose names were mentioned together with his, and the fifty other deputies of the Serbo-Croat coalition collectively sued the newspapers and the writers of the articles, and the case began in Vienna on December 9, 1909. Professor Friedjung unhesitatingly produced the documents he had received from the Austro-Hungarian Foreign Ministry and genuinely believed them to be authentic, though he showed a large amount of naïveté and negligence in the matter: the documents were copies and not originals and were in Serbian, a language he did not understand. Their phoneyness was demonstrated in the course of the trial.[62] Masaryk went to Belgrade to verify the facts and persuaded the Serbian politicians accused of plotting against Austria-Hungary—as well as Miroslav Spalajković, the head of the political department of the Serbian Foreign Ministry, who was stated to have borne the ultimate responsibility for the alleged sending of funds to Supilo and Pribičević—to come to Vienna to give evidence, and he once more played an outstanding part in demolishing the charges and demonstrating the inconsistency and contradictory nature of the alleged documents.[63]

Supilo was the principal target of the prosecution which produced an Austrian publicist and former high government official, Baron Chlumecky, who was close to the Belvedere and well known for his hatred of the Serbs. Chlumecky declared that earlier, when Supilo, like the rest of the Croat Right Party, had still been anti-Serbian, he had given him money. But he was unable to produce any evidence for this statement, and all the witnesses confirmed Supilo's integrity.[64]

As soon as he realized that he had been deceived, Professor Friedjung acknowledged the falsity of the documents on which he

[34]

had relied, with the result that the prosecution was withdrawn. Nearly a year later, a young Belgrade journalist named Vašić, fearing discovery by the Serbian authorities, wrote to Supilo confessing that he had forged them. He said that he had done so at the instigation of the Austro-Hungarian legation in Belgrade and of Count Forgách, the Minister, in particular, and that the legation had not kept its promise to recompense him by finding him a job in Vienna. He seems to have hoped that the Belgrade authorities, to whom he promptly gave himself up, would regard his letter to Supilo as an extenuating circumstance, but he was sentenced to five years' imprisonment.[65]

Interesting light on how the forged documents reached the Vienna Foreign Ministry is provided by the memoirs of Baron Szterényi, the Hungarian Under-Secretary for Trade and Communications.[66] An informer whom the Ministry kept in Belgrade because of the commercial war that Austria-Hungary was waging on Serbia—the man also worked for the Vienna Foreign Ministry—sent him a copy of a report that Spalajković was said to have submitted to his superiors in June 1907 on his contacts with Supilo, Pribičević and other members of the Zagreb Diet. Pašić, the Serbian Prime Minister, was said to have written on the back of the report an authorization to pay a certain sum of money to those men. Szterényi gave the document to F. Kossuth, who passed it on to Wekerle, the Hungarian Prime Minister, who showed it to Francis Joseph and then gave it to Aehrenthal, whose office put it in the hands of Professor Friedjung. This account of what happened, published by Szterényi at a time when he had no axe to grind—seven years after the end of the Habsburg empire and the Hungarian acquisition of national independence— seems to acquit Baron Aehrenthal of the suspicion of having deliberately made use of forged documents. According to Szterényi, Aehrenthal received them not only from Count Forgách, his subordinate, but also from an Hungarian official source independent of his own Ministry. This is now confirmed by F. Kossuth's letter to his brother of April 5, 1908, in which he states that at an audience with Francis Joseph a few days previously, he informed the Emperor that his Ministry had received information about payments to Supilo made by Pašić.[67] It might actually be supposed that the forgers were acting as *agents-provocateurs* at Austro-Hungarian expense.[68] L. Thallóczy, who was responsible for Bosnian affairs in the Austro-Hungarian joint Finance Ministry, was, as he states in his diary, aware that the documents came from agents of the Budapest government and that they were rumoured to be forgeries.

Whatever such theories may be worth, the Vienna trial ended in a defeat for the Austro-Hungarian Foreign Ministry, which was shown to have used documents, the authenticity of which it had checked so cursorily as to rouse the suspicion that it had actually forged them for the sole purpose of crushing the inconvenient political group that had a majority in the Croatian Diet. Conversely, the prestige of the Belgrade government, which had been the object of unfounded calumnies, was increased. Graver still was the fact that a rapidly growing section of student youth in Croatia and Bosnia drew the conclusion that against an enemy as unscrupulous as the Austro-Hungarian administration had shown itself to be, there was no alternative to resorting to violence. The attempts at assassinations carried out by young men in Croatia and Bosnia between 1910 and 1914 created the climate that culminated in the assassination of Francis Ferdinand, to whose 'military clique' responsibility for the accusations and persecutions was popularly (although erroneously) attributed.[69]

However, to the extent that the Austro-Hungarian government desired to divide the other leaders of the Serbo-Croat coalition from Supilo, whom both Vienna and Budapest regarded as their most dangerous enemy, their objective was attained, though with ultimate results very different from those for which they hoped.

The national coalition government in Hungary fell at the end of 1909. It had been in a state of crisis for some time. In spite of their 1906 undertaking to their country and their King, Wekerle, Andrássy and Apponyi opposed the introduction of universal suffrage, which in their opinion would represent the end, not only of the supremacy of the 'historical classes' to which they belonged, but also of the Magyar national character of the Hungarian state. As a counterweight to extension of the franchise, Andrássy's electoral reform plan, published at the end of 1908, therefore granted a plural vote to certain categories of electors possessing property or educational qualifications. The ballot was to be secret only in the towns. The Party of Independence and of 1848 was divided on the issue. One group, whose spokesman was F. Kossuth, was prepared to accept such manipulation of the franchise and, for the sake of remaining in power, was prepared to postpone indefinitely the party's demands for the financial and customs autonomy which it had proclaimed it wished to see exercised by a parliament elected by all of the country's citizens. The spokesman of the second group was Gyula Justh, a man of great honesty and courage and an excellent organizer, to whom the party primarily owed its election successes, though politically he was somewhat naïve and romantic. He wanted the introduction of universal suffrage, and placed even greater emphasis on the attainment of customs autonomy; if the latter were not practicable immediately, he wanted at least a step towards it in the form of the establishment of a Hungarian national bank independent of the Austro-Hungarian central bank in Vienna. This last project would have been difficult to carry out and its effects problematical. Even if the Vienna central bank had granted it a fair share of the joint gold reserves, an independent Hungarian national bank would have had difficulty in maintaining simultaneously the credit expansion which the Hungarians expected from it and the gold convertibility of its notes, behind which it would have been impossible immediately to create the confidence both at home and abroad that the Austro-Hungarian central bank had acquired in the course of a long and not easy process of development. But the idea seemed to kindle the imagination of those Hungarians who believed in a resurrection of the glories of 1848, besides making a more mundane appeal to the hearts of that section of the gentry and small peasant proprietors which constituted a vast class of debtors unable to rid themselves of their burden of debt.

On a more practical level, Kristóffy, the Minister of the Interior in the extra-parliamentary government of 1905, who in the meantime had become a confidant of Francis Ferdinand's, devised a plan with Brosch, Hodža and Vajda-Voevod to bring about a reconciliation between the dynasty and Justh's followers, on the basis of their common interest in the introduction of universal suffrage in Hungary. In spite of Francis Ferdinand's mistrust of Justh, in whose programme he saw a resurrection of the detestable political heritage of the older Kossuth, the obstacles were not erected by him. Kristóffy, Hodža and Vajda-Voevod had in fact assured Brosch that it would be possible and desirable to detach Justh from the small and intransigent (or anti-Habsburg) groups of Serbian radicals with whom the leader of the left-wing of the Independence Party had made contact—to the perplexity of many of his own followers.[70] Kristóffy's idea was that Francis Joseph should appoint a government similar to that of 1905, but this time reinforced by the participation of Justh's party, which in the event of an Independence Party split, would have been able to count on more than 100 deputies, besides the support of Slovaks and Romanian loyalists. This government would introduce an electoral reform bill, and if a majority for it were not forthcoming, would hold another election to produce a House willing to pass the bill. With the methods at the disposal of the executive power—which under the prevailing non-secret ballot was still the final arbiter of election results, at any rate in the non-Magyar provincial constituencies in which liberty of assembly was traditionally very restricted—the government would have no difficulty in bringing about this result with the support of Justh's followers behind them. This idea was laid

[37]

before Francis Joseph, who seemed to accept it, but on condition that Justh renounced the idea of establishing a Hungarian national bank. After months of vacillation and indirect negotiations, Justh, under the pressure of the nationalism of his own followers, who had meanwhile broken with those of F. Kossuth on this issue, ended by refusing to accept the condition.[71] If Francis Joseph had decided to dissolve the Hungarian parliament, he could of course have appointed a government to carry out the reform without previous agreement with Justh's party. But it was exceedingly difficult to find a Prime Minister capable simultaneously of inspiring Francis Joseph's confidence and of facing the violent opposition of the Magyar oligarchy. Kristóffy was out of the running because of his links with the Heir Apparent; the aged monarch had never forgiven his nephew's disobedience in regard to his marriage, and would never appoint one of his confidants Prime Minister. Moreover, Francis Ferdinand himself did not want Kristóffy—of whom he expected to make full use when he succeeded to the Imperial throne—to draw too close to his uncle, and thus be excessively influenced by him.[72] Two candidates were put forward. One was L. Lukács, a former Liberal Finance Minister known for his expertise in economic matters, and the other was Count Khuen-Héderváry. Both declared themselves convinced of the necessity of the extension of the franchise desired by the dynasty. At first, as long as there was hope of an agreement with Justh, the King's man was Lukács, who was supported by Francis Ferdinand at the suggestion of Kristóffy and also of Hodža. But when the negotiations with Justh broke down, Lukács wavered and did not dare undertake to dissolve parliament and hold an election.[73] On the advice of Aehrenthal, who was related to the Magyar aristocracy and wanted to prevent the Hungarian crisis from making difficulties for his foreign policy, in January 1910 Francis Joseph gave the post to Khuen, who undertook to put through the electoral reform.[74] Hodža and Vajda-Voevod warned Brosch that Khuen was perfectly capable of coming to terms with Tisza and Andrássy. Nevertheless, seeing that the royal choice had fallen on Khuen, Hodža persuaded Francis Ferdinand to put pressure on him to ensure that he would extend the franchise and repeal Apponyi's legislation restricting the educational rights of the non-Magyar nationalities.[75]

So far as dissolving parliament and holding an election was concerned, Khuen did not disappoint the hopes placed in him. In other respects he did the exact opposite of what he had undertaken to do. With the cynicism that had characterized him as Ban of Croatia, he reached a secret agreement with Andrássy, Tisza and F. Kossuth with a view to checkmating the parliamentary candidates

[38]

who favoured universal suffrage and preventing both any under-standing with the non-Magyar nationalities and everything else considered pleasing to the heir to the throne.[76] Khuen's political operation attained its objective as a result of the split in the Party of Independence and of 1848, which presented itself to the electorate in the form of two rival organizations, the country's disappointment with the results of four years of government by the national coalition, the financial resources mobilized by the new government to influence voters by propaganda or corruption, and the perplexity roused among nationalist voters by Justh's public contacts with representatives of the Slav and Romanian nationalities. These resulted in nothing specific, but were denounced as anti-Hungarian by the spokesmen of the 'historical classes'. In the old House, the Party of Independence and of 1848 had had 253 seats; in the new, F. Kossuth's party had fifty-five and Justh's fifty-one. Tisza's party of National Work secured an absolute majority. The non-Magyar nationalities, whose candidates were subjected to exceptionally severe harassment by the govern-ment, were left with only eight seats as compared with their former twenty-six.

Count István (Stephen) Tisza's stubbornness and brutality were deplored even by his father, Kálmán Tisza, who had been Liberal Prime Minister for fifteen years after abandoning the 1848 position in 1875 and accepting the 1867 Settlement. He lacked his father's extra-ordinary ability which incidentally had a systematic recourse to petty corruption. The younger Tisza did not like corruption even as an art of government, though he too obeyed the unwritten law of Hungarian political life of the time which reserved all remunerative offices to members of the party in power. Istvǎn Tisza took things to heart and made them move in the direction that he desired, if neces-sary by violence. Like his father, he believed that Magyar nationalism had every interest in defending the existing structure of the dual monarchy, which assured Hungary of a privileged position and gave it the military protection of one of the great powers of Europe. He could not of course foresee that one day the Vienna diplomatists and soldiers would drag Hungary into a war that was senseless from the point of view of the blessed class of Magyar landowners, and that when things came to that point, his opposition would be in vain because it was both late and inconsistent. What he regarded as certain was that universal and secret suffrage would mean the end of the supremacy which the Magyar historical classes had managed to maintain for many centuries, in spite of endless difficulties. That was why he dryly remarked to Kristóffy that his electoral reform plans were a way of 'killing the nation'.[77] If Francis Ferdinand persisted in his

[39]

plans to undermine the privileged position of the Magyars when he ascended the throne, Tisza was determined to fight to the last ditch.

Faced with a man of such violence and strength of character, Khuen carefully refrained from trying to put into practice the extension of the franchise which Francis Joseph had given him a mandate to carry out. The aged sovereign was daily giving up more and more of the detailed control of affairs that had formerly made him omnipresent. Also, in view of international complications, which were now aggravated by the annexation of Bosnia-Hercegovina, Francis Joseph's primary concern was to be able to depend on the Hungarian parliamentary majority to vote him the military supplementary estimates that he needed.

The Khuen–Tisza agreement had immediate consequences in Croatia. Khuen began by practising the policy of the smile. In the past he had favoured the Croatian Serbs against the Croats, but now he declared himself ready to collaborate with the Serbo-Croat coalition if it would agree not to go beyond the limits set by him.[78] His first step was to dismiss the Ban, Baron Rauch, who was greatly disliked by the coalition, and to have a bill passed increasing the number of voters in Croatia from 45,000 to about 200,000.[79] This measure still left the great mass of workers without a vote, and, as the minimum voting age remained twenty-four and in some cases thirty, it left student youth voteless too. Its beneficiary was the Church, which was stronger among the enfranchized peasants than among the landowners, notables, retailers, professional men and white-collar workers. At the elections held at the end of October 1910 the government supporters retained a small majority in the Diet, but a Christian Social alliance formed by Dr Frank with the declared clericals, won several seats from the Serbo-Croat coalition, depriving it of its absolute majority.[80] In their claims to autonomy the members of the Christian Social Party were no less advanced than the coalition, which was now moving towards a policy of caution and gradualism. Supilo, who won a triumphant victory in his constituency but was becoming increasingly isolated politically, considered these developments a victory for the 'clerical-opportunist trend'.[81] Magyar nationalism was still too inflamed, however, for Khuen to dare grant the Croats the concessions necessary to bring about a *détente*. In the Hungarian parliament the forty-eightist opposition again resorted to obstructionism against the increased military estimates, and the government thought it unwise at such a moment to take a step in Croatia, which in Hungary would have been denounced as weakness towards those who did not recognize the essentially Magyar nature of the territories subject to St Stephen's Crown.

[40]

In November 1911, the Ban dissolved the Diet, but the election that followed, in which government intervention was more unbridled than it had ever been, did not bring about any radical change in the situation. The Serbo-Croat coalition lost several more seats, which went to the intransigents of the Right Party, who had first broken away from the 'pure' Right Party led by Dr Frank (who, out of dynastic zeal and hatred of the Serbs, had actually declared himself publicly against the accused in the Zagreb trial of 1908–9), but had then, after Dr Frank's death, briefly reunited with his followers. The Right Party was revived by men loyal to the memory of Starčević, the intransigent leader who had founded and led it from 1868 to 1895, but no longer maintained the Croat particularism that had characterized it in a now obsolete historical situation. Under the leadership of a nephew of Starčević and of Dr Ante Pavelić (not to be confused with the Ustaša leader of the Second World War, who later began his career as a follower of Dr Frank's son), it made an agreement for political co-operation with the Slovenian Catholic Popular Party, thus breaking down the barrier that divided the Croats from the Slovenes, who were concentrated entirely in Austrian territory.[82]

Khuen, having failed to secure a majority in the Diet, once more appointed in the place of the Ban an official, S. Cuvaj, giving him the powers of a royal commissioner, as well as authority to suspend the constitution, which he exercised in March 1912 in order to forbid political meetings and to introduce censorship in Croatia.[83] The students at Zagreb, followed by their fellows throughout Croatia, Dalmatia and Bosnia, declared a strike, went out into the streets and put up barricades. Finally, one of them, a young Croat of Bosnian extraction, fired at Cuvaj's car, fatally injuring one of his colleagues and a guard. The young man was sentenced to death, and the Serbo-Croat coalition appealed to the Hungarian parliament to avoid irreparably exacerbating the situation. A meeting of Southern Slav deputies to the Austrian parliament and the diets of the various Austro-Hungarian territories organized by the Slovenian Popular Party and the Croat Right Party submitted a memorandum to Francis Joseph asking that Croatia be withdrawn from Hungary and united with the Austrian Southern Slav territories.[84] According to the reports of the governors of Trieste and Zara, young Yugoslavs, who proclaimed themselves to be in favour of a most violent struggle on the Adriatic coast in particular, were still divided between Catholic supporters of a tripartite reform of the Habsburg monarchy and anti-clericals (progressives, Social Democrats, anarchists) who favoured a revolutionary union with Serbia.[85]

[41]

Khuen, caught between two fires both in Hungary and in Croatia, and having lost the royal confidence as a result of the promises on military matters which he had made to the Hungarian forty-eightists, resigned in April 1912. He was succeeded by L. Lukács, who had an undeserved reputation as a progressive, as he was to show. To prevent him from carrying out a democratic policy, Tisza had himself elected president of the Budapest Lower House. In that capacity he quickly set about smashing the obstructionism by which the forty-eightists were holding up the passage of the increased military estimates. He suspended the obstructionist deputies and put police in the Chamber to remove them by force.[86] In protest against this step, a deputy fired at Tisza but missed; he then turned the weapon against himself but not fatally. This incident roused a wave of demonstrations of sympathy with him among forty-eightist enthusiasts throughout the country. Much more important was the fact that Justh's party, in protest against Tisza's brutality, allied itself with the Social Democrats for a joint campaign in favour of an extension of the suffrage. This was virtually the birth of the coalition that overthrew Tisza in 1917 and proclaimed the Hungarian Republic in 1918.

The working class, strengthened by the rapid growth of industry in Budapest and increasingly organized in Social Democratic trade unions and the political party based on them, showed clear signs of restlessness and fighting spirit. The Social Democratic trade unions reached a membership of 112,000 workers. After a series of political strikes in favour of electoral reform, on May 23, 1912, the Social Democrats called a general strike throughout the country for universal secret suffrage. Huge processions of workers advancing into the centre of Budapest were met by police and troops who, apparently on Tisza's advice, were given authority to use their arms. (Tisza's election to the presidency of the Chamber had incidentally led to the most violent popular protests.) The workers resisted, formed barricades of overturned trams, took complete charge of outlying quarters of the city, tore up gas lamps, and held out until the following day. The cost of restoring order was six killed and more than 200 wounded. The employers in the metal-working industries declared a lock-out in order to be able to dismiss the agitators, but they had to abandon the idea because the exasperated workers broke down the factory gates.[87]

Lukács's electoral reform plan, made public at the end of 1912, and the Minister of Justice's solemn undertakings did little to improve the situation. The bill increased the number of voters by a little more than a million to about 1,600,000. When it was presented to parliament in March 1913, the Social Democrat Party wanted to reply by proclaiming an unlimited general strike, but was dissuaded by its forty-eightist allies, who were alarmed at the strength of the troops concentrated in the capital by the government in order to suppress the movement, and by Kristóffy, whose advice was to await the accession of Francis Ferdinand, which could not be long delayed.[88] The postponement of the showdown and the enactment by parliament of the disappointing bill had the consequence of embittering and radicalizing both the socialist workers and the non-Magyar nationalities.

True, a forty-eightist deputy succeeded in enforcing Lukács's resignation by a specific accusation of corruption. But the task of forming a new government in June 1913 went to Tisza. The Balkan wars brought Austria-Hungary within a hair's breadth of deciding to invade Serbia. Invasion was advocated by Conrad, the Chief of the General Staff, but was opposed by Francis Ferdinand who wished for no adventures until he had tried to re-establish friendship with Russia. Francis Joseph decided in favour of peace. Meanwhile, he had become firmly convinced that in internal affairs he must rely on men with iron fists, such as Tisza, who promised to spare him trouble.[89] Count Stürgkh, the Austrian Prime Minister, was a friend and admirer of Tisza whose methods of violence against the parliamentary opposition he would have adopted if he could. In fact he checkmated it by governing without the Reichsrat.

In view of the outcome of the Balkan wars, which ended in July 1913 with the triumph of Serbia and Romania, and the disturbing jubilation with which the Slavs in the southern territories of Austria-Hungary greeted the news of Serbian victories (which caused the Austrian authorities to dissolve the councils of Sebenico (Šibenik), Spalato (Split) and other places, which had openly associated themselves with pro-Serbian demonstrations), Tisza, who was not lacking in political acumen, saw the necessity of reaching a *modus vivendi* both with the Serbo-Croat coalition and with the political and ecclesiastical representatives of the Romanians in Transylvania. Such an agreement was warmly desired by Francis Joseph himself and by the new Foreign Minister, Count Berchtold. Tisza's negotiations with the Romanians failed however. He came from an area very near the Romanian ethnic zone, and he refused to make concessions that reflected the reality of the situation in Transylvania, where the Romanians formed a majority of the population. He was willing to give financial aid to a larger number of Romanian elementary schools, to subsidize various economic activities of interest to the Romanians, to admit a certain number of Romanians to public offices, and to give an understanding that the Hungarian authorities would not (as they were able to do with the non-secret vote and the

[43]

control they exercised over the voters' list) prevent the elections of several more Romanian deputies. But all such concessions must remain within limits that did not infringe on Magyar supremacy. For their part, the Romanians wanted their language put on an equal footing with Hungarian in the local administration, and insisted that it should be made obligatory for all officials and magistrates throughout Transylvania to be able to speak Romanian. They demanded full liberty and equality of treatment in educational institutions on all levels, a substantial extension of the franchise both in local and general elections, and secrecy of the ballot. Tisza rejected these demands, which he described as 'indigestible to a Hungarian stomach'.[90]

Francis Ferdinand, who was on terms of friendship with the Emperor of Germany, complained to him that Tisza's rejection of the Transylvanian Romanians' justifiable demands risked alienating Romania, whose King was a Hohenzollern, from the Central Powers, and William II informed the Hungarian Prime Minister (who had incidentally made an excellent personal impression on him) that he considered greater concessions necessary.[91] But the fact that the Transylvanian Romanian politicians enjoyed the Archduke's favour had an exacerbating effect on Tisza, who described the advocates of federalism as dangerous lunatics.

He succeeded, however, in coming to an agreement with the Serbo-Croat coalition, and he did so the more easily as the latter did not enjoy the sympathies of the Heir Apparent, who had confidence only in those Croats whose Catholic and dynastic feelings kept them aloof from the Serbs. After the annexation of Bosnia-Hercegovina and the demonstrations of Yugoslav feeling that it provoked, the Archduke, as he came to be known in Hungary, was led by his fear of the pan-Serbian movement to drop all previous plans to reorganize the monarchy on the basis of trialism. He was supposed to favour now the idea of a reorganization of the whole of Austria-Hungary on the principle of ethnic autonomy in every province, with simultaneous reinforcement of the dynasty's central powers. Rightly or wrongly, the Archduke's ideas on the subject were considered as not very far from those suggested in a book by the Romanian Popovici in 1906 which, after it had been read at the Belvedere, led to its author being included in the circle of Francis Ferdinand's intimates. This seems to have persuaded Tisza to take the opportunity of administering a check to his formidable opponent by making appropriate concessions to the Serbo-Croat coalition, which had plainly shown willingness to come to terms with the Hungarians in 1905 and had again done so in 1910.[92]

[44]

As a matter of fact Brosch's 1911 'programme for the new reign', recommended that trialism should be used only as a means of putting pressure on Hungary and not carried out failing a simultaneous invasion of Serbia (which Brosch did not consider practicable in the immediate future), it being no longer possible to trust the Croats, who were too inclined to fraternize with the Serbs. The Zagreb coalition, unlike a section of the Right Party, looked, not to Vienna, but to Budapest, in part because the Hungarians had given up trying to divide the Serbs from the Croats. For the rest, Brosch's programme contained the same ideas as the almost simultaneously drafted memorandum by Hodža and Maniu on the advisability, with regard to the reorganization of the empire as a whole, of giving precedence to the introduction of universal suffrage in Hungary, relying on an alliance between the Crown and the non-Magyar nationalities. In Brosch's view, there need be no fear of a Hungarian insurrection of the 1848 type, because, while half Europe had then been shaken by revolution which had weakened the monarchies that remained in the saddle, this time the dynasty would take the initiative, would be stronger from the outset, and would be able to take advantage of its success to bolster the unity of its army and increase its strength.[93] In fact, in 1913, before and after the second Balkan war, Francis Ferdinand, as appears from his letters to Berchtold, the Foreign Minister, was primarily concerned with preventing Austria-Hungary from being involved in a European war. Unlike Conrad, he did not believe that a war with Serbia could be localized. He too believed in the existence of a Yugoslav threat, but proposed to neutralize it by a consolidation of the Austro-Hungarian alliance with Romania, which had been compromised by the imprudent sympathy with Bulgaria that had been demonstrated by the Austrians, and still more by the Hungarians.[94]

At the beginning of 1914, the Archduke was on the point of deciding to limit the reorganization of the empire to a mere revival of the historical states of the Crown in Cisleithania and perhaps also in Croatia, believing he would be able to resist Czech nationalism by a policy of firmness and get his way in relation to Hungary merely by postponing his coronation in Budapest until the introduction there of universal secret suffrage.[95] This would have eliminated the threat to the Hungarians of a federal division of their state on ethnic lines, but it would have lost them their supremacy in Croatia and Transylvania. Thus the understanding with Croatia was extremely important to the Hungarians.[96]

Before Tisza took up the matter, the idea of making concessions to the Croats and the Serbs as a whole (not only to those in Croatia) had been advocated by J. Baernreither, a former Austrian Minister of

Commerce and one of the most respected personalities in the Upper Chamber, who for many years had been studying the problems arising from the Southern Slav revival and advocated a policy of understanding in relation to Belgrade. At the end of 1912, Masaryk informed him that Count Berchtold, the new Austro-Hungarian Foreign Minister, had rejected an offer that Pašić, the Serbian Prime Minister, had asked him to transmit. Pašić had wished to inform Berchtold through political channels more open than the usual diplomatic channels that, if Austria-Hungary granted Serbia a port on the Adriatic even in Albania, perhaps, with a corridor to it of which it could make free use, and a commercial agreement to assist Serbian exports, he would be willing to come to Vienna for the purpose of re-establishing good Austro-Serbian relations.[97] This was not the first proposal of the kind. Serbia had made a similar proposal, also through Baernreither, at the end of 1909, and in the three years that had since elapsed, Serbia had grown stronger, so that it would have been only reasonable to negotiate with her. But Berchtold rejected the offer, and 1913 opened with a revival of the latent conflict between Austria-Hungary and Serbia. The dispute over Albania brought the two parties to the brink of war.

Baernreither persisted in advocating a more far-sighted Austro-Hungarian commercial policy in relation to the Balkan states in general and Serbia in particular, and regarded it as exceedingly important to put an end at least to the Hungarian disregard of the economic needs of Croatia, Dalmatia and Bosnia, and therefore to develop the railways in these territories. In February 1913, he discussed the matter with Wekerle and Szterényi, the Hungarian politicians best qualified on economic questions. Wekerle said that he was willing to make small concessions to Serbia, provided they did not increase Serbian competition with Hungary in agricultural exports, and also to the Southern Slav and Romanian nationalities subject to St Stephen's Crown.[98]

When this came to the knowledge of Bogdan Medaković, the chairman of the Serbo-Croat coalition, who was a Serb but a very flexible one, he went to Budapest in May 1913 to state the demands of the political majority in Croatia. They amounted, broadly speaking, to an annulment of the rule requiring railway workers to have a knowledge of Hungarian, a more generous economic and financial policy, the dropping of a policy of persecuting those who had resisted government absolutism, and the granting of widespread opportunities of public employment to supporters of the Serbo-Croat coalition.[99] In return, the coalition offered to shelve its demand for the autonomy of Croatia whereas, eight years before, Supilo, now in open conflict

[46]

with his Zagreb colleagues, had formed the coalition for the specific purpose of securing that objective on the basis of Serbo-Croat reconciliation.

During the summer, Count Tisza, now Prime Minister, informed the coalition that he was willing in principle to meet Medaković's demands, beginning with the abolition of the language rule on the railways. To win the Serbo-Croats over even more completely, he dangled before them the prospect of a reunification of Dalmatia with Croatia; this, as we have seen was an Hungarian interest, and was therefore capable of being exploited as a joint Hungarian-Croatian claim in relation to Vienna. Cuvaj was dismissed, and was succeeded by a new Ban, Baron I. Skerlecz, who was *persona grata* to the coalition, and an agreement duly followed.[100] Constitutional guarantees and liberties were restored throughout Croatia. In December 1913, free elections to the Diet were held and were won by the Serbo-Croat coalition, which obtained an absolute majority with forty-seven seats.[101] Thus it became the government party, as it remained during the war which broke out a few months later. Tisza, who did not want the war, but hoped frantically for victory when once it had begun, believed that by his agreement with the coalition he had divided not only the Croats but also the Croatian Serbs from Serbia. His critics were to point out that he handed over Croatia to a force that, when the real crux came, ultimately backed if not Serbia, an independent Yugoslavia.[102]

II

Negotiations with Italy, 1914–1915

The assassination of Francis Ferdinand marked the end of plans to reform the Habsburg empire. The Austro-Hungarian government now believed that a victorious war was essential for the survival of the monarchy. On July 2, 1914, Count Berchtold, the Foreign Minister, said to Francis Joseph that Austria-Hungary had no alternative but to act resolutely against Serbia if she wished to maintain her status as a great power.[1] Tisza, the Hungarian Prime Minister, saw the international situation more realistically than his Austrian colleagues. Unlike them, he was convinced that Russia would intervene in spite of German solidarity with Austria-Hungary, and was opposed to war at that moment. But he fatally weakened his case by admitting that he would be in favour of war in a situation in which Austria-Hungary were assured at least of Bulgarian participation in an attack on Serbia.[2] Also, he was notoriously more opposed than anyone else to the only real alternative to war, i.e. satisfying the national demands of Austria-Hungary's Southern Slavs within the framework of a reorganized Habsburg monarchy. Thus it came about that during the very fortnight in which developments began to show that his anxieties were justified, and that Germany and Austria-Hungary, alone, would have to fight Russia, France, Serbia, and perhaps also Britain, Tisza changed his mind and accepted the case for a preventive war.[3]

The British entry into the war greatly reduced the chances of a German victory and excluded any possibility of Italy's joining in on the side of her fellow-members of the Triple Alliance. Indeed, with the supplies that the British Navy would be able to assure her, she might well think of turning against Austria-Hungary. Thus it was plain that Austria-Hungary could avoid defeat only if Italy maintained indefinitely the neutrality that she proclaimed on August 2, 1914. At a meeting of the Joint Council of Austro-Hungarian Ministers on August 8, Berchtold announced that Rome was asking for compensation in view of the prospect of an Austro-Hungarian advance into the Balkans, and that Berlin advised negotiations on the matter, and General Conrad, the Chief of the General Staff, said that he would not have enough troops for a third, i.e. Italian front.[4] Conrad, who before Sarajevo, had been in favour of a preventive war against Italy, but then had failed too long to draw the conclusion that the military situation warranted, namely that adequate concessions must be made to prevent being attacked by her, always insisted subsequently that Italian intervention would get Austria-Hungary into a situation of hopeless military inferiority.

Why Austria-Hungary, which staked everything on war with Serbia even at the cost of having to fight Russia as well, did not consider winning the war to be the overriding consideration and— when it realized that it could not win if it had to fight Italy too— did not do everything humanly possible to secure the continuation of Italian neutrality while there was still time, is a question worthy of further study. Hugo Hantsch's biography of Berchtold is reticent on the matter, though the Austro-Hungarian Minister was forced to resign in January 1915, because he at last realized that it was essential to make Italy the concessions that might still prevent her intervention.[5]

The question requires re-examination in the light both of already published diplomatic documents and of the Austrian, Hungarian and Italian archives,[6] the latter including Sonnino's personal papers, which we have been able to consult.

At the Joint Council of Ministers on July 7, Berchtold, after reporting that William II and the Reich Chancellor had assured him of 'Germany's most determined support' in the event of war, added that 'now we should also have to reckon with Italy and Romania' in that matter. In agreement with the Berlin Cabinet, he thought that it would be better to act and await possible requests for compensation.[7]

The wait was shorter than he expected. On July 14 the Marquis di San Giuliano, the Italian Foreign Minister, laid down the lines of Italian policy as follows for the benefit of Bollati, his ambassador in Berlin, and the Duke d'Avarna, his ambassador in Vienna, at the same time communicating part of them to the German ambassador. 'The whole of our policy,' he said, 'must be aimed at preventing . . . any territorial aggrandizement of Austria without a corresponding territorial compensation in our favour.'[8] At the time, as appears from the whole context of the message, he was not yet sure that the imminent Austro-Serbian war would develop into a European war, and therefore agreed that for the time being Italy should remain in the Triple Alliance, though this was not to exclude the possibility of her leaving it 'within a few years, to join another grouping or to remain neutral'.[9] It was therefore his opinion that, in the interests of the 'solidity and efficiency of the Triple Alliance', Germany should appreciate the Italian point of view in relation to the compensation

[49]

to which Italy would be entitled in the event of an Austro-Hungarian advance.[10] On July 18, now convinced that Russia would enter the field in defence of Serbia (on the previous day he had instructed the Italian ambassador in St Petersburg to suggest to the Tsarist government that it should make its intentions in the matter very plain to Vienna, in the hope of persuading the latter to adopt more moderate counsels), San Giuliano instructed Bollati as a matter of urgency to make the following point plain in Berlin. If Austria-Hungary invaded Serbia, in accordance with Article VII of the Triple Alliance treaty, Italy was entitled to compensation for any occupation of territory, whether temporary or permanent, that Austria-Hungary might carry out in the Balkan regions.[11]

Things were still at the stage of discussion between allies, even though there was a sharp conflict of interest between two of them on which the third (Germany) should have arbitrated. On July 22, the Russian ambassador reminded San Giuliano that, as it wished to prevent Austrian domination of the Balkans, 'Italy has an interest in not allowing Serbia to be crushed'. The Italian Foreign Minister replied that 'that is true, but within certain limits we can help Serbia by diplomatic means, but we shall certainly not go to war with Austria to save her'.[12] The primary concern of the Italian government, which desired to play the part of a great power no less than did the Austro-Hungarian, was in fact to secure Italian domination of Albania and to prevent the Austrians from dominating Montenegro and the Balkans in general.

On July 24, the day after the presentation of the ultimatum to Belgrade, Italian diplomatic aid to Serbian independence took the form of the following telegram sent by San Giuliano to his ambassadors in Berlin and Vienna:

I request your Excellency immediately to inform the Minister of Foreign Affairs that if Austria-Hungary proceeds to territorial occupations, even temporary ones, without our specific consent, it will be acting in violation of Article VII of the Treaty of Alliance, and that we therefore reserve our position in every respect. Furthermore, I believe it advisable to point out that a step such as that taken by Austria-Hungary, which may lead to dangerous complications should not, in my opinion, have been taken without the previous agreement of the allies. . . . It is our desire to conduct policy in agreement with our allies, but in Balkan questions . . . this will not be possible if we are not assured of agreement on the interpretation of Article VII, in the absence of which our policy will have to be directed to the aim of preventing Austrian territorial aggrandizement and we should necessarily therefore have to proceed in agreement with those powers that share this interest. . . .[13]

The Italian government was officially informed of the ultimatum only after its delivery. The war in prospect could not be described as defensive, as Austria-Hungary declared it without being forced to do so by an act of aggression against her, and, according to the terms of the treaty, the alliance was a defensive alliance. Italy was therefore under no obligation to join in on her allies' side. On July 15, the day after Austria-Hungary decided to resort to arms, Berchtold sent a telegram to Mérey, his ambassador in Rome, instructing him to inform San Giuliano of the ultimatum on the day before it was delivered to the Serbian government, but on July 20 he changed his mind and instructed Mérey to do so on the day after.[14] Obviously he did not want to allow the Italian government even a single day in which to express its opposition to the step. Mérey, who was considered to be more anti-Italian than was appropriate in an ambassador accredited to Rome, thought it would have been better to stick to the original proposal and give Italy at least a day's notice. There is no doubt that in failing to give its Italian ally advance notice of the ultimatum, the Austro-Hungarian government failed to carry out an obligation implicit in the Treaty of Alliance. Mérey nevertheless hoped that a successful invasion of Serbia (a project which he now favoured, though he had previously opposed it) would re-establish Austro-Hungarian prestige in Italy.[15] Without excluding the possibility that in the event of a European war, the Italian government might consider it advisable to march with Germany, it seemed plain to him that for the time being, faced with war between Austria and Serbia, Italy would take advantage of the fact that she had been neither consulted nor informed to remain on the side-lines, ready to demand compensation for every Austro-Hungarian occupation of Serbian territory. He feared that Berlin would support Rome in the matter, but nevertheless suggested that Vienna should refuse all concessions. He reported:

In my opinion, no serious danger can result from this. The bad state of her army and her finances, the frequent disorders at home, the weakness of the present government, and the difficulties of the Italian position in Libya, the Dodecanese, and Asia Minor do not, in my opinion, permit the country any major action. . . . Italy will not abandon the Triple Alliance, if only because three quarters of the population would not agree to this. The worst that could happen would be an Italian operation in southern Albania.[16]

C   [51]

Mérey obviously wrote this in ignorance of the terms of San Giuliano's directives of July 24. Had he known them he would have realized that the Italian Foreign Minister had stated his demand for compensation under Article VII of the Triple Alliance treaty in such a way that, if it were rejected, Italy would already be virtually on the side of Austria-Hungary's enemies. Another who failed to realize this was former Italian Prime Minister Giolitti, a firm supporter of Italian neutrality, who (also in ignorance of San Giuliano's directives) declared himself during these days to be in full agreement with the attitude of the Italian government, and subsequently with its interpretation of Article VII, without suspecting that that interpretation contained in embryo the possibility of war with Austria-Hungary.[17]

San Giuliano in fact felt that he would be justified on principle in siding with the powers hostile to Austria-Hungary if she failed to grant Italy satisfactory concessions under Article VII.

It would certainly have been more honest if he had openly informed Austria-Hungary that he would denounce the Triple Alliance in the event of insuperable disagreement. Also (if it had been done before July 28) that would have been an effective means of putting pressure on Austria-Hungary to dissuade her from declaring war. But San Giuliano considered such frankness too risky for Italy, and instructed his ambassador in Vienna to submit the considerations contained in his July 24 directive in adulterated form.

Berchtold, however, could not ignore the gravity of the warning that reached him a few days later from the King of Romania, who had tried in vain in the Crown Council to persuade his government to march with Austria-Hungary in accordance with the alliance between Vienna and Bucharest. On August 6, Czernin, the Austro-Hungarian Minister to Romania, telegraphed as follows to Berchtold from the Romanian Royal residence at Sinaja:

> King informs me he does not consider it impossible Italy might similarly attack us. Italian public opinion said to be enormously against us. Local Italian minister here said to have contributed greatly to Crown Council decision, inasmuch as shortly before meeting he reported to all its members Italy did not accept *casus foederis*. Italian role and influence seems to have been decisive for negative attitude of Crown Council. Italian Minister informed the King in greatest secrecy in Italy everything would change at once in our favour and Italy might actively co-operate if we ceded Trent.[18]

Berchtold mentioned Italian aspirations to the Trentino at a meeting of the Joint Council of Ministers on August 8, but concluded correctly that even if this demand were met, Italy would merely remain benevolently neutral without making war on France and Britain. Tisza, who desired above all to avoid a precedent for similar Romanian aspirations to Transylvanian (i.e. Hungarian) territory, said that, if Italy obtained something from Austria-Hungary today, she would certainly ask for more tomorrow.[19] He did not, however, consider the possibility that, if Austria-Hungary satisfied the mounting claims of which he was so afraid, Italy would be forced willy-nilly into the position of wanting a victory for the Central Powers and fearing an Entente victory. Nevertheless, it was obvious that the Entente powers, and primarily Russia—which, though she too was motivated by imperialist considerations, proclaimed they were fighting in defence of a Slav nation in the Balkans such as Serbia was—would bear resentment against Italy if she backed Austro-Hungarian acquisitions of Balkan territory in exchange for concessions of Austrian territory which, if not confined to the Trentino, could consist only of ethnically mixed areas on the Adriatic inhabited by Yugoslavs as well as by Italians. Any Italo-Austrian agreement that consolidated the Triple Alliance would necessarily have identified Italy with the Central Powers in the eyes of the Entente. It could only be a question of time before the Italian government realized that, just as an incurable breach with Austria-Hungary over Article VII would lead her inevitably to the side of the latter's enemies, so a satisfactory agreement on that article would lead her to the side of the Central Powers.

Refusal at the outset to yield the Trentino of course excluded any consideration of the possibility that Italy might eventually be persuaded to side against the Entente. Instead it suggested the opposite possibility, which was mentioned at the meeting by Stürgkh, the Austrian Prime Minister, who wondered whether it would be wise passively to await an Italian attack. Would it not be advisable instead 'to deceive her with a kind of secret agreement?' he asked. 'Against brigands such as the Italians are now, no diplomatic swindle would be excessive.'[20] Justifying in advance the Italian insistence in the spring of 1915 on the immediate granting of the concessions that Austria-Hungary then offered, he suggested that Germany should make a secret treaty with Italy, promising her the Trentino on condition that she sided with her fellow-members of the Triple Alliance and accepted the steps that Austria-Hungary would take in the Balkans when the war was over. As one of these would be the elimination of Montenegro, to which Victor Emmanuel III could never consent for family reasons, Italy would then have to renounce the Trentino herself. Tisza and a fellow Hungarian, Burian, the Minister accredited

[53]

to the Crown, rejected this idea, pointing out that Italy would not so easily be taken in.[21] However, the fact that such an idea could germinate in the mind of the Austrian Prime Minister is further evidence of the lack of realism that prevailed among the leaders of the Central Powers. On August 9, the Austro-Hungarian ambassador in Berlin telegraphed Berchtold that both William II and the Chief of the German General Staff had suggested to the Austro-Hungarian military attaché that Italy should be promised the Trentino, but that when the war had been won, a way of not keeping the promise should be found.[22] At the meeting of the Joint Council of Ministers on August 19 Berchtold—faced with information from German sources according to which Italy had not only 'already spoken the word Trentino' but had also taken 'huge military measures' putting her into a position to attack at any moment—said that, in view of the desirability of making the possibility of war with Italy as remote as possible, he was conducting conversations with the Italian government, causing them to believe that some concessions might perhaps be made. At the meeting on September 7 Berchtold said that he had in mind the possibility of making concessions in Albania. This, as well as the necessity of preparing defences against Italy, was agreed to by Tisza, who also said that nothing should be done that Italy might regard as provocative.[23]

Meanwhile Mérey, whose nerves did not stand up to the tension resulting from the war that he had wanted Austria-Hungary to plunge into, had suffered a breakdown, and his place in Rome had been taken by Baron Macchio.[24] The negative judgement that Prince Bülow and also other, more disinterested, personalities formed of his inflexibility and lack of enterprise weighs justly on him, but in his reports he does not show himself to be without real political understanding. He saw the Secretary-General of the Foreign Ministry immediately after his arrival in Rome, and the next day, August 15, telegraphed that in that city 'the public seems still to be wavering, the desire to maintain the prevailing neutrality and the fear of complications with her allies being at least as strong as the desire to provoke them'.[25] He deplored the reports by the German military attaché that caused the Berlin government to believe that an Italian attack might be imminent.[26]

The truth of the matter was that the Germans were deliberately exaggerating, hoping that the Vienna government would take alarm and make concessions that might result in Italy's entering the war on the side of the Triple Alliance. That might have tipped the scales in France, where the German offensive was in progress. The Italian documents show clearly, however, that the Italian government had not the slightest intention of fighting the Entente, with whom it was already conducting secret conversations with a view to possible intervention against Austria-Hungary. The choice which the Italian leaders believed they were faced with was always between neutrality and war on Austria-Hungary. They finally made their choice at the end of February 1915, when they decided that Austria-Hungary was going to make no substantial territorial concessions. Thus, though Macchio was right in deflating the illusions of his German colleagues, and also in saying that the time for an irrevocable Italian decision had not yet come, he was wrong in overlooking the fact that time was working against Austria-Hungary in Rome, and that his instructions from Vienna to delay the Italian decision were profoundly mistaken. With the passing of time, Italian demands increased instead of diminishing. Austria-Hungary under the pressure of the Russian offensives was in no position to deploy large forces on the Italian frontier, and the Italian army took advantage of the interval to fill the gaps in its material and technical preparations. It was mere chance that the Russian defeat at Gorlice on May 3, 1915, which preceded the denunciation of the Triple Alliance by Italy by one day and her intervention by three weeks, enabled the Austro-Hungarian High Command hurriedly to transfer a few divisions to the Italian theatre. The time thus gained, precious though it was, was not owing to any foresight on the part of Vienna, but to the desire of Baron Sonnino, the new Italian Foreign Minister, to extract the maximum territorial promises from the negotiations in progress with the Entente and also to justify his rejection of Giolitti's neutralism.

What Macchio and the Vienna government should have foreseen, however, was that Entente propaganda, and French propaganda in particular, was bound, sooner or later to gain the upper hand in Italy unless countered by a courageous Austro-Hungarian diplomatic move. The Giolittian deputies most attached to the party of neutrality, such as Guido Fusinato and Camillo Peano, saw this plainly, and eloquently denounced the danger in their letter to Giolitti dated August 19 and 25.[27] Giolitti, however, inasmuch as he continued to stay away from Rome, did not attach much importance to the warning. Macchio, whose country was in mortal danger and who saw with his own eyes the anti-Austrian student demonstrations that took place in September outside his embassy, also did not believe there was any urgency in the matter.[28] On November 29, he wrote to Berchtold that he could not believe that Baron Sonnino, who had the reputation of being a man of great integrity, apart from having always been a supporter of the Triple Alliance, would begin his work at the Foreign Ministry (where he had succeeded San Giuliano, who had died the previous month) with an act of treachery. Macchio was aware that General Cadorna was anti-Austrian, but did not believe that the Italian Chief of Staff would be in a position to impose on his government a policy different from the one on which it had decided.[29] The Austrian diplomatists overlooked the fact that, as Article VII was well known in Italy, public opinion, which has a decisive influence in a genuinely parliamentary régime (such as then existed in Italy but not in Austria), would not have permitted the Rome government to remain empty-handed.

When the Italian parliament reopened, Giolitti—speaking ostensibly in support of Salandra's statement on behalf of the government that Italy was under no obligation to take up arms to support its partners under the Triple Alliance, who had not been attacked, while one of them had been the first to attack Serbia—disclosed that Vienna had asked him in August 1913 to support an operation against the Serbians, but that he had refused.[30] Macchio expressed to Salandra surprise that such a disclosure, of a kind unusual among allies, had been made, and the Italian Prime Minister replied that he too had been 'pained' by it. 'He added confidentially,' the ambassador reported, 'that personal considerations always had to be taken into account with Giolitti.'[31] Salandra, in other words, interpreted the revelation as being intended to reaffirm the decisive influence that Giolitti intended always to exercise on Italian politics. According to further information gathered by Macchio, Giolitti was jealous of the success of Salandra's statement, and made the disclosure to prevent the government from adjourning the Chamber *sine die* (the former Prime Minister could count more surely on the parliamentary majority than he could on the government), and to force it to fix a date for recalling it; this was fixed for February 18, 1915. Macchio added that Giolitti 'informed me through a confidential friend that he was well aware of the unusual nature of his so-called disclosure. His sole purpose had been to show in a demonstrable fashion that the question of the *casus foederis* had already been discussed in his time in connection with a possible European war, from which he wished it to be deduced that in certain circumstances Italian neutrality was compatible with the terms of the alliance. At the same time he had wished to recall that Italy must remain loyal to the Triple Alliance in the future also and make the Chamber more clearly aware of this.'[32]

As for Salandra and Sonnino, Macchio liked to think that 'taking everything into account, the consolidated position of the government is a guarantee against violent actions by irresponsible elements. The cabinet, however, in view of the increased economic depression, must show the country, which is faced with the raising of 1,000 million lire voted for military preparations, some countervailing factor that will be considered sufficient to make the neutrality policy seem satisfactory to the Italian mathematical instinct.'[33]

That was Macchio's answer to Berchtold's message informing him that the Italian ambassador in Vienna had told him in Sonnino's name that the Austro-Hungarian advance into Serbia, which had recently begun, raised the question of the application of Article VII. Macchio did not deny that the Italian government was under the necessity of producing tangible results. Nevertheless, in his view, Italy had no serious intention of intervening, preferring to gain something by threats at Austro-Hungarian expense if things went badly for the Central Powers, or from the Entente if things went badly for the latter.[34] Bülow, who arrived in Rome at this moment, decided that the situation was much more serious, and did not conceal his belief that cession of the Trentino was essential to ensure the continuation of Italian neutrality. In a letter to a friend who was also a friend of Giolitti's and occupied a high place in the Italian financial world, and in whose judgement both rightly had a great deal of confidence, he nevertheless wrote on January 3, 1915, that 'Salandra makes an excellent impression on me: he is both gracious and cultivated.'[35]

The objective situation favoured the maturation of the Italian choice. To universal surprise, the Austro-Hungarian expeditionary force was defeated by the Serbians and had to evacuate Belgrade. Italy, as Macchio noted, so far from deciding that this made an agreement on Article VII less urgent, concluded that the Habsburg monarchy had been sufficiently weakened for war against it not to be excessively risky.[36] Bülow and his colleagues had read the situation more correctly. At the end of 1914, Count Berchen, counsellor of the German embassy in Rome, made a personal approach to Count Hoyos, Berchtold's *chef de cabinet*, telling him that, unless the Trentino were ceded to her, Italy would certainly go to war, and that her example would be followed by Romania.[37] Also the Austro-Hungarian military attaché telegraphed to the High Command that he had learned from a reliable source that General Cadorna had said that, in view of the cost and the magnitude of Italian rearmament, Italian intervention was inevitable. According to the German military attaché, intervention would take place in the spring; however, unlike his Austrian colleague, he still believed that it would be possible to turn Italy against France by sacrificing the Trentino and Albania.[38]

Without sharing the illusions of the German military—which merely played into the hands of those in Vienna who refused any concession to Italy because, being easily able to demonstrate the impossibility of her attacking the Entente, they used that proof as

[57]

an argument to refute the possibility of her attacking Austria-Hungary—Macchio and his colleague at the Vatican, Prince Schönburg, came to the conclusion that Italian policy was moving in the direction of intervention.[39] On January 6, Sonnino reminded the Austro-Hungarian ambassador that settlement of the question of the compensation provided for under Article VII could no longer be deferred and gave him to understand, without specifically mentioning it, that Italy insisted on the Trentino.[40]

On the same day, Macchio wrote a long private letter to Berchtold, advising him in the interests of safeguarding the monarchy to reconcile himself to a sacrifice of territory, possibly in exchange for a commitment by Italy to render some service to its ally in the future. Otherwise he was convinced that sooner or later Italy would attack Austria-Hungary, if only because of the government fear of a republican revolution by the interventionists.[41]

A few days later, Sonnino, as is recorded in his personal papers, told Bülow that Italy had decided to ask for the Trentino and for a part of Istria and that a settlement should be reached very quickly because only substantial Austrian concessions could enable the Italian government to resist the pressure of those who wanted intervention on the side of the Entente. His papers confirm that in January 1915, although the King, Victor Emmanuel III, wished the victory of the Entente, Sonnino was still ready to reach an agreement with Austria. He made a definite option for war only at the end of February.

Similar pressure was put on Berchtold by the German ambassador in Vienna, who gave him Bülow's alarming secret reports to read, and Berchtold gave in. On January 9, he suggested to Francis Joseph that the Trentino should be ceded to Italy. But the Trentino was particularly precious to the House of Habsburg, and the Emperor would not hear of it.[42] Next day, a message arrived from General Conrad recommending, with the inconsistency typical of soldiers trying to intervene in politics, that in view of the delicacy of the situation no concessions should be made, because they would only be interpreted as a sign of weakness. In spite of this, Berchtold repeated to Stürgkh, Tisza and Burian the arguments he had put to the Emperor. Tisza said it was premature to talk of concessions; the military situation on the Russian front was not so grave as to justify them. After lunching with the German ambassador, who returned to the charge, warning him that stubbornness in the matter would lead Vienna to ruin, the Hungarian Prime Minister informed Berchtold that he was going to ask for his resignation. Berchtold replied that he would be only too happy to resign. The Emperor offered the post to Tisza, who declined it, however, on the ground that he could influence

Vienna from Budapest but could not govern Hungary from Vienna. His recommendation that Burian be appointed was accepted.[43] Before his resignation was made public, Berchtold received the Italian ambassador on January 11 and had to answer in the negative Sonnino's enquiry about Austria-Hungary's willingness to yield some of her own territory to satisfy her obligations under Article VII. In the view of the Vienna government, Italy ought to be satisfied with the occupation of Valona in Albania, which had already been carried out.[44]

Berchtold himself said of Burian, his successor, that it was not true, as some alleged, that he was merely a docile tool of Tisza's; on the contrary, he was a courageous man with a mind of his own.[45] That, indeed, is what he shows himself to be in his diary, which we have already had occasion to quote several times; it confirms that he was frequently at odds with Tisza, particularly in 1917–18. Forgách, the departmental head in the Vienna Foreign Ministry, wrote to Macchio on February 3 that it was difficult to imagine a greater contrast than that between the always hesitant Berchtold and the excessively self-confident Burian, but he concluded that 'at all events we now have effective leadership'.[46] But it was not leadership in the right direction. The Italian ambassador, the Duke d'Avarna, said that Burian had the 'mentality more of an argumentative and domineering lawyer than of a diplomat'. On February 24, Forgách confessed that he was very worried by what Burian was doing. 'If he goes on like this, in two months' time we shall be at war with Italy and Romania', he wrote. 'He says that he would prefer that to voluntarily yielding a square metre!'[47] This, however, was merely an outburst by an official who, having played a decisive part in the decision to make war on Serbia, was now particularly anxious that no chance should be missed of emerging victorious from that war. What Burian would never have agreed to was the cession of any Hungarian territory; he would not have refused to yield the Trentino to Italy, and perhaps Austrian Bukovina to Romania, if he had really believed that that was the only way of avoiding their intervention. Both he and Tisza indicated this at the Joint Council of Ministers on February 2, when Tisza insisted on the greater gravity of the Romanian threat. According to information given to the meeting by Burian, the Italian army was not yet ready to fight, and the Italian government was not foolish enough to decide on war before its army was ready.[48] Tisza and Burian hoped that in the meantime a great improvement would take place in the situation on the Russian front.

This putting off a painful payment in the hope that something would turn up to wipe out the obligation before the final day of reckoning was obviously a sheer gamble. The German leaders, beginning with the Chancellor, Bethmann-Hollweg, saw more clearly that the war could be won only in France. To Germany the assurance of Italian benevolent neutrality would be of enormous aid; it would save her the necessity of sending more troops to the aid of Austria-Hungary and—when an Austro-Italian agreement was made public —would force France to take steps to protect her Italian frontier. On February 6 and 10, Bethmann-Hollweg had long conversations with the Austro-Hungarian ambassador, appealing to him to use his best efforts to persuade Vienna to reach an agreement with Italy to prevent an Italian intervention which, he reiterated, would be disastrous to the Central Powers.[49]

Macchio's reports now spoke of a growing war-like trend within the Italian government. On January 27, a few days before the publication of Giolitti's letter on the *parecchio*, i.e. the 'substantial consideration' that he claimed was obtainable by Italy without going to war, Macchio wrote that the conflict between the former Prime Minister and Salandra was increasing. The Giolittians wanted to get back into power. Giolitti himself, however, who was used to being a kind of autocrat, seemed 'to have lost some of his energy with advancing age' and had little desire to shoulder the burden of government in a situation in which Salandra, if he succeeded in enforcing his resignation, would have little difficulty in criticizing him for having neglected military preparations since the Libyan war without having succeeded in consolidating the Italian finances as a result. He was probably awaiting an opportunity to put someone more amenable to his wishes in Salandra's place without himself assuming office.[50] On February 10, Macchio added that the neutralism displayed by a number of Giolittian parliamentarians and the success of socialist demonstrations for peace showed that the Italian people did not want war, but there was a danger that the weakening of Salandra's domestic position might result in his 'resorting to foreign policy to maintain himself in the saddle under the banner of nationalist aspirations'.[51] On March 2, he reported that Salandra, having created the illusion among his supporters that he would succeed in extracting something from Austria-Hungary, was now in difficulties as a result of not having obtained anything yet. 'Giolitti, however, with his flair for domestic political situations, which more than ever form the cornerstone of this country's foreign policy', had no desire to jeopardize his prestige by extricating Salandra from his difficult position and taking his place in the negotiations with Austria-Hungary. So far from desiring to form a government himself, he 'is taking pleasure in the role of a kindly uncle towards the Salandra cabinet, to whom he is once again promising his support, glad not to be the man caught by an evil destiny in the Prime Minister's chair at this unrewarding moment.'[52] As Macchio did not fail to point out, the fact was that the unanimous rejection of Giolitti's point of view by the Vienna government newspapers—they rejected it from the opposite point of view to that of the Italian interventionist press, on the ground that it required Austrian sacrifices—had persuaded the former Prime Minister of the difficulty of obtaining satisfaction for Italian demands by means of friendly negotiations.[53] Thus, while Macchio believed Salandra to be ambitious enough to make war in order to remain in office, Austrian public opinion, by its hostility to any concession, expressed itself in such as way as to discourage the friends on whom the Triple Alliance could still count in Italy from openly assuming responsibility.[54]

The German government had no doubts in the matter. Sonnino himself admitted to Bülow that, in view of the expectations of Italian public opinion, if Austria made no concessions, 'c'est la guerre'.[55] The Pope made the same statement to the German Catholic deputy Erzberger, who went to Rome in support of Bülow's mission.[56]

On February 27, the Prussian cabinet agreed to Bethmann-Hollweg's proposal that Austria-Hungary should be offered the Polish mining area of Sosnovice in compensation for yielding the Trentino to Italy, and, if Vienna were not satisfied with this, a frontier rectification in Prussian Silesia as well.[57] These offers were never made, however, for on March 6, the day on which the German Emperor approved his Chancellor's idea, the Austro-Hungarian leaders were making up their minds to yield the Trentino. On March 3, Burian noted in his diary: 'Today the Italian claim does not seem refusable, because the military situation is bad.' On the same date, Tisza told him that, in spite of the gravity with which he still regarded the loss of the Trentino, he had decided to consent to it, there being no other way of preventing an Italo-Romanian alliance.[58] Though he had previously opposed negotiations with Italy for fear of establishing a precedent for Romania, he now realized that Italian hostility made the Romanian attitude dangerous; and, as the real enemy in his eyes was Romania, he now set out to regain Italian friendship, but without following to the end the road which, however painful it might be, was the only one that could lead to it.

Macchio's report of March 5 on a conversation he had had with the deputy Facta, who had been sent to him by Giolitti, arrived in Vienna soon afterwards; Tisza had a copy of it within a few hours (as he did of all diplomatic correspondence of any consequence). Giolitti wished it to be known that he would support the Italian government in its negotiations with Vienna, and he advised the latter to 'make haste' to settle matters. Facta claimed that Italy did not want to go to war, but if Austria-Hungary failed to make the necessary concessions she would be under 'an implacable necessity' to do so.[59] This warning, coming from the most consistent advocate of Italian neutrality, was the graver in view of the fact that—as Macchio had several times pointed out—the strongest card in Giolitti's hand for keeping Salandra and Sonnino under control—namely his ability to compel their resignation at any moment by a revolt of the parliamentary majority devoted to him—was about to lose a lot of its force by the adjournment of the parliamentary session, which was likely to be decided on in March. What it amounted to was that the Austro-Hungarian government had only two or three weeks left. Sonnino was of the same opinion; on March 10, he instructed Avarna to propose that negotiations should be concluded within a fortnight.

In Vienna a decision was made, but an inadequate one. The Joint Council of Ministers approved the cession of the Trentino on March 8. Burian, proposing this, said that according to his information the Italian army would be ready for action by the middle of April, while since February 14 the Italian government had imposed a veto under Article VII on any further Austro-Hungarian military action in the Balkans that was not preceded by an agreement on the compensation due to Italy under the treaty. As the German government was ready to guarantee that, if Vienna made their necessary concessions, it would obtain from Italy 'a free hand in the Balkans' for Austro-Hungarian plans in that area, he believed Italy could no longer be denied the Trentino. Tisza associated himself with the proposal, admitting that the certainty that the great fortress of Przemyśl in Galicia was about to fall to the Russians, the Anglo-French attack on the Dardanelles, and the probability of Romania's following Italy into intervention, had convinced him of the necessity of making sacrifices that he had refused to consider in January. These sacrifices, he believed, should be made on the understanding that the maintenance of good relations with Italy 'will be a vital question for us after the war too'. The Austrian Ministers, whose country had to make these sacrifices (while none were required of Hungary), were not willing to go so far. Stürgkh said he was willing to sacrifice the Trentino, but not the Isonzo line, which was now known to be the minimum that Italy would require, and he added that he 'was willing to put a good face on the matter' only up to the end of the war, after which, 'we shall see'. Krobatin, the War Minister, agreed, but with the reservation that after the war he would like to see the expulsion and expropriation of all Italians from Trieste and elsewhere, even if they were Austrian citizens. Burian said that irredentism would be subdued, but by less draconian methods, and that the Italian counterpart should be taken into account; 'Germany has informed us that Italy offers us a free hand in the Balkans', which might even imply Italian renunciation of Albania. Conrad, who was now reconciled to the loss of the Trentino but was ready to fight 'to the death' against yielding the Isonzo line, doubted whether Italy would ever give Austria-Hungary *carte blanche* in Serbia; 'in his opinion, when the war was over the first opportunity should be taken to teach Italy a lesson'. Stürgkh also 'took the view that in the future there would be a fight with Italy over the Serbian question'. Tisza and Burian disputed this, however, and reiterated that it would be politic to reach a lasting understanding with Italy. But their position was weakened by two circumstances. As Hungarians, they rejected the idea of any concessions to the Romanians in Transylvania, and since July 1914 they had made it clear that, to avoid increasing the Slav population of the dual monarchy, they opposed the annexation of Serbia and Montenegro that the Austrian generals and Ministers wanted, though they were well aware that it would be very difficult indeed for Italy to consent to it. Burian ended by accepting authorization to offer the Trentino only.[60]

On the same day, Burian noted in his diary: 'The Trentino, but with a good strategic frontier. There can be no question of the Isonzo. To be handed over only after the conclusion of peace.' Nevertheless, Avarna had warned him on February 22 that, '*l'accord préalable doit être non seulement initié, mais terminé.*'[61] Sonnino, if he could have seen the report of the Austro-Hungarian Ministers' meeting just quoted, would have regarded it as completely justifying his insistence on the immediate handing over of the territory. The Vienna decision to postpone carrying out the agreement until the end of the war in fact implied a German commitment to persuade (or, as would certainly be feasible if the Central Powers won the war, to force) Italy to give Austria-Hungary *carte blanche* in the Balkans. Tisza, though he was aware that Hungary (though for different reasons) shared Italy's interest in not permitting Austria to annex a large amount of Serbian territory, did not realize that he should have advocated the immediate hand-over of the Trentino for that very reason, quite apart from the fact that it was the only way of reaching agreement with Rome.

Nor was Sonnino acting loyally on March 3, when Italy was still a member of the Triple Alliance, in deciding to inform London of the conditions on which Italy would intervene on the side of the Entente.[62] (These included demands on strategic grounds, or at any rate on grounds not in conformity with the nationality principle, to territories such as the South Tyrol and Dalmatia, which were inhabited almost exclusively by German Austrians and Yugoslavs respectively.) But it had been obvious to Salandra for months that Italy could not remain neutral in the absence of substantial territorial gains, and that, if Austria-Hungary refused them, they would have to be obtained from the Entente. San Giuliano in his time had also accepted this requirement of *sacro egoismo*, which Salandra proclaimed in a public speech before appointing Sonnino to the Foreign Ministry. Sonnino's subsequent haste was owing to the Anglo-French attack on the Dardanelles, which brought the war into the Mediterranean. If he had waited a little longer, he would have realized that nothing had occurred to justify his being forced, as he was on Salandra's insistence, to negotiate simultaneously with both belligerent blocs. Italy could have denounced the Triple Alliance first and negotiated with the Entente afterwards. In that event, the Entente would probably not have promised Italy Dalmatia, which was also claimed by Serbia, and Italy would have been spared the disappointments of the peace conference. But if he had waited only until March 27, when Burian informed Avarna of what was expected of Italy in exchange for the Trentino, in other words 'benevolent neutrality from the political, military and economic point of view', as well as 'full and complete liberty of action in the Balkans' for Austria-Hungary except in Albania, Sonnino might have concluded that the Trentino was not worth so much.[63] To Rome the Austrian refusal to hand over the Trentino immediately, though qualified by Burian's offer of a German guarantee that it would be handed over after the end of hostilities, meant that she would have had to commit herself to remaining neutral merely for the sake of obtaining a province at the end of a European war, the outcome of which might be such as to induce the Habsburg monarchy, in the event of victory, to make the execution of the agreement subject to conditions that might be excessively onerous, while defeat might make it unable freely to dispose of its territory.

The point of view of the Italian Foreign Ministry had been expressed in the reports which its general secretary, De Martino, prepared for Sonnino at the beginning of the negotiations with Vienna. In his report of January 9, 1915, De Martino stated that it was essential for Italy not to find herself, at the end of the war, on the side of the defeated. At that moment De Martino still believed in the possibility of a victory of the Central Powers and was therefore ready to settle

[64]

with Austria for the Trentino and to receive eventually Tunis, at the expense of France, in place of Trieste. In March 1915, however, De Martino too persuaded himself that the Entente was going to win the war.

Sonnino in fact drew Macchio's attention to the circumstance that, while the Italian parliament would have to ratify the agreement with Vienna immediately, its Austrian counterpart, which had not met since the beginning of the war, would be called on to ratify it only when the war was over. What would happen if the Reichsrat then refused ratification? In fact, only an agreement that was carried out immediately made sense to Italy.[64] Although on March 14 the Italian ambassador explained still more clearly to the State Secretary in the German Foreign Ministry—who immediately passed on what he said to the Austro-Hungarian ambassador—that the negotiations for an immediate hand-over must be concluded within a fortnight, failing which the Rome government would consider them to have broken down, Burian, egged on by his ambassador in Berlin, who was still more intransigent in the matter than he, stood firm on the ground that he had taken, namely that an immediate hand-over was 'out of the question'.[65] According to Avarna's reports, he maintained this stand until the end of April. On April 16 the Austro-Hungarian government, in its reply to the demands finally formulated by Sonnino (which, in addition to the Trentino, Bolzano included, embraced Gradisca, Gorizia, the establishment of Trieste as an independent state, the Curzolari (Korcula) islands and Valona), reiterated that, while leaving Italy Valona, it was willing to cede the Trentino as far as Salorno, and might, according to what Burian said to Avarna, consent to a rectification of the frontier on the Isonzo, but only when the war was over.

Sonnino might well conclude that further negotiations with Vienna were pointless, and in fact did so, swiftly completing the Treaty of London.[66] We have found more documents in the Austrian archives that seem to justify Sonnino's conclusion. After the revolution of the autumn of 1918, the head of the cipher office in Vienna felt it to be his duty to inform Otto Bauer, the new Secretary of State in the Foreign Ministry of the Austrian Republic, who was planning the unification of Austria with Germany, that he had learnt from experience that the Entente powers were able to decipher the German diplomatic codes. He was convinced that in April 1915 the French had deciphered and communicated to Tittoni, the Italian ambassador, a telegram sent by the Berlin government to its embassies in Rome and Vienna in which it expressed the hope that 'Austria would make those concessions to the Italians which the latter desired, inasmuch as

[65]

after the attainment of victory what was yielded might well be taken back'.[67]

Although we failed to find any trace of this telegram, we found in Vienna another which tends to confirm the correctness of the assertion by the head of the Austrian cipher office. On May 9, 1915, Schönburg, the Austrian ambassador to the Vatican, who, in agreement with Benedict XV, was trying to make the final concessions submitted by Bülow and Macchio acceptable to the Italian government, sent a telegram to Berlin suggesting that the post-war execution of the commitments that Austria-Hungary proposed to assume in relation to Italy might be guaranteed by the Pope. Prince Hohenlohe, the Austro-Hungarian ambassador in Berlin, who saw the text of this proposal by his colleague, telegraphed to his government on May 11: 'If we have to make a mental reservation in relation to certain concessions, going as far as proposing to take back what has been extorted from us when a suitable occasion arises—a matter of which Prince Schönburg is evidently unaware—it is unthinkable that we should actually invite the Pope to guarantee the maintenance of the concessions made on our part.'[68]

Thus there was indeed a mental reservation in the Austro-Hungarian Foreign Ministry about the offer to Italy, and the ambassador in Berlin, who would obviously in due course have to explain this to the German government on whose insistence Vienna had made the offer, was aware of it. It can be assumed that, so far as Burian was concerned, the mental reservation applied, not to the Trentino, but only to the 'extras' (the frontier on the Isonzo, autonomy for Trieste, etc.) that Bülow extracted from Austria-Hungary at the last moment. But, even if it was limited to that extent, it shows that Italian insistence on the immediate execution of the agreement was justified.

The papers of Sonnino disclose that at the beginning of March 1915 the Italian Intelligence Service succeeded in decoding the cipher with which Burian communicated with the Austrian ambassador in Rome. It also decoded the cipher used by the Vatican in its communications with the papal nuncios.

The Austro-Hungarian documents also provide additional information on how it came about that at the beginning of May (when it was too late, though Vienna could not know this) a final offer was made to Italy (and communicated to Giolitti before it was submitted to Sonnino) which, if made two months earlier, might have changed the course of events. The first to realize the inadequacy of the concessions agreed to on March 8 was Tisza, who undoubtedly possessed greater political flair than any of his colleagues. On March 28, he

[66]

wrote to Burian suggesting that Italy should be informed that, if she renewed her friendship with Austria-Hungary in return for the cession of the Trentino, the latter would reciprocate her friendship, and would there and then provide her with a German guarantee of the faithful post-war execution of the territorial concessions agreed on. If, in spite of this, Sonnino insisted on an immediate hand-over, he suggested that contact should be made with Salandra, Giolitti and the King of Italy.[69] By that time it was probably a little late to change the course of events. The Italian Chamber had been adjourned until May, and the government, not having concealed its dissatisfaction with the Vienna offer, felt itself in possession of full liberty of action. Moreover, Burian wasted more precious time. On April 16, on receiving the negative reply to Sonnino's demands, Avarna admitted to Burian that, to his extreme regret, Italy would decide on war.[70] Next day, Forgách wrote to Macchio that a sudden change had taken place in Burian's state of mind; he was excited and worried, and said that peace must be asked for, and that he would discuss it with Conrad and the Germans.[71] On the same day, April 17, Tisza wrote to Burian, by whom he had been informed about the situation, that Italy had obviously been irritated by the dilatory tactics employed, and that she must now be told that Austria-Hungary might be willing to yield practically everything for which Sonnino asked, with the exception of Trieste.[72] The German government persisted in pointing out the urgency of making concessions to the Austro-Hungarian ambassador in Berlin.[73]

The files of the Austro-Hungarian Foreign Ministry contain, under the name of Chlumecky, an unsigned report dated April 30, 1915, stating that on April 23 'our confidential emissary' had met Alfredo Frassati, the editor of the great newspaper *La Stampa*, in Turin, who had gone to see his friend Giolitti the same evening. Giolitti, who happened to be in Turin, advised the cession of the Trentino and of a part of Austrian Friuli, and the full autonomy of Trieste and Fiume, the citizens of which should be exempted from military service in Austria-Hungary.[74] From the Sonnino–Salandra correspondence, the recollections of Senator Frassati, of Senator Luigi Albertini, the editor of the *Corriere della Sera* in Milan, who was aware of the approach, of which he sharply disapproved, and of Olinda Malagodi, the editor of the *Tribuna*, in Rome to whom Alberto Bergamini, the editor of the *Giornale d'Italia*, also in Rome, gave Sonnino's version of his conversation with Frassati, it can be taken for granted that the intermediary was Roberto Prezioso, the deputy editor of *Il Piccolo* of Trieste. Baron Chlumecky's papers include a file on 'activity in Italy between 1914 and 1915' that provides hitherto unknown details.[75]

[67]

On December 12, 1914, Chlumecky's emissary, after thanking him for having intervened with the Austrian authorities on behalf of a woman who was close to him and was being persecuted because she was suspected of irredentism, wrote to him from Trieste: 'I have decided to go to Rome as soon as possible to try to conduct a campaign there among the politicians and, if possible, in circles close to the government itself, to explain to them how absurd it would be to listen to "irresponsible elements" in regard to Italo-Austrian relations.'[76] On December 30, he reported to Chlumecky that he had been to Venice and, without mentioning names, gave him information about the lines along which Italian public opinion was divided.[77] On March 2, 1915, he informed Chlumecky that he had been to Rome and had several times seen Bergamini, the editor of the *Giornale d'Italia*, 'without, however, succeeding in persuading him'.[78] On April 12, after reporting that he had been to Milan and seen Luigi Albertini's brother, whose interventionism was unshakable, he wrote as follows:

However, I left Senator Frassati, the editor of *La Stampa*, in quite a different frame of mind. . . . He confirmed that Giolitti is definitely opposed to intervention and is in fact very much in favour of a peaceful agreement with Austria-Hungary. Giolitti wants Italy to accept the Trentino and Friuli and also to obtain from Austria-Hungary an absolute guarantee of the Italian-ness of Trieste and Fiume, which would be declared free cities, though under Austro-Hungarian sovereignty.[79]

On April 22 he wrote:

As I have telegraphed you, I am leaving at five o'clock tomorrow morning, and I shall telegraph to F. from the first station beyond the frontier, asking him to keep the evening for me. I shall try to persuade him to leave on Saturday morning for the place where G. now is, and I hope I shall succeed.

On April 30 he wrote:

I have just returned from Venice, where I went yesterday, summoned by a telegram from Senator F., who gave me an appointment there yesterday evening. . . . In Venice yesterday Senator F. (who came from Turin especially for the purpose) said this to me:
'I saw Sonnino the day before yesterday (Thursday) and told him what you informed me the Austro-Hungarian government is willing to grant, and I gave him the statement made by G., who

[68]

undertakes to secure the approval of parliament if the government presents itself to the Chamber and the Senate with these Austrian concessions as the outcome of its negotiations.

'Sonnino was taken aback by what I told him. He said that it appears from the official negotiations that the concessions which the Austro-Hungarian government seems willing to make are so disproportionately smaller that it is impossible either to reconcile the two communications or explain the difference between them.'[80]

Frassati, the emissary went on, informed Giolitti that 'the Italian government is sure that it will be unable to obtain from Austria-Hungary what it regards as essential in order to be able to preserve neutrality and is on the point of reaching an agreement with the Triple Entente.' Consequently, according to the emissary, Frassati had said:

> G. has decided to make a last effort. He asked me to meet you in Venice and to ask you to appeal to your friends in Vienna to persuade the Austro-Hungarian government to accept his programme and to inform the Italian government officially of this as quickly as possible.[81]

Frassati had added that:

> G. is not willing to influence the Italian government in any way towards reducing its demands. . . . As the government is considered interventionist and Giolitti is a neutralist, it is the government, and not G., who must be satisfied by the Austrian concessions. Because G. must remain in the shadow.[82]

The emissary grew pessimistic because, among other things, Chlumecky's replies (which are not in the files) must have caused him to believe, in contrast to his first impression, that the Austro-Hungarian government had not yet decided to make the concessions that even Giolitti considered indispensable for the maintenance of Italian neutrality. In the letter dated April 30, which we have already quoted, he in fact warned Chlumecky that within a few days Italy would probably choose the path of war.[83]

Prezioso took refuge in Italy after the Italian intervention, and in a memorandum he submitted to Luigi Albertini he coloured what he had said to Frassati and Chlumecky to suggest that he had not really wanted any agreement between Austria and Italy to be reached, but had preferred Italy to decide to liberate his native city of Trieste by force of arms.[84] Whether he really played this unlikely Machiavellian double game or only imagined it in retrospect is immaterial; what is of interest is the written reports that Chlumecky received about Frassati's views and what he said to Sonnino and Giolitti.

What the reports to Chlumecky make clear is that at the middle of April, Vienna was aware of the conditions (the cession of Friuli as well as the Trentino and guarantees for some kind of autonomy for Trieste and perhaps also for Fiume) that the neutralist Giolitti regarded as indispensable if intervention was to be avoided, and that it was the dilatoriness of Vienna in accepting them that made it impossible for Giolitti to take timely action in relation to the government and in parliament, where the majority of members backed him. Giolitti, having advised Sonnino through Frassati to accept certain definite Austrian concessions if they were made, obviously could not move until Austria-Hungary officially confirmed its willingness to make those concessions.

On May 4, the day on which Italy denounced the Triple Alliance, the German ambassador in Vienna formally asked Burian for authority for Bülow to offer Italy the Trentino, the Isonzo line, the autonomy of Trieste, and Albania. Burian replied that he would authorize Macchio to discuss these concessions together with the Italians and Bülow.[85] On May 9, Bülow persuaded Macchio to take the unusual step of drafting and submitting to Giolitti, who had arrived in Rome on that day, and subsequently to Sonnino and Salandra, a list, signed by the diplomatic representatives of both the Central Powers, of concessions more far-reaching than those previously formulated. They included the cession of the Trentino and of the right bank of the Isonzo—i.e. those parts of them that were inhabited by Italians; the establishment of Trieste as a Free City, with municipal autonomy, an Italian university, and a free port, though within the framework of Austria-Hungary; Valona; Austria-Hungarian disinterest in the rest of Albania; protection of the interests of those whose mother-tongue was Italian who remained in Austria-Hungary; a benevolent examination of Italian demands in relation to Gorizia and the Curzolari islands; and a German guarantee of the loyal execution of an agreement on these lines.[86]

Macchio explained as follows to his government (all the members of which, including Tisza, thought he had gone too far, particularly in the penultimate and previous points) why he had been persuaded to accept the Bülow draft: 'It was plain, in view of the arrival of Signor Giolitti and the intense activity of the Holy Father, who has exposed himself in the interests of peace to the extent of having now made contact with Giolitti, that it was necessary to take decisive steps immediately.' The list of concessions 'was submitted to his

[70]

Holiness and sent by the Pope to Giolitti', who showed it to the King.[87] The Pope told the Austro-Hungarian ambassador to the Vatican that he had persuaded Grippo, the Education Minister, to resign, in order to provoke a government crisis and Giolitti's return to power.[88] Giolitti, though he told the King, and others as well, that the last Austro-Hungarian offer made it absurd for Italy to enter the war against her former allies, and though the majority of the parliament was behind him, was unwilling to resume the reins of government. Macchio had foreseen that Giolitti 'will not consider it politic to come forward as an Austrophile Prime Minister'.[89] According to the ambassador, Giolitti proposed merely to get rid of Sonnino and to negotiate with Salandra acceptance of the Central Powers' proposals.[90]

Giolitti's refusal to return to power, though its consequence in Italy was to leave the way open for a further period of office for Salandra, was certainly based on the fact that Austria-Hungary had still not declared itself willing to hand over immediately the territory it offered, but had merely expressed willingness immediately to exempt from military service citizens of the territories that it offered to give up after the war. As a result Italy would still have had to face difficult negotiations before reaching the stage of signing an agreement (even if her hands had not already been tied since April 26 by the Treaty of London, a fact of which, it now seems certain, Giolitti was still unaware).[91] If his and Bülow's offer had been accepted, Macchio proposed, for instance, to submit to the Italian government a document, to be made public immediately after its signature, that would certainly have included the concessions listed above (except for the postponement until later of negotiations about the future of Gorizia and the islands), but would have stipulated that Italy not only undertook to pay an indemnity for the territory that would be yielded to her, but also renounced taking further advantage of Article VII of the Triple Alliance treaty (which obviously would have to be revised) 'aussi concernant avantages territoraux ou autres qui résulteraient pour l'Autriche-Hongrie du traité de paix terminant cette guerre'.[92] Although the draft would have stated that Italy committed herself to une parfaite neutralité (Sonnino had stated on March 31 that to avoid incurring British economic reprisals, the Italian government could not in any event give a public undertaking to maintain 'benevolent' neutrality), Macchio said in an explanatory memorandum written on his return to Vienna that the Italian counterpart to the Austro-Hungarian concessions would in fact have had to consist of 'benevolent neutrality for the whole duration of the war . . . and a completely free hand for us in the Balkans'.[93]

The Entente, who were obviously mistrustful, undoubtedly would have interpreted an agreement between Italy and the Central Powers (even if the Italian government had not been already committed under the Treaty of London) as indeed implying the tacit Italian promise of aid to their enemies that the Austro-Hungarian ambassador thought should constitute the counterpart to the concession it was proposed to grant. Even in the absence of the Treaty of London, the least that the Italian government could have expected from the Entente would have been an attitude of diplomatic ill will and open support for the political forces in Italy opposed to the Triple Alliance. After the signature of the Treaty of London, the Entente would obviously have had at their disposal the powerful means of exercising pressure represented by the threat to publish it, with a view to provoking an interventionist revolution in Italy which it would support. On the other hand, if Austria-Hungary won the war, in which event its strength would be enormously increased (thanks among other things to the previously given Italian consent to its enjoying a free hand in the Balkans), Italy could hardly have expected from it the benevolence that it would itself have had to promise for the duration of the war. On May 15, the Austro-Hungarian Foreign Minister (who, being a Hungarian, was much less anti-Italian than his Austrian colleagues) again telegraphed to his ambassador in Rome that he proposed to carry out 'without any second thoughts the cessions agreed to by us', i.e. those he had approved before the compilation of Bülow's list on May 9. But, as for these subsequently added (he specified them as Gorizia, the islands, the status of Trieste as a free city and the rights of Austria-Hungary's Italian citizens) 'this hasty extension forces us for the protection of our vital interests to think of limitations, now or later'.[94]

It is possible, as Giolitti said to Malagodi, that, if Italy had resumed negotiations and continued them, Austria-Hungary might have ended by giving Italy the guarantees required to prevent her intervention. Macchio himself telegraphed to Vienna on May 16 suggesting the immediate hand-over of the city of Trent.[95] Tisza, according to Forgách, was now 'completely convinced that war with Italy must be avoided at all costs; this is also the opinion several times expressed by Conrad'.[96]

But, apart from the fact that on May 18 Bülow was again informed by Berlin that the Vienna government was still opposed to the immediate hand-over that was also supported by the Pope, the time for negotiations had run out.[97] The last Austro-Hungarian offers, apart from the question of whether they were to be carried out immediately or after the end of the war, undoubtedly met a substantial part of the demands that Italy had put forward two months earlier. If they had been made before the negotiation for the Treaty of London, an agreement of the kind that Giolitti wanted might yet have been possible and Italian intervention might have been prevented. But once more Austria arrived an hour too late.

III

Prelude to the Self-determination
of the Nationalities

The declaration of war on Serbia, the news of the intervention of its powerful German ally and its first resounding victories, the departure to the fronts of the first regiments of recalled conscripts, were greeted in Austria-Hungary by demonstrations of popular enthusiasm. Of those in Vienna we have the evidence of Trotsky, who was sarcastic about them, but recognized their spontaneity.[1] A fortnight after the beginning of hostilities, the enthusiasm of the Magyars was still just as vociferous, according to the observations of Josef Redlich, who travelled through the country in mid-August 1914.[2] M. Buchinger, the secretary of the Hungarian Social Democratic Party, who from long experience as organizer of a party execrated by the authorities and kept under supervision by them as a gang of 'vagabonds without a fatherland', knew the agents of the political police very well, noted their presence in the ranks of the demonstrators.[3] His party opposed this bellicose jubilation, sharply in its newspaper and much more cautiously in the official statements of its executive committee, but he admitted that it was swimming against the current.[4] The Social Democrats were not represented in the Budapest parliament, but the non-Magyar nationalities in Hungary had half a dozen deputies who, however, did not dare raise a dissentient voice when Count Apponyi on July 28 expressed the solidarity of the opposition parties with the decision to inflict punishment on Serbia that Hungarian public opinion not only believed to be thoroughly deserved but, according to the speaker, also awaited with impatience.[5] The Budapest Social Democratic newspaper was still reiterating its opposition to the imminent war when diplomatic relations with Serbia were broken off, which led to Tisza's denouncing it as the 'only exception' in a country vibrant with patriotism. When hostilities began, however, though it did not make a leap comparable with that of its Vienna counterpart, which celebrated lyrically the vote cast for military credits by the Social Democratic deputies in Germany, it adapted itself to the requirements of the military censorship and justified the principle of national defence by the necessity of facing up to the threat represented by the Tsarist Russian armies.[6]

[74]

Massive and unopposed pro-war demonstrations also took place in Zagreb and Prague. In Croatia, they were fed by the traditional anti-Serbian feeling which existed in part of the population because of religious conflict and material rivalry, which the 'pure' Right Party systematically cultivated. However, the demonstrations in the streets of Prague, in which both Germans and Czechs took part on August 7 and 8, 1914, were organized by the Austrian authorities, as Count H. Clam-Martinic, who made prodigious efforts to assure their success, admitted a few days later to J. Redlich, and were not conclusive evidence of the genuineness of Czech loyalty.[7] On the other hand, Count Stürgkh, the Austrian Prime Minister, unlike his counterparts in Berlin and Budapest, failed to summon his national parliament, with which the government arbitrarily dispensed from the spring of 1914 onwards. This saved the Czech deputies and those of other centrifugal nationalities from having to show their hand on a war credit vote.

During the first few weeks, the sharpest opposition to the war in Austria-Hungary was displayed by the Italian socialists in Trieste. In spite of the censorship, they opposed the line taken by the central organ of the Social Democratic Party in Vienna, and reaffirmed their loyalty to the principles of proletarian internationalism and their rejection of the 'sacred union'.[8]

No sooner had military operations begun than signs of sympathy with Austria-Hungary's enemies appeared in the frontier zones of Bosnia-Hercegovina, southern Hungary, Galicia and Bukovina, where many people were Serbs and Ukrainians. On August 31, 1914, the Hungarian cabinet had to take note of the fact that a whole town, Pancsova, the population of which was predominantly Serbian, had displayed its sympathy with the enemy and, in spite of the measures taken, was still giving refuge to deserters from the Austro-Hungarian army who had taken to the woods to avoid having to fight fellow-Serbians.[9]

In political circles in Budapest it was taken for granted that the military authorities succeeded in putting down the pro-Serbian movement in southern Hungary only thanks to many thousands of arrests and many hundreds of summary executions.[10] These figures may have been exaggerated, but Tisza, who was known for his iron fist, though he respected the principle of legality (he ordered Hungarian and Croatian Serbo-Croat deputies imprisoned by the military to be released, while the Austrian authorities let the Czech and Southern Slav deputies, who had been arrested in similar circumstances, remain in prison), actually protested against the excessive number of arrests carried out on grounds of military security among

[75]

the Serbians in southern Hungary and in Croatia, as well as among Slovaks in the north-western part of the country, which was still remote from the area of the Russian advance. 'The most incredible things have happened', Tisza wrote on September 21 to the Archduke Frederick, nominally the Commander-in-Chief of the Austro-Hungarian armed forces in the field, to whom he had already written on the same subject a week earlier. On October 3, he addressed a similar protest to Krobatin, the Minister of War.[11]

On October 27, 1914, A. Scheck, the head of the Bosnian Department of Justice, told Redlich that in all the areas in Bosnia-Hercegovina adjoining the frontiers of the kingdom of Serbia, the Serbian part of the population had in fact rebelled, and that suppression of the rebellion had caused the Austro-Hungarian command a great deal of trouble.[12] To the north, a few desertions and demonstrations of pro-Russian feeling took place among the Czechs during the same autumn. Manifestos either of Russian origin or written by the National Socialist followers of Klofáč (who was imprisoned soon after the outbreak of war) were distributed in Bohemia and Moravia; the latter called for a railway strike.[13] Incidents of this kind during the first six months of the war led to 121 Czechs being sentenced, eighteen of them to death.[14]

The Austro-Hungarians, however, had their most disagreeable surprise in Galicia and Bukovina. In spite of the bureaucratic nature of the Vienna government and the chauvinism of the German parties—to whom Germany's entry into the war at the side of the Habsburg empire seemed to be a definite guarantee of the *de facto* supremacy in Austria that they were losing with the extension of the franchise—political, cultural, religious and social liberties for all citizens of whatever language, denomination or class were far greater in the Austrian territories than in the autocratic Russia of the Tsars. In particular, the Poles in Galicia, who for class reasons were the dominant local nationality and on whose strong representation in the Reichsrat the Vienna government constantly relied to pass almost any legislation, as well as the Ukrainians or Ruthenians of that region, whose peasant masses had been so useful to Vienna against the independence movement of the Polish nobility in 1846–48, and those of the adjacent Bukovina, enjoyed political and trade-union rights that their brothers in Russian Poland and the Russian Ukraine were very far indeed from possessing, in spite of the concessions made to them in the 1905 revolution and the advances made by the bourgeois industrial economy at Kiev, Warsaw, Lodz and elsewhere. In Tsarist Russia, the Orthodox Church, though it tolerated Polish Catholicism, had jurisdiction over all Ukrainians, who in the

[76]

Austrian territories enjoyed full freedom of religion and were divided between Uniates and Orthodox.

Immediately after the outbreak of the war, however, though the Poles and Ruthenians dutifully obeyed the call to arms and accepted the exigencies of military life, only a minority of those nationalities showed any enthusiasm in the cause of the Central Powers. Pilsudski, the leader of the 'activist', nationalist revolutionary, wing of the Russian Polish Socialist Party, took refuge in Galicia, where he could count on the support of the strong Austrian Polish Social Democratic Party led by the popular deputy I. Daszynski, and on August 3, 1914, formed a company of Polish volunteers to fight against Tsarism.[15] Ten days later, however, the Austrian authorities incorporated the company into the Galician territorial militia, which greatly reduced its potentiality as an inducement to the Polish troops in the Russian army to desert. On August 16, a national committee of all the Polish political parties in Galicia was formed at Cracow.[16] It was intended to follow the policy announced by the Polish deputies' 'club' in the Reichsrat, which at the beginning of the war called for the reunification of so-called 'Congress Poland' (subject to Russia), with Galicia to form a kingdom of Poland which would be part of the Habsburg monarchy. Of the forty members of the national committee, twelve belonged to the National Democratic Party, whose counterpart of the same name, led by Roman Dmowski, was the strongest political party in Russian Poland. On October 20, the National Democrats withdrew from the committee, thus aligning themselves, though they could not publicly say so, with the position taken in Warsaw by Dmowski who, believing the chief enemy of the Poles to be the Prussians—who, in his view, were using methods more effective than those of the Tsarists to denationalize the Poles of the province of Poznan—desired a victory for the Entente, from which he expected a permanent diminution of St Petersburg absolutism and the re-establishment of Polish unity and autonomy within the Russian framework.[17] Had Russia won the war, she would indeed have been able to detatch Galicia from Austria and Poznan and Upper Silesia from Germany, whereas victory for the Central Powers would at most have enabled Austria (always assuming the consent of Germany on the one hand and of Hungary on the other) to add Russian Poland to Galicia. She certainly would not have been able to incorporate the predominantly Polish provinces of the German empire.

The assumptions on which the Cracow committee was based turned out to be tenuous. During the first days of the war, L. Bilinski, the Austro-Hungarian Joint Finance Minister, who was of Polish origin, proposed that a proclamation should be made promising the Russian Poles liberation and reunification with their Austrian brothers in an autonomous Poland under the Habsburg sceptre. In the second half of August, he believed he had secured Francis Joseph's consent to this, but it was vetoed by Tisza, who regarded it as a step towards 'trialism' (as distinct from 'dualism') or federalization of the Habsburg monarchy. Tisza argued that a commitment to the liberation of Congress Poland would exclude any possibility of a negotiated peace with Russia.[18] This was the origin of all the rumours that circulated about an alleged Hungarian desire for a separate peace.

Because of centuries-old common traditions, the Magyars were in general favourably inclined to the Polish cause, but such an obdurate supporter of the dualist principle as Tisza regarded it as vital to the maintenance of the privileged position of the Magyar governing classes—and to him the overriding consideration was preservation of the existing system, no matter how attractive an alternative might be in any other way. He would have accepted the detachment of Russian Poland from the Tsarist empire only on two conditions: firstly that it was purely and simply annexed to Austrian territory, becoming part of it just as Galicia was, i.e. without the reunified Polish provinces being granted any special autonomy that might lead to their promotion to the rank of a third Habsburg kingdom on a par with Austria and Hungary; and secondly that Hungary was compensated for this aggrandizement of Austria by the restoration of Dalmatia and Bosnia-Hercegovina to the St Stephen's Crown, which had possessed them at various times in the Middle Ages; it was through St Stephen's Crown that the House of Habsburg had inherited its sovereign rights over them.[19] The Austrian Prime Minister feared that any move in the direction of autonomy would weaken the power of the central government in Vienna, and he supported Tisza, with the result that Bilinski's proposal was shelved and the Austro-Hungarian high command limited itself to a general, non-committal appeal to the Poles. The matter naturally came to the knowledge of the Polish deputies to the Reichsrat and served to justify the mistrust felt by the National Democrats. After their departure, the Cracow committee consisted of representatives of the feudal nobility on the one hand and the Social Democrats and the Polish Peasant People's Party on the other, and they were irreconcilable for social reasons. With the entry of German troops into Warsaw in August 1915, the Polish problem was revived, but in the meantime the Habsburg monarchy had lost a favourable opportunity.

The Petrograd government was more timely, at any rate in words. At the end of July 1914, even before Russia was involved in the war,

Sazonov, its Foreign Minister, gave to Prince G. Trubetskoy the task of drafting a manifesto to the Poles promising them the reunification of all Polish territories (i.e. including those in Austria and German possession) within the Tsarist empire, with their own administrative autonomy and guarantees of freedom of worship and education.[20] The manifesto was published on August 14, not over the signature of the Tsar, but over the much less binding one of the Commander-in-Chief, the Grand Duke Nikolai Nikolaievich, who took the step the more willingly inasmuch as he hated the Germans and, married as he was to a Montenegrin princess, had for a long time, in contrast to the pre-war cautiousness of Sazonov himself, favoured the idea of war on Austria-Hungary in defence of the Slav minority nationalities. Goremykin, the Prime Minister, incompetent and hostile in principle to any reform, had talks with Maklakov, the Minister of the Interior, a man who was so reactionary that he regarded as a radical even a man like Sazonov. (Sazonov's devotion to Orthodoxy should have been sufficient to safeguard him from the slightest suspicion in this respect, but he had more intelligence and greater experience than his colleagues.) The talks resulted in Goremykin and Maklakov hastening to declare their opposition to the granting of any real autonomy to Russian Poland.[21] Nevertheless, the manifesto had a certain importance because it seemed to confirm the soundness of Dmowski's policy. The representatives of the large Polish colony in the United States, who were anti-German both because many of them were immigrants from East Prussia and because their competitors in American life were Germans and not Russians, quickly approached the Russian High Command with an offer to finance a strong corps of Polish volunteers to fight for the liberation of Poznan and Upper Silesia from German domination.[22] This offer was too democratic for the tastes of the Tsarist High Command, which declined it, but General Yanuskievich, the Chief of the General Staff, asked the government for instructions on whether and how practical application should be given to the Grand Duke Nikolai's manifesto.

The cabinet discussed the question several times. Sazonov, supported by two colleagues, argued the necessity of granting administrative autonomy to Poland, but the Ministers of the Interior, War and Justice and the Deputy Minister of Education, on whom the application of such measures would have depended, rejected the idea, either because they regarded it as dangerous to the unity of the empire or because they secretly aspired to a separate peace with Germany.[23] At all events, one of their most effective arguments was that, for ethnic and religious reasons, Russia's primary concern should be the Ruthenians in Austro-Hungary, who were notoriously hostile to the re-establishment of Poland in its historical frontiers, which included large areas inhabited by Ukrainians. A few days after the appeal to the Poles was issued, Sazonov himself asked Trubetskoy to draft another, addressed to the Ruthenians of the Habsburg empire, announcing that the Russian armies would bring them emancipation from the foreign yoke.[24] There was a certain inconsistency between the two manifestos, but that did not prevent the second from being even more disturbing to Austro-Hungarian plans than the first.

At the suggestion of the Austrian Social Democrats, the Vienna Foreign Ministry had given financial support to the Ukrainian Socialists who took refuge in Galicia after the defeat of the 1905 revolution. In August 1914, the latter formed a league for the liberation of the Ukraine that put itself at the disposal of the Austrian authorities in the struggle against Tsarism.[25] The Uniate Metropolitan of Lvov openly took up a pro-Austro-Hungarian position. Some Vienna diplomatists believed that in the event of victory the Poles, only too delighted at the emancipation of their country from the Russian yoke, would be satisfied with the reunification of Congress Poland with western Galicia, whereas eastern Galicia, inhabited predominantly by Ruthenians, would constitute a centre of attraction for the Russian Ukraine.[26]

The Ruthenian peasants, however, as J. Redlich noted on the spot in the second month of the war, listened readily to the Russian promises; in Galicia they felt oppressed by the administrative and social preponderance of the Poles, and both there and in Bukovina by the greater economic and commercial strength of the Jews, while in sub-Carpathian Hungary they were still more exploited and deprived of political and educational liberties.[27] General Conrad told Redlich that a large number of Ruthenians (seemingly also including members of the Galician Uniate Church), had been influenced by the propaganda of Orthodox priests in Bukovina, were solidly pro-Tsarist, and wanted the enemy to win. Some went so far as to give direct aid to the Russians by carrying military information across the lines, and many had been caught and hanged by the Austro-Hungarians. Fortunately for the latter, once the Russian police authorities, who desired the Russification of the Ukraine and the reconversion to Orthodoxy of the members of the Uniate Church, had established themselves in large areas of Galicia and Bukovina, occupied by the Russian army, they treated the Ruthenians far worse, forbidding newspapers in the Ukrainian language, controlling or closing their schools and persecuting the Uniate Church. The

Tsarist police response to Ruthenian protests was to arrest those who complained, beginning with a number of Uniate priests. The Grand Duke Nikolai protested in vain against this trampling on the contents of his manifesto.[28]

Until the truth about the brutal and senseless behaviour of the Tsarist police administration became known to those Austro-Hungarian Slavs who had so far been prevented by the course of the war from seeing it at work, Russian propaganda had the upper hand. It was able to take advantage of the open support of the Czechs and Slovaks living in Russia, who came out in favour of their host country. Most of these people were artisans or farmers who had reached a relatively high degree of prosperity, particularly in the Ukraine. In the towns, and especially in Moscow, there were a large number of Czech teachers, principally of Latin and Greek, whom the Tsarist government had brought to the country in the belief that a classical education would be an antidote to revolutionary ideas.[29] On August 4, 1914 (according to the western calendar), the Czechs in Moscow asked Sazonov for permission to raise volunteers to fight for the liberation of their country and held out the prospect of St Wenceslas's Crown being offered to the Tsar.[30] Sazonov had not forgotten similar possibilities suggested to him before the war by Klofáč, Kramář and other Czech politicians, and within a few days he obtained his colleagues' agreement in principle to the raising of a Czech volunteer force.[31] On August 20, talking to the French ambassador in Petrograd, Sazonov made a first reference to Entente war aims. Apart from the destruction of German military power and the aggregation to Russian Poland of the Central Powers' Polish territories, he suggested that these might include the liberation of Bohemia.[32]

Meanwhile a congress of Czechs living in Russia met in Petrograd and offered the Tsar the crown of the ancient kingdom of Bohemia. The Tsar must have considered the offer purely platonic, but immediately received the delegation that sought an audience with him. The Russian command formed the Czech volunteers into a so-called *družina*, which left for the front in October. However, Sazonov, when he received the committee appointed by the Czech congress, recommended caution on the question of St Wenceslas's Crown. In his opinion, it would not be advisable for an Orthodox prince to mount the throne of a Catholic country.[33]

He nevertheless promoted the launching of another manifesto on September 16, 1914, again signed by the Grand Duke Nikolai, addressed to 'all the peoples of Austria-Hungary'. One hundred thousand copies in nine languages were distributed at the time of

[81]

the big Russian advance on to Austro-Hungarian soil. 'Russia brings you liberty and the realization of your national aspirations,' it said, and it invited the Slavs and other nationalities subject to Austria-Hungary to receive fraternally the Russian troops who were fighting 'for the emancipation of the nations from the foreign yoke'.[34]

Later editions of the manifesto printed by the Russian propaganda services were adapted for clandestine distribution, and were illicitly introduced into Austria-Hungary besides being dropped from the air, and some impact was made on the Czechs, Ruthenians and Serbians serving in the Habsburg armies.[35] There were many Czechs among the huge mass of prisoners captured in the Russian advance, and a number of them promptly volunteered to serve with the Tsarist armies. But the Russian government hesitated to accept them, not so much because it was contrary to international law as because of the difficulty of establishing the genuineness of the many who hoped to escape from prisoner-of-war camps by this means. When Russian troops approached the Bohemian and Moravian frontiers, General Alexeyev, the Chief-of-Staff on the southern front, asked in a memorandum dated November 29 that another manifesto should be aimed specifically at the Czechs. He wanted the latter to be specifically informed about Russian war aims, to remove their fear that their country would remain a mere governorship under Russian rule, as it was now under Austrian rule; and he also asked that Czech and Slovak prisoners-of-war who were ready to fight on the Russian side should be organized in national regiments.[36] To Petrograd this proposal was excessively audacious. The question was revived by news of the desertion to the Russians of part of the 28th Prague Regiment (of which, incidentally, Victor Emmanuel III was honorary colonel), which apparently took place on April 3, 1915.[37] On April 13, the recently organized Association of Czech Clubs in Russia made another request for the setting up of a Czech legion, but this was again rejected by the Tsarist government, in which Sazonov alone supported the Czech cause. The *družine*, or companies of Czech volunteers, remained part of Russian regiments. At the beginning of May, the military situation was suddenly reversed by the Austro-German victory at Gorlice. The surviving Czech nucleus of the Austro-Hungarian 36th Regiment seems to have gone over to the enemy on May 27. After that, the Russian retreat made Czech desertions impossible until the next great Tsarist offensive in the summer of 1916.

In the diplomatic field also, the position of the Russian government in relation to Bohemia was at first anything but firm. Those Petrograd Ministers who were virtually in favour of a negotiated peace did not want to compromise future possibilities by irrevocable commitments to the Czechs. Thus, though Sazonov mentioned the liberation of Bohemia in his conversation on August 20 with Paléologue, the French ambassador, on September 14, in the deliberately still unofficial survey of possible war aims that he submitted to Paléologue and his British colleague Buchanan, he proposed the destruction of German supremacy and a series of territorial changes that would be justified by the nationality principle, but carefully refrained from deducing all the possible consequences in relation to the Danubian monarchy.

Sazonov said that his government expected to reunite western Galicia, Silesia and Poznan with Congress Poland. Serbia would be given Bosnia-Hercegovina, Dalmatia and northern Albania; Bulgaria would be compensated by Serbian concessions to her in Macedonia. According to Paléologue's telegram to his Foreign Minister, he said that 'Austria should form a triple monarchy, consisting of the Austrian empire, the kingdom of Bohemia and the kingdom of Hungary. The Austrian empire should include only the hereditary states. The kingdom of Bohemia should include present-day Bohemia and Moravia. Hungary should come to an understanding with Romania about Transylvania.'[38]

Sazonov insisted that this was merely an outline of possibilities which the Russians had not yet finally considered and worked out, but he obviously did not contemplate a break-up of Austria-Hungary. The Habsburg monarchy, after losing Galicia and Silesia in the north and Bosnia-Hercegovina and Dalmatia in the south, but reorganized internally on a basis acceptable to the Czechs and Romanians, and retaining its own great ports on the Adriatic, might actually have gained in cohesion what it lost in territory. Nor would the Czechs necessarily have regarded this as a breach of the Russian promise to free them from the foreign yoke because, if Bohemia and Moravia had been granted the degree of independence that Hungary had enjoyed since 1867, they would have been entitled to consider themselves masters in their own house.

In the autumn of 1914, very few Czechs indeed had come out definitely in favour of total national independence. The Croats who wanted such independence were even fewer. To them, Sazonov's scheme, if it had come to their knowledge, would have been a terrible disappointment because, with the detachment of Bosnia and Dalmatia, the Southern Slavs of the other Austro-Hungarian provinces would have been left in a position of reduced political strength.

The fact is that not even the government of Serbia, which, having been deliberately attacked by Austria-Hungary, had a maximum interest in seeing her total and irrevocable defeat, raised the question of the other Slav nationalities of the Danubian empire, apart from the annexation that it desired of some provinces inhabited wholly or in part by its co-nationals and co-religionists. Pašić, strong in the Serbian army's initial defensive success and suspecting that the question of territorial aims was in the air, telegraphed to his Minister in Petrograd on September 21, instructing him to inform Sazonov of the Serbian war aims. In addition to Bosnia-Hercegovina and Dalmatia, the Serbian government wanted two rich regions in southern Hungary, the Bačka and the Banat, as well as Gorizia and its surrounding district, and Istria in the Austrian part of the Habsburg monarchy, though it was willing to share the latter with Italy if she sided with Austria's enemies.[39] A week later, having got wind of the nature of possible Italian demands, Pašić again telegraphed to Petrograd, asking Sazonov not to promise Italy Dalmatia, to which Serbia believed herself entitled, though she was willing to leave Istria to Italy (and, as it remained unmentioned, presumably also Gorizia).[40] He referred to Croatia too in order to point out that if excessive concessions were made to Italy, the Serbo-Croats in Austria-Hungary would take the Austro-Hungarian side.

Pašić was naturally not unaware that, since the Bosnian crisis, some Croats, beginning with Supilo, had adopted the idea of dissociating themselves (and the Slovenians) from the state of which they had formed part for many centuries and of combining with the Serbs to form an independent Yugoslavia.[41] It is to be assumed that he knew that, in January 1913, under the impact of the first Balkan war, the most radical representatives of the Dalmatian Croats—J. Smodlaka and A. Trumbić, who were friends of Supilo—had met the political representatives of the Serbs of Bosnia-Hercegovina—N. Stojanović and A. Šola—at Spalato (Split) and had agreed, in the event of war between Vienna and Belgrade, to fight for Serbian and Yugoslav independence.[42] But, as can be deduced from his messages, the Serbian Prime Minister thought it unwise to complicate his basic claims with others more difficult to justify. The events that immediately followed the outbreak of war plainly revealed the feelings of the Serbs in Bosnia and southern Hungary, and Dalmatia was the natural area in which Serbia sought the access to the sea that Austria-Hungary stubbornly denied her, but Pašić of course had no right to act as spokesman for the aspirations of Croatia, the government of which, as the result of free elections to the Zagreb Diet, was in the hands of a coalition of Serbo-Croat parties which during the previous year had come to an agreement with Hungary and continued to co-operate loyally with her even after the declaration of war.

Supilo was little more than an isolated individual when he left his home in Fiume in the middle of July 1914 on the pretext of taking a holiday in South Tyrol, but in reality as a precaution, and went from Trent to Venice on July 26.[43] The outbreak of war made his exile permanent. Trumbić, and the great Dalmatian sculptor Ivan Meštrović arrived in Venice at about the same time; Meštrović, having recently returned from abroad convinced that war was imminent, had decided to emigrate to Italy, where he intended to remain, remembering the success of his 1911 exhibition in Rome.[44] 'Yugoslavia or nothing,' Supilo and Trumbić said to each other when they met in St Mark's Piazza.[45] They were joined in Venice by H. Hinković, who had acted as counsel for the defence at the Zagreb trial of 1909, and by a small number of compatriots and friends from Dalmatia. Gina Lombroso Ferrero, to whom Supilo wrote immediately, invited him to stay with her and her husband in Turin, but he replied that he preferred to remain in Venice, where it was easier to meet people coming from or going to Fiume.[46] Guglielmo Ferrero gave him an introduction to Antonio Fradeletto, the Radical deputy for Venice. We have no certain knowledge of his other contacts with Italians during those weeks.

In the latter part of September, Ljuba Mihajlović, the Serbian Minister to Italy, learned from the French embassy that, in the event of its intervention, the Italian government was proposing to claim Dalmatia, and he passed on the information to Meštrović, who had meanwhile settled in Rome. Meštrović immediately sent for Supilo and Trumbić, who reached the Italian capital on September 27. Meanwhile Supilo had written to Wickham Steed, the foreign editor of *The Times*, who had advised him to come to London.[48] Thanks to an introduction by the Serbian Minister, Meštrović, Supilo and Trumbić were received on the 28th by C. Barrère, the French ambassador, and the next day by Sir Rennel Rodd, the British ambassador, and A. Krupensky, the Russian ambassador. The Croatian exiles assured the Entente envoys of their desire to fight against Austria-Hungary and pointed out to them that the great majority of the population of their native Dalmatia was not Italian, but Slav.[49]

Of the three Entente representatives, Sir Rennel Rodd, who remembered the part played by Supilo in the Friedjung trial five years before, and who also knew the east coast of the Adriatic from his travels, was the only one to unbosom himself to his interlocutors. He gave them to understand that Italy was claiming Istria and Dalmatia, and said that, if the Croats wanted their rights to those provinces to be fully represented to the Entente, they should send a representative delegation to the West.[50] Barrère and Krupensky were cool and reserved, however, and confined themselves to listening to the three Croats.

The differences in attitude among the ambassadors of the three great powers certainly reflected, among other things, their personal temperaments. During the battle that raged over Italian intervention, Leonida Bissolati, the leader of the interventionist democratic left, wrote on March 21, 1915, to his brother-in-law, Luigi Campolonghi, the Paris correspondent of the Milan newspaper *Il Secolo*:

> Here I have been able to make use only of Rodd—the British ambassador, the only one of the three Entente ambassadors who immediately saw the utility of getting in touch with me. The other two simply might not exist. Barrère remains shut up in his *palazzo*, sees only one or two caryatids of the aristocratic world, is a sick man—and, moreover, is incapable of appreciating the responsibilities that devolve upon him at this hour. Krupensky is to be replaced—alas, how late![51]

Probably more important than personalities, however, was the fact that persuading the Italian government to intervene was a matter of life and death to France and Russia. Consequently, in spite of their long-standing goodwill towards Serbia, they had to satisfy Italian demands, if necessary at the expense of the Southern Slavs. To Britain this situation was less painful than to Russia, the natural protector of the Serbs in the negotiations with the Italian government, and she was able to look at the matter with greater detachment.

Also Krupensky, who interpreted his government's instructions too broadly, though in pursuit of its immediate aim, had already made extensive promises to Italy. Because of the vital part played by Luigi Albertini, the editor of the great Milan newspaper, the *Corriere della Sera*, in 1914–15 in influencing Italian public opinion towards intervention, we quote here a letter written to him on August 24, 1914, by Giovanni Amendola, his political correspondent in Rome, about a conversation he had had three days previously with the Russian ambassador:

> Some days ago I decided to try to find out exactly what point had been reached in regard to us.
> Barrère had talked to me in general terms about Franco-British goodwill towards Italy. This was too little and too vague. In relation to the Adriatic, the greatest obstacles could not come from Britain and France, but from Russia, which might have plans favouring Serbia. I therefore called on Krupensky, and had the

good fortune to be received by him immediately after he had seen Witte, and I talked at length with him. Was Witte here in Rome on a political mission? There are some who say so and others who deny it. At all events, if he was, what Krupensky said to me undoubtedly reflected what he may have heard from Witte. He talked to me in the strictest confidence; he told me that if I made our conversation public, he would repudiate it in the most categorical fashion; his purpose was purely to provide information to enable the chief organ of Italian public opinion to form a view.

First of all, I asked him what were the limits to the support that Russia would give Serbia in the Adriatic. He replied that Russian support extended to her obtaining an outlet to the sea adequate to her commercial needs, but was not intended to enable her to become an important naval power. I then asked him about the position that Italy might have in the Adriatic. He replied: 'If you enter the war now, you will be able to be the *Masters of the Adriatic*. You will be able to establish yourselves in Dalmatia, apart from the Serbian outlet to the sea. You will also be able to secure possession of Valona. All this, of course, in addition to the Trentino and Istria.' With regard to Valona, I gathered there was only one reservation, namely that Greece would be allowed to extend her coast-line to the north of it. Valona would become an Italian Gibraltar in Greek territory.

Finally I asked him whether the coalition powers would be willing to undertake to sign a peace treaty only when Italy signed it. He said that that seemed to him to be a very reasonable stipulation, and he could not believe that Russia, France and Britain would refuse it.

After seeing Krupensky, I wanted to get confirmation of what he had told me. I went to see Cav. Biancheri, San Giuliano's private secretary, from whom I have often had very secret information, and I told him what I believed I knew about proposals that had been made to Italy to recompense her for armed intervention on the Entente side. *He confirmed the existence and nature of these offers.* I then asked him why on earth the negotiations were not leading to any results. He replied that that *depended on us*—that we were in no hurry.

That statement, together with innumerable signs in the political atmosphere, makes me certain of one thing: that Italy remains undecided (I do not say *inactive*, because a decision would not necessarily imply immediate action), not because objectives worthy of action are denied her, but because of the state of mind, the views, and the mental reservations of her statement. The objectives that are offered us exceed what it was legitimate to hope for,

[87]

as we shall be given the opportunity not only to solve our national problems to the east and the question of our natural boundaries in the east, but also to prevent another naval power from taking the place of Austria-Hungary on the opposite shore. Mastery of the Adriatic, with the key of Valona in our hands, would lead to a strengthening of our position in the Mediterranean, for from Valona and Tobruk we should control one of the world's great sea routes.

Krupensky said to me: 'But you must intervene quickly. Today we need you; today you would bring us, not only your military aid, but also a political influence that might be decisive with regard to Romania and for the re-establishment of the Balkan League. The quicker you enter the war, the more generously will the terms on which we shall agree be later interpreted in your favour.'

Nevertheless everything points to the conclusion that we are in no hurry to come to any decision. Why?[52]

Albertini and Amendola were among the first important Italian journalists to appreciate the complexity of the Adriatic question. Amendola plunged resolutely into the heated controversy with a political despatch from Rome on 'The Adriatic Problem and Italy' in the *Corriere della Sera* of October 6, 1914. It reflected the line which his editor had decided on, as is evident from his correspondence. Some articles, obviously written by Wickham Steed, an old friend of Albertini's, had appeared in *The Times*, calling on Italy to fulfil the mission of the Risorgimento and complete the task of achieving her national unity in defiance of Austria-Hungary, but simultaneously warning her that she would be ill-advised in such an eventually to embark on annexations of Istrian or Dalmatian territory inhabited by Yugoslavs. To this, the Rome correspondent of the *Corriere* replied that 'the ideas put forward by *The Times* on the relations between Italians and Slavs on the Adriatic coast are the well-known ideas of Mr Steed, a publicist who has studied the problems of the Danubian monarchy with seriousness and acumen, but has come to conclusions with regard to the Southern Slavs which will meet with much disagreement in Italy.' In spite of Steed's criticisms, there was no question in Amendola's mind but that Trieste and Istria should pass to Italy if Austria were no longer able to hold them. He added, however, that 'there would be room for discussion, we admit, about Dalmatia'. After enumerating strategic, political and cultural reasons for an Italian presence on the east coast of the Adriatic, he added that, when the 'Yugoslav state' that Steed desired came into being, it would be in the interests of everybody for its relations with Italy to be those of 'permanent tranquillity'. But that would be impossible if Italy failed to observe solid guarantees for her security, so that that she would no longer have to fear such attacks either by land or sea on her eastern frontier and coastline as she had always had to fear with Austria-Hungary intact. In conclusion, and here he agreed with Steed, he said that the Adriatic problem depended on the fate of the Habsburg empire. Unlike Steed, however, he regarded as premature the debate that Steed wanted to open in order to establish the case of his Yugoslav friends.

Supilo seemed to have better fortune with Izvolsky, the Russian ambassador to France. From Rome he went to Marseilles, where he had a friend in the Russian Consul-General, A. Salviati, who had earlier been in charge of the consulate at Fiume. Salviati gave him an introduction to Izvolsky, who on October 5 received him at Bordeaux, the temporary seat of the French government and the diplomatic corps. To the Tsarist ex-Foreign Minister, who had never forgiven the annexation of Bosnia-Hercegovina and the trap into which he believed he had then been led by Aehrenthal, the dismemberment of Austria-Hungary by means of the emancipation and unification of the Yugoslavs was exactly what was wanted. He therefore arranged for Supilo to be received by Delcassé, the French Foreign Minister.[53]

Izvolsky's message to Sazonov of October 13 raised the question of the dissolution of Austria-Hungary for the first time in all its amplitude.[54] He had discussed with Delcassé the territorial reorganization that would result from an Entente victory. Apart from the restoration to France of Alsace-Lorraine, the French Foreign Minister had in mind the permanent weakening of Germany by depriving her of certain regions, the acquisition by Britain of the German colonies, and the full satisfaction of Russian claims. As for the future of the dual monarchy, Delcassé was more reserved. In Izvolsky's opinion:

> In spite of Delcassé's assurances to the contrary, certain undoubted French sympathies for Austria-Hungary must be borne in mind. They are based on the totally erroneous view of an Austria that would try to emancipate herself from Germany and had rendered services to France at Algeciras. Similar sympathies exist to an even greater extent in Britain.

Izvolsky therefore thought it important that Russia's position on this matter should be defined and her allies informed. He continued:

> When speaking in my own name I neglect no opportunity of emphasizing here that an end must be put to the Habsburg monarchy, which is a total anachronism, and that the peoples who

[89]

form part of it, with the exception of the Poles, must be educated to independent political life.[55]

Izvolsky was too intelligent not to see that the exclusion of the Poles —that is to say, the nation best known to the West and the most highly regarded because of its past struggles for liberty—from the peoples who were to acquire or re-acquire independence would make acceptance of the policy he advocated more difficult than it was already. It can therefore be assumed that Supilo's appearance on the scene gave him a splendid opportunity to play the Yugoslav card in a game in which the Polish card might have been used against Russia. His message to Sazonov went on:

> One of these problems, and perhaps the most important, is the future of the kingdom of Serbia. I am trying here to spread the idea of a strong Serbo-Croat state, including Istria and Dalmatia, as a necessary counterweight to Italy, Hungary and Romania. To that end, I have introduced to Delcassé the well-known Serbo-Croat politician and former deputy to the Hungarian parliament, Supilo, who has arrived here and is a zealous advocate of this idea.[56]

The opinion that Asquith, the British Prime Minister, formed of Supilo when he met him a few weeks later was, according to Count Sforza, that he was a 'force of nature', and that explains the impact Supilo made on Izvolsky.[57] Russia might be interested in the break-up of Austria-Hungary, but the immediate task was to prevent the Central Powers from winning the war. As the Russian ambassadors well knew, the Petrograd government, like its allies, was doing everything in its power during that period of anxiety on the various fronts to draw into the Entente camp the two states that either formed part of the Triple Alliance or had been connected with it but had nevertheless declared their neutrality. That is to say, Italy and Romania, against whose future influence in central eastern Europe, Izvolsky, evidently influenced by Supilo (who was concerned to prevent the cession to Italy of his native Dalmatia and Istria—it was no accident that these were separately mentioned in Izvolsky's report, which merely implied the other Serbian territorial claims), thought he could erect a bulwark in the form of the future Yugoslavia. His concern with finding a counterweight for a future independent Hungary may well have been planted in his mind by Supilo. The Hungarians, once detached from Austria, would obviously have far graver territorial conflicts with the Romanians than with the Russians, and it was hard to conceive that the two could become friends and allies. Meanwhile, Croatia was under Hungarian sovereignty, from which it could free itself only if Hungary were weakened.

[90]

Strangely enough, the idea of playing the card of the traditional Hungarian independence movement arose at that very moment. At the beginning of October, Kudashev, the head of the diplomatic office at the Tsarist general-headquarters, informed Sazonov that the Magyar troops were dismayed by the Russian advance and worried about the possibility of their country's being invaded from the east by the Romanians; their state of mind suggested that, if they were given an assurance that the Russians would not cross the Carpathians, they might withdraw behind that mountain chain, which protected their country, without orders from the Austro-Hungarian High Command. General Yanuskievich, the Chief of the General Staff, therefore wished to know whether he would be authorized to treat with any Hungarian officers who might possibly bring him proposals of the sort.[58] Sazonov withheld authorization. He feared that such Magyar emissaries might not be in a position to commit their colleagues, and that conversations with them would merely have a detrimental effect on the negotiations in progress with the Romanians, to whom Transylvania had already been promised as an inducement to declare war on the Central Powers; also, Russia would be deprived of freedom of action in relation to the Slav nationalities of the kingdom of Hungary, and without the certainty of any substantial recompense.[59] Six weeks later, Sazonov was again faced with the question as a result of information originating with neutral diplomats and reports from a Russian army corps commander reiterating that discontent was increasing among the Magyars: their best troops had been sacrificed in Galicia and Serbia without adequate supplies and arms and with unsound operational orders, for all of which they held the Austrian command responsible. Thus, when the British Foreign Ministry informed the Russians in January 1915 that an influential member of the Hungarian opposition 'has made certain proposals for a separate peace with Hungary', Sazonov, though reiterating his objections, was willing to admit that it would be unwise to discourage the Hungarians. He therefore suggested that it should be made known to them 'that the Entente powers are prepared for the desires for independence of the Hungarian people and, if the latter succeeded in proclaiming its independence, they would listen benevolently to any proposals made by the Budapest government'.[60] Approaching the enemies of the Central Powers was, of course, the last thing that would have occurred to the Hungarian government in power, which consisted of men who, like their leader Tisza, were the soul of loyalty to Francis Joseph and their German ally. Feelers at most could have come from their most violent opponents, or from persons who represented only themselves. Whichever they were, and

[91]

whether they failed openly to reveal themselves because they could not or because they would not, the Croatian exiles, few though they were, offered something more solid to work on.

Supilo, after going to London, saw Izvolsky again in November 1914, bringing with him, among other things, a memorandum by Masaryk on conditions in Bohemia. This gave the Tsarist ambassador the idea of asking both Supilo and Salviati to draw up memoranda on the Yugoslavs, and when he received these, he supplied copies to Delcassé.[61]

Salviati's memoranda gave statistical details about the Southern Slavs, analysed their political parties in detail, and concluded by recommending the establishment of an independent Yugoslavia, though with the retention by Hungary of guaranteed access to the sea through what would become the Free Port of Fiume. Supilo's memoranda, only too animated by nationalist fervour, claimed that all the Austro-Hungarian territories inhabited to a sufficient extent by Serbs, Croats and Slovenes, from southern Carinthia to the Banat, from Gorizia to Istria and Dalmatia, should be included in the state, that was to arise from the unification of Croatia-Slavonia, Slovenia and Bosnia-Hercegovina with Serbia and Montenegro. He admitted that a Yugoslav state embracing all that territory would, according to the statistics he used, include about 1,300,000 Italians, Germans, Magyars and Romanians, but he justified that by the impossibility, in view of the many ethnically mixed areas, of otherwise ensuring the independence of all the 12,700,000 Yugoslavs.[62] He recognized the undoubted Italian majority in Trieste, though he emphasized the Slav character of the city's surroundings, and asked that it should be made a Free City.[63]

In backing Supilo's memoranda, at any rate to the extent of forwarding them to Delcassé, Izvolsky probably did not realize that acceptance of the proposals, apart from disappointing Romania, which claimed the Banat, would have made Italian intervention on the allied side impossible. The Vienna government itself ended by offering Italy more (in the Gorizia area) than the Yugoslav agitator was willing to grant her. Izvolsky must have realized this barely three months later, when he had to transmit to his government the insistent appeals of Delcassé, who had taken alarm at the information he had received about Bülow's promises, that the Italian demands should be accepted immediately.[64]

Supilo's first stay in London, from the middle of October to the middle of November 1914, made him excessively optimistic. Thanks to Steed and Seton-Watson, he quickly saw Sir William Tyrrell, private secretary to Sir Edward Grey and Sir Arthur Nicolson, the

Permanent Secretary at the Foreign Office, and subsequently he also saw Lloyd George.[65] The instinctive political talent that, according to Steed's character sketch of him (which erroneously dates his stay in London as September 1914), resided in Supilo's big, robust peasant's body, his dignity, his frankness, and above all his firm confidence in an Entente victory, won him the esteem of British diplomats and politicians.[66] His political attitude is fully stated in the letter he wrote from London on October 20 to Pašić, the Serbian Prime Minister, to encourage him to pursue the objective of Yugoslav unity. Supilo made no concealment of the depth of the conflict with Italy that would ensue from the proclamation of this objective, but he believed that in spite of it a community of interests between Italians and Yugoslavs would emerge in opposition to the Teutonic domination of the Adriatic, from which both parties had everything to fear.[67] That, however, was a question for the future. Of more immediate consequence, in spite of appearances to the contrary, was the fact that he was in London in the second half of October when Masaryk, who had been his ally in the political struggle against the dominant caste in Austria-Hungary, met Seton-Watson in Rotterdam. Seton-Watson had become Steed's closest colleague on Slav questions, and he went to Rotterdam on Steed's behalf as well as on his own. He had two days of intense conversation with Masaryk, who was able to give him full information about the situation in Austria-Hungary after two and a half months of war as seen by a Czech parliamentarian who had many contacts with representatives of the other centrifugal nationalities.[68]

During the first few weeks of the war, Masaryk had noted that Czech conscripts had no desire to spill their blood fighting their Russian fellow-Slavs. Several battalions had left Prague singing 'I've got to fight the Russians, but I don't know why'.[69] After hearing about the first, still small-scale and sporadic Czech desertions on the Russian front, he had become convinced that the national struggle would end by assuming revolutionary characteristics, and that it must be conducted with resolution. The imprisonment for an indefinite period of his Reichsrat colleague Klofáč and of a number of Serbo-Croat deputies confirmed the frailty of the judicial guarantees enjoyed by the Slavs in Austria, including those who should have been protected by their parliamentary mandate, and reinforced both his pessimism and his determination. At the end of August, through Voška, an American citizen of Bohemian origin and proprietor of a Czech-language newspaper in New York who was returning from Prague to the United States by way of London, Masaryk had sent Steed information about political, financial and military conditions in Austria-Hungary, asking him to forward it to Lord Kitchener, the War Minister, and to the Russian embassy, and to take the opportunity of asking the Russians to give a friendly reception to Czech deserters.[70] Masaryk was perfectly well aware that in taking this step he exposed himself to a possible charge of high treason. As a progressive democrat, he disliked the Tsarist government, but he believed that anyone who wished to help the Entente to the victory from which the liberation of the Czechoslovak nation was to be expected, could not avoid contacts with the representatives of Russia.

Steed and Voška passed on his message to Benckendorff, the Russian ambassador, who was very willing to receive it, as he, Izvolsky and Sazonov formed a trio of Russian diplomatists who were resolutely anti-German and anti-Austrian.[71] Through this channel, Masaryk was told that Czech deserters should reveal their identity by singing the popular song *Hej Slovene!* The distinguished historian Sir Bernard Pares, who was an observer on the Russian front in 1914–15, later told Steed that he had often heard prisoners singing that song, and had never understood why the Russian command permitted it, as the tune was that of the Polish national anthem which was normally forbidden under the Tsarist régime.[72] It would seem from the Austro-Hungarian military records that the first desertions took place at the end of September 1914, when small groups belonging to the 26th Division of the Bohemian Territorial Militia went over to the enemy lines. On October 20, six companies of Czechs belonging to the 36th Infantry Regiment were alleged to have surrendered to the Russians.[73]

In spite of the state of war, Masaryk, as a member of the Reichsrat, possessed a passport valid for neutral countries, and on September 12 he went to Holland on the pretext of accompanying his sister-in-law, an American citizen, who was returning to the United States, to the port of embarkation. From there he wrote to Steed as well as to Professor Denis, the great French scholar in Czech history.[74] As he received no reply from Steed, who was away from London, he wrote to Seton-Watson; he had read a letter which the latter had written to *The Times* inspired by what Supilo had written to him from Italy in defence of the Yugoslav cause.[75] Masaryk had left Holland before Seton-Watson received the letter, but he returned to Rotterdam on October 14, and the conversation then took place.

The more radical of the two at that time was Seton-Watson, who already advocated the principle of unlimited self-determination for all nations, young and old. Whereas Masaryk had left Prague, to which he proposed to return, holding the pre-war view that only nations which had existed historically had a right to independence.[76] At the end of their conversations, Masaryk outlined a programme that Seton-Watson drafted as a memorandum. This was submitted by Steed to the British and French Foreign Ministers, by Professor Vinogradov to Sazonov, and by Supilo to Izvolsky.[77]

At that time, Masaryk still considered complete independence a maximum demand. He believed that if the future Bohemian state was to be viable, it would have to include the whole of Slovakia, including its ethnically Magyar zones, as well as the Sudeten provinces that were inhabited by Germans but were surrounded by Czech territory. He also believed that it should have a common frontier with Russia, which, he thought, would annex the sub-Carpathian Ukraine, which belonged to Hungary. He suggested that a Danish or Belgian prince, not a Russian grand duke, should be made King of Bohemia. Using a rather specious argument because of his desire not to insist on the political motivation of his mistrust of Tsarism, he said that a Russian grand duke would irritate the three or four million Germans who would pass under Czech sovereignty.[78]

As is known, of course, in 1919 the Czechoslovak Republic, taking advantage of the weakness of revolutionary Russia, in fact absorbed the Ruthenians of the sub-Carpathian Ukraine. But, even apart from that, the inclusion for historical, geographical, strategic and economic reasons of the three million Germans mentioned above, and of just under a million Magyars which Masaryk's programme demanded, violated the principle of self-determination. Convinced as they were of the Germans' and Hungarians' war guilt and of their incorrigible desire for domination or revenge, Steed and Seton-Watson overlooked the inconsistency at the time. Had they pointed it out, Masaryk would have been able to reply that without those frontiers Czechoslovakia could not emerge as an independent state. Rather than renounce the historical frontiers of Bohemia and the geographical frontiers of Slovakia, the Czechs and Slovaks would have preferred the federalism under the old Danubian monarchy that he had himself advocated up to the outbreak of war. Professor Denis was more cautious than his British colleagues. When he wrote to Masaryk on October 31, inviting both him and Supilo to Paris, he advised him to confine himself to calling for the transformation of Austria-Hungary into a confederation of administratively autonomous nations (including Bohemia, Moravia and Slovakia on the one hand and the Yugoslav regions on the other).[79]

Another man who in the first few weeks of the war did not envisage the destruction of Austria-Hungary was the Italian historian Gaetano Salvemini. Writing about the struggle between Austria and Serbia in *Unità* at the beginning of August, he sided with Serbia, saying that, because of the democratic nature of the Yugoslav national movement he did not fear she would be reduced to being a mere tool of Russia. In his view, defeat of the Habsburg monarchy should result in the transfer to Italy of the Trentino, Trieste and the towns or townships of Istria, and he regarded it as inevitable that Dalmatia, whose minute Italian enclaves would in any case not long survive the pressure of the vast Slav majority, would form part of a 'greater Serbia'. Although he thought that victory for the Central Powers would be disastrous, for they would reduce Italy to vassalage, he nevertheless believed that a break-up, or even an excessive weakening, of Austria-Hungary would be dangerous. Even without the Italian provinces, Dalmatia, Bosnia, Croatia (the unification of which with Serbia he approved of), Transylvania (which he believed should go to Romania), and Galicia (which should be transferred to a reunited independent Poland), he believed that the Danubian monarchy could exercise a useful balancing function, containing the conflicting drives of Germany and Russia towards the Adriatic and the Balkans.[80] Four months later, Salvemini reiterated this opinion, hoping that the war would result in a reduction of the population of Austria-Hungary from more than fifty million to about thirty.[81]

Italy however was not to enter the war, and face all the risks and accept all the sacrifices that she subsequently faced, only for the sake of Trent, Gorizia (which Austria would have offered her—on terms thought acceptable by Giolitti—in exchange for her neutrality) and Trieste (the possibility of which becoming a Free City was eventually not excluded by Austria); nor was Romania to do so for Transylvania alone. On the other hand, but for the Italian and Romanian intervention, Austria-Hungary would have been able to hold out against her enemies, with the result that Germany would have been able to concentrate all her strength on winning the war in the west. Thus, Italy intervened either for the specific and deliberate purpose of destroying the Habsburg empire, or in order to obtain territorial acquisitions far greater than any the Vienna government would offer her.

The Romanian government, which had ambitious territorial aims in Hungary, extending far beyond Transylvania, as well as in Bukovina, and was unembarrassed by any feelings of genuine respect for the nationality principle, which it regarded merely as a tool, having discarded the idea of remaining loyal to its alliance with the Central Powers, was well aware of the far-reaching consequences of the decision with which it was faced; it intended making war on the Central Powers only if it could be sure that an Entente victory would reduce Hungary to such small proportions as to make it impossible for her to try to regain what she had lost. Otherwise, as it did not fail to whisper into the ear of Berlin while negotiating with the Entente, its interest was to seek compensation from Germany, which was willing to promise it Bessarabia at Russia's expense and also to put pressure on Austria-Hungary to persuade it to yield a part of Bukovina and to give some political satisfaction to the Romanians in Transylvania. Thus, on September 14, 1914, Baron Fasciotti, the Italian Minister plenipotentiary in Bucharest, was able to report to the Marquis di San Giuliano that Brătianu, the Romanian Prime Minister, had said to him that 'the best thing would be for Italy and Romania to set about the liquidation of Austria-Hungary (if liquidation there must be) in their favour'.[82] The Italian Foreign Minister's reply authorized secret conversations with the Romanian government, but avoided going into the question of the future of the Habsburg empire. We know that neither San Giuliano nor his successor, Sonnino, believed that such a large-scale liquidation of the Habsburg monarchy would be in the Italian interest. In any case, before it entered the war, the Romanian government waited for a time when the intervention of fresh forces on its side was so vital to the Entente that its governments would accept its maximum claims without stopping to consider how they would be able to implement them.

Salvemini had no sympathy with nationalist annexationist aims, as he made clear in regard to Romanian nationalism in the first place, but he would not have hesitated to abandon his concern for the maintenance of a balance of power and to champion the right of self-determination of the nations if it formed an integral part of a democratic reorganization of Europe. On August 28, he stated that he wanted intervention, both for the sake of Italian national aims and in order to overthrow the militarist and imperialist Hohenzollern and Habsburg dynasties and bring about the democratization of Germany and Austria, which, in his view, would cease to be a constant threat to the peace of Europe only if they were so democratized.[83]

The attitude towards the war of Leonida Bissolati, the leader of the small but influential reformist group which seceded from the Socialist Party in 1912, was identical with that of Salvemini, his long-standing friend. In the middle of November 1914, he openly advocated Italian intervention, which, he said, should take place in such a way as to enable 'Italy to appear in the eyes of the Balkan peoples as the sincere and disinterested supporter of the nationality principle', disclaiming Dalmatia for herself. But he too hesitated before drawing conclusions about the future of Austria-Hungary.[84]

The first Italian to declare that the Austrian empire should be

[97]

liquidated was Cesare Battisti, a socialist deputy for the Trentino who took refuge in Italy immediately after the outbreak of war. The socialist organ, *Avanti!*, on September 14 printed an 'open letter' to its editor, Benito Mussolini, signed by 'a refugee from the Trentino', explaining the reasons why that area 'insists on separation from Austria'. The author of the letter was Battisti. This is not the place to recall the dispute he had a few weeks later with Mussolini which contributed to hasten the latter's conversion to interventionism. What concerns us in this context is that when Oddino Morgari, the secretary of the Socialist parliamentary group, said at a meeting that the Trentino and specially Trieste, where economic conditions were good, were not worth 'redeeming' at the cost of war, Battisti dropped his anonymity and wrote another open letter, this time longer and more explicit, published by *La Stampa* of Turin on September 27. 'Austria,' he wrote, 'lives by maltreating and denying the nations.'[85] Why not democratize and revolutionize her? he asked. 'The Austrian socialists have tried, but have not succeeded. The domestic struggle has showed itself to be vain. Because of national differences and the complex of other economic and social dissonances, it is impossible to coalesce all the forces necessary to strike down the old Austria. This is the view of a socialist who agreed to co-operate with all the other socialists in Austria in the task of regenerating the state on a democratic basis, and has been forced to the conclusion that the best will in the world and the most complete good faith on the part of the socialist representatives of all nationalities have not sufficed and do not suffice for this purpose,' so much so that, after threatening to make war on Serbia in 1912–13, the Vienna government had been able to declare war on her in 1914 without taking any notice of parliament.[86] Battisti concluded by saying that anyone who did not believe that Austria would disintegrate as a result of the war did not know her.

Battisti's passionate irredentism caused him to believe that what he ardently desired was already true. The majority of his Tridentine compatriots, as represented by the Catholic Party, which was Italian but not irredentist, did not yet think as he did, though they came round to his point of view in 1918. The same can be said of the Austrian socialists as a whole. Although animated by motives different from those of Battisti—that is to say, by international Marxism instead of irredentism of the Risorgimento type—Friedrich Adler, the organizing secretary of the Austrian Social Democratic Party, took the view, according to what he said at his trial for the assassination of Count Stürgkh in 1917, that, in spite of universal suffrage, the Austrian government had shown by the way it declared war, that the Habsburg monarchy was still autocratic. In the manifesto of the

Austrian internationalists published in socialist newspapers abroad at the end of 1915, Adler denounced (as bitterly as Battisti had done the previous year) the existence in Austria-Hungary of a despotism no better than that of the Tsars.[87] Though this was an obvious exaggeration, it does not alter the fact that these feelings were destined to spread as a result of the sufferings and passions to which the Habsburg government had opened the gates by its recklessness in unleashing the conflict.

Although Battisti did not exactly reflect the present, he had an inkling of the future when he said in an interventionist speech at Bologna on October 13, 1914, that Austria had been able to last so long only because the 'peoples without a history' had been asleep. But now they had awakened. 'National consciousness has been awakened in them too, and with it the irredentist spirit has vibrantly emerged.'[88] The Croats, like the Italians of the Trentino and Venezia Giulia who had been sent to Galicia in the ranks of the Austrian army to die fighting an enemy that was not theirs, were, in Battisti's view, bound to detest the power that had made them fight against their 'blood brothers'.

Battisti's attitude certainly influenced Salvemini, who was an old friend, and Bissolati also; and some English writings worked in the same direction, particularly on Salvemini. On January 29, 1915, Salvemini's journal, *Unità*, published a long article by G. M. Trevelyan on 'Post-War Europe'. In it, the distinguished historian of Garibaldi supported the Italian claims to Trent and Trieste and advocated the establishment of an independent Yugoslavia, to include Serbia and all the Austro-Hungarian territories inhabited by Southern Slavs, whose democratic outlook he emphasized on the basis of his own personal knowledge of them. A fortnight later *Unità* reprinted in full a pamphlet by another British historian, Ramsay Muir, on 'The National Principle and the War'. His ideas were similar to those of Seton-Watson, to whose journal he was to contribute in 1916; he advocated Czech and Yugoslav independence, the accession to Italy and Romania of territories inhabited by Italians and Romanians, and, in short, the right to self-determination of all the nations of Austria-Hungary, including the right of the German Austrians to join a democratized Germany.[89] In April, *Unità* summarized the chapters on the Danubian monarchy contributed by Seton-Watson to a book by various authors published in London at the end of 1914.[90] Seton-Watson must have written his contribution at the latest at the beginning of November, because in the second half of that month he arrived in Rome with G. M. Trevelyan. After calling on Trumbić and Meštrović and giving them news of Supilo, they

[99]

went on to the Balkans on a Foreign Office mission, from which they returned only in February.[91] The book entitled *War and Democracy*, quoted a phrase of Mazzini's on the need to redraw the map of Europe in conformity with the mission and the geographical, ethnic and historical conditions of the various peoples.[92]

In his contribution, Seton-Watson said he had long believed in the utility of Austria-Hungary because of its balancing function in Europe and because it was a place of peaceful cohabitation by different nationalities that for centuries had mingled in the same territorial area. The mission of the Habsburgs had been to hold their peoples together on a basis of equity, but this they had betrayed by abandoning the Slavs and Romanians of Hungary, Transylvania and Croatia to oppression by the Hungarian oligarchy (which the author, not without obvious exaggeration, denounced as the 'evil genius of Austria'), and now by the aggression on Serbia. If Austria lost the war, as Seton-Watson hopefully foresaw, inasmuch as that would also ensure the defeat of Germany, its dissolution was inevitable. It could be saved only by a compromise peace, but Seton-Watson opposed the supporters of such a peace, who were numerous among the British ruling class, on the ground that a stalemate would merely be the prelude to another war.[93] As for Hungary, Seton-Watson observed that on paper it had a very admirable and enlightened nationality law which, however, had been a dead letter for forty-six years, the Hungarian practice being to deprive the non-Magyar masses of political, and also to a large extent, of their educational, rights. Hungary should be given the right to choose between unification with Austria and independence (just as German Austria, in Seton-Watson's view, should have the right to choose between union with Hungary or union with Germany), but would have to be reduced to the purely Magyar provinces. The principal beneficiaries of the change would be the Magyar peasants, for the revolution of the oppressed nationalities, implying democracy and agrarian reform in the new states, would liberate them from exploitation by the Magyar oligarchy as a result of the break up of the latifundia.[94]

While an Austro-Hungarian victory would mean the end of independent Serbia, her defeat would bring about the reunification of all the Southern Slavs into an independent state. Yugoslav, Czechoslovak and Polish independence, and the separation from Austria of the irredentist Romanians and Italians, particularly the latter, which would deprive her of the ports of Trieste and Pola, would seal the dissolution of the Habsburg empire.[95]

Salvemini, returning to the theme in *Unità* of March 12, said he had overcome his previous doubts and become convinced that 'the destruction of Austria is the only guarantee that the Triple Alliance, in the event of victory, can have against the resumption of war by Germany'. Austria-Hungary, being the weakest link in the chain, was the point at which the Central Powers could be most easily defeated. Germany, even if defeated, would not cease to be potentially very powerful, and disarmament could not be imposed on her indefinitely. On her south-eastern frontiers, therefore, she must not be allowed to have as a neighbour another empire that shared her aspirations for revenge, but must have states opposed to the latter. The defeat of Austria-Hungary, the interventionist Salvemini continued, would of course mean the 'annexation to Italy of Venezia Giulia, the Quarnero (Kvarner) islands and the Zara peninsula'.[96] The editor of *Unità* was also concerned about Fiume, which the British publicists tacitly assigned to the future Yugoslavia. Salvemini, however, claimed that 'Fiume should be re-established in its traditional autonomy under the joint guarantee of Italy and Serbia, or added to Italy, according to what the majority of its citizens decided by plebiscite'.[97]

Neither Trumbić, who remained in Rome until the end of April 1915, nor Supilo, who returned to Italy at the end of November and again in January, made contact with Salvemini, Battisti or Bissolati during this period, though they had some contact with two officials of the Foreign Ministry; Supilo with an unindentified Italian diplomatist and Trumbić with the consul Carlo Galli. The latter had been sent to Trieste by Sonnino on an information-gathering mission, and in January he met the Italian irredentist leaders as well as such representatives of the Slovene parties as O. Rybař, a Reichsrat deputy, J. Vilfan, a future deputy to the Italian Chamber, and the lawyer J. Mandić, who travelled backwards and forwards between Rome and Trieste and kept Trumbić informed about the situation. On his return to Rome, Galli himself expressed a wish to meet Trumbić.[98]

Supilo, writing from Florence, where he spent a few days, wrote to Gina Lombroso Ferrero on November 28, 1914:

I have understood the government situation from his letter. But the Italians are known as a nation—as a people of good sense, commonsense, and I hope it will be possible to do a great and fine work that will last for centuries. The Adriatic must be our field of understanding against the common enemy, never a field of battle or of poisonous hatreds. That is my *idée fixe*—not dating just from today. . . . I have not been able to see from Guglielmo's articles how he sees things in detail, but in general he thinks as I do and we agree on many things.[99]

Guglielmo Ferrero in his newspaper articles did not hesitate to argue the necessity of agreement with the Yugoslavs, which would be possible only if Italy refrained from claiming Dalmatia, which had belonged to Venice in the past, but was now Slavonic. Even if it were granted to Italy by treaty, the historian said, she would not have the authority to hold it that only popular consent could give; and it was dangerous to have more strength than authority based on consent.[100]

But this voice like those of Salvemini and Bissolati himself, was a dissentient one without influence on Italian diplomacy. Salvemini later regretted that Bissolati and Amendola did not publicly campaign against the claim to Dalmatia at that time. Up to May 1915, the cause of interventionism was by no means secure, and they were afraid of weakening and blunting it against the strong forces of neutralism in parliament and in the country. Sonnino, not believing in the end of the Habsburg monarchy on which he was preparing to make war, did not think it necessary to worry about future relations with the Southern Slavs, whom he regarded as enemies of Italy in any case. Significantly, however, the consul Galli, who had informed himself on the eastern Adriatic question at Trieste, where he had lived from 1905 to 1911, came to the conclusion that an Italo-Yugoslav agreement was necessary and possible. According to his diary, he suggested this to Sonnino in a report dated February 15, 1915, in which he said that the Yugoslavs might side with Italy if she went to war with Austria, and would resign themselves to the accession to Italy of Trieste and Istria provided the Rome government gave them assurances about Dalmatia.[101]

In Galli's opinion, 'encouraging the extreme nationalism' of those who claimed Dalmatia for Italy would be an 'unpardonable' error. He himself was 'very much tied to nationalism', but examination of the situation on the spot had convinced him that on the question of the ethnical composition of the Dalmatian population 'Salvemini unfortunately was right'.[102] Sonnino left Galli's reports unanswered and sent him no instructions, with the result that he decided that it was his duty to break off his contacts with Trumbić, who continued supporting the Slav claims to Istria but seemed willing to reach a compromise with Italy, being well aware that without Italian intervention the Habsburg empire would retain the disputed territories.[103]

For lack of any understanding with the Rome government, by which it was deliberately ignored, the Yugoslav movement made the mistake of putting polemics against the Italian claims, including those to the indisputably Italian towns of Istria, on a par with propaganda against Austria-Hungary.

[102]

Trumbić and Meštrovič approached Pašić with a view to persuading him to send to Italy a Serbian delegation with whom the Croat exiles proposed to form a Yugoslav committee.[104] The Serbian Prime Minister sent two Bosnian refugees, N. Stojanović and D. Vasiljević, who conferred in Florence with Trumbić and Supilo on November 22–25. Stojanovič brought a message from Pašić, who took the view that his government already represented all Serbs, whether liberated or not, and he advised the refugees to set up a committee for the sole purpose of advocating the separation of Croatia from the Austro-Hungarian monarchy and its unification with Serbia. Use of the term 'Yugoslav' seemed to him to be premature. The meeting decided to set about forming a Serbo-Croat committee with headquarters in London as an organ of Yugoslav propaganda.[105] Two days later, Trumbić urgently summoned Supilo and Stojanović, who had remained in Florence, to Rome. Meštrović had learned from the British ambassador that Italy had decided to claim Dalmatia.[106]

The refugees found a single friend in the diplomatic circles of the Italian capital with the arrival there on a propaganda mission of the French publicist Charles Loiseau, whom Barrère, the French ambassador, charged with following Croatian affairs, a task to which he was the better disposed by reason of the fact that he was the brother-in-law of another exile, Count Lujo Voinovich, who soon moved to Rome also.[107] But Barrère, according to F. Charles-Roux, who in 1916 became his closest colleague, remained opposed for a while to the idea of the destruction of Austria-Hungary, and accepted it only when he was satisfied that in the event of a negotiated peace, the Vienna government would deny Italy even the concessions that Bülow and Erzberger had extracted from it in 1915, to the rejection of which he himself had powerfully contributed.[108] The Russian embassy had accentuated its previous position. On October 23, Krupensky informed Salandra that his country was willing to release the ethnic Italians (Tridentines, Triestines, Istrians, etc.) from the camps of its Austro-Hungarian prisoners-of-war if Italy undertook not to return them to their place of origin until the end of the war. This offer was intended to embarrass the Rome government, as its acceptance would immediately bring it into conflict with Austria-Hungary, whose citizens these prisoners were. Salandra therefore did not reply. Krupensky left no doubt about the propagandist nature of the offer, which was intended to emphasize the advantages that would accrue to Italy from intervention. On the day after his conversation with the Italian Prime Minister, he gave the *Corriere della Sera* an interview in which he said:

[103]

Above all, I hope that the chief significance of the Tsar's proposal will not escape your notice. It represents official recognition on the part of Russia that the territories inhabited by Austro-Hungarian subjects of Italian nationality whom we have made prisoner are Italian territories.[109]

Thus, though his government did not wish to give the gesture this meaning, the Russian ambassador by implication dismissed to Italy's advantage the Yugoslav claims to the mixed Italian-Slav areas of the Adriatic.

Faced with these events, Pašić, who had had to broaden the base of his government by including representatives of the Serbian democratic and progressive parties which had hitherto been in opposition, made a public statement in favour of the Yugoslav idea. Presenting his coalition government to the Skupština, which, like the government itself, had taken refuge in Niš in southern Serbia, the Prime Minister, speaking at a time when a major victory for the Serbian army was in sight, announced that the war had 'become a struggle for the liberation and unification of our enslaved brothers, Serbs, Croats and Slovenians'.[110]

The Croatian refugees took the first opportunity of following up this gesture with one of their own. In a speech in Budapest on January 31, 1915, at a meeting held in connection with the Red Cross services of the Central Powers, Count Tisza spoke of the loyalty demonstrated by the various Austro-Hungarian nationalities in wartime, and of the bravery of the Croats in the army of the dual monarchy. Their self-sacrifice, he said, showed that the Croat nation had forgotten its pre-war political differences with the Hungarian nation and remembered only the centuries of common history that united them. Trumbić sent to the *Corriere della Sera* a letter, which he signed in the name of a 'committee of action of Croat *émigrés*', consisting solely of himself, Voinovich, and Hinković, denying the Hungarian Prime Minister's statement. Croatia, he said, had no liberty of speech, but in spite of that, Tisza's attempt to divide the Croats from Serbia would fail, as the war was being fought by the Magyar and German oppressors of the Southern Slavs. The Croatian people and the Serbian people had always been ethnically a single nation, linked with other Slav nations, and above all to Russia.[111]

Some days previously, at a meeting held on the occasion of a visit to Rome by Supilo, the exiles had decided to launch the idea of a legion of Adriatic Yugoslav volunteers to be recruited wherever possible, but especially in America, to fight with the Serbian army. An appeal for funds and volunteers was published in February in

London, and Trumbić sent a memorandum to the Serbian legation in Italy informing it of the action taken.[112] Although without any encouragement from the Entente countries, who were aware how displeasing the step must be to the Italian government, volunteers indeed presented themselves, some in America, but more among prisoners-of-war in Russia. Unlike its Czech counterpart, however, the progress of the Yugoslav movement depended on international political developments rather than volunteers. When political reasons caused the Entente to give serious consideration to the idea of a Yugoslav nation, the heroism of the Serbian army, which had beaten the Austrians at the end of 1914, was sufficient to give the Yugoslavs military prestige.

Supilo had persuaded Izvolsky to draw the attention of Delcassé and Sazonov to his memorandum.[113] Austria-Hungary was being defeated on every front at the time, and the possibility of destroying Austria-Hungary was dawning on the Russians. On November 21, the Tsar himself, after enumerating the Russian, French, Serbian, Italian and Romanian claims in conversation with Paléologue, remarked that, if it had to yield all the territories that were claimed from it, Austria-Hungary would no longer be in a position to prevent the secession of Bohemia and Croatia.[114] The French ambassador also thought that the Habsburg monarchy would be unable to survive such amputations, but he could see no advantage to his country in encouraging such a development. So when, he discussed the prospects ahead with Sazonov and Buchanan on New Year's Day 1915, he suggested that an attempt should be made to divide Austria-Hungary from Germany by offering her a separate peace in return for the cession of Galicia and Bosnia-Hercegovina only. Sazonov replied that, to do justice to the Slav nations of Bohemia and Croatia, Austria-Hungary must be dismembered.[115] Paléologue pointed out that it would be possible to satisfy the Czechs and Croats by the grant of regional autonomy, and that the primary interest of the Entente was the defeat of the German empire, which the defection of Austria-Hungary would greatly facilitate. Sazonov agreed that this was an argument worthy of consideration. But, in reply to Paléologue's report of the conversation, Delcassé asked him to say nothing in future that might lead Russia to believe that France did not leave the fate of Austria-Hungary completely to her.[116] The idea of a separate peace on the basis of a voluntary limitation of Russian ambitions was obviously a double-edged weapon; it could be offered to Russia by the Central Powers just as it could be offered to Austria-Hungary by the Entente. As long as they could count on the efficacy of the Russian army, it was in the interests of the western powers to encourage

[105]

Russia to persevere in her anti-Austrian and anti-German ambitions. In a despatch antedating the above-mentioned conversation by three days, the British Foreign Secretary informed his ambassador in Petrograd that it was Russia's business to decide whether a separate peace with Austria-Hungary were possible. If Russia decided that such a peace would be to her advantage, her allies would certainly not oppose it, but it was not for them to take any initiative in the matter.[117]

In view of this attitude of Sir Edward Grey, it is not surprising that on March 11, 1915, he received Supilo, who made good use of his relations with Izvolsky in London also. Soon afterwards, Supilo was received by Asquith, the Prime Minister.[118] The Croat agitator submitted to Sir Edward Grey another memorandum which he wrote in Italian and which Steed translated into English. In this, after reiterating his arguments for Yugoslav unity, he dealt with what he knew to be the most delicate question of all and therefore the more likely to interest the British Foreign Secretary.

The first of these questions [he said] is that of the relations between the Yugoslavs and Italy.

In this respect, Italy has aspirations which are just and others which are unjust. The just aspirations are those which coincide with the real national feelings of the majority of the population. The others, the unjust aspirations, as those which go beyond the limits of that majority, claiming national rights among Yugoslavs for whom the Italian language is only the language of culture, and has been so since ancient times. Italy would lose nothing to which she is entitled if in relation to these areas she restricted her national programme to what is ethnically hers and that of her people. On the contrary, she would gain, as we Yugoslavs, particularly on the Adriatic coast, are well-disposed towards the Italian spirit and inclined to open all our doors to the Italian language as an element of Italian culture and Italian civilization and as our natural ally against the pernicious influence of so-called German culture.

Also the very necessity of things and of our geographical position should induce Italy to seek, not merely a more or less platonic friendship with the Yugoslavs on the other side of the Adriatic, but actually a formal alliance, which would be no mean reinforcement of our joint defence against the Teutonic offensive. Few in Italy yet see this common necessity and, unfortunately, hardly anyone yet feels it. They generally consider us 'barbarians' unworthy of negotiating with them. . . . The only party who could intervene in this difficult situation with undisputed authority and success is Britain. The question of pushing Yugoslavs and Italians

[106]

along the right road of broadly based understanding is also worth some attention from the exclusively British point of view.[119]

The second problem, according to Supilo, was that of bringing about a merger between the Croats, who were western by tradition and Catholic by religion, with the Serbs, who were eastern and Orthodox. The third problem he considered to be the promises of autonomy which, he was convinced, Austria-Hungary would herself eventually make to the Croats and other Slavs peoples in her empire in order to keep them within it. But after the war, he argued, Austria-Hungary would gravitate towards Germany even more than before because she would emerge from the conflict much more weakened than the German empire which, even if defeated, would objectively remain a great power, capable of exploiting even the Slavonic part of Austria. A new bulwark must therefore be established against the German advance, and the 'liberation and unification of the Yugoslavs and a good understanding between them and Italy' could provide it. 'If your Excellency deigns to consider these few lines,' Supilo concluded, 'I am convinced that I shall have done something useful for my country. And that is all I seek.'[120]

All that those to whom Supilo addressed himself in London could do was to refer him to the power whose overriding interest in Austro-Hungarian matters they had recognized, i.e. Russia, Supilo promptly took their advice. He returned to Rome at the end of January, and then set off for Petrograd, stopping on the way at Niš.[121]

IV

Yugoslav, Czechoslovak and Hungarian Independence Movements, 1915–1916

At the beginning of 1915 the Russian government, whose new Minister in Niš was a diplomat of the calibre of Prince G. Trubetskoy, put great pressure on Pašić to persuade him to grant territorial concessions in Macedonia to Bulgaria, whose intervention on the allied side Petrograd still hoped to secure, thus hastening the similar decision expected of Romania.[1] The greatest importance was attached to this, as the British and French had decided to force the Dardanelles, and were preparing a landing at Salonica, with a view to opening another front in the Balkans. Trubetskoy tried to establish the compensation that the Serbian government would require for agreeing to pay the price asked by Bulgaria for falling in with Russian wishes. According to the information he was able to gather, Pašić, who was opposed on principle to any concessions to the Bulgarians, proposed asking, if need be, for the Banat and Dalmatia, in addition to Bosnia-Hercegovina, which his government had already been promised—this apart from the possibility of uniting Croatia-Slavonia with Serbia herself. But these ambitions hardly facilitated the plan, as the Banat was already claimed by Romania, and Dalmatia by Italy. The three Entente powers accepted Delcassé's proposal that Serbia should be offered the western part of the Banat and the southern part of Dalmatia, but matters were cut short by Pašić, who told Trubetskoy that he had no confidence in Bulgaria, which, in his view, if granted one concession, would promptly ask for more.[2]

Supilo arrived at Niš at the end of January, armed with a letter from the new Russian ambassador in Rome, Giers, who at his previous post in Montenegro had become friendly with Count L. Voinovich and therefore gave a warmer welcome to the Croat refugees than his predecessor had done. Giers said in his letter of introduction that Trumbić, Hinković and Stojanović regarded Supilo as the 'plenipotentiary of all the Serbo-Croat émigrés'. Thus he managed to be received almost on equal terms, not only by Pašić and Prince Alexander, the Serbian Regent, but also by Trubetskoy.[3] When he learned about the diplomatic soundings in progress, he suggested to Pašić that he should raise the question of

[108]

the liberation of all the Yugoslavs of Austria-Hungary and their
union with Serbia, not as a mere counterpart to possible concessions
to Bulgaria, but as an objective necessary and desirable in itself.
This would enable Serbia to follow in the footsteps of Piedmont,
which had transformed itself into the kingdom of Italy by ceding
Nice and Savoy to France. In his report to Sazonov, Trubetskoy's
comment was that 'The soundness of the case put forward cannot be
doubted'.[4]

Trubetskoy believed that Russia had not only a sentimental but
also a practical, political interest in the liberation of all the Slavs, on
the ground that this would reinforce her position as a great power
in Europe. He naturally regarded it as essential that in a future
kingdom of Yugoslavia the Orthodox Serbs and not the Catholic
Croats should be dominant. But the immediate difficulty was Pašić's
obstinacy in refusing to cede to Bulgaria territory in Macedonia
(though it was of very recent Serbian acquisition).

Supilo, according to his correspondence with Trumbić, at first
believed that he had persuaded Pašić, but when he left to continue
his journey to Petrograd (with the Bosnian Serb D. Vasilievič),
Pašić merely gave him a letter of introduction to his representative
in Russia, Spalajković, whom Supilo knew well from the time of the
Vienna trial.[5] It is therefore not surprising that, arriving in
Petrograd practically empty-handed as he did, he had a cooler reception than he had hoped for. Sazonov, when he saw him on February
27, did not show much enthusiasm for the project of Yugoslav unification. For one thing, to the Tsarist Foreign Minister the Slovenes
were an unknown quantity. When Supilo brought the conversation
round to Italian ambitions in the Adriatic, Sazonov interrupted him
to say that his government was already giving sufficient support to
the Southern Slav cause, and that it was not he, but his British and
French allies that needed persuasion.[6]

The situation in fact was as follows. At the end of 1914 Sazonov
had decided that Krupensky, whose ability and breadth of vision
were not outstanding, and whom he replaced for that reason, had
promised Italy too much without obtaining any assurance of intervention in return. On the other hand, he had a great deal of confidence
in Trubetskoy, who had stopped at Bucharest on his way to Niš and
had informed him on December 9 that he had learned from Baron
Fasciotti, the Italian Minister to Romania, that Italy and Romania
not only were not yet ready to intervene but were in no hurry to make
a decision until they were better able to see which side was more
likely to win.[7] The Russian Foreign Minister therefore adjusted his
aim. He took the first opportunity of giving an interview to the

[109]

Corriere della Sera in which he said that he approved of Italian aspirations to Albania, which had begun to take shape with the occupation of Valona that had taken place some days previously, but added that this, assuming the defeat of Austria-Hungary, was sufficient to assure Italy of supremacy in the Adriatic, so that it would lose nothing in leaving room in Dalmatia for Serbia's 'imprescriptible rights' to access to the sea.[8] In a message from Niš a few days later, Trubetskoy confirmed that the Serbs were alarmed at the Italian claims to Dalmatia:

> If Italy avoids making the same mistake as Austria [he wrote], if she does not wish to raise a dangerous irredentist movement against herself on her own soil, and if, on the contrary, she tries to regulate her relations with Serbia on a basis of confidence, she will to a great extent inherit the advantages of the economic position of Austria in the Balkans. The proximity of the Italian ports, the cheapness of her products, will assure exclusive advantages to Italy. If, on the other hand, she does not take into account the national interests of Serbia and the Southern Slavs, she will run the risk not only of creating dangerous enemies for herself in the future, but of failing to secure all these advantages, because the Serbs are already talking of the possibility of an economic boycott of Italy.[9]

At one moment the Italo-Serbian conflict, the protracted negotiations with Romania, with which Italy was keeping in step, and the opposition of the Russian General Staff to the concession to Romania of a slice of the Bukovina that it wished to keep for itself, caused Sazonov actually to think of dropping the idea of Italian intervention. He raised the matter with the British and French on February 17, but a few days later, on the latter's insistence, he agreed that nothing must be left undone in trying to reach agreement with the Italian government.[10] The beginning of Anglo-French operations against the forts of the Dardanelles during the same few days had the effect of hastening Salandra's and Sonnino's decision.[11] On March 4, Marquis Imperiali, the Italian ambassador in London, informed the British Foreign Secretary of the conditions required for Italian intervention. In the area in which we are interested, Italy demanded Istria as far as Volosca and Dalmatia and including Spalato.[12] Sazonov regarded this as unacceptable. On March 20, Sir Edward Grey, in the name of the Entente, asked the Rome government 'to find a way of accepting the desiderata of the Yugoslav leaders' in regard to Dalmatia, but Sonnino pointed out in his telegram of March 21 to Marquis Carlotti, his ambassador in Petrograd, that seven months previously Russia had promised Italy the whole of Dalmatia.[13] The British government decided to accept the Italian demands. Negotiations continued for another month, but by the end of March it was clear that the Italian government was going to agree to drop its claim to Spalato and that the Russian government was going to agree to Italy's being granted the Dalmatian coast from Zara to Sebenico. Meanwhile, Russia obtained an undertaking from her allies that she could have Constantinople.[14]

Meanwhile Supilo was making strenuous efforts in political circles in Petrograd to advance his people's cause and to discover something about the highly secret diplomatic negotiations in progress. He saw Marquis Carlotti, who told Baron Schilling, Sazonov's deputy, the substance of their conversation. The Italian ambassador regarded Supilo as an 'intelligent and, it can be said, very understanding man'.[15] According to Schilling's report on what was told him, 'some of the arguments used by Supilo against the excessive Italian demands to Croatian territory and the Dalmatian coast actually seemed worthy of consideration to Marquis Carlotti. Among those particularly appealing to Carlotti was the idea of a community of interest between the Serbo-Croats and the Italians' against pan-Germanism.[16] Carlotti had, however, concluded by warning the Russians against favouring the Croats, pointing out that Italy would find 'the creation of a big and strong Southern Slav state on the shores of the Adriatic very difficult to accept'.[17] It was this that frustrated Supilo's efforts to win over the Tsarist political leaders. He was able to report to Trumbić that only Miljukov, the leader of the opposition Democratic Constitutional Party, had been completely won over to the Yugoslav cause.[18]

Finally, on March 25, when he was again received by Sazonov, Supilo, who had already gathered the substance of the negotiations in progress from a few words let slip by Baron Schilling, concluded that Italian intervention was already decided on, and that the price secured by Italy included the whole of Istria and part of Dalmatia.[19] When he protested, he was advised not to remain in Russia preaching to the converted, but to return to London and plead the Yugoslav case there.[20] He tried hard to secure an audience with the Tsar, or at least to be received by Grand Duke Nikolai, and he went to General Headquarters for that purpose, but all he got there were platonic assurances of Slav sympathy.[21] Three days after his conversation with Sazonov he succeeded in telegraphing to Pašić, and then to Trumbić, all that he had learned.[22] The Serbian government, alarmed at the prospect in store for Dalmatia, sent a note of protest to the Russian

[111]

government on April 9. Pašić wanted to go to Petrograd, but Sazonov informed him that the visit would be inopportune.[23]

A development of more far-reaching consequences resulted from Trumbić's contacts. He was in touch with the Slovene and Croatian politicians of Trieste, Gorizia and Istria, and he passed on to them the information that he had received from Supilo, which alarmed them greatly. They had always had greater conflicts of interest with the local Italians than with the Austrian government, and the idea of being transferred to Italian sovereignty was bound to be displeasing to them. To prevent it, they decided to take a step from which they had previously carefully refrained. At a number of meetings held in Trieste at the end of March and the beginning of April—attended among others by the deputies to the Reichsrat O. Rybař and G. Gregorin (Independent Slovenes), V. Spinčić and M. Laginja (Independent Croats), and the deputies to the Croatian Diet J. Lorković (Progressive), D. Hrvoj and A. Pavelić (Right Party)—it was decided to send Trumbić a letter announcing their solidarity with his action in siding with the Entente. Those who took this step were of course aware that their action, if it came to light, would expose them to severe penalties at the hands of the Austrian authorities. They nevertheless authorized Trumbić to organize a committee to fight for the independence of the Yugoslav territories, on condition that he would not agree to the cession of any Slovene or Croat territory to Italy. Rather than that, they said, they would prefer to remain under Austrian rule. G. Gregorin, D. Trinajstić, a deputy to the Istrian Diet, M. Marjanović, an Istrian journalist, and Professor B. Vošnjak of Gorizia, were sent abroad to work for the committee.[24]

A month earlier, Trumbić had received another encouragement to action. F. Potočnjak, a former deputy to the Croatian Diet, who had taken refuge in Italy at the same time as Supilo and Trumbić and had been sent by them to do propaganda in the United States with the co-operation of the Serbian consul in New York, Professor Michael Pupin (who was a well-known scientist and inventor and a friend of President Wilson's and, having been born in southern Hungary, took the problems of irredentism very much to heart), Father N. Gršković, an Istrian priest at Cleveland, Ohio, and Dr Biankini, a Dalmatian doctor very popular with the big Croatian colony in Chicago, succeeded in organizing in that city on March 10–11, 1915, a Yugoslav convention that was attended by 563 delegates. The meeting passed a resolution in favour of the national unity of the Croats, Serbs and Slovenes and the liberation, by taking part in the war against the Central Powers, of those who were Austro-Hungarian subjects.[25] As a beginning the sum of $5,000 was collected for the Yugoslav

Committee that was to be set up. In the course of time, particularly as the movement spread to Latin America, where many wealthy Croats lived, the propaganda of the American Yugoslavs provided Trumbić directly (that is, without any intervention by the Serbian government) with substantial funds.

Trumbić, after some hesitation, adopted the suggestion that Supilo sent him from Russia, namely that he should leave immediately for London and put pressure on the Foreign Office. He left Rome, and in Paris called a meeting of those of his friends who were willing to take the initiative in the organization of a Yugoslav Committee. This was duly established on April 30, 1915, and Trumbić became its chairman. Those asked to join it were Supilo, Meštrović, Hinković, Potočnjak, the representatives of the Trieste Slovenes and Istrian Croats whom we mentioned above, the two Bosnian Serbs appointed by Pašić during the previous November, some Dalmatian municipal councillors in exile, and the three chief organizers of the Chicago convention.[26]

Pašić informed his representatives in London and Paris that he agreed that a Yugoslav manifesto should be issued, and on his instructions, Vesnić, the Serbian Minister in Paris, introduced the committee to Delcassé. Meanwhile, the Serbian government protested (in its note of May 7 addressed to the three Entente powers) against the promise to Italy of territories inhabited by Serbs, Croats and Slovenes without taking into account their right to be reunited into a single kingdom, and asked his allies to guarantee that that right would be respected.[27] The French Foreign Minister replied evasively to the remonstrances of Trumbić's delegation. Trumbić was also received by Izvolsky, who admitted that Russia's concern in Dalmatia was with the Serbs; because they were Orthodox, their unification with Catholic Croatia did not seem desirable to his government.[28] Wickham Steed, who was in Paris at the time and was fully informed of developments by Hinković, immediately called on Delcassé and Izvolsky and argued the justice of the Yugoslav claims. To Delcassé he said that the Italian demands would strengthen the loyalty to Austria-Hungary of the Croats and the Slovenes, but the French Foreign Minister replied that though that might well be true, it counted for less than the million troops that Italy could throw into the scales on the Entente side.[29] That, indeed, was the reality of the situation, and it was a grave mistake on the part of the Yugoslav Committee not to have taken it into account from the outset and not to have kept its claims within limits that the Entente might have considered seriously. In view of the irreconcilability of the Yugoslav maximum demands with the conditions on which Italian intervention depended, the only possible effect was to cause the Entente to lose interest in the former. Italian intervention was infinitely more important militarily than anything the Croat exiles could promise, let alone do. It is true that Trumbić's hands were tied. The claim to Gorizia, Pola, and even Trieste had been stated already in 1912 by the Slovene Popular Party and the Croat Right Party (Trumbić was himself one of the leaders of the corresponding party in Dalmatia) in a programme for the unification of all the Croat and Slovene provinces in the Habsburg empire. As we have seen, Slovene and Croat politicians willing to take the difficult step of repudiating their loyalty to that empire insisted on their maximum programme remaining intact. But the Yugoslav Committee accentuated its intransigence by submitting to the French government and to the Russian ambassador in Paris on May 6 (and to the British government on May 15) a memorandum which, while greeting Italy as 'a new collaborator in the work of liberation', claimed that the Yugoslavia which was to emerge from the struggle with Austria-Hungary and the unification of the territories subject to it with Serbia and Montenegro, should extend northwards into southern Hungary. This included not only the Bačka, which was to a large extent Magyar, but also the whole of the Banat, including its Romanian part, while in the Adriatic area it would incorporate the whole of Dalmatia and Istria, including Fiume, Pola and Trieste, and to the west it would include, not only Gorizia, but also half of Carinthia and a part of Styria, which were German-Austrian provinces.[30]

At that time the governments were secretly bound by the Treaty of London, which, it seems appropriate to point out, granted Italy a considerably smaller number of citizens of foreign—Slav or German-Austrian—stock than Trumbić's memorandum (what with Italians, German-Austrians, Magyars and Romanians) claimed for Yugoslavia. Even if the hands of the Entente diplomatists had not been tied, they could not have failed to notice how absurd it was that the Yugoslav exiles, who said that they wanted to establish their state after the defeat of Austria-Hungary, and should therefore have been thinking of ways of contributing to that defeat, proposed leaving to Italy—whose army would have to face the Habsburg army in the field—less than the Vienna government was offering her during those very days to preserve her neutrality. This nationalistic refusal to face facts worked gravely to the detriment of the Slovenes and Croats at the end of the war, when they came into sharp conflict with Italy, in spite of Trumbić's co-operation in 1918 with those who tried to mediate between them, and, against his wishes, they had to accept Serbian supremacy in the organization of the new Yugoslavia.

That the Yugoslav Committee was able to survive the mistakes

[114]

caused by its exaggerated nationalism in 1915 was due to the few but tenacious friends it had in England. We have already mentioned Steed. Seton-Watson, whom Trumbić kept informed of Supilo's messages from Russia, was, according to what he wrote to W. Miller, the Rome correspondent of the *Morning Post*, more or less fully aware of the situation even before the signature of the Treaty of London.[31] Supilo, who had meanwhile returned to Niš, telegraphed an appeal to Sir Edward Grey on April 29. Seton-Watson, who had already pleaded the Yugoslav cause at the Foreign Office, saw a copy of the telegram and decided that public action was necessary. A personal interview with Sir Edward Grey failed to yield results; the Foreign Secretary reiterated that, in the opinion of the British and French generals, Italian intervention would clinch the outcome of the war.[32] While Trumbić, who eventually came to London, was still hesitating about what to do, Seton-Watson decided that the situation must be brought before the widest possible public opinion. He drafted a manifesto to the British parliament and people which Trumbić signed in the name of the Yugoslav Committee on May 12 and which was published by the British press.[33]

Thanks to Seton-Watson and Steed and to an exhibition of Meštrović's sculpture (the opening was attended by Lord Robert Cecil, the Under-Secretary of Foreign Affairs) the Committee was able to establish its headquarters in London. On July 2, Lord Crewe, the Permanent Secretary in the Foreign Office, received a delegation from the Committee. His advice to its members was to take another look at European history, which showed that no nation had secured its complete freedom in a single war, but that all had attained their unity gradually, one step at a time.[34] Seton-Watson and G. M. Trevelyan gave similar advice. The latter wrote to his friend from the Italian front, to which he had gone with a British ambulance unit, advising him not to annoy the Italians by condemning their claims, but to allow them time to realize who the Yugoslavs were; they might do so before the conquest of the disputed Dalmatia, which meanwhile remained firmly in Austrian possession.[35] Sensible though these suggestions were, the interested parties had no intention of stopping half-way. Fortunately for the Yugoslav exiles, the Czech independence movement kept open the high road of priority for the common struggle against the Habsburg empire, which they were able to follow.

On December 17, 1914, Masaryk, who was not yet seriously suspected by the Austrian authorities and was on good terms with Prince Thun, the governor of Bohemia, was able to leave Prague for Rome, where he called on Trumbić and his colleagues.[36] His contacts

E

with the Croatian exiles were noted by agents of the Austro-Hungarian embassy and, according to information gathered by Masaryk's friends, were reported to Vienna, and that made it impossible for him to return home. In Rome, Masaryk also met Svatkovsky, whom he knew by repute from the time when the latter had been a Russian newspaper correspondent in Austria. Svatkovsky immediately sent a report of their conversation to the Petrograd government.[37] Shortly before, he had received and passed on a message from his old friend Kramář, who, unlike Masaryk, had decided not to leave Prague, but to await the arrival of Russian troops there.[38] At the beginning of November, a *družina* volunteer succeeded in crossing the lines and bringing Kramář a message from the Czechs in Russia. As a result of this incident, the leader of the Young Czechs decided to resume contact with Svatkovksy by sending to Switzerland a deputy named Franta belonging to his party. Kramář informed Svatkovsky that he still supported the plan, outlined at his request in the late spring of 1914, that in the event of a war ending with the defeat of Austria-Hungary, Bohemia would join a greater Slav empire if it were supported by Russia. Although his expectation that Vienna might rashly plunge into war had come true, to Kramář this was still a maximum programme to which no one was committed. His message to Svatkovsky through Franta shows that if the Habsburg monarchy had made its peace with the Romanovs, he would still have been willing to accept an autonomous Bohemia forming part of a federal Austria.[39]

Masaryk was more resolute, however. He informed Svatkovsky that it was his intention and that of his colleagues to form a secret organization capable of military co-operation with the Russian army when it entered Bohemia, the sole condition being that the Russian troops must behave as liberators and not as invaders, and that after the war, with or without a Russian king (a point on which Masaryk who, unlike Kramář, was no friend of Tsarism, remained reticent) a strong and completely independent Czechoslovakia must be established with strategic frontiers including the Sudetenland and northern Hungary as far as the Danube, and connected by a corridor to the future Yugoslavia.[40] Masaryk also informed Svatkovsky that he had had useful exchanges of view on this matter with representatives of the principal Czech parties, with whom, as with some Slovak leaders, he thought he would be able to form a national committee when Russian troops approached Prague. In fact, before leaving Prague the future President of the Czechoslovak Republic had communicated his plan to the ablest of his followers, Dr Beneš, whom he had put in contact for the purpose with Scheiner, the leader of the Sokols, who

[116]

was politically a moderate (and a Russophile) like Kramář, but whose co-operation was essential for any serious paramilitary preparations.[41]

With regard to support by the Czech political parties for his plans, Masaryk's claim, though it optimistically anticipated events, was not without foundation. For all their social and ideological differences, the dissensions about tactics and the acute rivalries that prevailed between them, Kramář's party, Švehla's Agrarian Party, the National Socialist Party led by the imprisoned Klofáč, the small Progressive Party, and the Realist or Popular Party consisting of the radical democrats who followed Masaryk, all shared in varying degree the hope that the war would result in the independence of Bohemia. On the other hand, the Czech Social Democratic Party, which had the greatest following and the best organization among the masses, was led by Marxists who regarded the national independence movement as ideologically reactionary and practically dangerous. Their most prominent leader, Šmeral, believed at any rate in the economic vitality of Austria-Hungary and, prudent organizer that he was, had no desire to risk the material acquisitions of the labour movement in a struggle bound to lead to severe repressive action by the state, whereas the left wing of his party looked to the revolutionary pacifism of the socialists in other countries who remained loyal to internationalism.[42] Masaryk owed his election as deputy to Social-Democratic support. He was considered to be an ethical socialist, and in spite of his criticisms of Marxism, enjoyed high prestige in the movement, in part because of the help he had given in founding the party newspaper and the Prague Labour Academy.[43] The section of the party that at its last pre-war congress in 1913 had called for a more patriotic, i.e. anti-Austrian, attitude in reaction against the loyalty to the state of the Vienna socialist leaders was to find its ideologist in Masaryk. As the war went on, their strength naturally increased.

Masaryk's identification of the Slovaks with the Czechs had less correspondence with political reality. He mentioned to Svatkovsky two journalists of Slovak origin, A. Štepanek and V. Šrobar, as possible members of the proposed national committee. Štepanek was a member of the Czech Progressive Party (a small group that rivalled the National Socialists in extremism, but lacked their popular support), and had no connection with Slovakia.[44] Šrobar, who, besides being a journalist, was an effective speaker, had, however, been a member of the staff of the Slovak political and cultural periodical *Hlas*, which had been founded in 1898 at the instigation of Masaryk (of whom Srobar considered himself a disciple) and which, until it ceased publication after four years of struggle, proclaimed the ethnic identity of Czechs and Slovaks, advocated agrarian Social Democracy, and declared that intellectuals should go to the people. The party's intellectual influence was by no means negligible, but politically it could count only on the still very small Slovak Social Democratic organization, which tended to prefer the ideas of *Hlas*, which were better adapted to the conditions prevailing in Slovakia under Magyar domination, to the rather superficial Marxist internationalism of the Hungarian Social Democratic Party, of which it had formally been a branch.[45] A party that could claim to speak for a considerable number of Slovak peasants was the Catholic Popular Party led by the priest A. Hlinka, whose anti-Hungarian agitation among the most backward peasants had led to the bloodthirsty act of repression by the authorities at Csernova in 1907. The anti-clerical Šrobar, a Protestant by birth, had courageously sided with Hlinka and had been sent to prison with him, but this was not sufficient to bridge the gap that divided Slovak Catholicism from the lay or Hussite traditions of Czech patriotism. At the outbreak of war, Hlinka and F. Juriga, a deputy belonging to his party, had publicly expressed their hopes of a victory for the Catholic and Apostolic Habsburg monarchy.[46] The other Slovak party represented in the Hungarian parliament, the National Party, was predominantly the party of the Slovak bourgeoisie, and it still remained loyal to Austria-Hungary although it fought Magyarization and demanded the setting up of Slovak schools and universities. In December 1915, Hodža, who was the most democratic and the most anti-Magyar of the National Party leaders and therefore lived in exile in Vienna, assured J. Redlich that the Slovaks were completely loyal to the dynasty and rejected the 'artificial ideals' of the Czech independence movement.[47]

The big colonies of Slovak immigrants in Russia, France and America had in recent years been swollen by a continual influx of newcomers seeking to escape from poverty and unemployment, which were especially acute in Slovakia. Some of these colonies were very hostile to Hungary as a result of the world-wide repercussions of the Csernova massacre of 1907, and for that reason favoured the Entente just as the Czech colonies did, though they kept themselves distinct from the latter. A Czech committee formed in Paris at the end of 1914 started publishing a journal called *L'Indépendance tchèque*, and under the honorary presidency of Professor E. Denis organized a meeting at which the name of Masaryk, whose definite expatriation was announced by Trumbić, was received with acclamation.[48] Denis, was in close contact with Étienne Fournol, who worked

[118]

for Delcassé and with Professor Moysset who worked for Tardieu. Both were long-standing friends of students of the Slavonic world. In Denis's opinion a firm stand by Masaryk for the dismemberment of Austria-Hungary would be useful at that moment, since the French government was inclined to leave *carte blanche* in the matter to Russia.[49] Masaryk had moved from Rome to Geneva, choosing a neutral country to avoid prematurely exposing himself to a charge of high treason. In spite of his anxiety not to compromise his friends in Prague, and although he had less confidence in the Russians than the latter had always had he accepted the suggestion of the aged French historian of his people. Through a member of the staff of *L'Indépendance tchèque* whom Denis sent to him, Masaryk came to an agreement with the Paris committee on his taking an irrevocable public step, which he marked by a trip to the French and British capitals.[50] On May 1, 1915, *La Nation tchèque*, edited by Denis, took the place of *L'Indépendance tchèque*, which ceased publication. In its second number it printed a map of the future independent Czechoslovakia, showing the frontiers that were in fact drawn in 1919. In the third number, Denis, having learned of the arrest of Kramář, who had been his friend for many years, published an article entitled *Austria delenda est*, justifying this objective by the persecution to which the Czechs and Southern Slavs were subjected in Austria-Hungary.[51] Denis made no concealment of the fact that he borrowed this slogan from the Yugoslav *émigré* movement. He was a veteran student of Serbian affairs. He followed the latter just as he did the Czech movement, giving it just as much space in his journal, and used it to rally to the cause his fellow students of Slav and Austro-Hungarian affairs, including Louis Léger, Émile Haumant, Louis Eisenmann and André Chéradame. In his review of the French edition of a lecture by Salvemini in December 1916 which was printed as a pamphlet under the same title of *Delenda Austria*, Denis recalled that, like those colleagues of his, he had believed up to 1914 that the preservation of the Danubian monarchy, provided it were reformed in a manner satisfactory to the Slav majority of its population, was necessary to the balance of Europe, but the war on Serbia had convinced him of the impossibility of leaving the Slavs under the Germans and the Hungarians. He recalled that in 1872, when he had first visited Prague, loyalty to the dynasty had been universal among the Czechs, but on each of his frequent subsequent visits to Bohemia he had seen a diminution in that loyalty. Having realized in 1914 that it no longer genuinely existed, he had drawn the logical conclusion.[52]

When Denis wrote this in the middle of 1918, it reflected the attitude of practically the whole of the Czech population. But three years previously, except among a group of conspirators that included some authoritative personalities but had no opportunity for expansion, the slogan he launched was not yet current in Prague. The turning-point in the development of the clandestine organization came with the two visits that Beneš, who still had a regular passport, paid to Masaryk in Switzerland in February and April 1915. Beneš, Šamal, Masaryk's successor in the leadership of the Realist Party, Kramář, Rašin, another Young Czech leader, and Scheiner, the Sokol leader, with a few of their friends founded a secret society known as the Mafia which survived the expatriations and arrests that followed.[53] Thirty years earlier the name 'Mafia' had been used to designate a group of students and publicists, including Masaryk, who had met at a literary café and supported the campaign conducted by the latter—as soon as he was appointed to the chair of philosophy at the Czech University of Prague—to expose the inauthenticity of certain Czech medieval manuscript poems that had been consecrated by uncritical tradition.[54] The activities of the Mafia in 1915 were in fact restricted to the establishing of contacts, among others with the Southern Slav deputies Rybař, Lukinić and Lorković (to the last of whom, who were members of the Croatian Diet, Beneš brought messages from Masaryk and Pašić), and to the collection of funds. The money raised was used to pay the expenses of Masaryk's trips to the western capitals, and to finance the expatriation of the Agrarian deputy Dürich (who was sent abroad in order further to commit his party, which had the strongest parliamentary representation of all the Czech parties, but had not yet compromised itself by patriotic conspiracy). Subsequently, in September 1915, it was also used to finance the expatriation of Beneš himself when his position in Prague grew precarious after the arrests of Kramář and Scheiner at the end of May and of Rašin in July. The arrests did not mean that the existence of the Mafia came to the knowledge of the Austrian authorities; all that had happened was that Thun, the governor, was replaced by an official who had less confidence in the possibility of agreement with the Czech politicians, who were subjected to discreet surveillance. Towards the end of April, Kramář had been seen repeatedly talking to the Italian consul at a Prague hotel, and this caused him to be arrested when Italian intervention became a certainty. A copy of *La Nation tchèque* was found in his possession, and correspondence with Denis was confiscated at his home.[55] At his trial by a military court, he said that he believed dependence on Germany to be ruinous to Austria's historical position and that he had worked for reconciliation among Austrians, Russians, Serbians and Poles with a view to avoiding war. Stürgkh, the Prime Minister, and Berchtold, the former

Foreign Minister, gave evidence in his favour, recalling that in the last pre-war parliament the budget and military estimates had been passed thanks solely to Kramář's loyalty to the régime. In spite of this, he was sentenced to death on June 3, 1916, and a similar sentence was imposed on his colleague Rašin. After the death of Francis Joseph, these sentences were commuted respectively to fifteen and ten years' imprisonment.[56]

Repressive measures certainly hampered the activity of the Czech patriots, but the trial of parliamentary deputies (Kramář was actually vice-president of the Reichsrat) without parliament's having had an opportunity of deciding whether or not to raise their immunity —the Vienna government persisted in not summoning it—was invaluable to *émigré* propaganda, far outweighing any discouragement it caused to the conspirators at home. Denunciation to western public opinion of the persecution of his colleagues at home in Bohemia gave Masaryk a political advantange of which he had the greater need inasmuch as, in spite of the activity of Denis and his academic colleagues, of whom the most learned, Professor Louis Eisenmann, actually established close relations with the military authorities, the Quai d'Orsay was in no hurry irrevocably to compromise itself in an anti-Austrian sense. Many French diplomatic circles believed that the survival of the Habsburg empire was essential as a potential obstacle to the spread of pan-Germanism in central eastern Europe. Among Masaryk's papers there is a note dated March 28, 1915, in which he observes that the London and Paris governments did not want to use the Czech exiles' movement, and that therefore the only hope was to appeal to public opinion, especially in Britain.[57]

After the expatriation of Beneš, who settled in Paris, Masaryk moved to London, where Seton-Watson obtained for him a chair at the newly founded School of Slavonic Studies.[58] Meanwhile the drying-up of funds from Prague had been compensated for elsewhere. Czechs living in the United States held a pro-Entente convention on March 13 and 14, 1915.[59] The Slovaks living in the United States acted in the same way, but claimed full autonomy for their country in the future Czech-Slovak Confederation. The result was the formation of a working committee that set about raising funds for Masaryk. The latter rightly decided that the time had come to encourage the movement by public announcement of the formation of the Czech Committee Abroad, and this was done in a statement issued in Paris on November 14, 1915, signed by him and Dürich and by representatives of Czech *émigrés* in France, Russia and America at an earlier date.[60] The statement called for the total independence from Austria-Hungary of the Czechs and Slovaks, whom it regarded as forming a single nation. The president of the committee was Masaryk and its secretary Beneš. The latter was aided by the journalist L. Sychrava, who had been in contact with Klofač in Prague and went abroad immediately after the latter's arrest; and a few weeks later he also had the assistance of a Slovak, Milan Štefanik, who had just returned from the Serbian front, where he had been serving as a volunteer in the French air force. He was a scientist and explorer of great distinction and fascination and a self-willed, bold and ambitious man of action. He was the son of a Calvinist pastor, had been a pupil of Masaryk's, and for more than ten years had been secretary of the Paris Astronomical Observatory. He had become a naturalized Frenchman, and his *entrée* to highly-placed circles produced unexpected support for his country in France as well as in Italy.[61] In the spring of 1916, Masaryk, feeling that his position had been strengthened by an interview granted him, thanks to Štefanik's contacts, by Briand, the French Prime Minister, took the responsibility of changing the committee's name to the more binding one of National Committee of the Czech Countries.

Supilo, having returned from Russia and the Balkans in June 1915, also settled in London after conferring in Geneva with Masaryk; a deep mutual respect existed between the two. The Foreign Office, though it had ignored Supilo's protests against the undertakings given to Italy, had not ceased to keep its doors open to him. The British knew that at Niš, Supilo had tried to persuade Pašić to agree to make concessions in Macedonia to Bulgaria in exchange for Entente support for Yugoslav unity. With the failure of the operations in the Dardanelles and Gallipoli, the Russian defeat in Galicia, and the failure of the Italians to achieve a breakthrough on the Austro-Hungarian front on the Carso, it had become probable that, so far from siding with the Entente, Bulgaria would join in the war on the side of the Central Powers. In this event, Serbia would be caught between two fires and crushed (as indeed she was at the end of the year). At Russian suggestion the Entente governments again put pressure on Pašić to make concessions to Bulgaria sufficient at least to secure her neutrality and to renounce the Serbian claim to the Banat, so that the latter could be promised to Romania if she intervened. On Supilo's advice, Pašić's formal protest of May 7 against the cession of Slav territory to Italy included a statement of the principle of Yugoslav unification. The latter could now be useful to the Entente, for Serbia could be offered the prospect of unification with Croatia in compensation for renunciations elsewhere. But after the Italian entry into the war, any assurance that might be given in this respect needed the consent of Rome. After some vain soundings

[122]

of Sonnino by Delcassé, at the beginning of August 1915, Sir Edward Grey asked the Italian Foreign Minister whether he agreed that Serbia should be guaranteed the right to incorporate Croatia-Slavonia, including Fiume, as well as Dalmatia south of Sebenico (Šibenik) and Montenegro (in addition to Bosnia-Hercegovina, which had already been promised her), assuming that the population concerned explicitly showed their wish for this solution.[62] Sonnino informed both the British and the French ambassadors that he was opposed to giving Croatia to Serbia. He believed the creation of a big Yugoslav state on the Adriatic to be contrary to Italian interests, and he pointed to the possibility that Hungary might sooner or later dissociate herself from Austria and put out feelers for a separate peace, in which case it would be necessary to be in a position to allow her to keep Croatia and its coastline.[63] In the first phase of the negotiations for Italian intervention, Sonnino had in fact suggested that 'in the interests of Hungary and Croatia' the fate of Fiume and the coast from Volosca to Dalmatia should be left open, and, though, on the insistence of the French ambassador in London, who was very hostile to the Hungarians, he subsequently renounced mentioning Hungary in the Treaty of London (Hungary was, after all, Austria's full partner in the dual monarchy on which Italy was about to declare war), he did not for that reason cease to take that country into account.[64] The British ambassador in Moscow, though he knew no details, believed himself to be in a position to state on May 25 that a Hungarian emissary had been to Rome.[65]

We are now in a position to throw more light on the conversations between Italians and Hungarians which took place in 1915 and later. It was in the Risorgimento tradition to rely on the Hungarians against the Habsburgs. When San Giuliano, recalling this in September 1914, advised Malagodi, the editor of the *Tribuna*, to accept Tisza's invitation to send a war correspondent to Hungary, he remarked that 'though they march together, the Hungarians do not have too much liking for the Austrians'.[66] Tisza's initial stubborn opposition to the Italian demands was, as we have already noted, due to his fear that concessions to Italy would open the way to similar concessions to Romania.[67] In March 1915, when the Austrian Prime Minister Stürgkh had nearly reached the point of agreeing that, if it was absolutely essential, Romania might be granted a part of the Bukovina, Tisza not only agreed to the idea of yielding the Trentino to Italy but also, as we have seen, became the most determined advocate of a genuine agreement between Vienna and Rome.

Meanwhile the section of the Party of Independence and of 1848

[123]

most attached to the Kossuth tradition had decided to by-pass the Vienna Foreign Minister and the Budapest government and to make a direct approach to the Italian government. In 1913 Count Mihály Károlyi who, after his election to the chairmanship of the 1848 party, moved to the radical wing of the latter, had criticized Austria-Hungary's unconditional alliance with Germany in the foreign affairs committee of the joint delegations of the Austrian and Hungarian parliaments; and at the beginning of 1914 Károlyi paid a visit to Paris and called on some French statesmen, from Poincaré to Clemenceau.[69]

The young Hungarian aristocrat, in whose illustrious lineage Francophilia had been the rule (his ancestors included *condottieri* who had been allies of the King of France in the seventeenth and the beginning of the eighteenth centuries) did not realize that these French statesmen detested each other and were profoundly divided on matters of policy. Chance had it that he rendered a great personal service to Caillaux, a supporter of Franco-German reconciliation (on whose political gratitude the Hungarian independence movement could therefore not rely) by revealing to him that the Paris newspaper that attacked him most violently was subsidized by the Austro-Hungarian government. Károlyi, a man of great courage and tenacity, persisted in his efforts, however, aided by his party colleague and cousin, Count Theodore Batthyány, a grandson of the Hungarian Prime Minister of 1848 who was shot by the Austrians after the defeat of the revolution. Count Batthyány was much more conservative in his ideas than Károlyi, who developed in the direction of democratic radicalism and, after 1918–19, revolutionary socialism, but he shared Károlyi's belief that Germany was dragging Hungary into a war that would be disastrous to the Magyars. In 1913–14 they therefore informed the Russian consul-general in Budapest that as a token of their desire to free Hungary from Austro-German tutelage they wanted to send a delegation of parliamentarians of their group on a goodwill visit to Petrograd. As, however, they were members of a party which included political democracy in its programme, the consul-general regarded the offer with mistrust.[70]

When the war broke out, Károlyi, and some of his aides were in the United States on a propaganda tour to raise funds for his party among Hungarian immigrants. On the way home, he and his colleagues were interned in France. The French offered to release them if they gave an undertaking not to bear arms against the Entente; Károlyi did not accept this condition, but was released all the same. Meanwhile in Budapest the parliamentary representatives of their party, led by Count Apponyi, had joined the 'sacred union' that supported the government at war. When Károlyi reached home, he could not publicly repudiate this position which, as he did not conceal from Apponyi, he rejected because of his instinctive aversion to German militarism and also because the Battle of the Marne had shown the Germans not to be invincible. He therefore intended to resume his liberty of action at the first suitable opportunity and, when it seemed likely that Italy was going over to the side of the enemies of Hungary no less than of Austria, he decided that the time had come.

Károlyi, Batthyány, and two other deputies, Beck and Lovászy, as they have described in their memoirs, decided to make an approach through an emissary to Sonnino, whom Károlyi knew personally, and to suggest to him the possibility of a future Italo-Hungarian alliance.

Actually, Sonnino made the first move. As we have already mentioned, towards the end of 1914 there were rumours in London about moves or desires on the part of Hungarian aristocrats to extricate Hungary from the war by means of a separate peace. It is now clear that this was wishful thinking, but when Sonnino heard of the rumours, he telegraphed the Italian ambassador in Vienna and the consul-general in Budapest asking them to make enquiries. Both the Duke d'Avarna and the consul-general replied that they believed them to be without foundation.[71] But on January 20, 1915, Sonnino sent them another telegram, saying that rumours about an Austro-Hungarian or a Hungarian separate peace continued to circulate and asking them to 'intensify enquiries and report to me all clues in the matter'.[72] To the Italian Foreign Ministry, which was weighing up the pros and cons of coming to terms with Austria-Hungary or making war on her, all information relating to the secret attitudes of Austrians or Hungarians was a matter of great interest.

Meanwhile the consul-general in Budapest, Martin Franklin, had approached the individual who was in a better position than anyone else to give him information on the matter.

I have [he telegraphed to Sonnino on January 22] had a long, confidential conversation with Count Michael Károlyi, the Independence Party leader. He told me that there was no trace of any separatist movement in Hungary, and that rumours circulating abroad, including the rumour that emissaries had been sent to England, were false. All the parties had supported the government out of patriotism. But he and a part of his party are not satisfied with the latest change of government because, while it seems a satisfaction granted to Hungary, it conceals grave dangers.[73]

Franklin went on to say that Károlyi believed that

> neither of the two power groups is in a position to defeat the other
> and that therefore the war is likely to end out of exhaustion without
> changes of frontier, provided Italy and Romania do not enter the
> field. He is therefore of the opinion that it is absolutely essential
> to satisfy Italy by ceding the Trentino and granting autonomy to
> Trieste. He believes that, with Italy eliminated, Romania would
> decide not to move, or at any rate would not represent a vital
> danger. He naturally considers that this, in addition to avoiding
> a catastrophe for the whole monarchy, would be in the direct
> interest of Hungary, because Austria, after losing the Trentino and
> probably also part of Galicia and the Bukovina, would be
> weakened and Hungarian supremacy would be further consoli-
> dated.[74]

Károlyi also said to Martin Franklin that Count Berchtold would
have been willing to negotiate the cession to Italy of the Trentino,
but that Burian and Tisza still hoped that a decisive victory on the
Russian front would make it possible to avoid this. In Károlyi's
view, these tactics were highly dangerous, and their probable effect
would be to push both Italy and Romania into intervention.

> He would therefore like the government to decide immediately
> to negotiate the cession of the Trentino. He told me that among
> the influential personalities in his 1848 party, Justh and Batthyány
> share his views. Apponyi is opposed to them, and so is Aladar
> Zichy, the leader of the clerical opposition. His father-in-law
> Andrássy, the sixty-seven party leader, is wavering.[75]

Franklin pointed out that Károlyi, who was always extremist in his
views, detested Tisza (who was also detested by Károlyi's father-in-
law, Andrássy) and resented his having given to Burian the place of
Berchtold, who was a relative of his. For this reason, in Franklin's
view, Károlyi could not be regarded as completely objective. Nevertheless he proposed to see him again, and did so, as he reported to
Sonnino on February 10. He said that Károlyi agreed that Tisza
desired to secure Hungarian supremacy in the dual monarchy, but
believed that this could be achieved by means of a decisive contribution to the victory of the Habsburg armies. This, according to
Károlyi, was a Utopian idea, for:

> The real interests of Hungary lie in increasing her autonomy,
> and this is possible only if for the time being Austria does not

[126]

win a complete victory and is weakened by the cost of the war. He hopes that Italy will obtain the Trentino and possibly also Trieste, but will renounce Fiume, which must remain Hungarian. Though he believes that too much reliance should not be placed on promises, he does not exclude the possibility that Italy might obtain its ends without war. . . . To Hungary, good relations with Italy are absolutely essential if she is not to be overwhelmed by Germanism and Slavism. Károlyi told me he has written a confidential letter to your Excellency, whom he met years ago at Scipione Borghese's; he has entrusted it to a priest named Török, who is going to Rome. He asked me for a letter of introduction to your Excellency for this priest. I did not agree to do this, but said that the priest might present himself to Count Aldrovandi.[76]

The Greek Catholic priest J. Török went to Rome and made frequent journeys between the Italian and Hungarian capitals. He was received by Sonnino, and saw the Italian *chef de cabinet*, Count Aldrovandi, several times, the first time on March 12, and then again on March 24, April 9 and April 22, and twice in the middle of May. At any rate, those are the dates mentioned by Károlyi in the first volume of his memoirs, published in 1923. The Sonnino papers confirm the accuracy of this part of Károlyi's recollections. On March 24, Sonnino, according to Károlyi, told Török that his principals would be well advised, to try to reconcile Hungary with Romania, if necessary making contact with Bratianu, to whom he would be willing to introduce the Hungarian forty-eightists.[77] As we know, however, this was not in conformity with the line of the Party of Independence and of 1848 which, so far as Romanian claims to Transylvania were concerned, shared the prevalent intransigent Magyar nationalism of which Count Apponyi was the most eloquent spokesman. On April 22, Sonnino (still according to Károlyi) said to Török: 'If God does not make miracles, he makes war.' Károlyi informed his father-in-law, Count Andrássy, of this, and the latter, though a supporter of the 'sacred union', was also, as a leader of the most moderate of the opposition parties, i.e. the 1867 Constitutional Party, Tisza's most influential political (and personal) rival. Andrássy suggested that Sonnino should be informed that he was working for a change in the composition of the Hungarian government with a view to the opposition being represented in it. On Török's return from his last visit to Rome, Károlyi and his colleagues handed Andrássy a memorandum on his conversations with Sonnino. We cannot be certain that this faithfully reflects what Sonnino said to Török, but it certainly corresponds with what the latter reported to the leaders of the Hungarian Independence Party. Here is a translation of the most interesting passages:

The deputies Count Mihály Károlyi, Count Tivadar Batthyány, Lajos Beck, and Márton Lovászy, who have been observing events in foreign policy with great concern since the beginning of the war, have felt it to be their duty to follow the attitude of the neutral states, and among them primarily Romania, Italy, and Greece, with the greatest attention, and have tried to obtain information based, not only on public opinion in those countries, but if possible also on the plans and proposals of their official circles.

In the course of this activity, through a friend of theirs who was repeatedly sent to Rome before the outbreak of war with Italy, they succeeded in gaining information months in advance, but always confirmed by events, on the plans and proposals of official Italy. . . . The above-mentioned deputies, knowing that on the most important question to our country, the Romanian question, Italy was acting in harmony with Romania as long as she remained neutral, believed it to be their imprescriptible duty to make use of their valuable and now consolidated contacts in Italy in the interests of their country and their King, and have again sent their friend to Rome. . . . Both during and since the end of the Italian political crisis, the emissary has found ways and means of communicating with Sonnino, who told him substantially what follows.

In spite of the fact that Italian opinion unanimously demands the fusion with Italy of the areas inhabited by Italians, he nevertheless gives a positive undertaking to drop the aspirations concerning Fiume and the Hungarian coast and to use all his influence to try to modify Romanian demands in relation to Transylvania, if he is met on the Hungarian side by the formation of a cabinet that includes all the political parties of the country—thus including the supporters of a policy of peace—and that demonstrates its desire for peace by excluding from the cabinet Count István Tisza, who is considered abroad to be the leading spirit behind the war.

Sonnino will adhere to this statement up to the end of June.

As it is in the pre-eminent interest of the dynasty, Hungary, and the dual monarchy that Romania should not attack us, the above-mentioned deputies consider it to be their patriotic and dynastic duty to submit the above information so that the most discreet use may be made of it, and they also do so because the consequences of a failure to communicate information of such vital interest would weigh on their conscience.

Should it be so desired in competent quarters, amplification of

[128]

the contents of this communication and answers to possible questions can be obtained.

N.B. On the evening of May 29, at 7.30, Mihály Károlyi and I called on Andrássy at his home in Buda and, in reference to our previous communications, informed him of our emissary's last mission and its results, asking him to make use of this information as he thought best in the country's interest.[78]

The memorandum must have been drafted by Count Batthyány, with the assistance of Károlyi, Beck and Török. While the known diplomatic documents confirm Sonnino's assurances to the Hungarians about Fiume and the Croatian coast (which the Hungarians had called the Hungarian coast since the time of the elder Kossuth), it seems at first sight hard to believe that the reticent, traditionalist Sonnino could have gone so far as to undertake to intervene in the Hungarian–Romanian dispute and explicitly to ask, even as a guarantee of a genuine desire for independence on the Hungarian part, for the exclusion from the Budapest government of Tisza, who was its legitimate leader backed by a parliamentary majority. The personal papers of Sonnino confirm only that he advised the Hungarians to reach an agreement with the Romanians. However, ostracisms of men assumed to be responsible for the outbreak of war, were proposed by the Entente governments, and by Sonnino himself, in the second half of the war, when the objective was to counter Austro-German moves for a stalemate peace, based on the *status quo ante* in the case of Austria and her military successes in the case of Germany. Moreover, the fact remains that in the atmosphere of desperation created in Budapest by the Italian intervention and the threat of Romanian intervention, a veteran politician such as Count Batthyány accepted as genuine the statements attributed to Sonnino by the young priest Török, to the extent of putting them in writing for the use of a personality such as Count Andrássy, who was to be received in audience by the monarch with a view to his possible appointment to a key post either in joint Austro-Hungarian affairs or in the Hungarian government.

At Batthyány's suggestion, Andrássy, Apponyi and A. Zichy (the last representing the relatively small Catholic Popular Party) asked Tisza on May 18, 1915, to hand over the Hungarian Prime Ministership to a less exposed personality (the name of the former Prime Minister Wekerle was mentioned), with a view to making possible the inclusion in a government of a national concentration of representatives of their respective parties. This would give it greater authority both abroad and at home than that possessed by the one-party

[129]

government headed by Tisza. The latter, whose habit it was to face up to situations without delay, promptly informed his cabinet of the proposal that he should resign which had been made to him in the name of the 'sacred union'. The cabinet unanimously opposed its leader's resignation, but decided that a number of portfolios, including some important ones, should be offered to the non-government parties, provided that they would agree to serve under Tisza. The Prime Minister informed Apponyi of this on May 21, and the latter, after consulting his colleagues, rejected the offer.[79] The opposition aim was the formation of a government whose policy would be directly or indirectly guided by Andrássy (who was also a candidate for the Foreign Affairs portfolio in Burian's place). Tisza himself reported these negotiations to Francis Joseph, who received in succession Andrássy, Apponyi and Zichy but refused to drop Tisza. A general election should have taken place in 1915, but it could not be held easily in wartime, so the opposition resigned itself to waiting. Károlyi left for the front as a volunteer, which earned him sharp attacks in the French press.

In the middle of 1916, as the result of an apparently desperate step taken by Károlyi, the situation changed. We shall anticipate events by giving an account of what happened, as it will make possible a better understanding of the consequences that the approach to the Entente in general and to Italy in particular of the Hungarian forty-eightists had in the process of the break up of the dual monarchy. These were no less important than the activities of the Czech and Croat *émigrés*. They led indirectly to the fact that in October 1918, on the eve of the final Italian offensive, the first troops of the Habsburg army to mutiny on the Italian front were the Hungarians. Several Magyar units decided then to go home and to fight, if necessary, for the independence and the integrity of their fatherland only.

In 1916, except on the Austro-Russian front, where a big Tsarist offensive resulted in a breakthrough that cost the Austro-Hungarians very heavy losses but was eventually stopped by the arrival of German reserves, the second anniversary of the outbreak of war took place in conditions of military stalemate. This increased the desire for peace among the peoples of all the belligerent countries, and was reflected in all the democratic parties. The governments reacted by trying to show that they were doing everything possible to attain peace and by blaming the enemy for the impossibility of doing so. At the beginning of 1917 the picture was clear; Russia and Austria-Hungary were militarily exhausted, and the western powers, hoping for American intervention, which might also have the effect of putting fresh life into the Russians, redoubled their intransigence towards the Hohenzollern empire, on which Italy too had meanwhile declared war. This situation had been intuitively foreseen by Károlyi since the middle of 1916. He had come to the conclusion that it was now impossible for the Central Powers to win the war (a factor that helped him to reach it was the information he gathered in the course of his intermittent military service—as a deputy he was always able to take leave to attend parliament), and that Hungary was likely to have to pay heavily for being Germany's ally. He decided openly to resume the struggle for his country's independence. The task was, or seemed to be, urgent in view of the imminent end of the Settlement between Austria and Hungary, which was subject to renewal at ten-year intervals, and the pressure being exercised by Germany for a thirty-year alliance, economic as well as military, between the two empires. This last point shows, incidentally, that Károlyi's impulse came from his own inner convictions and was not, as his detractors were later to maintain, the result of the influence of radical and socialist intellectuals, generally of Jewish extraction, whose advice he persistently sought after the outbreak of the Russian Revolution. During the previous year those intellectuals were divided among themselves about the desirability, from the point of view of Hungarian economic development and the interests of the working class, of the German *Mitteleuropa* plan for a customs and economic union between Germany and Austria-Hungary.[80] The radical socialist who in 1917–18 was to have the greatest influence on Károlyi was the well-known historian and sociologist Oscar Jászi, who was a *Mitteleuropa* supporter, and who hoped that an enlargement of the economic area would encourage the Hungarian bourgeoisie, with the support of the worker and peasant classes, to engage in a serious struggle against the semi-feudal supremacy of the big landowners, most of whom (including Tisza and Apponyi) were in fact opposed to *Mitteleuropa*. Though Károlyi himself belonged to the landowning class, his opposition to *Mitteleuropa*, derived from his opposition to a military alliance with Germany, and its motivation was exclusively political, both patriotic and pacifist. For these reasons he was repudiated, condemned and vilified by the aristocracy, who regarded him as a traitor.

The dispute, still on an amicable basis, began in the forty-eightist party between Károlyi and Apponyi. In his speeches (and he was a very fine speaker), Apponyi had for many years been calling for a radical revision of the Settlement between Austria and Hungary, that is to say its transformation into a 'personal union'; in other words, the two countries would share only the reigning dynasty. In the 1917 negotiations for a new ten-year agreement, however, in view of the

[131]

fact that the war was raging, he was opposed to asking for more than a number of advantages for Hungarian finances and for the display of Hungarian emblems in the joint Austro-Hungarian army as a prelude to its post-war division into two separate armies owing allegiance to the same sovereign. Tisza and Andrássy, realizing the inherent weakness of Apponyi's position, succeeded in securing his agreement to the setting-up of an inter-party consultative council for foreign affairs, the various committees of Austro-Hungarian parliamentarians being unable to function because the Vienna Reichsrat had not met since the outbreak of war. In Károlyi's absence, Apponyi arranged for the forty-eightist parliamentary group to be represented on this council, thus tying its hands in regard to the existing foreign policy, i.e. unconditional alliance with Germany. This was one way of making the forty-eightist opposition appear loyal to the 'sacred union' in the eyes of the general public. Károlyi resigned his chairmanship of the party in protest, and on July 18, 1916, a meeting of party militants who had decided on a split passed a resolution calling for denunciation of the Settlement with Austria at the end of its ten-year term; for the negotiation of a provisional *modus vivendi* to govern Austro-Hungarian relationships until the end of the war; for the transformation of the existing dual system into a personal union; for the immediate setting-up, while the war was still in progress, of a separate Hungarian army for the defence of the country's frontiers; and for a declaration that when the war was over, independent Hungary would no longer be bound by existing military alliances.[81] The resolution also called for peace without annexations, for the introduction of universal secret suffrage, and for agrarian reform.

In the Hungarian parliament, Károlyi took an early opportunity of interrogating the government on the conditions on which it would be willing to make peace with the Entente. He said that in his view it was in the Hungarian interest, whatever the Austrian and German attitudes might be, immediately to declare itself in favour of peace without annexations. Tisza declined to answer this disgraceful question. In reply, Károlyi repudiated the government's war policy and said that an autonomous peace policy was the essential prerequisite for the realization of the traditional aspirations of the Hungarian people to genuine independence and the maintenance of its historical integrity.

This radical statement completed the split in the Party of Independence and of 1848. Apponyi repudiated Károlyi's speeches and claimed that the essential preliminary for effective action leading to Hungarian independence was victory for the Central Powers.[82] In the party at large, Károlyi, who had the support of Justh, the aged leader of the movement, who was now seriously ill but still had great moral authority, had a majority, but only about twenty deputies sided with him in the Chamber. The others, numbering about eighty, sided with Apponyi and formed a party known as the Reunited Independents.

To Károlyi and his friends the split was not unwelcome. Modelling themselves on the revolutionary tradition of Louis Kossuth in 1849 and during his exile, they were now willing to resort to anything for the sake of Hungarian independence. The Romanian declaration of war (August 27, 1916) and invasion of Transylvania, which the Austro-Hungarian High Command had left unguarded, was quickly repulsed by the arrival of German troops, who in their turn penetrated deeply into Romania and actually advanced as far as Bucharest. But the episode had an extraordinarily embittering effect on Magyar public opinion, for it seemed to be a visible confirmation of the correctness of Károlyi's warning about Hungary's precarious position. Unless it found a way of extricating itself from the war until it was in a position to rely, in case of need, on strong military forces of its own (which could be formed of the many regiments recruited in Hungary, which had shown themselves to be the best at the dual monarchy's disposal but were now mingled with units raised in Austria on the Italian and Russian fronts, etc.), it would be at the mercy either of the Entente allies of Romania and Serbia or of Germany's unlimited will to expansion (demonstrated immediately after the capture of Bucharest by the organization of exclusively German control of the agricultural and mineral exploitation of Romania and the practical subordination of the Hungarian railway system to the requirements of the latter). It would still have been possible to regroup the Hungarian units and recall them to Hungary, and this was indeed done, though too late, when the Hungarian revolution of October 31, 1918, broke out. It should be pointed out, however, that the many Hungarians who called for this underestimated the difficulties of carrying it out. They believed in it because of a historical precedent they had all learned to venerate in their school days, namely, the initial success of the struggle for independence in 1848–49 (the defeat of the Austrians until the arrival of the Tsar's army), brought about by Kossuth's successful appeal to Hungarian troops in Cisleithania to return to their country, then threatened by Austrian invasion and the Serbian and Romanian revolt. Thus, when the Romanian invasion dramatically demonstrated the dangers to which Hungary was exposed and the grievous dependence on Germany into which she was stumbling, immediate concern about the outcome of the war worked hand in hand with historical memories that had always been assiduously cultivated. The result was that the influential and widely read liberal democratic Budapest press began shifting its position from support of Tisza's policy to policies close to Károlyi's. The process was completed within a few months. That this took place in spite of the military censorship is not surprising. The national and local government franchise was very restricted in Hungary in order to preserve the monopoly of central and local power (the latter being largely independent of the former) of the historical classes of the aristocracy and gentry, and for the same reason, trade-union rights (particularly in the countryside) were subject to arbitrary police interference. But the Magyar-language newspapers (unlike those of the Slav and Romanian nationalities, which were regularly persecuted) could be said to be free. The press had also been free in Austria, but it had ceased to be at the outbreak of war and resumed its freedom again only after the revival of parliamentary activity in the middle of 1917. But in Hungary, as parliamentary debate continued freely there in wartime, the press could not be said to be gagged.

The Hungarian Marxist economist Varga, editor of the Budapest Social Democratic newspaper, wrote to Kautsky in October 1914:

'Censorship is pretty liberal here and, apart from purely military matters, of course, we can write whatever we like.'[83]

In practice, the Hungarian opposition parties, including the Social Democratic Party, stopped attacking the monarchy's foreign policy at the outbreak of war and refrained from urging the masses to express rejection of the government's domestic policy by demonstrating in the streets. At the beginning of 1917, when they resumed doing both, the censorship grew much stricter in regard to those newspapers which opened their columns to such attacks and appeals, but political criticism stated in non-agitatorial terms was still tolerated.

This helps to explain the atmosphere in which the independence movement of the forty-eightist type was able to develop to its logical conclusion. Tisza's correspondence, published in Budapest in the inter-war period, and the still unpublished documents in the historical archives of the Italian Foreign Ministry, enable us to state that for more than a year after the Italian intervention, Károlyi's party continued its efforts to resume the contacts it had tried to establish with Sonnino during the last period of Italian neutrality.

In October 1917, the Hungarian Prime Minister was informed by the Chief of the Austro-Hungarian General Staff that at the beginning of the previous month a Hungarian subject named Holló had approached the Italian legation in Switzerland. Tisza immediately ordered a secret enquiry. The police established that, acting on

behalf of Károlyi and two deputies who were members of his party—
L. Beck and L. Holló—a son of the latter, B. Holló, who was exempt
from military service for health reasons and possessed a regular passport, had called on the Italian Ministry in Berne in company with the
priest J. Török. This had come to light because the Austro-Hungarian
counter-esponiage service had intercepted and partially deciphered a
telegram from the Italian diplomatist concerned (Marquis Paulucci
de' Calboli) to the Italian ambassador in Petrograd informing him of
a conversation he had had with two Hungarian emissaries (he mentioned Holló by name), who had come to put forward feelers for a
separate peace on behalf of the Hungarian independence movement,
which declared itself willing to satisfy Italian claims in the event of
its success.[84]

Tisza, perhaps because he was convinced at heart of Károlyi's
patriotic motivation and good faith, though he could hardly have
admitted this in public, was in no hurry to exploit this information
at the expense of his political opponents, and limited himself to having them watched.[85] In any case, they were protected by parliamentary
immunity, and their emissaries for the time being remained in
Switzerland. Török returned to Hungary and was arrested only in
September 1917, and the prosecution tried to involve Károlyi in the
case against him. But after Tisza's fall from power in May 1917, it
was not easy to indict Károlyi, who, with the consent of the new
sovereign, Charles, who desired a separate peace no less than he did
(and admitted this to him), was at the end of that year given a passport
to travel to Switzerland, where, as he partly describes himself and as
we shall later further particularize with the aid of more diplomatic
documents, he personally resumed the previous peace feelers, though
on this occasion in relation to the United States, which then had
intervened in the war.

The files of the Italian Foreign Ministry contain some information
about these soundings. On September 7, 1916, the Italian Minister in
Berne informed Sonnino's government that the son of the deputy
Holló, who belonged to Count Károlyi's and Count Batthyány's
party, had called on him to say that it (that is to say, the Party of
Independence and of 1848) 'no longer has any illusions about the
outcome of the struggle between the two great groups of European
powers' and realized that a German victory would be as disastrous to
Hungary as a defeat. On October 3, Carlotti, the ambassador in
Petrograd, telegraphed to Sonnino that the Russian Foreign Minister
had known about Holló's call on Paulucci de' Calboli and 'in view of
the interest that Russia also has in Hungarian questions' desired to
be informed about the matter. Sonnino answered Carlotti the next

day, authorizing him to confirm to the Russians that the conversation with the Hungarian emissary had taken place, but adding that 'we did not accept his approaches and refused any discussion of the matter, and informed him that before anything else the Hungarian people must demonstrate by deeds that it recognizes the mistakes of those who caused the war and must suffer the consequences'.[86]

Sonnino was obviously reluctant to do anything that might weaken Italy's claims against Austria-Hungary in the eyes of the allies. Apart from that there is no need for us to dilate on his conservative mentality—he obviously did not wish—as Cavour had done in 1859–60, when he gave his support to the exiled Kossuth and established a legion of Hungarian exiles and deserters—to reach a deal with conspirators unless they had actually secured power in their country. However, as his papers disclose, in his message to the Italian Minister in Switzerland Sonnino authorized him to tell the Hungarian emissary that Italy 'would not forget the friendship which has existed between the two countries'. In the light of this 1916 correspondence we can interpret the hint that, according to Török, Sonnino gave to the Hungarian independence party in May 1915 that they must first of all put themselves in the position of being able to speak in the name of the Budapest government. Sonnino, like everyone else not in a position to know exactly how war had been decided on in Vienna in July 1914, might well consider Tisza to be one of those who bore a major share of the responsibility, but, as appears from other sources, he would not have refused to negotiate with him if Tisza had decided to separate the fate of his country from that of Austria, and it is in these terms rather than in those of a veto on Tisza that we should perhaps interpret the references to necessary changes in the Hungarian government reported by Török in 1915 with implications that do not seem to have corresponded to the intentions of the Italian Foreign Minister, who in fact simultaneously agreed to enter into negotiations with Tisza.

As is stated in his correspondence, Tisza informed Burian on April 27, 1915, that he had been approached by a friendly personality who had given him a message from Sonnino. What happened was this. Professor Luigi Maria Bossi, a former socialist deputy who worked for the newspaper *Lavoro* of Genoa and was a keen interventionist, invited a distinguished Hungarian physician Dr R. Temesváry, a friend and fellow-gynaecologist, to Italy for a confidential political conversation. Temesváry, who asked for and received Tisza's approval before he made the trip, left Budapest on April 19, met Bossi at Genoa, and went with him to Rome, where he arrived on April 22. In Rome, Bossi was received by Sonnino, and immediately after their conversation he dictated to Temesváry a 'verbal message' for the Hungarian Prime Minister.[87]

The message said that Italy and Hungary, which shared the Risorgimento tradition, had a common interest in preventing either German or Slav supremacy in Central Europe. It would therefore be advisable for the Hungarian government to make itself independent of Germany and Austria, coming to a secret understanding to that end with Italy and Romania.[88]

In 1929, in a letter to the *Corriere della Sera*, Antonio Salandra, whose attention had been called to the message attributed to Sonnino printed in Tisza's correspondence, categorically denied that such a message could have been given by his deceased former government colleague, who had never mentioned it to him and was not a person likely to believe that a powerful and honourable personality such as Tisza was capable of agreeing to the idea of secret negotiations with potential enemies of the empire of which he was one of the principal political leaders.[89] Sonnino, Salandra said, might well have given a friendly reception to Bossi, who, being an influential Freemason, worked hard for Italian propaganda abroad, but could never have dictated to him such a message for Tisza.

Salandra added that the price of agreement with the Bucharest government could only have been Hungarian concessions to Romania, which (as we can confirm) had notoriously already been rejected by Tisza when they had been suggested to him by his Austrian associates and German allies, and it must be said that his argument is convincing. Tisza, in forwarding the message to Burian, said that he did so only as a curiosity, as he could not be sure how much of the contents was Bossi's and how much was Sonnino's.[90]

But Salandra's denial does not alter the fact that the message transmitted by Professor Bossi coincides, according to the testimony of Károlyi and his colleagues, with Török's report to them on his first conversations with Sonnino, and that Tisza thought it incumbent upon him to reply to it in writing, which he almost certainly would not have done if he had not believed that it originated with Sonnino, even though it contained some additions by Bossi. The letter, written in French, is published in Tisza's complete works. In it, Tisza restated the ideal and political reasons for the traditional friendship between Hungary and Italy, but said that it could survive only if 'all hostile designs on Austria' were excluded. 'Hungary can serve as a bulwark against the Slav tide that threatens the western coast of the Adriatic only if it is united with Austria,' he said. 'Hungary's fate is linked with the existence of Austria-Hungary as a great power.'[91]

Although Bossi's letters to Sonnino, which are preserved among the

[137]

latter's personal papers, do not establish that he actually dictated the message that Tisza received, they at least confirm that he authorized the intermediaries to sound out the views of the Hungarian Prime Minister on the future of Italo-Hungarian relations. In a 'personal and private' letter to Sonnino dated at Genoa on April 29, 1915, Bossi said:

> I have today received your telegram and hasten to reply. You will remember that the basis of the agreement with my friend Temesváry, who represents the whole of the liberal element in Hungary, was that Tisza should come to a secret understanding with Italy, that is with you, with a view to establishing a strong Hungary, and that the latter should subsequently remain linked with Italy, France, Britain . . . Russia.

On May 7, Bossi, again from Genoa, forwarded to Sonnino the message Temesváry had sent him from Budapest. That this was Tisza's reply is shown by the following sentence: 'I enclose the letter I found waiting for me at Genoa on arriving from Rome. From this it is evident that Tisza is sincere towards us, though he cannot act for the time being because of the situation he is in.' In the same letter, Bossi informed Sonnino that he was going to Lugano two days later to meet Dr Temesváry. After his return to Genoa, he wrote to Sonnino on May 10 as follows:

> I spent many hours yesterday with my friend D. Temesváry, who was sent to Lugano by Tisza for discussions with me. The substance of what he told me and of the various conversations he had with Tisza in Budapest is as follows: (1) Tisza is very, very angry with the Germans at the present moment, but cannot and must not reveal this in any way . . . (3) Tisza showed himself prepared, when the moment comes, to make peace separately from Germany, knowing that you will support Hungarian aspirations, but wants this to be, not a betrayal, but a genuine consequence of events . . . (5) Tisza insisted that I should express his gratitude and that of the Hungarians to you for your sympathies with Hungary and that I should tell you that this will bring fruits of great mutual utility. . . .[92]

Bossi's letters as a whole show that he had too much imagination. Just as he did not hesitate to attribute to Tisza a statement (relating to a separate peace) in obvious conflict with the whole of Tisza's policy, as is evident also from his private papers, so he may well have told him in Sonnino's name things that the latter did not by any means intend. But that does not alter the fact that he constantly gave information to Sonnino, who did not repudiate him or forbid him to continue his contacts with the Hungarians.

Thus it seems established that Sonnino had in mind the possibility of a Hungarian alternative. This can have made him only more reluctant to accept the idea of a greater Yugoslavia, which could be established only at the expense primarily of St Stephen's Crown.[93] Faced with the insistence of the British and Russian governments, on August 9, 1915, he at last agreed to Serbia's being promised Bosnia-Hercegovina, the part of Dalmatia not claimed by Italy, and a small slice of territory in southern Hungary, but only on condition that the fate of Croatia and Fiume should be left open until the end of the war.[94] Sir Edward Grey therefore drafted a note taking account of Sonnino's reservations, but modifying them slightly, which was presented to the Serbian government on August 16 by the British, French and Russian ambassadors. It asked Serbia to cede a part of Macedonia to Bulgaria, but, in addition to what Sonnino had agreed should be promised her, it offered her a larger slice of southern Hungary (that is to say Srem and the Bačka, but not the Banat, which was reserved for Romania) and Slavonia. It further stated that the fate of Croatia, with its coastline from the Bay of Volosca to the Dalmatian frontier, including Fiume, was reserved without prejudice for a final decision to be taken when peace was signed, though the allied powers for their part renounced any claim to these territories.[95] Next day, the Italian ambassador delivered a similar note to Pašić's government without, however, mentioning Slavonia.[96] In not wishing to promise the latter Sonnino was merely being consistent. For geographical reasons, the assignment of Slavonia to Serbia would have prejudiced the fate of the whole of Croatia.

Pašić refused the compromise, however. He expressed willingness to sacrifice a slice of Macedonia to the Bulgarians, though a substantially smaller one than the Entente governments had asked for, but said he would do so only after receiving the territories promised to Serbia, i.e. after final victory over Austria-Hungary. Furthermore, he demanded that Croatia-Slavonia, including Fiume, Slovenia and the western Banat, should be added to the territories offered to Serbia.[97] Supilo, who, like Pašić, feared the pro-Habsburg and pro-Hungarian particularism that was still strong in Croatia, had again insisted on restating the principle of the unconditional and irrevocable union of Croatia-Slavonia, including Fiume, and of Slovenia.[98]

The negotiations led to nothing. Though, as we have seen, the reasons underlying Sonnino's reluctance to sacrifice the Magyar card were not entirely without foundation, his critics are justified in

[139]

pointing out that these negotiations should have made clear to the Italian government the necessity of reaching a direct agreement with the Serbian government on the basis of recognition, in the event of total victory, of Yugoslav unity, at any rate in the territories not assigned to Italy (or it should have tried to keep Fiume Italian by offering concessions in Dalmatia, as Count Sforza did five years later).[99]

As Salvemini and Battisti foresaw, and as Albertini and Bissolati later made clear to the more sensible section of public opinion and the government itself, and as events themselves confirmed in 1918, Italy could not gain a partial victory over Austria-Hungary. After Italy had demanded compensation from her former ally and refused it as totally unsatisfactory when it was offered, though it was the maximum that Austria-Hungary could offer without beginning the process of its own dismemberment along national lines, and after the Entente had accepted Italy's claims, which were on a scale that made a separate peace with the Habsburg empire impossible (as was seen in 1917), the terms on which Italian intervention took place ensured that the war that Italy declared on May 24, 1915, would end in decisive victory for one side or the other. The final defeat of Austria-Hungary, which went to war in July 1914 for the specific purpose of stifling the Yugoslav movement, was bound to make that movement uncontainable. Sonnino's idea that Austria-Hungary could survive the mutilations from the Brenner to Sebenico implied by the Treaty of London was an unfounded illusion, even though at the beginning of 1915 no Entente statesman, with the possible exception of Sazonov, believed in the end of the Danubian monarchy.[100]

An American scholar has rightly pointed out that Sonnino's deficient understanding of the historical development that the Italian intervention set in train contributed to throwing the Croats into the arms of the Serbs within a framework of unification which—let us recall—ceased to be democratic, as a result of fear of Italy, opened the way to power in the new Yugoslavia to a militarism that far exceeded that of pre-war Serbia, almost as a response—both before and after the short prevalence of good sense represented by the Treaty of Rapallo of 1920 and the agreement of 1924—to the spread of an unlimited nationalism, anti-Yugoslav *par excellence*, in Italy herself.[101]

Supilo, who at the beginning of 1915 would have agreed to combine the Croat and Slovene cause with that of the projected Serbo-Bulgarian agreement, was kept informed about the course of negotiations by Sir Edward Grey's secretary, E. Drummond. During the summer he realized that Italian opposition put large-scale negotiations out of the question. Disappointing his British friends, he therefore advised Pašić to refuse any arrangement other than that of complete Yugoslav unity. He was received by the British Foreign Secretary at the end of August 1915. He told the latter frankly that the Yugoslav nation was not offering itself to Serbia in fragments, but only complete and in one piece, in a process of complete liberation.[102] Supilo's openness favourably impressed Sir Edward Grey, who at the end of their conversation said he would adopt the following formula: 'After the war, Bosnia, Hercegovina, southern Dalmatia, Slavonia and Croatia will be free. They will be able to decide their own fate.'[103]

Though the Foreign Secretary did not mention Slovenia, which would only have aggravated the disagreement with Sonnino—who not wishing to agree even to the union of Croatia with Serbia, had informed the Russian ambassador in Rome about ten days previously that he would prefer leaving Ljubljana and the Slovene provinces bordering on the frontiers claimed by Italy under Vienna rather than seeing them added to a Yugoslavia in which (because of the number of Slovenes and Croats transferred to Italian sovereignty under the Treaty of London) irredentism might well turn against the Italian state—Supilo, as appears from a message he sent to Pašić, wanted the Serbian government to pronounce itself immediately in favour of Sir Edward Grey's formula. The important thing was that it contained the principle of self-determination, which it would be impossible to refuse the Slovenes at the end of a war won in the name of the freedom of the nations. But Pašić disliked the formula since by offering them the right of self-determination it put the territories that with Italian consent had already been promised to Serbia on the same footing as Croatia, the fate of which, at the Italian request, it had been agreed to leave undecided until the end of the war. The Niš government therefore dropped Sir Edward Grey's and Supilo's idea of reconsidering the whole Yugoslav programme in terms of the principle of self-determination. Pašić and his Minister in London resented Supilo's independent intervention with the Foreign Office. To them the primary consideration was the danger that consistent application of the principle of self-determination would put a question-mark against some of the acquisitions to which they aspired in southern Hungary, as well as territory in Macedonia that they did not want to give up. The result was that the Serbian government took action with a view to cutting off Supilo's diplomatic contacts and setting against him those of his colleagues on the Yugoslav Committee who were under the influence of, or subsidized by, Pašić.[104]

Sir Edward Grey's statement, however, remained in the Foreign Office files, capable of being dusted off and revived in the future.

In the autumn of 1916, Asquith, faced with diplomatic and propaganda moves by the Central Powers for a peace based on the *status quo*, asked his Foreign Secretary—who had already proposed such a step to prevent Russia from detaching herself from the Entente after Sazonov's fall—to draw up a memorandum on the territorial aims that the Entente should declare in the name of the principles for which it was fighting.[105] The officials charged with drafting it, Sir William Tyrrell and Ralph Paget, the first of whom had often received Supilo whereas the second—who had served in Belgrade before the war—was in contact with Masaryk, pointed out, when they came to deal with the Yugoslav problem, that the Serbs, Croats and Slovenes desired to emancipate themselves completely from Austria-Hungary and merge into a single state to be established by free consent and with no supremacy on the part of anyone.

> The statement made by Sir Edward Grey to M. Supilo on September 1, 1915, that, provided Serbia agrees, Bosnia, Hercegovina, southern Dalmatia, Slavonia and Croatia shall be permitted to decide their own fate, is therefore far more in accord with Yugoslav ideals than the assurance previously given, and should be the determining factor in guiding our policy on this question.[106]

For the same reason, when they came to consider the fate of Austria-Hungary in the event of Entente victory, the memorandum concluded that

> there seems very little doubt that, in accordance with the principle of giving free play to nationalities, the dual monarchy, which in its present composition is a direct negation of that principle, should be broken up, as there is no doubt that all the non-German parts of Austria-Hungary will secede.[107]

Lloyd George and Balfour were more energetic in the prosecution of the war but less idealistic (and the former was more Austrophile) than Asquith and Grey, whom they were shortly to displace, and the British government took no action on the memorandum. Nevertheless, the idea of a break up of Austria-Hungary by the decision of its own nationalities, a possibility previously stated only as a matter of personal opinion by a Russian Minister, by Czech and Croatian exiles, and by some Italian, French and British radical publicists, took its place in the calculations of the Entente powers.

V

From the Central Powers' Peace Offer to the Corfu Agreement

The first statesman who publicly declared himself in favour of the inclusion in the Entente war aims of the dismemberment of the Habsburg empire was Leonida Bissolati, Italian Minister without Portfolio in the Boselli cabinet and responsible for liaison with the High Command.[1] His friend and colleague Cesare Battisti had been taken prisoner some months previously in Italian officer's uniform and, being an Austrian citizen, had been court-martialled and hanged for high treason. Taking up an idea that had been first put forward in Italy by Battisti, Bissolati, speaking in his friend's memory in his own native town of Cremona on October 29, 1916, spoke of what he considered should be the fate of Austria-Hungary:

> As long as that monstrous structure exists, that state which is a negation and suppression of all nationalities that are not German or Magyar, imperial Germany will always be able to stretch out her arm and use it as a weapon and exploit its enormous power for another trial of strength. The hydraheaded monster must be slain, and from its dead body must arise all the living stocks that have been painfully compressed into its artificial unity; some, such as the Tridentine and Adriatic Italians, the Romanians and the Yugoslavs, to rejoin their mother stock; others, such as the Czechs and the Poles, to revive their ethnic personality. A living wall of nations that want a life of liberty and peace, and will watch jealously over their peace and liberty, will force Germany to rid herself of her mania for brutal domination. Until this aim is attained, talking of peace is a most dangerous trap for peace. . . . Those who now talk of peace in the name of socialist proletarian solidarity should remember that the German socialists have repudiated Liebknecht, just as those of Austria have repudiated, not only the gesture, but also the ideas of Friedrich Adler. . . .[2]

The view that any idea of a compromise peace was playing the German game was very widespread among the Entente nations, no matter whether it was openly advocated by deputies of the Italian Socialist Party or put forward much more cautiously by statesmen known for their moderation, such as Lord Lansdowne in Britain, Caillaux in France and (according to public repute unsupported by any public gesture by him) Giolitti in Italy, or favoured by personalities outside the fray, in the neutral states or in the Vatican. Apart from the fanaticism prevalent in wartime, from which even Bissolati was not immune, there was an element of truth in his otherwise very exaggerated contentions. The resources of manpower and industrial and agricultural raw materials at the disposal of the Entente empires—which also had command of the seas—in the last resort greatly exceeded those of the Central Powers. If the morale of the Entente nations remained firm and aggressive in spite of the innumerable sacrifices of a war that became more and more bloodthirsty, its prolongation—provided their armed forces did not collapse under the enemy's blows—necessarily increased the probability of their final victory. On the other hand, German soil was practically free of enemy occupation, and the area of Austria-Hungary under enemy occupation had been greatly reduced by the end of 1916 after the final failure of the great Russian offensive of the summer of that year and the defeat of Romania. But troops of the Central Powers, and of Germany in particular, were in occupation of the whole of Belgium, a considerable portion of northern France, Russian Poland, and other areas of Tsarist Russia, Serbia, Montenegro, and a large part of Romania. The Italian army had taken Gorizia, but had not attained the other objectives for which Italy had entered the war. In negotiations for a stalemate peace, the positions actually occupied by the respective military forces could not possibly have been ignored, and Germany would therefore have remained in possession of far greater material pledges than those in the hands of the Entente, which at bottom could boast only of the seizure of the German colonies in Africa.

Nor was Bissolati wrong in suggesting that if, after years of bloodshed, a peace were to leave the Central Powers with their material potential and political and military structure intact, it would be far easier for a nation like Hohenzollern Germany—governed autocratically, though sometimes with the enthusiastic consent of most of its population (which, despite its high degree of culture and its legal system's provision of a number of guarantees of liberty, was brought up to worship militarism)—to make war again when its leaders believed the situation opportune than it would be for such nations as Britain, France and Italy, which had democratic institutions and were largely peaceful by inclination.

However, the German High Command, whose authority in the political field actually exceeded that of the Reich Chancellor (and a year later was to become greater still), and imposed itself even on the

Emperor William II, whose will was as weak as his love of martial poses was strong, did not want a compromise peace. Russian Poland had been occupied thanks chiefly to the German army, and the High Command insisted on setting it up as a new kingdom (proclaimed on November 5, 1916) under the protection of the Central Powers, though Bethmann-Hollweg, the Chancellor, pointed out in a report to the Prussian cabinet on October 24 that the step would probably make a separate peace with Tsarist Russia impossible. But Hindenburg and Ludendorff wanted it for military reasons of highly questionable validity—they were under the illusion that it would greatly facilitate the raising of Polish recruits.[3] Nevertheless there were representatives of the top flight of the great German steel industry, such as Thyssen, who favoured a compromise peace with the Petrograd government, though they held that the annexation of the Briey basin, which precluded the possibility of any such peace in the West, as essential to Germany.[4]

The plea that Germany should take the initiative in proposing a negotiated peace in a military situation in which this could be done without its seeming to be a sign of weakness came, not from the Prussian militarists, but from the Social Democratic Party. The deputy Südekum, who maintained liaison between the Chancery and the Social Democratic parliamentary group, on November 10, 1915, suggested in a memorandum to Under-Secretary of State Wahnschaffe that a German peace offer should be made in a speech in the Reichstag and followed by diplomatic activity for which he hoped the discreet backing of the Pope could be obtained.[5] Südekum, as a politician used to taking public opinion into account, realized that the Germans needed a moral strengthening of their cause, particularly abroad. But, though he was one of the least disinterested and most chauvinistic of the parliamentarians who took the German Social Democrats into the 'sacred union' with the imperial government now that all the documents are available it cannot be argued that either he or Bethmann-Hollweg thought of peace as an interval for the better preparation of another war. As for the leaders of the German Social Democratic Party, who, after all, were farther to the left than Südekum—whose action in the service of the government in 1915 was deplored by Ebert himself—Bissolati's charge was even wider of the mark.[6]

The Social Democratic leaders, under pressure of competition from the secessionists from their party who, in token of their loyalty to the principles of proletarian internationalism, were setting about founding the Independent Socialist Party, in August 1916 circulated a popular petition for a peace without annexations.[7]

To the Austro-Hungarian government, which now at heart regretted its plunge into war and was pressing for a peace move to be made, the idea of another war was even more remote. In a report to Bethmann-Hollweg on September 28, 1916, which he immediately forwarded to Hindenburg, Tschirschky, the German ambassador in Vienna, openly expressed his fear that the Habsburg monarchy might be facing a military and economic collapse which would drag Germany down to ruin in its wake.[8] Burian, the Austro-Hungarian Foreign Minister, said at a meeting with the Chancellor on October 17, 1916, that it was essential 'to make an effort to bring about the end of the war without abandoning any vital interests', but on a basis of reason.[9] Burian did not deny 'that the chauvinists would condemn a peace concluded on that basis as an act of cowardice and a renunciation of conquests gained by our armies' blood. But we shall never succeed in satisfying those people, and they constitute only a minority, whose fury no statesman must take into consideration. The great mass of the people, at any rate in the monarchy, will greet such a peace with joy.'[10] In the event of a negative reply by the enemy governments, he hoped that the move would at least serve to turn the pacifists in the Entente countries as well as the neutral states and the peoples of the Central Powers themselves against those responsible for the refusal (this, incidentally, was exactly what Bissolati feared).[11]

The peace terms that the Austro-Hungarian Foreign Minister had in mind, however, were not so reasonable as he believed. He demanded that the territorial integrity of the Central Powers should be respected, but he asked Germany to respect only that of France (and, it may be assumed, Britain). Belgium would be re-established as a sovereign state 'subject to guarantee of the legitimate interests of Germany,' but it would have to yield the Congo to Germany, which would of course regain all her own colonies. Germany would acquire Lithuania and perhaps also Courland from Russia; while Russian Poland would become an independent kingdom. For itself, Austria-Hungary asked only for frontier rectifications, minimal in relation to Italy, but substantial in relation to Serbia, Montenegro and Romania, and she also wanted a protectorate over Albania. Bulgaria would be entitled to greater territorial cessions from Serbia and Romania. Turkey in exchange for the abolition of the Capitulations, would have to grant Russia freedom of navigation through the Straits.[12]

These terms would in fact have meant victory for the Central Powers, though partial and not complete victory, but to the German High Command they were completely unacceptable. In a memorandum to the Chancellor, Hindenburg stated on a far more ambitious scale the conditions that he considered indispensable from the point

[146]

of view of German military security. He wanted the whole of the Longwy and Briey basin and other minor cessions of French territory; substantial annexations in Belgium, including Liège and a part of the Flemish coast, and the 'close dependence' of that country on the German empire; the Baltic coast and other Russian territories (some of which would go to Austria-Hungary), so as to encircle the Poland that was to be separated from the Tsarist empire and to reduce the Russo-Polish frontier to a minimum; the transformation of a part of Romania (Wallachia) into a German dependency 'practically on the lines of an ancient Roman province', and the transfer to German administration of the port of Constanza. He also stipulated that Germanys' new frontier with Russia must be as advanced as possible, so as to 'obtain thereby a good area of deployment for further warlike developments in the east against the centres of the Russian state, as well as a large area for the benefit of the public food supply.'[13]

Hindenburg and his mentor, Ludendorff, obviously knew that the Entente powers would never agree even to discuss such terms unless they were forced to do so by total and irrevocable defeat. No doubt for that reason, the Field-Marshal warned his government on December 8 that any peace feelers must be carried out without impeding either operations in progress, or the unrestricted submarine warfare projected for the end of January 1917 (and in fact begun then), or the plans for the strategic invasion of neutral countries, i.e. Denmark and Holland (which, as a result of the February revolution and the consequent hopes of a Russian capitulation, and also because of Bethmann-Hollweg's opposition, were never carried out).[14] Also the German Admiralty informed the Chancellor on December 24 that, in agreement with the High Command, it believed it to be its duty to insist on terms that would provide bigger and better operational bases against Britain in the event of another war. It therefore demanded nearly the whole of the Belgian coast (as well as the Lithuanian and Latvian coasts for use against Russia), as well as oceanic bases in the Azores, at Dakar and in Tahiti.[15]

Although proposals such as these amply justified Bissolati's hostility to Prussian militarism, it is by no means certain that peace negotiations based on them would have advanced the Central Powers' cause. Claims which would have satisfied Hindenburg and Ludendorff (to say nothing of the German Admiralty) could not have been put forward without alienating the democratic section of German public opinion and nearly the whole of Austro-Hungarian opinion, and if the governments concerned ignored their demands they would have run the risk of being overthrown by the military leaders, whose prestige was still high. (That, indeed, was what happened in July of the following year to Bethmann-Hollweg, who in his heart of hearts, as he confessed to one of the Emperor's private secretaries, would have been willing to accept peace on the basis of the *status quo ante*.)[16] In December 1916, President Wilson of the United States called on all the belligerents to declare their war aims, and Berlin and Vienna, after some hesitation, failed to give an adequate reply because they were unable to state their terms in public.[17] True, on December 12, 1916, anticipating the note from President Wilson that they knew was being drafted, they publicly offered peace to their enemies, but on the tacit understanding that negotiations on territorial matters would take place through secret diplomatic channels. Thus William II was able to claim in the eyes of the general public, and also for the benefit of the army, that being a victor he had offered peace.

Bissolati was motivated not merely by his hatred of German militarism, which was the reason why he had always insisted that Italy should declare war on Germany, as in fact she did in August 1916, two months after his entry into the government—he was also convinced that no agreement with Austria-Hungary, but only her total defeat would lead to the full satisfaction of Italian national claims, even if, as he intended, they were kept strictly within the limits of the ethnic principle. From the beginning of his campaign for intervention he had always stated that he did not want Italy to claim either the Dalmatian coast or any other territory to which she was not entitled by the 'genuine and disinterested application of the nationality principle'. (He accordingly strongly deplored the post-war annexation by Italy of the German part of the South Tyrol, from Bolzano to the Brenner.)[18] He also believed, as early as the end of 1914, that the nationality principle would have the effect of 'dissolving the Danubian empire as it is constituted today'.[19] As we have seen, in May 1915 Austria was willing to give Italy the Trentino and the area up to the Isonzo, but not Trieste (though she might have agreed to make the latter a Free City), and still less Istria, including Pola, which was the empire's chief naval base. To those who had wanted war to secure these territories for Italy, which were ethnically Italian but were economically and militarily essential to the Habsburg empire, the danger was that, in the event of negotiations for a compromise peace, the major Entente powers, seeing that, contrary to their hopes, Italian intervention had not sufficed to put Austria-Hungary out of action, might advise their Italian ally to content herself with what Vienna had offered in May 1915 and Giolitti had found acceptable. In fact, on December 27, 1916, the Papal Nuncio in Vienna informed Wedel, the German ambassador, of peace terms which, according to Cardinal Gasparri, the Papal Secretary of State, would be acceptable to the Entente. The Holy See's informant (concerning whose identity Cardinal Gasparri revealed only that *évidemment ce n'est pas un concierge*) had described these terms as follows so far as Italy was concerned: 'Trieste a Free City. A free hand in Albania. Cession of those territories in which the Italian language predominates.'[20] Substantially, with the addition of recognition of Italy's establishing herself in Albania (which was already taking place with the occupation of Valona and other strategic points), this amounted to the cession of the Trentino and of that part of the province of Gorizia in which Italian could be regarded as the dominant language. Leaving out of account Trieste, which was to become a Free City, in the rest of Istria the Slav population of the countryside outnumbered the Italian inhabitants of the small towns. The British and French statesmen might also have considered that, in the event of a separate peace with Austria-Hungary becoming possible, it would be only reasonable for Italy, which so far had failed to win either Trent ot Trieste by force of arms, to accept a compromise of this sort. As is shown by Giolitti's conversations with Malagodi, he himself believed this. But to those like Bissolati who had fought bitterly at the beginning of 1915 for the rejection of Giolitti's *parecchio*—the substantial gain the former Prime Minister believed Italy could have made without sacrificing her neutrality—and had wanted her to enter the war at all costs, acceptance, after eighteen months of enormous bloodshed, of a compromise similar to that which they had denounced, in opposition to Giolitti, as a betrayal of national interests, would have been a political impossibility.[21]

Unfortunately the difficulties of his position caused Bissolati to become so exasperated with the pacifism of the Italian Social Party as to make him appear in 1916–17 to be a supporter of severe measures against the pacifist and internationalist propaganda of the labour movement. The result was to strengthen the intransigents in the Socialist Party, to whom Bissolati's democratic, anti-nationalist foreign policy was no better than that of Sonnino and of the Nationalist Right. Between 1918 and 1921 the democratic opposition to nationalism consequently did not have the support of the labour, socialist and internationalist forces, even when the differences between neutralists and interventionists were overcome in 1920 with Sforza's entry, as a Foreign Minister, into Giolitti's last government.

Theoretically, opposition to any compromise with Austria-Hungary need not have been synonymous with the destruction of the Habsburg monarchy. Throughout the war the Italian Foreign Minister, Baron Sonnino, firmly insisted on Entente respect for the Treaty of London, which assigned to Italy, not only Trent, Gorizia, Trieste,

[149]

Pola and Zara, but also territories predominantly inhabited by Germans, as in the South Tyrol, and by Slavs, as in the interior of Istria and on the Dalmatian coast as far as and including Sebenico. Nevertheless, Sonnino did not regard the dissolution of Austria-Hungary as a necessity. He not only did not want it, he actually feared it, on the ground that it might bring Russia, as the patron of the Southern Slavs, to the Adriatic and Germany to the Brenner.[22] In practice, however, Sonnino's policy was even more contradictory than Bissolati's. Application of the nationality principle in Bissolati's sense, involving the assignment to Italy of all the undoubtedly Italian territories that had been left under Austrian rule in 1866, implied the elimination of Austria-Hungary from the ranks of the great powers. But if the amputations were limited merely to the Trentino, Gorizia, Trieste and the small Italian towns of Istria (excluding Pola) and, let us assume, the cession to Serbia of Bosnia-Herzegovina and a port on the Dalmatian coast (with which Pašić, as became clear later, would have been satisfied in the event of a compromise peace), Austria-Hungary would have been able to reorganize herself democratically and transform herself into a peaceful federation of nations, always assuming that these nations agreed to keep it in being for reasons of dynastic loyalty, community of economic and cultural interests, and the impossibility in areas of mixed population of drawing frontiers in harmony with the ethnic criterion. Today this may seem Utopian, but to the most authoritative 'realist' statesmen in Britain and France up to the beginning of 1918 it seemed to conform with the existing relation of forces, whereas the *Delenda Austria* campaign struck them as Utopian and senseless. Had Italy been satisfied with a solution of this kind in 1917, the problem would have remained of making it acceptable to Russia and Romania. But at the beginning of 1918 both these countries stopped fighting, conceded defeat, and accepted the truly brutal and monstrous terms imposed by the Central Powers. Thus the only certain allies in the campaign for the break up of Austria-Hungary on whom Bissolati and others in Italy who harked back to the principles of Mazzini could rely were—apart from Wickham Steed, Seton-Watson, and a few other British and French publicists— the Czech and Serbo-Croat exiles. They, however, were motivated, not so much by Mazzinian idealism as by aspirations for independence not devoid of nationalism and preoccupation with strategic considerations and, far from sharing Bissolati's 'renunciationism' and respect for the nationality principle, claimed for their future states territories which were ethnically German (such as the Sudetenland) or Magyar (in southern Slovakia and northern Hungary). Leaving aside Beneš and Trumbić, not even Masaryk or Supilo, who were undoubtedly rather more idealistic than they, would have agreed unless forced to do so by the relation of forces, to the renunciations in favour of the ethnical principle which Bissolati declared himself willing to make. Such were the paradoxes of the situation in which he put himself when he began his crusade for the dismemberment of Austria-Hungary.

Sonnino's position, on the other hand, was bedevilled by the fact that he took for granted the survival of Austria-Hungary in spite of the fact that he had made this *a priori* impossible by the terms of the Treaty of London. The Southern Slavs and German Austrians would never have forgiven the Habsburg dynasty for sacrificing their fellow-nationals in Istria, Dalmatia and the Southern Tyrol. With its military strength gravely diminished and weakened by the loss of strategic points such as the Brenner and the Monte Maggiore and the naval port of Pola, humiliated by the inevitable explosion of the Hungarian independence movement that would have taken place (and would almost certainly have resulted in the transformation of the monarchy into a mere personal union with the grant of military and financial independence to the kingdom of Hungary), the Habsburg empire would have been unable to counter the gravitation to Germany of the German Austrians. The consequence of an Austro-Hungarian defeat would inevitably be the loss of Bosnia-Hercegovina. This would immediately raise the question of the formation of a Yugoslav state, which would exercise a far more dangerous gravitational pull on the Slovenes and Croats, which the Habsburg empire would also have been unable to counter. Above all, it would not have been able to counter the independence movements of the Poles and Czechs.

With Supilo's return to Italy at the beginning of April 1916, the conflict between Bissolati's ideas and Sonnino's came to a head. Supilo, disappointed at Pašić's rejection of the idea—which Sir Edward Grey had accepted in the summer of 1915—that Croatia and the other Yugoslav territories of Austria-Hungary should be given the right to self-determination at the end of the war, including the right to decide the conditions of their possible unification with Serbia, in February 1916 asked the Yugoslav Committee to declare that the future national state must include all the Southern Slavs (not only those in the provinces conquered by Serbia or assigned to her by Russia or the other powers) and must be organized on the basis of self-determination and democratic federalism, thus with an implicit guarantee against pan-Serbian hegemony.[23] The Committee, some members of which were in the pay of the Serbian government, whereas others, such as its chairman, Trumbić himself, thought it unwise to risk a rupture with Pašić, rejected Supilo's proposal at a number of meetings held in Paris, and reiterated that it supported Yugoslavia unconditionally. Later meetings between Supilo and Pašić, and with the Regent Prince Alexander, whom Steed and Seton-Watson believed to be more committed to the Yugoslav cause than his Prime Minister, did not change the situation.[24] It was thus that Supilo, no longer committed to the Serbian government and in a position that would have enabled him to collaborate freely with the Italian government, approached Sonnino.

This time he made careful preparations for his trip to Italy. During the first half of March he succeeded in securing an interview with Tittoni, the Italian ambassador in Paris. Tittoni's report to Sonnino says that Supilo, who spoke excellent Italian, had become very friendly with deputy Fradeletto during his stay in Italy on the eve of the outbreak of the European war.[25]

Tittoni then goes on to recall that Supilo had had conversations in Petrograd in 1915 with Sazonov and with the Italian ambassador, Carlotti, and that in Britain he was

> received by Asquith, Grey, and Cecil, who listened to him very attentively and showed sympathy for his cause. From them he received the advice, which he is now following, to go to Italy and confer with the principal politicians and members of the government. On his way he stopped in Paris, but met with greater indifference there. . . . In Rome, Supilo will present himself to your Excellency, to whom he has a letter of introduction. In Rome, he proposes to advocate close union between Italians and Slavs in the Adriatic and the unification of Croatia with Serbia. After listening without interruption to what he had to say at this point I said that I advised him to mention only the first point in Rome and to refrain from mentioning the second. He told me that Briand, by whom he has been received, gave him the same advice.[26]

Gina Lombroso's letters to Supilo show that he asked her husband, Guglielmo Ferrero, and Professor Gaetano Mosca, who was a close friend of Ferrero's and was Under-Secretary of State for the Colonies in the Salandra Ministry at that time, to give him introductions to the Italian government. In an undated letter obviously written in March 1916, Gina Lombroso replied that during his previous stay in Italy she had spoken about him 'at length to Mosca, and he is consequently in a position to understand the importance that words have in your mouth. As for introducing you to Salandra and Sonnino, neither he nor Guglielmo will be able to do so—it seems that the leaders have no desire to see or listen to anyone.'[27] In reply to a telegram from Supilo

[152]

announcing the date of his arrival, she said that if Professor Mosca, who was frequently away, were not in Rome, he would be able to talk to Bissolati and Ferri, who would introduce him to someone in the government. She also suggested that he should see Nathan, the former mayor of Rome and Grand Master of the Freemasons.[28]

Bissolati received him on April 2, 1916. An entry under that date in his only partly published notes contains the following among other things:

> He showed me a 'pass' issued by all the governments of the quadruple alliance. . . . He said he was travelling with the consent of the British government to sound out whether it were possible to change the basis of the Russo-Italian compromise.
>
> According to this compromise:
>
> (a) The whole of Dalmatia would be assigned to Italy;
> (b) Serbia—with a small outlet to the Adriatic—would be separated from Croatia;
> (c) Serbia would have Bosnia and Hercegovina.
>
> This, he said, was contrary to the irresistible trend to Yugoslav unity and autonomy and would make both Croats and Serbs enemies of Russia and Italy.
>
> It was accepted by Russia because Russian policy, dominated by the Holy Synod, feared that in a Serbo-Croat union the Orthodox Serbian element would be dominated by the Catholic Croatian element; by Italy because in the division of the Yugoslav strength it hoped to see a guarantee of its Dalmatian possessions; by Britain because it feared that a strong Yugoslavia might be a tool of Russia in its plan for supremacy in the Mediterranean.
>
> Supilo of course wants Italy to see that her interests lie in the development of Yugoslavia (with a large part of Dalmatia) in alliance with Italy.
>
> I answered frankly that I agreed. I reminded him that I had already publicly stated my ideas.
>
> Supilo would like to talk to Sonnino. He came to see me again after talking to Mosca—the Under-Secretary for the Colonies—who said to him: 'The only one who can secure the interview is Bissolati.'
>
> I talked to Sonnino on the last day when the Chamber was in session. I gathered the impression that the compromise was as Supilo described it to me. I began arguing—he said to me: 'If we did not get what the Yugoslav agitators want to deny us, it would not have been worth while going to war.'

What pettiness. So he does not believe that the real guarantee of our independence is the formation of a Yugoslavia that would be independent of Russia and would hold the pass against Germany.

Here I see disagreement with the government, but it is not yet time to say so. Just as it is not yet time to say that one of the great advantages of the vote of March 19 was that it freed us from joint responsibility with the nationalists.[29]

As is apparent, Supilo's information about the Treaty of London was not entirely correct. Not the whole of Dalmatia, but only the northern part of it, with the islands, had been assigned to Italy. No decision had been made about central and southern Dalmatia, though the Russian government reserved the right to assign it to Serbia. Also, it had not been agreed that Croatia should remain divided from Serbia. True, the Italian government assumed that Croatia-Slavonia would remain part of the kingdom of Hungary: for that reason it agreed to leave the latter the city and port of Fiume, which was a Hungarian enclave. But neither Russia nor the other Entente powers had undertaken any commitment in regard to the future of the Croats. In spite of this erroneous information, the points in Supilo's argument of immediate interest to Bissolati were sound. The Entente governments were not fighting the war for the consistent application of the nationality principle which they had inscribed on their banner, and the Italian government ignored it in demanding the annexation to Italy for strategic reasons of relatively compact Slav territories such as Dalmatia. Bissolati, in opposition to these violations of the Mazzinian ideal of self-determination of the nations, which was the primary source of his interventionism, developed the political line that was to lead to an irreparable clash with Sonnino.

The latter had special reasons for not receiving Supilo. On April 10, 1916, the organ of the nationalists, the *Idea Nazionale*, denounced Supilo as an enemy of Italy because of the whole of his pre-war activity at Dubrovnik and Fiume. The attack originated with Italian refugees from Dalmatia, who in fact detested Supilo, not so much because of his past, whatever it might have been, as for his activity devoted to safeguarding the whole of the Dalmatian coast for the Yugoslavia to which he aspired. But the fashion in which his past was presented by his enemies was intended to create the impression that he had been, and might still be, an agent of the Austria with whom Italy was at war. Both the records of public security headquarters and Salvemini's papers contain copies of a long document (undated and unsigned, but certainly dating from 1915–16—Salvemini's copy must have been given to him by Bissolati) giving an account of Supilo's career that accepted as true the accusations made against him at the well-known Vienna Trial of 1909, which the whole of well-informed international public opinion believed to be based on the desire of some Austro-Hungarian officials to damage the Serbo-Croat coalition at Zagreb, of which Supilo had been one of the most influential leaders until, in spite of his opposition, it set out on the path of compromise with the Hungarian government.[30] Not only had Supilo never for one moment sided with Austria against Serbia, he had broken completely with those of his compatriots who, as deputies to the Budapest parliament or the Zagreb Diet, continued to support the Hungarian government even during the war. Nevertheless the document concluded, against all the evidence, as follows:

That is why [Supilo] was with Austria against Serbia when the Serbian programme did not seem to him to be vast enough, or at any rate Serbia seemed incapable of carrying it out; that is why today, being still uncertain about the final result, he sits on the fence between Austria and her enemies; he visits the Entente capitals calling for Yugoslav unity, and his friends in Austria-Hungary (*with whom he has frequent contacts*) collaborate with Vienna and Budapest so that, in the event of victory by the Central Powers, the Yugoslav idea may triumph with *trialism*.

Which of the two solutions would be more pleasing to Frano Supilo? If Italy renounced nine-tenths of her Adriatic programme, he would certainly prefer an independent Yugoslavia. But Italy is not renouncing it, cannot renounce it, the Italophobia that is the most powerful instinct in his mind shows him the way. His present desire for an understanding is not a matter of mental or cultural preference, is not a political idea, but calculation. The Yugoslav propaganda in London, Paris, and Petrograd while Croats and Slovenes give their votes for military credits in Austria-Hungary and fight fiercely against the Russians, Serbs, and Italians is nothing but a *precaution*.[31]

There is no point today in rebutting these charges, which are abundantly refuted by the whole of Supilo's activities, which can now be followed in both Russian and British documents, as well as in Austrian documents and the papers of the Yugoslav Committee.[32] But it is worth mentioning in passing that the anonymous informer, in the haste resulting from his desire to make his denunciation the more poisonous, besides erroneously attributing the voting of military credits to the Slovene deputies (the majority of whom would certainly not have refused to do so, but had no opportunity, as the Austrian parliament did not meet) includes the Budapest government among

[155]

the supporters of the 'trialist' solution of the Yugoslav problem, whereas in reality it was its most determined opponent. Incidentally, this was not the first denunciation of Supilo of this kind which reached the Italian police. A shorter and similarly unsigned document dated April 23, 1915, states:

> Someone, whom we presume to be well-informed, claims to see in Supilo an agent of Pan-Croatia or perhaps of a trialist Austria. In any case it is certain that the intentions ascribed to him in a much discussed anti-Italian article in the *Novoje Vremia* are consistent with the suspicion that, apart from the Pan-Croatian idea, he may be a direct agent in the European capitals acting in favour of Austria in the Adriatic.[33]

The nationalist deputy Foscari and the deputy Colonna di Cesaro (a nephew of Sonnino's) followed up the attack in the *Idea Nazionale* in political quarters;[34] and the Foreign Minister also received a report from Vigliani, the director-general of public security, who on April 14, 1916, pointed out that, though Supilo was travelling on an allied pass, legally he was an enemy subject, and suggested that he should be interned, or alternatively expelled from Italy.[35] Sonnino, who obviously did not believe Supilo to be an Austrian agent, declined the suggestion, but he instructed Vigliani to have Supilo discreetly watched and have his movements and contacts reported.[36] Thus we know from public security department telegrams that before Supilo left Italy in May 1916 he met the radical deputy Agnelli and the republican deputy Colajanni, and went to Turin to confer with Guglielmo Ferrero.[37] In Rome, Lujo Voinovich introduced him to Umberto Zanotti Bianco.[38] He also met the liberal economist Antonio De Viti De Marco, Dr Falbo, editor of the *Messaggero* (which then belonged to the proprietor of the radical *Il Secolo*), the liberal deputy Andrea Torre, and perhaps also Giovanni Amendola and Luigi Albertini.[39]

Supilo's contacts with the representatives of non-nationalist Italian democracy left him with some hope.[40] He had need of it, because his dissension with Pašić was becoming more serious and was turning to his disadvantage. The Serbian Prime Minister indicated, among other things in an interview with journalists, that, apart from Bosnia-Hercegovina and the Hungarian provinces inhabited by Serbs—which he wished to annex independently of the fate of Croatia —Macedonia was closer to his heart than the Yugoslav territories of Austria-Hungary. When Supilo met Miljukov, the leader of the progressive *bloc* in the Russian Duma, who in May 1916 went to Paris and London (where he also saw Beneš and Masaryk), he did not conceal either his disappointment at the Tsarist government's coolness towards the Croats or his belief in the necessity of a preliminary guarantee of the federal rights of Croatia-Slavonia in the event of its unification with Serbia. This earned him criticism from the Serbs, but he wanted to start a public debate with Pašić on the nature of the future Yugoslavia, and therefore took the dispute into the bosom of the Yugoslav Committee. Finding himself again in a minority, he then resigned.[41]

At the same time, Bissolati joined the Italian government.[42] He privately asked Salvemini (who disagreed with his dilatoriness in openly attacking Sonnino's policy but remained his best friend) to study the Yugoslav question for him, and took the opportunity of an interview with *Le Matin* of Paris to state that he had agreed to enter the government in order to serve two ideals. The first was a lasting agreement between France and Italy. 'The other is an understanding with the Yugoslavs . . . we can thus create a kind of moral and economic unity in southern Europe.'[43] The interview led to renewed attacks by the nationalist press on the Yugoslav *émigrés*, who were accused of playing the Austrian game by their opposition to the Italian claims to Dalmatia. While the socialist deputy Claudio Treves was speaking in the Chamber, expressing his desire for a general peace which, he pointed out, would make possible an equitable settlement of the Italo-Yugoslav dispute on the eastern shore of the Adriatic, the accusation was repeated in an interruption by the deputy Foscari, who as Under-Secretary for the Colonies was a member of the new government set up, which Bissolati had entered without, as he had hoped he would, first ridding it of the nationalists.[44] The Republican deputy Pirolini spoke in defence of Bissolati's position. He defended the Yugoslav exiles from the charge of being Austrian tools and called for 'a profitable alliance' with them 'that would serve as a barrier against Germanism'.[45]

Bissolati's attitude in the matter formed part of a definite view of the strategy by which he believed the war could be won. On December 20, 1916, he wrote to his brother-in-law, the Paris correspondent of *Il Secolo*, that it was no longer possible to believe in the possibility of breaking through the German front in France. The Entente forces should be concentrated on the Carso, to break through the Austro-Hungarian lines, or 'the positions nearest the vital centres of the monarchy, which is the weakest part of the *bloc*'. He added: 'I have been fighting for this idea for two months—I started with the Cremona speech.'[46] In fact, believing that Cadorna, the Chief of the Italian General Staff, was favourably disposed to the idea, he raised the question in the cabinet, but was opposed by Sonnino, who said that

Italy could and should win the war on her own front with her own forces, without calling on her allies for military aid.[47] The Foreign Minister was in conflict with those allies about the future partition of Asia Minor, and about Greece, which the British and French wanted to bring into the war on their side in spite of King Constantine, while Sonnino, who regarded the Greeks as possible rivals of Italy, would have preferred leaving them out of the fray.[48]

The idea of bringing Austria-Hungary to her knees by a great concentration of Entente strength, particularly in artillery, on the Carso had also occurred to Lloyd George, the new British Prime Minister, who may have had knowledge of some feelers on the subject put out by the Italian General Staff to its British counterpart. When the heads of government and military Ministers of Britain, France and Italy, together with the commanders of the Salonica expedition, met in Rome on January 5–7, 1917, with a view to agreeing on the ultimatum to be delivered to the King of Greece (as indeed they did, overcoming Sonnino's reluctance), Lloyd George warmly backed the project. But the opposition of Briand, the French Prime Minister, who was already committed to the decision of his army commanders, in agreement with their British colleagues, to launch another major offensive in France in the spring of 1917, caused the idea of joint action on the Italian front to be dropped.[49] When Bissolati visited France and Britain at the end of February and the beginning of March 1917, Lloyd George took advantage of the opportunity to invite him to attend a meeting of the War Cabinet to enable him to state the case for his plan, based on his experience of the war in Italy.[50] The British military leaders nevertheless continued to oppose it. Incidentally, there was a latent, but not unimportant, political difference between Lloyd George's and Bissolati's approaches to the question. Bissolati was warned by Wickham Steed about the existence of strong Austrophile tendencies in Britain, and he argued at the meeting of the War Cabinet that one reason for striking at the Habsburg army on the Italian front was to encourage the rebellion of the Slav nationalities in Austria-Hungary. Although Lloyd George assured his guest that 'there is no public opinion in Britain favourable to the preservation of Austria', he would in fact have been glad to accept an Austrian request for a separate peace if the Emperor Karl, Francis Joseph's successor, had made up his mind to make it.[51] A defeat in Italy would have forced the young Emperor to take such a step. That this was Lloyd George's secret idea even before the mission of Prince Sixtus—whom he received with great favour, as is well known—also appears from a message from Marquis Imperiali, the Italian ambassador in London, which came to the knowledge of

[158]

Bissolati, among whose papers a copy was found. Imperiali, writing on January 22, 1917, a few hours after being received by Lloyd George, reiterated that 'he attaches special importance to the operations on our front, pointing out that if by any chance a time came when Austria was obliged to sue for peace, it was obvious that she would more easily resign herself to giving up territory already taken by us, but would put greater difficulties in the way of surrendering territories still in her hands'.[52] When Bissolati said to Lloyd George that 'it is well known that in France and Britain there is a section of opinion that would like to save Austria. This is the greatest danger that can threaten Italy,' it is clear that his anxiety was not without foundation.[53]

At the inter-allied meetings in Rome, a political document had been agreed to which apparently reflected Bissolati's ideas. This was the Entente reply, delivered to the diplomatic representatives of the United States on January 10, 1917, to the appeal to the belligerents made by President Wilson to declare their war aims with a view to mediating between them. The Entente governments had rejected the Central Powers' peace offer. Knowing President Wilson's strict adherence to the principles of universal democracy, they stated that their countries were fighting to 'save Europe from the brutal greed of Prussian militarism', without for that reason desiring 'the extermination of the German peoples or their political annihilation'. Their war aims therefore included 'the restoration of Belgium, Serbia and Montenegro and the indemnities due to them; the evacuation of the invaded territories in France, Russia and Romania, with just reparations; the reorganization of Europe guaranteed by an equitable régime and based at the same time on respect for nationalities. . . . The restoration of the provinces and territories previously taken from the allies by force and against the will of their populations; the liberation of the Italians, Slavs, Romanians and the Czecho-Slovaks from foreign domination; the liberation of the peoples subjected to the bloodthirsty tyranny of the Turks. . . .'[54]

As for Poland, the Entente or, more accurately, the western Entente powers—for the Russian government, though represented at the Rome meeting by its ambassador in Italy, did not take part in its decisions—declared that they trusted 'in the maintenance of the recent proclamation by the Tsar concerning the restoration of Poland'.[55]

The whole question of a possible liberation of the Slav nationalities of the Central Powers was in fact, as far as the Paris and London governments were concerned, based on their relations with the Petrograd government. After the German occupation of Warsaw in

[159]

August 1915, the idea of using as a weapon against Russia the restoration of independence to Poland, which their troops had conquered, had naturally occurred to the Berlin and Vienna governments. With the opening up of practical prospects of large-scale recruiting for their legion, those Poles who, like Pilsudski, had offered to fight for Austria-Hungary at the outbreak of war, pressed the Germans and Austrians to give political and juridical sanction to the promises that had been given them. But, because of the differences between Berlin and Vienna on the one hand and between Vienna and Budapest on the other on the question of whether or not to incorporate the new Poland (to be reunified with Galicia and put constitutionally as a third kingdom on an equal footing with Hungary) in the Habsburg monarchy, no action was taken for a long time. When at last a decision was made, and the proclamation of November 5, 1916, established Russian Poland alone as a separate kingdom, formally under the protection of both Germany and Austria-Hungary but in fact under predominantly German military administration, it was a severe disappointment to the Poles, both those who were Russian subjects and those who were subjects of the Central Powers.[56] In the meantime, however, the expectation of Austro-German action in the matter had stirred up the waters, among both the Poles who remained in Russia and those who had migrated to the west. Dmowski, the leader of the National Democrats, the strongest political party in Russian Poland, was an advocate of reconciliation between his people and Russia, and thus had a passport enabling him to travel. In a memorandum that he submitted in February 1916 to Izvolsky, the Russian ambassador in Paris, he urgently recommended that the Petrograd government should anticipate a probable move to incorporate Poland into Austria by proclaiming the independence of Poland reunified within its pre-partition frontiers but still connected with the Russian empire.[57] Izvolsky, however, did not like the term 'independence', and he liked even less the internationalization of the Polish question being carried out by Poles resident in the west, among whom the great pianist (and future President of post-war republican Poland) Paderewski—whom Dmowski had sent on a mission to the United States—stood out because of the extraordinary effectiveness of his propaganda among the Americans, especially highly placed Americans.[58] But the pressure of the supporters of reconciliation with the Poles in Russia herself, in both neo-Slav and in liberal circles (among the latter Miljukov's Constitutional Democratic Party—the 'Cadets'—had put forward a plan for Polish autonomy which had been adopted in principle by a majority in the Duma), and that of western public opinion, expressed among other ways in a manifesto

[160]

signed by French intellectuals and a warning to Izvolsky and Sazonov by Briand of the importance that was attached to the matter, combined to force the Tsarist government to a show of goodwill.[59] Sazonov replied to Briand that it was extremely dangerous for France to take an interest in the matter, as her sympathy with the Polish revolt of 1863 had led her to Sedan. Nevertheless, he seems to have read Dmowski's successive proposals very carefully, and he declared himself in favour of a plan by which Russian Poland would be reunified with the Polish territories of Austria and Germany and enjoy internal autonomy under the sovereignty of the Tsar. Russia would be responsible for foreign, military and financial affairs, but internal affairs would be in the hands of a Polish government appointed by a Viceroy and responsible to an elected Polish parliament.[60]

The great progress made by the Russian offensive in Galicia at the beginning of the summer of 1916, in which huge numbers of Austro-Hungarian prisoners (estimated at 350,000) were taken, among whom those of Slav nationalities were especially numerous, encouraged Sazonov to ask the Tsar to promulgate his plan for an autonomous Poland. However, another opinion was upheld by Stürmer, the Prime Minister.[61] He was opposed to any concessions to the Poles before the end of the war. The most intelligent commanders in the field, such as Alexeyev, the Chief-of-Staff, General Brusilov, and General Gurko, favoured Sazonov's plan, which Nicholas II accepted in principle on July 12 (according to the Western calendar).[62] But a week later, to the general surprise, the Emperor dismissed Sazonov. This seems to have been the result of intervention by the Tsarina, who detested Sazonov, considering him to be an enemy of Rasputin and a supporter of the alliance with republican France.[63] The cabinet shelved Sazonov's plan and put in its place a draft manifesto vaguely promising the 'resurrection' of a united Poland.[64] Meanwhile the Russian offensive on the Austrian front was brought to a halt by the arrival of German reinforcements, and its failure to achieve final success seemed to make the problem less urgent. The result could only increase the bitterness of the Poles, as well as that of the Russian Liberals. On the other hand, the collapse of hopes of a victorious conclusion of the war intensified the underground revolutionary ferment in Russia. Paléologue, the French ambassador, noted the strike that stopped work in all the factories in Petrograd on October 29, 1916, a subsequent mutiny in the suburb of Vyborg, which ended in the shooting of 150 soldiers, and another protest strike.[65]

The British and French governments, alarmed at the situation in Russia and the repercussions to be expected from an Austro-German proclamation of a kingdom of Poland, which would enable the

Central Powers to raise a huge Polish Legion, once more put pressure on the Tsarist government to do something to regain the sympathies of the Poles and tacitly also those of the Russian Liberals, whom the Entente regarded as its surest friends. Immediately after Sazonov's dismissal, the British Foreign Secretary told the French ambassador, Paul Cambon, that he wondered whether this did not mean a victory for the supporters of a separate peace in Russia, who notoriously came from the most reactionary quarters. In his opinion, it was urgently necessary to agree on war aims that would make impossible a reconciliation between the Russian and the German and Austrian governments. Paléologue wrote from Petrograd in a similar strain. He said that a counter to the Austro-German move in Poland that, by proclaiming the separation of the conquered territories from Russia, showed the abyss that divided the war aims of the Central Powers from the vital interests of Imperial Russia would provide a good opportunity for re-establishing the solidarity of the allies.[66]

At the reopening of the Duma, Miljukov violently attacked Stürmer's government, as well as Rasputin and the Tsarina, whom he accused of sabotage in preventing Sazonov's 'wise' attempt to give satisfaction to the Poles. Although the newspapers were not allowed to print the speech its effect was such that General Alexeyev, the Chief of the General Staff, who was himself being replaced, succeeded in persuading the Tsar to dismiss Stürmer.[67] The policy statement by his successor, Trepov, included a phrase about the autonomy and reunification of Poland.[68] General Gurko, the new Chief of the General Staff, also favoured Sazonov's plan, and urged the Tsar to accept it.

The problem became more acute when Paléologue received from Briand and submitted to the Russian government the draft reply that in the opinion of the French Prime Minister should be submitted by the Entente to President Wilson.[69] This draft served as the basis of the reply subsequently agreed to in Rome. Its reference to the liberation of the Slavs under Austrian and German domination and to the restoration of Poland by the Tsar forced Russia to take a stand in the matter. The Petrograd government was the less able to extricate itself from the necessity because the rest of the document, which the French had drafted with the certainty of British approval, included the expulsion of Turkey from Europe among Entente war aims and gave thus satisfaction to the obvious Russian interest in the proclamation of the undertaking, long since secretly given, that the Straits should be transferred to her control. For that reason, immediately after receiving the Austro-German peace offer of December 12, N. N. Pokrovsky, the new Russian Foreign Minister, insisted to the British ambassador that the reply should make it clear that 'peace must be made on our terms'.[70] The western governments now took him at his word. In order to be able to state publicly, without offending their Russian ally, their desire that the Tsar should commit himself to Polish reunification—which would once and for all make impossible a separate peace between Petrograd and Berlin and Vienna because, unless they were forced to do so by military defeat, the Central Powers would never consent to renouncing their eastern territories inhabited by Poles—the western governments came out in favour of the 'liberation' of the other Slav nationalities of Austria-Hungary, though the question of what would happen to Danubian Europe in such an event had never been asked and was not asked yet.

General Gurko seized the opportunity to persuade the Tsar to announce to the troops in an order of the day dated December 25, in which he rejected the Austro-German peace offer, that Russia was fighting for Constantinople and the Straits, as well as for the 'creation of a free Poland with all the three parts of it at present dispersed'.[71]

When the Doumergue mission went to Petrograd in February 1917, the Russians undertook, to support when the war was won, the French demand for the annexation of the Saar (in addition to Alsace-Lorraine) and for the separation from Germany of the left bank of the Rhine; and in return the Quai d'Orsay assured the Russians that it would back them in fixing their own western frontier as seemed best to them.[72] This might have led to the Poles being sacrificed if everything had not been changed a few days later by the Russian Revolution. At all events, the incident shows how fluid the contents of the Entente's reply to President Wilson were in the minds of the Entente itself. As a result of the Russian Revolution, Poincaré had no difficulty in June 1917 in authorizing the setting up of a Polish Legion in France, but only a year later the French government recognized the right of the Polish National Council to political control of the legion.

At this point in the story we must turn back to trace the steps that led to the statement in the above-mentioned Entente document of the aim of liberating the nationalities subject to Austria-Hungary. A factor of great importance was the Treaty of Bucharest, under which Romania on August 17, 1916, committed herself to enter the war a few days later. Negotiations with the Romanian government, conducted chiefly by the Russians, had been dragging on since the autumn of 1914. At the outbreak of the war, Romania was still an ally of Austria-Hungary. She was hesitant about abandoning her neutrality, which had been very difficult for her to proclaim, and Austro-German offers were made to induce her to maintain it,

[163]

though these were insufficient in view of Hungarian reluctance to make substantial concessions to the Romanians of Transylvania. Also, she was determined to intervene only in the event of large-scale successes by the Tsarist army. Apart from all this, however, her price for an alliance with Petrograd (involving the implicit renunciation of her claim to Bessarabia, which might have been satisfied by the Central Powers in the event of a Russian defeat) was a very high one.[73] She demanded the whole of Bukovina, including the area inhabited almost exclusively by Ruthenians (or Ukrainians), which Russia wanted to reserve for herself, as well as Transylvania, about one-third of the inhabitants of which were Magyar, though Romanians constituted a majority (53·9 per cent), a large part of the Hungarian plain, in which Romanians constituted a small minority, as well as the Banat, which was also claimed by Serbia and had the most mixed population imaginable, consisting of Saxons, Magyars, Romanians and Serbs. After nearly two years of pulling this way and that, the Russian victories of June 1916 finally persuaded Bratianu's government to intervene. Under the pressure of France, which was planning an offensive by the Salonica army to coincide with her intervention and expected Austria-Hungary, whose forces were fully engaged on the Russian and Italian fronts, not to be able to resist a Romanian attack alone, with the result that Germany would have to hurry to her aid, thus withdrawing troops from the Western Front, practically all the Romanian demands were accepted.[74] After some initial successes, however, the intervention, which took place too late to help the Russian offensive, which had petered out, turned into a disaster as a result of the arrival of a German army corps, which made a victorious entry into Bucharest before the end of the year. Nevertheless, the Romanian army succeeded in maintaining an unbroken front for more than a year. The first division of Yugoslav volunteers, raised in Russia in 1916, fought with the Romanians in Dobrudja, with some support—in spite of objections by the Serbian High Command—from a delegation from the Yugoslav Committee in Petrograd. This division, which had been recruited partly from Austro-Hungarian prisoners-of-war of Yugoslav stock and was officered by Serbians, among them many ardent advocates of Yugoslav unity, ended up on the Salonica front side by side with the Serbian regular army, and took part in the victorious offensive of the autumn of 1918.[75]

The Treaty of Bucharest, though neither the French nor the British or at bottom even the Russians realized it—for, as Miljukov says in his diary apropos of Sazonov, they were wondering at the time whether a greater danger to them did not lie in the possible absorption of Austria into a German *Mitteleuropa*—constituted a decisive step towards the dismemberment of the Danubian monarchy.[76] The loss of Bukovina would not have affected Austria greatly. But the amputations with which Hungary was threatened were so enormous that, if they had been carried out, the Hungarians would have had no more interest in remaining united with an Austria that had turned out to be incapable of giving them effective aid in defending their historical frontiers.[77] There is no need to remind the reader that in 1849 the Hungarian war of independence had been crushed thanks only to the intervention of the Tsar's army. In 1867 the Magyars had been recognized as the second dominant nationality of the monarchy, and in the 1914 war, thanks to their agricultural resources, the valour of their troops and the ability of their Prime Minister, Count Tisza, to get his way in Vienna, they became more powerful than the German Austrians themselves. If the Habsburg dynasty were defeated in the war, it would have no way left of exercising pressure on Hungary and would be dependent entirely on her goodwill. A factor that might have continued to hold the Hungarians and the German Austrians together (even before the war it had been a restraining influence on the Hungarian independence movement) was fear of the secession of the non-Magyar nationalities of Hungary in the wake of the non-German nationalities of Austria. The potentially separatist nationality that the Magyars feared most, because of its numbers, its economic vigour, and its political awareness, was the Romanian, which as long before as 1848–49, when it was much more backward, had risen in arms against the Hungarian government.[78] The mere news of the Romanian invasion of Transylvania at the end of August 1916 led to tumultuous scenes in the Budapest parliament. All the deputies who were not close supporters of the government violently attacked Tisza for having compromised the defence of the Hungarian frontiers by its loyalty to the Austrian war leadership (the Habsburg military leaders were mostly Austrians),[79] and Tisza's position, though his parliamentary majority survived, was irretrievably shaken by the debate.[80] For one thing, in 1914–15 he did not meet the demands of the Romanians of Transylvania, who would have been satisfied at that time by being given more Romanian schools, more Romanian-speaking public officials, and an equitable reform of the electoral system giving them parliamentary seats proportionate to their numbers; for another, he had allowed all the Hungarian regiments to be sent to the Russian, Serbian and Italian fronts, thus denuding the frontier with Romania, which Vienna, relying on Romanian fear of a trial of strength with the Central Powers, had regarded as less threatened.[81]

The Hungarian Social Democratic Party, though not represented in parliament as a result of the electoral law which excluded the workers, and non-property owners in general, from the vote, which was non-secret into the bargain, successfully intervened in the debate by addressing an open letter to the whole of the opposition; though the censorship suppressed the complete text, it later had to authorize publication of a summary. It proposed a joint campaign to all Tisza's opponents to secure the introduction of universal secret suffrage. Károlyi's party immediately agreed.[82] The revolutionary alliance of exacerbated Magyar patriotism with an internationalist working-class party, which eventually on March 21, 1919, as a consequence of the unanimous refusal of these socially so diverse forces to yield ethnically Magyar territories to the Romanians, led to the passing of power from Károlyi's democratic republic to Béla Kun's Soviet Republic, thus took shape in 1916 without its tragic outcome being foreseen by anyone.[83]

With this, the Magyars were the first in Austria-Hungary to conduct a radical, open and sustained opposition, maintained by legal political parties regularly organized on a national scale and having a real and rapidly growing mass following, while the war was still in progress. In view of the barriers to the spread of news in wartime and the rarity of knowledge of the Magyar language, little was known abroad at the time about events in Hungary, and the Czech national movement, which in 1916 was still far more timid and cautious than its representatives abroad, made much more noise in the world. Up to the Russian Revolution of March 1917, all the Czech political parties, including the nationalist parties and especially the Czech Social Democratic Party, were far less radical in their opposition to the government than were Károlyi's party and the Hungarian Social Democrats.

The formation of the Czechoslovak National Committee in Paris, though it failed to have any immediate visible effects in Bohemia, galvanized into activity the association of Czechoslovak societies in Russia, which since the beginning of the war had been recruiting volunteers among Czech pre-war immigrants in the Tsarist empire and had been urging the Petrograd authorities to release from the prisoner-of-war camps Czechs and Slovaks who had been serving in the Austro-Hungarian army and to allow them to enrol in a national legion. On April 21, 1916, the Tsar undertook to grant the first of these requests. The association also asked the Russian Foreign Ministry to put it in contact with the Italian ambassador, to whom it wished to propose the setting up of a similar Czech Legion in Italy.[84]

In June, when Sazonov heard that in France, where 4,000 Czech prisoners had arrived from the Serbian front, the government had permitted Masaryk's National Council to carry out propaganda among them, he decided to anticipate the inevitable request that Czechoslovak ex-prisoners in Russia should be enabled to rejoin their fellow-nationals, and he thus obtained the agreement of the Minister of War to the setting up of a Czech Legion in Russia.[85] At that time, the number of Czech and Slovak prisoners was being swollen by those taken during General Brusilov's big offensive, and the two regiments of Czech *Družine* volunteers could easily have been multiplied many times if all prisoners-of-war had been allowed to join them. But, particularly after Sazonov's dismissal, the Russian authorities wanted to be absolutely sure that the legion they had promised but had not yet begun to organize would be completely under their control. The Agrarian deputy Dürich, one of two members of the Czechoslovak National Council on a mission to Russia, agreed to put himself in the service of the Russian government, in disagreement with the leaders of the association of Czechoslovak societies, who had been elected at a congress at Kiev and looked to Masaryk, who was a friend of Miljukov and the Russian Liberals. Štefanik, the other delegate of the National Council, took up an intermediate position, securing the support of General Gurko, the Chief of the General Staff.[86] Confidential notes sent by the Russian Foreign Ministry in September–October 1916, to the diplomatic office at army headquarters clearly foresaw the danger that in the event of an Entente victory a Czechoslovak state entirely independent of Russia, would come into being under French influence and led by Masaryk, whose advanced democratic opinions were well known to Petrograd.[87] The notes, while recommending the formation of a legion of Czech prisoners in Russia under Russian command, foresaw three possible alternatives: (1) The Czechoslovak territories might remain under Austria-Hungary; (2) They might be annexed to Russia, retaining a certain amount of autonomy, but with a Russian viceroy; (3) They might become a sovereign state. Of these the third was regarded as the most probable, and the prospect was considered acceptable provided that the kingdom to be established were under Russian influence, preferably with a sovereign of Russian stock.[88] In the last note (of October 30, 1916), the idea that had been considered by the Tsar and Russian diplomacy in the winter of 1914–15 but then shelved, namely that dismemberment of Austria-Hungary would be in the Russian interest and that a number of predominantly Slav states devoted to Tsarist Russia should be established in its place, was revived.[89]

The French authorities were certainly aware of the Russian attitude to the Czech problem, if only through the Czechoslovak National Council, which worked in close contact with them. In the spring of

1916, permission to carry out propaganda among Czech prisoners, followed a few months later by their separation from German, Austrian and Hungarian prisoners, was granted to the National Council by the French War Ministry, in exchange for an undertaking by the Czechoslovaks to pass on to them all information that came to them through this or any other channel.[90] This agreement was brought about by Professor L. Eisenmann, the French historian of Austria-Hungary, who had become a close friend of Masaryk and Beneš and was an officer seconded to the Ministry of War.[91] Before leaving for Russia, Štefanik had introduced Beneš to Mme de Jouvenel's *salon*, where, in addition to many politicians, he met Philippe Berthelot, director of European affairs at the Quai d'Orsay, who became *chef de cabinet* to Briand when the latter became Prime Minister and Minister of Foreign Affairs in October 1915.[92] Berthelot, according to the testimony of his closest colleagues, though he received Beneš a number of times at the Quai d'Orsay and caused him to be received in September 1916 by Briand himself, did not yet believe that the *Delenda Austria* propaganda being conducted by the Czech *émigrés* and their friend Professor E. Denis (whom Berthelot had been consulting ever since the beginning of the war as the greatest French expert on the Slav world) should yet be adopted by France and the Entente;[93] the Prime Minister and Jules Cambon, the Secretary-General of the Foreign Ministry, were even less inclined to the idea.

The view that Austria must be supported against Prussia had been a principle of French diplomacy since at least 1870. On November 23, 1916, two days after the death of Francis Joseph, Jules Cambon, talking to Prince Sixtus of Bourbon-Parma, the brother-in-law of the new Austrian Emperor, said that France had commitments to Italy, Romania and Serbia, but that, when these had been satisfied (he minimized them, referring only to Trent and Trieste, Transylvania and Bosnia-Hercegovina), so far from wishing further to weaken Austria in relation to Germany, he would like to strengthen her, e.g. by helping her to acquire Prussian Silesia.[94] The experts of the Quai d'Orsay were well aware, however, that the essential condition for detaching Austria from Germany was the internal re-organization of the empire, involving a diminution of German Austrian and Magyar supremacy in favour of the Slav majority of the population. In particular the Magyars, whose ruling class (which in the eyes of Paris monopolized its political will) were completely devoted to the German alliance, were considered to be dangerous enemies by French diplomacy, which was aware of their hostility to the federal reform of the dual monarchy, or even of Austria alone, and of their ability to block it, thanks to the 1867 Settlement, and of the vital

[168]

importance of Hungary as a source of food supplies in wartime.[95] When they overcame their last hesitation in the first few months of the war, Masaryk, Beneš, Štefanik, and Denis abandoned all idea of federalism within the Habsburg empire, but naturally still regarded as an irreducible enemy the Magyar oligarchy, which since 1871 had succeeded in Austria in blocking all constitutional reform in favour of the Czechs, and in Hungary refused political and educational liberties to the Slovaks, whom it oppressed economically and socially. Hence, in the drafting of the Entente reply to President Wilson, Berthelot took account of the ardent desire of his Czech and pro-Czech friends that their cause should be mentioned and backed; he also knew that it would be likely to make a favourable impression on the President of the United States, who was devoted to the principles of democracy (and also wanted the support of the large Slav vote in the United States). Thus among the nations to be liberated he did not just mention Bohemia, but specified the Czechoslovaks. Nevertheless, in 1916 no voice, even among the bitter opponents of the Budapest government, had yet been raised among the Slovaks in Austria-Hungary except to express unconditional loyalty to the Habsburg dynasty.

Berthelot's draft reply to President Wilson was submitted to the French ambassadors in Petrograd and London on December 23, 1916. Paléologue liked it as being satisfactory to the Russians, but Paul Cambon, who did not like Berthelot, regarded it as too long and rhetorical.[96] None of the few who saw the original draft has quoted the exact wording, but from all that is known about it it would seem that, among other things, it mentioned the liberation of the Slavs in general without going into details.[97] The Czechs, in whose cause Steed and Seton-Watson exerted themselves in London, with the aid of Masaryk and of some experts being used by the Foreign Office (including the future Sir Lewis Namier, who was born in a Slav area of Austria) who contributed also to the periodical *New Europe* founded by them in October 1916, were immediately mentioned in a draft submitted to Washington by Balfour, the new British Foreign Secretary, as one of the nations whose aspiration to self-determination the Entente should satisfy.[98] In fact on November 4, 1916, Balfour, not yet Foreign Secretary but a member of the government, in reply to a question put by the Prime Minister to his colleagues on what they thought of Lord Lansdowne's proposal that, in view of the military stalemate, peace negotiations should be opened with the Central Powers, had written a memorandum that was very intransigent in relation to Germany but said of Austria-Hungary: 'I should myself desire to see the dual monarchy maintained, shorn indeed of a large

[169]

part of its Italian, Romanian, Polish and Serbian territories (in Bosnia-Hercegovina) and also of Bohemia, which might become independent if it were considered economically viable and capable of holding up against German pressure'.[99] Rather than see an Austria reduced to its German areas uniting with Germany, Balfour would prefer the survival of the Habsburg empire which, he said, should be left with an adequate outlet to the sea. This, assuming the granting of the Italian claims to Trieste, could mean only that Hungary as a part of the Habsburg monarchy would retain Croatia and Fiume.[100] Balfour's friendliness to the Czechs, though it was only conditional and referred only to Bohemia (the problem of Slovakia was not present in his mind), was not immediately noticed by his government colleagues. His cousin Lord Robert Cecil, who was then Under-Secretary of State for Foreign Affairs, admitted in his memoirs that he had never thought about the Czechoslovaks until a French delegate to the Anglo-French conversations that were held in London on December 26–28, 1916, suggested that the liberation of that people should be included in the document to be drawn up. [101]

France was represented at the London talks by Ribot, the Finance Minister (who in the following March was to succeed Briand as Prime Minister and Foreign Minister), the socialist Albert Thomas (with whom Bissolati was on very friendly terms) who was Armaments Minister, and Berthelot. The French were very worried about the Russian crisis, the Romanian defeat and Caillaux's visit to Rome, where he was said to have seen Giolitti's lieutenants, if not Giolitti himself.[102] He had certainly seen Cardinal Gasparri, and perhaps the Pope himself, with a view to securing the compromise peace with Germany, a desire for which had been clearly stated in Benedict XV's Christmas address to the cardinals.[103] The French delegation therefore wanted the greatest intransigence in the statement of war aims. The American ambassador in London had informed the British government that the people of the United States still knew nothing of the democratic spirit that animated the Entente.[104] Balfour therefore said that a more specific statement, incapable of being interpreted by President Wilson as an evasion intended to conceal obscure aims of conquest, would be preferable to the draft sent from Paris.[105] Ribot agreed, and Lord Robert Cecil and Berthelot were charged with the task of drafting definite war aims, including a clause hastily proposed by the French on the 'liberation of the Italians, Slavs, Romanians and Czechoslovaks'.[106]

The illogicality of mentioning the Slavs in general and then adding the Czechoslovaks, as if they were not Slavs, was caused by the fear that, if all the Slav nationalities to be liberated, including the Yugo-

[170]

slavs, had been mentioned, it would not have been acceptable to Italy. The British and French were well aware of Sonnino's reluctance to identify Italian war aims completely with those of the Entente, and that made them all the more eager to associate him with their reply to President Wilson. On the other hand, they were of course aware of the danger of playing into the hands of Vatican pacifism, which was certainly capable of making an impact on the Italian masses, and wanted to do nothing that might weaken the position of the Italian Foreign Minister.[107] The British and French heads of government went to Rome on January 5, 1917, and Sonnino agreed to associate himself with the joint reply to President Wilson, believing that the omission of any specific mention of the Yugoslavs indicated tacit acquiescence in the stipulations of the Treaty of London which assigned a substantial number of Slovenes and Croats to Italy.[108]

The Paris and London governments were also well aware of the Italian–Yugoslav clash. Some weeks previously, Marquis Imperiali, the Italian ambassador in London, acting on Sonnino's instructions, had expressed Italian displeasure at the fact that a number of eminent personalities, beginning with Lord Cromer, a former governor of Egypt, who had agreed to become its president, had associated themselves with the Serbian Society of Great Britain. This had been founded in October 1916 at the instigation of Steed and Seton-Watson, who made no concealment of their intention of using it as a centre of propaganda for the establishment of a Yugoslav state to include all the territories (including those assigned to Italy by the treaty of April 1915, the contents of which had come to Seton-Watson's knowledge) inhabited predominantly by Serbs, Croats and Slovenes.[109] It should be noted that, while Steed and Seton-Watson went on working for an Italian–Yugoslav agreement based on equity and mutual understanding, and Supilo himself in his isolation continued to advocate it in letters to his Italian friends, in spite of the attacks to which he continued to be subjected by the Italian nationalists, the official bulletin of the Yugoslav Committee continued to claim both Trieste and Gorizia.[110] Salvemini thought it his duty at that time to warn *La Serbie* of Geneva, which had expressed indignation at an article (written by one Marini) in Bissolati's and Bonomi's party journal which spoke of the *italianità* of Dalmatia, that, though this article exceptionally opposed the consistently anti-nationalist line followed by that journal, no one among the Yugoslavs openly took a stand against the nationalism of his own compatriots.[111]

The Italian–Yugoslav conflict faced the Czech exiles with a choice. As a result of Štefanik's Italian contacts, he was the first of the latter to realize this. He decided that the Czech movement must necessarily

[171]

regard the support of a great power such as Italy, whose army was exerting pressure on the Austrian frontiers, as far more important than solidarity with the Croat *émigrés*. On the eve of his departure for Russia, he clashed with Professor E. Denis, who, as editor of *La Nation tchèque*, refused his suggestion that it should print no more criticisms of the Italian attitude to the Yugoslavs.[112] In the autumn of 1916, Colonel Brancaccio, head of the information section of the Italian military mission in Paris, with whom Štefanik had established terms of friendship, and the diplomatist Gino Scarpa, secretary to Ubaldo Comandini, the Minister responsible for war propaganda, called on Beneš to ask him to supply the Italian authorities with the information that he already supplied to the French.[113] Beneš agreed. Denis resigned the editorship of *La Nation tchèque*, which was taken over by the Czechoslovak National Council. His intransigence in relation to Italian policy was not shared by all the French students of Slavonic affairs. Louis Eisenmann, in a debate on the problem of the Southern Slavs organized in Paris by the Société de Sociologie, said that the *Bulletin Yougoslave* was making a grave mistake in claiming Trieste and the whole of Istria, thus clashing, not only with Italian nationalism, but also with that section of Italian liberal and democratic opinion whose sympathies it ought to set out to gain.[114]

Beneš, at the invitation of Gino Scarpa, went to Rome in January 1917 and was received by Comandini, and by De Martino, the Secretary-General of the Foreign Ministry, who told him that Italy was willing to take an interest only in the Czechs because, apart from being unable to renounce Dalmatia, she did not consider the birth of a Yugoslav state to be in her interest.[115] Although Sonnino declined to receive him personally, Beneš succeeded in making friends in the most diverse circles in Rome, ranging from the nationalists to followers of Salvemini. He established an office of the National Council in the Italian capital and laid the foundations for an Italian Committee for Czechoslovak Independence, the chairman of which was to be the former Under-Secretary Lanza di Scalea, a nationalist highly regarded by the Foreign Ministry. On the question closest to his heart, that of recruiting a legion among the Czech and Slovak prisoners-of-war in Italy, the only satisfaction he obtained was a promise that his fellow-nationals would be separated from the German Austrians and the Hungarians.[116] Sonnino was opposed to making military use of enemy subjects against their country of origin, which was contrary to the traditional laws of war. Štefanik, who had succeeded in securing this in Petrograd, vainly appealed to Carlotti, the Italian ambassador, to enable him to go to Rome again and secure an interview with Sonnino.[117] When Beneš returned to Rome at the beginning

[172]

of September 1917 and at last secured an interview with the Italian Foreign Minister, he succeeded neither in persuading him to change his mind about the legion nor in inducing him to favour the recognition of the Czechoslovak National Council which he wanted from the Entente governments. Sonnino agreed only to authorize him to visit the prisoner-of-war camps in Italy where Czech and Slovak prisoners were confined, to their separation from Austro-Hungarian prisoners, and to their use for special duties, but not for combatant service. The Prime Minister, Boselli and General Cadorna would have been willing to grant him more than that, but left the decision to Sonnino.[118] Beneš appealed to Bissolati, who pleaded the Czechoslovak cause at the War Ministry, and only his insistence, and the sustained advocacy that Luigi Albertini, Ugo Ojetti and Umberto Zanotti Bianco directed at Orlando when he became Prime Minister, resulted in eventual Italian acceptance of the idea of a Czech Legion.[119]

To recapitulate, then, the Entente proclaimed in their reply to President Wilson that one of their war aims was the liberation of the oppressed Slav peoples, but the representatives of the latter obtained no political recognition as a result. In February 1917, Lansing, the American Secretary of State, asked for an explanation of various points in the reply, and in particular enquired whether it amounted to a plan for the dismemberment of Austria-Hungary, but Lloyd George categorically denied that that was his government's intention. Britain, he said, was committed only to the detachment from Austria-Hungary of the Italians, Romanians and the Serbs of Bosnia-Hercegovina, and he took the view that Bohemia and Hungary would be able to remain with Austria.[120] When Professor G. A. Borgese, the distinguished writer, returned from Paris in March, he drew the attention of Luigi Albertini, to whose newspaper he was a valued contributor, to the Austrophilia still prevalent at the Quai d'Orsay. The result was that Luigi Campolonghi, the correspondent of the newspapers associated with Bissolati, was more or less regarded with hostility there, in spite of his excellent relations with the parliamentary left that formed the basis of the French government.[121] Borgese, an acute observer, foresaw, however, that the French attitude was bound to change sooner or later, and he suggested that Italian propaganda abroad should present itself to European opinion in an anti-Austrian guise.

In Austria-Hungary the censorship considered the reply to President Wilson to be so counter-productive to the Entente cause that it allowed it to be published by the newspapers in full, naturally with comments that emphasized its imperialistic and bellicose nature, as demonstrated by its support of the extreme claims of Italian and

[173]

Romanian nationalism; the talk of liberating nations that enjoyed full constitutional liberties under the Habsburg monarchy was described as totally devoid of realism.[122] One after another, in the Reichsrat the parliamentary representatives of the various nationalities, led by Mgr Korošec for the Slovene and Croat Catholics, Mgr Faidutti for the Italian Clericals of Gorizia and Gradisca, Štanek for the Czech Agrarian Party, Mastralka for the Young Czechs, Šmeral for the Czech Social Democrats, Vassilko for the Ruthenians, as well as the representative of the Romanians in Bukovina, handed to Count Czernin, the new Austro-Hungarian Foreign Minister, vigorous protests at the illegitimate Entente speculation on their respective nationalities, which remained completely loyal to the House of Habsburg.[123] This demonstration did not—as is believed by some authors desirous of demolishing the legends woven by the *émigrés* at the time—necessarily mean that the leaders of the Czech parties genuinely desired the survival of Austria-Hungary. The rapidity of their switch to radical demands for independence towards the end of the year, though the military situation of the Central Powers had in the meantime greatly improved as a result of the Russian collapse and the Italian defeat at Caporetto, shows that the loyalty to the Habsburgs at any rate of the Czech politicians, and also some of those of other nationalities, was merely tactical. The leaders of the Czech political parties, having declined the suggestion that they should emigrate illegally which was sent them by Masaryk in the summer of 1916, were bound to go on playing the legal political game in Austria,[124] and that was possible, before the repercussions of the Russian Revolution made themselves felt, only on the basis of loyalty to the monarchy. The Czechs in particular were interested in securing a general political amnesty from the new Emperor. Among the Slovenes, the Liberals and the Social Democrats were opposed to the declaration of loyalty to the dynasty, and in the Catholic Popular Party, which was far the strongest party among the Slovene peasants, Father I. Krek, the leader of the Christian Socialist wing, was critical of it.[125] On the other hand, it should be borne in mind that the Entente statement was indeed arbitrary in putting the desire for liberty of Belgium, Serbia, and even the Poles of Poznan—who could not hope to escape from the conditions of inferiority in which they were kept in certain respects in Germany—on the same plane as that of the various Slav peoples in Austria-Hungary, it not having been demonstrated that the aspirations of the latter could not be satisfied by democratic federal reforms under the Habsburgs.[126]

In fact, the Zagreb *Agramer Tagblatt*, a German-language newspaper which had come under the control of friends of H. Hinković,

[174]

a former deputy and an influential Freemason and a member of the Yugoslav Committee in exile, had stated on February 25, 1917, that Austria-Hungary's Slav troops were fighting bravely, not for German and Magyar supremacy, but in the hope of protection and justice from the dynasty against the oppression that weighed down on the Slav majority in the empire. A few days later, these feelings were expressed in the debate in the Croatian Diet on the address to be presented to Charles IV, the new King of Hungary and Croatia-Slavonia.[127] The democratic opposition parties, i.e. the Right Party led by a nephew of its dead founder Starčević and S. Radić's Peasant Party, proposed a resolution deploring that the King had found his coronation in Budapest sufficient and had not also been crowned in Zagreb, and declaring that in 1527, Croatia, as an independent state, had bestowed its crown on the Habsburg dynasty and had in consequence lost its independence, which had been arbitrarily repressed by the Hungarian supremacy that betrayed itself in economic and political oppression of the Croats. The resolution recalled that since 1912 the democratic deputies of Croatia and Slovenia had unanimously declared themselves in favour of the unity, over and above the frontiers between Austria and Hungary which kept them divided, of 'all the Croats and Slovenes, a single people by blood and language', and therefore called for unification, 'in accord with the nationality principle', of all the Croat and Slovene territories and their formation into a state that would be independent of both the Vienna and the Budapest governments, though still forming part of the Habsburg monarchy.[128] Although it said nothing about the Serbs, whom Starčević in particular, but Radić also had in the past regarded, not as brothers, but as strangers to the Croats (and almost as their enemies), the resolution was an act of open political protest against the existing dual system, which would be struck a fatal blow by unification of the Slovenes, living in parts of Austria which the German Austrians regarded as sacrosanct, with Croats subject to Hungary, which would never renounce Croatia except under compulsion.[129] Radić said in the Diet debate that it was essential to persuade the dynasty to accept the nationality principle, which he interpreted as meaning the democratic right to self-determination stated by President Wilson, and to dismantle the dual system which prevented its adoption.[130] A member of Starčević's party went so far as to call for the unity of all the Southern Slavs, including the people of Serbia.[131] The majority in the Diet consisted of members of the Serbo-Croat coalition, and the resolution that it put through limited itself to calling for a political amnesty, the re-establishment and enlargement of democratic rights in Croatia, and reunification of the latter with Dalmatia and Bosnia-

[175]

Hercegovina, still under St Stephen's Crown, but with autonomy greater than that granted in 1868 at a time when the Croat nation was weak.

The Croats were still considered completely loyal, and the young Emperor Charles I, who was undoubtedly animated by genuine humanitarianism and had a horror of avoidable bloodshed, met those of their desires which he could satisfy without substantial political reforms. In April 1916, a long trial of about 100 Serbs charged with high treason ended at Banjaluka, in Bosnia. Sixteen, including two deputies to the Diet and four Orthodox priests, were sentenced to death.[132] Cardinal Gasparri, as in the case of the Czech deputy Kramář, who was sentenced to death in June 1916, secretly intervened to save the lives of those sentenced at the Banjaluka trial, but, while he was successful in the former case, he was not in the latter.[133] Their sentence was confirmed on appeal. But in March 1917 it was commuted by Francis Joseph's successor.

Meanwhile, revolution was triumphing in the capital of all the Russias, and before long the whole world was to be shaken by the repercussions. On March 16, the Tsar was forced to abdicate, and the Russian Democratic Republic was proclaimed. What concerns us here is that on March 24, Miljukov, the Foreign Minister in the Provisional Government, who had always cultivated relations with the Czech and Yugoslav *émigrés*, and who was concerned with preventing the revolution, which had been sparked off by the exasperation of the Russian troops and working masses at the long duration of the war, from leading republican Russia into a separate peace with the Central Powers, said in a statement to the Russian news agency: 'We wish for the liberation of the oppressed nationalities of Austria-Hungary. Russia intends to establish a solidly organized Yugoslavia around glorious Serbia.'[134] A few days later, he made a similar statement in favour of Czechoslovak independence, and repeated that Austria-Hungary must be dissolved into its constituent parts.[135] This became known immediately in the Danubian monarchy. The Czech newspaper *Narodni Listy* printed the statement, observing, however, that it was a theoretical formula lacking in reality because it assumed the dismemberment of Austria-Hungary and not its reorganization, which was what the people concerned wanted. The news, together with the Prague newspaper's comment, was copied by the *Agramer Tagblatt*.[136]

In the Central European empires, things began to move, as a result, not of Miljukov's words, but of the huge waves of revolution. Among the first to be swept away by them in the next few weeks was the leader of the Russian Constitutional Democratic Party himself.

The entry into the war of the United States, in the name of resistance to Prussian militarism and the struggle for the victory of democracy throughout the world, and the proclamation made by the Russian revolutionaries of the peoples' right to be masters of their own destiny, contributed to making insoluble the crisis of the old order in Austria-Hungary, the weaker of the two Central Powers.

When the Russian Revolution broke out, the Habsburg empire was in a state of severe exhaustion. The total cereal crop in Austria fell from 91 million quintals* in 1913 to 49 million in 1916 and to 28,100,000 in 1917; in Hungary (including Croatia-Slavonia) it fell from 146 million quintals in 1913 to 78 million in 1916, though it rose again to 98 million quintals in 1917. Nevertheless, the Hungarians refused to increase supplies to starving Austria.[138] The Austro-Hungarian coal output fell from 57 million tons in 1914 to 52,800,000 in 1916 and 50,100,000 in 1917. Production of military blankets fell from 9,500,000 in 1914 to 7,000,000 in 1916 and 2,900,000 in 1917.[139] The Austro-Hungarian armaments industry did not collapse until the first half of 1918, but the shortage of manpower and raw materials had made catastrophe foreseeable a year earlier.[140] Eight million men had been called to the colours, and by the end of the war, casualties amounted to 1,200,000 killed, nearly 3,000,000 wounded or incapacitated, and more than 2,000,000 taken prisoners-of-war. Inflation was in full swing. In spite of rationing and the consequent restraint on prices, the cost of living of an average working-class family had increased from 100 in July 1914 to 302 in July 1916; in July 1917 it jumped to 616, and a year later to 1,560. Those were among the reasons that induced Charles I, immediately after his accession, to entrust his brothers-in-law, Princes Sixtus and Xavier, who were officers in the Belgian Army, with the task of putting out peace feelers, for which we refer the reader to Appendix I as well as to the recent critical study by R. A. Kann on the subject.[141] Czernin, the Foreign Minister, admitted in his memorandum of April 12, 1917, which was forwarded by Charles I to William II and came to the knowledge of some representatives of the German political parties, that Austria would be unable to go on fighting beyond the end of the year.[142]

The fall of Tsarist absolutism, which tripped up on the banana peel of its conflict with the Duma, made the summoning of the Austrian parliament inevitable. Stürgkh, the Prime Minister, had refused to recall it since the outbreak of the war, and his persistence in doing so, even when a majority of German Austrian deputies called for its reopening in the summer of 1916 was Friedrich Adler's motive for

* Translator's note: a quintal is 220 lbs.

assassinating him.[143] Charles I's new ministers decided to revive constitutional life, and the Reichsrat was summoned for the end of May 1917. According to J. Redlich's diary, a return to constitutionalism was the condition laid down by the Austrian Social Democratic leaders for declaring their confidence in the peace policy that the Foreign Minister assured them he wished to pursue and for agreeing to back it at the socialist international conference that had been called in Stockholm for the month of May by a committee formed by the Dutch and Scandinavian Social Democratic parties and the Petrograd Soviet.[144]

The Reichsrat debates were, however, inevitably dominated, as they had been in the last years before the war, by the claims of the nationalities, starting with the Czechs, who felt themselves to be deprived of their rights. On the eve of the Russian Revolution, Šmeral and Tusar, the leaders of the Czech Social Democratic Party, who had always opposed the inflamed nationalism of the Bohemian 'bourgeois' parties, told J. Redlich that, if the Vienna government did not quickly set in motion the necessary administrative and language reforms on behalf of their people, the latter's hopes would turn to the exiled Masaryk, compelling the Social Democrats to demand Czech national independence too.[145] The Austrian German national parties, among whom even a man of Redlich's intellectual prestige—as a deputy he was a member of their parliamentary group—was regarded as a potential capitulator, would not hear of such concessions.[146] Time might have been against making some concessions to the Southern Slavs to begin with, for they were reputed to be much more loyal than the Czechs. That was the course advocated by Field-Marshal Conrad and Clam-Martinic. Although the new Austrian Prime Minister, like Czernin, was opposed to any concessions to the Czechs, whose demands, he feared, would only increase with every concession,[147] Tisza, the Hungarian Prime Minister, was opposed to any concession to the Southern Slavs, a large proportion of whom lived under St Stephen's Crown.[148] In view of this state of affairs, the Southern Slav deputies to the Reichsrat overcame the previous divisions among Serbs, Croats and Slovenes, and the no less acute divisions between Clericals and Liberals, and, at the suggestion of Professor Krek, organized themselves into a single parliamentary group, which came to an agreement on a common policy with the Czech deputies.[149] The defection of the Slovene and Croat Catholic deputies, who had always supported the government, weakened the majority on which it relied. Moreover, the effect on the Polish parliamentary group (which constituted an essential basis for any possible majority in the Reichsrat) of the

[178]

Russian Revolution, which resulted in the recognition of the Polish right to independence, was to cause the democrats who supported the (virtually anti-German) demand for the reunification of the three Polands into a single independent state with access to the sea, to prevail over the conservatives, who had previously always controlled the policy of the Poles in Austria, where the Galician aristocracy traditionally formed part of the ruling class.[150] Since May 1917, the Ruthenians of Galicia who were in conflict with the Poles, by whom they felt themselves oppressed, had been demanding unification with their brothers on the other side of the frontier.

The Austrian government, which could not secure a majority in the Reichsrat without the Poles, was forced to go back on its previous acceptance of the German request, made in January 1917, that Russian Poland should be left to Germany in the post-war settlement. The Austro-Hungarian Crown Council had agreed on March 22, 1917, to leave to the Germans the new kingdom of Poland, the fate of which had been left unsettled the previous November. Since the meeting of January 12, Tisza, with whose views Field-Marshal Conrad came to agree, had argued that Poland should be bartered for Romania. Germany, whose military leaders thought it essential to retain the Polish territories wrested from Russia, as that would give them the strategic advantage over both the Russians and their now unreliable Austro-Hungarian allies, was willing to grant Austria-Hungary political control of Romania (as well as of Serbia and Montenegro) at the end of the war in exchange for Poland, provided that Romanian oil, railways and shipping routes remained under German control. Czernin believed that an offer to add Galicia to the new German-dominated kingdom of Poland would make it easier to persuade the German government to make a general peace possible by consenting to the restoration of Belgium and the cession to France of a part of Lorraine. The detachment of Galicia from Austria would result in a German government majority in the Reichsrat and enable the Vienna government to extricate itself from the otherwise ultimately inevitable necessity of making concessions to the demands for autonomy of the Slav nationalities, which would become a minority instead of a majority of the population of Cisleithania. Hence, during the very days when the Austrian Polish parties were adopting their pro-independence position, Czernin reached an agreement at a secret meeting with Bethmann-Hollweg at Kreuznach (May 17–18) which left Russian Poland to the German empire and Serbia, Montenegro, and Romania to the Habsburg empire, on the assumption that Germany was in a position to secure Courland and Lithuania for herself.

Political developments in the Habsburg monarchy, however, were against the Kreuznach agreement. In Hungary, Tisza fell. Of the leaders of the Hungarian national coalition whose campaign against Tisza persuaded Charles I to dismiss the man who had been the most powerful politician in the dual monarchy under Francis Joseph, Count Andrássy had since September 1915 favoured the incorporation of Poland in Austria-Hungary, whereas Count Batthyány and Count Károlyi actually favoured Polish independence. The reduction of Romania to a vassal state was a pleasing idea to most Magyars, but whether she became politically a vassal of Germany or of Austria-Hungary did not make a great deal of difference to them (only Tisza thought he would do better than the Germans at reducing the Romanians to docility). Romanian oil and other mineral products would have been important to the Austro-Hungarian economy, but these the Germans had reserved for themselves. Romanian agricultural produce would only provide additional competition for Hungarian produce, which was in any case faced with the prospect of competition from Serbia in view of the proposed economic incorporation of that country. The Austrian government therefore had to fear that if the Poles now turned to the Hungarians, they would, in view of Tisza's elimination, be able to count on Hungarian support. Czernin failed to persuade the Germans to respond to the peace appeal made by Benedict XV in August by agreeing to surrender a slice of Lorraine to France, or even to restore the full independence of Belgium. In the meantime popular pressure for peace was mounting in Austria-Hungary. The behaviour of the German military authorities as the absolute masters of occupied Poland made it clear what the fate of that country would be in the event of victory by the Central Powers, but the Vienna statesmen had to take into account the certainty that on the day when Poland's future under Germany was announced, rebellion would break out, not only in Russian Poland, but also among the Poles of Galicia, who could be assured of the sympathy of the Hungarians, Czechs and Yugoslavs. So it was necessary to return to the Austro-Polish solution. If this took the form of 'trialism', it set in train the process of the federal transformation of the whole of Austria and the consequent transformation of Hungary into an independent kingdom tied to the Habsburg throne only by a personal union. Thanks to the war, Hungary had grown relatively too strong for 'trialism' to be imposed on her by force. But the Polish independence movement reminded Czernin that there was a third possible solution, namely that of establishing a personal union under Habsburg sovereignty with the kingdom of Poland, to which Galicia would be added. To this the Hungarians

[180]

would agree, and the departure from the Reichsrat of the Galician deputies would leave it with a secure German majority, making federal reforms no longer essential. At the end of September 1917, Czernin therefore asked Germany to review the Kreuznach agreement and, in spite of the reluctance of the German military leaders, it was agreed at meetings held on October 22 and November 6 that Russian Poland, except for those areas which the German High Command considered strategically indispensable, would be left to Austro-Hungary. In exchange, Romania would be left to the Germans, and Austria-Hungary agreed to accept a new twenty-year military alliance, closer than its predecessor, and a kind of economic union with Germany. But that plan was not carried out either: it was upset by the peace of Brest-Litovsk, by which the Central Powers recognized the independence of the Ukraine and assigned to it a slice of territory it claimed from Poland. At this point we must return to the events of the spring of 1917, the narration of which we interrupted to indicate the enormous permanent difficulties that the Polish question caused the Vienna government.

The Emperor, at the suggestion of Count Polzer-Hoditz, his private secretary, who realized the gravity of the situation, proposed that the Speech from the Throne in the Reichsrat should promise the concession of far-reaching national autonomies. Clam-Martinic and Czernin refused to agree to this, believing that it would be interpreted as a sign of weakness.[151] On the other hand, probably out of regard for the pro-Austrian activity that the Vienna Social Democrats promised Czernin to carry out in Stockholm (they duly carried it out, but without success), the censorship permitted the publication of the speech made by Friedrich Adler in his own defence at his trial for the assassination of Count Stürgkh, which began on May 18.[152] His eloquence and his passionate invocation of internationalist socialist anti-war feeling, made a tremendous impact. In Vienna, where, as throughout Austria-Hungary, but not in Germany, May 1 was again celebrated as a holiday after a lapse of two years, sporadic strikes began taking place in armaments works, railway workshops, among tramwaymen, etc.[153] Among the crowds that celebrated May 1 in Prague, shouts for Masaryk were heard. At the end of May, a series of strikes led to the formation of a workers' council in Prague under Social Democratic leadership. Incidents of fraternization with the enemy were continually reported from the Russian front.[154]

The reopening of the Reichsrat took place on May 30. The event was keenly awaited; interest centred above all on what the Czech attitude was going to be. It was known in both Vienna and Prague, that Masaryk has gone to Petrograd, where the Czechoslovak Legion being set up had recognized him as its political leader. Beneš had secretly suggested to the representatives of the national parties that they should boycott the Reichsrat, but the suggestion was not even considered. A manifesto by Czech writers called for Czechoslovak unity and liberty, and in the Czech parliamentary group a resolution was passed, not without difficulty, claiming the right of the Czechs to form a single nation with the Slovaks.[155] The Slovak journalist Šrobar had been pressing for this, and he succeeded in putting it through in spite of the indifference to Slovakia of most of the Czech deputies.[156] Thus the Czech statement, read in the Reichsrat by the Agrarian deputy Stanek, aimed straight at the heart of Austrian-Hungarian dualism, which it declared to be the source of oppression of the non-dominant nationalities. It called for the reorganization of the Habsburg monarchy into a federal state of free and equal nations, among which the Czechoslovak nation would take its place.[157]

Federalism was not necessarily incompatible with the survival of the Habsburg empire—it might actually have given it a new lease of life by winning it the support of the majority of the population, which was neither German nor Magyar. Francis Ferdinand himself had toyed with the idea for years, and it had figured in the programme of the Austrian Social Democrats since 1899. The Czech Social Democratic delegation, led by Šmeral, who wanted to preserve the unity of the peoples of the Danubian monarchy, included it in the memorandum it presented to the Stockholm conference.[158] In view of the determined opposition of the German Austrian parties and the Hungarian government to any reform of this kind, calling for Federalism as a matter of urgency in front of an international assembly in wartime could have been interpreted as having a latent revolutionary significance, so the Austrian Social Democratic delegation restricted itself to calling for the grant of national autonomy to all the peoples of Austria-Hungary, emphasizing that this was a domestic matter for the monarchy and attacking anyone who wanted its dismemberment.[159] In fact, only one of the two deputies of the insignificant Czech Progressive Party spoke in revolutionary (i.e. of course, national revolutionary) terms in the Reichsrat on May 30. Mgr Korošec, the Slovene Catholic deputy, was certainly not revolutionary in outlook, but he read a statement by the Yugoslav parliamentary group which, relying on the nationality principle and the historical rights of the Croat state (a matter on which, as a result of the dual system, the Reichsrat had no more competence than it had on Slovakia), put forward claims that were an exact counterpart to the Czechoslovak claims. In other words, it called for the reunification of all the Slovenes, Croats and Serbs of the monarchy into an 'inde-

[182]

pendent and democratic state, free from domination by any foreign nation, under the sceptre of the dynasty of Habsburg and Lorraine'.[160] The representatives of the Poles and the Ruthenians also stated the claims to national unity and self-determination of their respective peoples, who were split up among several states.

These statements on behalf of the various nationalities still reiterated their loyalty to the Crown, provided it promoted the federal reforms at which they aimed. Taken in conjunction with the interest that Paris, London and Washington were showing in the secret peace feelers that Charles I had authorized—the western powers actually advised the young monarch to carry out the federal reform of his empire, which would have enabled him to dissociate himself from Germany with the enthusiastic support of the majority of his people— this was probably the Habsburg monarchy's last chance of saving itself by audacious action. Serbia and Romania had been defeated and, though they fought on with what was left of their armies, they would have been in no position to impose all their claims on the Entente, and still less on the United States, which was not bound to them by treaties or undertakings of any kind. Russia was on the verge of disintegration. Italy alone still represented a major threat, but her defeat at Caporetto in October was to show how unsubstantial it was. Unfortunately for the dynasty, Charles I, a well-meaning but volatile monarch, was not of the calibre which the situation required. The most intelligent of his ministers, Count Czernin, who was the *de facto* leader of all the Austrian governments that succeeded each other between January 1917 and April 1918, was fittingly described by J. Redlich as having the mentality of a man of the seventeenth century. He was undoubtedly highly skilled in the practice of politics in the traditional sense, and, though he possessed a marked personality, he was unprejudiced to the point of lack of character. But he was ill-adapted to seeing the urgency of recognizing that the age of popular self-government had arrived.[161] As a shrewd politician Czernin should at least have realized that, so long as the Habsburg army remained an effective fighting force, the introduction of federalism might have strengthened the empire, dividing the Slovaks, who wanted autonomous self-government for themselves, from the Czechs, instead of uniting them, and that it would have divided the Croats and the Slovenes from the Serbs for the same reason. It was the Austro-Hungarian refusal of any kind of federalism, until it was too late, that made inevitable the union between Czechs and Slovaks, and between Croats, Slovenes and Serbs.

Some mitigatory circumstances must of course be granted both to the Emperor Charles and to Czernin. As Foreign Minister, Czernin

[183]

represented both Austria and Hungary, and was responsible for relations with their ally, Germany. The Germans, as is shown by the reports of their ambassador in Vienna, supported Czernin, who was in a very shaky position in mid-1917 in view of Tisza's fall and the unresolved government crisis in Vienna. If the Austrians made a separate peace, the German reaction was very much to be feared. The German army might actually have invaded Austria, though probably it would have been able to do so only in periods in which potentially decisive battles were not raging on the Western Front. It would hardly have run the risk of doing so while the British and French offensive of the summer of 1917 was at its height; after Ludendorff's last great offensive in March 1918, it would no longer have been able to do so. In any case, Austria-Hungary could have dissociated itself from Germany only if it had been relatively united. In 1917, the desire for peace was certainly very strong among the Hungarians and the German Austrians as well as among the other nationalities, though the German Austrians had a strong feeling of solidarity with Germany. In 1917 democratic reforms could still have saved the monarchy from disintegration, but a peace that would have been equivalent to a confession of military defeat would have been opposed by both the majority in the Hungarian parliament and the German Austrian parties in the Reichsrat, with the sole exception of the Social Democrats.

The Slavs, Italians and Romanians, plus the Social Democrats, outnumbered the German Austrian nationalists in the Reichsrat, however, even if the Christian Socialists were included with the latter, as they were rightly included at the time. As the Austrian régime, unlike the Hungarian, was not parliamentary, effective power being in the hands of the Crown, it was up to the latter, if it had the courage, to take the initiative in decreeing reforms. In spite of the parliamentary system in Hungary, the monarch's powers were even greater there than those of any crowned head in any of the western democracies. But Charles I did not have the stature to assume responsibilities far graver and more difficult than those which devolved upon Francis Joseph in 1849 and 1867. Clam-Martinic and Czernin among his ministers came from Francis Ferdinand's intimate circle, but neither believed in the large-scale reorganization of the empire to which he had aspired. The Austrian Prime Minister shelved as inconsistent with each other all the reforms called for by the various nationalities, and limited himself to inviting their parties to be represented in a government enlarged to include them.[162] The Slav parties, not trusting him, rejected the proposal, which forced him to resign. Several weeks of negotiations followed. The Emperor desired to show his goodwill by granting, against Czernin's advice, a general political amnesty, which included those sentenced for high treason.[163] The next day, Charles I sent for J. Redlich, who had distinguished himself in the Reichsrat a few weeks earlier by speaking in favour of large-scale national autonomies, to the applause both of the parties of the various nationalities, including the Czech, and of the Social Democrats. Redlich's appointment had been recommended by Polzer-Hoditz, but above all by two personalities, the pacifist Professor Lammasch, a member of the Upper House, and the great industrialist and administrator Meinl, who with a view to a peace feeler were looking for a thread that might lead them to President Wilson.[164] (For this episode we refer the reader to Appendix I.[165])

In Redlich's second audience with the Emperor, the latter approved his plan to include in the cabinet representatives of all the nationalities and the Social Democrats on the basis of a programme of autonomist reforms. But a few hours later the Emperor changed his mind. According to Lammasch, Czernin alarmed him by telling him that, in the event of a separate peace, the German High Command would invade Bohemia.[166] This was certainly a possibility, but as secret negotiations with the Entente, in view of the difficulties in the way of coming to an agreement with Italy, would in any case have been protracted, a government with a strong parliamentary base such as that suggested by Redlich would have regained the confidence in the empire of the majority of the population, which was not German in Austria (or Magyar in Hungary).

Like nearly all the German-Austrian politicians—with the exception of the Social Democrats and a few relatively isolated personalities such as Redlich, Lammasch and Mgr Seipel—Czernin was very much opposed to autonomistic reforms in favour of the Czechs. Also, as a German-Austrian politician he felt a sense of solidarity with Germany, combined with fear of her. Thus Austrian Prime Ministership was entrusted to Seidler, a former Minister of Agriculture, a bureaucrat competent in economic and administrative matters but obtuse in other fields. While immobility perpetuated itself in Vienna, a brigade of the Czech Legion being formed in Russia was taking part in the summer offensive launched by Kerensky, and fought very bravely. On the other side, a predominantly Czech division of the Austro-Hungarian army abandoned its section of the front line.[167] The opportunity that Austria turned out to be incapable of seizing was seized by her enemies.

Things were no better in Hungary. There the monarch at least had the courage to dismiss Count Tisza, whose arrogance at the solemn coronation ceremony in Budapest had annoyed him.[168] After the

Entente note to President Wilson, Hodža and Vajda-Voevod informed the King that he could rely on their continued loyalty if he introduced universal suffrage in the territories of St Stephen's Crown.[169] Polzer-Hoditz, the Emperor's private secretary, who detested the proud Magyar aristocracy, encouraged him in that direction. He was aware of the insuperable opposition of the Hungarian parliament in its existing form to any far-reaching extension of the franchise. He therefore suggested to his master that he should do what Francis Ferdinand had planned to do, i.e. entrust the Prime Ministership of Hungary to someone completely loyal to the throne (there were such persons among the Magyars), dissolve parliament, hold a general election (which would have been possible in spite of the war, as after the failure of the Romanian invasion, no enemy troops remained on Hungarian soil), take advantage of the existing electoral law, which was based on the open vote, to exercise pressure, as all Hungarian governments always had done, in favour of its own candidates, besides favouring the nationality parties and the Hungarian democratic parties, principally that of the small landowners, but also the Social Democrats. The new parliament so elected would then adopt universal secret suffrage.[170] Charles dismissed this proposal, however, believing that, apart from being very risky, it would be an infringement of the Hungarian constitution, which he had sworn at his coronation to respect and defend.[171]

But he needed a Hungarian government that would support him if the peace feelers he had put out to the Entente came to anything. The party in the Hungarian parliament which campaigned openly for universal suffrage and for a peace without annexations, not disguising the fact that this would have to be paid for by sacrificing the German alliance, was Count Károlyi's. Czernin therefore received Károlyi on March 9 and told him that he was convinced of the absolute necessity of a speedy peace.[172] The monarch, acting constitutionally, informed Tisza that he was granting an audience to his greatest opponent.[173] The royal invitation reached Károlyi immediately after he had made a speech in parliament in which, taking as his cue the news from Russia—he declared the revolution there to be of equal importance with the French Revolution of 1789—he castigated the imperialist policy pursued by Germany since the fall of Bismarck. He condemned the annexationist designs both of the Germans and of the Magyar nationalists, and pointed out the necessity of a reconciliation with the non-Magyar nationalities as a basis for the desired independence of Hungary.[174]

Political and social antagonisms had been so exacerbated in Hungary, and the immense war effort that had devolved on her—

[186]

being less industrialized than Austria, she had sent proportionately more conscripts to the front—had caused so much mourning and suffering that the first news of the Russian Revolution had awakened an ardent desire to bring the war to an end. The will to struggle for democracy, social justice and peace was widespread, and was necessary felt with special acuteness in Budapest, the country's political capital and only big industrial city. Intellectuals and students, particularly the very numerous intellectuals and students of Jewish descent, were no less radicalized than were the workers.[175] Károlyi who, since dissociating himself from the traditionalists and conservatives of the forty-eightist party and coming out in favour of universal suffrage and (still more disinterestedly, as he himself was a big landowner) agrarian reform, had surrounded himself with radical and also socialist journalists who gave a voice to the rapid evolution of the proletariat towards hopes of a new life. They gave clear expression to the irruption of the proletarian masses on to the political stage even before the Social Democrats did so.

When Károlyi was received in audience by the King on March 22, he did not foresee that little more than eighteen months later he would be the leader of a republican revolution. Some months previously he had said to J. Redlich that, in spite of his party's independence programme, if the dynasty decided to make peace, he would agree not to question Hungary's link with Austria.[176] He saw plainly that to Hungary continuation of the war was far more ruinous than its lack of diplomatic and military independence. On the one hand, war increasingly subordinated the Habsburg monarchy to imperial Germany, and on the other it was pushing the Entente into adopting the Serbian and Romanian aspirations to Hungarian territory. Thus, after he had urged on Charles the necessity of dismissing Tisza to enable universal suffrage to be introduced in Hungary and to make it possible to conclude a separate peace (which Tisza, a convinced supporter of the German alliance, would certainly have opposed), and had received Charles's assurance that it was his intention to carry out this reform and end the war within the year, Károlyi left with the impression that he was to be appointed Prime Minister. But in parliament his party was in a tiny minority. His appointment would have required either a general election or the adjournment of parliament until the end of the war. His own temperament being if anything excessively audacious, he failed immediately to see that the monarch to whom he had been talking was too slight a man to undertake such a risk.

Tisza had a better understanding of the young monarch's inner weakness. He had repeatedly been invited by the latter to extend the

[187]

suffrage in a manner 'corresponding to the great times and the sacrifices made by the people', but had stubbornly refused to bow to the royal will.[177] When he was finally forced to resign, he outlined in a letter to his brother a resistance programme that he subsequently carried out tenaciously. They must see to it, he said, that parliament postponed debating universal suffrage until the end of the war, and that the Prime Ministership went to Count Andrássy, i.e. the most conservative of their opponents, if he would agree to this course. Otherwise the post must go to Wekerle, the ex-Prime Minister who (let us recall) had before the war postponed indefinitely the radical extension of the suffrage then desired by Francis Joseph.[178] Tisza's grave mistake, which subsequently cost him his life, was that—as he wrote to a friend on April 26, 1917—he believed that the Hungarian people were basically tranquil and that universal suffrage was wanted only by Social Democrats, radical Freemasons and the agitators among the various nationalities. He proposed that the penal code should be applied more rigorously than in the past to these agitators, and that Serbian and Romanian language schools and teachers should be watched.[179] He did not believe that the Central Powers were going to be defeated (though it fell to him on October 17, 1918, to announce their defeat to the Hungarian parliament). Consequently, it did not occur to him that the result of elections conducted under universal secret suffrage, in which the real and indisputable feelings of the people in every constituency would be revealed (among other things, by the nationality of their elected representative), might, in the absence of a plebiscite, be invaluable to the Hungarians at the peace conference as a weapon to prevent excessive mutilation of their country's territory, of which large and even predominantly Magyar areas were claimed by their enemies.

Károlyi's party, however, believed, as its newspaper openly stated, that the collapse of Tsarism and the intervention of the United States had changed the character of the war. The Hungarian people had no reason to fight against the new Russian democracy, and every reason to embrace President Wilson's anti-imperialist and anti-militarist peace principles, to prevent these from being applied at their expense.[180] Knowing that the monarch was going to ask Tisza to introduce universal suffrage and that he would refuse, Károlyi and his followers had held meetings all over the country with the declared aim of forcing the government to resign.[181] The Social Democratic Party could not allow itself to be left behind. Abstention from work on May 1 was complete, and perhaps 100,000 persons took part in a mass meeting in Budapest.[182] The next day, at the instigation of the representatives in the factories of the Social Democratic Party (which was organized on a trade-union basis, not unlike the British Labour Party, but in a situation saturated with class hatred), all factory workers in the Hungarian capital downed their tools from 11 a.m. to midday in support of the demand for universal suffrage, social security measures, the dismissal of Tisza, and peace without annexations.[183] A week later, the Social Democratic Party, Károlyi's party, the 'bourgeois' Democratic Party, the Christian Social Party and all the trade unions formally organized themselves into an electoral *bloc*. Tisza countered by adjourning parliament and increasing the severity of the censorship. But Charles was already aware that the situation in Hungary was getting out of hand, and on May 21 he summoned up sufficient energy to force Tisza to resign.[184] When the news was known, a long procession of workers paraded through the streets of Budapest shouting 'Down with Tisza!'[185] Strikes for better pay, which had practically ceased since the outbreak of war, began again. On May 23, a strike broke out in all the railway workshops in Hungary; it ended nine days later in a victory for the workers. The number of subscribers to the journal of the Social Democratic railway union increased from 5,000 to 12,000.[186]

During those days, the Hungarian Social Democratic delegation left for Stockholm; they were given passports by Czernin, who believed them to be as loyal as the Austrian delegation.[187] In Stockholm, the delegates saw the complete text of the appeal issued by the Petrograd Soviet on May 25 for a peace based on the right of nations to self-determination, without annexations or indemnities. The reply of the Hungarian Social Democrats to the questionnaire that the organizing committee of the conference submitted to all the socialist parties took as its starting-point the economic, political and cultural necessity of rejecting the dismemberment of Austria-Hungary implied by the Entente in its note to President Wilson, and insisted on the maintenance of Hungary's territorial integrity for the same reason. It committed itself, however, to fighting, as it claimed it had always done, even during the war, when it had rejected the 'sacred union', the system of national and social oppression that existed in Hungary. It recognized the urgent necessity of granting democratic administrative autonomy to the 'oppressed nations' of Austria-Hungary and accepted the justice of the demand for the re-establishment of the independence and the material reconstruction of Serbia and Belgium (in the case of the former with access to the sea), but rejected the claim of the socialists of the Entente countries that Germany bore the sole responsibility for the war. It attributed that responsibility to the dominant classes in all countries, from the French financial oligarchy to the Prussian Junkers, from Tsarism to

[189]

Austro-Hungarian feudalism. As for the question of Alsace-Lorraine, it expressed the hope of a solution on autonomistic lines to be peaceably arrived at on the basis of the agreement reached in 1913 by the German Social Democrats and the French Socialist Party on the principle that all disputes between nations should be settled by arbitration.[188] The Hungarian delegation associated itself with the peace aims proclaimed by the Petrograd Soviet, specifying that the conclusion of a peace without annexations or indemnities was not to be expected from the victory of either of the two belligerent power *blocs*—both of which were imperialist—but must be achieved by the peoples with a peace without victors or vanquished. To that end, the Hungarians suggested consideration of the idea of concerted action by all the European socialist parties, to take the form of peace meetings and demonstrations, and also a twenty-four hour protest strike.[189]

Kunfi, who in the Hungarian Social Democratic leadership had for years represented a radical trend that was pacifist throughout the war, and was also the most ardent supporter of the political alliance with Károlyi, had succeeded in swaying his fellow delegates in the drafting of this memorandum. The papers of the Swedish Social Democratic leader Branting, whose Entente sympathies were well known, include a letter written to him by Kunfi on the day of his departure from Stockholm. It contains the following passage:

At all events, it was a great pleasure for me to meet you and to note that in our high esteem of western democracy and the way in which I visualize the progress of humanity and desire the development of socialism we have many points of contact. With Comrade Huysmans we discussed the fact that in a note about their war aims by the Entente powers it would be of great importance if account were taken of the fears of Hungary in regard to Transylvania and access to the sea [Croatia and Fiume].[190]

Although the whole careers of Kunfi and Károlyi show the genuineness of their revolutionary feelings, they shared the illusion, which was to be fatal to both in 1918–19, that it would be possible for a democratic Hungary to retain areas which, like Transylvania, were not predominantly inhabited by Magyars. But the inclusion by the Hungarian Social Democrats of the Central Powers in their denunciation of imperialism, and their denunciation of the national oppression prevailing in Austria-Hungary, the existence of which was categorically denied by Victor Adler, the Austrian Social Democratic leader, pleased Branting and Huysmans, the Secretary of the Socialist International, who hastened publicly to express his approval.

Neither of the two, however, was in a position to gain Hungary the sympathies of the Entente. The favour of the western powers could have been won only by a speedy accession to power of the Magyar independence movement and a weakening of the military position of Germany by a Hungarian move for a separate peace. That was certainly Károlyi's and Kunfi's aim. The Austro-Hungarian legation in Stockholm, which closely followed the activities of the Social Democratic delegations, immediately reported the non-conformist behaviour of the Hungarians to the Vienna and Budapest governments.[191] Tisza, though he had submitted his resignation, was still in office pending his successor's appointment, and threatened to take criminal proceedings against the socialists who signed the memorandum.[192] The difference between the positions of the Hungarian Social Democrats and their Austrian and German colleagues (meaning, in the case of the latter, that of the majority Social Democratic Party, for the minority Independent Socialist Party expressed itself in Stockholm in terms even more radical than the Hungarians), was also noted by the Italian Minister in Stockholm, who informed Sonnino. The latter thought the matter sufficiently interesting to inform the Italian ambassador in London.[193] To the Slovak Social Democrats, the radicalism of the Hungarian party seemed insufficient. They constituted a branch of the Hungarian party, and complained that none of their number had been included in the delegation to Stockholm, and that their federal claims were not even mentioned in the document presented there. Their dissatisfaction with the limitations of the internationalism of the Hungarian Social Democrats caused them to gravitate towards the Czechoslovak independence movement, which they were the first to represent in Slovakia in the following year.[194]

When the Social Democratic leaders reached home, they called on the proletariat to go into the streets to campaign for universal suffrage, declaring the struggle to be also one for a democratic peace.[195] On June 8, 1917, Charles arrived in Budapest to settle the ministerial crisis. At 2 p.m., a half-day general strike broke out, paralysing factories, public transport, the shops and the public services. Processions of perhaps 150,000 persons marched through the city centre, calling for universal suffrage, an end to the war, and for Tisza to be sent to the gallows.[196]

A new government, a national coalition for electoral reform, was formed a few days later, and hopes were dashed. It included representatives of parties notoriously hostile to universal suffrage—the new Prime Minister was a deputy belonging to one of the moderate parties (the Constitutional Party, led by Count Andrássy), Prince

[191]

Maurice Eszterházy, a well-intentioned young man obviously too weak for the task of leading a government of reform—and Károlyi was not a member of it. At the last moment the post of Minister accredited to the Crown, which Charles had ended by promising him was given to another, more moderate representative of his party, Count Batthyány.[197] Those who had worked for Károlyi's exclusion were Charles's private secretary, probably also the German government, and Vázsonyi, the leader of the Hungarian 'bourgeois' Democratic Party, who was given the Justice portfolio. Vázsonyi, who was an effective speaker and was very able in his way, but was in reality more moderate than genuinely democratic, could count on the votes only of the sizable Jewish bourgeoisie of Budapest, consisting of traders and artisans. This, however, enabled him to be on excellent terms with the Social Democratic leaders, who always needed the goodwill of the Budapest municipality which, in view of the restricted suffrage, was controlled by Vázsonyi's party. In a series of secret conversations that were withheld from Károlyi (who was mistrusted both as an aristocrat and an extremist by the reformist trade-unionist leaders) Vázsonyi persuaded a majority of the Social Democratic leadership to agree that the extension of the franchise should be kept within the limits that Count Andrássy, the new Minister of the Interior, was willing to propose. The vote would be given to all male literates who had reached the age of twenty-four and to illiterates who had won the War Cross by three months' service at the front. Workers in industrial establishments would not be required to prove their literacy.[198] This would increase the number of voters from 1,600,000 to about 3,900,000, and would include the great majority of the workers likely to vote for the Social Democrats. The ballot was to be secret in all urban constituencies and in one-third of the rural constituencies. The Social Democrats did not place much reliance on securing the vote of the illiterate agricultural proletariat or semiproletariat, a substantial proportion of whom were of non-Magyar nationality. Most of the Social Democratic leaders accepted the reform framed in such a way as to provide some hope of its being passed by parliament.

Although they were not aware of this electoral compromise, the masses, who had been radicalized by the news of the Russian Revolution, felt instinctively that Tisza, the leader of the parliamentary majority whom the conservative state apparatus continued to consider its real master, had not really been displaced. On the evening of June 28, after nearly 30,000 workers had attended a meeting addressed by Kunfi, about 2,000 youths stormed and wrecked Tisza's party headquarters, broke the windows of a newspaper that supported him and those of a number of luxury shops, and dispersed only after violent clashes with the police.[199] The Social Democratic Party leadership repudiated those responsible for these excesses and succeeded in preventing a repetition. But the situation remained tense. Károlyi realized that the formation of the new Hungarian government had done nothing to reinforce Charles's uncertain will for peace and began to have doubts about Czernin's firmness in relation to the German supporters of 'war till victory'. In a speech in parliament, he openly attributed the chief responsibility for the continuation of hostilities to the unrestricted submarine warfare begun by Germany at the beginning of 1917 and declared that peace presupposed the effective democratization of Germany and Austria-Hungary.[200] The majority in the House did not share his view. At the end of August, Prince Eszterházy felt no longer able to bear a burden that exceeded his strength, and resigned. In accordance with Tisza's plans, his place was taken by Wekerle. This made it probable that not even Vázsonyi's electoral compromise would be fully carried out. Few of its more democratic stipulations in fact survived when parliament at last passed a sham extension of the franchise in mid-1918.

Discontent among the Hungarian working class, made acute by the continual rise in the cost of living and the inadequacy of the rations, made itself strongly felt at the National Congress of Social Democratic Trade Unions held in Budapest in the second half of August 1917. Working-class organizations had been growing rapidly in Hungary since the Russian Revolution. In the last year before the war (which was a year of economic crisis), they had had 110,000 paying members. Mobilization caused this figure to fall to about 51,000 by the end of 1914 and 43,000 by the end of 1915. At the end of 1916, it increased to 55,000, and at the end of July 1917 it was estimated at 125,000. This figure almost doubled in the following six months. The most significant increase was in the trade-union organization of the metal-working industries, which rose to about 50,000 in July 1917 from the December 1916 figure of 20,000. The miners' organization, which was still forbidden by the police, had increased from 3,000 to 9,000; that of the white-collar workers from fewer than 2,000 to 9,000; and that of the tramwaymen from a negligible figure to 6,000.[201] A number of left-wing spokesmen, politically close to Kunfi or farther to the left than he, criticized the union leaders for their reluctance to use the strike weapon for pay claims in war time, though the masses wanted this, and wanted to see the prospect of a vigorous class struggle for democracy, peace and socialism restored to the whole movement. According to one of them, D. Biró of the bookbinders' union, whom the opposition succeeded in electing to the Trade-Union's Central Council, they should not be afraid of force in relation to either the employers or to the government.[202] The aggressive spirit that prevailed at the congress also reappeared in the international sphere. At the conference of the International Trade Union Secretariat summoned in Berne in October 1917 by its German leaders (a French delegation that wished to attend were not given passports, and the British refused to resume contact with the Germans), the Hungarian delegation, of which Biró was a member, to the great surprise of the German delegation, which caused it to be rejected, proposed that a declaration be made in which the following words occurred:

> This conference expects the workers of all countries, in order to secure the most rapid possible conclusion of peace, to use all the means of the class struggle against governments conducting an imperialist policy.[203]

Months passed in Hungary before these words were followed by deeds, but in the end the deeds came, with the result that this pronouncement came to seem prophetic. In Croatia-Slavonia, the Eszterházy government promptly appointed a new Ban in the person of A. Mihalović, a member of the Serbo-Croat coalition, with which his predecessor, Baron Skerlecz, had already collaborated.[204] Now it obtained control of local affairs, on the tacit understanding that it would not demand any change in Croatia's relationship with Hungary, which was certainly one of dependence; that is to say, it would not call for a 'trialist' system among Austrians, Hungarians and Southern Slavs in the Habsburg empire or have any truck with an independent Yugoslavia.[205] This was not sufficient for the most ardent Croat patriots, who did not see why they should not claim for their country at least the degree of autonomy and equality of rights which Hungary herself enjoyed in relation to Austria, though the Magyar independence movement was not satisfied with them.

On June 5, 1917, A. Pavelić, the leader of the Croat Right Party, adopting the declaration made by the Southern Slav deputies in the Reichsrat, asserted in the Zagreb Diet that 'the right of every nation to manage its own affairs is the basic right that has been more than ever put into relief during the course of this war by all the belligerent peoples', and that it was therefore necessary 'to reorganize the Habsburg monarchy . . . excluding the supremacy or domination of one people over others . . .' now that 'the democratic spirit of great, enlightened Russia has begun to spread its wings with irresistible force over the other countries of Europe'.[206] For his part, Radić said that he considered the section of the coalition to which the new Ban

[194]

belonged, to be socially conservative, indeed reactionary, and he called on the monarch to take account of the fact that he must introduce democracy throughout Austria-Hungary if he wished his subjects, who looked to the Russian Revolution, to remain loyal to him. In another speech, on August 4, Radić did not hesitate to say that the Entente, by adopting the principle of self-determination of nations proclaimed by the new Russia, would force Austria-Hungary to regulate her national questions in accordance with that principle, which Germany alone still refused to accept. To Croatia this would mean separation from Hungary and reunification in an independent state, even though it was a Habsburg state, with the Southern Slavs of Austria.[207] The Croat Social Democrats went even farther. In their memorandum to the Stockholm conference they said that the Serbs, Croats and Slovenes ethnically constituted a single people, and that the proletariat was the class that suffered most from the division of the Yugoslav nation into various states and its oppression in Austria-Hungary. They therefore called for the unification of all the Southern Slavs into a Balkan republican confederation.[208] The author of the memorandum, Mijo Radošević, knowing that he would run the risk of criminal proceedings because of his republican statements if he returned to Zagreb, went from Stockholm to Petrograd. Franjo Markić, the representative of the socialists of Bosnia-Hercegovina, did the same. In the memorandum that he and a comrade presented in Stockholm, he adopted the cause of Yugoslavia and accused Austria-Hungary of having deliberately made war on Serbia in 1914 in order to stifle the aspirations of the Southern Slavs. From Stockholm he went to Paris.[209]

On the other side of the lines, the Serbian government had lost its principal backer with the collapse of Tsarism. Even Miljukov, during the few weeks he was at the Russian Foreign Ministry, showed that the cause he favoured was the birth of Yugoslavia, not that of a Greater Serbia. His successors, adapting themselves to the progressive radicalization of the revolution, could show no sympathy for the Serbian monarchy. The United States, now in the war, was not committed to respecting the undertakings given to Pásic by the Tsarist government or to the Paris and London governments. According to the memoirs of I. Meštrović who, as a sculptor of international repute was one of the members of the Yugoslav Committee with easiest access to the Entente governments, Supilo's representations to the Foreign Office resulted in the British cabinet's not pronouncing itself on Pašić's request—put forward after Bulgaria's intervention on the side of the Central Powers had relieved him of the pressure previously put on him to yield a part of Macedonia—that in the event of victory, southern Dalmatia and southern Hungary should be assigned to Serbia in addition to Bosnia-Hercegovina.[210] This must have been the more disturbing to Pašić inasmuch as he probably had wind of the peace feelers being exchanged between London and Paris and the Habsburgs. If these had come to anything, it would certainly have been at the expense of Serbia's claims. On the other hand, Ljuba Davidović's Serbian Democratic Party had resigned from Pašić's government in Corfu, where the Skupština, the Serbian parliament, was meeting in exile, believing that they could more effectively influence affairs by threatening to withhold their parliamentary support and thus destroy the government's majority. The Democrats, among whom there were some friends of Supilo, were far more willing than Pašić to merge the kingdom of Serbia into a Yugoslav state.[211] Pašić, taking these things realistically into account, sent his lieutenant, S. Protić, to Nice to come to an agreement with Trumbić and Meštrović, who had moved to Cannes, on the broad lines of a declaration to be signed and issued jointly by the Yugoslav Committee and the Serbian government.[212] After difficult negotiations, agreement in principle was reached. Protić, though he was even more of a Greater Serbia man than Pašić, agreed that the future kingdom of the Serbs, Croats and Slovenes should be named Yugoslavia. Trumbić, who had begun by insisting that the constitution of the new state should be settled by a constituent assembly requiring a two-thirds majority, ended by agreeing that a simple majority would be sufficient, which meant putting control in the hands of the Serbian parties which, because of the size of the population, were bound to have a majority.[213]

A delegation from the Yugoslav Committee arrived in Corfu in mid-June,[214] and the so-called Corfu agreement was signed on July 20, 1917. Trumbić, who signed it with Pašić, regarded it as completely satisfactory, and Supilo, who followed these developments with passionate interest from London, where he was suffering from a fatal illness, received the news with joy.[215] The Croats in America, however, to whom the document was presented by Hinković, did not like it; they feared that a Yugoslav state on such lines would not offer sufficient guarantees against Serbian centralization and supremacy,[216] and the future showed that their fears were justified. The fact of immediate importance to the Croat *émigrés*, however, was that Serbia had formally committed herself to fight, not merely for the provinces she might hope to annex directly from Austria-Hungary, but also for the unification of all the Serbs, Croats and Slovenes into an independent Yugoslavia.[217] The Yugoslav Committee, having committed itself irrevocably to the campaign for the dissolution of

Austria-Hungary, could no longer put the claim to democratic federalism (theoretically attainable within the Habsburg monarchy) on a level of importance with complete national unity. An accurate summary of the Corfu agreement was published on August 5, 1917, by the Budapest democratic newspaper *Az Est*, which had received it from its correspondent in Switzerland. The news was immediately taken up by the Zagreb newspapers.[218] The priest Professor Barac, who, being a personal friend of Field-Marshal Boroević, had a passport enabling him to travel abroad, was sent to Switzerland to obtain more definite information. At Lausanne, Trumbić assured him that the interests of the Croats and Slovenes were fully safeguarded by the agreement. The Yugoslav deputies to the Reichsrat and to the Croatian Diet to whom Barac repeated this assurance were not completely convinced, but thought it useful to them to be able to play the card of an independent Yugoslavia.[219]

A few weeks previously, Korošec and Krek, the leaders of the Slovene Popular Party, had gone to Prague to propose to the Czech politicians that they should press for a reconstruction of the Austrian government which would enable both to enter it.[220] The Czechs, however, declined. But, as Vienna showed no signs of willingness to make substantial concessions, Korošec, who had previously been one of the most moderate leaders of his party, came out in September for firm opposition to the government in office.[221] Apparently with the aid of funds provided by the Czechs, the Croat Right Party, which was allied to the Slovene Popular Party, founded a newspaper at Zagreb, the *Hrvatska Država*, which in its second number printed an article by Krek singing the praises of the future independent state of the reunited Slovenes, Croats and Serbs, which the writer did not necessarily assume would be under the Habsburg sceptre.[222] Soon afterwards, the same newspaper published a highly laudatory obituary of Supilo, who had died in London, mentioning his revolutionary work for the Yugoslav cause abroad and his contribution to the Corfu agreement.[223] When the Diet reopened, Radić earned himself a thirty-day suspension by declaring that the Croats would not remain loyal to the Crown if the price of loyalty were servitude.[224] In the Reichsrat, the Slovenes, like the Czechs, refused to vote for the budget. The Dalmatian deputy Tresić-Pavičić, whose reputation as a poet and translator extended to Italy (he was a friend of Guglielmo Ferrero) dramatically denounced the barbarous treatment inflicted on Slav detainees and civilian internees, among whom he had spent three years in spite of his parliamentary mandate.[225]

The German and Austrian victory at Caporetto, which was greeted with pleasure by the apolitical masses of Croats and Slovenes,

Austrian propaganda having succeeded largely in imposing the picture
of a treacherous Italy thirsty for Slav territory, had a temporarily
depressing effect on the independence movement among all the
nationalities of the Habsburg empire. A memorandum on the Yugoslav question dating from the end of 1917 preserved in the records of
the German Foreign Ministry expressed the view that the Yugoslav
parties in Austria and the Right Party in Croatia wanted a federal
Yugoslavia under the Habsburg sceptre, and that the Serbo-Croat
coalition wanted merely the unification of Dalmatia and Bosnia-
Hercegovina with Croatia within the existing framework of the
monarchy.[226] Meanwhile, the Vienna and Budapest governments,
which should have been much more accurately informed, were nurs-
ing the illusion that, with Russia out of the war, the problem of their
Slav subjects had become less urgent and acute.

VI

The Rome Congress

On November 27, 1917, Count Czernin received the parliamentary representatives of the Austrian Christian Social and German national parties. He said that, after the collapse of the Italian front and the armistice in Russia, 'the military situation is so good that the war could be regarded as won in that respect, were it not for the situation in the back areas, or the food, heating, and transport situation, in which conditions are critical in many respects'.[1] He reiterated his desire for a rapid peace, without annexations, but honourable. As for relations with Berlin, he embellished the picture, saying that 'the sky is cloudless', as he was bound to do for an audience of German Austrian nationalists who regarded all talk of a possible dissociation of Austria-Hungary from Germany as high treason. There was a danger that the notorious annexationism of the German High Command might cause the imminent peace negotiations at Brest-Litovsk to fail. Austria-Hungary, however, was hungry for Russian or Ukrainian cereals, and to her it was vital that the negotiations should end quickly and successfully. To indicate the necessity of her having a free hand in the matter Czernin said: 'We will march to the end with our German brothers for the defence of Germany, but not for conquests.'

But he reserved the right not to regard as coming under the heading of conquests all those areas which could be incorporated without any more fighting, i.e. those which had now been occupied for several years or months by the armies of the Central Powers. The absorption into the Habsburg empire of Russian Poland in one way or another, with the consent of the Poles, now seemed to him once more to be a practicable proposition in exchange for the definite recognition that Lithuania and Courland fell within the German sphere of influence. He concluded:

As for the future set up of the Balkan states, this is evidently a power problem, which will be solved in a manner corresponding with the situation. What we desire is possession of the Lovcen, together with a coastal strip connecting it with Albania, as well as some frontier rectifications at the expense of Serbia and Romania.

We also aspire to a common frontier with Bulgaria. If the Kara-georgevich dynasty were to disappear, *tant mieux*.

In relation to Italy, he said, Austria and Hungary would be satisfied with the *status quo ante bellum*.[2]

Compared with what he and his government colleagues said at the Crown Council meeting on March 22, 1917, that is, when it was still hoped that unrestricted submarine warfare would win the war for Germany and that revolutionary Russia would be only too delighted to consolidate its new democratic set up by coming to terms rapidly with the Central Powers, this new programme of Czernin's could be described as relatively moderate.[3] At the March meeting, after he had announced that Germany intended to have an absolutely free hand in annexing former Tsarist territories, including Russian Poland, it had been agreed, in order to counteract this aggrandisement of the Reich, to aim at vast Austrian-Hungarian annexations in Romania, possibly sharing them with Russia (if she wanted compensation for leaving the Entente in the lurch and for being deprived of the Baltic or other territory she would have to yield to Germany), and at the inclusion in the Austro-Hungarian customs union of Serbia—minus all the territory in Macedonia desired by Bulgaria—on terms that would have involved the end of her national independence.[4] However, a few days after this maximum programme was approved, Czernin was forced to realize that the hopes on which it was based were illusory. He had himself admitted to Bethmann-Hollweg that Austria was at the end of her resources, though without doubting that Germany would win the war. But unrestricted submarine warfare, for all the losses that it inflicted on the British, yielded no decisive result other than drawing the United States into war with Germany, while the Russian Provisional Government obstinately tried to go on fighting on the side of the western democracies.

Eight months later, peace with a disintegrating Russia and a virtually prostrate Romania really seemed likely. Czernin, knowing that those in Russia and Romania who wanted peace at any price had strong opposition to contend with, was anxious not to prejudice by excessive ambitions the outcome that his country needed. He paid lip-service to the slogan of peace without annexations based on the principle of self-determination of the nations, which had been launched by the Russian Revolution, but could in fact be used to justify the dismemberment of the former empire of the Romanovs. But even this more moderate programme would have been realistic only if the scales of war had tipped definitely in favour of the Central Powers. In April 1917, Czernin had stated in his famous memorandum to Charles I, which had come to the knowledge of many people, that Austria-Hungary would not be able to go on fighting beyond the autumn. But when that season arrived without the appalling food situation's leading to hunger riots, and the military situation greatly improved with the Italian defeat and the Russian quest for peace, Czernin acted as if final victory had been won. On November 30 he received the parliamentary leaders of the Czech parties, who were now united in opposition to the government but had not yet formally repudiated loyalty to the dynasty. The Czechs demanded the right of self-determination for their people. At that time they might still perhaps have been satisfied with the exercise of that principle within the framework of the Habsburg monarchy, which would have meant its reorganization into a free federation of equal nations and abolition of the dual system which gave supremacy to the German Austrians and the Hungarians. But Czernin, who was preparing to use the principle of self-determination as a tool at Brest-Litovsk, replied by reaffirming the untouchability of the dual system under which, in his opinion, the peoples already enjoyed all the democratic liberties they were entitled to demand. He was of course too intelligent not to know—nor did his interlocutors conceal from him—that this reply made final the breach between the Vienna government and the Czech parties.[5] But, as he wrote from Brest-Litovsk on December 26 to the former Prime Minister Clam-Martinic—who wanted some satisfaction to be given to the similar demands by the Yugoslavs of Austria-Hungary, whom he regarded as more loyal than the Czechs, though unlikely to remain so for long —he believed that no reform of the dual system would really satisfy the nationalities of the monarchy, for the satisfaction of one would cause the dissatisfaction of another, and it was therefore better, at any rate while the war lasted, to leave things as they were. Moreover, he did not really believe there was any danger that the Yugoslavs of the Habsburg empire would follow the Czechs in the struggle for independence: he considered the Croat politicians too corrupt for a struggle of that kind, and the Serbs of Hungary too demoralized by the assignment to Romania of the Banat, a substantial proportion of the population of which was ethnically Serbian, in the treaty concluded between Romania and the Entente, which the Bolsheviks had published, together with other secret treaties.[6]

When Czernin spoke like that he already knew that in order to pave the Habsburg dynasty's way to a compromise peace, which they would obviously prefer to be a separate peace, involving her dissociation from Germany, the major Entente powers were suggesting that Austria-Hungary should show goodwill by reorganizing herself into a democratic federation of its constituent nations. Such a move, by putting an end to the supremacy of the German Austrians and the Magyars, most of whom were reputed to be fanatically loyal to the alliance with Germany, would on the one hand have weakened that alliance, and on the other would have relieved the Entente of the moral commitment to fight for the 'liberation' of Austria-Hungary's Slav and Latin nationalities. Czernin did not attach much practical importance to this commitment, which in fact was still very vague and easily revocable, for he believed that Germany was going to win the war. His chief concern was therefore to leave no doubt about the solidity of the alliance with her. Nor did he attach much importance to the contacts that the Vienna industrialist J. Meinl had had in Geneva with the American Professor Herron, which he considered an amateur intrusion into his domain.[7] But through the instrumentality of some Egyptians living in Switzerland he had himself sent to Switzerland the former Austro-Hungarian ambassador in London, Count Mensdorff (a relative of the British royal family and therefore *persona grata* in high circles in London) for a secret meeting with the South African statesman General Smuts, a member of the British Imperial War Cabinet. The meeting, at which Philip Kerr, the British Prime Minister's private secretary, was also present, took place on December 18 and 19, 1917. In his instructions to Mensdorff, Czernin laid his cards on the table. 'No question of a separate peace, talking about it would be a waste of time', is a phrase that occurs in the notes. They add that negotiations, in which Germany must be included, must be for a general peace on the basis of the *status quo ante*; Austria-Hungary's nationality questions were her own domestic affair, though the Crown had recognized the necessity of bringing the rights of the nationalities in Austria up to date and reforming the electoral system in Hungary.[8]

Mensdorff's report on his conversations was published many years ago.[9] But his complete notes, which are now accessible, as are General Smuts's full report and the reports by Kerr, throw more light on the affair.

Czernin wanted to display his diplomatic skill, and he succeeded. But skill is useful only to the extent that it is applied to realistic aims. In the existing military situation, which Smuts himself recognized as favourable to Germany, it would certainly have been very difficult for the Austro-Hungarian Foreign Minister to entertain the Entente aim, which Smuts repeated to him, of destroying Prussian militarism (though this, he indicated, did not necessarily exclude the possibility of making peace with the Hohenzollerns), or the Entente suggestion that substantial territorial concessions should be spontaneously made

[202]

by Germany (Alsace-Lorraine) and Austria-Hungary (Bosnia-Hercegovina, Transylvania, Bukovina, and the Trentino). But Mensdorff, on Czernin's instructions, told Smuts at the outset that there could be no question of any territorial concessions by Austria-Hungary, particularly to Italy, and this was by no means wise at a moment when Italy and Serbia would probably have been satisfied with much smaller concessions than at almost any other time.[10] Smuts's emphasis on British sympathy with the preservation of a 'great Austria-Hungary' which, if it granted full liberty of federation to its constituent nationalities, would, after the war, particularly in view of the collapse of the power of Russia, be 'a strong factor for peace and the surest counterweight to the bellicose ambitions of an excessively strong Germany', and his warning not to underrate the immense resources of the United States, had an immediate political significance that it was a grave error on Czernin's part not to examine closely.[11] Italy had not yet recovered from the blow of Caporetto. France—against which the Germans were at last able to throw the whole of their strength—was awaiting the arrival of American reinforcements in anxiety mingled with uncertainty, and Britain was in a position to pursue an agreement with Austria-Hungary with greater resolution than on the occasion of Prince Sixtus's mission, which had come to nothing because of Sonnino's opposition and Ribot's decision to side with his Italian colleague, though even then Lloyd George had been more in favour than the other Entente leaders of conversations with Vienna. This political constellation, which a far-sighted observer should have realized was basically more important to the survival of Austria-Hungary than the military situation that subordinated its destiny to the fortune of German arms, would not of course last indefinitely.

Charles I and Czernin certainly had reason to fear that the Germans might invade Austria in the event of a separate peace. But a beginning could have been made by decreeing the federal reorganization of the empire (the Crown could have done this by a royal decree in Austria, while in Hungary it could have achieved the same purpose by appointing a government committed to the introduction of universal secret suffrage), thus paving the way for an agreement with the Entente, which through General Smuts had suggested such a reorganization. Germany could hardly have committed military aggression against her ally to prevent her carrying out such a reform, which, after all, would have been her own domestic affair. Moreover, after the beginning of their final offensive in France (March 21, 1918) the Germans would have been unable to invade Austria-Hungary, even if the latter had left her in the lurch by making peace with her enemies; the failure of that offensive of course meant that the Entente was no longer interested in a separate peace with Austria, but only in the complete capitulation of the Central Powers.

Meanwhile General Smuts, after his return to London, remained confident of Vienna's genuine desire for peace, and did not even exclude the possibility that it might agree to yield the Trentino to Italy, while he regarded it as certain that, in the event of peace, it would cede Bukovina to Romania. Lloyd George immediately presented his report to the War Cabinet, which instructed Smuts, Kerr and Lord Robert Cecil, the Under-Secretary of State for Foreign Affairs, to prepare a draft of British war aims.[12] Pacifist pressure, represented by liberal and radical intellectuals, militant socialists (including the whole of the Independent Labour Party and other minority groups), and a Conservative personality such as Lord Lansdowne, was strong in Britain at the time. The original decision of the Labour Party to take part in the international socialist conference in Stockholm, the resignation from the government of Arthur Henderson, the Labour leader, in protest against the refusal to grant passports for the conference, the strikes, often led by small revolutionary groups, in some centres of armament production, and, in short, the whole process of radicalization of the British working-class movement which the Russian Revolution had sparked off and accelerated, all encouraged the peace movement. Even those members of the Labour Party who agreed that the war must be continued until final victory over Germany and approved of trade-union representatives remaining in the government after Henderson's resignation, believed that victory would be hastened by the declaration of peace aims acceptable to the peoples of the enemy countries.[13] A number of influential moderate Conservatives and Liberals took the same view. The entry of the United States into the war, which could not be won without it, worked in the same sense. President Wilson's aversion to imperialist conquests and secret treaties, and his enthusiasm for the idea of a League of Nations to settle all future international disputes were well known; as was his belief in disarmament and in the right of nations freely and democratically to choose their own destiny. Through his special counsellor in the American embassy in London,[14] he was in close contact with the Union of Democratic Control, a small but intellectually and politically influential group of liberal and radical intellectuals.

The view that Austria-Hungary, with whom Britain had had no recent conflicts of interest, should be preserved as a bulwark against pan-Germanism in eastern Europe—an indispensable one since the disappearance of the military counterweight exercised by Russia for many years past—was held alike by the pacifists and by the many who supported the war as a war for international democracy or were motivated by traditional power politics.[15] When the nature of the Italian claims was revealed by the publication of the Treaty of London in the Soviet press, they were considered excessive by nearly the whole of British public opinion, either because they made peace-making with Austria difficult or because they conflicted with the interests of the Southern Slavs; these, since the Corfu agreement, were associated in the public mind with Serbia, whose military valour had gained her a great deal of sympathy.[16] In that respect, the Labour Party's change of attitude towards Italy was significant. On August 10, 1917 the party conference had adopted a memorandum on allied war aims drawn up by a sub-committee, of which Henderson (then still a Minister) and Sidney Webb were the moving spirits; it put Italian aspirations on the same level as the return to France of Alsace-Lorraine, recommending only that Italy should come to an agreement with the other nations bordering on the Adriatic. The conference declared 'its warmest sympathy with the people of Italian blood and speech who have been left outside the inconvenient and indefensible boundaries that have, as a result of the diplomatic agreements of the past, been assigned to the kingdom of Italy, and supports their claim to be united with those of their own race and tongue'.[17]

The memorandum was then submitted to the inter-allied Labour and Socialist conference that met in London on August 28. Because of disagreement on the representation of the minorities of various parties (these minorities were mostly internationalist and revolutionary), the conference did not proceed to a vote and was adjourned *sine die*. With Arthur Henderson's resignation from the government, the internationalists in the Labour Party became more determinedly pacifist, while the belligerence of some trade-union leaders increased. In France, the left-wing internationalist trend was gaining ground in the leadership of the Socialist Party, which indicated that it might perhaps agree to the idea of a plebiscite in Alsace-Lorraine instead of insisting on annexation pure and simple. On the eve of a conference of the Labour Party held jointly with the parliamentary committee of the trade unions on December 28, the memorandum on war aims was amended to take account of the new situation.[18] The revised version, which the conference adopted and agreed to submit to the next inter-allied socialist conference to take place at the end of February 1918, called for a plebiscite in Alsace-Lorraine, but Italy's claims suffered more severely. While stating that the 'unredeemed' territories inhabited by Italians should be restored to Italy, the document declared that it had 'no sympathy with Italian imperialism's far-reaching aims of conquest'.[19] On the same evening the executive committee of the Labour Party and the parliamentary committee of the trade unions personally submitted the document to Lloyd George, with whom 'a frank discussion took place on the points of greater importance included in the memorandum'.[20] In the opinion of the trade-union leaders, the Prime Minister 'in many respects accepted the principles' of the memorandum.[21] In fact, in regard to the question of interest to us in the present context, Lloyd George did not accept the document's indiscriminate anti-imperialism, which he regarded as completely Utopian, but did not reject its reservations about the maximum Italian claims, the modification of which would have been very helpful to him in his dealings with Austria, besides being desired by President Wilson, then engaged in drafting his Fourteen Points.[22]

In a speech to a meeting of trade unionists on January 5, 1918, Lloyd George called for an international organization for the limitation of armaments, stated the principle that territorial adjustments must not take place without the consent of the peoples concerned, declared (among other things, to reassure those who feared an indefinite prolongation of the war) that the Entente desired the dismemberment neither of Germany nor of Austria, and reiterated, as a matter to which he attached special importance, that he agreed with President Wilson that 'the destruction of Austria-Hungary does not form part of our war aims'. There must be a complete restoration of Polish unity and independence, and this embraced both Russian Poland and the Polish territories under Germany and Austria. So far as the other nationalities of Austria-Hungary were concerned, the Prime Minister (in contrast to the Entente reply to President Wilson of January 1917) merely called for genuine self-government on truly democratic lines, adding, however, that he considered 'vital the satisfaction of the legitimate claims of the Italians to union with those of the same race and language'; and he said that justice must also be done to the Romanians within the same legitimate bounds. 'If these conditions were fulfilled,' he concluded, 'Austria-Hungary would become a power whose strength would contribute to the permanent peace and liberty of Europe' instead of being a tool of Prussian militarist autocracy.[23]

To those who knew what had gone before, it was clear that, to meet Wilson (and the British supporters of Wilson's policy) and to offer a bait to the Austro-Hungarian government, Lloyd George, in quoting the words of the Labour memorandum on the application of the ethnic principle, was indicating that he was willing on a number of important points to sacrifice the treaties with Italy and Romania, which contemplated large-scale annexations of territories inhabited by peoples of non-Latin stock and language, and that he was not interested in the aspirations to national independence of the Czech and Yugoslav *émigrés*. The American President, who had neither signed nor recognized those treaties, was naturally even more explicit. Furthermore, he regarded the new leaders of Soviet Russia as rather crazy Utopians who, though they had been deceived by the Germans, were not yet irretrievably lost to the alliance with the democracies, and he did not exclude the possibility of persuading them that the United States was by no means imperialistic, and that from the point of view of safeguarding the achievements of the Russian Revolution, it was a bad thing to favour brutal German imperialism by withdrawing from the war.[24]

During the last days of 1917 and the first of 1918, the attitude of the Soviet leaders was still fluid. The debate that took place in Soviet Russia some weeks later on whether or not to accept the greedy and pitiless terms that the Germans laid down at Brest-Litovsk is well known. Here we shall confine ourselves to mentioning a telegram, dated January 1, 1918, from the Italian Minister in Stockholm reporting some information received by the Tridentine socialist Antonio Piscel, who had been sent by Bissolati as an observer to the projected international socialist conference. Huysmans, the secretary of the Bureau of the Second International, had told Piscel on December 31 that shortly beforehand the Bolshevik delegate Vorovsky had called on him and had said on behalf of the maximalist government that, if the Stockholm socialist conference took place, as a mere delaying expedient, that government would interrupt its peace negotiations with the Central Powers, would itself take part in the conference without objecting to the presence of pro-war socialists, and would then refuse to make peace and would continue the war if the Central Powers refused to accept the principal decisions of the conference.

Huysmans added that, as a result of recent contacts with him, he was sure of Arthur Henderson's willingness to take the Bolsheviks at their word. Axelrod, the veteran Russian Menshevik, who also discussed the matter with Piscel, was even more optimistic about the possibility of reaching agreement with the Bolsheviks in that way.[25]

The Stockholm conference was to be attended by socialists from all the belligerent and neutral countries, ranging from the German 'majority' Social Democrats who supported their government, to Italian, French and Polish revolutionary internationalists. President Wilson however could not fly in the face of the categorical opposition of the Entente governments and the big trade unions in his own country by establishing contacts with it. But he wanted his words to reach the ears both of the Bolshevik leaders and of the militant German socialists, and hoped to encourage the latter to vigorous opposition to the annexationism prevalent in Germany.[26] He knew that Clemenceau and Sonnino did not share his confidence in the German socialists, or some of them, and were actually opposed to it. But events, beginning with the general strike of January 1918 and culminating in the German revolution in the following November, confirmed that the Fourteen Points indeed had great repercussions among the working masses, not only in Austria-Hungary, but also in Germany herself.

Though some of its members were in contact with the Czech *émigrés*, the committee that Wilson had set up some months earlier to study the question of American war aims recommended in a memorandum submitted to him on January 2, 1918, that Austria-Hungary should be allowed to survive, that Italy should be granted only the Trentino, while Trieste should be made a Free City, the South Tyrol and Dalmatia (and presumably also Istria) should be left to the Habsburg monarchy, and the other nationalities (unlike the Italian) should remain under the Habsburgs, provided that their democratic demands were met.[27] In his Fourteen Points, announced on January 8, the President adopted these recommendations, adding, however, that Poland should be made independent and should be reunited in all its parts. In accord with his democratic vision of the post-war world, the President repudiated secret treaties and secret diplomacy and announced the principles of the freedom of the seas, disarmament and collective security. He declared that the territories invaded and occupied by the Central Powers must be restored, that Alsace-Lorraine must be returned to France, and that Serbia must be given access to the sea. He concluded by proposing the establishment of a League of Nations to guarantee the independence of all nations, great and small. So far as the nationalities of Austria-Hungary were concerned, he limited himself (except in the case of the Poles) to calling for 'the widest possibility for autonomous development' for them (Point 10). In the case of Italy he called only for the rectification of her frontiers with Austria according to 'clearly recognizable lines of nationality' (Point 9).[28]

Not that all American politicians agreed that the Habsburg monarchy should be preserved. Lansing, the Secretary of State, as a jurist and a diplomatist, was better aware of the grave difficulties that would face the Entente powers if they were really to repudiate the secret treaties they had negotiated, above all, that with Italy. On January 10 he wrote a private memorandum, pointing out that perhaps it would be better to renounce the preservation of Austria-

Hungary and—as a barrier to future German ambitions in central eastern Europe—to encourage the establishment of independent states, not only by the Poles, but also by the Czechs, the Yugoslavs and the Ruthenians, and to give Transylvania to Romania and the Austro-Italian provinces to Italy.[29] The spokesmen of large numbers of Czech, Slovak, Croatian and Ruthenian immigrants in the United States were in fact agitating for the independence of their countries of origin.[30]

But the President, in agreement with the British Prime Minister, was determined to continue his efforts to induce Vienna to make peace, regarding that as the quickest way of weakening Germany or causing the pacifist forces in Germany to prevail.

The American ambassador in Rome kept him fully informed of the Italian government's concern, but the ambassador in Paris and the envoys to the neutral countries (Switzerland, Denmark, Spain) encouraged his peace feelers towards Austria-Hungary.[31]

Meanwhile, the opening of peace negotiations with Soviet Russia, which proclaimed the right to national, political and social self-determination, revived and gave increased aggressiveness to the opposition in Austria-Hungary to the traditional system of dominant classes and nationalities and to the alliance with German imperialism. The first to move were the Czechs. At Brest-Litovsk on December 25, 1917, Czernin declared that the right to self-determination which the Soviet delegation put forward as a universal principle did not apply to nationalities belonging to states that granted them full constitutional liberties and in return had the right to demand from all its citizens respect for the untouchability of the state sanctified in its constitution.[32] This restriction of the right to self-determination to the peoples of the former Tsarist empire obviously referred primarily to the Czechs. On December 16, Poincaré, among other things to encourage the Czech Legion in Russia to oppose the Bolsheviks, had announced the administrative arrangements for the Czech Legion that was to be organized in France, and this was reported in the Vienna newspapers on the same day, December 25. The effects of Czernin's rejection of the possibility of granting concessions to the Czechs were the opposite of what he intended.

On January 6, 1918, the Czech deputies to the Reichsrat and to the Diets of Bohemia and Moravia met in Prague. They proclaimed the right to self-determination of the Czechs and the Slovaks (emphasizing the graver oppression to which the latter were subject in Hungary) and called for the independence of the historical state of Bohemia.[33] There was an inconsistency between the two claims, because nearly three million Germans lived on the territory of historical Bohemia and, in the event of its complete territorial restoration, they would be denied the self-determination claimed for the Czechs and the Slovaks, as indeed happened in 1919, with consequences for which Czechoslovakia paid in 1938. That, however, was an issue with which the deputies who attended the Prague meeting did not concern themselves. Instead, to ensure that the Catholic deputies, who were reluctant to abandon the dynasty, should vote for the resolution, they watered it down, declaring it to be the logical outcome of the statement made in the Reichsrat on May 30, 1917, which had called for Czechoslovak independence under the House of Habsburg and Lorraine. But then the aim had been a federal reorganization of the state which (like the 1867 Settlement with Hungary) would have left wide powers to the centre, particularly in the fields of defence and diplomacy, whereas what was now proposed was a reduction of the link with Austria to a personal dynastic union on the lines of what the left wing of the Party of Independence and of 1848 wanted in Hungary. The Prague resolution in fact called for independent representation of the Czechoslovak nation at the peace conference.

Formally this was not an ultimatum, but merely a statement of principles which could have led to negotiations, if Vienna had been willing. But the fact of immediate practical importance was that the meeting had been initiated by the strong Czech Social Democratic Party, which thus made its official entry into the struggle for national independence. Up to then, that struggle had been waged primarily by the predominantly bourgeois nationalist parties, but now it had the support of the Czech working masses, who were among the best organized in the empire. In the autumn of 1917, when the social-patriotic wing of the Czech Social Democratic Party prevailed over its Austro-Marxist wing, the National Socialist Party, led by Klofáč and Strbrný, promptly renamed itself the Czech Socialist Party and proposed a merger with the Social Democrats on the basis of an amalgamation of the traditional principle of the class struggle with that of the self-determination of nations proclaimed by the Russian Revolution. Because of the opposition of the left-wing Social Democrats, whose position approximated to that of the Bolsheviks on the socialist revolution and the dictatorship of the proletariat as well as on the question of self-determination, the two parties did not merge. But they formed an alliance which became a major political force, both in the Reichsrat, in which it greatly outnumbered the Agrarians, previously the strongest Czech party and above all in the industrial towns and mining areas of Bohemia and Moravia.[34]

This move by the Czechs galvanized into action the Yugoslavs in the Reichsrat. For the most part they were fervent Catholics, and they were believed to be much more loyal to the Habsburg monarchy, having reason to fear an Italian victory in view of Italian aspirations to territories inhabited by Slovenes and Croats. On January 31, Mgr Korošec, the chairman of their united parliamentary group, sent an open letter to the chairman of the Brest-Litovsk conference calling for an immediate, general and democratic peace and claiming the right of the Slovenes, Croats and Serbs to be represented at the conference, and to unification into an independent state by virtue of the principle of self-determination. Yugoslav unity, he said, could be achieved under the sceptre of the Habsburgs, but 'a peace that tried to sanction the present situation' in Austria-Hungary, which the Yugoslavs considered oppressive, 'would be the beginning of a life-and-death struggle by the Slavs of Austria-Hungary'.[35]

This shift by the nationalist movement to implicitly revolutionary positions raised the question of its relations with the proletarian, pacifist and socialist revolutionary movement that was rumbling among the German Austrian and Hungarian workers in particular, stimulated by the appeals launched from Brest-Litovsk by Trotsky and Kamenev.[36] The Austrian and Hungarian (and at first also the German) Social Democratic press had applauded the Soviet seizure of power, which it regarded as the dawn of peace, and, as the Austro-Hungarian government also wanted peace with Russia, the censorship allowed the first rejoicings over the Bolshevik Revolution to pass. On November 11, 1917, in Vienna and November 25 in Budapest, the Social Democrats organized mass meetings to call for peace with the Soviets. On November 15, the *Arbeiter Zeitung* noted the grim revolutionary tension prevailing among the workers. The Social Democratic press was allowed to give a great deal of space to the speeches of the Soviet delegates at Brest and to criticize (as, for instance, the *Arbeiter Zeitung* did on January 12) the imperialist attitude of the German General Hoffmann, who did not hesitate brutally to block the diplomatic manoeuvres of Czernin at the conference itself. Moreover, the armistice facilitated Bolshevik propaganda in the Austro-Hungarian lines, and a constant refrain in soldiers' letters to their families was that if they were not able to come home yet, that was not the fault of the Russians, who had ceased to be enemies. The Social Democratic leadership organized mass meetings in Vienna and in Budapest on January 13 to call for an immediate democratic peace with the Soviets, and at some of these meetings speakers belonging to extreme left-wing revolutionary groups succeeded in addressing the crowd.[37]

In this overheated atmosphere it was announced that from Monday, January 14, the flour ration in Austria was to be reduced from

200 to 165 grammes a day. In the industrial town of Wiener-Neustadt, where a small group of revolutionary socialists, future communists, already in contact with the internationalist Zimmerwald movement, had been active for months, the workers downed tools on January 14 in protest against this measure, which undoubtedly meant real hunger, and went out into the streets, supported by groups of soldiers in a mutinous frame of mind. A local workers' council was formed immediately.[38] The Austrian Social Democratic leaders did not think the strike opportune. Victor Adler, the veteran party leader, certainly had said at its congress two and a half months before that, as the Russian Revolution had finally removed the Tsarist menace, the Social Democrats could now revert to the class struggle, but he had added that for Austria the war on the Italian front was a war of legitimate self-defence and that he still believed 'firmly in Count Czernin's intentions to make peace'.[39] One of the Social Democratic leaders, Karl Renner, went to Wiener-Neustadt on January 15 to urge moderation on the strikers. In the previous, non-political, strikes that had broken out in the course of 1917, the workers had always ended by acknowledging the authority of the Social Democratic Party, in which the trade-union leaders had always held key positions,[40] but this time the appeal for moderation failed. On January 16 the strike spread to Vienna, involving large numbers of workers, including men employed in militarized armament factories, and later also newspaper printers.[41] Leaflets were distributed among the strikers who thronged the streets of the city's industrial suburbs, calling on them to follow the Bolshevik example and demand an immediate armistice on all fronts and the election by the people of delegates to the peace conference.[42] The Social Democratic leadership hastily changed its line and took steps to take charge of the movement. In Vienna it organized a workers' council for the city, consisting of factory representatives who were members of the party and trade unionists, and subsequently did the same in other places. It demanded that the Austro-Hungarian delegation at Brest-Litovsk should show a genuine desire for peace and called for an improvement in workers' rations, equal suffrage in local elections and an end to the militarization of armaments factories.[43]

In Hungary, rations were higher because of the predominantly agricultural nature of the country, and no reduction in the flour ration was threatened, but on January 17 and 18 when news of the strike reached Budapest and then spread to the rest of the country, the Budapest workers began downing tools too. The strike spread to Brünn (Brno) in Moravia and Cracow in Galicia, and later to Pola and Trieste, where it lasted longer and where the atmosphere was especially violent and tense.[44] The Austrian government was taken by surprise. When the strike broke out, it had only 2,500 police in Vienna, and among the troops stationed in the capital perhaps 3,000 officers and men could have been depended on to obey a possible order to fire on the crowd, but the great majority of the garrison would probably not have obeyed and might actually have mutinied rather than shed the blood of their fellow-citizens. The numbers whom the Vienna Social Democrats could mobilize, including their families, were estimated at 300,000 persons by the deputy chief of the political police department.[45] After the strike, when Seidler, the Austrian Prime Minister, was criticized at a meeting of leaders of pro-government parties for having capitulated to the Social Democrats, he replied that 'forcible suppression of the working-class movement was made impossible' by the relations of strength existing at the time in the capital, but that the authorities were taking steps to suppress another possible general strike.[46] The police in fact arrested the most active revolutionary socialists, and Bosnian, Romanian and Ruthenian troops, who were considered the least 'subversive', were sent to Vienna. The Emperor asked two generals to work out a plan for military government in the event of a revolutionary out-break.[47]

Between January 16 and 19 the Social Democrats could in fact have become masters of the situation in Vienna if they had dared. The arrival of military reinforcement was compensated for by the spread of the strike to Hungary, where it was particularly bitter and enlisted workers in the public services, including the tramways and local railways, as well as the depots and workshops of the state railways, thus paralysing several important lines of communication. Here again the initiative came from below. The first demand of the Hungarian workers was for an immediate peace, the second for universal secret suffrage. According to the German Consul-General in Budapest, the demand for peace among the strikers assumed a violently anti-German note.[48] If the Austrian and Hungarian Social Democrats had proclaimed an all-out strike and had appealed to all the railway workers to come out, and if the workers in Bohemia, the most developed industrial and mining area in the empire, had joined in too, the authorities would not have had enough troops to suppress the movement without withdrawing units from the Italian front, because those on the Russian front, who were being subjected to Bolshevik propaganda, could not be relied on.[49] But on January 19 the leaders of the Czech Social Democratic Party, who, aided by the traditional discipline in that country, had its members better in hand than either the German Austrian or Hungarian parties had at the time, decided

[213]

to restrict themselves to declaring a twenty-four hour protest strike on January 22.[50]

According to Franz Borkenau, the unique opportunity that the Austro-Hungarian working classes had of extricating their country from the war by means of a political and social revolution for peace was thrown away by the reluctance of the Austrian Social Democratic leadership to come out in favour of the right of the Czech and Slovak territories to self-determination and national independence, for, after the Prague meeting of January 6, the Czech Social Democrats would have agreed to calling an unconditional general strike only for the conquest of that right.[51] Most of the Austrian Social Democratic leaders were certainly very reluctant to accept the Czech national claims. At the party congress at the end of October 1917, Renner had been applauded for a report recommending a moderate federal reform of Austria, which he conceived of, not on a territorial basis, but on one of 'personal' and cultural autonomy.[52] Above all, the Czech claim to the historical frontiers of independent Bohemia was violently opposed by the then very strong German-speaking Social Democratic Party in the Sudetenland and in the Moravian region. Otto Bauer, the outstanding leader of the Austro-Marxist left wing, had recently returned from Russian imprisonment convinced that all the Slav nationalities would dissociate themselves from Austria-Hungary. He had seen his expectations confirmed by the conversion to the independence movement of the Czech, Polish and Slovene Social Democratic parties (the last of which was regarded as the most loyal supporter of the principle of 'personal' autonomy), which was one of the reasons why he defended the line taken by Lenin and Trotsky against the criticisms of his more moderate colleagues. Nevertheless, in his reminiscences of the events of January 1918 he said that 'we ourselves did not want the strike to be intensified to the point of revolution'.[53]

At the beginning of 1918, Bauer believed that a popular revolution for peace in Austria-Hungary would lead to the irruption of German troops into Bohemia in order to suppress it. The Czech Social Democratic leaders regarded that possibility with even greater alarm. In the event of a declaration of a strike of unlimited duration, the military headquarters in Prague had in fact decided to proclaim a state of siege.[54] On the other hand, the Czech Social Democratic leaders could not act without the Czech National Socialist Party, both because of their alliance with it and because of the dynamism of its militants, who in Bohemia took the most vigorous part in the patriotic conspiracy; and the National Socialists believed that it was not in the Czech interest for Austria-Hungary to make peace before

[214]

being militarily defeated. Unlike the more moderate parties in Bohemia, who early in 1918 would still have been satisfied with a compromise peace, they feared that such a peace would rescue Austria-Hungary, possibly an Austria-Hungary transformed into a democratic federation of nations. The establishment of Czecho-slovakia as a totally independent state with frontiers corresponding to the maximum claims of the most ardent nationalists could be assured only by the defeat of the Austro-Hungarian armies in the field.[55]

The only politician who had clear ideas for the immediate situation and the energy and adroitness necessary to ensure that they were carried out was Czernin. While the Emperor and the Austrian government hesitated between the idea of crushing the strike by military force and that of asking Czernin, who was at Brest-Litovsk, to sign a peace treaty at all costs, even without Germany, on January 17 the Foreign Minister telephoned a high official of his ministry and told him to make contact with the Vienna Social Democratic leaders and tell them in the greatest secrecy that he was on the point of making peace with the Soviets, but could do so only if the domestic politico-social situation returned to normal. To calm the masses, he would persuade the Germans to send all cereal supplies from Poland and the Ukraine to Austria.[56] The reformists who were still in charge of the Social Democratic Party in Vienna asked for nothing better than for a prospect of this kind to look forward to.[57] However, they insisted that the Austrian government, in addition to reaching a rapid agreement with Russia on a peace without annexations, must undertake to introduce equal and direct suffrage in local elections (to which the electoral reform of 1907 did not apply) and take steps to demilitarize the armaments industry. Seidler, the Prime Minister, promptly gave the required undertakings, which were represented by the Austrian Social Democratic and trade-union leaders as a satisfactory outcome of the strike. On the night of January 19–20, after tumultuous debates, they succeeded in persuading the Vienna workers' council to agree to a resumption of work on Monday, January 21.[58] The Hungarian Social Democratic leaders succeeded in obtaining similar undertakings from the Budapest government, and at a meeting of factory representatives secured a majority in favour of a return to work on the same day.[59]

The German ambassador to Austria-Hungary described the agreement with the Social Democrats as a government capitulation.[60] The workers however were very reluctant to give up the struggle and, in spite of the decision to go back to work, the strike continued in most Vienna and Budapest factories on January 21, and in many places it

[215]

went on for another two or three days. The Social Democratic leaders who tried to calm down the strikers were received with cries of 'traitor' and were pelted with snowballs. In Vienna the party had great difficulty in dissuading the workers from marching through the centre of the city. In Budapest the party leadership thought it prudent to resign and submit itself for re-election at an extraordinary congress, at which it obtained a vote of confidence after a bitter debate.[61] According to the German ambassador, the chief cause for concern was that 'the masses had realized their power and the weakness of the government'.[62]

That the militant workers were not wrong in resenting the trust placed in the government by their leaders on the question of a democratic peace is confirmed by a very thoughtful private letter, written by Bethmann-Hollweg, the former Reich Chancellor, to Prince Max of Baden, who was to become Chancellor the following October. Bethmann-Hollweg said that he was convinced on the basis of his experience that 'peace will come only when it is seized, in one way or another, by the popular masses out of war-weariness'.[63] That a substantial proportion of the armed forces of the Habsburg empire was war-weary is shown by the Austro-Hungarian naval mutiny at the Bocche di Cattaro (Kotor) on February 1, 1918. Discontent at the bad food and bad treatment was already rife and the mutiny was sparked off by the spreading of the news of the strikes in Vienna, Budapest, Trieste and Pola.[64] In this instance there was a spontaneous solidarity between Social Democratic seamen and seamen of Czech, Southern Slav and Italian nationality which was lacking between the socialists of Vienna and Prague. The principal leader of the mutiny, the petty officer Franz Rasch, was a militant German Social Democrat from Bohemia. At his suggestion, the chief demand of the mutineers was for immediate peace on the basis of the principles proclaimed by President Wilson and the Soviet delegation at Brest-Litovsk, and they sent telegrams, which were of course stopped by the censorship, to Victor Adler, Valentino Pittoni, the leader of the Social Democrats in Trieste, Stanek, the chairman of the Czech parliamentary union, and Count Károlyi, the Hungarian opposition leader.[65] On the third day the crews of the mutinous ships, which were isolated from the shore, were forced to surrender, but news of the event nevertheless spread through the country, particularly when the mutineers were court-martialled.

The repercussions in Germany of the mass struggle for peace that began in Austria-Hungary were much greater than might have been thought possible. The German Social Democratic newspapers that reported the news of the strike were confiscated, but it nevertheless

[216]

came to the knowledge of the leaders and many militant members of the German socialist parties, both the majority and the independent party. The fact that the Austro-Hungarian workers' protest had been sparked off by the crudely imperialist statements of the representatives of the German High Command at Brest, and that this had led to popular demonstrations against the German diplomatic missions in Vienna, and above all at Budapest, made a big impression in political circles in Berlin.[66] On January 19, a police report stated that the deputy Ledebour, a popular left-wing representative of the Independent Socialist Party, was planning a general strike with some of its comrades.[67] In fact, at Ledebour's insistence, the party leaders, all pacifists though not all determined revolutionaries, had already recognized the necessity of a general strike in Germany, though they had not yet fixed a date.[68] An appeal to the working masses to raise their voice in favour of an immediate democratic peace was issued by the Independent Socialist parliamentary group. In Berlin and elsewhere it was distributed illegally, but the socialist newspaper at Gotha managed to publish it without the censorship's spotting it in time.[69] The 'revolutionary' shop-stewards whom the left wing of the Independent Socialist Party had in the metal-working factories in Berlin, particularly among the turners, took the responsibility of opening the campaign. On January 27, they held a meeting attended by about 1,500 militants at which it was decided to down tools the next day.[70] On January 28 it was estimated that 400,000 men went on strike in Berlin and its industrial suburbs. A workers' council, formed by shop-stewards, elected a strike committee of eleven, which proclaimed the objectives of the movement to be a general peace without annexations in accord with the Soviet proposals at Brest-Litovsk; the presence of representatives of workers' organizations at the peace conference; better food for the working population; full restoration of political and trade-union liberties that had been hampered by militarization; a political amnesty; and universal, equal, and direct franchise in elections to the Prussian Diet.[71] The strike committee invited the Independent Socialist Party to delegate three of its parliamentary deputies to join it. A proposal to invite the majority Social Democratic Party to do the same was defeated by 198 votes to 196, but was later adopted by 360 votes to 40.[72] The three most authoritative leaders of the majority Social Democratic Party (Ebert, Scheidemann and O. Braun) accordingly joined the committee leading a strike that was unwelcome to them, and the result was to help to encourage the movement to spread throughout the country. The number of strikers increased to 500,000 in Berlin and its suburbs, bringing the tramways and local railways to a halt, and more than

1,000,000 in the whole of Germany.[73] On January 30, a deputation from the strike committee was received by the Under-Secretary for the Interior but, though the majority of Social Democrats were eager for a compromise that would bring the strike to an end as soon as possible, the government refused to make concessions. Next day the military authorities announced a minor state of emergency in Berlin. Many arrests were made (a deputy of the Independent Socialist Party was given a five-year sentence), meetings were broken up by force, factories were put under the jurisdiction of war tribunals, and on February 1 it was announced that work must be resumed on the following Monday, February 4, failing which the strikers would be sent to the front and agitators would be subject to imprisonment.[74] On February 3 the Berlin workers' council decided by a majority that it was not in a position to defy the ultimatum and decided to break off the strike.

It can be assumed that, if the strike had still been in progress in Austria-Hungary when it broke out in Berlin, it would have been much more difficult to suppress the latter. However, the German working masses had shown that they too wanted peace at any price. On February 13, three days after the negotiations at Brest-Litovsk were broken off, Hertling, the Reich Chancellor warned General Ludendorff that there would probably be another general strike if the demands of the High Command caused the negotiations with the Russians to fail.[75] Czernin took the same view. On January 22, in spite of the opposition of the Chief of the Austro-Hungarian General Staff, he had asked the Crown Council for authorization to conclude a separate peace with the Bolshevik government in case of need. His intention was not to leave Germany in the lurch. On the contrary, he proposed assuring her that Austria would continue the fight against the western powers. His object, he stated, was, in agreement with Kühlmann, the German Secretary of State at the Foreign Ministry, to have a weapon available for use against the unbridled annex-ationism of Hindenburg and Ludendorff.[76] At that same meeting of the Crown Council, however, he took an alternative course that enabled him to avoid a head-on clash with the German High Com-mand. As the great mass of Austro-Hungarian troops in the east was not deployed on Greater Russian soil, but on the Ukrainian and Romanian fronts, and the hoped-for corn supplies would in any case have to come from the Ukrainian plain, he suggested that Austria-Hungary might limit herself to concluding an immediate peace with the new government of the Ukraine which had proclaimed its independence, assigning the latter the Cholm district, which was inhabited by Ruthenians, but belonged to the Russian Polish district

[218]

of Lublin.[77] The German High Command liked the plan, which it had been considering on its own account, and it was duly carried out by the signature on February 8 of a peace treaty between the Central Powers and the independent Ukraine. At the January 22 council meeting, some ministers, including Burian, had pointed out that the cession of Cholm might lead to violent reactions from the Galician Poles, with disastrous consequences to Austria-Hungary. But in Czernin's view the Austro-Polish solution was no longer important. The economic guarantees that Germany intended to impose for her own exclusive benefit on the kingdom of Poland set up in 1916 were so burdensome that eventually Poland would have to be left to her completely, while Austria sought compensation in Romania. The Austrian situation, Czernin said on this occasion, flying in the face of his own optimism of a few weeks earlier, was that of a man trying to save his life by jumping from a third-floor window of a house on fire.[78]

As for the domestic situation, Czernin counted both on the relaxation of tension that peace with the Ukraine and Russia would bring to the majority of the peoples of Austria-Hungary (even though this did not apply to the Poles) and on the goodwill towards the Habsburg empire demonstrated by President Wilson. On January 24 he made a speech in reply to the President's Fourteen Points, and next day Hertling did the same. The latter reaffirmed Germany's right to her territorial integrity and the restoration of her colonies, but was reticent about the fate of the German-occupied territories in the west and still more in the east, whereas Czernin indicated his approval if not of all the Fourteen Points, at any rate of some of them, and expressed the hope that the United States and Austria-Hungary would become joint mediators in bringing about a general peace.[79] In view of the conversations that Herron, not without Lansing's backing, was conducting with Professor Lammasch, a member of the Austrian Upper House and an imperial candidate for the Prime Ministership, President Wilson in a speech on February 11 openly differentiated between Hertling and Czernin, rejecting *en bloc* what the former said and agreeing with a good deal said by the latter.[80] The Paris and London governments followed a similar course. In the summer of 1917 Count Armand, a captain in the Deuxième Bureau, had been sent to Switzerland to make contact with the Austro-Hungarian diplomat Count Revertera. The peace terms suggested by the French emissary were considered unacceptable by Czernin and he dropped the negotiations.[81] At the beginning of 1918, Armand again met Revertera and told him that the Paris government, which was aware of the Smuts–Mensdorff meeting, desired that Franco-

[219]

Austrian conversations should be resumed.[82] Czernin's reply was that France would have to abandon her claim to Alsace-Lorraine, whereupon Clemenceau decided that it was pointless to continue these exchanges. In the spring of 1917, Czernin had vainly tried to persuade the German government to yield at least Lorraine in order to secure a peace that would be satisfactory to Germany in other respects.[83] Now he did not feel inclined to repeat the effort.

The resumption of exchanges with the British was due to the impression gathered by a British emissary in Geneva from a conversation on January 10, 1918, with Skrzynski, the counsellor of the Austrian-Hungarian legation, that the speech made by Lloyd George a few days earlier had caused Czernin to desire a secret meeting between himself and the British Prime Minister in Switzerland.[84] At the time Czernin was afraid that the demands of the German High Command were going to lead to a breakdown of the Brest-Litovsk negotiations. But the making of peace with the Ukraine and Soviet Russia, which were successes for the German policy of strength, persuaded Czernin not to continue negotiations with London. It appears from the documents of the Austro-Hungarian Foreign Ministry that in their contacts with Skrzynski, the British emissaries had been urging upon him the necessity of resuming conversations between London and Vienna before peace was signed at Brest-Litovsk, and at the same time pointing out that the British government would encourage the Wilson–Czernin exchanges only on condition that the Austro-Hungarian representative discussed 'his own personal affairs'.[85] When, after several exchanges of telegrams, Czernin understood this to mean that the British did not want to include Germany in the conversations, he broke off the contacts.[86] Lloyd George was not, however, diverted from his aim of coming to an agreement with Austria, and in the first few days of March again sent Kerr, his private secretary, to Switzerland. In view of the emissary's importance, Czernin authorized Skrzynski to see him, and the meeting took place in mid-March. Kerr said that the British government wanted 'to find out if there were sufficient points of view in common between it and Count Czernin for a meeting to lead to a practical result'.[87] Czernin's reply was negative.[88]

The German High Command's victory over Bolshevik Russia, which had to accept terms even harsher than those which Trotsk had originally refused to sign; over Romania, which was also preparing to capitulate; and over its own Socialist opposition at home which, though it criticized the Brest-Litovsk *Diktat*, was not in a position or did not dare to call on the masses to strike again, and the Austro-Hungarian Social Democrats' similar self-restriction to verbal or

[220]

paper protests, reawakened Czernin's belief in German invincibility.[89] He also knew that the German army was on the eve of staking everything in the west. His decision, which turned out to be disastrous to himself and still more to his Emperor and his country, was expressed in an incredibly imprudent and provocative speech he made on April 2, 1918, when it looked as if the German offensive in France was going to succeed. His reckless words, followed by Clemenceau's revelations about the letters to the Entente that the Emperor of Austria had entrusted to Prince Sixtus, led a few days later to his enforced resignation, because of his inability to refute the 'Tiger's' denunciation of him as a liar.[90] With him disappeared the last chance of negotiations between Vienna and the western capitals.[91] Italy and the Slav *émigrés* from Austria-Hungary took immediate advantage of this.

The Italian initiative was put forward by Luigi Albertini, aided by contributors to the *Corriere della Sera*, G. A. Borgese, Giovanni Amendola, Andrea Torre, Guglielmo Emanuel and Ugo Ojetti. The last of these was a long-standing personal friend of Orlando (as he also was, incidentally, of Bissolati and Salvemini) and had drafted for the new Prime Minister the royal proclamation to the people of Italy made after the disaster of Caporetto. He had Orlando's ear, though as Minister of the Interior the latter had been severely criticized by the *Corriere*.[92]

Luigi Albertini, unlike Bissolati and Salvemini, whom he esteemed highly and defended courageously in the post-war period against the violent attacks of Nationalists and Fascists, belonged to the traditional ruling class of liberal Italy, though he often opposed the governments of the day. His newspaper was extraordinarily influential and widely read, and through it he had played a major role in persuading the ruling class of the necessity of Italian intervention in the war. He had enthusiastically taken the lead in interventionist propaganda, not out of sympathy with French democracy or Mazzinian romanticism or out of any desire for adventure, but because of his considered opinion of the benefits that would accrue to Italy from participation in the war. No one could suggest that to the editor of the *Corriere* the cause of the greatness of Italy and the interests of the Italian state, were secondary to ideological or sentimental considerations. His declaration, in the interests of the rapid and complete defeat of Austria-Hungary and future Italian collaboration with the successor states, that Italy should renounce Dalmatia (except for Zara, which, like Fiume, he always maintained should be annexed by Italy) was based on his knowledge of the private opinions of the army

[221]

Chief of Staff (until November 1917 this was General Cadorna, but General Diaz, his successor, agreed with him in the matter). Cadorna's view was that the occupation of the Dalmatian coast which the navy wanted would be militarily useless. As a matter of fact the navy wanted Dalmatia only because it was backward-looking and failed to see that after the collapse of the Habsburg empire the Italian fleet would have no serious rivals in the Adriatic.[93] Albertini therefore did not follow Bissolati and Salvemini when, in strict accord with the principle of self-determination, under which Italy should not have included German or Slav populations within her frontiers, they declared that a strategic frontier on the Brenner was unnecessary, and that Italy should acquire only the ethnically Italian part of the Habsburg empire.[94] But the factor that counted most in 1917 was the entry of the United States into the war. It had not signed the Treaty of London and President Wilson called for the renunciation of secret treaties. Italy therefore found herself in urgent need of gaining new friends abroad for her policies, whereas the collapse of Russia removed one of the anxieties, that of a pan-Slav empire taking the place of the Habsburg empire, the prospect which had persuaded Salandra and Sonnino in 1915 to insist on the assignment of a great part of Dalmatia.[95] The *Corriere* campaign for an Italo-Yugoslav understanding, with which *Il Secolo*, which followed the directives of Bissolati, naturally associated itself, thus came at a time when circumstances were favourable, in contrast to a year before, when Bissolati's efforts had failed.[96] Albertini was in contact with Trumbić and Supilo through his newspaper's London correspondent, G. Emanuel.[97] Through 'one of our newspaper correspondents, a serious, sensible and very patriotic individual' (who might have been either Emanuel or G. Chiesi, the correspondent of *Il Secolo*, who was also on excellent terms with him), Supilo in May 1917 had sought an interview with Marquis Imperiali, the Italian ambassador in London, in order to point out to him the urgent need of an Italo-Yugoslav agreement because of the growing tendency in England to look for a compromise with Austria-Hungary in view of the Russian collapse. Supilo would have been willing to accept Italian supremacy in the Adriatic if Rome would take a stand for the total dissociation of the Yugoslavs from the Habsburg monarchy and their unification in an independent state.[98] Trumbić, whom Count Sforza saw some weeks later, also said on his arrival in Corfu that he favoured a lasting agreement between the Italians and the Yugoslavs, though he reaffirmed that Dalmatia must go to the latter.[99]

Marquis Imperiali immediately reported Supilo's request to Sonnino, who was unwilling to negotiate with the Yugoslavs on that basis. When Pašić went to Rome at the beginning of September 1917 and proposed discussing the future situation in the Adriatic, the Italian Foreign Minister replied that the Corfu agreement, which claimed for the future Yugoslavia all the territories inhabited by Serbs, Croats and Slovenes, thus including areas claimed by Italy, made an agreement impossible in practice. For one thing the Catholic, Socialist and other (evidently Giolittian) supporters of a compromise peace with Austria would conclude from it that Italy should rather accept the territorial concessions that Vienna might offer and thus spare further bloodshed. Pašić replied that the Corfu agreement 'was necessary to defend ourselves against Austria's tempting the Slav populations with the offer of concessions of autonomy' and that in his own personal view Yugoslavia would be able to leave Italy Trieste, Pola, half of Istria, some islands in the eastern Adriatic and Valona. Sonnino said that 'that was far from enough'. The only concession he was willing to make as an 'equitable guarantee in regard to the respect of all . . . school and language rights and the free enjoyment of civil and political rights' of the Slav population assigned to Italy.[100]

Sonnino's papers disclose that the cipher with which Pašić corresponded with his diplomatists was known to the Italian Intelligence Service. Sonnino had thus the proof that Yugoslav nationalism was not less greedy than Italian nationalism.

A possible Italo-Yugoslav agreement would have had to be conceived of as part of a joint effort to rouse the Slav nationalities against Austria-Hungary with a view to their achieving total independence on the ruins of the Habsburg empire, but any such plan was totally alien to Sonnino's way of thinking. Luigi Albertini was of course aware of the ideas of Bissolati, whom he often saw at the High Command, and of Wickham Steed, of whom he had been a personal friend for twenty years.[101] 'It is not only a war. It is a revolution' aiming at 'international justice and national liberty', he had written in the *Corriere*, applauding the proposal to liberate the Slav and Latin peoples of Austria-Hungary which was contained in the Entente reply to President Wilson of January 1917.[102] Nevertheless he was accustomed to looking facts in the face, though fundamentally an idealist, as he showed himself to be through his opposition to the growth of nationalism in 1919 and to the Fascist dictatorship after 1924. When the independence movement of the Slav nationalities of Austria-Hungary started developing in earnest, he resolutely supported it.[103] Albertini was in fact in the Cavour tradition, but the event that caused him to write articles that Salvemini considered worthy of Mazzini was the signature of the Corfu agreement, for, unlike the great

[223]

majority of the Italian ruling class, he immediately saw that this inevitably implied the establishment of a Yugoslav state and realized the importance that it would have to Italy as a neighbour.[104]

He was strengthened in his attitude in the matter by the information brought back by G. A. Borgese from a study mission to Switzerland. When Borgese had learnt in mid-1916 that a propaganda office responsible to the Prime Minister had been set up, he had asked Albertini to ensure that it would make use of him in view of his mastery of German, for missions to Holland, Denmark or Switzerland.[105] We may assume that it was as a result of Albertini's efforts that Gallenga-Stuart, the Under-Secretary for Propaganda, and the special office of the High Command jointly entrusted Borgese and Gaetano Paternò, a diplomatist working in the propaganda office, with the task of making confidential enquiries about the Yugoslav émigrés in Switzerland.[106] The report on their mission, which was carried out in the second half of July and the first half of August 1917, was published by Borgese, with some small cuts, two years later in the course of the controversy that arose concerning the Rome Congress.[107] In Switzerland, Borgese and Paternò had conversations with several members of the Yugoslav Committee (Gazzari, de Giuli, Stojanović), with L. Marković, the editor of La Serbie, and with other leaders.[108] The conclusions that they drew anticipated the events of a year later. Far from being secretly pro-Austrian, as certain Italian nationalists maintained, the Yugoslav émigrés were confidently predicting that their fellow-nationals in Croatia and Slovenia would be forced to rise against the Habsburgs. As Hungary would block the introduction into the Habsburg empire of any kind of federalism or 'trialism', the consequence would be that the Southern Slavs would revolt, like the Czechs,[109] and an independent Yugoslavia would certainly ensue. Borgese and Paternò, referring explicitly to the Corriere argument, wrote that 'today there could be obtained from the Yugoslavs, in addition to Trieste and Gorizia, recognition of: (1) Italian Istria all the way to Monte Maggiore; (2) Albania as an Italian zone of influence in return for the cession to Yugoslavia of Dalmatia except Fiume and Zara, which would be Italian Free Cities. On that basis, Italy would be able to hasten the break up of Austria-Hungary to the advantage of its Slav nationalities.[110]

These conclusions, which Borgese repeated in his articles in the Corriere and in a letter [111] to Albertini of September 30 which laid down the whole programme that Orlando was to adopt, though hesitantly, between January and October 1918, met with no response until the gravity of the rout of Caporetto came to be fully appreciated. The replacement of Sonnino had been virtually decided on some days

[224]

previously by the political grouping that brought Orlando into power and displaced Boselli, but to those who wanted to fight on at all costs, including Bissolati and Amendola, the very magnitude of the disaster, which forced Italy to seek the aid of the western powers, made the dismissal of Sonnino look like a concession to Giolittian or Catholic or Socialist pressure for a compromise peace.

The situation remained extremely critical even after the huge numbers of disbanded Italian troops were rounded up and reorganized, Anglo-French reinforcements arrived, and the front was stabilized on the Piave. The losses of war materials and supplies of all sorts that followed the invasion of the Veneto were enormous. The Central Powers, no longer having to worry about their eastern fronts, might at any moment send forces, German as well as Austro-Hungarian, outnumbering those which, with their superior military capacity, had made the breakthrough at Caporetto. The idea spread that another Austro-German offensive might force Italy to sue for peace, and that she should therefore negotiate while she was still in a position to do so. Apart from the socialists, who were electrified by the Soviet Revolution, many remembered the Pope's message of August 1917 about the futile slaughter and looked to Giolitti, who in his last public pronouncement (in a speech on August 13, 1917, to the Provincial Council of Cuneo, which was widely reported in the press) had criticized 'foreign policy based on secret treaties'. It was this to which Albertini referred when he wrote to Emanuel on December 17, 1917, that 'the neutralists are raising their heads again and are making proposals of an audacity and infamy that one would never have thought possible'.[112]

Whether they were infamous or sensible, we know that the idea of diplomatic action with a view to dissociating Austria-Hungary from Germany—which, to be successful, required a compromise between Rome and Vienna—was proposed by Lloyd George at the inter-allied conference in Paris from November 27 to December 3.[113] Sonnino saw plainly that the success of such a project would involve the renunciation of everything that he had obtained from the Entente in 1915 except the Trentino, and he vigorously opposed the British Prime Minister's suggestion. The latter, however, had the support of Colonel House, representing President Wilson, and also the unenthusiastic support of Clemenceau, with the result that Orlando and Sonnino were isolated and had to swallow their objections.[114] Lloyd George's argument about the disastrous consequences that the now extremely probable peace between the Central Powers and Russia would have for the Entente if they were not counterbalanced by some initiative by the latter was not easy to refute. All that Sonnino managed to achieve was to prevent a new statement of common war aims, more elastic than that of January 1917, from being issued. It emerged from the discussion, however, that in relation to Austria-Hungary, Britain and the United States reserved the right not to adhere to the reply that the Entente had sent to President Wilson eleven months previously.[115]

Sonnino was a solitary and taciturn man, well known for his obstinacy. (A political journalist of the time considered that his repression concealed a basically passionate temperament that made him impervious to excessive worry about the future.) Not all the other Italians responsible for the political and military conduct of the war concealed from themselves, however, the fact that something ought to be done to anticipate future dangers. Some political and military leaders wanted to sound out Austria's intentions, apparently without Sonnino's knowledge.

In December 1917, the Austro-Hungarian military attaché in Berne twice reported that Italian agents had approached him with a view to a discussion of 'peace questions'. Czernin said in parliament that he was opposed to responding to such approaches, which he believed to be an Italian military stratagem aimed at finding out whether Austria-Hungary felt the need to make peace or to postpone another possible Austro-German offensive.[116] But at the beginning of 1918, Orlando was alarmed at the Smuts–Mensdorff meeting, which he had heard about from the British, who, though they did not give the Italians full information on the subject, did not either wish to keep them in the dark, as well as by rumours about other peace feelers, conversations between the Austrians and Serbs for instance. He therefore agreed that Nitti, the Minister for the Treasury and a member of the Italian War Committee, should approach the Vatican and enquire through that channel whether Austria-Hungary wanted peace with Italy and, if so, on what terms.[117] Nothing came of that, however, because the Vatican learned that Vienna was unwilling to negotiate on the basis of any territorial sacrifice by Austria, which after Caporetto considered herself to be the victor and Italy to be the vanquished.[118] Orlando indicated at the outset that an essential condition for an agreement was the cession to Italy of Trieste, in addition to what Austria-Hungary had promised in May 1915. It is safe to assume that he expected these feelers to be futile; he probably authorized them because, having criticized Sonnino's outright rejection at St Jean de la Maurienne in 1917 of the idea of conversations with Austria proposed by the British and French following Prince Sixtus's mission, he did not want to expose himself to a charge of still prouder intransigence at his country's expense in a situation as critical as Italy's was in the weeks that followed the invasion of the Veneto. Czernin, thus, lost the opportunity of negotiating with an Italy which, after the defeat of Caporetto, wanted, not a separate peace with Austria alone, but a general peace, and restricted herself to demanding—through the Vatican—Trento, Trieste and Gorizia, in return for which it offered some of its own colonies in Africa. But, however that may be, Orlando, who was sceptical about Austrian intentions to make substantial concessions, did not wait until the end of the Vatican soundings before giving the all-clear to the development of the opposite policy.

Albertini concluded the letter to Emanuel quoted above: 'I should like you to put these matters very plainly to our British friends, Steed in particular.'[119] Emanuel had already anticipated these instructions. On the day after the rout at Caporetto, General Mola, the Italian military attaché and head of the Italian military mission in London, together with some Italian journalists, who included Emanuel, had appealed to Steed to use his influence with *The Times*, of which he was foreign editor, and with other newspapers, to induce them not to comment on the news from the Italian front in such a way as to discourage public opinion from approving the sending of troops and supplies to Italy.[120] Steed did this to the full satisfaction of his Italian friends.[121] During those days, Trumbić admitted to Steed that he realized that a defeat of Italy would mean the end of all hope of Yugoslav independence. Some meetings between Italians and Yugoslavs at Steed's house gave rise to the idea of a private meeting between personalities of the two nations.

Two meetings took place, with Steed in the chair, on December 14 and 18, 1917.[122] They were attended by Sir Arthur Evans, Seton-Watson, General Mola, his aide-de-camp Captain Pallavicino, Emanuel, and, at the second meeting, Major de Filippi of the Italian propaganda office. Mola and Pallavicino attended in their personal capacities, but in any case it was understood that the meetings were unofficial, none of those present having any authority to speak for his government.[123] Those on the other side were Trumbić, Gazzari, Banjanin, Trinajstić and Gregorin, all members of the Yugoslav Committee. The minutes of the meeting were taken by Emanuel, who informed Albertini that those present agreed on the principles of a common struggle that would lead to the dismemberment of the Habsburg empire and the exclusion of Austria from the Adriatic, and also noted that the Treaty of London was a source of conflict between Yugoslavs and Italians.[124] Although it was obviously impossible to come to any decision about territorial demarcations, it seemed clear that agreement would be attainable only if Italy renounced Dalmatia, though with Zara as a Free City, and if the Yugoslavs renounced the Carso and Istria.[125] An agreement of that sort was the indispensable minimum required to induce the Yugoslav peoples of Austria-Hungary to side with the Czechs in a rising against the Habsburgs.[126]

After the end of the war, when the breach between Sonnino and Bissolati on whether the Treaty of London should be renounced or not had become unbridgeable, the Italian nationalists involved in their denunciations of those responsible for the so-called 'sell-out' the men who took part in those London meetings, particularly when an account of them was published by A. Gauvain, the well-known French journalist, who was pro-Yugoslav, and it was followed by the publication of the minutes by the Italian nationalists Preziosi and Giuriati. General Mola in particular was accused of having promised the Yugoslavs concessions that he had no right to promise.[127] The nationalists claimed that the minutes of the meeting had been sent to Orlando and Gallenga-Stuart, and also to the High Command, but not to Sonnino, from whom they alleged, it was carefully concealed, as it was from the Nationalist Party delegates to the subsequent Rome Congress (which they would have refused to attend if they had known of it).[128] The minutes in fact show that Mola merely expressed the personal view that the Treaty of London, which had been drafted when no one had in mind the possibility of the disintegration of Austria-Hungary or of the formation of a Yugoslav state, might well in those changed circumstances be liable to revision, provided that 'all the powers undertook a joint revision of their war aims'. He also observed in reference to Dalmatia, but not to Dalmatia alone, that 'there are grey zones which at the end of the war will not be easily assignable without mutual concessions and agreements'.[129]

At the end of the meeting, Mola said that he would report to the Italian ambassador in London what had taken place.[130] Emanuel believed he would do so promptly, but unfortunately, as he said in his letter to Albertini of January 27, he learnt later that Mola had had second thoughts and had decided that Imperiali might be nervous about giving his approval to a step taken without previous Foreign Ministry authorization. Mola did not therefore report the matter until the ambassador, who was himself becoming convinced of the necessity of a *rapprochement* with the Yugoslavs, had raised the question in his telegrams to Rome.[131] When he wrote this, Emanuel still believed that the Foreign Ministry had not replied to the ambassador's warnings. The ambassador, however, had increased his pressure after Lloyd George's speech of January 5, against which Sonnino protested to the British ambassador in Rome, as he informed Imperiali, who made a similar protest in London.[132] The similar protests made at the same time by the Yugoslav Committee to the British government (and also to the American government in regard to the Fourteen Points) created an objective coincidence that could not fail to interest the Italian ambassador in London, for both the Italians and the Yugoslavs were worried by the Anglo-American approaches to Austria. But Sonnino's reply to Imperiali was in the negative. On January 14 he telegraphed as follows:

> I do not believe it to be practically possible to reach agreement with the Serbs and Yugoslavs with any probability that after taking note of any renunciation on our part they would subsequently abide by it. . . . Furthermore, I think it dangerous to take today any initiative of the kind.[133]

On December 28, in fact, Sonnino had instructed Sforza to find out whether there was any possibility of coming to an agreement with Pašić 'on the basis of a general formula not implying any compromise detrimental to the basic postulates of the Italian position on the Adriatic question'.[134] Pašić's response was evasive. His visit to Rome in the previous September had made him mistrustful, and in any case he really cared only about the Serbian-populated provinces of Austria-Hungary and Bulgaria, which were far from the borders of Italy. Imperiali, like the Italian ambassadors in Paris and Washington, continued to urge the Foreign Ministry to come to an agreement with the Yugoslavs, but on January 31, Sonnino replied in a long telegram in which he said that he had no 'objections in principle to such an agreement', which he realized would be helpful in relation to Anglo-American public opinion, but believed that negotiations 'would help the Yugoslav agitators, some of whom are certainly acting in bad faith, to commit the Italian government to substantial renunciations on the Adriatic question without binding the Yugoslavs, who, when a suitable opportunity arose, would raise false and exaggerated claims'.[135] If there were to be negotiations, he would agree to their taking place, not with the Yugoslav Committee, but with the great western powers, from whom Italy could 'claim and obtain' compensations for any possible concession.[136]

Thus Mola would not have been able to obtain the approval of his ambassador, whose hands were tied by Sonnino. However the question remains whether, in his capacity as head of the Italian military mission, reporting what he did or learnt to the High Command, he had not been encouraged by the latter, or by General Alfieri, the Minister of War.[137]

Orlando went to London in the last week of January. He was

[229]

accompanied by Senator Crespi, the High Commissioner for Supplies, whose task was to draw the British attention to the urgent Italian need of large quantities of coal, cereals and other things, together with the shipping necessary to deliver them (because of the submarine warfare, it was much more difficult to secure the shipping than to buy the supplies required in America). Orlando's purpose was to discuss personally with Lloyd George all the Italian worries arising from the British Prime Minister's speech.

Crespi obtained ample assurances on the question of supplies. Lloyd George made apparently reassuring statements to Orlando with regard to his policy towards Vienna, which he explained as a war stratagem, for which reason he had no intention of dropping it.[138] Today we know that he was still determined to resume his exchanges with Czernin. During his stay in London, Orlando agreed to an Italo-Yugoslav agreement as a means of liquidating Austria-Hungary. Crespi, who, it is worth recalling, was a member of a family who were part-owners of the *Corriere della Sera*, noted in his diary:

> General Mola, the head of the Italian military mission, came to see me and talked about the possibility of an agreement between us and the Yugoslavs. I telephoned Wickham Steed . . . Steed ended by asking me to ask Orlando to have a conversation with Ante Trumbić.[139]

Next day Crespi noted: 'I talked to Orlando about my conversations with Mola, Steed and Emanuel. He replied: "What will Sonnino say?" '[140]

At all events, Orlando, encouraged, according to Emanuel, by Imperiali himself, received Steed, who talked to him about the conversations he had arranged between Mola and Trumbić and persuaded him to receive the chairman of the Yugoslav Committee. The meeting took place on January 26. Steed told Emanuel immediately afterwards that it was 'long' and 'very cordial'. At the end of their conversation, Orlando invited Trumbić to Rome.[141] Orlando later said to Emanuel: 'There is no doubt that Italy must take advantage of the opportunity offered her by the allies, in Lloyd George's and Wilson's speeches, to make good their apparent abandonment of the Yugoslavs and Czechs.'[142] The correspondent of the *Corriere* expressed the hope that Orlando had been convinced of the soundness of the case argued by his newspaper, but what Orlando had said had raised a suspicion in his mind that the idea of an agreement with the Yugoslavs was regarded in government circles as a secondary question, a mere diplomatic tool.[143] He therefore did not hesitate to say to Orlando that the carrying out of a democratic foreign policy

[230]

capable of gaining Italy the sympathies of the British, American and Slav peoples assumed the replacement of Sonnino, possibly by Bissolati. Orlando replied by pointing out Bissolati's unfamiliarity with the techniques of diplomacy.[144] This objection was sound in itself, but Orlando could have found a personality suitable for replacing Sonnino among the ambassadors who were advocating a new course in Italian foreign policy.

Orlando's intention was not to replace Sonnino, but to persuade him.[145] Steed was a long-standing personal friend of Sonnino's, and the Italian Prime Minister suggested that he should write to him direct, putting to him the advisability of reaching an agreement with the Yugoslavs. Steed did so, and entrusted the letter to the Minister of War, General Alfieri, who had arrived in London. Alfieri handed it to Sonnino during the later inter-allied meeting in Paris.[146] Sonnino did not reply. More than a month later, at the first cabinet meeting that Orlando caused him to attend, Crespi noted that 'Sonnino is opposed to any agreements with the Yugoslavs, foreseeing great difficulties when peace is negotiated. . . . Bissolati wants an agreement, even at the cost of possible sacrifices.'[147] Again on March 10, after Andrea Torre, not without Orlando's consent, had signed the agreement with Trumbić (to which we shall be referring in a moment) Sonnino telegraphed to Imperiali: 'For your information, the Hon. Torre had no instructions from the Ministry of Foreign Affairs and I believe an irredentist meeting in Rome to be inadvisable.'[148]

The Rome congress was first suggested by Borgese in a note enclosed with his letter to Albertini of January 10, 1918. He believed it necessary to reach an agreement with the Yugoslavs and to 'call a congress of the nationalities subject to the Habsburgs—Italians, Bohemians, Yugoslavs, Romanians, Poles, Ruthenians—and impose a just solution of the Austrian question on America. America will not resist the peoples' will.'[149] The same idea, and for the same reason— that is to say, to bring about a modification of President Wilson's position on the ground that it was too favourable to Austria-Hungary —occurred to Beneš. As he was living in Paris, he naturally thought of having the congress organized by the French parliamentary committee for action abroad, of which the chairman was the deputy Franklin-Bouillon. The French liked the idea. Barrère, the French ambassador in Rome, had realized that Caporetto would make the Austrians completely obdurate in relation to the Italian claims and, looking at the campaign in the *Corriere della Sera* and the news of the popular ferment in the Habsburg empire in that light, he had become convinced, and had suggested to his government, that it should take the lead in the anti-Austrian movement, among other things to

[231]

prevent a possible Italo-Yugoslav agreement from diminishing French influence on Serbia.[150]

In advance of the inter-allied socialist conference in London, to which both the Italian Socialist Party, which was highly regarded by the left wing of the French Socialist Party, and the interventionist socialists and the revolutionary syndicalists who were about to form the Italian Socialist Union, were invited, the latter sent a delegation to Paris. The irredentist socialists, who took the Bissolati line and formed part of the delegation, asked Beneš to put them in touch with the Serbian socialists who had taken refuge in France, and thus heard of the proposal to call a congress in Paris.[151] They, or Bissolati, whom they kept informed, suggested that it should be held in Rome because Italy was bearing the chief weight of the war with Austria-Hungary. When Gallenga-Stuart, the Under-Secretary for Propaganda, arrived in Paris at the beginning of February, at a gathering at which the principal representatives of the Czech, Polish and Romanian *émigrés* in France were present, he proposed to Franklin-Bouillon that the congress should be held in Rome.[152] In that event, he was told in reply, the participation of Trumbić would have to be assured. Trumbić indicated that he would not go to Rome in the absence of an Italo-Yugoslav agreement.[153]

Almost simultaneously, on February 2, at a meeting in Milan of the parliamentary group for national defence, which was formed immediately after Caporetto, Albertini proposed the calling of a conference in Rome of the nationalities subject to Austria-Hungary, including the Yugoslavs.[154] The question was adjourned to a subsequent meeting in Rome which was also attended by Amendola and Borgese and nationalist journalists such as Maraviglia and Preziosi, with a view to gaining the support of all the interventionists.

It was agreed (Luigi Albertini noted) to appoint an executive committee to organize the congress. Its members were Senators Ruffini and Scialoja, the deputies Barzilai, Arcà and Torre, and the publicists Amendola and Maraviglia, and 'my proposal to send Torre to London to make contact with Trumbić and reach an agreement with him in general terms which would enable us, the Yugoslavs, and the representatives of other oppressed peoples to meet in Rome, was accepted.'[155]

Torre, an influential parliamentarian, first assured himself of the Prime Minister's consent.[156] Two considerations persuaded Orlando to back the project in spite of Sonnino's hostility. Wickham Steed continued his representations to him, this time in agreement with the British government, which, in the same month, February 1918, had put Lord Northcliffe, the proprietor of *The Times*, in charge of

[232]

propaganda to enemy countries.[157] Steed, with Seton-Watson, was the head of the Austro-Hungarian section of the committee formed by Northcliffe for that purpose. On February 11, on the eve of the reopening of the Italian Chamber, he sent Orlando a telegram informing him that if on this occasion he would 'indicate what was the Italian national policy for the liberation of the peoples subject to Austria-Hungary in accordance with the principle of government with the consent of the governed and that he also favoured a solution of the Adriatic question by means of an agreement between the Adriatic nations, a speech to that effect would meet with a sympathetic reception from responsible circles in Britain.'[158]

Before Steed's telegram was sent, it was read by Lloyd George and Balfour.[159] They approved its being sent, but did not yet give up their sounding out of Vienna. A fortnight later Northcliffe submitted to Balfour a memorandum drafted by Steed on propaganda aims in relation to Austria-Hungary. This asked for a Foreign Office decision between two possible objectives: either a separate peace with the Habsburg monarchy, which had already been sought without success, or its break up by encouraging the nationalities subject to the German Austrians and the Magyars.[160] Steed himself of course favoured the latter. On February 26, Balfour replied that the two alternatives were not necessarily mutually exclusive. Propaganda directed to the anti-German nationalists of Austria-Hungary might force the Emperor Charles to sue for a separate peace.[161] In the second half of March, Bissolati, who went to London again, noted that Lloyd George did not dismiss either alternative.[162] The choice was imposed by events: the German offensive in France, Czernin's speech and the Rome congress.

In his speech in the Italian parliament on February 12 Orlando did what Steed asked him to do. He indignantly rejected the suspicion 'that our war aims are determined, not just by the ineluctable necessities of our national life, but also by ambitions to exercise imperialist rule', and said that 'no one in the world can have greater sympathy than we with the aspirations of the various nationalities still groaning under the oppression of dominant races'.[163] Steed was delighted with the speech and, having heard of Beneš's idea of holding a congress of the Austro-Hungarian nationalities, immediately pointed out to the Italian ambassador, Imperiali, that 'holding the meeting in Paris instead of in Rome would be a colossal error, since it would lend itself to the interpretation of being intended to exercise pressure on Italy'.[164]

The other factor that Orlando took into account was the inter-allied socialist conference; as Minister of the Interior in 1917 he had

[233]

shown his understanding of the socialist movement, which drew down much criticism on his head. In view of the Italian Socialist Party's opposition to the war, the public security authorities kept a watch on all the activities of the international socialist movement. On December 31, 1917, the public security commissioner attached to the Italian consulate in London submitted a report on the Labour conference held three days previously which, as we already know, condemned the 'far-reaching aims of conquest of Italian imperialism'. On January 13, public security headquarters submitted the report to the Prime Minister's office.[165] The Inspector-General of public security at the London embassy said of the inter-allied socialist conference in a report on January 26: 'I fear that the Italian aspirations—which in the socialist view in general are held in little esteem here or at any rate are regarded with little sympathy, and in public opinion at large rely here more on the sanctity of treaties than on agreement on what is right and just'—may meet with 'difficulties and criticisms' from the British Labour Party and the French Socialist Party.[166] British Labour was still represented in the government, and the French Socialist Party, which had left the government only a few months previously, might join it again at any moment, so their attitude could not be a matter of indifference to Orlando, and still less to Bissolati. In fact Imperiali saw both Barnes, the trade-union leader who had taken Arthur Henderson's place in the government, and Henderson himself, the real leader of the Labour Party, and tried to persuade them that the charge of imperialism in relation to the Italian claims was unjustified.[167] Bissolati approached Albert Thomas, the former French socialist minister. The interventionists who were to take part in the inter-allied socialist conference as delegates of the Italian Socialist Union, were flanked by the Irredentist Social Democratic movement.[168]

This organization, consisting of republicans and socialists refugees from Venezia Giulia and the Trentino, had been formed in Milan in October 1917 by a committee of which Angelo Schocchi, the former editor of *Emancipazione*, and Edoardo Schott-Desico, the correspondent of *Il Lavoro*—both Mazzinians from Trieste—were members.[169] The best-known socialist who joined it was Giuseppe Lazzarini di Albona, who before the war had led the opposition to Pittoni's Austro-Marxism in the Social Democratic movement in Istria. The Irredentist Social Democratic movement, which opposed the imperialistic demands of the most extreme type of Italian nationalists, who were obviously very numerous among the refugees from Trieste, Istria and Dalmatia, and was hated by them for that reason, had the support of the Ministers Chiesa, Comandini and Bissolati, and for

[234]

some time also that of Orlando, who aided its activities in the international field.[170] The meeting at which it was established took place in Milan on January 14, 1918, and was attended by the radical deputy Agnelli, Riccardo Zanella, the leader of the autonomist party at Fiume, and Hlaváček, the representative in Italy of the Czechoslovak National Council. It adopted a resolution declaring that the proletariat in the 'unredeemed' territories felt itself to be Italian, that propaganda must be carried out in international 'democratic and proletarian circles' and in inter-allied socialist meetings for 'the justice and equity of the Italian claims', the necessity of the break up of Austria-Hungary, and 'a sincere and genuine agreement between Italians and Slavs, in principle subordinating territorial problems to this main objective, and in any case affirming, with the claim to the Trentino and Venezia Giulia within the limits demarcated by the watershed of the Alps and the Carso, the right of the cities of Fiume and Zara to be annexed to Italy in the name of the nationality principle'.[171]

Orlando at any rate could not have disapproved of this position, for he arranged for the government to pay the travelling expenses of the delegates of the Irredentist Social Democratic movement to the socialist conference in London.[172] There they reached agreement with representative of the Serbian, Polish and Romanian Social Democrats and syndicalists who had taken refuge in the West and had set up in Paris under the chairmanship of Albert Thomas a 'socialist committee of understanding between the oppressed nationalities' which announced that 'the existence of certain collapsing empires such as Austria-Hungary' was incompatible with the right of self-determination of the new nations.[173]

At the inter-allied socialist conference, which took place in London on February 21–23, the Italian Socialist Union delegation, led by the deputies Canepa, Arcà and De Ambris, presented a memorandum claiming for Italy 'the Italian peoples and territories of the Trentino and the Upper Adige, the eastern Friuli and Istria', adding that in the Quarnero and along the eastern coast of the Adriatic 'the frontiers between Italy and the new Slav state must be based on the principles of justice and conciliation'.[174] The memorandum also stated that the 'indispensable condition for a genuine and lasting peace is the dismemberment of the Austro-Magyar empire' and the consequent establishment of an independent Czechoslovakia and Yugoslavia.[175] Canepa, introducing the memorandum to the conference, said that negotiations between Italy and the Yugoslavs were going well.[176]

Among the best-known Socialists who attended the conference were Arthur Henderson and Sidney Webb, the Frenchmen Renaudel and A. Thomas, the Belgians Vandervelde and de Brouckère, the Italian G. E. Modigliani, one of the organizers of the Zimmerwald international conference in 1915, and Huysmans, the secretary of the Bureau of the Second International, who came from Stockholm. A memorandum was adopted looking forward to a federation of the United States of Europe and the world; a League of Nations with international jurisdiction; the inclusion of the constitution of the latter (in accord with the wishes of President Wilson) in the peace treaties; the League to be given a mandate over all colonies, with a view to securing their liberation; and collective security against all acts of aggression.[177] The chapter on territorial questions was drafted by Sidney Webb in co-operation with A. Thomas. It declared in favour of the wiping out of the 'brutal' treaty of 1871 and the restoration of Alsace-Lorraine, following a 'consultation of the people' to be organized by the French under the supervision of the League of Nations. It condemned the 'aims of conquest of Italian imperialism', but was more moderate in this respect than the last statement made by the British Labour Party, which had spoken of the latter's 'far-reaching aims'. But it reaffirmed the Italian right to Austro-Hungarian territories inhabited by Italians and the necessity of guaranteeing 'the legitimate interests of the Italian people in the adjacent seas', and recommended that reciprocal guarantees be given to the 'Italian populations scattered along the eastern shores of the Adriatic' and the Yugoslav ethnic groups that would be included within the new Italian frontiers.[178] As for Austria-Hungary, the memorandum stated that it could not propose its dismemberment as a war aim, but at the request of the Italian Socialist Union, the Irredentist Social Democratic movement, and the Serbian, Bosnian and Romanian Socialists, said that it could not agree to treatment as a mere domestic political matter of the claims to international independence made by the Czechoslovaks and the Yugoslavs. 'National independence must be granted . . . to the peoples who claim it. . . . If they think it desirable, they can substitute a free confederation of the Danubian states for the dominion by the Habsburgs.'[179]

The conference then turned to the Social Democratic parties of the Central Powers, declaring itself willing to meet them at an international congress in a neutral country, provided that, in reply to the above-mentioned memorandum, which it forwarded to them, they made a public statement of their war aims in conformity with the principle of democratic peace, without annexations and based on self-determination of the nations.[180] In the name of the Italian Socialist Party, Modigliani proposed that the word 'democratic' should be deleted from the phrase 'democratic peace', in order not to

[236]

set 'limits to the peace that is the urgent aspiration of the peoples'. The Italian Socialist Party delegates in fact had instructions from their leadership to dispel the illusion that a democratic peace could emerge from an imperialist war. Arthur Henderson disagreed with this proposal, but agreed to add the word 'speedy' to the adjective 'democratic'. Modigliani, supported by the French Zimmerwaldians, proposed a resolution calling for the 'immediate conclusion of an armistice'. This was rejected, and Modigliani and his comrade Schiavi voted against the memorandum.[181] The Italian Socialist Union voted for it, however, stating that the phrase 'reunification with Italy of the Italians of Austria-Hungary' referred to the peoples of the Trentino, eastern Friuli and Istria.[182] At the concluding banquet, Albert Thomas said that 'the delegates have been able freely and fully to discuss the war aims of Italy. They have not hesitated, as their governments have, to support the demands of the oppressed nationalities and have given a definite answer to the appeals of the Czechoslovaks and the Yugoslavs.'[183] Beneš, applauding this, later wrote that 'the London conference was the logical and necessary predecessor to the Rome congress.'[184] In *The Times*, Wickham Steed, who in December 1917 had criticized the Labour war aims, warmly praised the memorandum.[185] Imperiali, forwarding the text to the Italian Foreign Ministry, drew attention to the paragraph concerning the right of self-determination 'for the Czechoslovaks and the Yugoslavs'.[186]

As a result, Andrea Torre found the atmosphere in London more favourable to Italy. Trumbić, at the invitation of Mario Borsa, the chief editor of *Il Secolo*, had already stated his attitude in a letter published by the Milan democratic newspaper. He emphasized that Austria-Hungary was not only worn out by the war, but was also riddled by the discontent of 30,000,000 Slav and Latin subjects, and said that 'between us and Italy there are no real differences, but only misunderstandings'.[187] During his conversations with Torre, which took place in the presence of Borgese, Steed, Seton-Watson, Evans and members of the Yugoslav Committee, Trumbić, pressed by these last, admitted the existence of grave differences on territorial questions. His intransigence threatened to lead to a breakdown of the talks,[188] but after five days of discussion he agreed on March 7, after lively remonstrances and pressure by Steed and his British colleagues —who on this point supported the Italian point of view—to exchange letters of agreement with Torre. The text agreed upon, in accordance with Italian wishes on the subject, left aside territorial questions and merely declared that 'individual territorial differences' must be resolved 'amicably' and 'on the basis of the nationality principle and

[237]

the right of the nations to decide their own fate, and in such a way as not to harm the vital interests of the two nations which will be established when peace is made.'[189] In Torre's opinion, which was shared by the Italian ambassadors in London and Paris, Trumbić, in recognizing the principle of 'vital interests', had implicitly admitted that Italy must have strategically sound frontiers.[190] For his part, Trumbić was able to believe that Italian acceptance of the nationality and self-determination principles was incompatible with the Treaty of London.[191]

Disagreement on frontier questions remained, but the letters made it clear that both sides were committed to the joint all-out struggle against Austria-Hungary and declared that 'the unity and independence of the Yugoslav nation is a vital interest of Italy, just as the completion of Italian national unity is a vital interest of the Yugoslav nation'.[192]

By signing this letter Trumbić committed an organization cemented by three years of struggle and dangers jointly faced; a committee sanctioned by the fact that the Serbian government had signed the Corfu agreement with it, thus laying the foundation of the future Yugoslavia. Both the Yugoslav Committee and the Serbian government gave their approval to the Torre–Trumbić agreement.[193] Torre, however, by his signature merely committed an *ad hoc* committee, which not only had no official or semi-official standing, but also could break up without even binding the individuals represented on it.[194] That, indeed, was what eventually happened when Sonnino's disapproval of the agreement signed by Torre turned out to be stronger than Orlando's initial approval of it.[195] Meanwhile, however, something had been done.

The congress of nationalities subject to Austria-Hungary took place at the Campidoglio in Rome on April 8–10, 1918, with Senator Ruffini in the chair. Many members of the Italian delegation could have been said to be represented politically on the committee on whose account Torre had acted (Senators Albertini and Della Torre, Deputies Ferdinando Martini, Agnelli, Di Cesarò, Federzoni and others, the journalists Amendola, Borgese, Forges-Davanzati, Mussolini, etc.). A delegation representing another Italian group, the Committee for Propaganda for Italo-Yugoslav Understanding, also took part; it had been set up at the beginning of the year as a result of the contacts that Arcangelo Ghisleri, a close friend of Salvemini, whose outlook on international affairs he completely shared, and the Tridentine refugee Professor Luigi Granello, who worked in the press office of the Italian legation in Berne, had made with the Serbo-Croat democratic *émigrés* in Switzerland. Among the Italians on this com-

[238]

mittee were Senator Volterra, Deputies Colajanni, De Viti De Marco, Ettore Ciccotti and Pirolini, as well as men of letters or economists such as Ghisleri, Salvemini, Ojetti, Prezzolini, Luigi Einaudi, Guglielmo Ferrero, Pietro Silva, Angelo Sraffa, Felice Momigliano, Carlo Maranelli, Umberto Zanotti Bianco and Ernesta Battisti.[196] Essentially they shared the views of Salvemini, who would not (and could not) have sat on a committee of which nationalists were members.

The outstanding members of the Czechoslovak delegation were Beneš, Štefanik and Osuský. The Yugoslav delegation included Trumbić and Meštrović, and the Polish the future Foreign Minister Skirmunt and the Reichsrat deputy Zamorski. The principal Romanians were Senators Mironesco and Draghicesco and Deputy Lupu. The Serbian parliament in exile at Corfu sent twelve deputies. France was represented by Franklin-Bouillon, A. Thomas, Fournol, and the journalist de Quirielle, and Britain by Wickham Steed and Seton-Watson. The American ambassador in Rome, Thomas Nelson Page, held a watching brief for the United States.[197]

The conference set about its work with the greatest enthusiasm and the aim of completely liberating the peoples oppressed by the Habsburgs was reaffirmed.[198] True, Zamorski claimed that the principal enemy of the Poles was Germany, but agreed with the struggle against Austria-Hungary. Incidentally the Poles in the Reichsrat in Vienna had now gone over into opposition. Senator Draghicesco said that the Romanian patriots repudiated the armistice concluded months previously and the peace negotiations that had been imposed on the Romanian government by the Austrian and German invaders, and intended to go on fighting on the Entente side.[199] On April 11, after the end of the congress, Orlando, accompanied by Bissolati, received the Yugoslav delegation alone as a token of friendship, and then solemnly received all the delegations.[200] Sonnino, whom Steed had tried in vain to persuade to attend the congress, did not follow suit, though he assured it of his sympathy.[201]

Salvemini wrote to his wife on the first day of the congress that the Italians who attended it could be divided into three groups: that of Ruffini, Albertini and Amendola, who wanted the congress to be 'a serious thing, to give rise to effective anti-Austrian action and create a stable organization for such action'; the nationalists, who accepted the congress as a provisional war weapon but did not intend that anything lasting should come of it, above all anything that might obstruct their territorial ambitions; and the *Unità* group, which was concerned with the future and wanted to take advantage of the opportunity to remove misunderstandings and lay the foundation for

[239]

a satisfactory demarcation of Italo-Yugoslav frontiers based on mutual concessions. Steed, Seton-Watson and Albert Thomas favoured the Salvemini line, and pointed out to Trumbić—who, like the Italian nationalists, was unwilling to commit himself on the frontier question, thus possibly surrendering his own country's maximum programme—that by so doing he was playing into the hands of both Italian and Serbian imperialism.[202] Salvemini greatly liked the Czech delegates. He thought the Romanian delegates weak, and the Poles resolutely anti-German, but 'Austrophile at heart'. The Yugoslavs struck him as suspicious and reluctant to be dragged too far in any direction 'out of fear of being cheated by the Italians'. Trumbić made an 'excellent impression of moral fibre, but he is a lawyer, fearful of being deceived; half a century of fierce local struggles weigh down on him, he does not want to be accused of letting down the Slavs by abandoning Istria to Italy'.[203] On April 7 and 10 Salvemini, De Viti De Marco, Ojetti and Silva (and on the second occasion also Bissolati and Canepa) met Trumbić and the other Yugoslav delegates in the presence of A. Thomas, Steed, Seton-Watson and Milner, the correspondent of the *Morning Post*. Salvemini tried to secure from Trumbić an assurance that he would support the Yugoslav renunciation of Istria as far as Monte Maggiore in exchange for an Italian renunciation of Dalmatia, but the chairman of the Yugoslav Committee 'obstinately' refused, though in subsequent conversations the Serbian delegates said that they agreed to Istria's being left to Italy. Salvemini concluded that out of fear of the Slovene and Croat nationalists, Trumbić wanted the necessary concessions to be forced on him by the Entente, in which case he would agree to them, but under protest.[204]

In spite of these symptoms of the gravity that the failure to reach a solution of Italo-Yugoslav differences was to assume after the end of the war, the Rome congress represented a mortal blow to Austria-Hungary. This opinion, which Professor E. Denis was the first to state, has been confirmed by several historians who have subsequently concerned themselves with the subject.[205]

Because of the Czernin–Clemenceau clash, which, with its revelations, caused an international sensation in spite of the fact that the terrifying German advance in France was in full swing, the Rome congress took place at the most favourable possible moment for those who approved of its purposes. The French ambassador in Italy was the first to suggest a 'declaration of collective recognition on the part of the allied governments of the result of the Rome conference'. Sonnino refused. He replied that he regarded with 'lively sympathy the whole movement towards liberty and independence of the peoples oppressed by the Austro-Hungarian empire', and that it was his genuine desire 'to reach an equitable agreement with the Yugoslavs which would reconcile and as far as possible assure the various essential interests of ours and theirs in the fields in which they might possibly come into conflict, but this was a question . . . exclusively between them and us, and neither could nor should in any way affect even in appearance the perfect validity and integrity of the agreements with France and Britain that were the basis of our alliance and our entry into the war. Any collective declaration of official recognition on the part of our governments of the aspirations and aims of the movement in question would create misunderstanding in this respect in the minds of the public' and would involve the risk of bringing it 'into conflict with our London stipulations'.[206]

In the Sonnino papers we have found the message which Sir Rennel Rodd delivered to the Italian Foreign Minister on April 18, 1918. 'The view of my Government,' the British ambassador wrote, 'is that they are prepared to recognize proclamations of independence made by subject nationalities in Austria-Hungary, though they cannot pledge themselves to secure such independence. We also approve of giving assurances to the troops belonging to those nationalities that in the event of their coming over to the allies, they would be treated not as prisoners of war but as friends and would be allowed to fight on our side.'

Sonnino agreed with this as far as the Czechs were concerned. As to the Yugoslavs he remained immovable. Consequently, when, at the inter-allied meetings in Paris and Versailles at the beginning of June the French proposed recognition of Polish, Czechoslovak and Yugoslav independence, though 'the creation of a united and independent Polish state with free access to the sea' was promptly approved of, Sonnino's opposition caused the Entente governments to restrict themselves to expressing their 'profound sympathy with the national aspirations to liberty of the Czechoslovak and Yugoslav peoples'.[207]

This was a bitter pill for the Czech and Yugoslav *émigrés* to swallow, and even the Serbian government regarded the Versailles declaration as unsatisfactory. Sonnino was not opposed to the Czech desire for official recognition, but did not want to create a precedent for the Yugoslavs and also—as appears from the end of his reply to Barrère, whom he admonished not to create the impression of wanting unnecessarily to prolong the war—at heart did not want the destruction of Austria-Hungary, but only its diminution. He addressed the same warning to Sir Rennel Rodd, the British ambassador, and it was echoed at the Foreign Office. On May 23, Lord Robert Cecil prepared a draft document recognizing the Czechoslovak National Council, but the Foreign Office pointed out that, if an under-taking were given to ensure the independence of Bohemia, it would be impossible to detach Austria from Germany. Nevertheless on June 5, the War Cabinet submitted the draft to Washington, explain-ing that the Czech legions in France, Italy and Russia must be taken into account.[208] Meanwhile the American administration, which a few weeks earlier had tried to rescue the Habsburg monarchy, had been won over to the cause of Czechoslovak independence. The American ambassador in Rome, who sympathized with Bissolati's and Albertini's idea of reconciling Italian policy towards the Yugo-slavs with President Wilson's new principles, reported to the State Department with approval the outcome of the congress, which he had attended.[209] Under the influence of Herron's conversion to the principles of the Rome congress, the head of the American legation in Berne, through whom a great deal of the previous contacts between Washington and Vienna had taken place, took the same line.[210] Lansing, the Secretary of State, had had doubts already at the time of the launching of the Fourteen Points about the wisdom of upsetting Italy and Serbia—that is, allied nations—in order to rescue Austria-Hungary, an enemy nation. He had finally been convinced by the Czernin–Clemenceau affair of the futility of counting on a separate peace with Vienna, and to him the Rome congress opened the way to resolute diplomatic action. In a memorandum that he submitted to President Wilson on May 10, he suggested that the United States should openly support the revolutionary independence movements of the centrifugal nationalities of the Austrian empire.[211] Next day he telegraphed to his ambassador in Italy that the American government had 'the greatest sympathy' with the principles stated by the Rome congress and instructed him to ask the Italian Foreign Minister what concrete suggestions he had for the 'active co-operation of the United States in the whole of this movement'.[212] Sonnino's reply as usual was negative. Opposed to the making of any new declaration, he drew a distinction between the Czechoslovaks, whom he regarded as definitely hostile to Austria-Hungary, and the Yugoslavs, whom he regarded as partly loyal to it and only partly desirous of following the Czechs. Moreover, he feared that a possible Yugoslav state would turn out to be an enemy of Italy and would eventually gravi-tate towards either Austria or Germany. Lansing reported Sonnino's reply to President Wilson, pointing out that the time was approaching when the United States would have to decide to support the Yugo-slavs, who in his view had a right to independence, even if this

[242]

implied the undesirable course of clashing with Italy.[213] In a public announcement on May 29 he said that the Washington government had followed the Rome congress 'with great interest' and 'that the national aspirations to liberty of the Czechoslovaks and Yugoslavs had the greatest sympathy of the United States government'.[214] It was already clear to Lansing, as appears from one of his memoranda, that 'Austria-Hungary must be wiped off the map of Europe as an empire. It must be divided up between the nationalities of which it is composed'.[215] But the final decision rested with President Wilson.

Wilson was influenced even more by the repercussions in the United States of the actions of the Czech Legion in Siberia and Masaryk's arrival from Russia than by the representations of his Secretary of State. Japanese troops had landed at Vladivostok on April 5, 1918. This had alarmed the government and public opinion in the United States.[216] In the second half of May, the Czech Legion in Russia, which Masaryk, before he left for America, had instructed to embark for France at Vladivostok, occupied the Siberian town of Chelyabinsk after some incidents had occurred which had displaced the local Bolshevik authorities.[217] This news roused the immediate sympathy with the Czechs of American public opinion, which had by then turned against the Bolsheviks, both because of their class revolution and because of the peace they had made with Germany. Wilson and Lansing had previously rejected Anglo-French proposals to intervene in Russia.[218] The desire not to allow the Japanese to become sole masters of Siberia and the possibility of intervening, at any rate in appearance, not as imperialists but as supporters of a democracy such as the Czech Legion proclaimed to fight for, eventually caused the United States administration to make up its mind. Masaryk was greeted at Chicago by a crowd of 100,000; at Pittsburgh on May 30 he brought about a pact of national unity between the representatives of the Czech and Slovak colonies in America. On June 19 he was received by the President.[219] On June 25, Lansing asked the President for authority to promise the independence, not only of Poland, but also of Czechoslovakia and Yugoslavia, not concealing that 'this would in fact mean the dismemberment of the existing Austro-Hungarian empire'.[220] Two days later the President gave his consent, suggesting also 'the recognition of Hungary as an independent state, completely detached from Austria'.[221] The Hungarian independence movement, active as it was at home, was not represented abroad, and therefore could not be taken into consideration by the American administration, apart from the fact that a step in favour of the Hungarians would have roused the vigorous opposition of the Czechoslovaks. Lansing's announcement on June 28

I

therefore stated that 'the position now adopted by the United States was that all the branches of the Slav race must be completely liberated from German and Austrian domination'.[222] It was not yet a formal pledge, as desired by Masaryk, but a step in that direction. On September 3, Lansing announced American recognition of the Czechoslovak National Council as the *de facto* government of Czechoslovakia.[223] On June 29 France had taken into consideration such a recognition as soon as Lansing's statement was made public in Paris.[224] Britain had done the same—although in a more cautious way—on August 9.[225] On October 4, the Austro-Hungarian government asked President Wilson for an armistice on the basis of his Fourteen Points. The American administration replied that the situation existing at the time when they had been drawn up 'had been radically altered by our recognition of the Czechoslovaks and our encouragement of the Yugoslavs'.[226] The publication of this reply in Austria-Hungary led in the course of a few days to the bloodless victory of the revolutions by the independence movements in Prague and Zagreb.[227] The imperial manifesto of October 16, 1918, had just announced (too late) the reorganization of Cisleithania into a federation of national states; Hungary declared herself henceforward to be bound to the Habsburg monarchy only by a 'personal union'. Militarily exhausted as she was, Austria-Hungary had no alternative but to accept President Wilson's terms.

Already, in October 1917, the Italian War Minister had ordered that Czechoslovaks and Poles were to be separated from other Austro-Hungarian prisoners, and that representatives of the Czechoslovak National Council were to be permitted to conduct propaganda among their fellow-nationals, who numbered many tens of thousands of men.[228] It was proposed for the time being to use volunteers from among those prisoners as a military labour force. But in a conversation with Albertini and Ojetti at Padua on March 8, 1918, Orlando said that he had decided on the immediate formation of a Czechoslovak Legion.[229] On April 11, immediately after the end of the Rome congress, the War Minister instructed General Andrea Graziani to set about forming such a legion. On April 21, Orlando, General Zuppelli, the Minister of War, and Štefanik signed a convention, the first point of which stated that the 'Royal Italian Government recognizes the existence of a single and autonomous Czechoslovak army, based from the national, political and juridical aspects under the authority of the National Council of the Czechoslovak countries'.[230] Orlando, who besides being a politician was a distinguished jurist, took the view that, by granting the Czechoslovak National Council the eminently sovereign power of exercising political and civil jurisdiction over the members of the Legion recruited in Italy, the Italian government had granted it recognition as a *de facto* government.[231] When the Czechoslovak Legion in France was formed, the Paris government had equally granted jurisdiction over the Legion (which was however subject to French military law and regulations) to the Czechoslovak National Council.

The first big Czechoslovak unit left for the Italian front at the end of May. On June 27, a Czechoslovak battalion was mentioned in despatches for valorous conduct on the Piave. In September the whole legion, then at a strength of 24,000 men (it was subsequently to be doubled), distinguished itself in fierce fighting.[232]

In February 1918, the War Minister ordered the Yugoslavs to be separated from the mass of Austro-Hungarian prisoners.[233] But, though about 20,000 Yugoslavs volunteered, because of Sonnino's opposition to the recognition of Yugoslavia, and also because of the difficulty of finding a form of oath acceptable to all the parties (the Italian government, the Yugoslav Committee and the Serbian government), no Yugoslav legion was formed. Only some infiltration companies recruited from courageous Yugoslavs were used on the Italian front. A declaration in favour of the Yugoslav national movement that Bissolati succeeded in extracting from the cabinet on September 8 was not equivalent to a *de facto* recognition of the future Yugoslavia and did not change the situation.[234] Italy went to the Peace Conference, in 1919, without having recognized the Yugoslav state, though it had by then been in existence for several months.

However, in 1918, the moral effect of the Allied promises on the Slav (and eventually not only the Slav) troops of the Austro-Hungarian army was very noticeable.[235] An important factor was the work of the Central Committee for Propaganda to the Enemy, which Orlando had formed in March 1918 and attached to the High Command. At the suggestion of Luigi Albertini, who knew him well and appreciated his organizing ability as well as his gifts as a writer, Orlando put Ugo Ojetti in charge of the committee's work. Ojetti worked not only in the back areas but also in the front line, and his committee maintained close co-operation with the representatives in Italy of the corresponding British, French and American organizations, as well as with the Czechoslovak, Yugoslav, Polish and Romanian committees.[236] Between May and October 1918, it distributed a total of about 60,000,000 copies of 643 leaflets in eight languages and a total of about 10,000,000 copies of 112 newspapers in four languages, by air and also by means of infiltration into the enemy lines and the back areas, as well as in Austro-Hungarian towns (Ljubljana, Zagreb, and, with d'Annunzio taking part,

[245]

Vienna).[237] During the June battle on the Piave, 800 of these leaflets were found on 350 Austro-Hungarian prisoners in a single day.[238] Desertions of Czechs and Yugoslavs from the Austro-Hungarian lines became very frequent, and on the eve of the enemy offensive in June, some deserters gave the Italian command detailed information about the place, date and even the time of the latter, and later, in October, they gave it the exact deployment and order of battle of the Austro-Hungarian troops.[239] On one evening in June, 300 Czechs crossed the lines in a group, shouting *Viva l'Italia!* A company of 200 Croats surrendered almost simultaneously, the lieutenant in command proving to be a friend of Jambrišak, the Yugoslav representative on Ojetti's committee, whose name appeared on the leaflets dropped by Italian aircraft.[240]

On the eve and during the first few days of the final Italian offensive in October, whole Austro-Hungarian regiments and even divisions mutinied, though this was not owing to Italian propaganda only, as the first units that refused to go up into the line were Magyar; they wanted to go home, and were only willing to fight, if at all, for the defence of the soil of Hungary, where a political and social revolution —headed by Károlyi—was now in full swing. But they represented an explosion of the feeling expressed by the slogans calling for the end of the Habsburg empire.[241]

We cannot here follow the story of the national or social revolutions that convulsed and dismembered Austria-Hungary in 1918.[242] We shall deal with the events in Hungary in a separate work. In the present context we shall confine ourselves to some especially significant incidents.

After a member of the Serbo-Croat coalition was appointed Ban of Croatia, liberty of the press increased at Zagreb. On January 21, 1918, *Hrvatska Država*, the organ of the Right Party, reported Trumbić's criticisms of Lloyd George's speech and President Wilson's Fourteen Points. On February 15, it copied from *The Times* the report of the Orlando–Trumbić conversation. In spite of the censorship, the Zagreb newspaper indicated that Italy was perhaps in the process of changing its 'imperialist policy' in relation to the Yugoslavs, which would be a fact of 'the greatest importance'.[243] On February 23, at a meeting of a Reichsrat committee in Vienna, the Slovene deputy Benković welcomed the rapprochement taking place between Italians and Yugoslavs. Three days later, the Tridentine deputy Alcide De Gasperi said in reply that he was a genuine and warm supporter of such a *rapprochement* and hoped for the triumph of the 'world trend' to liberty and democracy.[244]

On March 2 and 3, a meeting took place at Zagreb under the

chairmanship of Dr Ante Pavelić, leader of the Croat Right Party, attended by the deputies of that party to the Diet, two Serbian deputies to the Diet of Croatia-Slavonia, Mgr Korošec and two other Slovene deputies to the Reichsrat, two deputies (Laginja and Spinčić) from Istria, and two (Čingrija and Smodlaka) from Dalmatia, six deputies from the Bosnian Diet, and some other politicians, including the leaders of the Croat Social Democratic Party. They adopted a resolution declaring that the Slovenes, Croats and Serbs formed a single nation and demanded the right of self-determination.[245] At a meeting of Austro-Hungarian leaders in the Southern Slav territories, Lieutenant-General Sarkotić, the governor of Bosnia, pointed out how dangerous this was. Previous statements made by the Southern Slavs of Austria-Hungary had spoken of Yugoslav unity under the Habsburgs, but this had now been displaced by the claim to self-determination. Pupils in Croat, Dalmatian and Bosnian schools were collecting signatures in support of the statement and were distributing it.[246] Sarkotić believed that this was a result of influences from abroad, and that was partly true, though émigré propaganda would have been ineffective if it had not struck a responsive chord at home.[247] In a report to his government on the events at Zagreb, the German Consul-General in Budapest drew attention, not only to the popular support behind the independence movement, but also to the formation in the forests of Croatia-Slavonia of large units of deserters, called the 'green cadres', their numbers, we may add, greatly swollen by the influence of Bolshevism, pacifism or nationalism. In the Consul-General's opinion, the Serbo-Croat coalition at Zagreb was now playing a double game; it declared itself loyal to the Hungarian authorities, but was in reality staking everything on the success of Károlyi's revolutionary independence movement in Hungary. 'Things in Croatia,' he concluded, 'seem to be heading towards a violent explosion.'[248]

A few days after the Rome congress, several Zagreb newspapers reported it, copying from the Swiss newspapers long passages of the resolution it adopted.[249] Not as a result of this, but in reply to Czernin's speech, which greatly provoked them, the leaders of the Czech parties met in Prague for a national oath-taking ceremony on April 13. The poet A. Jirašek read the text of an oath of independence to a crowd of more than 10,000, and speeches in favour of the principle of self-determination were made by Stanek, Kramář, Habrman and Klofáč, and also by the Yugoslav leaders Korošec, Pavelić and Radić, who came especially with some of their colleagues from Ljubljana and Zagreb.[250]

May 1 was celebrated in Prague by big processions in which many members of the middle class mingled with the workers. Banners proclaimed 'End the war and long live peace'; 'No more slaves or masters'; 'We want self-determination of the nations'; and 'Long live the Czech state'.[251] In Zagreb, the Croat Social Democratic Party raised a crowd of 6,000, and deputies of the radical opposition addressed it as well as the Social Democrats. A resolution was adopted openly claiming Yugoslav unity and independence.[252] Even the relatively minute Slovak Social Democratic Party took similar action that was not without repercussions. At a May 1 meeting held at Lipto St Nicholas (it was the first time that a Slovak party subject to the harsh Hungarian police régime had dared to do such a thing) it proclaimed the struggle for the national liberty of the Slovak people, 'the branch of the Czechoslovak nation living in Hungary'. One of the speakers was Šrobar, a follower of Masaryk.[253]

The independence movements, which now included nearly all the 'subject' nations of Austria-Hungary and nearly all the social classes of those nations, held a joint demonstration on the occasion of the celebration of the fiftieth anniversary of the Czech National Theatre on May 16–18, 1918. This happened almost to coincide with the 300th anniversary of the Defenestration of Prague, which began the Thirty Years' War. Many Slovak, Slovene, Serbo-Croat, Polish, Romanian and Italian delegates attended, led by a number of deputies and mayors. Influential politicians, ranging from former conservatives to Social Democrats, and recent or long-standing supporters of the various independence movements (except those of the Magyars, who were hopelessly at loggerheads with the Czechs over Slovakia and with the Romanians over Transylvania, the Italians of the Adriatic region, who were at odds with the Yugoslavs, and the Ruthenians, who were at odds with the Poles) met in the presence of a huge crowd which ranged through the streets of Prague in defiance of the police. After their speeches, some of the speakers, beginning with Kramář, were carried about in triumph. The new political factors in the demonstration was the presence of leaders of the traditional Polish parties, who until a few weeks before had been supporters of the government, and Tridentine Catholics led by the Reichsrat deputy Enrico Conci.[254] Conci said that the Austrian Italians, breaking all residual Catholic attachment to the Habsburgs, were united to the Czechs by the same destiny and were subject to the same persecutions; common oppression made them brothers. The Poles, who in Galicia—like the Italians in Trieste, who, however, were not represented in Prague—were in fact a dominant and not an oppressed nationality, made similar statements. A resolution adopted unanimously said that the representatives 'of the nationalities who have

[248]

been groaning for centuries under the oppression of other foreign nations, meeting in conference, proclaim their unanimous purpose to do everything in their power to enable their nationality, after this horrible war, to obtain emancipation and to be resurrected to a new, free life based on the right of self-determination of the nations. Those present are unanimous in the belief that a better future will not smile on their nations except on the firm basis of universal democracy.'[255]

Beneš, writing to Amendola, regarded this as indisputably an echo of the Rome congress. 'I take the liberty of reminding you,' he wrote, 'of what I said when I left Rome after the congress. I said we should see similar demonstrations in Prague. They took place on May 16.' He enclosed a letter that he had received clandestinely from Bohemia, and said that he had informed his friends at home of what had happened in Rome and had asked them to do something similar.[256]

At the instigation of the German nationalists in the Tyrol, Conci was dismissed by imperial rescript from the post of provincial vice-captain which he had held for ten years. In the Vienna Reichsrat, Alcide De Gasperi, the future Prime Minister of the Italian Republic (the birth of which in 1946 no one could then foresee) protested against this arbitrary act. To the applause of the Czech and Yugoslav deputies, Conci spoke on the same occasion in protest against the persecutions to which the Italians in the Trentino, beginning with the Bishop, Mgr Endrici, were being subjected.[257]

Even before the Vienna government complied with the wishes of the German nationalists, Conci was severely criticized by the Italian nationalists in Trieste for having joined in a demonstration in which Slovene nationalists, who wished to make Trieste a Yugoslav city, took part.[258]

In an interview with the Trieste socialist newspaper, De Gasperi defended Conci against all the nationalists, stating the problem in its true terms. 'If Conci protested against oppression in Prague,' he said, he deserved the support of all those to whom what was at stake was 'the question of principle whether the cause of democracy and civil liberty shall emerge from this war vanquished or victorious. Conci went to Prague for the specific purpose of invoking its victory, which is the only thing that can guarantee the civil and social life of the nations now subject to German centralism'. This was not the time, he said, to make a 'stale distinction between clericals, socialists, bourgeois. . . . Persecution that has levelled them out has deprived those terms of all significance for the time being. . . . Let us today acquire the right to live and resume discussion about ways of living better tomorrow.'[259]

[249]

With the exception of Conci, none of the party leaders of any nationality who took part in the Prague demonstration seems to have been penalized in any way. The oppression denounced by De Gasperi, which had indeed been evident from 1915 to 1917, was now fading away. The Austro-Hungarian authorities were faced with constant mutinies in the back areas among units determined not to return to the front. On May 12–13, the 17th Regiment, consisting of Slovenes, mutinied at Judenburg; and the 88th Brigade (Magyars and Ruthenians) mutinied at Rimaszombat; on May 20, it was the turn of the 58th Regiment (Ruthenians) at Lublin and the 6th Regiment (Serbs and Magyars) at Pécs and on May 21 the 7th Regiment (Czechs) at Rumburg and the 15th Brigade (Slovaks) at Trencsén followed suit.[260] On May 27 the 97th Regiment (Italians and Slovenes) revolted at Radkesburg; on June 4 the 79th Regiment (Slovaks) mutinied at Krafujevac. Many of the mutineers were ex-prisoners-of-war who had returned from Russia after Brest-Litovsk and had seen Bolshevism put an end to the fighting. These mutinies could still be suppressed by force of arms, but the revolutionary propaganda made everywhere by the huge masses (almost 700,000 men) who returned from Russian prisoner-of-war camps could no longer be contained. The number of deserters grew tremendously.

Burian, the Foreign Minister, noted in his diary: 'Our offensive, which is now very urgent from every point of view, begins on June 15.'[261] His reference was to the Battle of the Piave, which ended in a great Italian victory and cost the Austro-Hungarian army, whose human and material reserves were already exhausted when it launched a strategically unsound attack, losses estimated at more than 150,000 dead, wounded and taken prisoner.[262]

The Austro-Hungarian monarchy survived the defeat on the Piave for another four months because its centripetal forces, though dying, had not yet lost all their strength. The state apparatus of oppression was still in being, as was demonstrated in Hungary, while the battle was raging on the Piave. On June 20, after a clash between the gendarmerie and trade unionists at the Hungarian state railway in which four workers were killed and five seriously injured, a violent protest strike broke out in Budapest which within forty-eight hours spread to the whole of Hungary, involving more than half a million workers, paralysing factories, mines, urban and inter-urban tramways and many railway lines. On June 22, the Social Democratic Party and the trade unions had a workers' council elected by the shop-stewards of the Budapest factories, this time declaring their objective to be that from which they had shrunk during the previous January, namely that of forcing the government to resign. The military authorities responded by announcing that militarized workers who did not return to work immediately would be tried by military courts, but this threat went unheeded. However, on the evening of June 27, the workers' council was forced to call off the strike which, in spite of its mass support, failed to shake the government. Instead, the latter went over to the counter-attack, arresting and charging agitators, but also promising pay increases.[263] In the Hungarian parliament, the strikers were defended only by the small group led by Károlyi. In the country the middle classes were hesitant and divided. At the end of June, many Magyars, who were to become revolutionary at the beginning of October, still hoped, if not for victory, at any rate for a compromise peace. The bourgeois and peasant classes of the non-Magyar nationalities felt they had nothing in common with the revolutionary movement of the socialist workers who looked to Bolshevik Russia. The decisive move should have come from the Austrian Social Democrats. The workers of Vienna, Graz and other Austrian centres had for weeks been wanting their party to lead them in a general strike for an immediate peace.

At the beginning of June, a national conference of Austrian Social Democrats, held behind closed doors, called on the militants to desist for the time being from mass strikes out of a sense of responsibility in view of the military situation in Europe (the Germans were on the Marne and not a few Social Democratic leaders still hoped for a German victory).[264] The bread ration, which had been increased after the January strike, was again reduced in Austria on June 17 to 650 grammes a week, and the workers' exasperation forced the Social Democratic leadership to resuscitate the workers' council which had been elected in Vienna five months previously, only to be quickly shelved again. In order to prevent further deterioration of the food situation, it appealed to the railwaymen and other transport workers not to join in the strikes that were breaking out spontaneously in many factories. On June 22, when the strike in Hungary was at its height (a fact known to very few in Austria, as the news was suppressed by the censorship), the Vienna workers' council called on the Austrian strikers to go back to work in view of the pay concessions promised by the government.[265] Many workers in Vienna did not resume work until two days later but, on the whole, Social Democratic discipline again prevailed over the spontaneous strike movement, though this time there was no fear of intervention by the German army, which was engaged in its last supreme effort on the Western Front.

Because of considerations similar to those of the Austrian Social Democrats, though with different ends in view, the political leaders

[251]

of the Slav nationalities of the empire, in spite of the news from the various fronts, which from their point of view should have been encouraging, refrained from playing the card of insurrection. In the summer and at the beginning of the autumn of 1918, apart from making bitter parliamentary speeches, their activities were confined to the organization—possible now legally—of the National Councils that were to constitute the first organs of their future independent states.

The new Austrian government, presided over (since the end of July 1918) by Max Hussarek, had just begun to discuss the long over-due federalistic reform of the empire. It was already too late, because all nationalities inside Austria-Hungary knew by then that the Central Powers had virtually lost the war and took for granted that the victorious Entente, and the United States, would secure independence and restore national unity to the Czechoslovaks, the Yugoslavs, the Romanians, the Poles and in general to the subject nationalities of the Habsburg monarchy. When the Imperial Manifesto of October 16, published on October 17, 1918 eventually transformed Austria (but not Hungary, the Hungarian government having refused to accept this settlement) into a democratic federation of free peoples, all nationalities, including those which had always asked for such a reform, interpreted it as the end of the old state and as the birth of separate national states.[266] Incidentally, the Manifesto gave no indication of how it was proposed to deal with the conflicts (in particular, those between Czechs and German Austrians in the ethnically mixed areas of Bohemia and Moravia) which had frustrated all reform in the past. It ignored this problem, because the Sudeten Germans still hoped that they would be able to avoid absorption into the Czechoslovak state, whether federal or independent.

The revolutionary wave, mainly nationalistic, but in Austria proper and in Hungary also socialistic, began shortly after the capitulation of Bulgaria at the end of September 1918. Nobody doubted any more that Germany too had been beaten on the Western Front. At the end of October 1918, during the very days when the revolutionary wave convulsed Austria-Hungary and overthrew the governments in Vienna and Budapest, and the state apparatus everywhere in the Habsburg monarchy, from Prague to Zagreb, the Italians finally destroyed its army at Vittorio Veneto.

Could Austria-Hungary have survived? Our reconstruction of the process of its disintegration shows that its leaders, after the introduction in 1907 of universal suffrage into the Austrian part of the dual monarchy only, did nothing positive to save it—unless Tisza's 1913

[252]

agreement with the Serbo-Croat coalition at Zagreb is considered a step that might have had lasting results but for the war. Francis Ferdinand had a reform programme that was restricted to Hungary, but it is impossible to be sure that, once on the throne, he would have had the determination necessary to carry it through in the teeth of the violent opposition of the Magyar 'historical classes'. After his assassination, the Austro-Hungarian government, without being forced to do so by any imminent external threat (for Serbia was weak and Russia undecided or unprepared) or by any immediate danger of internal disintegration (as, contrary to the hopes of the planners of the Sarajevo assassination, the immediate reaction to it was demon-strations of loyalty by the empire's Southern Slavs), sought security in a preventive war. Austro-Hungarian diplomacy forgot on this occasion that one reason why the Habsburg monarchy's position as a great power had been undisputed for the last forty years was that the two nations that could put forward the most dangerous claims at its expense, i.e. Italy and Romania, had had to seek alliance with the Central Powers. It was not appreciated in Vienna that, if war were declared on Belgrade without previous assurances of solidarity from Italy and Romania, both countries would be free to turn on Austria-Hungary, with the result that the latter, already at grips with Russia and Serbia, would automatically find herself in a desperate situation, no matter how great the valour of her troops might be.

During the course of the war, which was virtually lost by Austria-Hungary after its first big defeats on the Russian front, the Italian intervention, and then the Romanian intervention, the Habsburg government, in spite of the pacifist and humanitarian aspirations of Francis Joseph's youthful successor (which, however, produced no practical results, other than the 1917 amnesty), did nothing but wait for salvation from the fortune of German arms. Reversing Clause-witz's dictum that war is a continuation of politics by other means, the Austro-Hungarian government subordinated politics to the out-come of the war.

Although the successor states, by the mere fact of having risen again after the Second World War and preserved their spirit of national unity and independence in the very difficult twenty-five years that followed, have shown themselves to be more viable than Austria-Hungary was in the last decade of its long life, the governments that gave them real independence between 1918 and 1939 did not during that period show themselves more far-sighted, or even merely more reasonable, than the defunct Austro-Hungarian government.

In May 1918, Valentino Pittoni stated in the newspaper of the Italian Socialist Party of Trieste, of which he was the long-standing leader, that he had been invited to the Prague celebrations, but had not wanted to go. 'The Italo-Yugoslav fraternity proclaimed at the Rome congress,' he wrote, 'is an ephemeral product of the war, is one of the many vicissitudes of the war, and is not genuine and sincere.' He noted that the Rome congress had been attended both by Italian nationalists, who in the past had always denounced the Trieste socialists for the goodwill they showed to the Slovene workers and for their defence of the right of the Slovenes to their own schools in Trieste, and by Yugoslav nationalists, who claimed Trieste, un-questionably a predominantly Italian city, for their future state. The Prague celebrations had been attended by Czech, Yugoslav, Polish and Romanian nationalists, to whose aspirations to territories that were ethnically not theirs he confessed that he still preferred the old programme of the Austrian Social Democrats, who had wanted to transform the empire into a free federation of nations willing to co-exist peaceably in an area which, because of the large number of ethnically mixed zones that it included, and for deep reasons of economic and cultural interdependence, could not be dismembered without infringing the principles of justice and liberty which were being proclaimed, or without detriment to the peoples themselves.[267]

Pittoni was answered in the same newspaper, *Il Lavoratore*, by one of its editors, Edmondo Puecher, who deplored his failure to go to Prague to defend Bissolati's programme in order to prevent national-ism from prevailing. The overriding consideration, in his opinion, was the desire of the Slav and Latin peoples to free themselves from German and Magyar supremacy and to make use of the right of self-determination, which was the most significant outcome of the war. The struggle between the supporters of the new League of Nations or of possible democratic confederations on the one hand and nationalists of every colour on the other would have to be carried on inside the democracies when the war was won by them.[268]

The terms of the debate that began then and has been continued in Europe and America ever since, indeed include the opposite poles of the dilemma, as they do in the eyes of the many historians of the end of the Austro-Hungarian empire whom we have quoted in these notes.

A number of arguments can be adduced in favour of the view, now prevalent among Austrian and also American historians (though it is sharply contested by most historians of the countries of eastern Europe) that the harm done by the break up of Austria-Hungary distinctly outweighed the advantages derived from the attainment of national unity and independence by the peoples who ceased to feel free under the Habsburgs. Apart from the material damage done by the fragmentation of a vast unified economic area and the replacement of a conservative monarchy by dictatorships, first of the Right and then of the Left, in some of the successor states, perhaps the weightiest argument is that relating to the 1919 demarcation of frontiers. At the peace conference, the governments of the successor states allied to the Entente, obeying nationalist impulses, aimed at and succeeded in including within their frontiers territories inhabited by large, compact masses of Germans and Hungarians, provoking a virulent irredentism among them which played a part as important in the developments that led to the Second World War as Yugoslav irredentism had played in the developments that led to the tragedy of 1914.

But the historian who lingers over events, deploring that certain things happened, however catastrophic they may have been, instead of concentrating on his task of throwing light on how they happened, is making the mistake of implicitly or explicitly contrasting 'ifs', hypotheses about what might have happened 'if' . . . to what in fact happened. In reality the most perspicacious protagonists of the last phases in Austria-Hungary at the time of its break up, when they spoke with sincerity, acknowledged that military defeat merely set the seal on the inability of the Habsburg monarchy to keep pace with the requirements of the times. On October 27, 1918, Count Burian, who until three days previously had been the Austro-Hungarian Foreign Minister, noted in his diary: 'The whole of my political activity suffered from the fact that it was impossible to correct our internal and external conditions in a progressive direction and thereby prevent the catastrophe that is now taking place.' The German-Austrians and the Magyars, he went on, 'have never been willing to do what foresight, if not a sense of justice, commanded. Where there was understanding there was no courage; when understanding peeped out, it was immediately reviled, and this went on into our own time.' The peace efforts that should have been made were blocked by excessive pretensions or illusions, sometimes by Germany, sometimes by Austria-Hungary herself. 'We were not capable of internal reforms to the extent necessary', he concluded. And on December 19 of the same year, referring chiefly to Hungary, his native country, he wrote: 'A dreadful historical nemesis. The fruit of fifty years of bad and anachronistic policy.'

This frank confession by a man who had served Austria-Hungary in high office (with brief interruptions, he had been a leading member of the government since 1903) does him credit, but it nevertheless corroborates that it was the governing class of the Habsburg monarchy, though it was composed of very civilized people, most of

[255]

them highly cultivated and often also well-meaning, which made its end inevitable. Austria-Hungary, a multi-national state, could live only while the devotion to the dynasty of its governing class put the latter above the passions that agitated the nationalities to which its individual members belonged. In a period in which nationalism was reviving everywhere, as soon as the dominant groups in Austria-Hungary began to feel themselves to be German or Hungarian nationalists, the empire in which they represented no more than minorities was doomed.

APPENDIX I

German and British Documents on the Peace Feelers between the Entente and Austria-Hungary

The publication of the second volume, relating to 1917, of the German documents on the attitude of Germany, and also of Austria-Hungary, to the question of peace, and the fact that the British records for the whole period of the First World War are now accessible, call for a summary of the light they throw on the peace feelers that took place between the Vienna government and those of London and Paris.[1]

The German documents contain nothing previously unknown on the soundings for a separate peace carried out by Prince Sixtus and Prince Xavier of Bourbon-Parma, the brothers of the Empress Zita of Austria.[2] They merely confirm that Bethmann-Hollweg, the Reich Chancellor, was informed on May 13, 1917, on the occasion of a visit to Vienna, of the content of their conversations, but not of the two letters handed by Charles I to his brother-in-law Prince Sixtus (in the first of which the Austrian Emperor referred to the restoration to France of Alsace-Lorraine as '*les justes revendications françaises*').[3]

As is known, following the contacts that the new sovereign's consort made soon after Francis Joseph's death on November 21, 1916, through her mother, the Duchess of Bourbon-Parma, with her brothers, Prince Sixtus and Prince Xavier, who were officers in the Belgian army, the two princes went secretly to Vienna, where on March 23 and 24, 1917, they met their brother-in-law, Charles I, and his Foreign Minister, Count Czernin. (On March 5, Prince Sixtus had been received by Poincaré, the French President, who gave his approval to the seeking of a negotiated peace with Austria-Hungary. On his return to the West, Prince Sixtus was again received by Poincaré on March 31, and on April 18 by the British Prime Minister, Lloyd George.) Czernin did not inform the German government of this first approach. But he did not conceal from Bethmann-Hollweg his belief that a general peace could be attained only by the cession to France of at any rate a part of Alsace-Lorraine, and he said that in his opinion Germany would be acting in her own interests and those of her allies by not dismissing on principle the possibility of such a step, however painful it might be, and by seeking compensation for it in territories in eastern Europe that might be incorporated at the expense of Russia, where the revolution was in full swing.[4]

Prince Sixtus returned to Vienna, this time alone, in the first week of May. A few days later, Czernin informed Bethmann-Hollweg, according to what the latter wrote to William II the next day (May 14), that the Entente governments had offered Austria-Hungary a 'separate peace in exchange for the cession to Italy of the Trentino and some island or other'.[5] In Czernin's view a possible 'legitimate' separate peace, i.e. a peace that Austria-Hungary would conclude only with the consent of her German ally, would not be detrimental to the German military situation, for the Austro-Hungarian troops no longer required on the Italian front could be concentrated in Russia, thus enabling large German forces there to be transferred to the Western Front. Moreover, if the allied naval blockade were withdrawn from Austria-Hungary, the latter would be able to import foodstuffs by way of its ports on the Adriatic, and would be able to let Germany, which had great need of them, have some of these.[6]

Bethmann-Hollweg was not wrong, however, in describing this proposal as unclear and suspecting that the Entente's purpose was to divide Austria-Hungary from Germany in order to improve its own chances of defeating the latter.[7] Czernin was of course too intelligent not to realize that this was the Entente aim. What he did not know, perhaps, was that the proposal that only the Trentino and a few islands be ceded to Italy had been made without the Italian government's knowledge. (When Ribot, the French Prime Minister and Foreign Minister, without giving all the details about the soundings that had taken place, told the Italian Foreign Minister at St Jean de la Maurienne on April 19, 1917, that there was a possibility of a separate peace with Austria-Hungary, Sonnino refused to consider the possibility so as not to have to renounce the Italian claim to any of the Austro-Hungarian territories promised under the Treaty of London of 1915.)

On May 17, Czernin went to Kreuznach to meet Bethmann-Hollweg and Hindenburg for the purpose of jointly formulating the war aims of the Central Powers. It was agreed on that occasion that, in the event of peace negotiations, Austria-Hungary would insist on the complete integrity of her own territory, on the annexation of Lovcen, on rectifications of her frontier with Serbia, and on the military, economic and political dependence on the Habsburg monarchy of Serbia and Montenegro. In the event of Germany's being able to annex Courland and Lithuania and secure total domination over former Russian Poland, the Germans would recognize

[258]

Austrian-Hungarian political hegemony over Romania, though with safeguards for a German share in the exploitation of the Romanian economy.[8] So far from agreeing to concessions to Italy, the Kreuznach agreement laid down that 'Italy must be removed from Valona'.[9]

The Paris and London governments were of course unaware of the Kreuznach decisions, but it was evident to them that Sonnino's intransigence on the one hand and the Austrian refusal to make substantial concessions to Italy on the other meant that Prince Sixtus's mission was doomed to failure. What Lloyd George himself wrote about it is confirmed in substance by a memorandum on the peace feelers with Austria-Hungary drafted in May 1918 by Sir Maurice Hankey, the Secretary to the War Cabinet.[10] According to this memorandum, while on June 8, 1917, Lloyd George had proposed to the War Cabinet that there should be negotiations with Austria-Hungary for a separate peace on the basis of concessions to Italy similar to those which the Vienna government in May 1915 had been willing to make in return for Italian neutrality, at a meeting of the War Cabinet on July 20 he put the case for a joint allied offensive (i.e. by the Italian army reinforced by Anglo-French heavy artillery and other aid) on the Austro-Italian front. This, in Lloyd George's view, should have led to the capture of Trieste, thus forcing Austria-Hungary to yield that city and the Trentino if it wanted to secure peace.[11] This proposal was submitted to Paris on July 25–26, but was rejected by the French army commanders, with whom the British commanders were in agreement. At the beginning of September, however, the French generals changed their mind and said that they were willing to send 100 heavy guns to Italy, but this time General Cadorna decided that the autumn was too far advanced for a big offensive.[12]

On August 14, however, Lloyd George reported to the War Cabinet that peace feelers with Vienna were not yet at an end. He had had information from Paris about the existence of promising contacts between Painlevé (Minister of War in Ribot's Government) and Count Czernin.[13]

Except for the report published in a Paris newspaper in 1920 by Count Armand, one of the French emissaries, practically nothing has yet been found in the Quai d'Orsay archives about Painlevé's Austrian contacts, but the second volume of German documents previously quoted is full of them. The fact that Lloyd George considered the information he received about Painlevé's contacts with Czernin sufficiently important to mention them at a meeting of the War Cabinet means that the German documents on the subject cannot be ignored. Though some of them are based on unconfirmable facts, their wealth of detail is far greater than that in the recollections of Count Revertera, Count Armand's Austrian opposite number.

A sister of Julius Szeps, the editor of an authoritative Vienna newspaper, was married to Paul Clemenceau, a brother of the famous statesman. Sophie Szeps-Clemenceau's Paris *salon* was frequented by many eminent men, including Briand, and by Painlevé in particular. Julius Szeps's other sister, Berta, was married to a Vienna physician of high repute, Professor Emil Zuckerkandl, and knew Czernin.[14] The two sisters, one coming from Paris and the other from Vienna, met at Vevey in Switzerland. The German Minister in Switzerland was immediately informed of this through a friend of Frau Zuckerkandl's, the writer Harry Kessler. His long report, dated July 31, 1917, obviously relates what Frau Zuckerkandl told him she had been told by her sister. According to it, Painlevé who, like Lloyd George, was opposed to offensives in France because of their cost and their futility, had been wanting to inform Czernin since March that France wanted to make a separate peace with Austria-Hungary. (We do not know whether Painlevé, the Minister of War, had been informed of Prince Sixtus's mission, which was supposed to be a jealously guarded secret among Poincaré, Ribot and the Secretary-General of the Quai d'Orsay.) When Czernin reacted unfavourably to an invitation intended to divide Vienna from Berlin, Painlevé allegedly informed him that France would not be opposed to making peace with Germany too if Alsace-Lorraine were restored to her; in exchange she would be willing to grant Germany colonial compensations.[15]

From an Austro-Hungarian note on Czernin's meeting on August 1, 1917, with Michaelis, the new German Chancellor, and other representatives of the Reich, it appears that the Austrian Foreign Minister reiterated on this occasion that Austria-Hungary would in any case remain loyal to Germany, but feared that she would not be able to stand up to a fourth winter of the war, and that her collapse might drag her German ally down to ruin too. In view of the chaos that prevailed in Petrograd, Czernin believed a separate peace with Russia to be impossible, though peace with France might be possible if Germany made concessions in Alsace-Lorraine. To compensate Germany, Austria-Hungary would be willing to leave her the whole of Poland, adding Galicia to Russian Poland, while in turn Austria-Hungary would be compensated in Romania.[16] The Germans who four months earlier (under the pressure of their generals who, however, were not present at the August 1 meeting) had wanted Austria-Hungary finally to renounce Russian Poland in their favour, now objected that Czernin's offer represented a burden rather than

[260]

an advantage to them. On the other hand, though they did not exclude the possibility of discussing concessions, though very small ones, in Alsace-Lorraine, they did not believe that France would make peace independently of Britain.[17] In fact, General Ludendorff, at his meeting with Michaelis on August 9, caused it to be decided that Germany could yield nothing or practically nothing in Alsace-Lorraine; that she intended to secure for herself the economic advantages of the French mining area of Longwy-Briey and had no intention of surrendering her domination over Belgium; and that she was not interested in Galicia, but intended that the existing agreement that assigned Russian Poland to her in return for concessions to Austria-Hungary in Romania should be maintained.[18] Ludendorff's insistence on keeping Belgium in German hands (though with Belgian sovereignty apparently maintained) notoriously led to the failure in the next few weeks of Pope Benedict XV's proposal for a negotiated peace between the two *blocs*.[19]

On August 30, the Austro-Hungarian ambassador in Berlin told the German Secretary of State in the Foreign Ministry that Painlevé had informed Czernin that he was willing to meet him in Switzerland.[20] Some weeks later, the Germans discovered through Count Kessler that Czernin had been deceiving himself in believing that Painlevé, who in the meantime (on September 12) had become Prime Minister, would go to Switzerland himself; in his place he would send a personal friend, one Bernard, who has not been further identified, provided that Czernin sent Julius Szeps, Mme Clemenceau's brother, to meet him. Czernin had probably gathered his false impression as a result of the conversation that his emissary, Count Revertera, had had with Count Armand, on August 7–8 and on August 22, whether on the initiative of Vienna or that of Paris is uncertain.[21] Armand had submitted to Revertera a French proposal for peace negotiations on the basis of the restoration to their pre-war situation of Belgium, Serbia and Romania (except that Serbia would be granted access to the sea and union with Montenegro), the cession to France of Alsace-Lorraine in return for the transfer of some colonies to Germany, and of Trent and Trieste to Italy, in return for incorporation into Austria of the whole of Poland, restored to her 1772 frontiers.[22] Czernin, informing the Germans of this proposal, called it a 'bad joke' and said that Austria-Hungary would yield nothing to Italy.[23] But he suggested replying that the Central Powers would be willing to negotiate a general peace on the basis of the renunciation of annexations by all the belligerents, apart from some frontier rectifications, and on the basis of compensations for Germany in eastern Europe and for Austria-Hungary in the Balkans.

[261]

Czernin later confided to his German colleague Kühlmann that in the event of a separate peace with Austria-Hungary the French offered her, in return for the cession of the Trentino, not only supremacy over Poland and Romania, but also the incorporation into the Habsburg empire of Bavaria, Saxony and Silesia, in other words the dismemberment of Germany.[24] The Frenchmen who had drafted this proposal were obviously living in imagination in a distant and irrecoverable past, but it showed the importance they attached to the detachment of Austria-Hungary from Germany. Czernin assured the Germans that he had rejected all *ballons d'essai* of this kind, but added that he would nevertheless be willing to meet Painlevé if the Germans agreed. Kühlmann advised him against it, however.[25]

According to subsequent information from the German legation in Berne, a meeting between personal emissaries of Painlevé and Czernin (the latter's nominee would have been Julius Szeps) was to have taken place in Switzerland on October 10, but was called off at the last moment by the French Prime Minister, whose government was already in difficulties.[26] When she returned to Vienna at the end of October, Frau Zuckerkandl herself called on the German ambassador with her brother and told him that the state of mind in France, as reported to her by her sister, was such that no negotiations were possible that did not contemplate the cession of Alsace-Lorraine.[27]

Austria-Hungary continued to receive suggestions for a separate peace from France and Britain, and also from America. But at his meeting with the German leaders on November 6, 1917 Czernin tied his hands. He undertook to sign the post-war thirty years alliance with Germany that the Germans had been pressing upon him for sometime. Germany, compensating herself in Romania, which Austria-Hungary renounced, undertook to leave Russian Poland to Austria.[28]

The Bolshevik revolution was not of course foreseen in the Austro-German conversations, which actually took place on the day immediately preceding it, and the participants, though they took the Russian defeat for granted, did not mention the political consequences that might flow from it. Czernin did not immediately appreciate that the Bolshevik revolution, though it relieved the military situation of the Central Powers, confronted them with a materialization of the slogan of self-determination for all nations, which had previously been no more than propaganda. The Central Powers of course claimed to be applying that principle at Brest-Litovsk when they recognized the independence of the Ukraine, from which they expected large supplies of corn. But Austria-Hungary was obliged to give the Ukrainians the district of Cholm which it had occupied, thus irretrievably offending

[262]

the Poles, who claimed that district as an integral part of historical Poland.

Thus it was an illusion on Czernin's part to believe that he solved the Polish question in November 1917. This illusion, jointly with the euphoria resulting from Caporetto, the Russian armistice, and the probability of the consequent capitulation of Romania, played its part in persuading him to reject the further offers of a separate peace made to him by the British government, though these were much firmer and more authoritative than those made previously.

The Vienna documents date the beginning of the British feelers as of the beginning of November 1917.[29] The British Foreign Office documents show, however, that Anglo-Austrian contacts in Switzerland (there were others in Holland which we shall not discuss) dated back to the summer of that year. The British Minister in Berne, Sir Horace Rumbold, informed his government on July 17 and August 18, 1917, that the Pasha Djemil Tussun (a relative of the Khedive of Egypt) had been approached by Skrzynski, the counsellor of the Austrian legation in Switzerland, whom he knew well, and had been told by him that the Vienna government would be willing to send Count Mensdorff, the former Austro-Hungarian ambassador in London, to Switzerland to meet a possible British emissary.[30] The Austrian and German documents show that, coinciding with the first contacts of the Szeps sisters, but specifically at the instigation of Professor Haguenin, whom the Quai d'Orsay also used for contacts with German agents, Mensdorff had already gone to Switzerland in March 1917 to meet a French representative, but had been recalled to Vienna because no one of equal status had been sent from Paris.[31] Still according to a report (dated October 13) by the British Minister in Berne, Skrzynski reopened the matter, asking Tussun whether the British government would respond to the idea of sending Mensdorff to Switzerland.[32] Sir Horace Rumbold's message of October 31 is even more definite. Skrzynski had told Tussun that he had been instructed by Czernin to inform Britain 'that if she were prepared to have an *officieuse* conversation on the subject of peace, the Austrian government would pledge its honour to keep the matter secret. Czernin would be disposed immediately to make a declaration guaranteeing the integrity of Italian territory as it existed before the war, in spite of the favourable turn which events are taking for Austria on the Italian front'.[33]

This last phrase was undoubtedly a result of Austrian over-valuation of the Italian defeat at Caporetto. The stumbling-block that had led to the failure of Prince Sixtus's mission had been the Italian claims to Austrian territory. If, as seemed possible in the

[263]

first few days after Caporetto, Italy had been prostrate, she would have had to drop her claims and accept peace. On November 3, the British informed the French and Italian—and also the Russian—governments of this proposal by Czernin.[34] It can be taken for granted that the news helped to induce Orlando, the new Italian Prime Minister, to adopt the two-pronged policy which, as we have said, he set in train at the beginning of 1918, on the one hand trying to discover through the Vatican whether Austria-Hungary would be willing, in spite of Caporetto, to make concessions to Italy in order to secure peace, and on the other, in the expectation of an Austrian refusal of substantial concessions, of using the slogan of self-determination of the nations to encourage the revolution of the Slav nationalities within the Habsburg monarchy.

Sir Horace Rumbold was instructed by his government to inform Vienna that Britain was willing to negotiate only in agreement with her allies, but was ready to listen to any Austrian proposals.[35] According to Rumbold's telegram of November 23, Czernin replied that 'the Austrian nation is very favourably disposed towards the English nation' and that he was ready to send Mensdorff, or alternatively Count Mérey, another authoritative ex-ambassador, to Switzerland if an assurance were given that a personality of equivalent status would come from London. The Foreign Office informed Rumbold that the matter would be submitted to the inter-allied conference in Paris. We know from the Italian documents that it was so submitted, and that the Italian representatives noted that fact resentfully. On November 29, Balfour telegraphed to Rumbold that he had no objections to the meeting proposed by Czernin.[36] Thus it came about that Mensdorff went to Switzerland at the beginning of December and the British sent no less a personality than General Smuts, who was accompanied by Philip Kerr, Lloyd George's private secretary.

The choice of Smuts, a member of the Imperial War Cabinet, showed the importance that Lloyd George and Balfour attributed to the matter. Their instructions to the South African statesman were to tell the Austrians that, if they freed themselves from the domination of Germany, they could count on the 'full sympathy and support' of the British Empire.[37] When Rumbold asked whether he should inform his French and Italian colleagues of the course of the conversations, the Foreign Office at first instructed him not to do so.[38] Only after some indiscretions had leaked out (through Wickham Steed), did Lloyd George personally give information about them to President Wilson, Clemenceau and Orlando.[39]

Smuts's report was published in due course by Lloyd George. The conversations were abortive because the Vienna government refused to contemplate either a separate peace or cessions of Austrian territory. On the contrary, Mensdorff was instructed by Czernin to ask for the Italian evacuation of Valona and was authorized to give an assurance of the restoration of Serbia and Montenegro only subject to guarantees for the security of Austria-Hungary which, in the opinion of Mensdorff himself, might well imply the displacement of the Karageorgević dynasty.[40]

After Lloyd George (in his speech of January 5, 1918) and President Wilson (in his Fourteen Points) had publicly declared that they did not desire the dismemberment of Austria-Hungary, Skrzynski informed Rumbold that Czernin was willing to come to Switzerland himself for a conversation with the British Prime Minister.[41] This idea, which was suggested to Czernin by Mensdorff—who, like Smuts, believed it a mistake to break off the conversations—led to nothing, for one thing because in the weeks that followed, the Austro-Hungarian Foreign Minister was engaged in peace negotiations with the Russians at Brest-Litovsk and, with the Romanians at Bucharest. The outcome of those negotiations, so favourable to the Central Powers, made Czernin less willing than ever to detach himself from Germany. It was now the time of the Foreign Office to take the initiative and on March 2, Rumbold received a telegram: 'Have any developments taken place? We are anxious that the door shall remain ajar and that Austria should not think that there is no chance of further conversations.'[42] On March 6, the War Cabinet decided again to send Philip Kerr to Switzerland to find out whether Austria-Hungary would be willing to discuss peace and 'if so, the general line of the Austrian programme'.[43] On March 12, Lloyd George telegraphed to Kerr in Berne that, if the latter thought it advisable, he would again send Smuts to Switzerland to meet Czernin.[44] It was obvious, in view of the imminent German offensive, that for the time being it would be possible to discuss only a separate peace, so Czernin declined again to send Mensdorff to Switzerland, though the latter, according to his diary, was very insistent that the thread should not be dropped. Czernin informed Rumbold and Kerr through Skrzynski that there was no point in conversations so long as France and Italy failed to renounce their desire to annex German and Austrian territories respectively.[45] Kerr's comment was that in a few months' time, when Austria-Hungary's hopes, based largely on the amplitude of the corn supplies she expected from the Ukraine, had been disappointed, she would change her attitude.[46] This prediction turned out to be correct. Austria-Hungary indeed changed her attitude, but too late: at the end of the summer of 1918. In Rumbold's opinion, Czernin wanted a compromise peace as long as he feared that the food shortage might cause strikes and disorders which would lead to the collapse of Austria, but the peace of Brest-Litovsk and the German offensive on the Western Front revived his hopes of victory.[47]

In the memorandum that Kerr drew up on his return from Switzerland, he did not exclude an alternative theory, namely that Austria would rather negotiate with the United States than with Britain, as the United States was not committed by any treaty to the Italian claims.[48] We now know that, while this was not true of Czernin who, with his characteristic impressionability, was convinced that Germany was about to win the war on the Western Front and therefore thought it essential to repudiate even the conversations that his Emperor had tried to set in train with President Wilson, it was true of Charles I. The last Austrian Emperor intended to continue his contacts with the American President, though he could not summon up the resolution necessary to take the steps and make the concessions required to make them successful.

APPENDIX II

The Austro-Hungarian Pacifists and the United States

In the introduction to his book on the subject, the well-known Austrian historian Heinrich Benedikt observes that, while the memoirs and literature on the 1917 peace efforts are endless, insufficient attention has been paid to the talks that, in his opinion, had perhaps the best chances of success, that is to say those which the Vienna industrialist Julius Meinl had at Geneva at the end of 1917, with the consent of the Emperor Charles I, with the American publicist G. D. Herron, who was authorized by President Wilson and the State Department to engage in discussions with the Austrian emissaries and report to Washington and London.[1] Meinl was an able business man and industrialist who quite naturally became the organizer of one of the Austro-Hungarian supply services; he was a cultivated man, and also showed that he had political flair. The importance of the conversations derived from the fact that the American President, unlike the French and British governments, was, as we have seen, not bound by any treaty to support Italian, Serbian and Romanian claims to territories belonging to Austria-Hungary. Wilson would have been free, had he wished, to come to agreement with the Austro-Hungarian government without taking into account the secret treaties made by the Entente with Italy and Romania or the undertakings it had given to Serbia.

Herron gave a brief account of the final phase of the conversations in a volume published in 1922 in memory of the last Prime Minister of the Austrian empire, the distinguished jurist Professor Heinrich Lammasch, a member of the Vienna Upper House and the International Court of Arbitration at The Hague and a friend of Meinl, whose mission to Geneva he followed up in February 1918.[2] Herron's revelations, as well as those of one of his wartime colleagues, S. Osusky, who later became Minister of the Czechoslovak Republic in London, and the diary of the German democratic deputy Konrad Haussmann, one of the artificers of the new parliamentary régime in Germany in October 1918, whom Meinl put in touch with the American emissary, have been supplemented by his ample papers, which have been partially used by his biographer, M. P. Briggs, and

[267]

another American scholar, R. H. Lutz; the United States diplomatic documents which have been published; the voluminous biographies of President Wilson; the memoirs of Hugh L. Wilson, the American chargé d'affaires in Switzerland, and those of W. G. Sharp, the American ambassador in France, as well as by those of the German pacifist F. W. Foerster, a professor at the universities of Zürich, Vienna and Munich, who in the summer of 1917, authorized by Meinl and Lammasch, went to see Herron and began the peace feelers which we are discussing.[3]

Meinl's and Lammasch's families made their papers available to H. Benedikt, who has published the essence of them, consisting of the political letters that they exchanged and the memoranda on the Austrian economic and international situation written by Meinl between 1916 and 1918 for the use of his country's Foreign Minister and the Emperor himself. Benedikt has supplemented these documents by police reports of the discussions that took place in the Österreichische Politische Gesellschaft, a club formed in 1915 by Meinl, Lammasch and Professor Josef Redlich, the distinguished historian and student of politics, for the purpose of offering a forum to more responsible members of the educated class and political circles who, as a result of the press censorship and the closing of the Austrian parliament, had no opportunity of airing their views. Among those who took part in its discussions were some of the more moderate, but not least influential, leaders of the strong Austrian Social Democratic Party, such as Friedrich Austerlitz, the editor of the *Arbeiterzeitung*, the party organ, and Karl Renner, the future Chancellor (and after the Second World War the President) of the Republic, who was then the leading theorist of the Austro-Marxist movement on the burning nationalities question.

Benedikt also consulted—as we have done—the voluminous notebooks on Austria and Italy contained in the Herron papers at the Hoover Institution on War, Revolution and Peace, which had been inaccessible for twenty-five years.[4]

Meinl was the proprietor of a large firm engaged in foreign trade (in coffee and other food products), with an important branch in London, and his knowledge of the economic resources of the belligerent countries and his conclusion that the outcome of the world war depended on the state of them, resulted, from the middle of 1916 onwards, in his not disguising from himself or from others that time was working against the Central Powers. He knew only too well that their stocks of raw materials and food supplies were exiguous, and that in Vienna and in other Austrian industrial zones the situation was already approaching catastrophe. In a memorandum to Count

[268]

Burian, the Austro-Hungarian Foreign Minister, in September 1916, he therefore stated that it was vitally important to the Central Powers to make a peace move while their military strength was still great.[5]

Although they were completely in the dark about Prince Sixtus's highly secret mission and did not know that the young Emperor had confided to Count Mihály Károlyi, the leader of the parliamentary opposition in Hungary, his burning desire for peace, Lammasch, Meinl and Redlich, the last of whom was on terms of friendship with Count Czernin, were aware that, particularly after the Russian Revolution of March 1917, the policy in high places was to bring about as rapidly as possible an end to a war that threatened to over-whelm the Habsburg monarchy in a wave of revolution.[6]

Meinl, with the directness and logic characteristic of a man of action, stated in a discussion in the Politsche Gesellschaft in May 1917 and in a memorandum to the Foreign Minister the two preliminary conditions essential for any serious peace negotiations: the explicit renunciation of all annexationist intentions by the Central Powers and the granting of full autonomy to the non-German nationalities of the Austrian empire, recognizing their complete parity of rights with the German Austrians.[7]

As far as the first of these two conditions was concerned, Austria-Hungary would have to present Germany with a *fait accompli*; the initiative, Meinl pointed out, must therefore come from Vienna. At the time when Meinl wrote his memorandum, i.e. before any Entente government had granted recognition to the national committees of the Czech or Southern Slav *émigrés*, the second matter was a purely Austro-Hungarian domestic affair. We say Austro-Hungarian and not, with Meinl, simply Austrian because the Budapest government—which had no intention of making any autonomist concessions to the non-Magyars, who in Hungary enjoyed far fewer rights than those of their counterparts in Austria—was always able to obstruct—as it had done in 1871—any changes in the constitutional structure of the other half of the dual monarchy.[8] The Hungarian threat (which was indeed carried out when Charles I decided on October 16, 1918, to re-organize Austria into a multinational federal state) in that event to repudiate the 1867 settlement and to consider the historical inde-pendence of the kingdom of Hungary to have been revived, even if the dynasty of Habsburg and Lorraine remained on St Stephen's throne, had become a very real thing in view of the preponderance that the Hungarians had acquired since the beginning of the war because of their military significance and the importance of their food supplies; the Austrians seemed to have much more need of them than they had of the Austrians. The Budapest government would not have resigned itself to co-existence with an Austria in which all the nationalities had been made equal and autonomous. Redlich and Lammasch were acutely aware of this, the former because as a historian he had studied the development of the complex and difficult relations between Austria and Hungary, and the latter because, as one of Francis Ferdinand's political advisers, he had taken a prominent part in the working out of the Archduke's plans for breaking the supremacy of the Magyars in the kingdom of Hungary immediately after his accession. The Magyars, after all, constituted only about half of the population of Hungary.[9] But, because of the language difficulty and the difference in political environment, the Austrians found it hard in practice to find their way about in the Hungarian political world.[10]

The weakness of the Austrian advocates of a rapid peace was also shown by their lack of close co-operation with Károlyi, who not only shared their aim but also had not hesitated to proclaim his ardent pacifism in the Hungarian Lower House since the end of 1915, defying the insults and threats of Tisza's followers. Meinl, Lammasch and Redlich knew Károlyi personally, but did not dare establish political links with him.[11] They abided by the constitutional practice by which relations with Hungary must be conducted through the sovereign and those Ministers that were shared by the two governments. This weakness—which H. Benedikt himself does not take into consideration—was the graver in that Germany exploited the fact that the Hungarian dominant class shared the determination of its German counterpart to fight the war à outrance.

Polzer-Hoditz, the Emperor's private secretary, who by virtue of his office and his own belief in a peace policy put Charles I into contact with the Austrian and Hungarian pacifists, did not like Károlyi; he suspected him of being a revolutionary par excellence and feared he would lead Hungary, not to closer co-operation with the Habsburg dynasty but—like Kossuth in 1849—to total detachment from it. This was indeed what happened in November 1918, but not because of any long-standing aspiration for this on the part of Károlyi who, at any rate up to the end of the previous year, would, if Charles I had accepted his programme, have remained a loyal servant of the Crown to which his family was bound by long-standing ties, which had not been broken even by the unjust shooting of his illustrious great-uncle L. Batthyány, the Prime Minister of 1848.

Károlyi certainly made no concealment of his dislike of the alliance with the German empire, which he had criticized since 1912 and which, he was now convinced, was dragging Austria-Hungary down to ruin with itself. 'Károlyi,' wrote his closest colleague of the previous

[270]

two years, the historian O. Jászi, to R. W. Seton-Watson in 1919, 'is not only a man of noble and firm character—and how rare such persons are in Hungarian public life!—but he is also a sincere democrat and a true pacifist, and he was a true friend of the Entente even before the war and in the midst of the greatest German victories'.[12]

Polzer-Hoditz, in spite of his genuine desire for peace, was too much of a German patriot—as, incidentally, Redlich was also—to be able to share this view. Among the German Austrians, Lammasch alone was opposed to the alliance with Berlin. France and Britain would have been glad to conclude a separate peace with Austria-Hungary, but this presupposed the detachment of Vienna from Berlin. Károlyi, according to his memoirs, the accuracy of which is confirmed by the documents, as we shall see, frankly said so in his first audience with Charles I on March 22, 1917.

The Habsburg monarchy could have taken the wind out of the sails of the *delenda Austria* campaign being waged in the Entente countries by the Czech and Yugoslav *émigrés* by carrying out the required reforms, which would have enabled it to count on the loyalty of the great majority of its peoples in the inevitably difficult task of resisting the furious reaction of Germany to the defection of its ally. But to begin serious peace negotiations or to undertake the domestic reforms necessary to make them successful involved boldness (even at the cost of sacrifices), and Károlyi was alone in practising and preaching boldness. It was a grave error on Polzer-Hoditz's part to have made it difficult (as he himself says he did) for Charles I to accept the inclusion of Károlyi (whom he had previously promised to appoint his Minister *ad latere*) in the Hungarian coalition government that followed Tisza's dismissal in June 1917.[13]

When the Austrian parliament met in Vienna on May 30, 1917, the government of Count Clam-Martinic (who was of Czech origin but was opposed to granting autonomy to his fellow-nationals) had to resign. The Emperor consulted Lammasch and Meinl among others, and offered the prime ministership to the former because of his international reputation as a pacifist of long standing. Lammasch because he felt weak and ill and faced the hostility of Czernin, with whom he had always disagreed at the time when both were intimates of Francis Ferdinand, declined. Polzer-Hoditz, on Meinl's advice, then proposed that the post should be given to Redlich, with Lammasch at the Ministry of Justice and Meinl at the Trade Ministry. The Emperor received both Redlich and Meinl. The latter submitted a memorandum stating his ideas for the autonomous reform of the state. Under it, nationalities would be on an equal footing of 'personal' rather than 'territorial' self-government (to avoid the problem

[271]

of the ethnically mixed territories)—he had borrowed this idea from the Social Democrat Renner. At his last audience, on July 5, Meinl informed the Emperor that he had learnt from the manager of the branch of his firm at Pilsen that 40,000 workers (mostly Czechs) at the Skoda arms factory there had gone on strike, and that another strike in the neighbouring mining area had already led to bloody clashes.[14] Meinl considered Polzer-Hoditz intelligent but as acting with an amateurish impulsiveness similar to that which, alas, characterized his young sovereign, and he took away the impression that neither really liked the idea of giving the prime ministership to a man of Redlich's robust and solid background.[15] The latter was summoned that evening by the Emperor and was offered the appointment. He accepted it on condition that he kept the Home portfolio for himself and included representatives of the major parties of the various nationalities in the government.[16] Next day the appointment had been revoked. This was the result of the intervention of Czernin, who had stated that Redlich's programme would alarm and shock the German government. The biggest German Austrian party, the Christian Social Party, had also made known its reservations because of Redlich's Jewish origins.[17]

Charles I also received the pacifist German Professor Foerster, whom Lammasch and Meinl had invited to Vienna for a meeting of the Politische Gesellschaft. Foerster recalls in his memoirs that the sole subject of conversation during the audience was his own writings on the federal reorganization of Austria, which Polzer-Hoditz had drawn to the Emperor's attention.[18] A letter from Foerster to Lammasch written a few days later shows his hope that he had convinced Polzer-Hoditz of the urgent necessity of the Emperor's openly showing his will for peace. For that purpose he should have appointed Lammasch Prime Minister. Charles I in fact again offered Lammasch the post, but as soon as the latter expressed his hesitations (this time for the sole purpose of encouraging the Emperor to insist more warmly on his acceptance) Charles I dropped the matter.[19] The post in fact went to a bureaucrat, Seidler. Meinl had the impression that the Emperor's object was solely to gain time, and that after a few months the appointment of a Redlich–Lammasch government would be on the *tapis* again. He told his friends, however, that this presupposed the dismissal of Czernin, the Foreign Minister.[20] In fact Meinl secured Charles I's consent to his secretly approaching an influential British politician of pacifist outlook, Lord Lansdowne, with a view to concerting joint action.[21] According to Meinl, it was his correspondence with Lord Lansdowne that led to the latter's celebrated letter to the *Daily Telegraph*, published on November 29,

[272]

1917. But, as Lord Lansdowne wanted peace with the Central Powers as a whole, i.e. primarily with Germany, it could not fail to be rejected by the greater part of the British political world.

Meanwhile another peace move had repercussions on an entirely different scale. On August 12, Mgr Pacelli, the Papal Nuncio at Munich, handed the Germans Pope Benedict XV's peace note, which was also submitted to Charles I and the British and French heads of state. The consequences of this papal initiative have recently been reconstructed, as far as Austria-Hungary is concerned, by Professor Engel-Janosi.[22]

In Austria, Benedict XV's peace move was followed with intense interest. Meinl considered it to be 'one of the best opportunities for peace that have ever been offered', and undertook to do everything in his power to prevent the Vienna government from allowing Berlin to throw it away. Although foreseeing grave difficulties from Italy, he believed that the greatest concession Austria could make her was to postpone to the peace conference the decision on the future of the Trentino, for which he would agree to a plebiscite, whereas he would not in any event agree to the renunciation of Trieste.[23] Like all Austrians, including the pacifists, he obviously failed to appreciate that the refusal to grant Italy at least what Austria-Hungary had offered her in May 1915 made impossible any compromise with the Entente, which could not sacrifice Italian claims to that extent. This incomprehension vitiated from the outset the contacts with Herron which constitute the main theme of the book by H. Benedikt.

Foerster, besides seeing Herron in Switzerland in July 1917, in fact also saw a British agent, whom he told of his conversation with Charles I on the reorganization of Austria-Hungary into a free federation of peoples, with the possible inclusion of Serbia and Romania in a Habsburg confederation. It would, in his opinion, be a 'blessing in disguise' if the Entente demanded this in possible peace negotiations with Austria-Hungary, as it would be evidence of the dual monarchy's emancipation from Germany. We cannot be sure, but it is not impossible that this statement was the origin of the federation suggestions made by Smuts to Mensdorff in the following December. At all events, the British agent told Foerster that the Entente would not be able to make peace with the Habsburg monarchy unless Trieste were ceded to Italy. Foerster replied that that was out of the question, though the cession of the Trentino and Gorizia did not seem to him personally to be inconceivable. Foerster also met officials of the French legation in Switzerland on this occasion.[24]

But let us come to Herron, whose attention Foerster called in the

[273]

summer of 1917 to Charles I's, Lammasch's, and Meinl's desire for peace. George Davis Herron, a self-taught professor of Theology, was the son of a professional soldier. He grew up in poverty, educated himself, worked as a printer and became a Congregationalist minister, his great Christian socialist missionary fervour soon attracting attention. In 1899 he joined the American Socialist Party and became one of its most eloquent speakers, which caused him to lose his university chair. He left the church when he divorced his first wife and then married the daughter of the wealthy Mrs Rand, whom he later persuaded to found the School of Social Sciences in New York. At the end of 1904, the Herrons moved to Europe and settled at Fiesole, where they bought a villa.[25] The outbreak of war in 1914 caused Herron, who, like the many revolutionary syndicalists with whom he was on close terms, had an especially violent aversion to Prussian military imperialism, to leave Italy, which was still allied with the Central Powers, and move to Switzerland, where he settled in a villa in Geneva. His first political activity on Swiss soil which we have been able to trace has been insufficiently investigated both by his biographer and by H. Benedikt, so it seems worth while exhuming it.

The papers of Robert Grimm, the well-known Swiss Social Democrat and organizer of the international socialist conferences at Zimmerwald and Kienthal in 1915–16 and secretary of the International Socialist Committee established as a result, include a number of letters from Herron, who wrote to him as from one comrade to another. The first, in French, is dated July 1, 1916. Enclosed with it was the sum of 100 Swiss francs as Herron's contribution to the expenses of internationalist propaganda; according to the correspondence that follows, he continued to send this sum monthly for more than a year.[26] In a long letter in German dated September 20, 1916, Herron states that a victory for Germany would be the worst of disasters, for it would make the whole world subject to militarily organized German capitalism. In his view, the neutralism and pacifism that were flourishing in the United States ran the risk of playing into the hands of pan-German imperialism, since in the existing military situation a stalemate peace would be equivalent to a victory for the Germans, who were in occupation of vast territories in Europe which belonged to their enemies.[27] In another letter, dated September 30, 1916, he states his belief that the Internationalist Socialist Committee appointed in Zimmerwald—not the old secretariat of the Second International, which was in Belgian hands—was faced with the task of reconstructing the latter, on a basis different from that prevailing before the war, when it was dominated by the German Social Democrats, who had sullied their good name in 1914 by supporting a war of aggression. The committee should therefore not, like the Vatican, favour a compromise peace from which imperial Germany would benefit, but should back the German revolution.[28]

In 1916, as he did not conceal from Grimm, Herron was pursuing the aim of facilitating and, as a progressive democratic publicist, advocating the intervention in the war of the United States on the side of Germany's enemies; he foresaw this intervention at a time when few thought it possible. Consistently with this, he spoke at a meeting at Lausanne of the Union des Nationalités presided over by the Belgian Professor Paul Otlet. 'If America is to intervene,' he said, in the course of a speech that obviously favoured the cause of the Entente, which, he maintained, was fighting for the liberation of the subject nations, 'it will intervene to restore peace. There can be no peace as long as there are oppressed nations. The nationality principle must be recognized without compromises.'[29]

Herron was delighted at the re-election of President Wilson, and commented in the Swiss newspapers on the note that the American President sent to the belligerents in December 1916 calling on them to declare the terms on which they would be willing to make peace. In a letter to the *Journal de Genève* he said that the war aims of the Entente were the re-establishment of the independence of the countries invaded by the Central Powers, the restoration of Alsace-Lorraine to France, the return to Italy of the Italian territories still in Austrian possession, and the liberation of Bohemia. Germany's war aims were so vast, he said, that she could not confess them. This would force the United States to take up arms to impose a just peace.[30]

When he was approached by Foerster, whom he knew from the international pacifist movement, he immediately introduced him at his Geneva villa to the Italian minister in Switzerland, Marquis Raniero Paulucci de'Calboli, in whose presence he said that all those who desired peace must put their trust in President Wilson.[31]

After the American intervention, Herron published a collection of his own articles under the title *Woodrow Wilson and the World's Peace*,[32] and his interpretation of the Democratic President's universal mission pleased the latter greatly. At the President's request, the State Department asked him to submit regular reports on the European situation based on the many contacts he had in Switzerland, which was then the best neutral observation point. Herron's reports, which always reached the President's desk, were sent first by way of the American embassy in Paris and then through the American legation in Berne. Word of his valuable intelligence work came to the knowledge of the British, who wanted to have the benefit of it too, and he was authorized to send copies to the Foreign Office.

Consequently he came to be considered by many Europeans, including men in positions of high responsibility, as a confidant, of and almost a spokesman, for President Wilson. In fact he had no right to speak in the President's name, but, at any rate in public, Wilson never repudiated him. On the contrary, he several times adopted Herron's suggestions, and at the beginning of 1919 nominated him as one of the two American delegates to the meeting with the Bolshevik government which was to have been held at Prinkipo, but never took place.[33]

Herron had been in contact with the Italian Minister in Berne and his counsellor, Marquis Durazzo, since the end of 1916.[34] In arranging a meeting between Professor Foerster, who was a German citizen but was the spokesman on this occasion of highly placed Austrian circles, and the diplomatic representative of Italy, he was evidently motivated by the realistic belief that no Austro-Hungarian peace move could succeed without the consent of the Italian government which had the greatest interest in the matter on the other side of the barricades. He also saw plainly that if Italy wished to avoid isolation, she must recast and clarify her demands, harmonizing them with the broad lines of President Wilson's policy. This is shown by his letter of August 15, 1917 to Marquis Durazzo, which from the context seems to be in reply to a suggestion by the Italian legation that he should go to Rome to state his views to the Italian Foreign Ministry.[35] In it he advised Italy publicly to state her war aims, which should be laid down in the spirit of Mazzini and Cavour, and to reach an agreement, both with Serbia and with President Wilson, which would enable her to be regarded by the United States as its best ally in the new Europe that would emerge from the war.[36]

As is shown by Meinl's letter to Lammasch of September 2, 1917, Foerster had asked him as a matter of urgency to send him reports of the meetings of the Politische Gesellschaft for submission to Herron.[37] Herron had introduced Foerster also to Hugh Wilson, the American chargé d'affaires in Berne, and the two Americans gathered from their conversations with him that Austria would be willing to yield the Trentino and Trieste to Italy and reorganize herself into a confederation to satisfy her other nationalities, provided the Entente protected her from Germany and, in regard to the problem of confederation, helped her to overcome the resistance of Hungary.[38]

Their belief in the willingness of the Austrian Emperor to meet the minimum Italian demands was, however, unfounded. H. Benedikt's view is that Foerster said no more about Charles I's intentions than he was entitled to say with certainty, but that Herron, excited at the enormous prospects opened up by the glimmer of hope he saw, gave free rein with regard to Austrian federation to his imagination; the

Emperor was not then thinking of diluting his Empire into a con-federation.[39] However that may be, Herron was right in believing that the essential thing was to find a point of agreement with Italian aims. Let us recall that, since the cessation of hostilities on the Russian and Romanian fronts, the only army still fighting the Austro-Hungarians was the Italian.

We have already noted that neither Meinl nor Lammasch was willing to accept the obvious conclusion that Austria could secure peace only at the price of concessions to Italy not smaller than those of May 1915. Charles I and his Foreign Minister were even more reluctant. Nevertheless, that was the reason why Prince Sixtus's mission had failed. The second letter (on May 9, 1917) he gave his brother-in-law, the Emperor, to justify his rejection of the Italian claims of which he had been informed by Sixtus after his first mission, referred to an offer of a separate peace in return for the cession of the Trentino alone which had been submitted to him by Italian emiss-aries.[40] Czernin, to show that he was unaware of the Emperor's letter, denied two years after his resignation that any Italian approach had ever taken place.[41] The German documents show, however, that he knew about it. At all events, information about it was for-warded to Berlin in February 1917 by the German Minister to Switzerland. On March 26 the German leaders discussed it with Czernin, who told them that Austria-Hungary did not intend to yield any territory to Italy.[42]

We have succeeded in finding some traces of the affair in the Austro-Hungarian documents. In telegram No. 56 of April 2, 1917, Czernin informed his representative with the Austro-Hungarian High Command that 'Italy has made an offer of a separate peace in return for the cession of the Trentino. It has been rejected.' In consequence, the Austro-Hungarian Foreign Minister expected an early offensive by the Italian army.[43] The documents also contain a file entitled *Friedensverhandlungen*, in which various Italian feelers are reported, but their date and nature do not fit in with Charles I's and Czernin's statements.[44] A telegram of January 28, 1917, from the Austro-Hungarian ambassador in Madrid says that he had learnt from his German colleague that the Italian ambassador had asked the Spanish government whether it would be willing to mediate between Italy and the Central Powers,[45] but the documents do not suggest that this had any substance or consequences. An approach made by some agents of the Italian High Command to the Austro-Hungarian military attaché in Berne is mentioned, but this was only after Caporetto, in the first half of December 1917.[46] Czernin, when he was informed of this by the Austro-Hungarian High Command, replied that it should

[277]

not be rejected out of hand, but that the first thing to do was to make sure that it really came from Italy and not from unauthorized inter- mediaries, as had happened in the past. He feared that Italy did not seriously wish to make peace, but merely wanted to find out whether Austria-Hungary was or was not in urgent need of it.[47] But before receiving the Foreign Minister's reply, the Austro-Hungarian military attaché sent a message saying that the Italian agents had withdrawn; according to his information, Sonnino had instructed them to take no further action.[48] At all events, Czernin's telegrams show that, while he doubted the seriousness of the feelers attributed to Italy, he was—failing a general peace between the Entente and the Central Powers—opposed to the cession even of only the Trentino, even at the time when he admitted in his famous memorandum that Austria- Hungary was on the point of catastrophe. When this was avoided or postponed by the victory of Caporetto and the request for peace made by the new Soviet government, Czernin, speaking on January 24, 1918, in the Austrian Lower House in reply to President Wilson's Fourteen Points, categorically dismissed the idea of territorial con- cessions to Italy. He said that the only result of Italy's entry into the war had been her 'losing for ever a gain she could once have had'— that is, when it had been offered her in the spring of 1915 in return for the maintenance of her neutrality.[49]

A secret file by the Intelligence service of the Italian High Command on Austrian peace manoeuvres states as a piece of information sent by the Berne 'centre' dated May 24, 1917, that 'Austrian agents have tried to persuade us that the Vienna government is willing to yield us Trent and Trieste and to share Albania with us provided we renounce all Slav territories included in our claims, which are intended to be included in the famous Yugoslav state to be federally associated with the other two in the monarchy.'[50] A later secret file from the same source on other Austro-Hungarian moves states that 'immediately after the invasion of the Veneto, manoeuvres began to force Italy into a separate peace. . . . Many clues indicate that the principal activity in this connection took place in relation to the Vatican', but in November 1917 the British government was also informed that Austria was ready to make peace with Italy on the basis of the *status quo ante*. According to this source, it was believed in Vienna that the Rome government, with so many provinces invaded, and also because of the precarious domestic situation, might agree to this.[51] The writers of the file, showing themselves to be aware of the secret moves carried out in Switzerland, mention the approaches made by Foerster, Meinl and Lammasch, as well as those of Count Károlyi, who, in Berne in November 1917, had informed the Italian representatives that he was willing to meet them. They, however, considered him an emissary of his government, which was Italy's enemy.[52] The file states that the aim of Lammasch, Meinl and Foerster was 'to convert to their ends the noted journalist George Herron, then in Switzerland, who was the author of a good book on the "danger of peace"'. Herron is described as being allegedly a personal friend of President Wilson, who is said to be influenced by him to the extent that the United States declaration of war on Austria was said to have been owing to his representations.[53] The file says that Herron, unlike other Americans, had nevertheless turned out to be a loyal friend of Italy.

Herron himself claims that he played a part in the American declaration of war on Austria-Hungary on December 7, 1917, eight months after the declaration of war on Germany, and there is support for the contention, vague though it may be, in a report by the American ambassador in Paris.[54]

Following his conversations with the Italian legation which— according to what he himself says in the 'preparatory remarks' to his own papers—had asked him to go to Rome to explain the necessity of an Italo-Serbian agreement, Herron went to the Italian capital, where he arrived after Caporetto.[55] He was received by De Martino, the Secretary-General of the Foreign Ministry, who asked him to go to Paris to try to persuade the American ambassador to France (who was known to be unconvinced of the wisdom of the step) to declare himself in favour of the American declaration of war on Austria-Hungary for which the American ambassador to Italy was pressing at Sonnino's request.[56] Sharp, the ambassador in Paris, caused Herron to attend a meeting of a number of Americans who were in France at the time. 'I presented the whole Italian situation quite nakedly,' Herron wrote, 'and what I conceived to be the cause of the disaster, with the urgent reasons for an American declaration of war against Austria, and with what seemed to me the still more urgent reasons for sending a part of the American army to the Italian front.'[57] Sharp was not convinced, however; he considered a declaration of war on Austria-Hungary to be a 'useless complication', but reported to the State Department that a decision to that effect was considered necessary in various quarters.[58]

President Wilson said in his message to Congress on December 4, 1917, in which he announced the declaration of war, that 'we do not wish in any way to impair or to rearrange the Austro-Hungarian empire'.[59] This was sufficient for Herron to take the first opportunity of picking up the thread leading to Vienna which Foerster had offered him. Negotiations with Austria and American aid to Italy

[279]

were obviously not mutually exclusive in his view because, it is worth repeating, the Austrians still had to be convinced that they could not have peace without making concessions acceptable to Italy.

An opportunity for a series of meetings between Meinl and Herron arose with the conference 'for the organization of a future League of Nations' organized in Berne in November 1917 by the Central Organization for a Lasting Peace, an association of intellectuals of which a number of university professors such as Lammasch and the Italian Achille Loria were members. Its secretary was Baron de Jong van Beek en Donk, a former Dutch high official who lived in Switzerland and was a friend of Herron's, who took advantage of his presence and his mediation to arrange some of the conversations with the Austrians. Redlich, Lammasch and Meinl were invited to the conference, as were other Austro-Hungarian personalities noted for their pacifist views.[60] Among those who took part were Meinl, Károlyi and Jászi, who—the first independently of the other two—took advantage of their stay in Switzerland to make contact with the Americans and British. The Hungarian journalist Diner-Dénes, who accompanied Károlyi, met Louis Eisenmann, the distinguished historian of contemporary Austria-Hungary who was then working for the Intelligence service of the French War Ministry and, according to his memoirs, he also met G. A. Borgese.[61] In view of the accusations of high treason later levelled at Károlyi and his companions, by German and Hungarian nationalists in particular, it should be pointed out that the Austro-Hungarian government was informed of these contacts. Apart from the information given by Polzer-Hoditz and Benedikt about Meinl's connections with the Emperor's office and Czernin himself, we have other direct evidence of Meinl's and Károlyi's loyalty. In the first place, the latter's papers contain a letter from the deputy L. Beck, who had discussed his proposed trip to Berne with Wekerle, the Hungarian Prime Minister. Wekerle replied that, so far as the granting of the passports was concerned, he would submit the matter to Czernin, the Foreign Minister; he was afraid that Károlyi would make no secret in Switzerland of his well-known belief in the necessity of the restoration to France of Alsace-Lorraine.[62] At all events, Károlyi and his friends were granted passports. Even more significant is the fact that Baron Musulin, the Austro-Hungarian Minister in Berne, in his reports to Czernin, informed him in routine fashion that Meinl, Károlyi and Diner-Dénes had called on him and told him that they had seen Hugh Wilson, the American chargé d'affaires, and Whittal, the British Vice-Consul. Károlyi had reiterated that he considered it absolutely essential that Austria-Hungary should urge Germany to agree to the renunciation of Alsace-Lorraine, which was the necessary prerequisite to any general peace. He undertook to report to Charles I all that he had learnt in Switzerland.[63]

As a member of one of the wealthiest aristocratic families in Europe and leader of the parliamentary opposition in Hungary, Károlyi had no need of any introduction to the British and American diplomats, to whom he spoke with great frankness. If the war ended in a German victory, in his view, the probable consequence would be pan-German domination of Austria-Hungary and the consequent stifling of the Hungarian nation. On the other hand, if the war ended in a disastrous defeat of the Central Powers, it would be Austria-Hungary that would pay. He believed that the escape from this dilemma might lie in an Austro-Hungarian separate peace. Czernin, repudiating his original policy, was opposed to this, but Károlyi hoped to be able to overthrow him by appealing to the popular masses, who were largely organized in the Social Democratic movement (let us recall that their numbers both in Budapest and in Vienna had swollen enormously since the Russian Revolution). In Hungary there might be a general strike. But the Entente must secretly assure Austria-Hungary that excessively severe peace terms would not be imposed on her, and that she would be granted the economic aid necessary to save her from material disaster. Károlyi admitted that 'just Italian claims' must be satisfied and that Galicia must become part of a genuinely independent Poland.[64]

In December 1917, Meinl met the representatives of the United States and Britain whom Károlyi had met a month earlier, but his dealings were chiefly with Herron, whose reports reached not only President Wilson but also Balfour, the British Foreign Secretary.[65] The possibility that he was aware of the simultaneous conversations between Smuts and Mensdorff can be excluded. Nevertheless he frequently saw Mensdorff in Vienna, and the latter told him that he shared his desire for an early peace.[66] Meinl had the courage to inform the German Minister in Berne, Baron Romberg, of his conversations with the Americans and British and succeeded in obtaining the latter's goodwill, with the result that he was able to introduce to Herron and the British representatives a German deputy, Konrad Haussmann, the leader of the Progressive parliamentary group which, though small, had been represented in the Imperial government by the Vice-Chancellor since the so-called peace resolution of July 9, 1917, had resulted in a democratically inclined majority in the Reichstag.[67] Meanwhile, Herron obtained from the State Department an assurance of economic aid to Austria in the event of her making peace, while in view of the contact made with Vienna, President Wilson, both

[281]

in the drafting of the celebrated Fourteen Points (which for this very reason were so disappointing both to Italy and Romania and to the Czech and Yugoslav *émigrés*) and in his speech of February 11, 1918, in which he replied in very benevolent terms to Czernin's very ambiguous comment on the Fourteen Points, offered the Austro-Hungarian empire the chance of survival at the cost of not unreasonable territorial sacrifices and internal concessions.[68] A week before Wilson's speech, Herron met Lammasch, who was sent to Switzerland for the specific purpose, with instructions to report personally to Charles I on the results of his journey.[69]

Herron had tried to meet the objective difficulties with which the Austro-Hungarian and German seekers for peace were faced. He urged them to seek agreement, not to outright territorial concessions (which would immediately have run into opposition in Vienna, and still more in Berlin), but to the principle of self-determination of the nations which Czernin and his German colleagues were simultaneously proclaiming at Brest-Litovsk and which they wished to see applied in the not totally Russian territories of the former Tsarist empire.[70] Democratic application of the principle would, of course, have led to the separation from Germany and Austria-Hungary of at any rate some of the territories inhabited by nationalities other than those of the dominant Germans and Magyars. It was for this reason— apart from his confidence in the outcome of the next big German offensive on the Western Front—that Czernin broke off the contacts that he had himself made, or allowed to be made, with the Entente. The American President who, unlike the British and French governments, was not bound by any secret agreements (such as the treaties with Italy and Romania, or the undertakings given to Serbia), of course had full freedom of movement, whereas the Austro-Hungarian Foreign Minister had to take into account the bitter opposition that possible acceptance of the Wilson formula would arouse both in Germany and among the German-Austrian and Hungarian dominant classes in his own country.[71] No voice had been raised among the German-Austrians or the Magyars agreeing to territorial renunciations based on the right of the subject nationalities to self-determination at the cost of Austria or Hungary, as the case might be. During the impressive general strike in the second half of January 1918, which had broken out independently of their will, partly as a result of the food shortage, but still more because of the sympathy of the working masses with the peace principles proclaimed by the Bolsheviks from the platform provided by the Brest-Litovsk Peace conference, the Social Democratic leaders in Vienna and Budapest had every opportunity of seeing that the situation was pre-

[282]

revolutionary. But they too had no intention of declaring, as Lenin had done—and as Otto Bauer alone had been doing inside his own party, since his return from imprisonment in Russia, though he was not yet doing so in public—that the right of the nations to detach themselves from the state structure of which they formed a part should be applied to Austria-Hungary.[72] Károlyi and his party made no secret of their belief that Austria should resign herself to some sacrifice of territory, at any rate within the limits promised to Italy in 1915, but the integrity of Hungary was still a dogma to them. In a report to the Foreign Office on June 3, 1918, the British Minister in Berne said that he believed it to be in the interests of the Entente that Károlyi should become Prime Minister of Hungary, but he added that, according to his information, no one in Károlyi's party was willing to admit the right to independence of the Hungarian Slovaks, Romanians or Serbs.[73] As for Meinl, in his memorandum of January 7, 1918, he proposed, not complete self-determination, but merely federal autonomy, both for Alsace-Lorraine and for Austria's Italian territories.[74]

As a consequence of the Lammasch–Herron conversations, President Wilson authorized Herron if necessary to go to Vienna incognito to discuss on the spot the federal reorganization of Austria-Hungary for the benefit of its Slav nationalities if the Emperor decided to carry it out and Charles I took one further step.[75] As soon as he had heard Lammasch's report, he sent to the King of Spain, for transmission to President Wilson, a telegram in which he declared himself to be in agreement with the peace principles stated in the President's speech of February 11.[76] He added, however, that Austria-Hungary continued to insist on respect for the pre-war territorial *status quo* in relation to the Italian claims, which he described as contrary to the rights of the Slavs loyal to the Empire.[77] In reply to an enquiry by Colonel House, Balfour, the British Foreign Secretary, pointed out that the Vienna government was trying to reject the Italian claims on principle and at the same time to discourage the Slav peoples who were already looking to the Entente.[78] The American President, replying to Charles I on March 5, asked him to state his concrete proposals for 'the satisfaction of Slav national aspirations' and specify the 'precise concessions to Italy' that Austria-Hungary would be willing to make.[79]

Charles I could not conceal in his answer that he had no intention of making any territorial concessions to Italy—the Austrians obviously believed that after Caporetto there was no chance of an Italian military recovery[80]—and that brought all negotiations to an end.

[283]

Herron himself came to the conclusion that the future was on the side of the Italians, Czechs and Yugoslavs (and, independently of them, the Hungarian revolutionaries), who banked on a rising by Austria-Hungary's subject nationalities. Although he reserved the right to change his mind if circumstances called for it, he argued this in a long letter dated April 19, 1918, to the American chargé d'affaires in Berne.[81] He described as the alternative to the detachment from Germany of the Austrian-Hungarian empire—and thus to its survival as the result of a separate peace as a bulwark against the pan-Germanism of Berlin—the agreement between Italy and the Czecho-slovaks and Yugoslavs which he assumed had meanwhile been arrived at.[82]

For the rest, it is legitimate to assume that Herron's negotiations with Meinl and Lammasch may have contributed to strengthening the Italian Prime Minister, Orlando, who was exceedingly alarmed at the possibility of a separate peace with Austria of the kind aimed at by Wilson and Lloyd George, in his decision to give free rein for the time being to the 'nationality policy' advocated by Luigi Albertini and Leonida Bissolati which led to the Rome congress. Marquis Paulucci, the Italian Minister in Berne, got wind of Lammasch's meeting with Herron and, according to the latter's reports, went to see him several times at the end of February 1918 to tell him that he was aware of the Austrian emissary's visit and insisted on being kept fully informed.[83] The Sonnino papers disclose that he eventually received all the information he asked for.

Herron was given a first-hand account of the proceedings of the Rome congress by one of the participants, the Bosnian deputy N. Stojanović, who was a member of the Yugoslav Committee and leader of the Geneva colony of Serbian émigrés, and he expressed an entirely favourable opinion on it in his report of May 3 to the American chargé d'affaires. He deplored at length the publication by Clemenceau of Charles I's letter, insisted on the urgency of President Wilson's summoning the League of Nations, and noted that 'more significant in certain respects . . . is the evidence that reaches me of the very important congress of Italian and Slav nationalities which has just ended its week-long session in Rome. Allow me to say in passing that this congress resulted in a complete and happy agreement between Italy and all the Slavonic peoples who, like the Romanians, remain loyal to the allied cause.'[84]

This report of Herron's, like its predecessors, was forwarded to the State Department and submitted to President Wilson.[85] Lansing, the Secretary of State, must certainly have read it carefully, for one thing because he had known Lammasch from before the war and had followed his conversations with Herron with great interest, and it may have played a part, of course in conjunction with many other far more important considerations, in persuading him publicly to back the unequivocally anti-Austrian resolution at the Rome congress, as he did a few weeks later, thus inducing the London and Paris governments to do the same.[86]

Having lost any hope of a separate peace with Austria-Hungary, the government of the United States decided also, in August 1918, to break off the conversations which Herron had begun with some Bavarian pacifists.[87] War was to be won by the force of arms.

The politico-constitutional decisions in Vienna were not taken until more than two weeks after the defeat of Bulgaria, whose capitulation opened the southern frontiers of Austria-Hungary to the armies of the Entente. The effort to rescue the Habsburg monarchy led to the manifesto of October 16, 1918, in which Charles I proclaimed the federal reorganization of Austria, and recognized the right of its nations to self-determination.[88] This attempt to introduce federalism on the pattern of Foerster's ideas, according to Mensdorff's diary, which we have already quoted, was decided on by the Emperor *in extremis*. He believed that by doing so he might yet gain the favour of the United States and the Entente, who had advised him to take that course ten months earlier. But it was too late. Granting, belatedly, the principle of self-determination to the peoples of Austria (and even then not to those of Hungary), when the Central Powers had already lost the war, merely made it easier for them to proclaim themselves independent states.

Lammasch's appointment as Austrian Prime Minister on October 28, 1918, a step on which Charles I decided after Mensdorff, according to his diary, had been advising him to take it for at least two weeks, was made only on the eve of the Italian victory, in the illusion that it might yet be possible to gain American favour. The appointment contributed to ensuring that at the very end, the residual Austro-Hungarian military units received orders not to oppose by force of arms the national independence revolutions that started that day in Prague, spread next day to Zagreb, Cracow and Lvov, and culminated two days later in Budapest.[89]

APPENDIX III

French Documents on Italy and the Yugoslav Movement

In June 1968 I received permission to consult the French diplomatic documents of the years 1914–18 concerning Italy, Austria-Hungary and the Czechoslovak and Yugoslav national movements.[1] Although their contents do not substantially affect the results of my previous researches included in the Italian edition of this book (1966), they throw an interesting light on some details. I therefore thought it appropriate to summarize them here, in conjunction with the contents of similarly unpublished British and Italian documents.

We mentioned (in Chapter III) that Camille Barrère, the French ambassador in Rome, received the Dalmatian exiles Supilo, Trumbić and Mestrović on September 28, 1914. In the message he immediately sent to his Foreign Minister he put his impressions in a nutshell: '*Ils préféreraient rester sujets de l'Autriche que devenir sujets du roi Victor-Emmanuel.*'[2] To a French envoy who was devoting all his energies to trying to persuade Italy to declare war on Austria-Hungary, Croatian politicians who seemingly hated Italy more than Austria were of no interest. If anything, what they said reinforced him in his belief, which prevailed in the French diplomatic world and was shared by the British and the Italians, that Austria-Hungary, though an enemy in the war in progress, nevertheless constituted an indispensable stabilizing force in central and eastern central Europe, which without it would be rent by national divisions and would fall under the sway of Germany, if not of Russia.

One of those who did not take this view was Charles Loiseau, an assistant to Barrère. He was connected by marriage with a family of Croatian aristocrats in Dalmatia, and in 1898 had published a book on the Balkan Slavs, taking the part of the incipient Yugoslav national movement. He contrasted it with Hungarian chauvinism, which in foreign policy was pro-German, and regarded it as a potential bulwark against the pan-German push to the south-east. In the following year the Austrian authorities expelled him from Dalmatia.[3] After that, he was a frequent visitor to Italy, wrote about Italian foreign policy, and took a lively interest in the problem of tunnelling the Alps between Italy, France and Switzerland. At the outbreak of the First World War, Barrère had him attached to the

[286]

Rome embassy and gave him the task of maintaining contact with the Vatican, where he was *persona grata*, being a practising Catholic and having connections with eminent personalities in the Croatian Catholics world.[4]

Supilo's return to Rome in April 1916 gave Loiseau the opportunity of writing reports on the Yugoslav question for the use of Barrère and the French Foreign Minister, who highly appreciated the information they contained and their lucidity.[5] If in 1914 Supilo had ever had bitter feelings towards the Italy that was setting about claiming his native Dalmatia as the price of intervention, now, when the Italian army was fully engaged against the Austro-Hungarians, he placed his hopes on an Italo-Yugoslav agreement. On the other hand, though he knew that Serbia was France's surest ally in the Balkans, he was very dissatisfied with the Serbian government and did not conceal his dissatisfaction from Loiseau. He feared at the time that the Belgrade government was thinking, in the event of victory, of annexing Croatia as well as other territories that it desired, but not for the purpose of establishing a Yugoslavia democratically based on the right of self-determination of the Serbs, Croats and Slovenes. Loiseau, though he approached the question from the point of view of the overriding French interest in winning the war at all costs, had full confidence in Supilo's intentions.[6] In his view, the Croats and Serbs would end by coming to an agreement, and this would be a fatal blow to the Central Powers on the Balkan front, where, incidentally, a French expeditionary force was fighting in the Salonica sector. The French embassy in Rome considered the reaching of the agreement an event useful to the Entente cause, though it was aware that the Italian Foreign Ministry resented it because of the Yugoslav claim to territories assigned to Italy under the secret Treaty of London. To discredit the future Yugoslav state, some Italian diplomatic spokesmen suggested that after the war it might gravitate towards Germany.[7]

Barrère himself was in two minds on the matter. On the one hand, he realized that, as Loiseau (and the Czechoslovak *émigrés* Štefanik and Beneš when they reached Rome) argued, to encourage the rebellion of the Czechs, Croats and Slovenes was the concrete alternative to the separate peace with Austria-Hungary desired by Lloyd George, the British Prime Minister, and by influential personalities in France, though he himself was opposed to it, being only too well aware that such a peace could be achieved only at the expense of the Italian claims for the attainment of which the Rome government, thanks among other things to propaganda promoted and financed by the French embassy in Rome, had entered the war.[8]

On the other hand, in his opinion, by far the most valuable friend, both because of his loyalty and his strength of character, that the Entente had among the Italian statesmen was Sonnino. In his messages Barrère never tired of reiterating that Italian intervention had been due to Sonnino even more than to Salandra, the Italian Prime Minister from 1914 to 1916, and that, if he were displaced, the Foreign Ministry would probably go to Tittoni, who had several times held the post in the years between 1903 and 1909 and had been Italian ambassador in Paris from 1910 to 1916. According to Barrère, Tittoni, who was close to the Vatican and also to Giolitti, to whom he owed his political career, was still at heart a neutralist. (According to the ambassador's information, the fact that Italy had declared war on Germany in 1916 instead of in 1915 was ultimately owing to Tittoni, who was said to have advised the Rome government not to hurry in the matter.) At all events he was the candidate of the majority of these Italian parliamentarians who secretly favoured a compromise peace between the Entente and the Central Powers and who regretted that the Prime Minister was not Giolitti, or wanted Nitti in that position.[9] Barrère objected to Nitti in particular because of his friendship, based on their common scepticism about an overwhelming Entente victory, with men in the Vatican who did not like France, and because as Minister of the Treasury he had opposed investigations into what the former French Prime Minister Caillaux, who was accused of pacifism and defeatism in France, might have done or concealed on the occasion of a stay in Italy.

It was obviously wrong to say that in Italy only Sonnino was totally committed to fighting on until victory. In 1914 the cause of intervention against Austria had been advocated by Bissolati and Luigi Albertini, for instance, several months before Sonnino took it up, and with feelings of much more genuine friendship for the democratic or liberal western nations. They had been also the first to advocate the Italian declaration of war on Germany. On December 18, 1916, the French Prime Minister's office forwarded to Barrère a Foreign Office note that spoke highly of Bissolati, who was known in London to favour both a reconciliation of Italian and Yugoslav claims in the Adriatic and Lloyd George's plan for an offensive in Italy supported by a concentration of Anglo-French forces. Sonnino was cool, if not actually hostile, to both these objectives.[10] Barrère, however (as he several times wrote to Paris), considered Bissolati unsuited to high office (in which, in view of the latter's well-known naïvety and over-idealism, he may well have been right), and also believed that the criticisms of Italian policy made by Bissolati and Albertini (whom he could not describe as naïve, but for some reason

[288]

did not like) could only have the involuntary effect of playing into the hands of the real oppositional forces, those of Giolitti and his followers, the Vatican and many Catholics, and the Italian Socialist Party.[11] These forces, in Barrère's view, wanted a compromise general peace, while Sonnino totally rejected the idea of anything but a victorious peace. He believed that Italian opinion would interpret Sonnino's displacement as a first success for the pacifists, towards whom, in his opinion, Orlando, the Minister of the Interior in 1916–17, had been too tolerant. Sonnino shared this opinion, but, as Barrère could not fail to know, though it did not fit in with his argument, it was held even more strongly by Bissolati and Albertini.

After Caporetto, Sonnino at first did not want to join Orlando's new government. But Barrère took the rather unusual course of strongly urging him to remain at the Foreign Ministry and suggested to the French government that it and the British government should inform the new Italian Prime Minister that '*les Alliés attachent une importance particulière à ce que M. Sonnino soit maintenu à la Consulta*'.[12] Barrère was convinced that Tittoni, in agreement with Giolitti and some diplomatists who had grown up in the old anti-French tradition of the Italy that had been a member of the Triple Alliance, was hatching a plot to get rid of Sonnino.[13]

Meanwhile the control of French policy had passed into the hands of Clemenceau and Pichon, who were determined to imprint on it a note of inflexible determination. They accepted Barrère's arguments, and frankly told Orlando, who went to Paris at a time when Italy after Caporetto was in extreme need of its allies' help, that they wanted Sonnino to remain.[14] This had grave consequences, for one thing because it was based on a series of misunderstandings. Clemenceau, in spite of his Jacobin nationalism, was above all the man of the British and also of the American alliance. To avoid breaking up this alliance, he refrained at the peace conference from an all-out fight for the French frontier on the Rhine, Marshal Foch's unyielding demand which had Barrère's support. Underlying the latter's liking for Sonnino there was also the fact of the latter's insistence on the sacrosanct nature of the stipulations of the Treaty of London which violated the nationality principle, in the interest of strategic frontiers. The Treaty represented a useful precedent for similar French demands.[15] Soon afterwards, Orlando realized that Sonnino's refusal of all agreement with the Yugoslav movement made it more difficult for Italy, at a time when it could not take any military initiatives, to take the lead in fomenting the revolt of Austria-Hungary's Slav nationalities, besides being damaging to Italian relations with the United

States. But the fact that Sonnino had the support of the Italian nationalists as well as of the French government certainly weighed with Orlando, who was a man of remarkable political sensitivity but was weaker and more impressionable than his Foreign Minister, and strengthened his reluctance to clash with him.

Even before his clash with Wilson at the peace conference, but with doubled force after it, Orlando realized that the inconsistency of demanding the part of Dalmatia that was assigned to Italy by the Treaty of London and simultaneously demanding Fiume, which that treaty reserved for Croatia, was to lead to the isolation of Italy, while Sonnino's stubbornness in refusing to yield an inch of Dalmatian territory for the time being made impossible the compromise—that is to say Italian renunciation of Dalmatia, with the exception of Zara, in exchange for the establishment of Fiume as a free city—which was advocated by Bissolati and Albertini and was put into practice by Giolitti when he returned to power in 1920 with their friend Count Sforza at the Foreign Ministry, in the Treaty of Rapallo. In 1920, of course, the fact that Yugoslavia could no longer count on President Wilson's support worked in Italy's favour. Orlando always denied in public (and in his memoirs) that a reasonable compromise might have been attainable at the Peace Conference of 1919 that would have spared Italy the virtual rupture with the United States which was to be so harmful to her financially and economically, and the terrible blow struck at the fragile organism of the liberal Italian state by D'Annunzio's Fiume adventure. But he implicitly admitted it in May 1919 in a confidential talk with an influential Italian deputy who went to see him in Paris. 'Perhaps,' he said to him, 'my gravest error was that of not having had the courage to get rid of Sonnino in good time. I should have done it. I did not do it in order not to create agitation in the country. I regret it.'[16]

At the time when victory still had to be won—and, indeed, in the months after Caporetto, still seemed exceedingly remote—Orlando could easily have taken advantage of his position as Prime Minister of a country engaged in a mortal struggle to get rid even of a Minister as authoritative as Sonnino. But Sonnino, to Barrère's surprise, at that time had the support of the newspapers associated with Giolitti and those Catholic circles which, the French ambassador believed, were plotting to get rid of him. In February 1918, Barrère sent to Paris a memorandum written by one of his colleagues which contained the information, which subsequently turned out to be correct, that since Albertini's *Corriere della Sera* and *Il Secolo*, which was associated with Bissolati, had begun criticizing Sonnino for not committing himself to the break up of Austria-Hungary, the friends of Giolitti and of the Vatican who wanted the Habsburg monarchy to be preserved had decided to support him.[17]

By this time Barrère was convinced of the soundness of Loiseau's view that it was in the Entente's interest to back the rebellion of Austria-Hungary's Slav nationalities. On December 1, 1917, he suggested to the French Foreign Minister that he should try to persuade Sonnino, who had gone to Paris for an inter-allied meeting, of the merit of the idea. On December 21 Pichon replied to Barrère, agreeing with his proposal as far as the Czechs and Yugoslavs were concerned.[18] The approval was in general terms, making no specific commitments. It later turned out that the Polish National Council in exile was advising the French government not to show excessive animosity towards Austria-Hungary. The Poles in fact knew that the Vienna government was at odds with the Berlin government, and still more so with the German High Command, about the future of the kingdom of Poland, which the German military leaders intended to keep indefinitely under their own exclusive control. If this kingdom of Poland had been added to Austria, whose government claimed it in order to satisfy the many and influential Polish deputies in the Reichsrat, this, besides representing a beginning of the re-establishment of Polish unity (the kingdom of Poland within the framework of the Habsburg monarchy could have been reunited with Galicia, where the Poles were the dominant class), would also have meant that an area of great strategic and industrial importance would have been removed from the sway of Prussian militarism, which France regarded as her mortal enemy.

In the autumn of 1917, Beneš, on a visit to Rome, assured Barrère that Sonnino, who at the beginning of the year had been totally opposed to the organization of prisoners-of-war in Italy into a Czechoslovak Legion, now seemed amenable to the idea in view of the prospect of the formation of such a legion in France and of the fact that Czech and Slovak prisoners in Italy were asking to be sent to France so that they could join it.[19] Barrère believed that, if Italy committed herself to the Czechoslovak movement, it would be possible gradually to bring Sonnino round to a policy implying support for the Yugoslav national movement, with which he was at that time determined to have nothing to do. The French Consul-General in Milan informed him on February 11 and 15, 1918, that the *Corriere della Sera* campaign for the disruption of Austria-Hungary by means of the Slav national movements was bringing about a change in public opinion, at any rate in northern Italy. On the other hand, the criticisms of Italian diplomacy which A. Gauvain was making in defence of the Yugoslav cause in the *Journal des*

[291]

Débats seemed totally counter-productive to the French ambassa-dor.[20]

Barrère was told by Štefanik after the latter's return to Rome from revolutionary Russia that Orlando had told him that he was deter-mined to form Czechoslovak and Yugoslav legions in Italy, even at the cost of having to get rid of Sonnino. The French ambassador still believed that Sonnino's departure would be a misfortune, as at that time (March 1918) his most probable successor was Nitti, whom he regarded as lacking faith in victory.[21] However, Barrère, quarrelling with the reluctance of his colleagues at the Quai d'Orsay to commit themselves in the matter, was pressing his government to encourage the Slav nationalities of Austria-Hungary, including the Yugoslavs. In view of the danger of another big Austrian offensive on the Italian front (which indeed took place on the Piave in June 1918), the Rome government would have no alternative but to fall into line with the French initiative.[22]

In fact, in spite of Sonnino's reluctance, Orlando, as we have already related, anticipated the Paris government in giving support to the calling of a congress of Austria-Hungary's subject nationalities, which took place in Rome on April 8–10. On the day the congress opened, Paul de Margerie, the director of political affairs at the Quai d'Orsay, informed Barrère that he was in agreement with the Polish delegation, which had gone to Rome with the intention of main-taining that the real enemy was not so much Austria-Hungary as Germany.[23] At the congress the Polish delegation and Franklin-Bouillon, the French parliamentarian who was closest to the Quai d'Orsay, opposed as premature the formal proclamation of the independence of the nations subject to the Habsburg dynasty.[24]

On the last day of the conference, Pichon telegraphed to Barrère that he had learnt that his British colleague Balfour approved of the anti-Austrian resolutions drawn up in Rome. Although he still thought the Polish preoccupations were justified, the French Foreign Minister thought it necessary to associate himself with the British point of view.[25] But in a conversation with Barrère after the congress, Sonnino persisted in his opposition to the recognition of the Yugoslav national movement in view of the incompatibility of its claims with the Treaty of London. Barrère therefore suggested to Pichon that the French and British governments should put pressure on the Italian government.[26] On the eve of the inter-allied conference at Versailles he asked Pichon to propose the recognition of Polish, Czechoslovak and Yugoslav independence.[27] But chiefly because of Sonnino's opposition to the very idea of Yugoslavia, and also because London and Paris were in no great hurry to proclaim the destruction of

[292]

the Habsburg monarchy, on June 3 the conference, though guaranteeing the independence of Poland, merely expressed its sympathy with the aspirations of the Czechoslovaks and the Yugoslavs.[28] At a meeting of the Supreme War Council a month later, also at Versailles, Pichon raised the question of forming a legion of Yugoslav prisoners-of-war, on the lines of the Czechoslovak legions. He suggested incorporating it in the Serbian army on the Salonica front. Orlando agreed with the idea of a Yugoslav legion, provided that it were used on the Italian front. Sonnino expressed a substantially different view, recommending caution. In fact a Yugoslav legion was never formed in Italy.[29]

Recognition of Czechoslovak independence had to wait for a few more months; the Yugoslav question remained in suspense until after the end of the war.

On September 8, 1918, the Italian cabinet, on Bissolati's insistence but against the opposition of Sonnino, agreed to issue a statement recognizing that the Yugoslav national movement was fighting for aims in harmony with those of the Entente.[30] But this was not a formal commitment, and after the victory, Italian diplomacy and the Italian military authorities ignored it. The Italian government took its place at the Peace Conference not only without having recognized the new Yugoslav state (the kingdom of the Serbs, Croats and Slovenes) established after the Austro-Hungarian collapse, but in acute conflict with it.[31]

In the summer of 1918, Orlando had promised Bissolati to carry out the policy of reconciliation between Italians and Yugoslavs which had been proclaimed at the Rome congress.[32] According to a report by the British ambassador in Rome, Orlando had in mind removing Sonnino from the Foreign Ministry, taking it over himself, and giving the Ministry of the Interior to Nitti.[33] Nitti, however, was understood to have refused, either because he wanted to remain at the Ministry of the Treasury, or because he believed that his time would come when the war was over. Some articles by Amendola, the Rome correspondent of Albertini's *Corriere della Sera*, openly criticized Sonnino for his hostility to the break up of Austria-Hungary and the birth of Yugoslavia, but the criticism was echoed only by *Il Secolo* in Milan, *Il Messaggero* in Rome and *Il Lavoro di Genova*, on which Bissolati had influence. By far the greater part of the Italian press, including the pro-Giolitti and Catholic press, supported Sonnino. Even the Liberal Association of Milan, traditionally the political group closest to the *Corriere della Sera*, deplored the attacks on Sonnino.[34] At that time, the news from the Western Front made it clear that the defeat of the Central Powers was certain and close at

[293]

hand. The nature of the Italian victory in the last few days of October exceeded the rosiest expectations, among other things because Austria-Hungary was disintegrating as the result of the revolutions of those of its constituent nations which were seizing independence. Theoretically this justified Bissolati's and Albertini's attitude, but in practice Italian public opinion was hypnotized by the fact that, with the disappearance of its powerful traditional enemy, Italy was militarily incalculably stronger than its new northern and eastern neighbours, with the result that it seemed only natural that she should take advantage of this superiority to secure the strategic frontiers that had been promised her in return for her entry into the war, and something extra as well. The something extra was Fiume, the Italian population of which outnumbered its other inhabitants. On October 30, 1918, the Fiume National Council asked to be annexed by Italy. The Yugoslavs, who naturally did not welcome the Italian occupation troops in Dalmatia and other Croatian or Slovenian areas, were by then regarded as enemies. For the same reason, the demand for strategic frontiers conforming with the Treaty of London (and also for Fiume) was taken up by the high officials of the still very influential Italian Freemasons, who dissociated themselves from the views of the Freemason Bissolati.[35]

When he realized the way things were going, Bissolati decided to confront Orlando with a choice. To make possible a lasting peace based on the right of self-determination of the nations and their amicable co-operation, particularly in central and east central Europe —where, with the collapse of the Habsburg monarchy and the fall of the Hohenzollerns a new system, acceptable to Italy, had to be established—he wanted the Italian government to renounce that part of Dalmatia and the ethnically German zone (north of Bolzano, which he wanted to be Italian) of the south Tyrol which the Treaty of London had assigned them, but to claim that Fiume was Italian and should be established as a free city under an Italian protectorate, its harbour to provide a guaranteed outlet for the trade of the Croatian and Hungarian hinterland.[36] But, in the hope of persuading Orlando to accept this, Bissolati waited for another month before he acted, and that, according to the British ambassador (who himself realized the importance of Bissolati's proposals too late) was a grave tactical error, because on the eve of the meeting of the Peace Conference it was too late to engage in a battle to change the Foreign Minister.[37] At all events, when he realized that Orlando did not intend, or did not dare, to get rid of Sonnino, Bissolati resigned on December 28, 1918. Barrère criticized him for this, declaring him to be *prêt à tous les renoncements*.[38] He certainly disliked Bissolati's willingness to renounce the strategic frontier of the Brenner, which was not a good precedent for French demands for strategic frontiers. He had, however, at last realized that Sonnino was going to make excessive territorial demands and now rested his hopes on Orlando, who *'redoute l'irrédentisme slave et préfère à la Dalmatia des compensations . . . c'est à dire Fiume et Zara'*.[39] According to Barrère's information, the Italian General Staff agreed with Orlando, foreseeing that in the event of war with Yugoslavia, the Italians would need 400,000 men to defend the Dalmatian coast. He noted, however, that Sonnino was *'actuellement entouré de la popularité nationale'*, while Orlando could not be sure that the Peace Conference would give Italy Fiume in exchange for Dalmatia, for Fiume had been promised to Croatia, and Yugoslavia was bound to fight stubbornly for it. In this situation it would have required *'beaucoup d'audace et risquer beaucoup'* for Orlando to have got rid of Sonnino.[40] The British ambassador's comment on Bissolati's resignation was: 'As for the present, Baron Sonnino's policy appears to receive the general support of the country.'[41]

Bissolati's colleagues took the same view. It was expected that at any rate Agostino Berenini, the Education Minister, a member of Bissolati's own party (the small Reformist Socialist Party) would resign out of solidarity with its leader, but he remained in the government. Bissolati's place in it was taken by his former friend and comrade, the future Prime Minister, Ivanoe Bonomi. The British ambassador reported that Nitti 'admitted to me that, although he considered Bissolati had been wrong in choosing the moment he had adopted to resign, instead of doing so several weeks before, in the main he agreed with Bissolati's view'.[42] In fact Nitti also resigned from the government, but two weeks after Bissolati, and without showing solidarity with him or giving any public reasons for his resignation. This tactical prudence made it easier for Nitti to become Orlando's successor in June 1919, but only after the dramatic clash at the Peace Conference between Orlando and President Wilson had put Italy in a situation of dangerous international isolation, accentuating the exasperation of Italian nationalist public opinion.[43]

Bissolati, who on January 4 had had a conversation with President Wilson (who was given a triumphal reception in Italy, where his views on the Adriatic question were not yet well known) and also had stated his views in an interview with the London *Morning Post*, which caused him to be denounced for lack of patriotism in the nationalist press, tried to appeal to the country in a speech in the Scala theatre in Milan on the evening of January 11.[44] But a dense group of nationalists, 'futurists', officers and ex-servicemen headed by the poet F. T.

Marinetti and by Mussolini, repeatedly made violent interruptions, denouncing Bissolati as a 'Croat', and when he tried to explain that the South Tyrol north of Bolzano was not ethnically Italian, he was prevented from finishing his speech.[45] According to the police report to Orlando, 'the demonstration against the Hon. Bissolati was obviously prearranged by Mussolini and other elements'. Referring to the socialist masses, whose ranks had increased enormously in Italy since the Russian Revolution, the police report added: 'It seems that a large part of the Milan population is in favour of the Hon. Bissolati's policy.'

Although the socialist parliamentary group and the General Confederation of Labour (though without mentioning Bissolati) declared themselves against the annexation to Italy of hundreds of thousands of Yugoslavs and German Austrians, *Avanti*, the Italian Socialist Party organ, control of which was in the hands of the extreme left wing, dogmatically announced that Bissolati, having wanted Italy to intervene in the war, deserved the fate that was now overtaking him, and therefore had no right to the solidarity of the proletariat.

The majority of the Italian Socialist Party, hoping for the early advent of a proletarian revolution of the Bolshevik type in Italy, was already withdrawing from real political issues, leaving the field open to nationalism. Orlando, in the words of the British ambassador, 'influenced by the general consensus of the press in favour of the extreme claims of Italy, and the almost universal condemnation of Bissolati's action', fell back on Sonnino. Nevertheless the ambassador foresaw that Bissolati's ideas would gain sympathy abroad and, in the course of time, also in Italy herself.

In a letter written in 1920 to Millerand, who was then the French Prime Minister, Barrère noted that Italy, disappointed by the Peace Conference, had again become anti-French and was in danger of again becoming pro-German. In his view, Italy's great concern was to prevent the formation of a confederation of Danubian states in the place of the dismantled Austria-Hungarian empire—in other words, the re-establishment of a substantial power on Italy's northern and eastern frontiers. Barrère too was obsessed by the principle of divide and rule which prevailed in nationalist Europe in the period immediately after a war, which, according to the Entente's official war aims, had been fought for democracy. Since 1898 he had worked with great skill in Rome for the re-establishment of Franco-Italian friendship, but the advice he now gave his country was not to favour any Danubian confederation, in order not to clash with Italian nationalism. His advice was in harmony with the short-sighted and

[296]

nationalistically inclined policy that then prevailed in France, in Italy and in nearly all the other interested countries. The confederation of Danubian states never came into being (the so-called 'Little Entente' never became such a confederation) and the end of Austria-Hungary left a void that was never filled.

Notes (I)

Centrifugal National Movements, 1905-1914

1. Henry Wickham Steed, *Through Thirty Years*, London, 1927; Italian ed., Milan, 1962. David Lloyd George, *War Memoirs*, six vols., London, 1934–36; *The Truth about the Peace Treaties*, two vols., 1938. T. G. Masaryk, *Die Weltrevolution. Erinnerungen und Betrachtungen, 1914–28*, Berlin, 1925. Edward Beneš, *Souvenirs de guerre et de révolution (1914–1918). La lutte pour l'indépendance des peuples*, two vols., Paris, 1928–29. Cf. also the works of the director of the archives of the Czechoslovak Foreign Ministry, Opočensky, which supplement those of Beneš: Jan Opočensky, *La fin de l'Autriche et la genèse de l'État tchécoslovaque*, Prague, 1928; *Umsturz in Mitteleuropa. Der Zusammenbruch Oesterreich–Ungarns und die Geburt der kleinen Entente*, Hellerau bei Dresden, 1931. Luigi Albertini, *Le origini della guerra del 1914*, three vols., Milan, 1942–43; English ed. *The Origins of the War of 1914*, three vols., London, 1957. *Vent' anni di vita politica*, Part II, *L'Italia nelle guerra mondiale*, three vols., Bologna, 1951–53. Apart from these of course strongly biased recollections by men involved in the developments with which we are concerned, we shall here restrict ourselves to quoting only a few studies of Austria-Hungary: Heinrich Benedikt, *Monarchie der Gegensätze*, Vienna, 1947; *Dir wirtschaftliche Entwicklung in der Franz-Josef Zeit*, Vienna, 1953. A. J. P. Taylor, *The Habsburg Monarchy, 1809–1918*, 2nd ed., London, 1948. Robert A. Kann, *The Multinational Empire. Nationalism and National Reform in the Habsburg Monarchy*, two vols., New York, 1951; German ed., amplified and revised, Graz and Cologne, 1967. Arthur J. May, *The Habsburg Monarchy, 1867–1914*, Cambridge, Mass., 1951; *The Passing of the Habsburg Monarchy, 1914–1918*, two vols., Philadelphia, 1966. C. A. Macartney, *The Habsburg Empire, 1790–1918*, London, 1968. Victor L. Tapié, *Monarchie et peuples du Danube*, Paris, 1969. Rudolf Schlesinger, *Federalism in Central and Eastern Europe*, London, 1945. Hans Mommsen, *Die Sozialdemokratic und die Nationalitätenfrage im Habsburgischen Vielvölkerstaat, 1867–1907*, Vienna, 1963. Jacques Droz, *L'Europe Centrale. Evolution Historique de l'idèe de Mitteleuropa*, Paris, 1960. Julius Miskolczy, *Ungarn in der Habsburg-Monarchie*, Vienna, 1959. Z. A. B. Zeman, *The Break-Up of the Habsburg Empire, 1914–1918*, London, 1961. Friedrich Walter-Harold Steinacker, *Die Nationalitätenfrage im altern Ungarn und die Südostpolitik Wiens*, Munich, 1959. As a contempoary document which contains the reflections of a great historian who took an active part in political life, I have found very useful the diary of J. Redlich, edited by Fritz Fellner, entitled *Schicksalsjahre Oester-*

reichs, *1908–1919. Das politische Tagebuch Josef Redlichs*, two vols., Graz and Vienna, 1953–64. Cf. the collections of essays *Nationalism in Eastern Europe*, ed. Peter F. Sugar and Ivo J. Lederer, Seattle–London, 1969. Cf. also *Oesterreich–Ungarn in der Weltpolitik 1900–1918*, Berlin, 1965; *Die Frage des Finanzkapitals in der Oesterreichisch–Ungarischen Monarchie, 1900–1918*, Bucharest, 1965; *Die Nationale Frage in der Oesterreichisch–Ungarischen Monarchie, 1900–1918*, Budapest, 1966. Eduard März, *Österreichische Industrie und Bankpolitik in der Zeit Franz Josephs I*, Vienna, 1968. We must also mention the list of doctoral theses on Austria-Hungary published by Professor Walter Rechberger in *The Austrian History News Letter*, No. 1, 1960, edited by Professor R. John Rath. Cf. the supplementary lists in later numbers of that publication, which has now become the *Austrian History Year-Book*, Vol. III, of which (1967) contains a very interesting discussion of the problems of economic development, and the social difficulties of the Habsburg monarchy. Cf. also the bibliographies published by the national historical committees—in particular the Hungarian, Polish, Czech, Slovak, Romanian and Yugoslav —on the occasion of the eleventh, twelfth and thirteenth International congresses of historical sciences (Stockholm, 1960; Vienna, 1965; and Moscow, 1970). Cf. of course F. R. Bridge, *The Habsburg Monarchy 1804–1918*. Books and pamphlets published in the United Kingdom between 1818 and 1967. *A Critical Bibliography*, London, 1967. Cf. now the *Austrian Historical Bibliography* published since 1965 by E. H. Boehm and Fritz Fellner at the Clio Press, Santa Barbara, California.

2. I am indebted to the courtesy of the following for allowing me access to documents in their possession: Countess Elena Albertini Carandini, Countess Catherine Károlyi, Mrs Nina Ferrero Raditsa, Professor Bogdan Raditsa, Professors Hugh and Christopher Seton-Watson, and other friends. Much help was given me by Dr Rudolf Neck and Professor Richard Blaas of the Haus- Hof-und Staatsarchiv, Vienna; Mr Noel Blakiston, the head of the Public Records Office, London; Professor Leopoldo Sandri, director of Archivio Centrale dello Stato, Rome, and his colleague, Dr Constanzo Casucci; Professor Renato Mori, director of the historical archives of the Foreign Ministry, Rome; Dr Pietro Gasser, deputy-director of the Allgemeines Verwaltungsarchiv, Vienna; Mr Arnold Dániel; Professor Georg A. Lányi; Dr Dragovan Šepić; Dr Ante Smith Pavelić; Professor Ben F. Brown at the Sonnino Archives, Montespertoli; and other friends and colleagues. To these I express my gratitude, as I do to a great number of Italian libraries, to the Institute of Historical Sciences of the Hungarian Academy of Sciences, the Institute for the History of the Socialist Workers' Party of Hungary, the Hungarian National Library, the Hungarian National Archives, the archives of the German Foreign Ministry in Bonn, the Austrian National Library, the Arbetarrörelsens Arkiv, Stockholm, the International Institute of Social History, Amsterdam, the Institut des Études Slaves, Paris, and in particular the *Rivista Storica Italiana* which allowed me to use articles of mine that appeared in its columns.

3. The Study of *Les problèmes nationaux dans la Monarchie des Habsbourg*, Belgrade, 1960, presented to the International Congress of Historical Sciences in Stockholm, by Professor Fran Zwitter, in collaboration with Professors Jaroslav Sidak and Vaso Bogdanov, states on p. 147 that 'the movements frankly opposed to the existence of the monarchy before 1914 were few'. This indisputable fact is the more significant when the ethnic composition of the empire is taken into account. According to the 1910 census, the population of Austria-Hungary, including Bosnia-Hercegovina, was in round figures 51,400,000. Of these about 12 million were (by language) German (10 million in Austria and two million in Hungary and Croatia-Slavonia), 10,100,000 were Magyars (nearly all in Hungary), 6,600,000 were Czechs, two million were Slovaks, five million were Poles, four million were Ruthenians, 3,200,000 were Romanians, 3,200,000 were Croats, 2,100,000 Serbs, 1,400,000 Slovenes, and nearly 800,000 Italians. The remainder consisted of 600,000 Slavs of the Muslim faith in Bosnia-Hercegovina, who could equally well be regarded as Serbo-Croats, and some unassimilated Jews, Turks, Bulgarians and Gypsies. Germans amounted to fewer than 36 per cent of the population of the whole of the Austrian territories, but to 37 per cent of the population of Bohemia alone, which explains their conflict with the Czechs. In Hungary (the population of which was 18,300,000) the Magyars were in a slender majority which, however, disappeared if Croatia-Slavonia (2,700,000 inhabitants) was considered, as it obviously should have been, as it formed part of the kingdom of Hungary. As to the social classes and professions which made up the population of Austria-Hungary, cf. the study of L. Katus in *Die Nationale Frage, op. cit.*

4. For Kossuth's attitude in exile, cf. Endre Kovács, *A Kossuth emigráció és az europai szabadságmozgalmak*, Budapest, 1967. György Szabad, *Forradalom és kiegyezés válaszutján (1860–61)*, Budapest, 1967. Of course the old edition of his works: Lajos Kossuth, *Irataim az emigrációból*, 13 vols., Budapest, 1880–1911, in particular Vol. VIII (the new critical edition of Kossuth's complete works has not yet reached the period of his exile). An excellent study is that of Gyula Szekfü, 'Az öreg Kossuth, 1867–1894,' *Magyar Történelmi Társulat. Emlékkönyv Kossuth Lajos születésének 150. évfordulójára*, two vols., Budapest, 1952, Vol. II, pp. 341–434. For a general picture of Hungarian politics, cf. Gusztáv Gratz, *A dualizmus kora. Magyarország története 1867–1918*, two vols., Budapest, 1934; Oscar Jászi, *The Dissolution of the Habsburg Monarchy*, Chicago, 1929. Gratz, a Liberal, and Jászi, a Radical, lived through the last twenty years of Austria-Hungary both as active politicians and historians of their time. Cf. also Nicola Asztalos-Alessandro Pethö, *Storia dell' Ungheria*, Milan, 1937, though it is fiercely nationalist in tone. For the relations between the Magyars and the Crown, cf. the memoirs of Albert Apponyi, *Emlékirataim. Ötven év*, Budapest, 1922–24 and of József Kristóffy, *Magyarország Kálváriája Politikai emlékek, 1890–1926*, Budapest, 1927. On a small republican movement founded in Hungary in 1911, cf. the historical review *Századok*, No. 4, 1960, pp. 661 ff.

5. The dynastic (Habsburg) union between Austria and Hungary was finally accepted by the Party of Independence in 1884. Previously it was torn by dissension on this question between extremists and moderates. Cf. Gyula Mérey, *Magyar politikai pártprogrammok (1867–1914)*, Budapest, 1934, pp. 99 ff.

6. Johann Christopher Allmayer Beck, *Ministerpräsident Baron Beck*, Vienna, 1956. Cf. p. 157 for the relations between the Austrian government and the Social Democratic Party at the 1907 general election. This life of Baron Max Wladimir Beck, under whose Prime Ministership (1906–8) universal and equal suffrage was introduced into Austria, being based on ample documentation, is full of valuable details, even though these are not always sufficiently worked out. It shows that Baron Beck, an excellent example of the best kind of Vienna bureaucrat, was the first to suggest in a 1903 memorandum to Francis Ferdinand, whose tutor he had been, that the franchise should be extended in Hungary in the interests of the dynasty (cf. *op. cit.*, pp. 99 ff.). Francis Joseph therefore made a good choice in appointing him to carry out the electoral reform in Austria. The idea of giving workers the vote as a way of diverting attention from national conflicts to social questions in Cisleithania had been recommended to the Emperor as early as 1893 by Emil Steinbach, Finance Minister in Count Taaffe's government, under which the problem of a first extension of the suffrage arose. Cf. Rudolf Sieghart, *Die letzten Jahre einer Grossmacht. Menschen, Völker, des Habsburger Reiches*, Berlin, 1932, pp. 24 ff.; cf. also Joseph Maria Baernreither, *Der Verfall des Habsburgerreiches und die Deutschen. Fragmente eines politischen Tagebuches 1897–1917*, Vienna, 1939, ed. Oskar Mitis. Baernreither points out on p. 168 that Steinbach wanted to keep the reform within limits that would not affect the privileged position of the landed aristocracy that, unlike finance capitalism, of which he was critical, he revered for traditional reasons. However, the conflict of 1905 led to a clash between Francis Joseph— an aristocratic sovereign if there ever was one—and the Hungarian nationalist aristocracy. He was therefore in a favourable frame of mind for accepting the idea put forward by Kristóffy, the Hungarian Minister of the Interior, of overcoming its opposition by resorting to universal suffrage. The decisive factors that led to the introduction of the latter in Austria were the identical resolutions in its favour proposed by the Christian Democrats, the Christian Social Party and the Young Czechs which were passed by a majority, though not the required two-thirds majority, in the Reichsrat on October 6, 1905, the anxieties roused by the Russian Revolution of that year, which extracted from the Tsar his manifesto of October 30 which made that democratic promise, and the demonstrations staged by the Social Democratic working class, which were especially violent in Vienna and Prague and owed their success to the enthusiasm roused by the news from Russia. Cf. William Alexander Jenks, *The Austrian Electoral Reform of 1907*, New York, 1950, pp. 30 ff.; Charles A. Gulick, *Austria from Habsburg to Hitler*, two vols., Berkeley, 1948, Vol. I, pp. 33 ff.; and Ludwig Brügel, *Geschichte der österreichischen Sozialdemokratic*, five

[301]

vols., Vienna, 1922–25, Vol. IV, pp. 349 ff. Cf. also R. Mommsen, *op. cit.*, pp. 366 ff.; J. F. N. Bradley, 'Czech Nationalism and Socialism in 1905', *American Slavic and East European Review*, February 1960, which give further details about the struggle for the vote in Bohemia, the liveliness of which was pointed out by Edvard Beneš in one of his first articles, which appeared in the *Revue Socialiste*, 1908 (2), pp. 97 ff. If it is true that universal suffrage would not have been passed in Austria without socialist pressure, nevertheless Francis Joseph, who looked to it for a reinforcement of the strength of the Crown—to which the peasant masses of all nationalities, which were particularly favoured by the reform, were more devoted than the various bourgeoisies among whom nationalist influences prevailed—was convinced that he must hasten its introduction, and in 1905 and 1906 he twice changed his Austrian Prime Minister in order to find a man determined and able to secure the passage of the bill. On the Emperor's personality, cf. Albert von Margutti, *Kaiser Franz Joseph*, Vienna and Leipzig, 1924; Joseph Redlich, *Kaiser Franz Joseph von Österreich*, Berlin, 1928; on the last period of his reign, cf. Friedrich G. Kleinwächter, *Der Untergang der österreichisch–ungarischen Monarchie*, Leipzig, 1920; also the memoirs of Alexander Spitzmüller-Harmersbach, *Und hat auch Ursach es zu liehen*, Vienna, 1955, and those of Baron J. von Szilassy, *Der Untergang der Donau-Monarchie*, Berlin, 1921. Cf. also *Erinnerungen an Franz Joseph I*, ed. Edmund Ritter von Steinitz, Berlin, 1931, which contains contributions by M. W. Beck, A. Spitzmüller and other statesmen.

7. The theorist of co-operation between the Social Democrats and the dynasty with a view to the reorganization of Austria on the basis of concessions to national autonomies on modern lines not detrimental to the necessary economic unity of the empire was Karl Renner, the future Prime Minister of the Austrian Republic after the First World War and its President after the Second World War. He was then merely a scholar and a librarian in the Reichsrat library, who at first had to write under a pseudonym to conceal his membership of the Social Democratic Party. For his ideas, and for those of his fellow and rival, Otto Bauer, another socialist student of Austrian national questions—Bauer put more emphasis on the class struggle than Renner, but was not averse to advocating Social Democratic support of a possible solution of national conflicts from above —cf. H. Mommsen, *op. cit.*, R. A. Kann, *op. cit.*, and J. Droz, *op. cit.* Renner's ideas for a modern system of autonomy for the empire (on a 'personal' as distinct from the old territorial basis) had behind them a whole evolution of political thought to which Droz draws attention, *op. cit.*, p. 173, and were supported by experiments in autonomous organization on a not purely territorial basis in ethnically mixed provinces (Moravia, Bukovina), on which cf. F. G. Kleinwächter, p. 57. They gained a great deal of prestige, and were submitted to Francis Ferdinand. In practice, however, in conformity with the sceptical Austrian maxim of thinking of the most rational possible solution and betting on its opposite, it was national antagonisms that made a breach in the organization of the Social

Democrats in spite of their efforts to prevent this. Since 1897 they had been organized as a federation consisting of as many socialist parties as there were nationalities in Austria, and in 1899 they had adopted a programme, still on very general lines, for reorganizing the state on federal principles. Cf. (in addition to the contemporary press and congress reports, which we take for granted and shall quote only for less familiar points) Arthur S. Kogan, 'The Social Democrats and the Conflict of Nationalities in the Habsburg Monarchy', *Journal of Modern History*, September 1949. In 1910 a split between Czechs and Germans took place in the trade-union movement in Bohemia and Moravia. The Czech organizers decided against continuing to send to the Vienna headquarters the very considerable sums they collected from their branches. Their attitude was encouraged by their flourishing popular education centres, which were very sensitive on the language question. The Czech Social Democratic Party, which had more than 130,000 paying members, with 400,000 votes and twenty-six deputies, made common cause with the secessionists, who seceded from the central committee in Vienna, the authority of which extended to the whole empire, and acknowledged instead the authority of the already existing Prague committee which had hitherto had little influence. Most Czech Social Democrats now joined in the demand for the adoption of Czech as a second official language in Bohemia, including the predominantly German districts in the Sudetenland. As very few German Austrians knew Czech while all Czechs who wanted a career in the public service knew German, such bilingualism would necessarily favour the Czechs. A small group of socialists who described themselves as centralists in turn broke away from the Czech Social Democrats, whom they described as separatists. Up to the war, however, and in some cases up to the last year of the war, the Czech Social Democratic leaders, for all their 'separatism' in trade-union organization and also in parliament, remained opposed, not only to the detachment from Austria of Bohemia and Moravia advocated by the most extreme National Socialists, but also to the claim to the 'historical rights of the Bohemian state' which were supported by nearly all the other Czech parties but had been rejected by the Social Democratic Party in 1897. Cf. Emil Strauss, *Von Hainfeld bis zum Weltkrieg. Geschichte der deutschen Sozialdemokratic Böhmens (1889–1914)*, Prague, 1926; L. Brügel, *op. cit.*, Vol. II, pp. 77 ff. Zdenek Šolle, 'Die Sozialdemokratie in der Habsburger Monarchie und die tschechische Frage', *Archiv für Sozialgeschichte*, Vols. VI–VII and 'Die tschechische Sozialdemokratie zuischen Nationalismus und Internationalismus', *ibid.*, Vol. IX, where Šmeral's speech is extensively quoted.

8. Cf. Giuliano Gaeta, *Trieste durante la guerra mondiale. Opinione pubblica e giornalismo a Trieste del 1914 al 1918*, Trieste, 1938. Cf. also Silvio Benco, *'Il Piccolo' di Trieste. Mezzo secolo di giornalismo*, Milan, 1931. Though Benco simply identifies the Trieste National Liberal Party, which *Il Piccolo* supported, with irredentism, he himself reminds us that Teodoro Mayer, the proprietor and editor of his newspaper, from 1902 onwards spent part of the year in Rome, where he was on intimate terms

with members of the government who, though they feared and disliked Austria and therefore supported Italian rearmament, did not desire a clash with it, and on some occasions, as in 1913, when the governor of Trieste came into conflict with the Italians over the continuation of the employment of citizens of the kingdom of Italy in the communal offices, successfully acted as mediators, causing Berlin to exercise pressure on Vienna to induce it to give way. Cf. S. Benco, *op. cit.*, p. 192, and in particular William C. Askew, 'The Austro-Italian Antagonism, 1896–1914', *Power, Public Opinion and Diplomacy. Essays in Honor of Eber Malcolm Carrol by his former students*, Durham, Duke Univ. Press, 1959, especially p. 217. Mario Alberti, *L'irredentismo senza romanticismi*, Como, 1936, pp. 31–32 in fact estimates the conscious irredentists at about 2 per cent of the population, but believes that their number increased with the approach of the European war. His estimate is accepted by Theodor Veiter, *Die Italiener in der österreichische–ungarischen Monarchie*, Munich, 1965. Irredentism was of course latent among a great many more who did not openly profess it. Hans Kramer, *Die Italiener unter der österreichische–ungarischen Monarchie*, Vienna, 1954, is, however, of the opinion (cf. p. 36) that with the aggravation of social problems irredentism was on the decline. For conflicting contemporary estimates, cf. Angelo Vivante, *Irredentismo adriatico*, new ed., Milan, 1954, and Attilio Tamaro, *Trieste*, Rome, 1930. The Trieste socialists made big advances under the leadership of Valentino Pittoni. Apart from hostility to the idea of war, and economic and historical considerations of which Vivante was the mouthpiece, they were influenced by a strong desire to avoid the split in their flourishing labour, trade-union and co-operative movement which was always possible in view of the fact that, like the Social Democratic parties of other nationalities in the empire, the Italian and Slovene socialist parties were distinct. At the Italo-Austrian socialist conference against nationalism in 1905, at which his report was approved unanimously, even by the Slovene delegates present, Pittoni recalled that he had been an irredentist in his youth, but that now the irredentists seemed to him to be exactly like the anarchists and the intransigent republicans who substituted a prejudice for reality. Cf. *La nostra politica estera. I convegni socialisti di Trieste, 21–22 maggio 1905*, Trieste, undated. Cesare Battisti, who sent a colleague (Antonio Piscel) to the convention instead of attending himself, though one of the reasons for inviting him was the desire to enable the Austrian socialists to condemn in the presence of their Italian comrades (as in fact they did) the pan-German violence that in 1904 had prevented the establishment of an Italian faculty in the University of Innsbruck, announced in his newspaper, the Trent *Popolo* that 'to solve the problem of nationalities in Austria the Austria of the present day must be destroyed'. Cf. Cesare Battisti's *Scritti politici*, national edition, ed. Ernesta Bittanti, Florence, 1923, pp. 437 ff.; and cf. now Cesare Battisti, *Opere complete*, three vols., Florence, 1966. Cf. also Claus Gatterer, *Unter seinem Galgen stand Österreich. Cesare Battisti*, Vienna, 1967. Renato Monteleone, *Il movimento socialista nel Trentino 1894–1914*, Rome, 1971.

While the National Liberal press of Trieste denounced the international socialist conference as a crime against the ardently Italian feelings of the people of the city, the Italian Foreign Minister, Marquis di San Giuliano, used it to assuage Austrian concern about Italian irredentism. 'Talking of irredentism, which he said was gradually fading away, he'—that is to say, San Giuliano, according to a report of a conversation with him by the Austro-Hungarian Ambassador in Rome dated December 27, 1905—'mentioned that a chief contributory factor was the attitude of the Social Democrats. They regard agitation of the kind as a certain means of encouraging militarism and increasing the military budget—hence their aversion to it.'

9. For Bakunin's view of the necessity of the revolutionary destruction of Austria, cf. *Michail Bakunins Sozial-politischer Briefwechsel mit Alexander Iw. Herzen und Ogarjow*, ed. Michail Dragomanow, Stuttgart, 1895, pp. 39 ff. and 301. Cf. also Franco Venturi, *Roots of Revolution*, London, 1960, and Benoît P. Hepner, *Bakounine, et le panslavisme révolutionnaire*, Paris, 1950. For Bakunin's position in 1848–49, cf. Alfred Fischel, *Der Panslavismus bis zum Weltkrieg. Ein geschichtlicher Überblick*, Stuttgart, 1919; Josef Pfitzner, *Bakunin-Studien*, Prague, 1932; Boris Nikolaevsky 'M. A. Bakunin in der "Dresdner Zeitung"', *International Review of Social History*, Vol. I, 1936; Vaclav L. Beneš, 'Bakunin and Palacky's Concept of Austroslavism', *Indiana Slavic Studies*, Vol. II, 1958. Cf. now Stanley Z. Pech, *The Czech Revolution 1848*, Durham, 1969.

10. Yugoslav literature on the assassins and the youth movement from which they emerged is referred to in Vice Zaninović, 'Mlada Hrvatska uoči I. svjetskog rata', *Historijski Zbornik*, 1958–59, pp. 65 ff., and in Vladimir Dedijer, *The Road to Sarajevo*, London, 1966. For the Yugoslav independence movement see Ju. A. Pisarev, *Osvoboditel'noe dviženie jugoslavskih narodov Avstro-Vengrii*, Moscow, 1962. Cf. also R. W. Seton-Watson, *Sarajevo, A Study in the Origins of the Great War*, London, 1926; Josef Matl, 'Der Panslavismus als politische Idee in Südosteuropa im. 19. und 20. Jahrhundert', *Wirtschaft und Gesellschaft in Südosteuropa*, Gedenkschrift für Wilhelm Gülick, Munich, 1961. At the 1914 trial Čabrinović said he had been inspired by reading Stepniak's *Underground Russia*, described his activity in the Bosnian Social Democratic movement and the anarchist wing of the Serbian socialist movement, and gave an account of the steps that led to his conversion to 'radical nationalism'. Princip said he had read Bakunin and Kropotkin, but had adopted the Italian Risorgimento as his model. Grabež said that Herzen had pointed the way. Cf. Alfred Mousset, *Un drame historique. L'Attentat de Sarajevo. Documents inédits et texte intégral des sténogrammes du procés*, Paris, 1930, *passim*. Princip told the prison doctor that the writings of Kropotkin had inspired him with the end and Mazzini with the means. He hoped that the assassination of the Archduke would lead to a social revolution by the peoples of Austria-Hungary and to the birth of a Yugoslav republic. For his 'radical nationalism', cf. V. Dedijer, *op. cit.* It should be recalled that a populist tradition existed among Serbian students which

had originated in about 1870 with Svetozar Marković, a young socialist who knew Bakunin personally but was a follower of Chernishevsky and Marx. He played a part in the democratic and radical political reawakening of the Serbs of southern Hungary and advocated the disruption of the Habsburg monarchy and the unification of the Southern Slavs by the route favoured by the federalist socialists of the Italian Risorgimento, i.e. by the preliminary establishment of liberty and justice. Cf. Woodford McClellan, *Svetozar Marković and the Origins of Balkan Socialism*, Princeton, 1964; and the same author's 'Serbia and Social Democracy', *International Review of Social History*, 1966. Serbian populism had its baptism of fire in the revolt of Hercegovina and in the war against Turkey in 1876, in which numerous Italian libertarians took part (cf. my *Questioni di storia del Socialismo*, Turin, 1958, and more specifically Marcella Deambrosis, 'La partecipazione dei Garibaldini e degli internazionalisti italiani all insurrezione di Bosnia ed Erzegovina del 1875–76 e alla guerra di Serbia', *Studi Garibaldini e altri sagi*, Mantua, 1967). On the wars with Turkey cf. David MacKenzie, *The Serbs and Russian Panslavism, 1875–1878*, Ithaca, 1967. The democratic groups among the Southern Slavs in Hungary were accused of high treason and crushed by the repressive measures of the Hungarian government, which sympathized with the Turks. Serbian socialism made its first appearance with Marković in the form of political radicalism and agrarian populism. Later, after some of Marković's friends had found a home in Pašić's Radical Party, the real socialists with the exception of a small minority who chose anarchism, became Marxists. For the evolution from populism to Marxism in Serbia, Hermann Wendel's *Aus der Welt der Südslaven*, Berlin, 1926, can still be consulted. This not being the place for a survey of recent Yugoslav social historiography, we shall confine ourselves to referring to the documents assembled in the volumes *Istorijski Arhiv Komunističke Partije Yugoslavije*, devoted to the history of the labour movement in all areas inhabited by Serbs, Croats or Slovenes. That underlying the ideological tradition and the political contingencies of the day social pressures were at work is obvious. Even the right of trade-union organization, which had existed in Austria-Hungary for twenty years, was obtained by the Bosnian workers only after a bloodthirsty general strike in May, 1906. Cf. Peter F. Sugar, *Industrialization of Bosnia-Hercegovina, 1878–1918*, Seattle, 1963, pp. 173 ff. A twelve-hour working day for seven days a week, with no Sunday rest, was still common in Bosnia in 1908. At the trial (A. Mousset, *op. cit.*, p. 669), Čabrinović denounced the poverty in which Bosnia-Hercegovina had been left by the Austro-Hungarian failure sufficiently to reform the feudal agrarian conditions left behind by the Turks. On the resulting peasant exasperation, cf. J. A. Pisarev, 'Krestjanskie volnenija v Bosnii i Herzegovine v 1910 g. i agrarija reforma 1911', *Novaja i Novejšaja Istorija*, 1960, No. 6, cf. P. Mitrovic, in *Revue d'histoire moderne et contemporaine*, July–September 1964, and in particular V. Dedijer, *op. cit.*, who explain both the revolutionary populism of the Young Bosnian movement and the attraction exercised by Serbia because of the press freedom and freedom of assembly that existed there. In reality the Black Hand had militarist authoritarian inclinations which the Young Bosnians failed properly to appreciate. All they saw was that Austria-Hungary was governing their country with semi-colonial police methods.

11. Cf. again L. Albertini, *op. cit.*, Vol. II, on the origins of the war, based, so far as Sarajevo is concerned, on a study carried out in Yugoslavia in 1937 by L. Magrini on Albertini's behalf. Also, in spite of his obvious exaggerations, cf. Hans Uebersberger, *Öesterreich zwischen Russland und Serbien*, Graz and Cologne, 1958, particularly for the responsibility of the Tsarist military authorities, already documented by him in his earlier works. For the Black Hand, as the 'Unity or death' organization came to be called, cf. D. Čedomir Popović, 'Das Sarajevoer Attentat und die Organisation "Vereinigung oder Tod"', *Berliner Monatshefte*, 1932 (2), pp. 1097 ff. The author, who was a member of the central committee of the organization, was sentenced to ten years' imprisonment at the trial at Salonica instigated by the Serbian government in 1917 of Colonel Dragutin Dimitriević, known as Apis, and his colleagues, for an attempt to assassinate the Regent Alexander that probably never took place. His story, however, gives information only about the general attitude of the Black Hand, which called its newspaper *Pijemont* to emphasize that it aimed, not just at the aggrandizement of Serbia, but at the creation of a new state to include all the Southern Slavs. He knew nothing of the relations between Apis and General Artamonov, the Russian military attaché in Belgrade. Victor A. Artamonov, 'Erinnerungen aus meiner Militär-Attachézeit in Belgrade', *Berliner Monatshefte*, 1938 (2) tries to minimize these contacts. They have, however, been documented in a series of revelations, for which cf. H. Uebersberger, *op. cit.*, who confirms the theories of L. Albertini and L. Magrini. H. Uebersberger, however, acknowledges (*op. cit.*, p. 289) having (in 1943) mistranslated the 1917 document in which Apis mentions his relations with Artamonov. In reality Apis denied that he informed the latter of the preparations for the assassination of Francis Ferdinand. On this point, cf. Stojan Gavrilović, 'New Evidence on the Sarajevo Assassination', *Journal of Modern History*, December 1955, pp. 410 ff.

12. Cf. the posthumous work by L. Štur, *Das Slawentum und die Welt der Zukunft*, ed. Josef Jirašek, Bratislava, 1931. This was written in German in 1853, but remained unpublished. Štur pointed out with great clarity (e.g. on pp. 163 ff.) three possible solutions to the problem of the Slavs of Austria-Hungary: (1) a republican federation of the whole of east central Europe, including Serbia, which the author regarded as a dream dating back to the Dekabrists; (ii) a reorganization of the Habsburg empire on federal lines, carried out by the dynasty itself, in accordance with the ideas of Palacky, which Štur had originally shared, turning it into an Austro-Slav state; and (iii) the gravitation of all the Slavs towards Russia and their ultimate absorption by the Russian empire, which seemed to him the most rational outcome. For L. Štur during the two revolutionary years, cf. A. Fischel, *op. cit.*, and Daniel Rapant, 'Slovak Politics in 1848–

49', *Slavonic and East European Review*, December 1948, *et seq.* Cf. now *L'udovit Štur und die slavische Wechselseligkeit*, L. Holotik ed., Bratislava–Vienna, 1969. Cf. also *Studia Historica Slovaka*, and Vaclav L. Beneš, in *Austrian History Year-Book*, Vol. III, pt. 2. Štur's ideas made an impact in Moscow, where his work was published in Russian in 1867. Cf. Vladimir Matula, 'L'udovit Štur und Russland', *Jahrbücher für die Geschichte Osteuropas*, 1967, n. 1. Cf. also Michael B. Petrovich, 'L'udovit Štur and Russian Panslavism', *Journal of Central European Affairs*, April 1952. Konrad Pfalzgraf, 'Die Politisierung and Radikalisierung des Problems Russland and Europa bei N. J. Danilevskij', *Forschungen zur Osteuropäischen Geschichte*, Vol. I, Berlin, 1954. Cf. also Hans Kohn, *Die Slaven und der Westen*, Vienna, 1956, pp. 167 ff. On the Slovak national revival as a whole, see the work of J. Mésároš in *Historica*, X, Prague, 1965.

13. T. G. Masaryk, *op. cit.*, p. 13; Emil Strauss, *Tschechoslowakische Aussenpolitik*, Prague, 1936, p. 25. C. Jay Smith, Jr., *The Russian Struggle for Power 1914–17. A study of Russian foreign policy during the First World War*, New York, 1956, points out that the Russian consul in Prague, Zhukovsky, exceeding Sazonov's instructions (or rather, as would appear from the documents, not receiving any reply to his requests for instructions), did not refrain from encouraging the hopes of the Czech nationalists. But Zhukovsky, as appears from his reports published in *Die Internationalen Beziehungen im Zeitalter des Imperialismus. Dokumente aus den Archiven der Zarischen und Provisorischen Regierung* (the German edition, ed. Otto Hötzsch, thirteen vols., Berlin, 1931–42, from the well-known collection of documents made public by the Soviet government), and in particular on p. 289 of Vol. II of Series I, preferred Klofáč, who was indifferent to neo-Slavism but was ready to offer his services, to Kramář and his associates whom he accused of failing to understand the historical and religious factors underlying Russian policy and with being primarily interested in the Czech economic penetration of Russia. Cf. also of course Friedrich Stieve, *Iswolski e la guerra mondiale*, Bologna 1926, and his editions of Izvolsky's correspondence; *Rings um Sazonow. Neue dokumentarische Darlegungen zum Ausbruch des grossen Krieges durch Kronzeugen*, ed. Edmund Ritter von Steinitz, Berlin, 1928, a collection of first-hand evidence by Austrian politicians and diplomatists; and Erwin Hölzle, *Der Osten in ersten Welkrieg*, Leipzig, 1944, who was able to consult the documents at the Quai d'Orsay during the German occupation of Paris, thus increasing our knowledge of the subject, in spite of the anti-Russian polemical exaggerations he shares with other German and Austrian authors. For Sazonov, cf. *Der grossen Katastrophe entgegen. Die russische Politik der Vorkriegzeit und das Ende des Zarenreiches (1904–1917). Erinnerungen*, by Dr Michael Freiherr von Taube, second ed. Leipzig, 1937, as well as the memoirs of the former Russian Foreign Minister, *Les années fatales. Souvenirs*, by N. S. Sazonov, 1927. On neo-Slavism, cf. A. Fischel, *op. cit.*, and also the work of its most convinced advocate in the Tsarist diplomatic service, Fürst G. Trubetzkoi, *Russland als Grossmacht*, second ed., Stuttgart, 1917. The prince, writing in 1910,

dated neo-Slavism from the Austro-Hungarian annexation of Bosnia (*op. cit.*, p. 44) and thus regarded it as essentially anti-Habsburg, so much so that he drew attention to the resultant community of interests in the Balkans between Russia and Italy (p. 114). He nevertheless concluded that the existence of an independent Austria, though it must respect the *status quo* in the Balkans and the independence of the small nations of that area, was 'an absolute necessity for Russia as for Europe' (p. 147) as a counterweight to pan-Germanism. Izvolsky, who could not forgive Aehrenthal's action of 1908, even after his death, was certainly very hostile to Vienna, as were the pro-Serbian and anti-German nationalists and those who, like Count V. A. Bobrinsky, one of the right-wing leaders in the Duma, thought it necessary to 'liberate' the Orthodox, i.e. primarily the Ruthenians of Galicia, Bukovina and the sub-Carpathian Ukraine, from subjection to a Roman Catholic monarchy, and to reconvert the Uniate Church to Orthodoxy. These extremists were by reason of their very Orthodoxy unwilling to support the cause of the Catholic or Protestant Slavs of the Habsburg empire (Poles, Czechs, Slovaks, Slovenes, Croats). Cf. Horst Jablonowski, 'Die Stellungnahme der russischen Parteien zur Aussenpolitik der Regierung von der russisch-englischen Verständigung bis zum ersten Weltkrieg', *Forschungen zur Osteuropäischen Geschichte*, Vol. V, Berlin, 1957 (especially p. 67). The political testing ground of neo-Slavism was, however, the prospect of a Russo-Polish reconciliation, which would certainly have been a cause of concern to Austria, where the Poles in Galicia constituted a substantial political force; in the first place, however, it presented the St Petersburg government with very difficult problems indeed.

For the Slav meetings and congresses (Prague, July 1908; St Petersburg, May 1909; Prague, June 1912; St Petersburg, May 1914), cf. the Austrian information in H.H.St.A, XL–219–220. P. A. Interna XXXXV, partially used by Olga Heinz, 'Der Neoslavismus', thesis for the University of Vienna, 1963, and in H. Hantsch's article in the *Austrian History Year Book*, 1965, I. Cf. also A. Fischel, *op. cit.*, pp. 525 ff. These meetings put Russian politicians (ranging from conservatives to constitutional democrats) in contact with a number of Czech deputies (Kramář, Masaryk, Klofáč, Štanek, Dürich, etc.) as well as Croats (Radić, Lorković, Tresić-Pavičić), Bulgarians and a few Slovaks and Serbs from Hungary, but they were important only to the extent that they favoured the possibility of a favourable Russian response to the policy of the leader of the Polish National Democratic Party, Roman Dmowski, who was a member of the Duma and aspired to Polish autonomy within the Russian empire as a centre of attraction to all Poles, thus including those in Austria and Germany. A clear reflection of this appears in the report (apparently drafted by Trubetskoy) submitted by Sazonov to the Tsar on January 20, 1914, on the problems of the Slav nationalities in Austria-Hungary and of the Poles in Russia. Cf. *Int. Beziehungen*, *op. cit.*, Series I, Vol. I, pp. 48 ff. Cf. also Kurt Georg Haussmann, 'Dmowskis Stellung zu Deutschland vor dem ersten Weltkrieg', *Zeitschrift für Ostforschung*, 1964, Nos. 1–2; Erwin Hölzle, 'Prolog zum ersten Weltkrieg. Weltideologische Wandlungen in Amerika

[309]

und Russland', *Historische Zeitschrift*, 1955, especially pp. 517 ff. The Russian consul in Prague said in his report on Czech participation at the meeting in May 1914 (*Int. Beziehungen, op. cit.*, Series I, Vol. II, p. 287) that to the St Petersburg organizers of the meeting the vital problems were smoothing out the differences between Serbs and Bulgarians, Russians and Poles, Poles and Ruthenians, while the chief concern of Kramář and his Czech associates was the foundation of a Slav bank, which would have much less political significance. In fact, apart from some definite but limited economic and cultural objectives, neo-Slavism would have been politically important to Kramář if the increased weight of the Slavs in Austria had resulted in a reconciliation between the Habsburg and Romanov empires. That was the view of Aehrenthal. Cf. his conversation of January 1910 with J. Redlich, *Das politische Tagebuch, op. cit.*, Vol. I, p. 44. Radić, the leader of the Croat Peasant Party, although he had already seen the inside of his country's prisons, said that the Russians were blind if they believed that the Slavs enjoyed fewer liberties in Austria-Hungary than they did in Russia. The Slovene Popular Party did not conceal its disapproval of the presence of the mayor of Ljubljana, Dr Hribar, at these Slav meetings (cf. A. Fischel, *op. cit.*, p. 574).

14. This is shown by the documents produced by H. Uebersberger, *op. cit.* Cf. also *Der Saloniki Prozess*, Berlin, 1933. On the conflict between the Black Hand and the Serbian government at the beginning of 1914, cf. the reports of the Austro-Hungarian Minister in Belgrade, Baron Giesl, from March 8 to June 6, 1914, *in Oesterreich-Ungarns Aussenpolitik. Von der bosnischen Krise 1908 bio zum Kriegsausbruch 1914. Diplomatische Aktenstücke des österreichischungarischen Ministerium des Aeussern*, ed. by Ludwig Bittner, Alfred Francis Pribram, Heinrich Srbik and Hans Uebersberger, eight vols., Vienna and Leipzig, 1930, Vol. VIII, pp. 19 ff. and 77 ff. Baron Giesl concluded that those who hated Austria-Hungary out of Yugoslav fanaticism were the Serbian military, who had been bitterly opposed to Pašič's government for some time. Cf. also Wayne S. Vucinich, *Serbia between East and West*, Stanford, 1954; Hermann Wendel, *Der Kampf der Südslawen um Freiheit und Einheit*, Frankfurt, 1925, p. 719. The *Pijemont* criticized Pašić for his indifference to the Yugoslav idea. I. Ugron, the Austro-Hungarian Minister in Belgrade during the Balkan wars, incidentally said soon after they began to J. Redlich, *Das politische Tagebuch, op. cit.*, Vol. I, p. 169, that Pašić not only did not want war with Austria-Hungary but would not have fought Turkey either if he had not been forced to by circumstances. Obviously this does not diminish his responsibility for the negligence he displayed —whether out of cynicism, fear, or simply because he was engaged in a difficult election campaign—in the face of the organization of the Sarajevo assassination, which came to his knowledge. On this question cf. L. Albertini, *Le origini, op. cit.*, Vol. II, *passim*. For the primary economic conflict that existed between Serbia and the Habsburg empire, cf. the diplomatic documents, and J. M. Baernreither, *Fragmente eines politischen Tagebuches. Die südslawische Frage in Oesterreich-Ungarn vor dem*

Weltkreig, ed. J. Redlich, Berlin, 1928; Dusan A. Lončarević, *Yugoslaviens Entstehung*, Vienna, 1929; Maurice Schultz, 'La politique économique d'Aehrenthal envers la Serbie', *Revue d'Histoire de la guerre mondiale*, 1935, pp. 325 ff.; Dimitrij Djordjevii, *Carinski rat Austro-Ugarske i Srbije* (1906–11), Belgrade, 1962. See also Raymond Poidevin 'Les intérêts financiers français et allemands en Serbie de 1895 à 1914', *Revue Historique*, July–September 1964; Liljana Aleksič-Pejković, 'La Serbie et les rapports entre les puissances de l'Entente (1908–13)', *Balkan Studies*, 1965, No. 2. The Serbian documents confirm that Russia, on the advice of France, asked Serbia in 1909 and in 1913 to abandon for the time being her objective of obtaining access to the sea, since she could obtain this only by a war with Austria-Hungary for which Russia was still militarily unprepared. That Austria-Hungary, by discriminating against Serbian exports, bore the primary responsibility for Serbia's passing over to the side of her enemies was admitted in 1917 by Mérey and Czernin in conversations with Wedel, the German ambassador.

15. F. Zwitter, *op. cit.*, p. 146. Baron von Musulin (*Das Haus am Ballplatz*, Munich, 1924), p. 208, returning to his native Croatia in 1913 after a long absence, found that nearly all the Croat intellectuals were now pro-Serbian, while the mass of the peasantry remained loyal to the Habsburg dynasty. The political parties of course took this into account. For those in the Czech areas, cf. Willy Lorenz, 'Die tschechischen Parteien im alten Oesterreich', (typed) thesis for the University of Vienna, 1941.

16. Klofáč, after a secret visit to the Foreign Ministry in St Petersburg and the Tsarist General Staff in January 1914, in the following April asked the Russian government for financial aid. His view was that with funds available it would be possible to set up a secret organization in Bohemia, Moravia and Silesia consisting of military reservists and industrial and mining workers for the purpose of establishing a force which would collaborate with Russian troops in the event of war. Cf. *Int. Beziehungen, op. cit.*, Series I, Vol. II, pp. 290–91. Cf. also Ludwig Bittner, 'Zur Geschichte der techechischen Umsturzbewegung in den Jahren 1914 u. 1915. Nach den russischen Akten', *Mitteilungen der österreichischen Instituts für Geschichtsforschung*, Vol. III, 1938. The Russian consul in Prague tried to obtain an interview with Sazonov for Klofáč when he forwarded the memorandum to his Minister, cf. *Int. Beziehungen, op. cit.*, p. 289. In the absence of Sazonov's reply we do not know whether the interview took place or the financial aid was granted (the relatively modest sum of 10,000 roubles a year was asked for). Klofáč was considered to be personally greedy for money.

17. Cf. *Der Hochverratsprozess gegen Dr. Kramář und Genossen*, Vienna, 1918, pp. 147 ff.

18. Cf. Emil Strauss, *Die Entstehung der Tschechoslowakischen Republik*, Prague, 1934, pp. 73, 85, 345. See J. Redlich, *Das politische Tagebuch, op. cit.*, Vol. II, p. 66, for Milan Hodža's confidences about his colleagues Kramář and Masaryk. As appears from Redlich's own work, *Austrian War Government*, New Haven, 1929, in particular p. 72, he remained of the

opinion that up to the summer of 1914 Kramář did not seriously desire the dismemberment of Austria-Hungary. R. Sieghart, *op. cit.*, p. 330, who had close financial connections with Kramář, was of the same opinion. Also in the 1915 trial the prosecution was unable to prove anything subversive against him during the pre-war period. Cf. *Das politische Tagebuch, op. cit.*, Vol. II, pp. 77 ff. R. W. Seton-Watson, *A History of the Czechs and Slovaks*, London, 1943, when he comes to speak of Kramář and Masaryk, whom he knew personally, on p. 285 concludes that up to 1914 they substantially accepted the Habsburg empire. Thanks to the works of Ernest Denis, Seton-Watson and others, and to Masaryk's and Beneš's memoirs, the Czech political problem is well known. On Kramář, cf. Kurt Rabl, '"Historisches Staatsrecht" und Selbstbestimmungsrecht bei der Gründung der Tschechoslowakei 1918–19', *Zeitschrift für Ostforschung*, 1959, No. 3, and, on his great colleague (and opponent), Paul Selver, *Masaryk. A Biography*, London, 1940 (with preface by Jan Masaryk). On the attempts made to reach an agreement between the German Austrians and the Czechs and their failure, deplored by Kramář, in 1910, cf. Suzanne G. Konirsh, 'Constitutional Aspects of the Struggle between Germans and Czechs in the Austro-Hungarian Monarchy', *Journal of Modern History*, September 1955, pp. 231 ff.; Alexander Fussek, 'Die Frage des böhmischen Ausgleiches vor Beginn des Ersten Weltkrieges', *Österreich in Geschichte und Literatur*, 1967, No. 1. For Kramář's pro-Russian project, cf. Jaroslav Werstadt, 'Die tschechoslowakische Staatsidee in der Befreiungsrevolution während des Weltkriegs', in J. Malypeter *et al.*, *Die tschechoslowakische Republik*, Prague, 1937, Vol. I, pp. 129 ff.

19. A. Margutti, *op. cit.*, pp. 115 ff.

20. A. Hantsch, *Leopold Graf Berchtold*, two vols., Graz and Vienna, Vol. I, pp. 388 ff., Vol. II, pp. 555 ff.

21. Cf. in the papers of Franz Ferdinand, H. H. St. A, Depot Hohenberg, II, B–16a, the articles on the validity in Hungarian law of the Archduke's morganatic marriage published by a confidant of his, the former deputy G. Linder, in the authoritative Budapest *Pesti Hirlap*, 1904–5. These were publicly approved of by D. Bánffy, a former Hungarian Prime Minister. Cf. *ibid.*, Bánffy's letter of August 18, 1904.

22. The principal advocate of trialism, which, however, he wished to attain by making war on and annexing Serbia and incorporating it into a third (Southern Slav) Habsburg kingdom was General Conrad, the Chief of the General Staff. Cf. Oskar Regele, *Feldmarschell Conrad. Auftrag und Erfüllung, 1906–1918*, Vienna, 1955. Another supporter of the idea was General Potiorek, the governor of Bosnia-Hercegovina. Cf. the entries dated January 10 and 29 in the unpublished diary of L. Thallóczy, of whom we shall have more to say later.

23. Cf. Elfriede Putz, 'Die Delegationen von Oesterreich-Ungarn und die österreichisch-ungarische Aussenpolitik. 1908–1914', thesis for the faculty of philosophy of the University of Vienna, 1961. It was generally said that the Austrian delegation split into twenty parties, while the Hungarian consisted at most of two.

24. Cf. in H.H.St.A, Nachlass Franz Ferdinand (Depot Hohenberg), *op. cit.*, II, B–15a and II, B–16a, the numerous confidential political reports periodically sent to Brosch in particular by Hodža, Vajda-Voevod and Maniu, and also by the Hungarians Lányi, Linder and Kristóffy. It appears from this correspondence that the Archduke sometimes received the writers in secret audience. See also Vajda-Voevod's letters to Beck, the Austrian Prime Minister in 1906–7, to whom, shortly before the latter lost the Archduke's confidence, he owed his summons to the Belevedere. Cf. Allgemeines Verwaltungs-Archiv, Nachlass Beck, file 39. Vajda-Voevod expatiated on his relations with the Belvedere, apparently with a wealth of detail, in a manuscript of 1941–42 to which attention is drawn by Miron Constantinescu, 'Partisans et adversaires roumains de la "Grossösterreich" en Transylvanie (1905–1917)', abstracted from *Nouvelles études d'histoire*, Bucharest, 1965.

25. The basic work is Georg Franz, *Erzherzog Franz Ferdinand und die Pläne zur Reform der Habsburger Monarchie*, Brünn, 1943; the most detailed is Rudolf Kiszling, *Erzherzog Franz Ferdinand von Oesterreich Este, Leben, Pläne, und Wirken am Schicksalsweg der Donaumonarchie*, Graz and Cologne, 1953. Among the works of those who collaborated with the Belvedere, cf. Carl Freiherr von Bardolff, *Soldat im alten Oesterreich. Erinnerungen aus meinem Leben*, Jena, 1938; J. Kristóffy, *op. cit.*; Leopold von Chlumecky, *Erzherzog Franz Ferdinand, Wirken und Wollen*, Berlin, 1929; Edmund Steinacker, *Lebenserinnergungen*, Munich, 1937; Milan Hodža, *Federation in Central Europe*, London, 1942, and *Középeuropa utjan*, Bratislava, 1938; Friedrich Funder, *Vom Gestern ins Heute*, Vienna, 1952. Cf. also Magda Lammasch-Hans Sperl, *Heinrich Lammasch. Seine Aufzeichnungen, sein Wirken und seine Politik*, Vienna, 1922; Theodor von Sosnosky, *Franz Ferdinand. Der Erzherzog Tronfolger Ein Lebensbild*, Munich, 1929; Oliver Eöttevényi, *Ferenc Ferdinánd*, Budapest, 1942; Mihály Dömötör, *Ferenc Ferdinánd politikája*, Budapest, 1940.

The intelligence with which Brosch, who came of an old family of Austrian officials and was born in an ethnically mixed zone in south-east Hungary, picked men was demonstrated by the fact that after the war Maniu, Miron Cristea and Vajda-Voevod became Prime Ministers of Romania, while Hodža became Prime Minister of Czechoslovakia and Korošec of Yugoslavia, while in Austria since 1920 the reins of power have consistently been in the hands of the Christian Social Party. In Hungary the party of small landowners that Hodža and Kristóffy brought in contact with the Belvedere won the only two free elections conducted in conditions of universal secret suffrage that have ever been held there, in 1920 and in 1945. Both Kristóffy and Hodža were also in contact with the Hungarian Social Democratic Party. It is true that Francis Ferdinand was affected also by very different political influences, for instance that of Count Czernin, who was selected as his future Foreign Minister and in fact became Foreign Minister under the Emperor Charles (cf. M. Lammasch, *op. cit.*, pp. 87 ff., and Robert A. Kann, 'Count Ottokar Czernin and Archduke Francis Ferdinand', *Journal of Central European Affairs*, July

[313]

1956). Czernin, assuming that to facilitate his future task it would be better to avoid a clash with the Hungarian aristocracy (in fact he had to overcome Count Tisza's mistrust before being appointed Minister in Bucharest in 1913) had already begun advising the Archduke to advance very cautiously along the road to the democratization of Hungary though, as was to be shown by Charles's unhappy experience in 1917–18, this road could not be opened except by audacious action. His argument, which was that no Magyar politician was to be trusted, since all of them at heart wanted Hungarian independence, was well adapted to lodging in the Archduke's suspicious mind.

Brosch's opinion of Czernin was that he was a careerist, very intelligent, it is true, but too presumptious and lacking in balance. He believed Czernin found favour with Francis Ferdinand because the Archduke's wife, who was boycotted by the Habsburg court, liked him. Brosch believed that, if Czernin ever became Prime Minister, it would be disastrous for Austria-Hungary. Cf. his letter dated December 9, 1913 to a friend, a former Minister of War, published by Ludwig Jedlička in *Virtute fideque. Festschrift für Otto von Habsburg*, Vienna, 1965. Czernin's was not the only conservative influence. Paul Samassa said to J. Redlich (*op. cit.*, Vol. I, pp. 227 ff.) that if the Emperor of Germany, to whom the Hungarian aristocrats could have made representations, had advised Francis Ferdinand against democratization in Hungary, he would have hesitated. To the Archduke universal suffrage was of course merely a tool, and in Austria he would have revoked it if that had been possible. General Conrad, the Chief of the General Staff of the Armed Forces, was in favour of it for Hungary as a way of reinforcing the loyalty of the Slav and Romanian troops.

Another question is how much those outside the Belvedere knew about the Archduke's plans. The Hungarians were well informed about what concerned them and were preparing for a trial of strength (cf. G. Gratz, *op. cit.*, Vol. II, p. 283; cf. also Győző Bruckner, *Ferenc Ferdinánd trónörökös Magyarországi politikai tervei*, Miskolc, 1929). In September 1907 the Archduke frankly told Count Andrássy, then Hungarian Minister of the Interior, of his rooted aversion to the dual system (cf. O. Eöttevényi, *op. cit.*, p. 196). More information filtered through by way of G. Linder, a friend of Tisza's rivals in the Hungarian Liberal Party (cf. J. Szterényi, *op. cit.*, p. 24). Andrássy told Maniu that he was perfectly well aware that he and his Romanian colleagues in the Hungarian parliament had contacts with the Belvedere, and he deplored this because it made better relations impossible between the coalition government and the nationalities. Unless these contacts ceased, he said threateningly, 'We shall weaken you, so that the Viennese circles on whom you rely will be able to fight us with smaller chances of success'. Maniu replied that the non-Magyar nationalities owed to the Habsburgs what little they had ever obtained. Cf. Vajda-Voevod's letter to Brosch of March 19, 1909, in which the incident is mentioned (H. H. St. A, Nachlass Franz Ferdinand. II, B–16a). Khuen was aware of Vajda-Voevod's role at the Belvedere and tried to blackmail him; cf.

Vajda's letter to Brosch of June 27, 1910. Tisza himself (cf. his compete works, IVth series, Vol. II, pp. 197 ff.), writing to von Tschirschky, the German ambassador in Vienna, on October 6, 1914, indicated that he was aware of Popovici's relations with the Belvedere. Tisza was informed of the federation or trialism projects, submitted to the Archduke, by L. Thallóczy, a Hungarian who was head of a department in the Ministry for Joint Finances in Vienna. He had been a tutor of the Archduke's and maintained relations with his friends, such as Count H. Clam-Martinic, the 1917 Prime Minister, and Brosch himself. Dr Marta Tömöry, who is working on Thallóczy's papers, which are in the National Library in Budapest, has courteously put at my disposal the copy she made of his unpublished diary. (She has now published the part concerned with the years 1908–9, *Századok*, 1966, Nos. 4–5). Thallóczy, who was also a historian, recorded his conversations with many politicians in his diary. In 1912 he was most concerned at Hodža's activities at the Belvedere. A year later, because of the Balkan wars, his chief worry was the Archduke's pro-Croatian attitude. On April 5, 1913, he complained that Francis Ferdinand 'seriously wanted trialism', but not war with Serbia. Hodža, who, according to J. Redlich, *op. cit.*, Vol. I, p. 230, remained *persona gratissima* at the Belvedere to the end, must have given some information to Masaryk and Kramář. The attitude of Dr Frank towards the Archduke was well known in Croatia. H. Hinković, the deputy to the Croatian Diet, was aware that the Belvedere was faced with the choice between trialism and federalization, and wrote to Seton-Watson to that effect in 1913, stating, however, that, while federalization was the more likely of the two, he himself believed that Austria-Hungary was incapable of making up its mind and would therefore disintegrate. However, a journalist as acute as Wickham Steed, who spent so many years in Vienna, in his well-known book on the Habsburg monarchy that appeared in 1913, still considered the Archduke to be the leader of the war party. In his memoirs, *op. cit.*, Vol. I, p. 359, he attributes Francis Ferdinand's federalization projects almost exclusively to his ambitions for his sons. But the political intelligence of the Archduke seems to be confirmed by his correspondence with Professor Pastor (the historian of the Popes and director of the Austrian Historical Institute in Rome, whom he used to make his wishes known to the Holy See), Bishop J. Lányi and others (cf. Freiherr Ludwig von Pastor, *Tagebücher, Briefe, Erinnerungen*, ed. by Wilhelm Wühr, Heidelberg, 1950, and Friedrich Engel-Janosi's important *Oesterreich und der Vatikan*, 1846–1918, two vols., Graz and Vienna, 1958–60, and in particular Vol. II, pp. 122 and 154 ff). Cf. now the Franz Ferdinand–Berchtold correspondence, published by R. A. Kann, *Mitteilungen der Österreichischen Staatsarchivs*, Vol. 22, 1969.

26. Cf. the memorandum in H. H. St. A, Nachlass Franz Ferdinand, *op. cit.* Hodža's letters to Brosch have been published now (in Czech translation) in *Historičky Časopis*, 1970, n. 3.

27. J. Redlich, *op. cit.*, Vol. I, p. 283, cf. V. Klofáč, 'Souvenirs de prison', in *Le Monde Slave*, 1917, Nos. 3–4 and 7.

28. Cf. Frano Supilo, *Politika u Hrvatskoj*, new edition, Zagreb, 1953. This is a reprint of a collection of articles by Supilo that appeared in the Fiume (Rijeka) *Novi List*. The first edition appeared in 1911. The new edition contains a long introduction by Vaso Bogdanov on Supilo's life and work, as well as a bibliography of the writings about him. Cf. also Bogdan Radica, *Supilova Pisma Ferrerovima*, Buenos Aires, 1957; Dragovan Sepić, *Supilo Diplomat*, Zagreb, 1961 (which deals only with Supilo's work in exile, but on the basis of a very thorough documentation); cf. also R. W. Seton-Watson, *Die südslawische Frage im Habsburger Reiche*, Berlin, 1913; Carlo Sforza, *Yugoslavia, Storia e ricordi*, Milan, 1948. Supilo, who had just lost his mother, wrote from London on April 6, 1917, to Gina Lombroso Ferrero: 'If you knew how often I think of you, and Guglielmo, and all of you, but I cannot imagine you anywhere but in Turin, where we met fourteen years ago. Someone was missing, someone came and was welcomed. What a pleasure it was for me to come to that landing and ring the bell. Some sort of nostalgia makes me keep remembering it, especially now that I am alone, alone in the world . . .' Cf. Bogdan Radica, *Supilova Pisma Ferrerovima*, p. 48. Cf. also Gina Lombroso Ferrero, 'Frano Supilo u Italjii', *Nova Evropa*, 1926, No. 11; and now B. Raditsa, 'Guglielmo Ferrero et les Slaves du Sud', in G. Ferrero, *Histoire et politique au XXième siècle*, Geneva, 1966.

29. The Salvemini papers. In fact Supilo was always critical of Dr Frank's policy and welcomed the establishment of a new Right Party in Croatia in 1903. Cf. V. Bogdanov in F. Supilo, *Politika, op. cit.*, pp. 8–9. The old Right Party was based on irreconcilable opposition to the Hungarian-Croatian 'settlement' of 1868, which the Hungarians imposed when their reconciliation with Francis Joseph had put them in a position of strength. Control of Croat financial, commercial, agricultural, industrial affairs and railway and maritime communications was transferred to Budapest, as was the appointment of the Ban, the chief of the executive in the territory, who was left with responsibility for ordinary administration, the courts, schools, etc. Ante Starčević, the founder of the Right Party, a popular orator and a nationalist of Jacobin temperament but an ardent Catholic, could not forgive the Serbs for what he called their 'conversion' to Orthodoxy and fought for the restoration of the independence of the kingdom of Croatia-Slavonia. A few months before his death in 1896 his party split, as not all its members approved of a declaration of loyalty to the dynasty (actually a very vague one) which the now senile Starčević was persuaded to agree to in the hope of a possible tripartite reorganization of the empire. The secessionists especially disliked the personality of Dr Josip Frank, who had encouraged the pro-Habsburg trend and was to succeed Starčević as the leader of the party that was to be renamed the 'pure' Right Party. Frank, a skilful politician with a thorough grounding in financial matters in particular, was considered to be an ambitious opportunist because, among other things he, a converted Jew, had sought—and quickly obtained —Catholic Church support for his policy. In fact his objective was to obtain the backing of Vienna against the Budapest government which oppressed

Croatia, but his hatred of the Serbs, whom the Hungarians favoured from time to time in order to put them against the Croats, made him go too far. In 1903 Grga Tuškan, after negotiations for unification with Dr Frank that ended in failure, founded the Croat Right Party, with which the Dalmatian Right Party, from which Supilo himself came, aligned itself in a policy which, after the Hungarian government ceased favouring the Serbs, looked to a reconciliation with the latter based on the ethnic unity of the Southern Slaves. Cf. Ante Smith Pavelić, *Dr Ante Trumbić. Problemi Hrvatsko-Srpskih Odnosa*, Munich, 1959, pp. 12–13. Cf. also Maria Reuter, 'Die politischen Parteien in Jugoslawien von ihren Anfängen bis zur St Veits Verfassung', thesis for the University of Munich, 1942, as well the interesting articles by Mirjana Gross, 'Die nationale Idee der Kroatischen Rechtspartei und ihr Zusammenbruch (1883 bis 1895)', *Oesterreichische Osthefte*, 1964, No. 5, and 'Erzherzog Franz Ferdinand und die Kroatische Frage', *ibid.*, 1966, No. 4.

30. Cf. the report on Supilo that L. Voinovich sent from Rome on July 17, 1916, *Historijski Pregled*, 1963, No. 4.

31. B. Radica, *op. cit.*

32. *Ibid.*, p. 366.

33. R. W. Seton-Watson, *op. cit.*, pp. 134 ff. From 1901 *Novi List*, the newspaper that Supilo edited, was published in Fiume, a predominantly Italian town, instead of in the adjoining Croatian township of Sušak, where it was founded in 1900 and had the greater part of its circulation, because in Fiume, a Hungarian enclave, there was greater press freedom than in Croatia. Cf. V. Bogdanov, *op. cit.*, p. 8. The communal council of Fiume, the strongest party on which was Riccardo Zanella's Italian Autonomist Party, granted Fiume, and hence Hungarian, citizenship to Supilo, who by virtue of his birth in Ragusa was an Austrian citizen and would thus have been ineligible for election to the Croatian Diet, which came juridically under the sovereignty of the state of Hungary. Cf. the account by Antonio Luksich Jamini in *Fiume*, 1959, Nos. 3–4, p. 186. Cf. also Giovanni Dalma, 'Testimonianza su Fiume e Riccardo Zanella', *Il Movimento di liberazione in Italia*, No. 78. The political persecutions to which the Croatian opponents of the Hungarian régime were subjected were not of course remotely comparable with the practices of totalitarian governments of later generations. Svetozar Pribitchevitch, whose brothers were given heavy sentences (but later acquitted on appeal) in 1909, acknowledges in his *La dictature du Roi Alexandre. Contribution a l'étude de la democratie. (Les problèmes Yougoslave et Balkanique.) Documents inédits et révélations*, Paris, 1933, that respect for the human individual in Austria-Hungary was far greater than under the royal dictatorship established in Yugoslavia in 1929 which did not, however, amount to a truly totalitarian régime.On Khuen's personality, cf. Wickham Steed, *The Doom of the Habsburgs*, Bristol, 1933.

34. B. Radica, *op. cit.*, p. 36. Cf. Wickham Steed's account, *Through Thirty Years*, Vol. I, p. 204, of the proceedings taken in 1904 against Supilo, who was charged with having maintained the necessity of an Italo-Slav

understanding against pan-Germanism. Cf. in Allg. Verwaltungs-Archiv, Ministerium des Innern, Präsidiale, the charges that the Austrian governor of Zara made in 1904–6 against Trumbić and Supilo, whom he accused of subversive contacts (allegedly facilitated by membership of the Masonic movement with Italian irredentists). The governor also feared that Supilo, whom he described as 'very dangerous', intended with the aid of the Serbian government to provoke a revolt in Bosnia with a view to inciting the Hungarian independence party to rise and detach Hungary from Austria. Cf. the governor's report of February 17, 1906, *loc. cit.* Cf. now Peter Schurter, *Henry Wickham Steed und die Habsburge Monarchie*, Vienna 1970.

35. B. Radica, *op. cit.*, p. 366.

36. F. Supilo, *Politika, op. cit.*, p. 131; A. Smith Pavelić, *op. cit.*, p. 14. Cf. also L. V. Südland (Ivo Pilar in collaboration with Adalbert Shek), *Die Südslawische Frage und der Weltkrieg*, Vienna, 1918, p. 646. According to documents brought to light by Dimitrije Djordjević, *Carinski rat, op, cit.*, and *Révolutions nationales des peuples balkaniques, 1804–1914*, Belgrade, 1965, the Serbian government then placed its hopes on the Hungarian independence party. The author also confirms Supilo's contacts during this period with Pašič and Ljuba Stojanović, then the Serbian Prime Minister. Ivo J. Lederer, in a very good discussion of the question (cf. *Austrian History Year-Book*, Vol. III, pt. 2, p. 196) rightly stresses, however, that Djordjević overestimates the pre-war Serb government's interest in the Yugoslav idea.

37. *Ibid.*, p. 647; R. W. Seton-Watson, *op. cit.*, p. 169.

38. Mirjana Gross, *Vladavina Hrvatsko-Srpske Koalicije, 1906–1907*, Belgrade, 1960, pp. 12 ff.; A. Smith Pavelić, *op. cit.*, p. 15; P. Supilo, *op, cit.*, pp. 160 ff.; Jozsef Szterényi, *Régmult idök emlékei Politikai feljegyzések*. Budapest, 1925, p. 183. Cf. the text of the Fiume resolution in L. Südland, *op. cit.*, pp. 647–650.

39. G. Gratz, *op. cit.*, Vol. II, p. 161.

40. M. Gross, *op. cit.*, p. 14; L. Südland, *op. cit.*, p. 652. According to the 1900 census, the population of Dalmatia was about 600,000, of whom 81 per cent were Croats, 16 per cent Serbs, and 3 per cent Italians. In the same year Serbs constituted about 27 per cent of the population of Croatia-Slavonia. In Bosnia-Hercegovina, in 1910 they constituted 43 per cent if religion is taken into account, but in fact the proportion was higher, since there were also 600,000 Muslims who were ethnically Slavs. There were about 440,000 Croat Catholics in Bosnia-Hercegovina or 32 per cent of the total.

41. Cf. again Scotus Viator (R. W. Seton-Watson), *Racial Problems in Hungary*, London, 1903. Seton-Watson went to their country full of enthusiasm for the Kossuth tradition, which was his reason for learning their language, but the Hungarians accused him of distortion for the purpose of showing their régime in a bad light. In his memoirs, *op. cit.*, Vol. II, p. 54, Count Apponyi—very honestly subjecting himself to self-criticism—admitted that the ruling class of which he had been a representative had

been deeply convinced that it would have been a doctrinaire error to apply the liberal law of 1868 concerning the nationalistics and thus renounce Magyarization. Recent Hungarian historiography has tried objectively to reconstruct the development of the nationalities question. Cf. in the first place G. Gábor Kemény, *A magyar nemzetiségi kérdés története*, Budapest, 1946, and the valuable volumes of documents being published by him. On the development of R. W. Seton-Watson's ideas, awaiting the book his sons are writing on him cf. Gertrude Schopf, 'Die österreichisch-ungarische Monarchie und Seton-Watson', thesis for the University of Vienna, 1953, pp. 8–28. Up to Sarajevo he hoped that Francis Ferdinand would reorganize Austria-Hungary on the basis of trialism. Cf. Arthur J. May, 'R. W. Seton-Watson and British Anti-Habsburg Sentiment', *American and Slavic East European Review*, February 1961, pp. 40 ff. The Southern Slavs told him they would await the succession to the Habsburg throne, in the hope that the new sovereign would make decisions in their favour. Cf. J. M. Baernreither, *op. cit.*, p. 253, with whom Seton-Watson discussed the matter in June 1913.

42. For the Zara resolutions, cf. F. Supilo, *op. cit.*, p. 319, and L. V. Südland, *op. cit.*, p. 653. The text of the manifesto of December 11, 1905, is in *Istorijski Arhiv Komunističke Partije Jugoslavije*, Vol. IV, *Socialistički pokret u Hrvatskoj i Slavoniji, Dalmaciji i Istri, 1892–1914*, Belgrade, 1950, pp. 72–76.

43. R. W. Seton-Watson, *Die Südslawische Frage, op. cit.*, p. 171. An influx of Serbo-Croat students to Prague University began after some of them had been excluded (in 1895) from the University of Zagreb, a visit to which by Francis Joseph, accompanied by the Hungarian Prime Minister, led to an anti-Hungarian demonstration. One of the leaders of the demonstration was the future peasant leader, Sjepan Radić. At Zagreb in 1896 he and the future Serbo-Croatian coalition leader Svetozar Pribičević founded a united Serbo-Croat youth movement with a Yugoslav programme. Cf. S. Pribitchevitch, *op. cit.*, p. 17. The movement did not last long, however, and Radić reverted to Croat particularism.

44. *Garami Ernö Emlékkönyv, 1876–1935*, Budapest, 1939. At that time the Austrian socialists did not yet believe that the Emperor would grant universal suffrage but, when Victor Adler realized that Francis Joseph was in earnest, he skilfully intervened with his party and approved the precedent set by Garami, which Bebel himself subsequently defended against socialist left-wing criticism. Cf. now Ferenc Mucsi, *A Kristóffy Garami Paktum*, Budapest, 1970.

45. Cf. J. Kristóffy, *op. cit.*, pp. 187 ff., as well as his reports to Brosch in H.H.St.A, Nachlass Franz Ferdinand, *op. cit.*, 11, B–15a; Manó Buchinger, *Küzdelem a szocializmusért*, Budapest, undated (but 1946), pp. 243 ff., and Vol. III (1900–7) of the *Selected Documents on the History of the Hungarian labour movement*, published in Budapest in six vols. between 1951 and 1966. Kristóffy himself said (*op. cit.*, p. 186) that the idea of universal suffrage came to him from direct observation of the Social Democratic struggles. He was deputy for a multinational constituency in

which 'agrarian socialism' had had a wide following among the land workers since the 1890s. The Hungarian Social Democrats regarded Kristóffy as a man of not very wide horizons but well intentioned towards the workers. Cf. his obituary by M. Buchinger, the party secretary, in the periodical *Szocializmus*, 1928, pp. 169 ff.; J. M. Baernreither, *Der Verfall*, *op. cit.*, p. 164, and O. Jászi, *The Dissolution*, *op. cit.*, p. 193, footnote, who did not have a high opinion of Kristóffy, attribute his plan of action, the former to the head of his press office, the Liberal journalist J. Vészi, and the latter to a friend they had in common, the Radical sociologist K. Mérey-Horváth. The latter, an unusually strong personality according to G. Gratz, *op. cit.*, Vol. II, p. 115, certainly took part in working out the electoral reform project. This was drafted by Kristóffy's secretary, a conscientious young lawyer who showed in the preamble that under the existing law qualification for the vote varied enormously depending on the constituency, and thus left the door open to all sorts of abuses (cf. F. Funder, *op. cit.*, p. 391).

46. Cf. Johann Sassmann, 'Der Kampf un das allgemeine Wahlrecht und die Christlichsoziale Parte', thesis for the University of Vienna, 1948.

47. As he explained in his 1907 letters to Brosch referred to above, Kristóffy hoped by the grant of universal suffrage, not only to secure the loyalty to the dynasty of the Hungarian Social Democrats, but also to demonstrate that the forty-eightists opposition no longer had the masses in the Hungarian capital behind it. He hoped in the course of time to wean the radical and socialist peasant movements, which wanted to see the great estates broken up, from the revolutionary mythology of 1848–49. It should be borne in mind that while estates of more than 50 hectares constituted 40·72 per cent of the land in the whole of the Habsburg monarchy, the corresponding figure for Hungary only was 54·84 per cent. In Hungary estates exceeding 500 hectares accounted for 32·27 per cent of the cultivated land, and 91·4 per cent of the landowners were Magyars. Cf. *Die Agrarfrage in der österreichisch-ungarischen Monarchie, 1900–1918*, Bucharest, 1965.

48. According to his letter to Brosch of September 10, 1908, Kristóffy, before leaving the Ministry of the Interior (in 1906) secured an undertaking from the independence party that his programme for the introduction of universal suffrage would be adhered to. H. H. St. A, *loc. cit.*

49. A. Apponyi, *op. cit.*, Vol. II, p. 142; Julius Andrássy, *Diplomatie und Weltkrieg*, Berlin, 1920, pp. 228 ff.; Cf. now also J. Dolmányos, *A magyar parlamenti ellenzék történetéböl (1901–4)*, Budapest, 1963. For the favour with which highly placed representatives of the Hungarian economy regarded the nationalist demand for customs autonomy, cf. the conversations with the latter reported in J. M. Baernreither, *Der Verfall*, *op. cit.*, pp. 147 ff., Cf. also R. Sieghart, *op. cit.*, pp. 105 ff. On this point O. Jászi, *op. cit.*, pp. 208–212 ff., is unconvincing. He advocated Hungarian customs autonomy in the hope, subsequently disappointed by the social and economic development of independent Hungary between the two world wars, that in a predominantly agricultural country that had to industrialize the demand

for industrial labour would increase, while the cost of living would be kept down by the diminution of agricultural exports and the workers' real wages would increase. This was in fact the view of many socialists, though it was not shared by E. Garami, who had more confidence in the liberalism im- plicit in the customs union. More subtle was the argument of N. Asztalos and A. Pethö, *op. cit.*, p. 451, who attributed the conservatism of Hungarian agricultural methods to the assured market provided by the customs union with Austria. But with the financial separation that was bound to be the premise or the corollary of the end of the customs union it is hard to see where the Hungarian agriculturists, already heavily in debt, would have raised the capital necessary for increasing the productivity of their land. Pethö himself recognized—and Jászi had always maintained—that the root of the trouble lay in the latifundia system which, however, in Hungary sur- vived by twenty-seven years the end of the union with Austria. For the calculation of the Austrian and Hungarian gross domestic material pro- ducts cf. J. T. Berend, P. Hanák, L. Katus, Gy. Ránki, *Social-Economic Researches in the History of East-Central Europe*, Budapest, 1970. Cf. also Frederick Hertz, *The Economic Problems of the Danubian States*, London, 1947. A good evaluation of Austro-Hungarian economy is given by Kurt Wessely in *Donauraum* 1967 n. 1-2.

50. G. Gratz, *op. cit.*, Vol. II, p. 167. Cf. in B. Radica, *op. cit.*, p. 368, Supilo's letter of June 19, 1906, on the hopes roused by the first coalition success.

51. J. Szterényi, *op. cit.*, pp. 188–189. M. Gross, *op. cit.*, pp. 181 ff. Supilo later said to J. Redlich, *Das politische Tagebuch*, *op. cit.*, Vol. I, p. 12, Wekerle, the Hungarian Prime Minister, had suggested the language clause in order to wreck the good relations between the Party of Inde- pendence and of 1848 and the Serbo-Croat coalition. There is no certain evidence of this, though it is known that Wekerle was often disloyal to his forty-eightist allies.

52. Hodža informed O. Eöttevónyi, *op. cit.*, pp. 182–183, after the war that on the day after the Csernova incident he made an interpellation in the Budapest parliament and was urgently summoned by Francis Ferdinand, who wanted a complete account from him of the Slovak versions of the affair.

53. Solomon Wank, 'Aehrenthal's Program for the Constitutional Transformation of the Habsburg Monarchy. Three Secret "Mémoires"', *Slavonic and East European Review*, June 1963. H. Hantsch, *op. cit.*, Vol. I, pp. 72 ff. W. M. Carlgreen, *Iswolsky and Aehrenthal vor der bosnichen Annexionskrise*, Uppsala, 1955, p. 119.

54. I have consulted Burian's diary (handwritten in Hungarian in numerous notebooks) thanks to the courtesy of Dr I. Diószogi of the Uni- versity of Budapest. It covers the years 1886–1922. Cf. of course Stefan Burian, *Drei Jahre meiner Amtsführung im Kriege*, Berlin, 1923.

55. I have relied on Burian's diary and on Thallóczy's. Burian and Aehrenthal used Thallóczy to persuade Wekerle, by raising the spectre of a trialism, to agree to the territory's being annexed to Austria-Hungary

instead of to Hungary. On the whole question, cf. Jurij Križek's study, 'Annexion de la Bosnie et Hercégovine', *Historica*, IX, Prague, 1964. The author did not see the Hungarian sources, but used the Austrian, Croat and Bosnian sources and the most recent Russian literature. Cf. also the brief but well-informed work by K. B. Vinogradov, *Bosnijski Krizis 1908–1909. Prolog pervoi miroroi vojnii*, Leningrad, 1964. Cf. of course Bernadotte E. Schmitt, *The Annexation of Bosnia, 1908–9*, Cambridge, 1937, and Momtchilo Nincić, *La crise bosniaque (1908–1909) et les puissances européennes*, two vols., Paris, 1937.

56. Cf. H. Hantsch, *op. cit.*, and W. M. Carlgreen, *op. cit.*

57. J. Szterényi, *op. cit.*, p. 206. Cf. Jenö Horváth, *A magyar kérdés a XX. században*, Budapest, 1939, Vol. I, pp. 66 ff. for the report of the proceedings of the Hungarian cabinet of October 3, 1908. Wekerle had, however, already committed himself to Aehrenthal at the joint meeting of Austro-Hungarian Ministers on August 19 only making it a condition that there should be no infringement of the dual system by tripartite experiments for the benefit of the Southern Slavs. Cf. J. M. Baernreither, *Die südslawische, op. cit.*, pp. 82 ff. Tisza was also in favour of the annexation and said so to Wickham Steed (cf. *op. cit.*, Vol. I, p. 265), believing that Austria-Hungary should take advantage of the assurance of full German support.

58. The part that F. Kossuth played in the annexation of Bosnia is shown by his letters of 1906–9 to his brother (who remained in Italy after their father's death), published by R. Várkonyi Ágnes in *Századok*, 1961, Nos. 2–3.

59. A. Lončarević, *op. cit.*, pp. 343 ff.; R. W. Seton-Watson, *Die südslawische Frage, op. cit.*, pp. 207–240. According to J. M. Baernreither, *Die südslawische, op. cit.*, p. 135, after the crisis had passed Aehrenthal himself realized that it was a mistake to make martyrs and suggested to Wekerle that conviction of the Zagreb accused should be avoided, but Wekerle refused.

60. T. G. Masaryk, *Der Agramer Hochverratsprozese und die Annexion Bosniens und der Hercegovina*, Vienna, 1909.

61. F. Supilo, *op. cit.*, pp. 224 ff.; R. W. Seton-Watson, *op. cit.*, pp. 231–237. In a conversation in January 1910 with J. Redlich (*Das politische Tagebuch, op. cit.*, Vol. I, p. 44) Aehrenthal admitted that at a time when he believed war to be inevitable he asked Friedjung to use his prestige as a historian to begin an anti-Serbian press campaign, but he totally denied responsibility for the way in which this was carried out, attributing this to Jettel, head of a department in his Ministry. According to A. Lončarević (*op. cit.*, p. 375), who as Belgrade correspondent of the Austrian telegraphic agency was usually well informed, Jettel had doubts about using the documents in question, the source of which he was not sure of. The diplomatic papers published in *Oesterreich-Ungarns Aussenpolitik, op. cit.* (Vol. I, pp. 371–372) include a message from Forgách urging the use of documents forwarded by him for an anti-Serbian press campaign. For the subsequent course of events in Vienna, cf. Franz Graf, 'Heinrich Friedjung

und die Südslawische Frage', thesis for the University of Vienna, 1950.

62. R. W. Seton-Watson, *op. cit.*, pp. 250 ff.; P. Selver, *op. cit.*, pp. 224 ff.; cf. also H. Wickham Steed, *op. cit.*, Vol. I, pp. 227 ff., who attended the trial. The Austrian diplomatic authorities had realized that the 'documents' were not authentic from two months before the beginning of the trial. Cf. *Oesterreich-Ungarns Aussenpolitik, op. cit.*, Vol. II, pp. 483–484. Cf. *ibid.*, *passim*, the ensuing correspondence between the Ministry and the Austrian legation in Belgrade.

63. It is certain that Supilo met Pašić in Belgrade as early as 1905, but nothing has been found in the documents to support the charges made against him in Vienna. Cf. M. Gros, *op. cit.*, pp. 19 ff.; R. W. Seton-Watson, *op. cit.*, pp. 269–298. Before the Zagreb and Vienna trials Seton-Watson had no liking for Masaryk, of whose anti-clerical radicalism he disapproved. But, when he saw that he did not hesitate to stake his whole career on defending men belonging to a nationality different from his own, he realized he was an exceptional personality. *Ibid.*, p. 278, footnote.

64. *Ibid.*, pp. 258 ff. and 318 ff. Cf. Ingeborg Engerth, 'Leopold von Chlumecky', thesis for the University of Vienna, 1950. Redlich, who normally supported Aehrenthal's policy in the Reichsrat and at the beginning of 1909 would have been willing to see the dispute with Serbia settled by force of arms, which the Austro-Hungarian Foreign Ministry was trying to avoid, immediately felt that Chlumecky's accusation against Supilo was unfounded (cf. *Das politische Tagebuch, op. cit.*, Vol. I, p. 38). Supilo himself attributed the attack on him to the Christian Social Party in Vienna and to Dr Frank, who were united by a common clericalism. Cf. F. Supilo, *op. cit.*, pp. 211 ff. He was a Freemason, proud of his friendship with Ettore Ferrari, the secretary of the Italian Grand Orient Lodge (*ibid.*, p. 136). F. Funder, the editor of the Christian Social newspaper *Reichspost*, as he says in his memoirs (*op. cit.*, p. 442) in fact received the documents from Francis Ferdinand's military chancery. He realized during the trial that they were forgeries, but in his opinion the forger's first victim was Count Forgách (*ibid.*, pp. 443 ff.).

65. For Vašić's letter to Supilo, cf. R. W. Seton-Watson, *op. cit.*, pp. 342–343. A. Lončarević (*op. cit.*, p. 377) was informed at the beginning of November 1910 by Baron von Haymerle, the counsellor at the Austro-Hungarian legation in Belgrade, that Vašić had asked the legation for money. The latter suggested that he should go to Zemun, in Hungary. Fearing a trap, he refused. A few days later he gave himself up to the Serbian authorities. For his trial, which took place in Belgrade on December 22–23, 1910, cf. again A. Lončarević (*op. cit.*, pp. 378 ff.), who attended it. Masaryk, who had already raised the question of Vasić in the Reichsrat in an attack on Aehrenthal, also attended the trial (cf. T. G. Masaryk, *Vašić–Forgách–Aehrenthal*, Prague, 1911). According to A. Spitzmüller-Harmersbach, *op. cit.*, p. 113, J. Redlich, *op. cit.*, Vol. I, p. 238, A. Lončarević, *op. cit.*, p. 630, and others who knew him, Count Forgách, who in 1913 had become head of a department in the Vienna Foreign Ministry, was one of those who most wanted war with Serbia in

July 1914. The affair of 1909–10 might well have left him full of resentment against Belgrade. But it is well known that after the unexpected Serbian successes in the Balkan wars the trend in Vienna was definitely towards the 'settlement of accounts' that had been several times postponed. Cf. J. M. Baernreither, *Die südslawische, op. cit.*, p. 238, and J. von Szilassy, *op. cit.*, p. 218. Forgách's reports of the Belgrade trial express only anger and embarrassment. Cf. *Oesterreich-Ungarns Aussenpolitik, op. cit.*, Vol. III, pp. 115–117. A. F. Pribram, *Austria-Hungary and Great Britain, 1908–1914*, London, 1951, states on p. 74 that Forgách was very headstrong and ambitious.

66. J. Szterényi, *op. cit.*, pp. 195–200. The documents in *Oesterreich-Ungarns Aussenpolitik, op. cit.*, Vol. II, pp. 498–504, confirm Szterényi's recollections. The document with Pašić's forged signature had been first obtained from a Hungarian journalist named Horváth. It was forwarded to the *Reichspost* by the Belvedere before it reached Friedjung. *Ibid.*, p. 551. J. M. Baernreither was told about the matter at the time by Szterényi himself. Cf. *Die südslawische, op. cit.*, p. 288. At the Vienna trial Dr Spalajković was able to show that the report attributed to him was a forgery because its file number did not correspond with the numbering system used in 1907 by the department of the Serbian Foreign Ministry of which he was then the head. The numbering of other 'documents' was also not in accordance with the system in use at the time they were allegedly written. Cf. R. W. Seton-Watson, *op. cit.*, p. 291 (cf. *ibid.*, pp. 534–539, the text of the 'report' produced by Professor Friedjung).

67. R. Várkonyi, *op. cit.*, p. 354.

68. That is the theory adopted by H. Uebersberger, *op. cit.*, p. 50. It has the advantage of explaining why the forger wrote his letter of confession. If he had been a double agent, the Serbian government, having him at hand in Belgrade, could easily have forced him to make the admissions contained in his letter to Supilo. The theory that he was a double agent had previously been put forward by Seton-Watson (*op. cit.*, p. 366), who believed in the guilt of Count Forgách and Baron Aehrenthal. H. Graf in his thesis, *op. cit.*, p. 150, concludes that they acted in good faith. This had already been established by A. J Taylor, *op. cit.* Cf. also the diary of L. Thallóczy, *Századok*, 1966, Nos. 4–5.

69. On the actual facts, cf. V. Zaninović, *op. cit.*; V. Dedijer, *op. cit.*; A. Lončarević, *op. cit.*; R. W. Seton-Watson, *Sarajevo, op. cit.*; and L. Albertini, *Le origini, op. cit.*, Vol. II, *passim*.

70. Cf. the letters to Brosch in H. H. St. A, Nachlass Franz Ferdinand, II, B–15a and B–16a.

71. Cf. J. Kristóffy, *op. cit.*, pp. 600 ff.; L. von Chlumecky, *op. cit.*, pp. 231 ff.; and J. Redlich, *op. cit.*, Vol. I, pp. 14 ff.

72. R. Kiszling, *op. cit.*, p. 150. In view of the lack of firmness of character subsequently displayed by Kristóffy, who was undoubtedly energetic but of an intellectual and moral stature perhaps not adequate to the great task for which he offered himself, Francis Ferdinand's concern cannot be said to have been unfounded. In Kristóffy's letters to Brosch the most

frequently recurring note is in fact the problem of raising funds. In 1910 Kristóffy asked for and obtained from Lukács, the Finance Minister in the Khuen government, means for procuring funds for his and his friends' election campaign. When this came to Tisza's knowledge in 1913 he did not hesitate to exploit it against Kristóffy. Cf. J. Redlich *op. cit.*, Vol. II, p. 179, and *ibid.*, pp. 717 ff., for Kristóffy's defence.

73. In the opinion of G. Gratz (*op. cit.*, Vol. II, p. 206), who knew him well, Lukács regarded universal suffrage as inevitable but, sceptical and indifferent to political principles as he was, he had no intention of fighting to hasten its advent. In December 1909 Burian noted in his diary that Lukács had not been sincere in his negotiations with Justh who, however, was not taken in in the matter. Vajda-Voevod saw plainly that Lukács was not to be relied on. Cf. his letter to Brosch of January 11, 1910, in H.H.St.A, *loc. cit.*, II, B–16a.

74. Cf. Brosch's telegram of January 11, 1910, in H.H.St.A, *loc. cit.*, II, B–11. The Social Democratic leaders (who were violently criticized for it by their extreme left-wing opponents), the Hungarian Peasant Party, and Maniu among the Romanians, were also inclined to trust Khuen's promises. On the whole crisis, cf. F. Pölöskei, *A koalició felbomlása és a nemzeti munkapárt megalakulása*, Budapest, 1963.

75. Cf. Hodză's letters (of January 2 and 27, 1910) and Kristóffy's (of June 2 and October 3, 1910) to Brosch in H.H.St.A, *loc. cit.*, II, B–15a. These show that Khuen gave a definite undertaking to the Belvedere but —cynic that he was—failed to keep it.

76. This was said openly by Tisza in the euphoria of election success. Cf. R. Kiszling, *op. cit.*, p. 153. For the methods used to keep Hodža, the Slovak leader, Maniu, the Romanian leader, and other democratic personalities out of parliament, cf. R. W. Seton-Watson, *Ungarische Wahlen*, Leipzig, 1912; N. Asztalos and A. Pethö, *op. cit.*, pp. 501 ff. Cf. Tisza's Complete Works, Series IV, Vol. II, Budapest, 1937, pp. 166 ff., for a list of the occupations of the government deputies elected in 1910. Most were big landowners, indicating that the majority of the latter, fearing both being cut off from the Austrian market and an extension of the franchise, this time did not follow the politicians of the aristocratic opposition.

77. J. Kristóffy, *op. cit.*, p. 604. Count Apponyi, the leader of the right wing of the forty-eightist party, also thought that universal suffrage would lead to the breakdown of the old constitution. Justh, the leader of the left wing, took account of this and restricted himself, as Kristóffy also did, to demanding the vote for literates, among whom the Magyars were proportionately more numerous than other nationalities. The latter demanded the vote for everyone, including illiterates. According to M. Hodža, *op. cit.*, footnote 50, Francis Ferdinand took the same line, believing that granting universal suffrage would be basically a conservative measure.

78. On what he denounced as the capitulation of his colleagues in the Diet, cf. Supilo's letter of February 22, 1910, to Gina Lombroso Ferrero (B. Radica, *op. cit.*, pp. 378–380). Supilo remained in opposition in company with the only Croatian Social Democratic deputy. In his view, 'the

so-called common people would continue to struggle and resist', while the Croat bourgeoisie wanted only to put an end to the struggle. It is certain that it was the student youth movement that kept alive the most violent opposition, and continued to do so in the years ahead. At the congress at Spalato in the summer of 1911 it adopted a radical–progressive Serbo-Croat programme on lines close to those of Supilo. At the next congress (Fiume, September 1912) a vigorous nationalist trend emerged that soon secured a majority. Cf. V. Zaninović, *op. cit.*, pp. 73–76 and 97. In the towns, in which there was still little industrialization, the workers took up the radicalism of the students, with which the Croat Social Democratic Party initially sympathized. But the peasants seem to have followed either the clerical line or Radić's party, which had not yet adopted an anti-dynastic position (and did not do so until 1917), though it was in opposition to Budapest.

79. G. Gratz, *op. cit.*, Vol. II, p. 243; R. W. Seton-Watson, *Die Südslawische Frage, op. cit.*, pp. 335 ff.

80. Several seats were gained by Radić's Peasant Party, though the rural masses were still largely excluded from the vote. The party's representation increased from three to nine.

81. B. Radica, *op. cit.*, p. 376. The letter, apparently dated February 10, 1910, was nevertheless written in November of that year. For Supilo's criticisms of the coalition, again cf. his *Politika, op. cit.*, pp. 240 ff.

82. A. Smith Pavelić, *op. cit.*, pp. 24–25. Dr Frank's attitude is indicated by his letter of December 14, 1907, to the Chief of the General Staff. Out of loyalty to the dynasty he denounced what he considered to be the anti-state manoeuvres of the Serbo-Croat coalition. Cf. Conrad, *Aus meiner Dienstzeit*, five vols., Vienna, 1921–25, Vol. I, p. 525.

83. G. Gratz, *op. cit.*, Vol. II, p. 252; R. W. Seton-Watson, *op. cit.*, pp. 399–423. Francis Ferdinand himself wrote to Francis Joseph to protest against Cuvaj's dangerous and arbitrary methods in Croatia. Cf. G. Franz, *op. cit.*, p. 46; R. Kiszling, *op. cit.*, p. 234.

84. R. W. Seton-Watson, *op. cit.*, p. 398. Cuvaj's would-be assassin, who was already determined to do the deed, was given his pistol by Colonel Apis and Major Tankosić in Belgrade. Cf. L. Albertini, *Le origini, op. cit.*, Vol. II, p. 76. For the assassination attempt, cf. the report of the Zagreb public prosecutor's department in V. Zaninović, *op. cit.*, pp. 90–91.

85. Allg. Verwaltungs-Archiv, *loc. cit.* Cf. in particular the reports of July 22 and September 5, 1912. Cf. now Mirjam Gross, 'Die "Welle". Die Ideen der nationalistischen Jugend in Kroatien vor dem I. Weltkrieg', Oesterreichische Osthefte, 1908 n. 2.

86. G. Gratz, *op. cit.*, Vol. II, p. 255.

87. Tibor Erényi, *A vörös csütörtök. 1912 május 23*, Budapest, 1952. Ferenc Pölöskei, *Kormányzati politika és parlamenti ellenzék*, Budapest, 1970. This was the fourth general strike for universal suffrage organized by the Hungarian Social Democrats. The exasperation accumulated in years of frustration exploded in it.

88. J. Kristóffy, *op. cit.*, p. 701.

89. For the various phases of Austro-Hungarian policy towards the Balkan countries in general and Serbia in particular, cf. of course the diplomatic documents. For a good summary of the Vienna position, cf. Alfred Francis Pribram, *Austrian Foreign Policy* 1908–18, London, 1923. For the sake of brevity I refrain from mentioning the well-known works on the origins of the war and instead refer merely to the basic work of L. Albertini, to my review of the most recent publications in *Rivista Storica Italiana*, 1966, No. III, and in particular to the *Journal of Contemporary History*, 1966, No. 3, devoted to the crisis of July 1914.

90. G. Gratz, *op. cit.*, Vol. II, pp. 279–280. For Tisza's outlook, cf. his Complete Works. For criticisms in Berlin and Vienna of his insufficient generosity to the Romanians, cf. J. Redlich, *op. cit.*, *passim*. For the Romanian point of view, cf. Georges Moroianu, *La lutte des roumains transylvains pour la liberté et l'opinon européenne*, Paris, 1933; R. W. Seton-Watson, *Histoire des Roumains*, Paris, 1937, cf. now the report of the Romanian historians, *Die Nationale Flage*, *op. cit.* Some interesting detail about the background to the negotiations is given by Vajda-Voevod, in M. Constantinescu, *op. cit.* The question was brought up in the Hungarian parliament in February 1914. Cf. G. Kemény, *op. cit.*, p. 163, and Géza Supka, *A nagy dráma*, Miskolc, 1924, pp. 23 ff. Counts Apponyi and Bethlen (who was to be Prime Minister from 1921 to 1931) criticized Tisza for wanting to make too many concessions to the Romanians. Among the papers (at Oberlin College) of Count Mihály Károlyi, the future President of the Republic in 1918, whom the Party of Independence and of 1848 after its reunification in 1913 elected as its own president, there is a copy of a memorandum submitted to the monarch by the party in October 1914 warning him against making the concessions to the Romanians which were desired by Berlin in order to avoid a clash with Bucharest. The party reiterated that it stood for an extension of the suffrage and other democratic reforms, but wanted these for the population as a whole without any priority for non-Magyar nationalities. Priority should be given, if at all, the memorandum stated, to the just demands of the Hungarian working class and the Magyar national claims, both military and economic. The state of mind of the Magyars in Transylvania, Andrássy said to Baernreither (*Die südslawische, op. cit.*, p. 289), was such that if Tisza or anyone else 'made them [the Romanians] substantial concessions, he would be killed in the street'. Tisza, as appears from his Complete Works, Budapest, 1924–37, Series IV, Vol. II, pp. 272 ff., was willing to make concessions greater than those he had offered the year before (e.g. to agree to the election of thirty or forty Romanian deputies, to be chosen, however, from among the most moderate), but his offer was rejected by the Romanians, who insisted on full rights and representation proportional to their numbers.

91. R. Kiszling, *op. cit.*, p. 277; J. Redlich, *op. cit.*, Vol. I, p. 232. Baernreither (*op. cit.*, pp. 300 ff.) was told in government circles in Berlin that they were bound to put pressure on Tisza since the government of King Carol of Romania had given them an undertaking to counsel moderation to the Romanians of Transylvania. In Bucharest a month later

Baernreither found that hatred of the Hungarians had reached such a pitch that nothing less than the grant of democratic administrative autonomy to Transylvania would assuage it. Tisza for his part said to the editor of the *Reichspost*, whom he knew to be a member of the Belvedere circle, that every Romanian was a 'traitor to the country' (cf. F. Funder, *op. cit.*, p. 542). For William II's conversations with Tisza on March 23 and with Francis Ferdinand on June 13, 1914, in which the Romanian question was raised, cf. *Die grosse Politik der Europäischen Kabinette, 1871–1914*, Berlin, 1927, Vol. 39, *passim*. On the relations between the Austrian Heir Apparent and William II, cf. R. A. Kann, 'Emperor William II and Archduke Francis Ferdinand in their Correspondence', *American Historical Review*, January 1952, pp. 323 ff.

92. Cf. J. Andrássy, *op. cit.*, p. 250, for the influence of anxieties concerning the Archduke's intentions on Tisza's decision to make concessions to the Serbo-Croat coalition. According to L. Chlumecky (*op. cit.*, p. 178), the Archduke, faced with the agreement reached by Tisza, whom he detested, would have returned to the idea of setting up a system of trialism with the Croats if the latter had been successfully detached from the Serbs. On the federalization plan put forward by Aurel C. Popovici in his *Die Vereinigten Staaten Gross-Oesterreich*, Leipzig, 1906, and the Archduke's attitude to it, cf. C. Bardolff, *op. cit.*, pp. 152 ff.; T. Sosnowsky, *op. cit.*, pp. 71 ff.; and Hodža, *op. cit.*, pp. 26 ff. Popovici's plan foresaw the establishment of fifteen autonomous ethnical territories, two of them (the Trentino and Trieste) with Italian majorities. It is improbable, however, that Francis Ferdinand would have granted Italian autonomy in Trieste. He evidently liked Popovici's federalism to the extent that it revived, in a form adapted to the changed historical situation, the ideas put forward by the supporters of reform from above towards the end of the period of absolutism that followed the crushing of the revolutions of 1848–49. Popovici's ideas were based on the historical developments, both democratic and nationalist, that were taking place, but the aspects that the Archduke seized on were those that held out the prospect of restoring the power of choice between various administrative and political systems that the dynasty had possessed before the Settlement with Hungary. Also Popovici's plan opened up the possibility (advocated by some of his Bucharest friends who, in opposition to Bratianu, favoured a pro-Austrian policy) of absorbing the kingdom of Romania into a federal Greater Austria. Cf. O. Eöttevényi, *op. cit.*, p. 234. That the Belvedere's 'centralist federalism' was shared by some of the leaders of the Croat Right Party, and by the followers of the late Dr Frank, was confirmed to J. M. Baernreither in a conversation with one of them on May 9, 1913. Cf. his *Die südslawische, op. cit.*, p. 235.

93. Cf. H. H. St. A, Nachlass Franz Ferdinand, Thronwechsel.

94. Hugo Hantsch, 'Erzherzog-Thronfolger Franz Ferdinand und Graf Leopold Berchtold', *Historica. Studien zum geschichtlichen Denken und Forschen*, Vienna, 1965.

95. Cf. R. Kiszling, *op. cit.*, pp. 254 ff. The draft 'manifesto to the peoples of Austria-Hungary' which, according to a plan drawn up by Major

Brosch and Baron Eichhoff, Francis Ferdinand was to have issued immediately on ascending the throne, merely stated, however, that the new sovereign proposed to assure equality of rights and 'national development' to all his peoples, and an electoral reform that would give the vote to all citizens who did not yet possess it. Cf. the text in H.H.St.A, Nachlass Franz Ferdinand, Thronwechsel. To the oppressed nationalities in Hungary this would have been satisfactory for the time being. The reference in the draft to the necessity of a solution of the language question in Moravia and Bohemia was less clear. The Archduke had evidently not made up his mind on the matter.

96. Sazonov was well aware of the importance of Tisza's reaction to Francis Ferdinand's plans in relation to the Croats and Romanians, as is shown by the memorandum to the Tsar of January 29, 1914. Cf. also the reports from the Russian consul in Budapest in *Int. Beziehungen, op. cit.*, Series I, Vol. I, *et seq.*

97. J. M. Baernreither, *op. cit.*, pp. 182–184; J. Redlich, *op. cit.*, Vol. I, pp. 185–186. Pašić's offer, made at the beginning of December 1912, had been preceded by a visit to Belgrade by J. Redlich, who had been asked by Count Berchtold to sound out Pašić's intentions after the first Serbian victories in the Balkan war. Redlich used a letter of introduction from Masaryk and saw Pašić on November 6. What the Serbian Prime Minister said to him was almost identical with what he said in the message he sent to Vienna a month later by way of Masaryk, but he indicated his desire for a partition of Albania, which Serbian troops were then engaged in liberating from the Turks (J. Redlich, *op. cit.*, Vol. I, p. 166). The Austro-Hungarian Foreign Minister, after securing the support of Berlin and Rome for the independence of Albania, immediately protested vigorously to Belgrade against any Serbian aims on Albanian territory. Pašić promptly assumed an attitude of caution (J. Redlich, *op. cit.*, p. 177); he did not repeat his reference to Albania in the offer he submitted through Masaryk. Nevertheless Berchtold, believing he had succeeded in securing approval of his Balkan policy even from the British government, also rejected this more submissive Serbian approach (G. Masaryk, *op. cit.*, p. 2, and J. Redlich, *op. cit.*, Vol. I, p. 186). According to H. Hantsch, *op. cit.*, Vol. I, pp. 283 ff., Berchtold had been convinced by police and counter-espionage reports that Serbia was only awaiting Russian support to provoke a war with Austria-Hungary. On his way back from Paris in the following year Pašić stopped in Vienna (October 2–4, 1913) to talk to Berchtold. The latter, however, had decided irrevocably not to grant Serbia a port on the Adriatic, and said so to Redlich (*op. cit.*, Vol. I, p. 211). The aggrandizement of Serbia that resulted from the Balkan wars was now too worrying to the Austro-Hungarian leaders, who regarded it as having taken place at the expense of the prestige of their own country and were alarmed at its effects on the Southern Slavs of the dual monarchy. We know from the report of the meeting of the Joint Council of Austro-Hungarian Ministers of October 3, 1913, that it was informed by Berchtold of Pašić's new approaches. Though, because of the reluctance both of

[329]

Francis Joseph and of Francis Ferdinand, it again rejected the proposal by Conrad, the Chief of the General Staff, that Austria-Hungary should hurry up and 'swallow' Serbia, substantially it came to the conclusion that Count Stürgkh, the Austrian Prime Minister, summed up by saying that the 'humiliation' of Serbia had become 'vital to the existence' of Austria-Hungary, and that if such a humiliation could not be imposed immediately, active preparations for it must be made. Cf. *Oesterreich-Ungarns Aussen-politik*, *op. cit.*, Vol. VII, pp. 397–403, and Conrad, *op. cit.*, Vol. III, pp. 724 ff.; cf. also Carlo Sforza, *Pachitch et l'union des Yougoslaves*, second ed., Paris, 1938, pp. 108–111, which, however, is not very accurate about dates and excessively idealizes Pašić. At the very time when Pašić was passing through Vienna the Serbian army occupied some strategic positions inside the Albanian frontier to prevent the incursion of Albanian bands into Serbia. On October 18, 1913, the Vienna government sent Belgrade an ultimatum calling on it to withdraw its troops, and Serbia complied. Instead of sending an acceptable ultimatum, Austria might perhaps have invaded Serbia without further ado if she had not been dissuaded by the Italian, and also the German, refusal to support her three months previously. Cf. Corrado De Biase, *Le rivelazione di Giolitti del dicembre 1914*, Modena, 1960; Augusto Torre, 'Il progettato attacco austro-ungarico alla Serbia del luglio 1913', *Studi storici in onore di Gicacchino Volpe*, two vols., Florence, 1958, pp. 999 ff.; H. Hantsch, *op. cit.*, Vol. II, pp. 466 ff. Berchtold briefly embraced the idea (and mentioned it on April 29, 1913 to Thallóczy, who recorded the confidence in his diary, *op. cit.*) of attacking Serbia and partitioning it with Bulgaria without asking for Italian consent, but a few days later he had become convinced that Germany would consider the latter indispensable.

98. J. M. Baernreither, *op. cit.*, pp. 202 ff.

99. J. Szterényi, *op. cit.*, pp. 210–214.

100. G. Gratz, *op. cit.*, Vol. II, p. 279; L. V. Südland, *op. cit.*, p. 689.

101. The Right Party, led by Mile Starčević and Dr Ante Pavelić, won eleven seats. The 'pure' Right Party, which had again split with Starčević's party, which was now moving towards reconciliation with the Serbs but not with the Hungarians, declined in strength from eighteen seats to ten. Cf. Bajza József, *A horvát kérdés. Válogatott tanulmányok*, Budapest, 1941, pp. 28 ff.

102. L. Thallóczy wrote in his diary, *op. cit.*: 'The Serbo-Croat coalition has won, the only question is whether or not it will deceive us a second time.' The principal critic of Tisza, as previously of Khuen Héderváry on the Croat question, was the former Ban, Baron Rauch (the son of the architect of the 1868 Settlement), who advocated an agreement, not with the Serbo-Croat coalition, but with the 'pure' Right Party. After the 1908 secession from it of the intransigent anti-Hungarians and the death at the end of 1911 of Dr Frank, its leader, who had personal ties with Francis Ferdinand, the 'pure' party was in fact willing for an understanding with the Budapest government. (Dr Frank's son, who objected to union with Serbia, took refuge in Hungary after the war.) But Tisza did not trust this party, because

[330]

of its possible links with the Belvedere—at which however Baron Rauch himself was a *persona* not very *grata*—and, as he did not believe that now there was any more prospect of dividing the Croats from the Croatian Serbs, he proposed to neutralize both by keeping them away from Belgrade. For the criticisms made of him, cf. the publications previously referred to of J. Bajza, the Hungarian philologist and a specialist on Croatia and Montenegro, who had become the spokesman of the policy advocated by Baron Rauch, which was agreed to in principle by Count Andrássy. Cf. also the article by General Sarkotić, the Austrian High Commissioner in Bosnia during the war, in *Erinnerungen an Franz Joseph I, op. cit.*, pp. 341 ff. Sarkotić believed that Tisza, who needed Serbian votes for his party in southern Hungary, was taken in by the assurances of loyalty given by the youngest and most intelligent of the leaders of the Zagreb coalition, the Serb Dušan Popović. During the war even Burian, who had supported Tisza's policy, ended by believing that the leaders of the coalition at heart desired Yugoslav independence. Cf. S. Burian, *op. cit.*, p. 269. According to the present-day Yugoslav historians, the Serbian records show that from 1910 onwards Pašić advised the Zagreb coalition to try and reach agreement with Vienna or Budapest.

Notes (II)
Negotiations with Italy, 1914–1918

1. H. Hantsch, *op. cit.*, Vol. II, pp. 562 ff. Half a century later a Catholic historian such as Hantsch is still of the opinion that failing to make war on Serbia would have had disastrous consequences for Austria-Hungary, *ibid.*, pp. 576 ff. He does not explain what catastrophe as great as that of the First World War would have resulted from inaction. Though plans for making war on Serbia had been made in Vienna during 1913, the decision to invade her was in fact made under the impact of the emotion roused by the Sarajevo assassination and bore all the marks of improvisation. On the evening of the assassination Macchio, the future ambassador to Italy, saw his chief, Berchtold, at the Foreign Ministry in Vienna, and Stürgkh, the Austrian Prime Minister. The latter immediately declared himself in favour of war, regarding it as an opportunity to break the links between the Slav parties in Austria and the pan-Serbian and Yugoslav movements. In other words, he thought of war as being partly a domestic political operation. Berchtold said that an immediate attack on Serbia would bring in Russia, a risk that in his view ought to be accepted but not provoked. The immediate occupation of Belgrade urged by the military (though they did not have troops ready for a *Blitz* operation) had been renounced, but the Minister still believed it might be possible to confine the war to Serbia alone, though the Russian government, which was hesitant immediately after the assassination, had in fact been given time in which to consider intervention on the Serbian behalf. Cf. the typescript 'Momentbilder aus dem diplomatischen Leben des Botschafter A. D. Freiherrn von Macchio' (Ch. VIII), H.H.St.A, Nachlass Macchio.

2. H. Hantsch, *op. cit.*, pp. 560 ff.

3. Tisza agreed in the middle of July to war on Serbia on condition that she should be humiliated and that frontier rectifications should be imposed on her, but that she should not be annexed. On July 31 he agreed that the British mediation proposed should be rejected. Cf. *Protokolle des gemeinsamen Ministerrates der österreichisch-ungarischen Monarchie (1914–1918)*, ed. Miklós Komjáthy, Budapest, 1966.

4. *Ibid.*

5. H. Hantsch, *op. cit.*, pp. 715 ff.

6. Alberto Monticone, 'La Missione a Roma del principe Bülow (1914–1915)', *Quellen und Forschungen aus Italienischen Archiven*, Vol. XLVIII, Tübingen, 1968. Mario Toscano, 'Il libro verde del 1915', *Clio*, 1968, n. 2.

7. Cf. the report of the meeting in *Protokolle, op. cit.* Cf. also *Julikrise*

[332]

und Kriegsausbruch, 1914, ed. Immanuel Geiss, two vols., Hanover, 1964.

8. *I Documenti Diplomatici Italiani*. Fourth series, 1908–14. Vol. XII (June 28–August 2, 1914), Rome, 1964, p. 160. Cf. the correspondence 'Avarna-Bollati, luglio 1914—maggio 1915', *Rivista Storica Italiana*, 1949–50. For the literature on the subject, cf. Leo Valiani, *Il partito socialista italiano nel periodo della neutralità* (1914–15), Milan, 1963. Cf. also Brunello Vigezzi, 'La neutralità italiana del luglio-agosto 1914 e il problema del'Austria-Ungheria', *Clio*, 1965, No. 1.

9. *I Documenti Diplomatici, op. cit.*, p. 161.

10. *Ibid.*

11. *Ibid.*, pp. 207 and 221. On the Triple Alliance, cf. Luigi Salvatorelli, *La Triplice Alleanza, Storia diplomatica, 1877–1912*, Milan, 1939; Fritz Fellner, *Der Dreibund*, Vienna, 1960.

12. *I Documenti Diplomatici, ibid.*, p. 278.

13. *Ibid.*, p. 301.

14. Cf. Mérey's reports of July 22 and 29, 1914, in *Oesterreich-Ungarns Aussenpolitik*, Vol. VIII, pp. 584 and 886 ff. Cf. the memorandum of July 26 by Biancheri, San Giuliano's secretary, on his conversations with Mérey, *I Documenti Diplomatici, op. cit.*, pp. 354 ff. The Italian ambassador in Vienna had known since July 20 that Austria-Hungary was preparing an ultimatum to Serbia, and informed San Giuliano by telegram on the same day; those to whom he spoke, however, hoped that the Belgrade government would give way. Cf. *I Documenti Diplomatici, op. cit.*, p. 242. San Giuliano was glad not to have been consulted by Vienna about the ultimatum, because it saved him from having to repeat his veto of 1913 and having to make drastic decisions in the more than probable event of Vienna's this time taking no notice of the Italian opposition. Also, as Italy had not been consulted, she had freedom of action if war broke out. By presenting Italy with a *fait accompli* Austria in fact played into her hands.

15. 'I shall therefore consider it a piece of real good fortune if war with Serbia comes', Mérey wrote to Berchtold in a private letter on July 29. *Österreich-Ungarns Aussenpolitik, op. cit.*, Vol. VIII, p. 890. If a European war broke out as a result, in his opinion, it meant that it was inevitable, and it was better that it should come soon. Evidently he regretted his past opposition to General Conrad's desire for a preventive war on Serbia before Russia was ready. In the opinion of his colleague Maximilian Claar (cf. the latter's recollections, *Berliner Monatshefte*, 1932), his anti-Italian reputation did not accord with the facts.

16. Report of July 29, *op. cit.* The greater part of Italian public opinion most certainly did not take the line indicated by the Austro-Hungarian ambassador, but reading many Italian newspapers (with the notable exception of the *Corriere della Sera*) might well have given him the impression that it did. On this point, cf. B. Vigezzi, *op. cit.* Mérey's relative optimism was shared at the time by Berchtold, who on July 31 informed the Italian ambassador that Austria-Hungary was ready to reach agreement

with Italy in connection with Article VII provided that she should enter the war side by side with her allies (*I Documenti Diplomatici, op. cit.*, p. 484). Next day, when Mérey asked him whether Italy was going to join in the war, obviously on the side of the Triple Alliance, San Giuliano replied 'giving the known reasons why we are not under an obligation to do so, though reserving the right to decide later whether it is in our interests to do so and provided that these are safeguarded by clear agreements which Austria has hitherto refused'. *Ibid.*, p. 503.

17. It was, however, realized by the Italian ambassadors in Vienna and Berlin, who soon discovered, and deplored, that in Rome many highly placed people wanted war on Austria. Cf. the *Avarna–Bollati* correspondence, *op. cit.* Nevertheless Bollati must immediately have spoken plainly to the Berlin government, for San Giuliano wrote to Salandra on July 26: 'For the first time since the Kingdom of Italy came into existence a German Foreign Minister has said that this is the right time to gain the Trentino.' To gain something, in San Giuliano's view, the Italian government should not exclude the possibility of joining in the war on either side. On July 27 he informed Flotow, the German ambassador, that Italy had the choice between two different courses, and on July 29 he telegraphed to Bollati and Avarna instructing them to inform the Vienna and Berlin governments that, if Italy did not obtain satisfaction in regard to Article VII, 'we shall be compelled to follow a political course opposed to Austria-Hungary' (*I Documenti Politici, op. cit.*, pp. 350, 362, 413, 438, 443). For the attitude of the former Prime Minister, cf. Giovanni Giolitti, *Memorie della mia vita*, third ed., Milan, 1945, pp. 513 and 533, and O. Malagodi, *Conversazioni della guerra, 1914–1919*, ed. B. Vigezzi, two vols., Milan, 1960, Vol. I, pp. 24 ff.

18. H.H.St.A, rot 506–507, Italien, Liasse XLVII–5a. On the very skilful work by Fasciotti, the Italian Minister in Bucharest, cf. *I Documenti Diplomatici, op. cit.*

19. Tisza, replying on September 7, 1914 to Czernin, who had suggested concessions to the Romanians, said that no concessions would be sufficient to affect the Romanian attitude, which would be determined solely by the course of the war. Cf. I. Tisza, *Oesszes munkái* (Complete Works), Series IV, *op. cit.*, Vol. II, p. 126. Cf. also Graf Stefan Tisza, *Briefe, 1914–1918*, Vol. I, Berlin, 1928. (A number of letters concerning this period are missing from the German edition, which was never completed.) Up to March 1915 he based his opposition to concessions to Italy on the same argument. Later he realized that he was mistaken in this, but in regard to Romania his position remained unchanged. Cf. also Arthur Weber, 'Graf Tisza und der Eintritt Italiens in den Weltkrieg', *Berliner Monatshefte*, 1927, pp. 608 ff.; Iózsef Galántai, 'Stefan Tisza und der erste Weltkrieg', *Öesterreich in Geschichte und Literatur*, 1964, No. 10, and 'Die Kriegszielpolitik der Tisza-Regierung', 1913–1917', *Nouvelles études historiques*, Budapest, 1965, Vol. II, pp. 202 ff.

20. Cf. the report of the meeting in *Protokolle, op. cit.*

21. *Ibid.* It is well known how anti-Italian General Conrad, the Chief of

the General Staff, was. In 1911 he wanted to attack Italy, which was then engaged in Tripoli. Cf. the critical discussion of his memoirs and the literature about him in an excellent survey by Solomon Wank in *Austrian History Year Book*, 1965, No. 1. For their part, Victor Emmanuel III and Cadorna, the new Chief of the General Staff, would have welcomed intervention against Austria as early as August 1914.

22. H. H. St. A, Liasse XLVII–5a, *op. cit.* Szögyény to Berchtold.

23. Cf. the report of the meeting.

24. Freiherr von Macchio, *Wahrheit! Fürst Bülow und ich in Rom, 1914–15*, Vienna, 1931. Cf. of course Salandra's books on neutrality and intervention, the Italian Green Book, the Austrian Red Book and other documents.

25. H. H. St. A, Liasse XLVII–5a, *cit.*

26. Cf. *ibid.*, the reports of Prince Hohenlohe, the Austrian ambassador in Berlin. On August 21, 1914 he reported a telegram from the German ambassador in Rome doubting whether San Giuliano would be able to maintain neutrality in view of the success of Entente propaganda among the public. At that time, however, Sonnino, for instance, was still resolutely neutralist. This is shown by his papers, preserved at Montespertoli (Florence) and to be published by Professors Ben F. Brown and Pietro Pastorelli, and by his letters to Alberto Bergamini, the editor of the *Giornale d'Italia*, which I was able to read thanks to the courtesy of Professor Mario Gandini, the head of the G. C. Croce Communal Library at San Giovanni in Persiceto, where this correspondence is preserved. The first letter in which Sonnino does not totally exclude the possibility of war with Austria, though still without any enthusiasm for it, is dated September 4, 1914. Microfilms of Sonnino's official diplomatic correspondence are now available through University Microfilms, Ann Arbor, Michigan, U.S.A.

27. *Dalle carte di Giovanni Giolitti. Quarant' anni di vita politica italiana*, three vols., Milan, 1962, Vol. III, pp. 194 ff.

28. Macchio, *op. cit.*, pp. 40 ff.

29. *Ibid.*, pp. 57 ff.

30. Macchio noticed that Giolitti had mistaken the date. He telegraphed to Vienna on December 8 that the reference was to a Austro-Hungarian request made on July 4, 1913. H. H. St. A, Liasse XLVII–5a, *op. cit.* See Mérey's reports of July 1913 in *Öesterreich-Ungarns Aussenpolitik, op. cit.*, Vol. VI, pp. 881 ff.

31. H. H. St. A, *loc. cit.* Salandra knew nothing about the 1913 episode revealed by Giolitti, and admitted this to Macchio. On the whole of this question, cf. now Corrado De Biase, *L'Italia, dalla neutralità all' intervento nella prima guerra mondiale*, Modena, two vols., 1965–67, Vol. I, pp. 100 ff. But cf. above all A. Torre, *op. cit.*

32. H. H. St. A, 150 P.A. XI. Italien. Macchio to Berchtold, December 16, 1914. This was the interpretation put on the matter by the deputies and journalists close to Giolitti, to whom the latter said that Salandra's reference to Italy's 'just aspirations' had gone 'too far'. Cf. Corrado De Biase, '*La Libertà d'azione concessa dal Parlamento al Governo (dicembre*

1914–marzo 1915', *Rassegna Storica del Risorgimento*, April–June 1965. In fact Ferdinando Martini's *Diario 1914–1918*, Milan, 1966 (Martini was Colonial Minister in the Salandra cabinet) creates the impression that the pro-Giolitti feelings manifested by the parliamentary majority helped to persuade Sonnino not immediately to begin the negotiations with London with a view to Italian intervention for which he was preparing the ground, but instead to send a preliminary warning to Vienna about the Italian right to compensation under Article VII in view of the occupation of Belgrade, and thus give the Austro-Hungarian government an opportunity of disclosing how willing or unwilling it might be to meet the Italian claims, which Sonnino did not intend to specify until the Austrians asked him to do so.

33. H.H.St.A, *loc. cit.*

34. Macchio, *op. cit.*, pp. 64 ff.

35. Bülow to Otto Joel. Bülow expresses a highly flattering opinion of Giolitti in these letters. Otto Joel, who came of a family of Danzig Jews, a member of which (Levin Goldschmidt, Otto Joel's uncle on his mother's side), had attained high political and academic position under Bismarck, had founded the Banca Commerciale Italiana in 1894 and was its managing director. He had assumed Italian citizenship and was thoroughly Italian in feeling, though without forgetting his native country. In 1911–12 he played an important part in persuading the German government to give diplomatic support to Italy against the Turks and in inducing the latter to accept the peace treaty that gave Libya to Italy. Thanks to him, Giolitti had a direct secret line to Berlin during the crucial phase in 1912. Count Volpi, who acted as intermediary with the Turks, had financial connections with Joel. The latter had been a close friend of Giolitti for years, and he was on terms of friendship with San Giuliano also. Cf. now in B. Vigezzi, *Da Giolitti a Salandra*, Firenze, 1963, the 1914–15 correspondence of Joel with Bülow, Jagow and other statesmen. Cf. also the memoirs (very interesting for Italo-German relations) of Bogdan Graf von Hutten Czapski, *Sechzig Jahre Politik und Gesellschaft*, two vols., Berlin, 1936; Hans Fuerstenberg, *Carl Fürstenberg. Die Lebensgeschichte eines deutschen Bankiers*, Wiesbaden, undated, but new ed., 1961. Cf. also *Levin Goldschmidt. Ein Lebensbild. Briefe.* Berlin, 1898. On Prince Bülow in Rome cf. now A. Monticone, *La Germania e la neuralità italiana, 1914–1915*, Bologa, 1971.

36. Macchio, *op. cit.*, p. 71.

37. H.H.St.A, Liasse XLVII–5a, *op. cit.*

38. *Ibid.*, telegram of January 2, 1915. For the reports to Berlin by the German military attaché in Rome, Major von Schweinitz, and his timely warning of the Italian intervention, cf. Wilhelm Spickernagel, *Fürst Bülow*, Hamburg, 1921, pp. 211 ff., as well as Bülow's own memoirs.

39. H.H.St.A, *loc. cit.*, Macchio to Berchtold, January 3. According to Macchio (report of January 6), the German military attaché in Rome, regarding Italian intervention in the spring as inevitable unless agreement with her were reached, did not believe that in return for adequate compensation Italy would promptly turn against France. His calculation was simply this: Germany, having procured the Trentino for Italy, would have

the right to ask her to move her troops from the Austrian to the French frontier, which would force France to guard the latter, thus forcing her to withdraw troops from the Western Front. The Germans would also benefit because Austria-Hungary, freed of the Italian threat, would be able to commit herself more deeply on the Russian front. If this situation made possible substantial German successes in the west, Italy would be tempted to seize Tunisia. As his note to Sonnino of January 9, 1915, discloses, De Martino, the General-Secretary of the Italian Foreign Office, did not discard at that time this possibility. Cf. Sonnino papers, S. 104–C.1.

40. H.H.St.A, *loc. cit.*

41. Macchio, *op. cit.*, pp. 72 ff. In his opinion the pressure on Salandra and Sonnino, who were still hesitant, came from General Cadorna, who was now convinced that final victory would go to the Entente. Macchio to Berchtold, January 13, 1915. H.H.St.A, 151 P.A. XI. Italien.

42. H. Hantsch, *op. cit.*, pp. 705 ff. It appears from Gerhard Ritter, *Staatskunst und Kriegshandwerk*, Vol. III, *Die Tragödie der Staatskunst. Bethmann Hollweg als Kriegskanzler (1914–1917)*, Munich, 1964, that Forgách, the departmental head in the Vienna Foreign Ministry who bore primary responsibility for the drafting of the fateful ultimatum to Serbia, drafted a memorandum for Berchtold on the cession of Bukovina to Russia, or alternatively of the Trentino to Italy if the Tsarist government were unwilling to make peace. On the other hand, in a letter to Macchio of January 20 Forgách showed great indignation at Bülow's having dangled the prospect of the Trentino before Sonnino. He said it would be 'a futile enterprise, which would only stimulate their appetite and set the seal on our decline'. H.H.St.A, Nachlass Macchio, I, 4. But Forgách, who was a Hungarian, wrote this after Tisza had got rid of Berchtold. Not all Hungarian politicians took Tisza's line, however. Count Andrássy favoured the cession of the Trentino. Cf. H. Hantsch, *op. cit.*, p. 726, footnote.

43. *Ibid.*, pp. 716 ff. Cf. also Carlo di Nola, 'Documenti', *Il Risorgimento*, 1960, No. 2. As the Duke d'Avarna saw very plainly (he said so in a letter to ambassador Bollati on February 5, 1915, cf. *Rivista Storica Italiana*, 1949, p. 561). Tisza was opposed to the cession of the Trentino, which was after all an Austrian and not a Hungarian province, chiefly 'because of the precedent it would create for Romania, which is watching our steps here'. On December 17 Czernin had written from Bucharest that Romania would be guided by the Italian example; if Italy obtained concessions, she would ask for them too. H.H.St.A, Liasse XLVII–5a, *cit.* As long as the Russian army continued to exercise pressure on the Carpathians, as it continued to do until it was routed at Gorlice on May 3, Hungary would certainly have been in a difficult position if Romania had demanded concessions in Transylvania as a condition for her neutrality with the same insistence as the Italians. But for the Romanians, Tisza would probably not have been averse to concessions to Italy. On January 5, 1915, when he received the Italian Consul-General in Budapest, who informed him in Sonnino's name that Italian public opinion insisted on Italy's gaining some advantage from the war, he replied: 'Si les amis de l'Italie auront des

avantages, on pourra trouver les moyens de faire participer l'Italie.' His fatal mistake was to believe (as he wrote to Burian on the same day) that, as the Italian army would not be ready until the spring, there was no need to discuss possible concessions until then. Cf. I. Tisza, *op. cit.*, Vol. III, pp. 10 ff. It is possible that Tisza, who was opposed to Austrian annexations of Serbian territory which would diminish the weight of the Magyars in the Habsburg monarchy, at heart did not want Italy to give the Vienna government a free hand in the Balkans in return for satisfactory compensation. On January 17, rejecting the idea that Article VII implied cessions of Austrian territory, he informed the Italian ambassador that, 'it was not his purpose to increase the numbers of the Serbian peoples in the monarchy', and that any cession of territory to Italy for ethnical reasons 'might constitute a precedent' for Romania. Cf. A.S.M.E., Missione Avarna, political correspondence, which includes copies of the reports of the Italian ambassador in Vienna and other information sent by him.

44. H. Hantsch, *op. cit.*, p. 728. The Duke d'Avarna wrote to Sonnino on January 13, 1915, that Burian 'is undoubtedly intelligent, a man of wide culture and great political and administrative experience. He is frank but somewhat hard by nature, by no means expansive and very bureaucratic, like most Austro-Hungarian diplomatists.' When he had met him in Athens many years before he had not seemed to him to be very friendly to Italy, 'which he mistrusted', but later he had come round to favouring better Austro-Italian relations on the lines desired by Aehrenthal. A.S.M.E., *loc. cit.*

45. H. Hantsch, *op. cit.*, p. 724.

46. H.H.St.A, Nachlass Macchio.

47. *Ibid.* In fact on February 9 Burian had counter-attacked; he had told the Italian ambassador that it was Italy who owed compensation under Article VII because of her occupation of Valona and the Dodecanese. Cf. Avarna to Sonnino, February 9 and April 23, 1915, A.S.M.E., *loc. cit.*, as well as the Green Book and the Red Book.

48. *Protokolle, cit.* Vienna's military information was correct. In November 1914 Cadorna had informed the Italian government that the Italian army would be ready to fight only in April. Cf. Emilio Faldella, *La grande guerra. Le Battaglie dell' Isonzo, 1915–1917*, Vol. I, Milan, 1965, p. 27. The Vienna government's mistake was political. When its army was ready to move, the Italian government, if it was to remain neutral, would no longer be satisfied with concessions which it would probably have regarded as satisfactory a few months earlier. But in January 1915 the Austro-Hungarian General Staff was still hoping for a decisive victory over Russia. Burian (cf. his marginal comment of June 1915, on Erzberger's memorandum on his mission to Rome, *Ungarische Jahrbücher*, 1933) concluded that in that event all concessions to Italy could be avoided. He did not yet realize that, even if Russia suffered a major defeat (as in fact she did at Gorlice in May 1915) she would not so easily be eliminated from the war, with the result that Italian intervention was bound in any case to be fatal to Austria-Hungary.

49. H.H.St.A, Liasse XLVII–5a, *cit*. The ambassador in Berlin, Hohenlohe, to Burian.

50. H.H.St.A, 151. P.A.I. Italien. Macchio also explains why Giolitti then refused the offer to support his policy of neutrality made by the Socialist deputies (or some of them). Fearing the criticisms that Salandra would be able to make of him from the right (because of the precedence that previous governments led by him had given to social as against military expenditure, as well as because of a possible acceptance by a new Giolitti government of Austro-Hungarian concessions falling short of those claimed by the Italian nationalists), Giolitti thought it impolitic to be again linked with the Socialist Party, which was anti-militarist and opposed to any conquest.

51. H.H.St.A, Liasse XLVII–5a, *cit*.

52. *Ibid.*, Macchio to Burian, March 2.

53. *Ibid.*, Macchio's telegram of February 17. If he could have seen Avarna's reports, Giolitti would have concluded that his reluctance to return to power was justified. Avarna, though very anxious to prevent Italian intervention, duly reported to Sonnino, e.g. on February 22, that either Austria-Hungary would persist in refusing the Trentino and Friuli, or 'even assuming that for unforeseen reasons the imperial and royal government were persuaded to make us such a limited concession, which would certainly be insufficient to satisfy our public opinion, it is very unlikely that agreement could be reached on such a basis, because Austria-Hungary would not agree to the conditions to which this cession should in our view be subject'. On March 2 Avarna was aware that a change of attitude was taking place in Vienna, but pointed out that if it were true that Austria-Hungary were going to offer the Trentino and 'a small frontier rectification on the Isonzo', it would yield these territories 'only at the end of the war, assuming of course that the Austro-Hungarian troops were going to be victorious, and on condition that we maintained until then a neutrality that was both absolute and well disposed towards the monarchy'. A.S.M.E., Missione Avarna, *op. cit.* The realistic pessimism of his ambassador in Vienna may have carried great weight with Sonnino, who on March 3 decided to begin negotiations with the Entente.

54. H.H.St.A, Macchio to Burian, March 12.

55. *Ibid.*, Hohenlohe, the ambassador in Berlin (who had been told of this by Zimmermann, the State Secretary in the German Foreign Ministry), to Burian, February 19.

56. *Ibid.*, Hohenlohe's telegram of February 28. The Pope's statement had been reported to him by Zimmermann, the State Secretary in the German Foreign Ministry. Cf. also William A. Renzi, 'The Entente and the Vatican during the period of Italian Neutrality 1914–1915', *The Historical Journal*, 1970, n. 3.

57. G. Ritter, *op. cit.*, p. 80. Cf. also Egmont Zechlin, 'Das "schlesische Angebot" und die italienische Kriegsgefahr 1915', *Geschichte in Wissenschaft und Unterricht*, 1963, pp. 533 ff. At the beginning of April Bethmann-Hollweg was actually thinking of sending an ultimatum to the Austrian

government calling on it to make concessions to Italy (roughly correspond-ing to those that were made in May, but too late) and similarly calling on the Italian government to accept them immediately. Cf. the revelation in Alberto Monticone, 'Bethmann Hollweg e il problema italiano nell' Aprile 1915', *Dialoghi del XX*, 1967, No. 3.

58. I. Tisza, *op. cit.*, Vol. III, p. 144. Though he was of course unaware of the text of the Italo-Romanian secret agreement on mutual consultation concluded on September 23, 1914, and supplemented by a convention dated February 6, 1915 (on this, cf. Mario Toscana, *Il Patto di Londra. Storia diplomatica dell' intervento italiano, 1914–1915*, Bologna, 1934, pp. 52 ff.), thanks to Czernin's reports Tisza was aware of the probability that, once Italy had taken the risk of attacking first, the Bucharest government would make war on Austria-Hungary as soon as a suitable occasion arose. Cf. also Glenn E. Torrey, 'The Romanian–Italian Agree-ment of 23 September 1914', *The Slavic and East European Review*, July 1966.

59. H. H. St. A, Liase XLVII–5a, Krieg. P.A. rot. 510.

60. *Protokolle*, cit.

61. Burian diary, *op. cit.*

62. M. Toscano, *op. cit.*, pp. 82 ff. Cf. also L. Albertini, *Vent' anni di vita politica*, Part II, Vol. III, *passim*. Alberto Monticone, 'Salandra, Sonnino verso la decisione dell' intervento', *Rivista di studi politici internazionali*, 1957, No. 1. Cf. Salandra's letter to Sonnino dated March 16 quoted in this paper, in which he explains the reasons why it seemed to him to be essential to negotiate with both *blocs* simultaneously. The ambassador Bollati wrote to his colleague Avarna on March 9 that the negotiations 'will fail, because our side wants them to fail, because it wants war at all costs'. Cf. their correspondence quoted in *Rivista Storica Italiana*, 1950, p. 82. It can be pointed out in Sonnino's defence that he waited in vain for two months for Austria-Hungary to offer Italy the compensation to which she was entitled under Article VII and warned the Vienna government on February 12 that, having failed to receive serious Austrian proposals in the matter, he considered the negotiations to have been broken off.

63. Avarna to Sonnino, March 20 and 27. A.S.M.E., Missione Avarna, *op. cit.*

64. H. H. St. A, Liasse XLVII–5a, *op. cit.* Macchio's telegram of March 19.

65. *Ibid.*, Hohenlohe to Burian, March 14, Burian to Hohenlohe, March 15.

66. Jagow, the State Secretary in the Foreign Ministry, said to the Austro-Hungary ambassador, when the latter confirmed the refusal of an imme-diate hand-over, that in that case nothing was left but to 'fight to the last gasp'. *Ibid.*, Hohenlohe's telegram to Burian of April 6. According to Avarna's message to Sonnino of April 23, Burian did not yet believe that Italy would enter the war merely for the sake of what she had demanded in addition to the Trentino and its immediate hand-over. A.S.M.E., Missione Avarna, *cit.*

[340]

67. H.H.St.A, Nachlass Otto Bauer. K 262–X. Varia. Friedrich Probst, head of the cipher office, to O. Bauer, April 7, 1919.

68. Cf. the two telegrams in H.H.St.A, Liase XLVII–5a, *cit.* (P.A. rot. 507). On May 1 Stürgkh informed Berchtold that Tisza had told him that 'something *bona fide* and something *mala fide*' must be conceded to Italy. Cf. H. Hantsch, *op. cit.*, p. 738. It is not, however, certain that Stürgkh was quoting Tisza's exact words, as in all the latter's letters of the period he insisted on the necessity of not harbouring resentment against Italy if she remained neutral in return for Austrian territorial concessions. But it is certain that he considered exorbitant and impossible Italy's demand for the islands and for the detachment of Trieste from Austria-Hungary, and wrote to Burian to that effect. General von Falkenhayn, the Chief of the German General Staff, said much more cynically to the Austro-Hungarian leaders at a meeting on April 24, 1915, that after the war had been won it would certainly be possible to recover from Italy what had been conceded to her. Cf. now A. Monticone, *La Germania, op. cit.*

69. I. Tisza, *op. cit.*, Vol. III, pp. 201 ff. Avarna informed Sonnino on April 29 that in Vienna it was hoped that in Italy 'the neutralist trend of opinion would prevail and force it [the Italian government] to yield power to the Hon. Giolitti, who is regarded here as a sheet-anchor'. Cf. A.S.M.E., Missione Avarna, *cit.* Tisza had incidentally written very frankly to Avarna on April 11: 'En préservant sa neutralité elle [Italy] peut assurer la victoire de ses alliés, tandis qu'elle a des grandes chances de changer le résultat de cette guerre si elle se range du côté de leurs ennemis.' *Rivista Storica Italiana*, 1950, pp. 392–393. But if Avarna did not want the defeat of Austria-Hungary, many Italians thought it desirable and wanted it; and this state of mind was encouraged by the Vienna government's reluctance to yield to Italian demands.

70. Burian diary, entry under April 16. After this Burian began adapting himself to the idea of having to consent to an immediate hand-over of the Trentino. It does not, however, appear from the documents we have seen that he ever informed the Italian government that he was prepared to withdraw his previous refusal to hand over any territory before the end of the war.

71. Macchio, *op. cit.*, p. 108.

72. I. Tisza, *Briefe, op. cit.*, pp. 185 ff. Tisza had now so fully realized that this was the necessity of the hour that, though by nature a fighter to the last ditch, he wrote to Burian on April 27 that, failing an agreement with Italy, it would be necessary to ask the Entente for peace before there was 'aggression by Romania also'. I. Tisza, *op. cit.*, Vol. III, pp. 260 ff. His dismay was only momentary, however, and he soon returned to his advocacy of war until final victory, no matter what the cost.

73. Burian diary, April 14. H.H.St.A, Liasse XLVII–5a, *cit.* Report by Hohenlohe dated April 21.

74. *Ibid.*, P.A. rot. 509 Krieg. Baron Leopold Chlumecky, whom we already know from the Friedjung-Supilo case, was the son of a Minister of whom Francis Joseph thought highly. He was a deputy to the Diet and

editor of the review *Öesterreichische Rundschau*, and had been on terms of personal friendship with Francis Ferdinand. Immediately after the outbreak of war the Vienna government appointed him to the Foreign Ministry as an expert on Italian affairs, of which he had long been a student. He several times sent Prezioso, whose wife was a relative of his, to Italy as his confidential emissary. Cf. Alfredo Frassati, *Giolitti*, Florence, 1959, pp. 12 ff., as well as Frassati's own polemics with *Il Secolo* and with Prezioso's son in *La Stampa* of April 2 and May 8, 1952. Cf. also O. Malagodi, *op. cit.*, Vol. I, pp. 156 ff.; L. Albertini, *op. cit.*, Part II, Vol. I, pp. 488 ff. Frassati and Malagodi were editors of newspapers associated with Giolitti; Bergamini was very close to Sonnino and Albertini to Salandra. I was able to consult in the Albertini papers the memorandum dated Varese, July 22, 1915, that Prezioso submitted to the editor of the *Corriere della Sera*—it is briefly summarized by the latter in his *op. cit.*, vol. *cit.*, pp. 522 ff. In his letter to Senator Frassati written in June 1919 (cf. *La Stampa* of June 8) Prezioso states, though in edulcorated form, something of what he wrote in his memorandum to Albertini.

75. H. H. St. A, Nachlass Chlumecky. Meine Action in Italien. 1914–15. All the reports sent to Chlumecky by his Italian emissary (except for some telegrams in conventional terms) are handwritten in Italian and bear the signature of S. Benco (then a colleague of Prezioso's on *Il Piccolo* of Trieste). Prezioso is never mentioned in the file, which contains no letters or reports signed by him. The writer, however, describes point by point in the first person as things done, heard or seen by him some of the things that Prezioso himself describes in connection with his relations with Chlumecky on the one hand and with Senator Frassati on the other in the memorandum to Senator Albertini mentioned above. As there is no doubt that Frassati saw Prezioso and not Benco (the exact correspondence in dates and circumstances between the letters signed S. Benco and Prezioso's memorandum precludes their both having been given the same mission), it must be assumed that Chlumecky and Prezioso agreed that the latter's letters, which he sent by ordinary mail, should be signed S. Benco, of course without the latter's knowledge. Prezioso was naturally very anxious, as appears from another of his letters to Senator Albertini, that nothing about the background of his mission should come to light, and with good reason, since he had decided to take refuge in Italy in the event of war. He told Albertini he undertook it in order to be able to play a double game in favour of Italy. Indeed, a court of honour consisting of Trieste patriots was held after the war which, according to enquiries courteously made on my behalf by Dr Angelo Ara, acquitted him. The file also contains letters from a German Austrian correspondent of Chlumecky's at Naples who was in contact with the novelist Matilde Serao and other personalities who were in favour of neutrality, as well as receipts for substantial amounts earmarked for propaganda in Italy.

76. *Ibid.*
77. *Ibid.*
78. *Ibid.*

79. Though Prezioso states in his memorandum to Albertini that he also informed Teodor Mayer, the proprietor of *Il Piccolo*, who lived in Rome, he obviously did not know that as early as March 1915 Sonnino had asked the latter whether making Trieste a free city would be an acceptable solution, an idea which Mayer rejected. Cf. Mayer's article on Sonnino in the *Corriere della Sera* of April 14, 1926, and S. Benco, *Il Piccolo di Trieste*, *op. cit.*, p. 215. Prezioso claims in his memorandum that he told Chlumecky that Giolitti and Frassati wanted Trieste and Fiume to be given the status of free cities and (for the purpose of making an Italo-Austrian agreement impossible by such extreme demands) suggested to Frassati that he should actually ask for this. In his letter of May 5, 1915, published by Frassati in *La Stampa* on May 8, 1952, Prezioso anticipated the offer that Bülow and Macchio made to Giolitti several days later, with the additional proposal that national autonomy should be granted, not only to Trieste, but to Fiume also; this, however, was not mentioned in the official offer. The important point is that Giolitti, over and above the claim to the Trentino and Friuli, considered the establishment of Trieste and Fiume as free cities to be the indispensable minimum.

80. That Frassati's conversation with Sonnino followed the lines reported by Chlumecky's emissary is corroborated by O. Malagodi, *op. cit.*, who relied on conversations he had with Bergamini in 1917. It appears from the Sonnino papers that the Italian Foreign Minister considered the offers submitted by Prezioso as an Austrian manoeuvre against the Salandra government, having the purpose of preparing Giolitti's return to power. Frassati then went to see Salandra and tried to convince him to resume the conversations with Vienna, but without any result. Of course, Frassati could not know that Italy had already signed the Treaty of London.

81. Nachlass Chlumecky, *cit.*

82. *Ibid.*

83. *Ibid.*

84. On Prezioso (independently of his mission of April 1915 to which, to the best of my belief, he refers neither in this nor in his other books) cf. S. Benco, *op. cit.* Benco was interned by the Austrians in 1916, but was allowed to return to Trieste at the beginning of 1918.

85. H.H.St.A, Liasse XLVII–5a, *cit.*

86. Macchio, *op. cit.*, p. 117.

87. Macchio's telegrams of May 10 in H.H.St.A, *loc. cit.* For the criticisms of Macchio's final surrender to Bülow's pressure, cf. I. Tisza, *op. cit.*, Vol. III, pp. 290–291. Tisza asked Burian to forbid the ambassador in Rome to make further concessions. Bülow telegraphed to Macchio to this effect on May 15, rebuking him in particular for promising the islands 'for Giolitti had not asked'. H.H.St.A, *loc. cit.*

88. *Ibid.*, Schönburg's telegram, May 15.

89. *Ibid.*, Macchio's telegram, May 10.

90. *Ibid.*, telegram of May 11. Up to some weeks previously the Vatican, believing that Salandra would not go to war, had preferred him to Giolitti

for Italian domestic political reasons. Cf. F. Engel-Janosi, *op. cit.*, Vol. II, pp. 214 ff. On Catholic neutralism, cf. Klaus Epstein, *Matthias Erzberger and the Dilemma of German Democracy*, Princeton, 1959, which also throws light on Erzberger's mission to Rome.

91. On Giolitti at this time, cf. Luigi Salvatorelli, *Miti e storia*, Turin, 1964; also the testimony of O. Malagodi and V. E. Orlando, which are discussed, together with the book on Erzberger, in Leo Valiani, 'Recenti pubblicazioni sulla prima guerra mondiale', *Rivista Storica Italiana*, 1960, No. 3. Cf. also John A. Thayer, *Italy and the Great War. Politics and Culture*, 1870–1915, Madison, 1964 and now *Il diario di Salandra*, ed. G. B. Gifuni, Milano, 1969.

92. H. H. St. A, Liasse XLVII–5a, *op. cit.* Macchio's telegram of May 15.

93. H. H. St. A, Nachlass Macchio, Geheim. Italien. Undated memorandum.

94. H. H. St. A, Liasse XLVII–5a, *op. cit.* Burian to Macchio, May 15. Burian wrote in his diary on May 14: 'If Giolitti comes into office, the struggle will have to be continued in order not to yield Gorizia and the islands.'

95. H. H. St. A., *loc. cit.*

96. H. H. St. A, Nachlass Macchio. Forgách's letter of May 15. In fact on May 15 and 18 Tisza appealed to Burian urgently to ask Bülow and Macchio to do something through the Vatican to persuade the neutralist Italian Ministers to resign, induce Giolitti to set the socialists in motion, etc. The head of the Hungarian government, whose reputation in his own country was that of an expert in the violent suppression of workers' demonstrations, telephoned: 'Since the war party is using terrorist means, this should be countered by anti-war demonstrations by the workers.' Cf. I. Tisza, *op. cit.*, Vol. III, pp. 301 ff.

97. Cf. Macchio's telegram of May 18; the Pope was still insisting on the immediate hand-over of the Trentino as a way of avoiding intervention, but Bülow was convinced that he could not obtain this from Vienna in time. H. H. St. A, *loc. cit.*

Notes (III)

Prelude to the Self-determination of the Nationalities

1. L. Trotsky, *Ma Vie*, new ed., with introduction and appendix by Alfred Rosmer, Paris, 1953, p. 242.

2. Josef Redlich, *Das politische Tagebuch, op. cit.*, Vol. I, p. 247.

3. Manó Buchinger, *Küzdelem a szocializmusért, op. cit.*, p. 246.

4. *Ibid.*, pp. 246–247. *Népszava*, the official organ of the Hungarian Social Democratic Party, said on July 26, 1914, that 'today the voice of Social Democracy is the only one in the country that at this last moment is still raised in protest against the war'. The statement issued by the party leadership on July 29 limited itself to saying that 'after the war, whatever the outcome may be, there will be a different Hungary'. Cf. these statements in Carl Grünberg's compilation *Die Internationale und der Weltkrieg*, Vol. I, Leipzig, 1916, pp. 124 ff.

5. Gratz, *op. cit.*, Vol. II, p. 297. A. Vajda-Voevod, who was a Romanian deputy in the Hungarian Chamber, declared himself in the Vienna *Reichspost* in favour of the Habsburg empire at war. This former collaborator with Francis Ferdinand who later became head of the Bucharest government disclosed after the war that in the summer of 1914 he acted in agreement with Bràtianu, the Romanian Prime Minister, who wanted to avoid repressive action against the Romanians in Austria-Hungary. Cf. Imre Mikes, *Erdély utja Nagymagyarországtól Nagyromániáig*, Brassó, 1931, pp. 49 and 123. The attitude of the non-Magyar deputies was rewarded by Tisza's promulgation in November 1914 of a general political amnesty and concessions to the religious schools of the non-Magyar nationalities.

6. M. Buchinger, *op. cit.*, p. 247. In regard to the Austrian Social Democratic movement, it should be noted that, while on July 25 its central organ, the *Arbeiter Zeitung* published (with blank spaces due to the Austro-Hungarian military censorship which, however, did not prevent *Vorwärts*, its Berlin counterpart, from printing the document in full) a statement by the German Austrian Social Democratic deputies saying that they still repudiated 'all responsibility for this war', but next day it attributed responsibility for it to the fact that 'Serbia is animated by greed for the property of others' and expressed the hope that no other power would aid and abet the 'shameless appetites of the Balkan Serbs'. The attitude taken by the editor of the newspaper was immediately criticized by Friedrich Adler, but it was defended by his father Victor Adler, who was the undisputed leader of the Austrian Social Democrats; he caused a resolution condemning the bellicose articles that appeared in the newspaper, which in fact perplexed several of the socialist leaders, to be defeated. Cf. Max Ermers, *Victor*

Adler, Aufstieg und Grösse einer sozialistischen Partei, Vienna, 1932. Cf. also Robert Glock, 'Die österreichische Sozialdemokratie und der Weltkrieg', thesis for the University of Vienna, 1951. Friedrich Adler decided to resign all his party offices in protest against its support of the war, but when he discovered that his views were shared by many militant members, he decided to remain and continue his opposition within the party leadership. Cf. M. Ermers, *op. cit.*, p. 322; R. Glock, *op. cit.*, pp. 63 ff. and 84 ff. It escaped these authors' notice, however, that the first joint demonstration by Social Democratic officials who agreed with Friedrich Adler took place on October 16, 1914, on the occasion of Karl Kautsky's sixtieth birthday. Kautsky, who was considered the greatest living Marxist theorist, disagreed with the German Social Democratic vote for military credits in the Reichstag on August 4, 1914. Kautsky's attitude was not without its vacillations, as was in accordance with his doctrinaire nature, lacking in decision when faced with action. He gives his own account in his book *Sozialisten und Krieg*, Prague, 1937, pp. 446 ff. His attitude came to be known immediately, because he expressed it in the presence of numerous persons. The extremely interesting diary of Eduard David, a member of the executive of the German Social Democratic parliamentary group (*Das Kriegstagebuch des Algeordneten E. David*, Düsseldorf, 1966) gives further information on the subject. On August 1 Kautsky, with Hugo Haase, the chairman of the executive, drafted a resolution opposing the war credits which, however, was not approved by the committee. On August 3, at a full meeting of the parliamentary group to which Kautsky, though not a deputy, was invited, he would have liked to propose abstention from the vote but, as this would have been acceptable to only very few of those present, he suggested that the vote for the credits, on which the majority had already decided, should be made conditional on a government pledge that it would not aim at any kind of territorial aggrandizement. When David asked what they were to do in the foreseeable eventuality of the government's refusing to give such a pledge, Kautsky replied that they should vote against the credits. His proposal was rejected by the majority, of whom David, an old revisionist and ideological opponent of Kautsky's, henceforward became the principal spokesmen. Soon afterwards Kautsky let it be known that he regretted not having given unqualified support to his friend Haase's proposal that the party should vote against the credits. Cf. Victor Adler, *Briefwechsel mit August Bebel und Karl Kautsky*, ed. Friedrich Adler, Vienna, 1954, p. 635. In the telegrams and letters of congratulations they sent Kautsky on the occasion of his birthday, and in the articles written in honour of that event, Friedrich Adler in Vienna, M. Buchinger, and Z. Kunfi (the deputy editor of the Hungarian socialist newspaper), and E. Varga (the future economist of the Third International) in Budapest, and Haase in Berlin and many others who shared their views, praised him as the Marxist who showed the right way in relation to the war in progress. Cf. all these messages, and letters commenting on the published articles in the Kautsky papers at the International Institute of Social History, Amsterdam, and in particular the letter dated October 19, 1914 (Kautsky Archiv, D.I. No. 113) in which Friedrich Adler confirms the deep dissension on the question of the war that existed in the Austrian party, in which he initiated a debate on the subject. He succeeded in making the dissension public in the journal *Der Kamf* which he edited, in spite of the censorship. Meanwhile a far more determined and resounding demonstration was made by Karl Liebknecht, who on December 2, 1914, voted against the war credits in the Reichstag. This contributed to Friedrich Adler's adoption of a very determined oppositional line from 1915 onwards.

7. J. Redlich, *op. cit.*, Vol. I, p. 255. Both the Czech Catholic newspapers and the central organ of the Czech Social Democratic Party proclaimed their loyalty to the Austrian state at the beginning of August, the former out of loyalty to the dynasty, the latter because of fear of Tsarist invasion. This however, provided a mass base for Czech loyalism. Cf. Z. A. B. Zeman, *op. cit.*, pp. 43–44.

8. Cf. Ernesto Ragionieri and Leo Valiani, 'Socialdemocratici austriaci e socialisti italiani nell'agosto del 1914', *Studi Storici*, 1961, No. 1; cf. now *Il movimento natzionale a Trieste nella prima guerra mondiale*, ed. Giulio Cervani, Udine, 1968.

9. *Magyar Minisztertanácsi jegyzökönyvejk az elsö világháboru korából*, Budapest, 1960, pp. 85 ff. (Reports of Hungarian cabinet meetings 1914–18.)

10. J. Redlich, *op. cit.*, Vol. I, pp. 280 and 289.

11. Cf. Tisza's Complete Works, Vol. II, pp. 135–142, p. 184, and *passim*. Count Stürgkh too considered as excessive the arrests decided by the military authorities. Cf. Christoph Führ, *Das K. und K. Armeeoberkommando und die Innenpolitik in Oesterreich, 1914–1917*, Graz–Wien, 1968.

12. J. Redlich, *op. cit.*, Vol. I, pp. 285 and 289.

13. Paul Molisch, *Vom Kampf der Tschechen um ihren Staat*, Vienna, 1929, pp. 10 and 42. The trials for distributing Russian leaflets and propaganda urging desertion were reported and denounced in 1917 by the Social Democratic *Arbeiter Zeitung* of Vienna in the course of its campaign, after the accession of the Emperor Charles, for the withdrawal of civilians from the jurisdiction of military courts. On desertion at the front, cf. Karel Pichlik, 'Deutsche und tschechische Soldaten in der österreichischun-garischen Armee im Kampf gegen den Krief und die Monarchie', *Beiträge zur Geschichte der deutschen Arbeiterbewegung*, 1961, No. I, pp. 78 ff., which is based on the military records.

14. Emil Strauss, *Die Entstehung, op. cit.*, pp. 98 and 102.

15. J. Buszko, 'Die Arbeiterbewegung in Westgalizien, bis zur Revolution im Jahre 1917 (1880–1916)' in the volume of essays *Studien zur Geschichte der österreich-ungarischen Monarchie*, Budapest, 1961. Cf. Werner Conze, *Polnische Nation und deutsche Politik im ersten Weltkrieg*, Cologne and Graz, 1958, pp. 48 ff. On Daszynski, one of the first Social Democratic deputies to the Reichsrat, first Prime Minister of independent Poland in November 1918 and later an opponent of Pilsudski's dictatorial

trends, cf. A. K. Ružička, 'Geschichte des Klubs der sozialdemokratischen Abgeordneten 1879–1918', thesis for the faculty of philosophy in the University of Vienna, 1953.

16. W. Conze, *op. cit.*, p. 55.

17. On Dmowski's policy, cf. Titus Kormanicki, *Rebirth of the Polish Republic. A Study in the Diplomatic History of Europe*, London, 1957; Gunther Franz, 'Die Wiederherstellung Polens im Rahmen der russischen Kriegsziele', *Berliner Monatshefte*, 1930 (2); Louis L. Gerson, *Woodrow Wilson und die Wiedergeburt Polens 1914–1920*, Würzburg, 1956. Seton-Watson and Salvemini in spite of their aversion to Tsarism, still took the same view at the end of 1916. In connection with the views expressed by Seton-Watson's *New Europe* on the Polish question, Salvemini wrote to his friend and colleague Professor Pietro Silva: 'Russia, with the support and moral guarantee of the Entente, offers unity. . . . It is certainly difficult to make this proposal acceptable to the Austrian Poles, who in Austria were not only not deprived of their liberty but were also able to exploit the Ruthenians, but no great national enterprise is carried out without sacrifices. The Poles, when they have national unity, will be better able to fight for their liberty against the Russian bureaucracy than against Germany when they are divided between German and Austria.'

18. W. Conze, *op. cit.*; Louis L. Gerson, *op. cit.*; Tisza, *op. cit.*, *passim*; also Imre Lukinich, *Die ungarische Regierung und die polnische Frage in den ersten Jahren des Weltkrieges*, Budapest, 1938; Szokolay Katalin, *Az osztrák magyar Kormány lengyel politikája az elsö világháboru idején*, Budapest, 1967.

19. I. Lukinich, *op. cit.*, pp. 6 ff. Cf. the report of the meeting of the Hungarian government (October 1, 1915) at which the Polish question was fully discussed in *Magyar minisztertanáczi jegyzökönyvek*, *op. cit.*, pp. 189 ff. Only the Finance Minister pointed out, but in vain, that the rigid Magyar attachment to dualism would set all the nationalities of Austria–Hungary against them. *Ibid.*, p. 191.

20. Prince G. Trubetskoi, 'Souvenirs diplomatiques sur 1914', *Le Monde Slave*, 1937 (3), pp. 269 ff. Cf. the text of the manifesto in Giorgio d'Acandia (Umberto Zanotti Bianco), *La questione polacca*, Catania, 1916, p. 646.

21. C. Jay Smith, *op. cit.*, pp. 11 ff. Cf. of course M.S. Sazonov, *op. cit.*, though bearing in mind that the former Foreign Minister attributes to himself an understanding of national problems greater than that he had acquired before the revolution. On the limits of his neo-Slavism, cf. Paul Miljukov, 'World War and Slavonic Policy', *The Slavonic Review*, December 1927. On Russian policy during the war, cf. S. P. Melgunov, *Legenda o separatnom mir. (Kanyn revoliutsy)*, Paris, 1957. Cf. also George Katkov, *Russia 1917. The February Revolution*, London, 1967.

22. J. Smith, *op. cit.*, p. 14.

23. G. Franz, *op. cit.*

24. G. Trubetskoi, *op. cit.*, p. 289

25. Helga Grobing, 'Österrisch-Ungarn und die "Ukrainische Aktion" 1914–18', *Jahrbücher für die Geschichte Osteuropas*, *1959*, No. 3, pp.270 ff;

W. Bihl, 'Einige Aspekte der österreichisch-ungarischen Rutenenpolitik 1917–1918', *ibid.*, 1966, No. 4. Cf. also Z. A. B. Zeman and W. B. Scharlau, *Merchant of Revolution. The Life of Alexander Israel Helphand (Parvus)*, London, 1965, pp. 132 ff.

26. J. Redlich, *op. cit.*, Vol. I, p. 245. Cf. H. Lemke, 'Die Regierung Stürgkh und die Pläne zur Teilung Galiziens', *Oesterreich-Ungarn in der Weltpolitik, op. cit.*

27. *Ibid.*, pp. 254 and 265. Cf. in *Die Internationalen Beziehungen im Zeitalter des Imperialismus*, Series II, Vol. VI, p. 259, the memorandum by the diplomatic office attached to the Grand Duke Nikolai's General Staff on the friendly reception given to Russian troops in Galicia. On the Ruthenian pro-Russian movement, cf. Zeman, *op. cit.*, pp. 5–13. On the hanging of many pro-Russian Ruthenians by the Austro-Hungarians before the evacuation of Lvov, cf. the message from the spot by A. Fraccaroli in the *Corriere della Sera*, September 27, 1914.

28. J. Smith, *op. cit.*, p. 90. Cf. also Maurice Paléologue, *La Russie des Tsars pendant la grande guerre*, three vols., Paris, 1921–22, p. 221. It was, however, General Yanuskievich, the Chief of the General Staff, who suggested to the Prime Minister that the printing of Ukrainian newspapers in Galicia should be prohibited. Ukrainian in his view was not a real language, but an anti-Russian invention. Cf. *Int. Bez.* vol. *cit.*, p. 270. For the Russian responsibilities and the part played by Count Bobrinsky, the military governor of eastern Galicia, cf. G. D'Acandia, *op. cit.*, p. XLIV.

29. M. S. Sazonov, *op. cit.*, p. 293.

30. *Ibid.*, p. 294; J. Smith, *op. cit.*, p. 15.

31. E. Strauss, *op. cit.*, pp. 93 ff.

32. M. Paléologue, *op. cit.*, p. 93. Cf. also Erwin Hölzle, 'Russland und die Entstehung der Tschechoslowakei', *Jahrbuch des Collegium Carolinum*, 1960, Vol. I, pp. 221 ff.

33. J. Smith, *op. cit.*, p. 17. Cf. now Gerburg Thunig-Nittner, *Die tschechoslowakische Legion in Russland*, Wiesbaden, 1970.

34. Madeleine Levée, *Les précurseurs de l'indépendance tchéque à Paris*, Paris, 1936, p. 97. On October 1, 1914, Masaryk discussed with four Czech National Socialist deputies the problems raised by the manifesto, of which he had received a copy dropped by a Russian aircraft. He imprudently made a note of the conversation, which was found by the police when his house was searched when his definite expatriation became known. The four deputies were arrested and in 1916 received sentences varying from five to six years' imprisonment. The press was unable to report this until the following year, when the Reichsrat was reconvened. Cf. the *Arbeiter Zeitung* of July 21, 1917. A copy of the manifesto was taken to Slovenia, and to Trieste by the lawyer J. Mandić, who in 1915 paid several visits to Trumbić in Rome and received propaganda material from him. Cf. Milava Paulova, *Jugoslavenski Odbor. Povijest jugoslavenske emigracije zasvjetskog rata od 1914–1918*, Zagreb, undated (but 1925), p. 62.

35. J. Smith, *op. cit.*, p. 19.

36. M. S. Sazonov, *op. cit.*, p. 296; *Int. Bez.*, vol. *cit.*, pp. 487 ff.

[349]

37. K. Pichlick, *op. cit.*, p. 81. Cf. also Richard Plaschka, 'Aur Vor-geschichte des Überganges von Einheiten des Infanterieregiment Nr. 28', *Oesterreich und Europa, Festgabe für Hugo Hantsch*, Vienna, 1965, pp. 455 ff. The desertion of the 28th Regiment came to be known in political circles in Vienna. Cf. J. Redlich, *op. cit.*, Vol. II, p. 33. On the recruitment of Czechs in Russia, cf. Jaroslav Papoušek, *La lutte pour l'indépendance du peuple tchéchoslovaque*, Paris, 1928, p. 20.

38. *Int. Bez.*, vol. *cit.*, p. 193. The telegram in which Paléologue reported this statement of Sazonov's was deciphered by the Tsarist authorities, and against the passage mentioning what the kingdom of Bohemia was to consist of someone in the Russian Foreign Ministry wrote in pencil 'the Slovaks'. Thus the possibility of uniting Slovakia, which belonged to Hungary, with the Czech provinces belonging to Austria was present in the minds of the Russian diplomatic service.

39. *Ibid.*, p. 274.

40. *Ibid.*, p. 275. Cf. also Mario Toscano, *La Serbia e l'intervento in guerra dell' Italia*, Milan, 1939, p. 7. Pašić must have learnt from the Serb-ian Minister in Rome, who was told of it at the French embassy, that Italy was demanding Dalmatia. Cf. P. D. Ostović, *The Truth about Yugoslavia*, with an introduction by Ivan Meštrović, New York, 1952. The author was secretary of the Yugoslav Committee in London from 1916 to 1918 and was subsequently Trumbić's private secretary in the Yugoslav Foreign Ministry.

41. Dragovan Šepić, *Supilo Diplomat*, Zagreb, 1961, pp. 12–14.

42. Ante Smith Pavelić, *op. cit.*, p. 29.

43. D. Šepić, *op. cit.*, p. 15, footnote. The unpublished fragments of Bissolati's diary (Salvemini papers) has the following, dated April 2, 1916: 'Conversation with Supilo. . . . He was in Italy at the outbreak of the war. He was warned that if he returned to Croatia (he is from Ragusa—his mother is of Genoese origin and his father a Ragusan) he would be in-terned. The interned Austrian Croatian and Serbian politicians now num-ber more than 10,000.' There is no doubt about what would have happened to Supilo if he had remained in Austria-Hungary. Francis Kossuth's correspondence with his brother (*Századok*, 1961, Nos. 2–3, pp. 344 ff.) shows that Francis Joseph (on the basis of reports made in 1908 by a Hungarian government informer whom we have already mentioned) believed Supilo to be an agent of the Serbian government.

44. P. D. Ostović, *op. cit.*, p. 55.

45. D. Šepić, *op. cit.*, p. 11.

46. Radica, *op. cit.*, pp. 380–382. Cf. now D. Šepić, *Pisma i memoran-dumi Frana Supila (1914–1917)*, Belgrade, 1967.

47. D. Šepić, *op. cit.*, p. 19.

48. P. D. Ostović, *op. cit.*, p. 55. Steed, who was able to take advantage of his long-standing friendships in the Italian diplomatic and political world, called on the Italian ambassador to discuss the 'aspirations to a confederation of Southern Slavs' and the question of Istria and Dalmatia. Steed suggested to Imperiali 'bringing secretly to Rome the noted Supilo,

who is at present in Venice, and engaging in discussions with him with a view to arriving at an agreed solution to a most complicated problem'. Cf. Imperiali's telegram of October 2, 1914, in *Documenti Diplomatici Italiani*, Series V (1914–18), Vol. I (August 2–October 16, 1914), Rome, 1954, p. 515. Incidentally, having met the Italian ambassador a month previously at the Foreign Office in London, Steed had said to him that 'if Italy moves now and intervenes as the liberator of the Southern Slavs, she will acquire tremendous prestige which will save her from great troubles in the future in the event of the realization of her national aspirations to Trieste'. *Ibid.*, p. 301. For Supilo's gratitude to Steed for this, cf. his letter to Gina Lombroso Ferrero of April 6, 1917. 'I have a friend, Steed, whom I love as a brother'; he wrote. B. Radica, *op. cit.*, p. 48.

49. Cf. the note of his conversations with the Entente ambassadors made by Supilo on September 30, 1914, in *Arhivski Vjesnik*, 1958, Vol. I, pp. 252 ff., in the collection of documents published by D. Šepić, *op. cit.*, p. 23. Cf. also Trumbić's diary (*Trumbičev Dnevnik*, ed. D. Šepić) in *Historijski Pregled*, 1959, No. 2, pp. 171–175.

51. Salvemini papers. Part of this letter, but not the extract quoted here, was published by Raffaelo Colapietra, *Leonida Bissolati*, Milan, 1958, p. 220.

52. Luigi Albertini, *Epistolario, 1911–1926*, four vols., Milano, 1968. The Witte mentioned in Amendola's letter is of course the well-known former Russian Finance Minister, to whom intrigues for a separate peace were attributed. Cf. in *Int. Bez.*, vol. *cit.*, p. 116, the summary of Krupensky's telegram of August 21, 1914, on his conversation with the correspondent of the *Corriere della Sera*, who told him he was willing to campaign for intervention provided he had assurances about Italy's future position in the Adriatic. Cf. the copy of Krupensky's telegram sent by Sazonov to the Russian ambassador in France, *Iswolski im Weltkrieg. Der diplomatische Schriftwechsel aus den Jahren, 1914–1917*, ed. Friedrich Stieve, Berlin, 1926, p. 75. In reality Sazonov intended to offer less than his ambassador in Rome had done. In a memorandum probably drafted between August 20 and 22 he suggested promising Italy the Trentino, Trieste and Valona 'as well as a predominant position in the Adriatic, except for the granting of access to the sea to Serbia within limits to be decided on'. Cf. M. Toscano, *Il Patto di Londra*, *op. cit.*, pp. 50–51. This was a reiteration of what his deputy Baron Schilling had held out to the Italian ambassador in Petrograd on August 14. Cf. L. Albertini, *Venti anni di vita politica*, *op. cit.*, Part II, Vol. I, p. 347. After receiving Krupensky's message, Sazonov considered it advisable to restrict the scope of the promise given, as the Italian government had not hastened to accept the Russian ambassador's offer. On August 24, knowing that, if Italy entered on negotiations, she would do so in London, he telegraphed to his ambassadors to Britain and France: 'I consider it necessary during negotiations with Italy carefully to avoid premature undertakings concerning the Dalmatian coast, the whole of which is inhabited by Serbs.' L. Albertini, vol. *cit.*, p. 349.

[351]

53. Cf. Supilo's letters on his conversations at Bordeaux, *Arhivski Vjesnik*, Vol. I, pp. 254 ff.

54. Cf. the text in *Int. Bez.*, vol. *cit.*, pp. 394 ff.

55. *Ibid.*, p. 305.

56. *Ibid.*

57. Carlo Sforza, *Jugoslavia. Storia e ricordi*, Milan, 1948, p. 95.

58. *Int. Bez*, vol. *cit.*, p. 268.

59. *Ibid.*, p. 269.

60. *Ibid.*, Vol. VI, p. 564; Vol. VII, pp. 79 and 61. An official of the British embassy in Rome reported to the Foreign Office on January 16, 1915, that he had been approached by Count Paul Szapáry, of the Hungarian Party of Independence and of 1848, who had suggested to him the possibility of Hungary's making herself independent of Austria and signing a separate peace in return for a guarantee of her territorial integrity. The British Foreign Secretary informed his ambassadors in Paris and Petrograd of these proposals, which he considered too vague. Cf. P.R.O., Political, The War, File 1500. 1915–2505. On the Magyar independence movement, cf. Károlyi Mihály, *Faith Without Illusion*, London, 1956. Many items of news tending to create the belief in a Magyar desire to dissociate themselves from the Central Powers were published at the end of 1914 by the *Morning Post* (and repeated in the international press, including the Italian), accompanied by false information supplied by a Hungarian journalist resident in Britain who wanted to show his compatriots to the Entente in a favourable light and was unmasked by Steed and Seton-Watson. In connection with this matter, Amendola received from Icilio Baccich, a Fiume irredentist who took refuge in Italy and a future Italian senator, information that he summed up as follows in his letter to L. Albertini of January 11, 1915: 'Through his brother who lives in Fiume, Baccich has conducted an enquiry in Hungary. From this it emerges that there is no political ferment in Hungary against the Austro-German *bloc*; the Party of Independence (Apponyi, Andrássy) is more pro-war than others. On the contrary, there is discontent arising from military failures and there is worry about the future; which explain why there are those who are thinking of ways and means of keeping Hungary's access to the sea, or Transylvania, or other things.' L. Albertini, *Epistolario, op. cit.* At Fiume, of course, it could not then be known that Count Károlyi, who had recently returned from imprisonment in France, was preparing for independent action without regard to the bellicose attitude assumed by Count Apponyi in the name of the majority of his party.

61. Cf. Izvolsky's message to Sazonov of December 14, 1914, *Iswolski, op. cit.*, pp. 135 ff. Cf. Also D. Šepić, *op. cit.*, pp. 40 ff.

62. *Izwolski, op. cit.*,; pp. 136 ff. and 149 ff.; M. Toscano *op. cit.*, pp. 10 ff. Paul Henri Michel, *La question de l'Adriatique (1914–1918)*, *Recueil de documents*, Paris, 1938, pp. 30 ff.

63. *Iswolski, op. cit.*, p. 146.

64. *Ibid.*, pp. 176 ff.

65. D. Šepić, *op. cit.*, p. 33. Cf. Supilo's letter to Meštrović on his con-

versations with Tyrrell and Benckendorff in *Arhivski Vjessik*, Vol. I, pp. 261 ff.

66. H. W. Steed, *op. cit.*

67. *Arhivski Vjesnik*, Vol. I, pp. 256–260.

68. R. W. Seton-Watson, *Masaryk in England*, Cambridge, 1943. pp. 36–40. T. G. Masaryk, *Die Weltrevolution. Erinnerungen und Betrachtungen, 1914–1918*, Berlin, 1925, p. 7. For a discussion of Masaryk's policy and in general for a critical survey of the state of the researches, cf. now the very valuable collection of essays, *Aktuelle Forschungsprobleme um die erste Tschechoslowakischen Republik*, ed. Karl Bosl and others, Munich–Vienna, 1969.

69. K. Pichlik, *op. cit.*, *passim*.

70. T. G. Masaryk, *op. cit.*, p. 5. Cf. also E. V. Voška and Irwin Will, *Spy and Counterspy*, London, 1941, pp. 19–25.

71. On the Russian ambassador in London, cf. Wladimir V. Krostovetz, 'Graf Alex. Konst. Benckendorff', *Berliner Monatshefte*, 1936 (2), pp. 887 ff. Cf. his correspondence, *Graf Benckenderffs Diplomatischer Schrift Wechsel*, ed. B. von Siebert, three vols., Berlin, 1928.

72. H. W. Steed, *op. cit.*

73. K. Pichlik, *op. cit.*, pp. 81 ff. J. F. N. Bradley, *La Légion tchécoslovaque en Russie 1914–1920*, Paris, 1965, throws doubt, however, on the numbers involved in these desertions, which the Austro-Hungarian command tended to exaggerate in order to be able to attribute to the desertions responsibility for Russian military successes.

74. T. G. Masaryk, *op. cit.*, p. 6.

75. R. W. Seton-Watson, *op. cit.*, pp. 36 ff.

76. T. G. Masaryk, *op. cit.*, p. 7.

77. *Ibid.* Cf. R. W. Seton-Watson, *op. cit.*, *passim*; H. W. Steed, *op. cit.*, Vol. II, pp. 42 ff; *Iswolski*, *op. cit.*, pp. 135 ff.

78. R. W. Seton-Watson, *op. cit.*, p. 45.

79. *Ibid.*, pp. 52–53. Steed, though in practice giving every support to Supilo and Masaryk, as diplomatic correspondent of *The Times* could not then write in favour of the destruction of Austria-Hungary. Denis's caution is therefore not surprising, as the Quai d'Orsay was even more pro-Habsburg than the British. On Denis, cf. the obituary by his colleague Louis Eisenmann in the *Revue des Études Slaves*, 1921, pp. 138 ff. and the commemoratory speeches made at the Sorbonne on the tenth anniversary of his death, reported in *Le Monde Slave*, 1931 (1), pp. 459 ff.; also Ernst Birke, *Frankreich und Ostmitteleuropa im 19. Jahrhundert*, Cologne and Graz, 1960.

80. 'Fra la grande Serbia ed una più grande Austria', *l'Unità*, August 7, 1914. To Salvemini the decisive factor in the first few weeks of the war was the position taken by Luigi Albertini. On August 14, 1914, he wrote to Ugo Ojetti: 'The *Corriere della Sera* has shown itself to be the true Italian national newspaper. . . . There is only one kind of high politics today, and that is conducted by the *Corriere*.' The Salvemini papers. It should be borne in mind that since the Bosnian crisis of 1908–9 Salvemini and

Bissolati had backed the Southern Slavs against Austria and argued for the Italian nature of the Trento and Trieste.

81. 'Austria, Italia e Serbia', *l'Unità*, December 18, 1914. For a preliminary bibliography of the subject, cf. Arturo Cronia, 'Pubblicazioni italiane su gli Slavi meridionali nella prima guerra mondiale', *Südostforschungen*, 1956, pp. 458 ff. Cf. also Elio Apih, 'l'Unità ed il problema Adriatico (1911–1920)', *Scritti in onore di Camillo de Franceschi*, Trieste, 1951, pp. 253 ff., and Enzo Tagliacozzo, *Gaetano Salvemini nel cinquantennio liberale*, Florence, 1959.

82. *I Documenti Diplomatici Italiani*, vol. *cit.*, p. 389. On the proposals made to Romania by the Central Powers, cf. now Gerard E. Silberstein, *The Troubled Alliance. German–Austrian Relations 1914 to 1917*, Lexington, 1970. Cf. of course Ottokar Czernin, *Im Weltkriege*, Berlin, 1919; M. Erzberger, *Erlebnisse im Weltkrieg*, Stuttgart, 1920; K. Epstein, *Matthias Erzberger*, *op. cit.* Cf. also R. W. Seton-Watson, *Histoire des Roumains*, Paris, 1937; Nicolas Basilesco, *La Roumanie dans la guerre et dans la paix*, two vols., Paris, 1919. Glenn Torrey, 'Irredentism and Diplomacy. The Central Powers and Romania. August–November, 1914', *Südostforschungen*, 1966. According to this author, any Austrian or Hungarian concession to Romania would have been useless, because Romanian public opinion wanted war. But Romania waited two years before actually joining in war and in these two years Austria-Hungary, granting something substantial to Romania besides promising her Bessarabia, could have made some progress in Bucharest.

83. 'La guerra per la pace', *l'Unità*, August 28, 1914.

84. 'L'Italia e i Balcani', *Il Secolo*, November 14, 1914. The article is reprinted under the title 'L'Italia e gli stati Balcanici' in Leonida Bissolati, *La politica estera dell'Italia dal 1897 al 1920*, Milan, 1932.

85. *Scritti Politici di Cesare Battisti*, *op. cit.*

86. *Ibid*, pp. 193–198.

87. Cf. Friedrich Adler's appeal in *Avanti!* of December 3, 1915 under the heading 'Il manifesto della minoranza socialista austriaca'. It reached Italy through D. Riazanov, who maintained contact between the internationalist socialists of Vienna and Zürich, and Angelica Balabanoff, who represented the Italian Socialist Party leadership in Switzerland. Cf. A. Balabanoff, *Erinnerungen und Ereignisse*, Berlin, 1927, pp. 117–118.

88. C. Battisti, *op. cit.*, p. 210. The phrase 'peoples without a history' had been popularized by the Austrian Marxist Otto Bauer who, however, before the war looked to the democratization of Austria-Hungary and not its disruption as the result of their awakening.

89. Cf. *l'Unità*, February 12, 1915.

90. *Ibid.*, April 30, 1915.

91. R. W. Seton-Watson, *Masaryk*, *op. cit.*, p. 55; *Trumbičev Dnevnik*, *op. cit.*, pp. 182–183. Cf. Trumbić's letter to Supilo on these contacts in *Arhivski Vjesnik*, Vol. I, pp. 283 ff. During this journey, when he saw the immense damage that Austrian aggression had inflicted on Serbia, G. M. Trevelyan was converted to an all-out struggle against the Habsburg

empire and therefore be conducted propaganda to this effect both in Britain and the United States. Cf. Arthur J. May, 'R. W. Seton-Watson and British Anti-Habsburg Sentiment', *The American Slavic and East European Review*, February 1961, p. 42.

92. R. W. Seton-Watson, J. Dover Wilson, Alfred E. Zimmern, Arthur Greenwood, *War and Democracy*, second ed., London, 1915. The volume was aimed at the Labour or radical left wing for the purpose of inducing it to drop its traditional pacifism and regard the war as a struggle for democracy. The chapter on Russia therefore severely criticized the Tsarist régime.

93. *Ibid.*, pp. 251 ff. This is not the place to point out that the peace imposed by the victorious Entente failed to avoid sowing the seeds of another world war. Seton-Watson himself dealt with this in his *Britain and the Dictators. A Survey of Post-War British Policy*, Cambridge, 1938.

94. *War and Democracy, op. cit.*, pp. 274 ff.

95. *Ibid.*, pp. 264 ff.

96. Cf. *l'Unità*, March 12, 1915. The article is reprinted in *L'Unità di Gaetano Salvemini*, ed. Beniamino Finocchiaro, Venice, 1958, pp. 367 ff.

97. *Ibid.*

98. D. Šepić, 'Misija Carla Gallija u Trstu', *Anali Jadranskog instituta*, Vol. II, 1958, pp. 53 ff. Cf. Carlo Galli, *Diarii e lettere. Tripoli 1911– Trieste 1918.* Florence, 1951, p. 237; *Trumbičev Dnevnik, op. cit.*, p. 185. Cf. also Trumbić's letter to Supilo (February 4, 1915) in which he informed him of Galli's mission, *Arhivski Vjesnik*, Vol. II, 1959, pp. 353 ff. As Trumbić had heard, another Italiàn emissary, Gino Scarpa, had previously been sent to Trieste. Scarpa, a republican and ardent interventionist familiar with the Adriatic scene, having a Triestine mother and having been a student in Trieste, was an official in the Ministry of Agriculture, Industry and Commerce and when Ubaldo Comandini, a republican, entered the government he became his secretary in the propaganda department. Cf. Gino Scarpa, *Trieste, l'Italia e la Medioeuropa*, Rome, 1917, which made an effective case for an Italo-Slav alliance against German pressure, but contains only fleeting references to the author's personal contact at Trieste. Scarpa then entered the diplomatic service. In India he later became a close friend of Nehru's.

99. B. Radica, *op. cit.*, pp. 94–95.

100. Guglielmo Ferrero, 'Slavi e latini nell'Adriatico', *Il Secolo*, April 27, 1915.

101. C. Galli, *op. cit.*, pp. 248 ff. Trumbić told Galli he was a Croat who thought and spoke Italian; he wanted to remain a Croat, but wanted Italian to be his people's second language. Cf. Carlo Galli, 'La Serbia per un accordo con l'Italia', *Mondo europeo*, 1946, No. 1, p. 118. Cf. also 'Lettera di uno slavo a un amico italiano' unsigned, *l'Unità*, May 21, 1915. Trumbić wrote in excellent Italian to Seton-Watson (cf. the letters preserved among the latter's papers).

102. *Ibid.*, p. 254. According to Galli, the Italians in Dalmatia numbered no more than 10 per cent of the population. Austrian statistics put

the figure at only 3 per cent. Three and a half years later Galli noted in his diary that 'renouncing requires greater strength of character than demanding' (*ibid.*, p. 307). That Dalmatia was Slavonic when Zara was left out of account was admitted even by the greatest advocates of irredentism, such as Innocenzo Cappa and Giulio Gaprin. Cf. their letters in *Il Secolo* of October 23 and 26, 1914.

103. *Ibid.*, p. 255.

104. A. S. Pavelić, *op. cit.*, p. 34.

105. D. Šepić, 'Srpska vlada i počeci Jugoslavenska Odbora', *Historijski Zbornik*, Nos. 1–4. On this occasion Supilo must have been received by Ferdinando Martini.

106. The possibility of asking for a part of Dalmatia had been raised by San Giuliano in his telegram of September 25, 1914, to the Italian ambassadors to Russia and France. On this, cf. M. Toscano, *Il Patto, op. cit.*, pp. 52 ff. Toscano was of course unaware in 1934 of the still unpublished documents on Krupensky's offers. Comparison of the telegram mentioned, the original text of which can now be consulted in *Documenti Diplomatici Italiani*, vol. *cit.*, p. 475, with the offers that Krupensky mentioned to Amendola (who, as he wrote to L. Albertini, established that they really had been submitted to the Italian Foreign Ministry), shows that San Giuliano based himself exactly on what the Russian ambassador had proposed to him a month earlier and merely wondered whether it would be wise to put forward claims to Dalmatia 'bearing in mind the danger of future conflicts with the Slav states'. Carlotti and Tittoni replied advising against making claims to Dalmatia (the latter more strongly than the former). These were made (under pressure from the nationalists) by Sonnino, who, however, on September 4, 1914, had written to A. Bergamini, the editor of the *Giornale d'Italia*, that he did not think it advisable to ask for Trieste in addition to Trent, 'because Italian Trieste would be ruined'. Cf. the letter in the Bergamini papers in the Communal Library of San Giovanni in Persiceto. Sonnino was, however, entitled to say in the discussions that preceded the Treaty of London that in August 1914 the Russian government had been willing to give Italy the whole of Dalmatia. M. Toscano, 'Il negoziato di Londra del 1915', *Nuova Antologia*, November 1967. Sonnino actually decided for intervention in order to secure to Italy the eastern shore of the Adriatic sea.

107. On Loiseau's political activity in Rome, cf. Appendix III. Loiseau, who as a young man had been secretary to Strossmayer, the celebrated Bishop of Zagreb, married a sister of Ivo and Lujo Vojnovič. The latter, who as a publicist and historian spelled his name in the Italian manner (Voinovich), made many friends in Rome. Senator Umberto Zanotti Bianco—who with his *La Giovane Europa* and *La Voce dei Popoli* was the moving spirit of the movement for solidarity with the Slav and Romanian refugees—allowed me to see the letters written to him by L. Voinovich. Ivo Vojnović, who was one of the best Croatian poets, was arrested by the Austrians in 1914 and went blind in prison. Cf. his *Lettres de guerre*, written to Loiseau, in *Le Monde Slave*, 1931 (3), pp. 263 ff. On him, cf. the

Bulletin Yougoslave, No. 27, December 1917, and the *Agramer Tagblatt* of October 9, 1917.

108. F. Charles-Roux, *Souvenirs Diplomatiques, Rome-Quirinal*, Paris, 1958, p. 262.

109. For the drafting of the Russian offer, cf. *Int. Bez.*, Series II, Vol. VI, p. 252, Sazonov's proposals to the Tsar. According to Don Ernesto Vercesi, it was no other than Alcide De Gasperi, then a deputy to the Reichsrat and a frequent visitor to Rome during the period of Italian neutrality, who secretly suggested to Krupensky the idea of freeing the Tridentine prisoners in Russian hands. Cf. E. Vercesi, 'Ricordi quasi diplomatici', in the Anthology of the review *Civitas*, Rome, 1963, pp. 475 ff. De Gasperi visited Sonnino several times and on March 16, 1915, asked him to make a condition of an agreement with Austria (he was in favour of such an agreement) the immediate release of the Tridentine soldiers from the Austrian army. Cf. Sonnino papers. Krupensky's statement is in the *Corriere della Sera*, October 25, 1914. Cf. *Arhivski Vjesnik*, Vol. I, p. 265, for Trumbić's consternation, who wrote about it to Supilo. The refugees from Austria's Italian provinces hastened to submit to Krupensky a memorandum urging the speedy carrying out of his proposal, the result of which was an additional charge of high treason against Battisti. The refugees wanted their fellow-nationals to be allowed to fight the Austrians after their release by the Russians, but Krupensky, wishing to make his offer acceptable to the Italian government, which was still neutral, publicly refused this. The *Popolo d'Italia* of March 14, 1915, connected these vacillations of his with his being relieved of his post.

110. Cf. Pašić's statement in Ferdo Šišić, *Dokumenti o postanku Kraljevine Srba, Hrvata i Slovenska v. 1914–1918*, Zagreb, 1920, p. 10. For criticisms of the Serbian policy from the Croatian viewpoint, cf. Leopold Silberstein, 'Der Dreifrontenkrieg des Jugoslawischen Nationalausschusses', *Europäische Gespräche*, 1928, pp. 335 ff.; Charles Jelavich, 'Nikolas P. Pašić: Greater Serbia or Yugoslavia?', *Journal of Central European Affairs*, July 1951, pp. 133 ff. Light is now thrown on the question by D. Šepić, *Srpska Vlada, op. cit.*, based on Serbian government archives.

111. Cf. the Croat committee's letter in the *Corriere della Sera*, February 7, 1915. For Tisza's speech, cf. the Stefani agency summary in the *Corriere della Sera* of February 1, which was the version seen by Trumbić. Thus F. Šišić, *op. cit.* p. 12, is mistaken in attributing the Croat committee reply to December 1914, as does M. Paulova, *op. cit.*, p. 31, and following her Victor S. Mamatey, *The United States and East Central Europe 1914–1918*, Princeton, 1957, who in their basic works on the subject are under the impression that it was Tisza's New Year speech to which Trumbić was replying. To the Croat exiles the Hungarian Prime Minister's speech was the more disturbing inasmuch as it was one of a series of attempts on his part to strengthen his collaboration with the majority in the Zagreb Diet, to which he wanted to be able to point as an example to the more moderate Romanian politicians in Transylvania, with whom he hoped to come to a similar agreement. These efforts were denounced in a statement to *The*

Times of December 28, 1914 (reproduced next day by the *Corriere della Sera*) by a Croat *émigré* in London in whom we can recognize Supilo.

112. Cf. the appeal for volunteers, dated London and Rome, February 1915, F. Šišić, *op. cit.*, pp. 18 ff., and Trumbić's memorandum in M. Paulova, *op. cit.*, p. 35. Cf. also Trumbić's diary in which (on p. 185) he quotes the example of Garibaldi and Bixio.

113. Izvolsky submitted it to them on December 12, 1914.

114. M. Paléologue, *op. cit.*, Vol. I, p. 198; *Int. Bez.*, vol. *cit.*, p. 468.

115. M. Paléologue, *op. cit.*, p. 246.

116. *Ibid.*, p. 258.

117. *Int. Bez.*, Series II, Vol. VI, p. 567 footnote.

118. D. Šepić, *Supilo, op. cit.*, p. 57. Cf. *Trumbičev Dnevnik, op. cit.*, for the account written by Supilo for his colleague.

119. Cf. *Arhivski Vjesnik*, Vol. II, pp. 348–349.

120. *Ibid.*, pp. 350–351.

121. D. Šepić, *op. cit.*, pp. 66 ff.

Notes (IV)

Yugoslav, Czechoslovak and Hungarian Independence Movements, 1915–1916

1. Cf. Trubetskoy's report in *Int. Bez.*, Series II, Vol. VII, pp. 75 ff.
2. *Ibid.*, pp. 123 and 164.
3. *Ibid.*, pp. 179 footnote and 183 footnote.
4. *Ibid.*, pp. 183–184.
5. D. Šepić, *Supilo Diplomat, op. cit.*, pp. 71–73. On Supilo's stay in Russia, see D. Vasiljević's report to the Serbian Ministry in London, published by D. Šepić in *Historijski Pregled*, 1963, No. 4.
6. *Ibid.*, p. 80.
7. *Int. Bez.*, Series II, Vol. VI, p. 535.
8. Cf. the *Corriere della Sera* of January 8, 1915.
9. *Int. Bez.*, vol. *cit.*, pp. 649–651.
10. M. Toscano, *Il Patto di Londra, op. cit.*, p. 71.
11. An observer as acute as Anna Kuliscioff, the Russian-born companion of the Italian socialist leader Filippo Turati, immediately realized that the Dardanelles operation, which turned the Mediterranean into a theatre of war, made early Italian intervention inevitable, and said so in a letter on March 4, 1915, advising Turati, though vainly, to modify his neutralism in consequence. 'Certainly I do not want war either,' she wrote, 'but that does not prevent me from being vividly aware of the impending reality. . . . In short, Italy either marches within the next few days or she will remain isolated and badly damaged in the future.' The letter is included in the Turati–Kuliscioff correspondence, collected by the late Senator Alessandro Schiavi and due for early publication. For the Italian government's assessment of the Dardanelles operation, cf. the letters published by Monticone, *Salandra, Sonnino, op. cit.*
12. M. Toscano, *op. cit.*, pp. 83 ff.
13. *Ibid.*, pp. 90 ff.
14. Jay Smith, *The Russian Struggle, op. cit.*, p. 197.
15. *Int. Bez.*, Vol. VII, *op. cit.*, p. 321. According to the journalist Luciano Magrini, who was then in Petrograd and was present at a conversation in January 1915 between Carlotti and Spalajković, the latter appealed to his Italian colleague to do all he could to promote an Italo-Serbian agreement on military and political co-operation in the Adriatic. Luigi Albertini, to whom Magrini reported the incident, wrote that Carlotti was at heart convinced that a direct agreement between Italy and Serbia would enable Italian national aspirations to be achieved in such a way as to make possible good neighbourly relations between the two

countries after the war. But this view was not taken into account in Rome. Cf. L. Albertini, *Vent' anni di vita politica, op. cit.*, Part II, Vol. II, p. 6. The *Corriere della Sera* on March 23 published a message on 'The Croat deputy Supilo's work for an Italo-Slav understanding' which interpreted Supilo's trips to the Entente capitals as tending towards an Italo-Yugoslav agreement capable of preventing Dalmatia from becoming an obstacle to the joint struggle against the German drive to the Adriatic.

16. *Int. Bez.*, vol. *cit.*, *passim.*

17. *Ibid.* In a subsequent conversation (on April 4) with Schilling, who predicted that a hardening of the Italian attitude would sow the seeds of a future war between Italy and Serbia, Carlotti admitted that Sonnino was wrong to ignore Yugoslav needs.

18. D. Šepić, *op. cit.*, p. 84.

19. *Int. Bez.*, vol. *cit.*, p. 437; D. Šepić, *op. cit.*, p. 89. Supilo told Masaryk (cf. the latter's *Die Weltrevolution, op. cit.*, p. 151) that Sazonov believed that the Serbs who, because of their Orthodox religion were the only ones about whom he really cared, were concentrated in southern Dalmatia, and was surprised to learn that there were more of them in central Dalmatia.

20. *Int. Bez.*, vol. *cit.*, p. 445.

21. Sazonov informed General Headquarters in advance of Supilo's arrival and advised them not to hold out much hope to him, because Istria and part of Dalmatia had already been promised to Italy. Cf. H. Michel, *La question de l'Adriatique (1914–1918), op. cit.*, p. 74. Cf. *Arhivski Vjesnik*, Vol. II, pp. 363 ff., Supilo's letter, written in Athens on his return journey, describing his efforts in Russia.

22. Cf. R. W. Seton-Watson, 'Kako je postala Yugoslavja. II. Supilo u Rusiji', *Nova Europa*, 1926, No. 11, p. 358. Cf. also Milan Marjanović, *Londonski ugovor iz godine 1915*, Zagreb, 1969, pp. 215 ff.

23. *Int. Bez.*, vol. *cit.*, pp. 502 and 629. Cf. also M. Toscano, *La Serbia e l'intervento, op. cit.*, p. 21.

24. D. Šepić, *Misija Carla Gallija, op. cit.*, pp. 76–77 footnote; A. S. Pavelić, *Trumbić, op. cit.*, p. 37; M. Paulova, *Yugoslavenski Odbor, op. cit.*, pp. 62–63. The Slovene deputies who took part in these meetings were National Liberals. But the theologian Professor J. Krek, one of the most notable representatives of the Slovene Catholic Popular Party, the majority of whom remained loyal to the Habsburgs, notified his support. On the evolution of the Slovene parties on the eve of the war, cf. Dušan Biber's paper in *Istorija XX. Veka. Zbornik radova*, Belgrade, 1950, pp. 285 ff.

25. Cf. the text in F. Šišić, *Dokumenti, op. cit.*, pp. 20–21. According to a study by George J. Prpic, in *The Immigrants influence on Wilson's peace policy*, ed. Joseph O'Grady, Lexington, 1967, there were about 650,000 Croats, 250,000 Slovenes, and 100,000 Serbs in the United States. (These figures include those of the second and third generation.)

26. *Ibid.*, p. 75. Cf. also the *Bulletin Yougoslave*, No. 1, October 1, 1915. There are some differences between the list of names of members of the committee found by M. Paulova among its papers and those published in

the *Bulletin*, which was its official organ. We have found no evidence for the statement made by various authors that Trumbić was expelled from Italy. According to his biographer, A. Smith Pavelić, he left Rome of his own free will.

27. D. Šepić, *Srpska vlada, op. cit.*, pp. 31 ff. and *Supilo Diplomat, op. cit.*, pp. 118 ff. Cf. also M. Toscano, *La Serbia, op. cit.*, p. 44. On May 6, 1915, Sir Edward Grey had the impression from his conversation with the Serbian Minister in London that the Serbian government would be satisfied with Bosnia-Hercegovina, part of the Adriatic coast, and Bačka and the Banat in southern Hungary. Cf. P.R.O. Political—Balkan War Files 1915 u. 2257.

28. A. S. Pavelić, *op. cit.*, p. 66; P. D. Ostović, *The Truth, op. cit.*, p. 60; M. Paulova, *op. cit.*, p. 76.

29. H. W. Steed, *Mes souvenirs, op. cit.*, Vol. II, p. 60. French public opinion, so far as can be judged from the Paris newspapers, took the same line. Nevertheless the *Journal des Débates* and *l'Humanité* warned Italy against violating at the Yugoslav expense the nationality principle for which the war was being fought.

30. Cf. the text in F. Šišić, *op. cit.*, pp. 24 ff; H. Michel, *op. cit.*, pp. 113 ff; M. Toscano, *op. cit.*, pp. 59 ff.; also the map, plainly showing the territories claimed as Slav, in the *Bulletin Yougoslave*, No. 1.

31. R. W. Seton-Watson, *Kako je postala II, op. cit.*, p. 362; Arthur J. May, 'Seton-Watson and the Treaty of London', *Journal of Modern History*, 1957, No. 1 pp. 42 ff.

32. *Ibid.*, p. 44. Cf. Seton-Watson's account in his *Masaryk in London, op. cit.*, p. 62.

33. R. W. Seton-Watson, 'Kako je postala Yugoslavija. Yugoslavenski Odbor i Serbnjanska vlada i Londoni, za vreme rata', *Nova Europa*, 1927, No. 1, p. 7. Cf. the text of the manifesto in F. Šišić, *op. cit.*, pp. 36–37; H. Michel *op. cit.*, pp. 111 ff.; M. Toscano, *op. cit.*, pp. 56 ff. The existence of the Yugoslav Committee became known in Croatia as a result of its denunciation for high treason in *Hrvatska*, the newspaper of the pro-Austrian party of the followers of Dr Frank. The news was taken up by other Croatian newspapers. Cf. M. Paulova, *op. cit.*, p. 26.

34. P. O. Ostović, *op. cit.*, p. 61; M. Paulova, *op. cit.*, p. 86, dates the interview June 5, but D. Šepić, *Supilo, op. cit.*, p. 132, makes it July 2.

35. Cf. the letter, dated June 22, 1915, in A. J. May, *op. cit.*, p. 47.

36. T. G. Masaryk, *op. cit.*, p. 39; E. Beneš, *Souvenirs, op. cit.*, Vol. I, p. 36.

37. Cf. the text, *Int. Bez.*, Series II, Vol. VI, p. 590.

38. *Ibid.*, p. 566. Cf. Z. A. B. Zeman, *op. cit.*, pp. 157–158. For the hostility of the Czech middle classes to the Central Powers, cf. Bernard Michel, 'Le sabotage des emprunts de guerre autrichiens par les banques tchèques, 1914–1916,' *Revue d'Histoire moderne et contemporaine*, April–June, 1968.

39. E. Strauss, *Die Entstehung, op. cit.*, p. 86. *Int. Bez.*, vol. *cit.*, pp. 565 ff.
40. *Ibid.*, p. 590.

41. E. Beneš, *op. cit.*, Vol. I, pp. 30 ff.

42. C. F. P. Reiman, *Geschichte der Kommunistischen Partei der Tschechoslowakei*, Hamburg, 1931.

43. Cf. Fr. Modracek, 'Masaryk und der Sozialismus', *Festschrift Th. G. Masaryk zum 80, Geburtstage*, two vols., Bonn, 1930, Vol. II, pp. 291 ff. The author had been the spokesman of the patriotic faction of the Czech Social Democratic Party before 1914. In regard to Masaryk's attitude to socialism, a letter of his to Eduard Bernstein dated July 29, 1889, expresses what it was destined always to remain. He desired the development of the Social Democratic Party in the direction of Bernstein's revisionist ideas and wished this process every success. Cf. the Bernstein papers, D.40, International Institute of Social History, Amsterdam.

44. On the Czech Progressive Party, cf. Z. Zeman, *op. cit.*, p. 21.

45. Lajos Steit, *A tót kérdes*, Liptószentmiklós, 1912, pp. 150 ff.; Milos Gosiorovsky, *Adalékok a szlovák munkásmozgalom történetéhez*, Bratislava, 1952, pp. 25 ff.; G. Gábor Kemény, *Iratok a nemzetiségi kérdés történetéhez Magyarországon a dualizmus korában*, Budapest, 1952 et seq., Vol. I, pp. 768–769. Cf. Šrobar's article on Masaryk and the Slovak Populist students in 1897–98 in the *Prager Presse* of March 7, 1930, reprinted in Alexander Szama, *Die Geschichte der Slowakei*, Bratislava, 1930, pp. 123 ff. Cf. also Masaryk, *Staatsmann und Denker*, Prague, 1930, pp. 51 ff.

46. M. Gosiorovsky, *op. cit.*, pp. 63 ff. On the formation of Hlinka's party, cf. L. Steier, *op. cit.*, pp. 230 ff.

47. J. Redlich, *op. cit.*, p. 90.

48. M. Levée, *Les Précurseurs de l'indépendance tchèque à Paris*, *op. cit.*, p. 106.

49. *Ibid.*, p. 135. Étienne Fournol had been a fellow student of Kramař's at the École Libre de Sciences Politiques, which was attended by many students from Slav countries. Cf. Ernst Birke, 'Die französische Osteuropa-Politik 1914–1918', *Zeitschrift für Ostforschung*, 1954, No. 3, pp. 321 ff. In June 1915 several Czech deputies addressed some memoranda (signed, among others, by the Agrarian deputy Dürich, who fled shortly afterwards to Russia) to the French government, proposing the creation of a Kingdom of Bohemia. Cf. A.D.M.A.E. Guerre.Autriche-Hongrie 1914–18, Mouvement national tchèque.

50. M. Levée, *op. cit.*, p. 143.

51. Cf. *La Nation tchèque*, I, No. 4, June 15, 1915. Large scale persecution occurred, at that time, however, only in relation to the Serbs of southern Hungary and Bosnia-Hercegovina (4,000 of whom, according to J. Redlich's information, *op. cit.*, Vol. II, p. 21, were interned in cellars) and, after the intervention, to Italians.

52. *Le Monde Slave*, 1918, p. 564.

53. E. Beneš, *op. cit.*, Vol. I, pp. 43 ff.; Z. Zeman, *op. cit.*, p. 82.

54. P. Selver, *op. cit.*, p. 175.

55. E. Strauss, *op. cit.*, pp. 130 ff.; J. Redlich, *op. cit.*, Vol. II, p. 80.

56. *Der Hochverratsprozess gegen Dr Kramář*, *op. cit.*, pp. 169 ff. Cf.

Hermann Münch, *Böhmische Tragödie. Das Schicksal Mitteleuropas im Lichte der tschechischen Frage*, Braunschweig, 1949, pp. 581 ff.

57. Václav Kral, *A csehszlovákiai burzsoázia intervenciós háboruja a magyar tanácsköztársaság ellen 1919*, Bratislava, 1956, p. 55.

58. E. Beneš, *op. cit.*, Vol. I, p. 107, R. M. Seton-Watson, *Masaryk, op. cit.*, pp. 68 ff.

59. Cf. Charles Pergler, *America in the Struggle for Czechoslovak Independence*, Philadelphia, 1926, p. 23.

60. E. Beneš, *op. cit.*, Vol. I, p. 112; Z. Zeman, *op. cit.*, p. 89. The Archivio Centrale dello Stato, Rome (Affari Generali reservati, 1919, Pacco No. 18, Cat. A. 16 Stranieri) contains an interesting report dated February 15, 1917, by the Italian legation in Switzerland on the Czechs in the West. There were only about 500 Czechs in Switzerland, where Masaryk began his revolutionary organizing activity, but these, according to the report, consisted of skilled workers, who enjoyed a high reputation for industry and sobriety. They were Social Democrats and thus well disciplined, but were also very patriotic. Able militants were selected from these and sent to America by Masaryk's committee to conduct propaganda among the Czech immigrants there. The importance of this effort is to be judged by the fact that Czech and Slovak organizations in the United States had more than 300,000 paying members (cf. E. Voška, *op. cit.*, p. 33). The number of Czechs living in the United States was estimated at 540,000; that of the Slovaks at 284,000. On the latter, cf. M. Gosiorovski, 'Die Slovakische Frage bei der Entstehung der Č.S.R.', *Conférence Internationale du 50e anniversaire de la République tchèchslovaque*, two vols., Prague, 1968.

61. T. G. Masaryk, *op. cit.*, p. 98; E. Beneš, *op. cit.*, Vol. I, p. 128. I am indebted to the courtesy of Marchioness Giuliana Benzoni, Štefanik's fiancée and a personal friend of Masaryk and Beneš, for the text of the obituary of his celebrated colleague written by Leo Sychrava, a co-signatory with Štefanik of the convention of April 21, 1918, between the Italian government and the Czechoslovak National Council. 'In Italy', he wrote, 'I saw how useful Štefanik was to his country's cause, creating the impression among influential personalities of being an extraordinary, heroic and brilliant personality. The American ambassador in Rome, Nelson Page, became an enthusiastic admirer of his, and I heard him say that a country that had given birth to a Štefanik could not fail to gain its independence. The friendship of such men played a large part in his personal successes in the true sense of the word. It was said that diplomatists and soldiers carried out his wishes in order to please him personally. I should rather say that they really believed in the greatness of Štefanik's mission; he gave them the feeling that by helping him they were collaborating in a great work.' Štefanik rapidly gained an *entrée* to highly placed circles (in Rome he was received by Queen Margherita) as well as in democratic circles. In 1916 he met Salvemini, who introduced him to Ojetti. Cf. Ugo Ojetti, *Lettere alla moglie. 1915–1919*, ed. Fernanda Ojetti, Florence, 1964, p. 265.

[363]

62. *Int. Bez.*, Series II, Vol. VIII, pp. 390 ff.; M. Toscano, *La Serbia, op. cit.*, pp. 113–115.

63. *Int. Bez.*, vol. *cit.*, pp. 265 and 400. As early as April 8, 1915, Sonnino had said to F. Martini, *op. cit.*, p. 379, that it was not impossible that as a consequence of a Russian advance Hungary might wish for and take steps to secure a separate peace.

64. M. Toscano, *op. cit.*, and *Il Patto di Londra, op. cit., passim*; A. Depoli, *Fiume e il Patto di Londra, op. cit.*, L. Aldrovandi Marescotti, *Guerra diplomatica*, Milan, 1937, pp. 63 ff.

65. *Int. Bez.*, vol. *cit.*, p. 5.

66. O. Malagodi, *op. cit.*, Vol. I, p. 21.

67. Cf. J. Redlich, *op. cit.*, Vol. II, p. 27, for the confidences of the ex-Minister of Joint Austro-Hungarian Finances, the Pole L. Bilinski, who resigned from the government because of disagreement with Tisza. Tschirschky, the German ambassador in Vienna, also disagreed with Tisza. As early as September 21 the latter informed the Berlin Foreign Ministry that he had told Count Berchtold that 'something must be done for the Romanians by Herr Tisza'. In Tschirschky's view, concessions to the Romanians in Transylvania were essential, if only to guarantee Romanian neutrality. 'Count Berchtold', he continued, 'certainly has the best intentions in regard to meeting our expectations. He said he would immediately repeat his request to Herr Tisza to make the desired concessions as soon as possible. The Hungarian Prime Minister replied to his observations reiterated again yesterday here in Vienna that if special rights were granted to the Romanians, it would involve the risk of rousing the other nationalities in Hungary, particularly the Slovaks.' Tschirschky pointed out to Berchtold that 'perhaps it would be wise, and in the interests of the monarchy as a whole, to grant to all the other nationalities the political rights now desired by the Romanians. This argument definitely made an impression on the Minister. He again assured me at the end of the conversation that he would do everything to persuade Herr Tisza to make concessions.' P.A.A.A. Oesterreich, No. 85, Vol. VI. The support given by the Austro-Hungarian Foreign Minister to the German appeals on behalf of the Transylvanian Romanians was evidently a powerful factor in causing Tisza to resent the latter; he believed that he had already offered the Romanians (who had rejected them) all the concessions compatible with Magyar supremacy.

68. J. Redlich, *op. cit.*, pp. 23–26.

69. For Károlyi's criticisms of the Triple Alliance in 1913–14, cf. E. Putz, *op. cit.*

70. M. Károlyi, *Egy egész világ ellen*, Vienna, 1923 (German translation *Gegen eine gauze Welt*, Munich, 1924). Juhász Nagy Sándor, *Az októberi magyar forradalom története*, Budapest, 1945, pp. 41 ff. Cf. the reports of the Russian consul-general in Budapest, *Int. Bez.*, Series I, Vol. II, *passim*. On the proposed visit to Russia, cf. the article by J. Dolmányos, *Történelmi Szemle*, 1963, No. 2. In regard to Károlyi's and Batthyány's opposition to the German alliance from the time of the Balkan wars

onwards, what they said of it when they resumed their campaign to detach Hungary from it in 1916–17 should be borne in mind. For their speeches at that time, cf. their newspaper *Magyarország*, particularly January–June 1917. At a meeting held in defence of the deputy L. Holló, who was fiercely attacked for saying that Germany shared responsibility for the war, Károlyi said that, even if they lynched him for it, he would no longer conceal the fact that ever since the summer of 1914 he had considered the governments in power, beginning with that of his own country, to be equally responsible for a senseless war. Cf. *Magyarország*, June 25, 1917.

71. A.S.M.E., Missione Avarna. Avarna to Sonnino, November 21 and 22, 1914.

72. A.S.M.E., *loc. cit.*

73. *Ibid., loc. cit.* Telegrammi spediti 1915. Károlyi was of course referring to Berchtold's replacement by Burian.

74. *Ibid.*

75. *Ibid.*

76. *Ibid.*

77. M. Károlyi, *op. cit.*; T. Batthyány, *Beszámolóm*, two vols., Budapest, undated, German translation *Für Ungarn, gegen Hohenzollern*, Vienna, 1930, *passim*. Cf. Arnaldo Fraccari's interview with Károlyi in the *Corriere della Sera*, December 29, 1918. That Török was received by Sonnino is confirmed by L. Aldrovandi Marescotti, *Nuovi ricordi, Frammenti di Diario*, Milan, 1938, p. 227, footnote. Cf. also A. Depoli, *op. cit.*, pp. 23 ff. Among Sonnino's papers (A.S.M.E.) there is a letter from Török of April 24, 1915, which shows that he was not only received by Sonnino but that the latter also introduced him to another diplomatist. It appears from M. Károlyi, *Egy egész világ, op. cit.*, p. 165, that Sonnino arranged for Török a conversation with the British ambassador Sir Rennel Rodd. The latter saw the Hungarian emissary twice and informed the Foreign Office. Cf. his telegram of May 22, 1915, P.R.O., *loc. cit.* The Sonnino papers confirm that when Török went back to Hungary, the Italian Foreign Minister gave him a cypher with which he could cable him coded messages.

78. Károlyi papers (Oberlin College). M. Károlyi (*Egy egész világ, op. cit.*, pp. 152 ff.) and T. Batthyány (*op. cit.*, pp. 125 ff.) publish the memorandum without the annotation. According to M. Károlyi, *Memorie, op. cit.*, p. 72, the memorandum was submitted—presumably by Andrássy —to Burian, the Foreign Minister, and to Francis Joseph. A reference to Greece in the memorandum points to the assumption that the information about a Hungarian desire for a separate peace which, according to *Int. Bez., op. cit.*, *passim*, the Tsarist diplomatic service continually received either from Athens or from Greek diplomatists, also originated with the Hungarian independence movement.

79. T. Batthyány, *op. cit.*, Vol. I, p. 128; G. Gratz, *A dualizmus, op. cit.*, Vol. II, pp. 315–316. A copy of Tisza's letter dated May 21 addressed to the opposition leaders is among the Károlyi papers.

80. Cf. J. Droz, *op. cit.* The author in this valuable study summarises very well the ideas of Jászi besides those of the Austrian socialists and

liberals, but, not knowing Hungarian, is unable to analyse the debate that developed among the Hungarian left. This can be studied in the 1916–17 issues of the journals *Huszadik Század* and *Szocializmus*. The majority of the Hungarian Social Democratic Party, led by Kunfi, for reasons similar to those of the Austro-Marxist left, took up a position opposed to *Mitteleuropa*. Nevertheless there were many Hungarian socialists, both intellectuals and trade-union leaders, who believed that their country's labour movement would benefit from economic union with the industrially and economically more advanced Germany.

81. Cf. in *Magyarország*, May 10, 1917, a speech of Batthyány's asserting that the correctness of the independent party's resolution of the previous year had been confirmed by events. The Czech *émigrés* who intended to detach Slovakia from St Stephen's Crown immediately realized that the rupture of the 'sacred union' in Hungary and the campaign for separation from Austria and Germany were aimed at safeguarding Hungarian territory in the expectation of an Entente victory, and attacked Károlyi when he adopted this anti-German position. Cf. *La Nation tchéque*, July 15, 1916.

82. G. Gratz, *op. cit.*, Vol. II, pp. 331–332.

83. Kautsky papers (Amsterdam) D XII, No. 382. In 1908 Francis Joseph had complained to F. Kossuth, then a leading member of the Hungarian government, about the excessive press freedom that, according to his information, existed in Hungary. F. Kossuth took advantage of the opportunity to point out that it was the dangerousness of the Hungarian socialists, who were in his view much more revolutionary than their comrades in Austria or Germany, that made him oppose the introduction of universal suffrage that was favoured by the dynasty. As for the freedom of speech enjoyed by the Budapest newspapers, he explained to the Emperor that this was due to the liberal spirit of juries who regularly acquitted Magyar journalists accused of offences, with the result that the government avoided taking proceedings which resulted in defeats for the public prosecutor (cf. F. Kossuth's correspondence in *Századok*, 1961, Nos. 2–3, p. 354).

84. I. Tisza, *op. cit.*, Vol. V, pp. 385 ff.

85. Only in February 1917, when the deputy Holló put a question to the government on the possibility of making peace, did Tisza indicate in his reply that he had something in reserve against the questioner, whom he accused of wanting to stab the Central Powers in the back. In his *Egy egész világ*, *op. cit.*, Károlyi is necessarily reticent on this matter, because when he wrote the book he was under an accusation of high treason in Hungary. It was of course a trumped up charge, because Austria-Hungary no longer existed. But in a Hungary in which the counter-revolution had triumphed it was desired to punish Károlyi for his part in the revolution of 1918–19.

86. A.S.M.E., T. G. Gabinetto 1916–18.

87. Cf. the interview with Dr Temesváry in the *Corriere della Sera*, July 7, 1929.

88. Cf. the text in I. Tisza, *op. cit.*, Vol. III, p. 262. (*Briefe, op. cit.*, pp. 191 ff.)

89. A. Salandra, 'Una pretesa lettera di Sonnino', *Corriere della Sera*, June 12, 1929. Sonnino, after the conversation with Professor Bossi, said to Aldrovandi Marescotti: 'It was interesting.'

90. I. Tisza, *op. cit.*, Vol. III, pp. 260 ff. (*Briefe, op. cit.*, pp. 198 ff.)

91. *Ibid.*, pp. 193 and 263 ff.

92. A.S.M.E., Carte Sonnino. Cf. the *Corriere della Sera* of July 7, 1929, for Dr Temesváry's recollections of his meeting with Prof. Bossi at Lugano.

93. This point is well brought by Depoli, *op. cit.*

94. M. Toscano, *La Serbia, op. cit.*, p. 122; A. Depoli, *op. cit.*, p. 46; Ivo J. Lederer, *Yugoslavia at the Paris Peace Conference, A Study in Frontier-making*, New Haven, 1963. The Hungarian government's unwillingness to loosen its grip on Fiume is shown by its dissolution in June 1915 of the communal council, on which there was a majority of Italian autonomists, and Tisza's request to the War Minister not to allow Riccardo Zanella, the leader of the autonomist party, to return to Fiume on leave. Cf. *Magyar minisztertanácsi jegyzökönyvek, op. cit.*, pp. 139–140; I. Tisza, *op. cit.*, Vol. III, p. 105.

95. M. Toscano, *op. cit.*, pp. 129 ff.

96. A. Depoli, *op. cit.*, p. 205. Cf. in Ante Mandić, *Fragmenti zu historja ujedinjenji*, Zagreb, 1956, p. 192, the text of the telegram on Sonnino's proposals sent to Sazonov by the Russian ambassador in Rome.

97. M. Toscano, *op. cit.*, p. 148.

98. D. Šepić, *op. cit.*, p. 137.

99. M. Toscano, *op. cit.*, *passim.*

100. In August 1918 Orlando was still telling Malagodi, *op. cit.*, Vol. II, p. 373, that Sonnino did not believe in the break-up of Austria, and in any case did not want it. How Sonnino reconciled the survival of the Austrian monarchy with the stipulations of the Treaty of London, with the prospect of an independent Czechoslovakia to which the Italian government had virtually committed itself by the military convention of April 1918, and with the latent desire of the Foreign Ministry to aim at Hungarian independence, is difficult to understand. Sonnino probably regarded it as too soon to go into the problem, which would confront him with disagreeable alternatives.

101. J. Smith, *op. cit.*, p. 251.

102. D. Šepić, *op. cit.*, p. 144, who relies on the draft of the telegram sent by Supilo to Pašić on September 1, 1915, informing him of his conversations with Sir Edward Grey.

103. *Ibid.* J. Lederer, *op. cit.*, p. 18.

104. D. Šepić, *op. cit.*, pp. 146 ff. On the financing of some of the activities and some of the members of the Yugoslav committee by Pašić's government, cf. what was discovered by D. Šepić in the Belgrade files. Cf. also the exchange of telegrams between Pašić and the Serbian Minister in London in Marjanović, *op. cit.*, pp. 307 ff., and the documents published

in *Historijski Pregled*, 1963, No. 3. Cf. also A. Mandić, *op. cit.*, p. 195.

105. Cf. the summary of the report that Paul Cambon, the French ambassador in London, made to his government on September 10, 1916, on the concern expressed to him by Sir Edward Grey, who therefore insisted on a definition of war aims, in Hölzle, *Der Osten, op. cit.*, p. 56.

106. David Lloyd George, *The Truth about the Peace Treaties, op. cit.*, Vol. I, p. 38. According to this, Sir Edward Grey made the statement on September 1, but Šepić, relying on Supilo's papers, dates the conversation more accurately August 30. The previous assurance to which the memorandum refers is of course that promising Bosnia-Hercegovina and southern Dalmatia to Serbia. On the identity of the authors of the memorandum, cf. *The History of The Times. The 150th Anniversary and Beyond. 1912–1948. Part I. 1912–1920*, London, 1952, p. 320.

107. D. Lloyd George, *op. cit.*, p. 41. For the rest, the memorandum took account of the rights acquired by Italy, asserting that the Yugoslav claims would have to conform both with the stipulations of the Treaty of London and with the soundings carried out in Italy by the spokesman of the Hungarian independence movement. In this connection it noted that independent Hungary should be left with an outlet to the sea at Fiume and that it would not be wise to amputate her territorially more than was strictly necessary in accordance with the nationality principle (*ibid.*, p. 44).

Notes (V)

From the Central Powers' Peace Offer to the Corfu Agreement

1. As we have noted, in the winter of 1914–15, when the Russian armies seemed to be winning on the Austrian front, Izvolsky, the Tsarist ambassador in Paris, and Sazonov, the Foreign Minister, had aired the possibility of a dismemberment of the Habsburg empire. But it was merely an idea mentioned in the course of secret diplomatic exchanges to which no one was committed, and it was capable of being dropped without any difficulties ensuing. Thus it was not in any way comparable to a proposal made in a public speech by a member of a government responsible to a democratic parliament and public opinion, even though it was put forward only in his personal capacity.

2. Cf. the text in Leonida Bissolati, *La politica estera, op. cit.*, pp. 358ff. *La Nation tchèque* of November 15, 1916 immediately applauded Bissolati's speech. Bissolati's knowledge of the socialist movement in Germany and Austria was in fact neither objective nor deep. It was certainly true that at that time the majority of German and Austrian Social Democrats strongly disapproved both of Karl Liebknecht, who had voted against military credits at the end of 1914, had led an anti-war demonstration in Berlin on May 1, 1916, and had been arrested and sent to prison in consequence, and of Friedrich Adler, who on October 21, 1916 assassinated the Austrian Prime Minister, Count Stürgkh. But a section of the German Social Democratic Party (nineteen deputies out of 110) had in 1915–16 broken with the 'sacred union' policy and had gone over to open opposition to the war, going so far as facing expulsion from the old party and forming an Independent Socialist Party with a resolutely internationalist and pacifist programme. Another twenty-five deputies, without leaving the majority Social Democratic Party, had declared themselves opposed to the granting of further military credits. At the national conference of the Austrian Social Democratic Party held in March 1916, Friedrich Adler had indeed only a small minority in favour of his resolution to approve the declaration denouncing the imperialist war, made at the international socialist conference at Zimmerwald. But, though assassination was contrary to Social Democratic doctrine and traditions, Friedrich Adler's action, and his defence at his trial, earned him (with the aid of the Russian Revolution) an extraordinary increase in popularity among Austrian militant socialists, with the result that shortly before the end of the war the majority came round to his position. Cf. Friedrich Adler, *Die Erneuerung der Internationale*, Vienna, 1918; *Protokoll der Verhandlungen des Parteitages des sozialdemokratischen Arbeiterpartei in Oesterreich*,

[369]

October 19–24, 1917, Vienna, 1918; Julius Deutsch *Ein weiter Weg. Lebenserinnerungen*, Zürich and Vienna, 1960. A very useful guide is the *Bibliographie zur Geschichte der österreichischen Arbeiterbewegung, 1867–1918*, ed. Herbert Steiner, Vienna, 1962. For the attitude of the Austrian Social Democratic leaders, cf. V. Adler, *op. cit.* The literature on the German Social Democratic movement is very extensive. The basic work is Carl E. Schorschke, *German Social Democracy, 1905–1917*, Cambridge, 1955. We may also recall John L. Snell's acute paper 'German socialism and the Peace Crisis 1916', *Journal of Central European Affairs*, January, 1953. For the formation of the Independent Socialist Party, cf. Eugen Prager, *Geschichte der USPD.*, Berlin, 1921; Hugo Haase, *Sein Leben und Wirken*, Berlin, undated; Walter Bartel, *Die Linken in der deutschen Sozialdemokratie im Kampfe gegen Militarismus und Krieg*, Berlin, 1958.

3. *L'Allemagne et les problèmes de la paix pendant la guerre mondiale.* Documents extraits des archives de l'Office allemand des Affaires étrangères publiés et annotés par André Scherer et Jacques Grünwald. So far two volumes have been published (taking the record up to November 1917), Paris 1962–66. Cf. Vol. I, pp. 525 ff. On the Polish question, cf. W. Conze, *op. cit.* Hutten-Czapski's memoirs, *op. cit.*, should also be consulted.

4. Cf. Thyssen's letter of September 16 to Erzberger, the leader of the Centre Party, submitted by the latter to the Foreign Ministry, *L'Allemagn op. cit.*, pp. 467–468.

5. Cf. the text of the memorandum in Nachlass Südekum, No. 104, in the Bundes-Archiv at Koblenz. On Südekum's previous career, cf. L. Valiani, *Il Partito Socialista Italiano nel periodo della neutralità, op. cit.* On his political activity during the succeeding war years, cf. *Quellen zur Geschichte des Parlamentarismus und der politischen Parteien. First Series. Von der konstitutionellen Monarchie zur parlamentarischen Republik.* Vol. I/1. *Der Interfraktionelle Ausschuss 1917–18*, ed. Erich Matthias and Rudolf Morsey, Düsseldorf, 1959. The reports here collected are largely based on shorthand notes taken by Südekum, who was a big figure in the interparty meetings held during this period.

6. Georg Kotowski, *Friedrich Ebert, eine politische Biographie*, Wiesbaden, 1963, Vol. I, pp. 235 ff.

7. The petition, for which about 900,000 signatures were collected, was presented by the Social Democratic Party to the Reich Chancellor a few days after the peace offer of December 12, 1916. Cf. *Die Reichstagsfraktion der deutschen Sozialdemokratie*, ed. Erich Matthias and Eberhard Pikart, two vols., Düsseldorf, 1966, Vol. II, p. 213, footnote. A. Joseph Berlau, *The German Social-Democratic Party, 1914–1921*, New York, 1949, and other authors are of course correct in pointing out that collaboration with the Imperial Government resulted in the anti-annexationism of the majority Social Democratic leaders being not very determined. See the conversations with them recorded by Gustav Mayer, *Erinner-ungen. Vom Journalisten zum Historiker der deutscher Arbeiterbewegung (1871–1948)*, Zürich, 1949. Apart from a certain number of social-chauvinists such as

Noske and Südekum, the situation was not that the Social Democratic leaders wanted annexations; they merely did not wish to break the 'sacred union', either because they did not want to weaken Germany in war-time or because they hoped to obtain a democratization of Prussian politics as a reward for their loyalty (cf. the memoirs of Friedrich Stampfer, *Erfahrungen und Erlebnisse*, Cologne, 1957, and Philipp Scheidemann, *Der Zusammenbruch*, Berlin, 1921, and *Memoiren eines Sozialdemokraten*, two vols., Dresden, 1928). Scheidemann, the leader of the Social Democratic parliamentary group, being the party's best popular speaker, did most to popularize the demand for a peace without annexations after the Russian revolution of February 1917. Thus to the annexationists he became the symbol of 'renunciationism'.

8. *L'Allemagne, op. cit.*, pp. 477 ff. In his diary Burian foresaw as early as September 9, 1916, the probability of an Austro-Hungarian collapse as the result of famine unless peace were made quickly. On the critical economic situation of the monarchy, cf. Gustav Gratz-Richard Schüller, *Der Wirtschaftliche Zusammenbruch Oesterreich Ungarns*, Vienna, 1930; General von Landwehr, *Hunger. Die Erschöpfungsjahre der Mittelmächte. 1917–18*, Vienna, 1931.

9. Cf. Bethmann Hollweg's summary of the conversation, *L'Allemagne, op. cit.*, pp. 517 ff. On the whole question, cf. Fritz Fischer, *Griff nach der Weltmacht*, Düsseldorf, 1962. See Rudolf Neck's penetrating comment on the discussion roused by this work, 'Kriegszielpolitik im Ersten Weltkrieg', *Mitteilungen des Oesterreichischen Staatsarchivs*, Vol. XV, Vienna, 1962. Cf. also Wolfgang Steglich, *Bündnissicherung oder Verständigungsfrieden*, Göttingen, 1958.

10. *L'Allemagne, op. cit.*, p. 517.

11. *Ibid.*

12. The incorporation of Serbia into the Habsburg monarchy was proposed at the Joint Council of Austro-Hungarian Ministers on January 7, 1916. See the report of the meeting in *Protokolle, op. cit.*, as well as Helmut Rumpler, 'Die Kriegsziele Oesterreich-Ungarns auf dem Balkan 1915–16', *Oesterreich und Europa, op. cit.*, pp. 465 ff. Cf. also Alexander Fussek, 'Ministerpräsident Karl Graf Stürgkh', thesis for the philosophy faculty of the University of Vienna, 1959, p. 145. The defeat in Galicia in the summer of 1916 certainly limited Austro-Hungarian ambitions, which were then laid down in the document to be found in *L'Allemagne, op. cit.*, pp. 518–519. For later developments, cf. Klaus Epstein, 'The Development of German-Austrian War Aims in the Spring of 1917', *Journal of Central European Affairs*, April, 1957, and above all the reports of the meetings of the Joint Council of Austro-Hungarian Ministers in 1917–18. These show that the defeat of Romania and the news from Russia inordinately increased the annexationist ambitions of the Habsburg ministers. At the council meeting on January 12, 1917, and still more at that on March 22, 1917, some Austrian ministers insisted on the annexation of Serbia, Montenegro and Romania, though they were willing to leave a part of Romania to Russia in the event of a separate peace with Petrograd. Tisza again opposed

the annexation of Yugoslav territories, but gave his consent to the dismemberment of Romania, provided that the area to be taken over were annexed directly to Hungary which, he said, would govern it 'autocratically' to begin with. So far from being anti-annexationist on principle, Tisza was merely fearful of future Slav 'trialism' in the Habsburg empire, while Clam-Martinic, believing the unification of the Yugoslavs to be inevitable, wanted it to take place within the empire rather than outside and against it.

13. *L'Allemagne, op. cit.*, pp. 630–631.

14. *Ibid.*, p. 609.

15. *Ibid.*, pp. 633 ff.

16. Cf. *Regierte der Kaiser? Kriegstagebücher, Aufzeichnungen und Briefe des Chefs des Marine-Kabinetts*, Admiral Georg Alexander von Mueller, *1914–1918*, Göttingen, 1959. Cf. also Epstein, *op. cit.* F. Fischer, *op. cit.*; *Der Interfraktionelle Ausschuss, op. cit.* Also very interesting in this connection is the diary, *cit.*, of the Social Democratic deputy E. David (*Das Kriegstagebuch, cit.*). A few days after the dismissal of Bethmann Hollweg, he admitted that the supporters of a democratic peace had played into the annexationists' hands by allowing him to be dropped. At heart Bethmann Hollweg was certainly closer than his successor to the aims of the Social Democrats, but because he was looked at askance by the High Command he was unwilling to express all he thought. Cf. also the notes of another principal eye-witness, Conrad Haussmann, *Schaglichter. Reichstagsbriefe und Aufzeichnungen*, Berlin, 1924.

17. Bethmann Hollweg drafted some peace terms, which included the annexation by Germany of Liège, the Briey basin, Lithuania and Courland, as well as the separation of Poland from Russia, frontier rectifications in favour of Austria-Hungary and territorial acquisitions for Bulgaria, but he did not communicate these to Wilson. Cf. *L'Allemagne, op. cit.*, pp. 659–660. On January 7, 1917, Zimmermann, the Under-Secretary of State in the Foreign Ministry, instructed the German ambassador in Washington to go slow in defining German war aims, but giving an assurance that Germany would keep these 'within entirely reasonable bounds'. *Ibid.*, p. 669. Finally, on January 29, when unrestricted submarine warfare had begun, the Chancellor informed Wilson, that, if his peace offer had not been rejected by the Entente, Germany would ask only for frontier rectifications and strategic guarantees which it did not seem necessary to him to specify at that moment. *Ibid.*, pp. 685–687. As a matter of fact, on December 18 the German ambassador had warned Burian that the Chancellor had decided to refuse to announce his peace terms in advance. The Austro-Hungarian Foreign Minister insisted, however, that they should confidentially communicate their terms to each other in case the Entente were willing to negotiate. (Burian's diary.) Three days later Burian, who was opposed to unrestricted submarine warfare and was therefore disliked by William II, and had lost his principal supporter with the death of Francis Joseph, resigned. He was, however, told by Tisza that the new sovereign did not consider him sufficiently resolute in his desire for peace. Burian's diary, December 21, 1916.

[372]

18. In the conversation he had with Wilson on January 4, 1919, Bissolati, according to the notes made by a colleague of the President's, informed him that the areas he considered to be Italian were Gorizia, Trieste, the Istrian coast and Fiume, but not Postumia, 'which is entirely Slav', and, except for the annexation to Italy of Cherso (Cres) and Lussino (Losinj) and the autonomy of Zara, not Dalmatia. Cf. the Wilson Papers, VIII–A: 8, as quoted by Arno J. Mayer in his important work, *Politics and Diplomacy of Peace-making*, New York, 1967, p. 213. In the speech he made at the Scala a few days later Bissolati said he was also opposed 'to the annexation of the German Tyrol that extends from Bolzano to the Brenner' (cf. L. Bissolati, *op. cit.*, pp. 394 ff.).

19. *Ibid.*, pp. 332 ff. See also Salvemini's articles, now reprinted in *Opere* di Gaetano Salvemini, *Come siamo andati in Libia e altri scritti dal 1900 al 1915*, ed. Augusto Torre, Milan, 1963.

20. *L'Allemagne, op. cit.* pp. 643–644. Burian noted in his diary on December 17, 1916 the conversation he had on the same subject with the Papal Nuncio. The information about alleged Italian pacifism was based on statements made at Berne by a lady of the Italian court who said that a Giolitti government was a certainty. Cf. Burian's diary, October 8. For the activity of the Vatican, cf. *Benedetto XV, i cattolici e la prima guerra mondiale. Atti del convegno di studio tenuto a Spoleto nei giorni 7–8–9 settembre 1962*, ed. Giuseppe Rossini, Rome, 1963.

21. On this, cf. a long letter from Salvemini to Bernard Berenson dated November 27, 1917. (Copy in the Salvemini papers.)

22. Cf., e.g., O. Malagodi, *op. cit.* When the allies, as a result of Prince Sixto's soundings, at their meeting on April 18, 1917, raised the question of the possibility of making peace with Austria-Hungary, Sonnino said— in terms that he was to repeat two years later in connection with Dalmatia —that, if the war ended without Italy's gaining Trieste and the Dalmatian coast, the result would be a republican revolution in an Italy disappointed by the vanity of her sacrifices (cf. D. Lloyd George, *War Memoirs, op. cit.*, Vol. IV, pp. 2007 ff.). When Lloyd George proposed to start peace discussions with Austria, which—so he said—had asked for them twice already, the Italian Foreign Minister replied that he considered the Austrian feelers as a German manoeuvre. The British, French and Italian statesmen went over then to discuss the danger of a separate peace by revolutionary Russia. Sonnino asserted that Italy would go on fighting all the same, even in this case. Sonnino papers S. 106–C. 6. B. This assertion, of course, strengthened his position. On the meeting, cf. Mario Toscano, *Gli accordi di San Giovanni di Moriana. Storia diplomatica dell'intervento italiano. II. (1916–1917)*, Milan, 1936, p. 275. Salandra, more reasonably, partly perhaps because he was now free of the responsibilities of office, said to Malagodi in August 1918 that, in the new situation brought about by the collapse of Tsarism and the probable disintegration of the Habsburg empire, he could no longer see the value to Italy of Dalmatia, assurance of the acquisition of which he had wanted in 1915 as a means of containing Russian ambitions in the event of an Austrian defeat (O. Malagodi, *op. cit.*, p. 381). The

[373]

British Foreign Secretary, writing to his ambassador in Rome in March 8, 1915, summed up as follows the proposals made to him by the Italian ambassador in London: 'It would not be in the interests of Italy to free herself of Austrian supremacy in the Adriatic if this were replaced by Russian domination of the Dalmatian coast' (cf. G. M. Trevelyan, *Grey of Fallodon*, London, 1937, p. 296).

23. D. Šepić, *Supilo Diplomat, op. cit.*, pp. 160 ff. The known documents do not support Supilo's suggestion, made in a mood of bitterness, that Pašić did not want the union of Serbia with Slovenia and Croatia in order not to incur the disapproval of the Russian Holy Synod, which was opposed to a union of an Orthodox with a Catholic country. Pašić, who reasoned in the traditional diplomatic fashion, merely did not wish to do anything that might tend to weaken the force of the Entente undertaking assigning Bosnia-Hercegovina and a port on the Adriatic to Serbia by linking it with the right of self-determination of all the Southern Slavs in Austria-Hungary, who might have used it in a manner different from that hoped for by the Yugoslav unity movement (e.g. by pronouncing themselves in favour of a Habsburg confederation, which it would certainly not be in the Serbian interest for Bosnia to join). It should be noted that Sir Edward Grey, replying on May 3 to Seton-Watson's protests against the assignment of Slav territories to Italy, pointed out that without the Entente and Italy the Yugoslavs would have remained permanently under the Habsburgs, and once more made a distinction between Croatia, which he believed should in due course itself decide whether or not to unite with Serbia and those Austro-Hungarian provinces, the legitimacy of the Serbian claims to which had already been recognized (cf. G. M. Trevelyan *op. cit.*, p. 298). At the end of August 1915, however, the British Foreign Secretary agreed in conversation with Supilo with the formula suggested to him by the latter, that is, that the right of self-determination should be applied both to Croatia-Slavonia and to Bosnia-Hercegovina, as well as to the part of Dalmatia not assigned to Italy (cf. D. Šepić, *op. cit.*, p. 144). Thus the Serbian right to annex Bosnia was subordinated to the Bosnian right of self-determination, just like any other Yugoslav province. Supilo was, however, right in stating that a Greater Serbia was much more important than Yugoslav unity to Pašić, and that, once the essential claims of the former had been satisfied, he would not continue fighting for the latter; indeed, if a Yugoslav state were established, he would always try to impose Serbian supremacy within it (as indeed it was imposed after the war), though for political, economic and military and not for religious reasons.

24. *Ibid.*, pp. 170 ff.

25. Tittoni to Sonnino, A.S.M.E., Serbia 1913–17, fasc. 17. It is worth recalling that Tittoni, replying on September 28, 1914, to a question of San Giuliano's, said he was opposed to 'claims to Dalmatia where, only some coastal towns being Italian and the rest Slav, we should create an irredentism in our own house from which I forsee dangers for the future' (*Documenti Diplomatici Italiani, 1914–1918. Vol. I, August 2–October 16*

1914, *op. cit.*, pp. 495 ff.). This may be the reason why Tittoni did not hesitate to receive Supilo. When Supilo took refuge in Venice in 1914, Guglielmo Ferrero gave him a letter of introduction to Antonio Fradeletto, the Radical deputy for that city (cf. B. Radica, *op. cit.*, p. 380).

26. A.S.M.E., *loc. cit.*

27. Papers of the Yugoslav Committee (Yugoslavenski Odbor), Zagreb.

28. *Ibid.* This letter is also undated.

29. Some quotations from these notes (but only a few lines of the extracts quoted here) were published by R. Colapietra, *op. cit.* Colapietra believes that they consist of letters to unknown correspondents, but from the manuscript copies in the Salvemini papers they would seem to be pages from a diary. They were probably omitted from L. Bissolati, *Diario di guerra*, Turin, 1935, because the publication of anti-nationalist material would have run into difficulties at that time. In the parliamentary vote of March 19, 1916, the nationalist deputies lined up against the Salandra government, whose policy they did not consider sufficiently energetic and aggressive. During the previous days Bissolati had also criticized the government, among other things for its failure to declare war on Germany, but the article published by the editor of the *Corriere della Sera* on March 18 for the purpose of demonstrating the inexpediency of provoking a government crisis persuaded him not yet to withdraw his support from Salandra (cf. Luigi Albertini, *op. cit.*, pp. 168–175). Nevertheless the government was overthrown in June, after the Austrian offensive in the Trentino. Sonnino was uncertain whether or not to remain in office after Salandra's departure, but F. Martini, *op. cit.*, p. 725, persuaded him that it was essential that he should remain in the government to counter Giolittian pacifism. Bissolati's impressionability (for which Salvemini criticized him) thus lost him the only opportunity of easily getting rid of Sonnino. During the government crisis of October 1917 it seemed certain that Sonnino would go, but as a result of Caporetto it seemed inadvisable to get rid of a Foreign Minister in whom the Entente had confidence. *Ibid.*, pp. 1,019–1,021. In the second half of 1918 the approach of victory strengthened Sonnino's position. As for the Tsarist policy which Supilo mentioned to Bissolati, it appears from the report on his conversations with the former made to Sazanov by Prince Trubetskoy, the Russian Minister in Serbia on May 9, 1915, that the Russians wished merely to prevent Yugoslavia's being established on a basis of parity between Orthodox Serbs and Catholic Croats. In other words, Russia wanted a Yugoslavia under Serbian hegemony. (Cf. *Int. Bez.*, *op. cit.*, Series II, Vol. VII (2) p. 705.)

30. Cf. the report (or denunciation) in A.C.S., Direzione Generale di Pubblica Sicurezza, Direzione Affari Generali e riservati, 1919, busta 34, fasc. A. 16.

31. A.C.S., *loc. cit.*

32. A report by the police headquarters to the Minister of the Interior dated April 14, 1915, states: 'Francis Supilo, a deputy to the Croat Diet, born at Ragusa, head of the Serbo-Croat coalition and initiator of the well-

[375]

known Fiume resolution, the point of which is directed against Austria, is obviously employing his (somewhat involuntary) residence abroad for activity directed against the monarchy.' Cf. Allgemeines Verwaltungs-Archiv, Ministerium des Innern, Präsidiale. Other reports (*ibid.*) follow on the acts of high treason which the Austrian police attributed to him.

33. *Ibid.*

34. Cf. Charles Loiseau, 'Frano Supilo à Rome (avril 1916)', *Le Monde Slave*, May 1928. Supilo immediately sent to the *Idea Nazionale*, which published it on April 12, 1916, a reply to the accusations made against him, recalling the various occasions on which he had advocated Italo-Yugoslav understanding. He did not deny that in pre-war disputes between Italians and Croats in Austria-Hungary he had taken his own people's side, but he said that he had never considered the Italians to be enemies and that he wanted them as allies of the Yugoslavs in the Risorgimento spirit. The nationalist newspaper made an acid comment on this.

35. A.S.M.E., *loc. cit.*

36. *Ibid.* On May 6, when Supilo left Italy to return to London *via* Switzerland, Sonnino, describing him as a Yugoslav agitator, telegraphed to the Berne legation: 'Arrange to have him watched and report his activity to me.' The information which the Italian agents in Switzerland transmitted was however favourable to Supilo. Cf. the report of November 11, 1916, in Sonino papers. S. 112. C. 16.

37. *Ibid.*, and A.C.S., *loc. cit.*

38. Among Umberto Zanotti Bianco's papers is a letter from Voinovich, who was a close friend of his, inviting him to his home to meet Supilo.

39. Loiseau, *op. cit.*, *Il Secolo* and *Il Messaggero* of August 8, 1917. Cf. also Gina Lombroso's letters, *cit.* Among Supilo's Italian friends, Professor Giuseppe Lombardo-Radice, a brother-in-law of the Croat journalist's Fiume colleague Dr Lenaz, should not be forgotten. It was Lombardo-Radice who talked to him at length about Salvemini, whom Supilo did not meet but who later defended him with drawn sword (cf. B. Radica, *op. cit.*, p. 50; cf. also *l'Unità* of May 10 and 17, 1917 and March 9, 1918). Some information about Supilo's stay in Rome is also contained in the diary of the Serbian Minister in London, published by D. Šepić in *Historijski Pregled*, 1963, No. 4.

40. Cf. his letter from Milan to Gina Lombroso of May 2, 1916, B. Radica, *op. cit.*, p. 46. Supilo also expressed confidence about the future development of Italo-Yugoslav relations to the British ambassador in Rome (cf. Sir James Rennel Rodd, *Social and Diplomatic Memories*, 1902–19, London, 1925, p. 306).

41. D. Šepić, *op. cit.*, pp. 183 ff.; B. Radica, *op. cit.*, pp. 352–353. Cf. also the memoirs of the great sculptor Ivan Meštrović, *Uspomene na političke ljude i dogadjadje*, Buenos Aires, 1961, pp. 417 (especially pp. 64–68). On Miljukov's conversations with Supilo, cf. E. Beneš, *op. cit.*, Vol. I, pp. 213–214.

42. Bissolati gave Luigi Campolonghi advance information about the

declaration of war on Germany in a letter of July 28, 1916 (cf. R. Colapietra, *op. cit.*, p. 233).

43. Cf. *Le Matin* of September 30, 1916. Bissolati had asked Salvemini to make a careful study of the Yugoslav question shortly beforehand. Cf. R. Colapietra, *op. cit.*, p. 233. In an article in *Il Secolo* of September 9 entitled 'War for the Austrian succession', Salvemini stated the conclusions that Bissolati repeated in his obituary of Battisti. Incidentally, in a letter to Ugo Ojetti of April 6, 1916, Salvemini said he thought essential 'the most thorough possible demolition of Austria-Hungary as the only means of isolating Germany and making her innocuous' and the 'formation with the fragments of Austria of homogeneous and compact and strong states to the south-east of Germany capable of checking new German attempts in agreement with Italy and Russia'. Salvemini papers. Something of the sort was in fact achieved with the Little Entente, but the new states, instead of being compact, included conspicuous German and Hungarian minorities, and did not achieve co-operation neither with Italy, nor with Russia.

44. Cf. the report of the sitting of December 8, 1916, in *Atti del Parlamento Italiano*, Camera dei Deputati, Sessione 1913–16. Discussioni, Vol. X, Rome 1916, pp. 11,389 ff. The *Giornale d'Italia*, which was always close to Sonnino, on December 9 criticized Pirolini's 'somewhat naïve Yugoslavophilia'. Bissolati was also worried by the persistent rumours about 'trialism' under the Habsburgs, which the nationalist newspaper claimed was the aim, not only of the Croat people, but secretly also of the Croat exiles in Switzerland, and he asked for information about this in a letter to Supilo of October 10, 1916, which is preserved in the papers of the Yugoslav Committee at Zagreb. Cf. the reply of the Yugoslav exiles to these and other accusations in the *Bulletin Yougoslave*, No. 16, November 1, 1916. The Italian consul at St Gall in a report on the Yugoslav movement wrote: 'Grave harm has been done to Italy by the accusations against and attacks made on these Yugoslavs by nearly all the Italian newspapers, especially the *Idea Nazionale* and the *Popolo d'Italia*' (A.S.M.E., Svizzera 1917, Fasc. IV).

45. Cf. the *Atti del Parlamento*, *op. cit.*, p. 11,407, as well as the December 16 issue of *L'Iniziativa*, the republican periodical in which A. Ghisleri, a close friend of Bissolati's, gave publicity (as he also did in *Il Secolo*) to the positions taken by the Yugoslav *émigrés*.

46. Copies of these, and of other letters quoted, are in the Salvemini papers (cf. also R. Colapietra, *op. cit.*, p. 204).

47. *Ibid.*, *passim;* L. Bissolati, *Diario di guerra*, *op. cit.*, pp. 72 ff.; L. Albertini, *op. cit.*, vol. *cit.*, pp. 398 ff.; O. Malagodi, *op. cit.*, Vol. I, pp. 96 ff. Cadorna, independently of Bissolati, had already thought of the sort. Cf. E. Faldella, *op. cit.*, Vol. I, pp. 258 ff.

48. L. Albertini, *op. cit.*, vol. *cit.*, p. 343.

49. D. Lloyd George, *op. cit.*, Vol. III, pp. 1422 ff. and Vol. IV, pp. 2169 ff.; *Lord Riddell's War Diary, 1914–1918*, London, 1933, p. 267. A. J. P. Taylor, in his grand work, *English History, 1914–1945*, London,

1965, points out that, once his idea of an allied offensive on the Italian front had been discarded, Lloyd George himself favoured the Nivelle offensive in France. According to the British Prime Minister who, Sonnino himself admitted to Salandra (cf. the extracts from the Salandra diaries published by G. B. Gifuni in *Il Risorgimento*, October, 1965) was right in the matter, Cadorna's reservations about the length of time (which he wanted to be indefinite or prolonged) during which the Anglo-French heavy artillery was to remain in Italy turned out to be by no means helpful. Cf. Lord Hankey, *The Supreme Command, 1914–1918*, two vols., London, 1961, Vol. II, pp. 607 ff. According to the author, when Lloyd George went to see Cadorna, the latter had allowed himself to be impressed by the opposition of the British generals. A few weeks later Sonnino became aware of the harm his and Cadorna's hesitation had done and instructed the Italian ambassador in London to support Bissolati's mission. Cf. Sonnino papers, S. 112. C. 15. In June Cadorna himself revived the plan for an offensive on the Italian front with Entente artillery, but in September 1917, when the artillery had been promised and in part actually lent him, he decided that the season was too far advanced for a major offensive. He did not, of course, foresee that the advanced season would not prevent the Germans and Austrians from launching a major offensive. For Cadorna's viewpoint, cf. his conversations, and Bissolati's, with O. Malagodi, *op. cit.*, Vol. I, pp. 99 ff.

50. L. Bissolati, *op. cit.*, pp. 72 ff. Cf. also Bissolati's letter to L. Albertini, vol. *cit.*, p. 404.

51. On Lloyd George's assurances, cf. *ibid.*, p. 78. Cf. also O. Malagodi, *op. cit.*, Vol. I, p. 111 and p. 142 for Steed's warning. Mario Borsa, the chief editor of *Il Secolo*, who accompanied Bissolati, also met Supilo. Cf. B. Radica, *op. cit.*, p. 48.

52. A.C.S., Fondo Bissolati, Busta 1, Fasc. 6. Cf. Appendix I.

53. *Ibid.*, Busta 3, Fasc. 11. In London Bissolati talked in particular with Arthur Henderson, the representative of the Labour Party in the War Cabinet, and he explained the Italian position at a meeting of British trade union leaders and Labour politicians. Cf. *Il Secolo*, March 3, 1917.

54. Cf. the text in all the newspapers and in L. Albertini, *op. cit.*, vol. *cit.*, pp. 384–385.

55. D. Lloyd George, *op. cit.*, Vol. III, p. 1,113.

56. W. Conze, *op. cit.*; I. Lukinich, *op. cit.*; *Magyar minisztertanácsi op. cit.*, cf. also the Complete Works of I. Tisza, Series IV, Vol. VI. While the Austrian Ministers desired the union of Congress Poland with Galicia Tisza—among other things, to avoid replacement of the dual system by a system including a third Habsburg kingdom (Poland)—wanted to leave it to Germany which, he said, would crush any Polish irredentism with an iron fist. Cf. the report *cit.* of the Joint Council of Austro-Hungarian Ministers of January 12, 1917. The German High Command wanted Poland to raise troops there and for longer range strategic and economic reasons.

57. For Dmowski's activities, cf. Alexander Dallin, 'The Future of

Poland', *Russian Diplomacy and Eastern Europe. 1914–1917* (which contains a number of very useful papers), published by the Russian Institute of Columbia University, New York, 1963. Cf. also the critical review by V. S. Mamatey, *Journal of Central European Affairs*, October 1963.

58. L. Gerson, *op. cit.* There were nearly 2,500,000 Poles in the United States, most of them American citizens, for whose votes Wilson and his Republican opponent competed vigorously in the presidential election in the autumn of 1916. Paderewski, who gave innumerable concerts in America in aid of the Polish cause, was received by Wilson in the middle of 1916. During his previous stay in France he put pressure on the Quai d'Orsay. Cf. E. Birke, *op. cit.*, p. 321 ff.

59. M. Paléologue, *op. cit.*, Vol. III, *passim.*; Titus Komarnicki, *Rebirth of the Polish Republic*, London, 1957, p. 52; A. Dallin, *op. cit.*, pp. 39 ff. For the debate in Russia, cf. also V. I. Gurko, *Features and Figures of the Past*, Stanford, 1939; Thomas Rhia, *A Russian European. Paul Miljukov in Russian Politics*, London, 1969; Jay Smith Jr., 'Miljukov and the Russian National Question', *Harvard Slavic Studies*, Vol. IV; Georgii Adamović, *Vasilij Alekseovic Maklakov, Politik, Jurist, Čelovek*, Paris, 1960; and, of course, the works of Miljukov himself. On French policy in relation to the Poles, cf. Piotr. S. Wandycz, *France and her Eastern Allies, 1919–1925*, Minneapolis, 1962. Cf. also Andrzei Ajnenkiel, 'L'indépendance polonaise en 1918: faits et problèmes', *Acta Poloniae Historica*, 1969, Vol. XX.

60. A. Dallin, *op. cit.*, pp. 44 ff.; Jay Smith, *op. cit.*, pp. 391 ff.

61. A. Dallin, *op. cit.*, p. 47.

62. *Ibid.*, pp. 48 ff.; J. Smith, *op. cit.*, p. 401.

63. On the whole political crisis of 1916, cf. S. P. Melgunov, *op. cit.* For quite different findings, cf. Georg von Rauch, 'Russische Friedens-fühler 1916–17?' *Internationales Recht und Diplomatie*, 1965. In Rauch's opinion some Russian separate peace feelers had been made under Tsarism.

64. A. Dallin, *op. cit.*

65. M. Paléologue, *op. cit.*, Vol. III, pp. 66 ff. Cf. I. P. Leiberov, 'O revoliucionnih bistuplenijah petrogradskovo proletariata v godi pervi mirovoi voino i fevralskoi revoliucii,' *Voprosi Istorii*, 1964, No. 2.

66. A. Dallin, *op. cit.*, p. 68. E. Hölzle, *Der Osten, op. cit.*, p. 56. Cf. also Albert Pingaud, *Histoire Diplomatique de la France pendant la grande guerre*, three vols., Paris, 1938–41, Vol. III, p. 274.

67. A. Dallin, *op. cit.*, p. 70. J. Smith, *Miljukov, op. cit.*, p. 413.

68. M. Paléologue, *op. cit.*, Vol. II, p. 102.

69. *Ibid.*, pp. 116 ff. For the repercussions in Russia of the Entente reply to Germany and Wilson, cf. Wassili Gurko, *Russland 1914–1917*, Berlin, 1921, pp. 162 ff.

70. D. Lloyd George, *op. cit.*, Vol. III, p. 1103.

71. A. Dallin, *op. cit.*, p. 72. V. I. Gurko, *op. cit.*, pp. 254 ff.

72. *Iswolski im Weltkrieg*, Berlin, 1926, p. 213; T. Komarnicki, *op. cit.*, p. 56. Briand, in a letter written to Paul Cambon on January 12, 1917, for

him to read to the British Foreign Secretary, a copy of which he gave to Doumergue to show the Russians in Petrograd, enumerated only war aims relating to Germany's western frontiers. In regard to Germany's eastern frontier and Austria-Hungary, the French government, while recalling the undertakings given to the Poles and the commitments to Serbia and Romania, left the matter to the Russians (cf. Georges Suarez, *Briand. Sa vie, son oeuvre, avec son journal et de nombreux documents inédits*, six vols., Paris, 1938–52, Vol. IV, p. 128; cf. also A. Pingaud, *op. cit.*, Vol. VI, p. 288). E. Hölzle, *op. cit.*, p. 169, has established that the first draft of the letter was written on November 6, 1916, that is, on the day after the Austro-German proclamation of the Kingdom of Poland. The Poles naturally knew nothing of the secret Franco-Russian negotiations, but the Entente note to Wilson gave them the impression that they had been abandoned (cf. Paul Morand, *Journal d'un attaché d'ambassade, 1916–1917*, Paris, 1948, p. 146).

73. For the Romanian negotiations with Russia, cf. *Int. Bez., passim* Alfred J. Rieber, 'Russian Diplomacy and Rumania', *Russian Diplomacy and Eastern Europe, op. cit.* For those with the Central Powers, cf. O. Czernin, *op. cit.*; M. Erzberger, *op. cit.* Cf. also Tisza's Complete Works, especially Vol. V. Cf. F. Funder, *op. cit.*, p. 533, the account of the meeting that the author (editor of the principal organ of the Austrian Christian Social Party) and Erzberger had on March 25, 1916, with the political leaders of the Transylvanian Romanians, Maniu, Vajda-Voevod, Popovici and Pop-Cicio, who at that time would still have been satisfied with language, educational and administrative concessions. Funder immediately informed Tisza of the meeting. Tisza indignantly rejected his intervention in Hungarian affairs and sent Maniu (the future Romanian Prime Minister), who had previously been exempt from military service, to the front. For a general picture, cf. R. W. Seton-Watson, *Histoire des Roumains, op. cit.*

74. J. Rieber, *op. cit.*, p. 273; Iswolski, *op. cit.*, pp. 206 ff.

75. M. Paulova, *op. cit.*, pp. 253 ff., estimates the number of Yugoslav volunteers in Russia before the revolution as 20,000, i.e. about 7,000 Serbs from Bosnia and southern Hungary, 9,000 Croats and 4,000 Slovenes. According to a memorandum of June 15, 1918, of the Yugoslav Committee to the British government, at the end of 1916 there had been 42,000 Yugoslav volunteers in Russia; 19,700 of them had addressed themselves to the Serbian legation. P.R.O. Political, Austria-Hungary 3135. The delegate of the Yugoslav Committee in Petrograd, Ante Mandić, *Fragmenti za historiju ujedinienija*, Zagreb, 1956, p. 217, believed at the beginning of 1916 that the great majority of the volunteers were Serbs. Cf. also D. Ostović, *op. cit.*, 43 ff. The unit to which these volunteers belonged was called the Yugoslav Division only after the Pact of Corfu. Previously the Russian authorities called it the Corps of Serbian Volunteers. It had a chequered career. After the Salonica trial, as a result of which the famous Colonel Apis of the Black Hand and some of his comrades were shot, many Serbian officers resigned from the formation,

believing that these executions were intended by Pašić as a blow to the Yugoslav idea. The Croat officers who did not resign moved towards Supilo's position (cf. R. W. Seton-Watson, *Masaryk in England, op. cit.*, p. 102. On the trial, cf. Milan Z. Živanović, *Solunski Process hiljadu devetstvo sedamnaeste*, Belgrade, 1955).

76. On Milyukov's reference to Sazonov's alleged change of attitude to *Mitteleuropa* (entirely anti-German and no longer anti-Austrian), cf. Merritt Abrash, 'War Aims towards Austria-Hungary: The Czechoslovak Pivot', *Russian Diplomacy, op. cit.*, p. 99. On the *Mitteleuropa* question, cf. the works of Henry Cord Meyer, *Mitteleuropa in German Thought and Action, 1815–1945*, The Hague, 1955; J. Droz, *op. cit.*; Károly Irinyi, *A Naumann féle 'Mitteleurope' tervezet és a magyar közvélemény*, Budapest, 1963.

77. Romania demanded 121,744 sq. km. of Hungarian territory with a population of 6,600,000, of whom only 3,000,000 were Romanians and just under 2,400,000 were Magyars (nearly a quarter of the whole Magyar nation), while the rest were Serbs, Germans, Ruthenians, etc. (cf. *La Documentation Internationale. La Paix de Versailles*, Vol. I, *Questions Territoriales*, Paris, 1939, pp. 368–370).

78. For the Romanian viewpoint, cf., in addition to the works of N. Jorga, Georges Moroianu, *Les luttes des roumains transylvains pour la liberté et l'opinion européenne*, Paris, 1933; Constantin Kiritzesco, *La Roumanie dans la guerre mondiale 1916–1919*, Paris, 1934. Cf. now the contributions of the historians of contemporary Romania in the volumes published by their national committee for the XIth and XIIth Internation Congresses of Historical Sciences and for the Budapest conference (May 1964) on the end of Austria-Hungary; in particular, C. Daicovici, Miron Constantinescu and others, *La désagrégation de la monarchie austro-hongroise, 1900–1918*, Bucharest, 1965. Cf. also Sherman David Spector, *Romania at the Paris Peace Conference*, New York, 1962; and the review of this work in *Revue Roumaine d'Histoire*, 1965, No. 1.

79. Cf. the Budapest newspapers from August 24 to September 15, 1916, as well as the proceedings of the Hungarian parliament. A deputy representing the Szeklers (inhabitants of a part of Transylvania who claimed to be descended from the Huns) accused Tisza of having abandoned and betrayed them by his loyalty to Vienna. Counts Károlyi and Batthyány vigorously demanded the resignation of Tisza and Burian, the Foreign Minister. For a month, until the censorship began suppressing comments on parliamentary proceedings, the forty-eightist, radical and Social Democratic press of Budapest demanded the government's resignation. In fact Tisza, warned by Czernin of the probability of Romanian intervention, asked that troops should be sent to Transylvania immediately, but the High Command view was that they could not be spared from elsewhere. Cf. A. J. May, *op. cit.*, Vol. I, p. 216. However, as head of the Hungarian government he bore responsibility for decisions made, even though he did not agree with them.

80. Gratz, *op. cit.*, Vol. II, p. 337. During the parliamentary debate

Count Andrássy made a circumstantial attack on Tisza, whom he charged with having opposed the Austrian concessions to Italy that might well have prevented the Italian intervention instead of granting them in good time. Vienna had later agreed to grant them when it was too late and they served only to demonstrate in humiliating fashion that Austria was always late. Tisza's reply was inconsistent. He said that in his view Italy had in any case decided on intervention, so that the sole purpose of the concessions of April–May 1915 had been to gain Austria-Hungary time, which she needed militarily. Later in his speech he said that if Giolitti had returned to power the Austro-Hungarian government would have adhered loyally to the offer made *in extremis*. Cf. the Budapest newspapers of August 25 and September 6 and 22, 1916. The Italian question belonged to the past, however; they were now faced with the Romanian. When the Romanian attack began, about 25,000 Transylvanian Romanians went to meet the Romanian army and asked to be enrolled in its ranks. (Cf. V. Curti Capeanu, 'L'action de Octaviu Goga pour l'unité politique roumaine', *Revue roumaine d'histoire*, 1970, n. 1.) Tisza tried to induce the leaders of the Romanian National Party in Transylvania and Hungary to sign a manifesto condemning the territorial ambitions of the Bucharest government. Though the Austro-German troops were already victorious, the men appealed to refused, though protesting their loyalty to the Crown (cf. Imre Mikes, *op. cit.*, p. 125). Many Romanians in Bukovina, who were traditionally loyal to Austria, took the Romanian side when it came to war. (Cf. Erich Prokopowitsch, *Die rumänische Nationalbewegung in der Bukovina und der Dako-Romanismus*, Graz, 1965.)

81. The parties that at the end of August 1916 broke the 'sacred union' in foreign politics were Count Apponyi's forty-eightist party (the extremists of which, led by Károlyi had already seceded), Count Andrássy's Constitutional Party, the Catholic Popular Party and the 'bourgeois' Democratic Party.

82. *Népszava*, September 20, 1916.

83. The left wing of the forty-eightist party and the Social Democrats had taken part in a joint campaign for universal suffrage before the war. The reunification of the left and right wings of the Independence party in 1913 brought the alliance with the Social Democrats to an end. When Károlyi broke away from the right wing in 1916 he put the struggle for peace, universal suffrage and agrarian reform into his party programme. *Népszava*, the Social Democratic organ, immediately expressed pleasure at this (July 19, 1916), but added that it would be essential to include in the programme the giving of full equality to the non-Magyar nationalities of Hungary. Similarly the radical review *Huszadik Század*, 1916 (2), pp. 133 ff., pointed out that many members of Károlyi's own party still overlooked the fact that half of Hungary did not speak Hungarian. This was correct. On December 20, 1917, a member of the Romanian National Party in Transylvania, the former deputy L. Goldis, wrote to Károlyi proposing co-operation with a view to making Hungary another Switzerland, i.e. a multinational federal state (cf. the letter in the Károlyi papers, Oberlin

College. The term 'eastern Switzerland' had been put into circulation in Hungary by Professor O. Jászi, the great Hungarian student of the nationality problem.) But many months passed before Károlyi, hampered by the nationalism of his own followers, took some steps in the direction of accepting Goldis's invitation. He asked Jászi to open negotiations with the latter (cf. in the Károlyi papers the letter, dated October 8, 1918, from the radical Dr L. Varjassy, who called on Dr Goldis with Jászi). The Hungarian Social Democratic Party, which at the end of July 1914 was still openly opposed to the attack on Serbia, but after the Russian intervention held that the country must be defended against the aims of Tsarism, following the Italian Socialist Party campaign against intervention (to which *Népszava* gave a great deal of space in April–May 1915) started returning to its pre-war internationalist position. *Népszava* reported the Zimmerwald manifesto, which it received through the Swiss Social Democratic Party, on September 25, 1915. The Hungarian Social Democrats however interpreted working class internationalism as implying mistrust of the bourgeois and clerical parties of the non-Magyar nationalities and tried to discourage the spontaneous trend of the few socialists working among these nationalities towards supporting the right of self-determination—which Social Democracy theoretically recognized—under a bourgeois régime.

84. Cf. 'Tagesaufzeichnungen des russischen Aussenministeriums. 12 Januar bis 9 September 1916', *Berliner Monatshefte*, 1938 (2), pp. 632 ff.

85. J. Papoušek, *op. cit.*, p. 25. Cf. also M. S. Sazonov, *op. cit.*

86. Cf. 'La Russie tsariste et la question tchéchoslovaque', *Le Monde Slave*, 1924, pp. 123 ff. and 294 ff. According to M. Abrash, *op. cit.*, pp. 100 ff., the author of the confidential notes was M. G. Priklovsky, the former Russian consul-general in Budapest. On Štefanik's contacts, cf. W. Gurko, *op. cit.*, p. 182. Cf. now G. Thuring-Nittner, *op. cit.*

87. *Le Monde Slave*, *op. cit.*, pp. 125–126. The Petrograd government cannot have been pleased at Briand's reception of Masaryk, a friend of the democratic opponents of Tsarism. On the other hand, by the autumn of 1916 the number of Czech prisoners in Russia had increased to at least 210,000, and this represented a problem that could no longer be set aside. Cf. the figures mentioned in Z. A. B. Zeman, *op. cit.*, p. 131.

88. *Le Monde Slave*, *op. cit.*, p. 131.

89. *Ibid.*, p. 298.

90. E. Beneš, *op. cit.*, Vol. I, p. 221.

91. *Ibid.* The future joint editor of the *Revue Historique*, Louis Eisenmann, a friend of eminent Austrian historians such as J. Redlich and of their Hungarian colleague H. Marczali, had acquired a great reputation thanks to his *Le compromis austro-hongrois de 1867*, Paris, 1904, in which the history of the various nationalities of the Habsburg empire, including of course the Czechs and the Magyars, is related with great acumen and impartiality, though if anything with a marked sympathy for the courage shown by nineteenth-century Hungarian liberal patriotism. Eisenmann continued his Hungarian studies into later times (unfortunately leaving only the draft of his book, L. Eisenmann, *La Hongrie contemporaine*, Paris, 1921). His

original motive, like Seton-Watson's, was admiration for Kossuth. In a lecture given at the University of Paris in 1910 he revealed, however, the oppression inflicted by the dominant Magyar class on the Slav and Romanian minorities, as well as on the Magyar proletariat. He nevertheless declared himself in favour of the maintenance of the integrity of historical Hungary within its existing frontiers, while advocating the necessity of the introduction of secret and universal suffrage and honest application of the nationality law of 1868. (The typescript of the lecture, entitled 'La Hongrie et les Slaves', is at the Paris Institute of Slavonic Studies, of which he became secretary general after the death of E. Denis.) At the beginning of 1913 he was appointed to the Chair of Hungarian civilization at the Sorbonne, which had in its time been established by a Hungarian government subsidy. The review *Magyar Figyelö*, which was associated with the nationalists of the Hungarian government party, sharply criticized Eisenmann's appointment (in its issue of March 6, 1913), calling him a French Scotus Viator (Scotus Viator was R. W. Seton-Watson's pseudonym). Eisenmann, according to *Magyar Figyelö*, had shown himself to be an enemy of the Magyars, and the Hungarian government should therefore cease subsidizing his chair. With the outbreak of war it ceased to exist in any event. After the war Eisenmann succeeded E. Denis in the chair of Slavonic history and civilization (cf. his obituary in *Le Monde Slave*, 1937, pp. 193 ff.).

92. E. Beneš, *op. cit.*, Vol. I, p. 222. On the man who was for so many years the mentor of the Quai d'Orsay, cf. Richard D. Challeners 'The Era of Philippe Berthelot', *The Diplomats. 1919–1939*, ed. Gordon A. Craig and Felix Gilbert, Princeton, 1953. Auguste Bréal, *Philippe Berthelot*, tenth ed., Paris, 1937, is too apologetic.

93. Paul Claudel, *Accompagnements*, Paris, 1949, pp. 182 ff.; Jules Laroche, *Au Quai d'Orsay avec Briand et Poincaré, 1913–1926*, Paris, 1957, pp. 40 and 136–137. E. Beneš, *op. cit.*, Vol. I, p. 261, also testifies to the fact that at the end of December 1916 the Quai d'Orsay was unwilling to commit itself to the dismemberment of Austria-Hungary.

94. G. Suarez, *op. cit.*, Vol. V, p. 115, footnote. In fact Briand had again written to Paul Cambon on November 6: 'The western Slavs, Czechoslovaks and Serbo-Croats, can organize themselves strongly in autonomous groups, either as distinct states or as members of a federation.' Cf. E. Hölzle, *Russland und die Entstehung*, *op. cit.*, p. 228, footnote, who saw the letter in the Quai d'Orsay files. This shows that Briand did not exclude the possibility of Habsburg federalism as an acceptable solution.

95. Cf. also Geneviève Tabouis, *Jules Cambon, par l'un des siens*, Paris, 1938, p. 301. J. Cambon did not conceal from Prince Sixtus that France thought the Czechs useful as a counter-weight to the Budapest government, which was reputed to be extremely hostile to the separation of Austria-Hungary from Germany (cf. G. Suarez, *loc. cit.*). Moreover, one of the commitments that the secretary general of the Quai d'Orsay thought it essential to honour was that to Romania concerning Transylvania and other Hungarian territories.

96. M. Paléologue, *op. cit.*, Vol. III, p. 116; Paul Cambon, *Correspondence, 1870–1924*, three vols., Paris, 1946, Vol. III, p. 136.

97. M. Abrash, *op. cit.*, p. 118, shows convincingly that the document to which Paléologue refers, and which he quotes in the same terms as the note of January 10, 1917, must in reality have been vaguer than the latter, which was drafted in London immediately after Christmas and had the finishing touches put to it in Rome at the beginning of the New Year. That the Quai d'Orsay's first draft was in general terms is borne out by A. J. P. Taylor, 'The War Aims of the Allies in the First World War', *Essays Presented to Sir Lewis Namier*, London, 1956, p. 490.

98. Cf. the note in Blanche E. C. Dugdale, *Arthur James Balfour*, two vols., London, 1936, Vol. II, p. 189, and Kenneth Young, *Arthur James Balfour*, London, 1963, p. 377. For the activities of Seton-Watson and Wickham Steed, apart from their own works, cf. Harry Hanak, 'The New Europe. 1916–1920', *The Slavonic and East European Review*, June, 1961.

99. D. Lloyd George, *op. cit.*, Vol. II, pp. 870; B. Dugdale, *op. cit.*, Vol. II, pp. 435 ff.

100. *Ibid.*, p. 441.

101. Viscount Cecil of Chelwood, *All the Way*, London, 1949, p. 141; *A Great Experiment. An Autobiography*, by Viscount Cecil (Lord Robert Cecil), London, 1941, p. 46.

102. D. Lloyd George, *op. cit.*, Vol. III, p. 1,109. Cf. now Sterling Kernek, 'The British Government's Reaction to President Wilson's Peace Note of December 1916', *Historical Journal*, 1970, n. 4.

103. P. Morand, *op. cit.*, p. 113 and 137. According to Morand, *ibid.*, p. 272, the Pope said to all the Frenchmen he saw: *'Ménagez l'Austriche'*. For the Pope's speech, cf. also the impressions of the American ambassador in Rome, Thomas Nelson Page, *Italy and the World War*, New York, 1920, p. 279, which describes how the Entente felt the need to support the Italian government, whose war policy ran the risk of being weakened by the pacifism of Bendict XV. In fact the Vienna government had asked the Pope to support the Central Powers' peace offer (cf. Reinhold Lorenz, *Kaiser Karl and der Untergang der Donaumonarchie*, Graz, 1959, p. 244). It appears, however, from the documents consulted by F. Engel-Janosi, *op. cit.*, Vol. II, p. 291, that the Pope's attitude to this request was very reserved. On Caillaux's visit to Italy, cf. Raymond Poincaré, *Au service de la Francè*, Vol. IX, Paris, 1932, pp. 52 ff.; F. Charles-Roux, *Souvenirs Diplomatiques*, *op. cit.*, pp. 144 ff.; Giambattista Gifuni, 'Caillaux in Italia', *Nuova Antologia*, February 1959. It has not been ascertained which of the followers of Giolitti Caillaux saw, but it appears from this paper by the curator of the Salandra papers that the former French Prime Minister met some Socialist deputies, with whom he was unable to make headway, and then hit upon a supporter of fighting on to victory as enthusiastic as Ferdinando Martini. Cf. the account of the conversation in the latter's *Diario*, pp. 827 ff.

104. D. Lloyd George, *op. cit.*, Vol. III, p. 1,111.

105. *Ibid.*, p. 1,109 and A. J. P. Taylor, *op. cit.*

106. A. Bréal, *op. cit.*, p. 157 footnote. E. Hölzle, *op. cit.*, p. 169, footnote, saw a memorandum in the archives of the Quai d'Orsay in which, on Berthelot's return from London, the former foreign editor of the *Journal des Débats*, Robert de Caix, insisted on a commitment to the Czechoslovaks, whose cause, like that of the Yugoslavs, was invariably defended in that authoritative Paris newspaper by Auguste Gauvain. Both were close friends of E. Denis, with whom R. de Caix in 1917 founded the review *Le Monde Slave*.

107. G. Suarez, *op. cit.*, Vol. IV, p. 114. T. N. Page, *op. cit.*, p. 279.

108. Salandra, however, had reservations about the wisdom of the Entente declaration, which in his view tended to make the Central Powers fight to the last gasp. Cf. his diary, *op. cit.*

109. H. W. Steed, *op. cit.*, pp. 446 ff.

110. Up to its tenth issue the *Bulletin Yougoslave* printed a small map showing as Yugoslavia all the territories east of the existing Italo-Austrian frontier. The map then vanished, but the journal continued to write in the same sense. Seton-Watson, however, wrote: 'I was brought up in the love of Italy and her language and in admiration of the heroes of her Risorgimento; the sympathy I had for her ideas *a fortiori* inspired me with sympathy for the resurrection of the Yugoslavs.' Cf. *La Serbie*, January 21, 1917.

111. Cf. the letter in *La Serbie* of September 24, 1916, and in G. Salvemini, *Dal Patto di Londra alla Pace di Roma*, Turin, 1925, pp. 28 ff. Salvemini returned to the subject in a letter of February 10, 1917, to Seton-Watson, who had invited him to associate himself with *New Europe*. The editor of *l'Unità* hesitated because, he wrote, 'while there are people in Italy who openly oppose Italian imperialism, and insist on the necessity of an Italo-Slav compromise, and declare the imperialist claims to Split, Šibenik and all the islands of Dalmatia to be iniquitous and dangerous, there is no movement corresponding to ours on the Yugoslav side. Not a single voice has been raised among them—either in the Geneva *La Serbie* or in the *Bulletin Yougoslave*—to deplore the excesses of their nationalism, explicitly admit that the basis of an Italo-Slav compromise must also be based on Yugoslav renunciation of Gorizia, Trieste and western Istria—except, of course, that they must receive a formal Italian assurance, guaranteed by international treaty, that Slavs incorporated into the new Italian frontiers shall be granted liberty of education and full juridical equality.' (Copy in Salvemini papers, original in Seton-Watson papers). (Cf. now the complete text in Roberto Vivarelli, *Questione adriatica e politica estera italiana nella prima guerra mondiale*, Siena, 1964). After the Rome Congress in April 1918, Salvemini agreed to allow his name to appear in the list of editors of *New Europe*, but on January 7, 1919, in protest against the silence preserved by that journal in the face of the resumption of propaganda for the maximum Yugoslav programme, he asked Seton-Watson to remove it, together with those Giretti, De Viti De Marco and Bruccoleri. (*Ibid.*) He then knew that Trumbić, the Foreign Minister of the Kingdom of the Serbs, Croats and Slovenes, was about to demand (as indeed he did at the

February 18 meeting of the Council of Ten) the cities of Trieste, Gorizia, Pola, Fiume and Zara; he admitted that the majority of their inhabitants were Italian, but described them as oases in what was otherwise Slav territory. Cf. *Zapisnici za sednica delegacija kraljevine SHS na mirovoj konferenciji u Parižu, 1919–1920*, eds. Bogden Krizman and Bogumil Hrabak, Belgrade, 1960; I. Lederer, *op. cit.* The same point about the Yugoslav movement was made by O. Jászi's review, which in Hungary stood for the most radical anti-nationalism. *Huszadik Század*, 1918, pp. 293 ff., noted that, while the Southern Slavs bitterly opposed Magyar nationalism, no one among them criticized the nationalism in their own ranks. The coincidence of Salvemini's and O. Jászi's positions was noted by Armando Hodnig, *L'Ungheria e i magiari nella guerra della nazioni*, Milan 1925, p. 21.

112. E. Beneš, *op. cit.*, Vol. I, p. 169.

113. *Ibid.*, p. 271.

114. *La Serbie*, November 5, 1916.

115. E. Beneš, *op. cit.*, Vol. I, p. 291.

116. On Beneš in Rome, cf. also Amelie Posse-Brazdova, *Roman Roundabout*, London, 1933, pp. 40 ff.

117. A.S.M.E. 1917—Ambasciata Londra, Fas. II. 12. Propaganda Yugoslava, Carlotti's telegram of April 16, 1917. According to Masaryk, Sonnino still had hopes of the Magyars and was therefore not only anti-Yugoslav but tended also to be anti-Czech. Cf. R. W. Seton-Watson, *Masaryk in England, op. cit.*, p. 83. In July 1917, when the deputy Agnelli, who in July 1917 interrogated him about the Czech Legion, Sonnino replied that the proposal was contrary to international law (Arnaldo Agnelli, *Gli czecoslovacchi al fronte italiano*, Milan, 1918, p. 3).

118. Cf. the correspondence between Sonnino (or De Martino, the secretary general of the Foreign Ministry), Boselli, and Giardino, the War Minister, A.S.M.E. 1 50—Cecoslovacchia 1916–19.

119. A.C.S. Carte Bissolati, Busta 3. Fasc. 12; E. Beneš, *op. cit.* Vol. II, p. 418.

120. A. J. P. Taylor, *op. cit.*, p. 491. Balfour, on a visit to the United States at the end of April 1917, reiterated the view that the Habsburg empire might be able to survive with Austria, Bohemia and Hungary (cf. *The Intimate Papers of Colonel House*, ed. Charles Seymour, four vols., London, 1926, Vol. III, p. 46). The British Foreign Secretary had doubts about the independence of Poland, though the Russian revolution had now made this inevitable. He wondered how, in the event of another European war, Russia would be able to help France without crossing Polish territory, for an independent Poland would be free to refuse the Russians transit.

121. A copy of G. A. Borgese's report, consisting of 135 typed pages, dated Paris, March–April 1917, largely devoted to Franco-Italian relations, is among Bissolati's papers in the Salvemini papers; Borgese himself, or Luigi Albertini, who had become a close friend of Bissolati's, must have given it to him.

122. The Social Democratic *Népszava*, which on January 16, 1917, published the manifesto of the international socialist committee set up at Zimmerwald, which denounced as expressions of imperialism both the Central Powers' peace offer and the Entente refusal to discuss it, had stated on January 13 that the notes from Berlin and Vienna were at any rate more reasonable than the Entente reply. Next day it pointed out that, if it were desired to dismember a multinational state such as Austria-Hungary was along national lines, the same should be done with Russia, the British Empire, and even Switzerland and Belgium. The Austrian Social Democratic *Arbeiter Zeitung* pointed out on January 13 that it was not possible to separate territorially the nationalities that lived together in the numerous and extensive mixed areas of the empire. Any attempt to split the multinational state into national states would end in the oppression of one nationality by another. The Slavs, the newspaper went on, far from being politically oppressed in Austria, formed the majority in the Vienna Lower House; if there were any economic oppression, it was by the Italian bourgeoisie in the Adriatic provinces. However, the Social Democratic newspaper went on to weaken its argument by comparing the French claim to Alsace-Lorraine to a hypothetical Habsburg claim to recover Lombardy and Venetia. The *Lavoratore* of Trieste, quoting Marx and Engels, stated on January 18 that 'the dismemberment of great centralized states extending beyond the limits of nationality would undoubtedly lead to an unhappy political and economic regression. To the Austrian state, a state structure embracing many nationalities, the rise of independent "Slav republics" would mean a retrograde step in the level of civilization that had been established.' The *Lavoratore*, unlike its Viennese counterpart, had never supported the 'sacred union'. Nevertheless it continually attacked the Yugoslav and Czech nationalists.

123. R. Lorenz, *op. cit.*, pp. 303 ff.

124. Emanuel Victor Voška and Will Irwin, *Spy and Counterspy*, London, 1941, p. 57. Only the lawyer Šamal, Masaryk's successor as leader of the small Realist Party, who headed the secret organization known as the Mafia, and the two deputies of the Progressive Party opposed the 'wait and see' attitude of practically all the Czech politicians at this period. (Cf. Z. Zeman, *op. cit., passim.*)

125. Radonia Yovanovitch, *Les Croates et l'Austriche-Hongrie*, Paris, 1918, p. 137. Cf. the obituary of I. Krek in the *Bulletin Yougoslave* of October 10, 1917.

126. E. David noted in his diary that in Germany it was thought that the Entente reply 'has now justified the policy of the majority of the [Social Democratic] party'. At the meeting on January 18, 1917, of the central committee of the Social Democratic Party Ebert, who until recently—in spite of the reputation for 'hardness' that subsequent events created for him—had been more conciliatory towards the minority, declared that the Entente rejection of the Central Powers' peace proposals so fully justified the policy of national defence that the prospect of the secession from the party of those who opposed it could now be accepted. The minority group

was in fact expelled from the party at this meeting. Cf. G. Kotowski, *op. cit.*, p. 265.

127. The sovereign assumed the title of Charles I as Emperor of Austria and of Charles IV as King of Hungary.

128. *Agramer Tagblatt*, March 1, 1917. Cf. also *La Serbie*, of March 18. The Peasant Party leader Stjepan Radić, who was still a convinced monarchist, told his deputy Dr V. Maček when the latter was called up for military service that either a German victory or a Habsburg collapse would have disastrous effects on Croatia. The former would mean victory for German imperialism, the latter victory for Russian imperialism. When he returned from the front in the middle of 1917, Maček found Radić full of confidence in the new sovereign, to whom he looked for peace and the reorganization of Austria-Hungary into a free confederation. Towards the end of the year, seeing that these hopes were vain, he became a republican (cf. Vladko Maček, *In the Struggle for Freedom*, New York, 1957, pp. 58 ff.).

129. It would similarly be struck a fatal blow by unification of the Czechs and Slovaks; federal autonomy only for Bohemia, which was situated entirely in Austria, would theoretically have left the dual system unchanged, provided it were not granted equal rights with Austria and Hungary in determining the joint policy of the monarchy.

130. *Agramer Tagblatt*, March 8, 1917.

131. *Ibid.*, March 6.

132. *Der Banjaluka-Prozess*, ed. Stephan Freiherr Sarkotić von Loveen, two vols., Berlin, 1933.

133. F. Engel-Janosi, *op. cit.*, Vol. II, pp. 282–283.

134. *Bulletin Yougoslave*, No. 21, April, 1917. Cf. A. Mandić, *op. cit.*, pp. 59 ff. and *passim*, on how Miljukov arrived at the decision to make the declaration asked for by the delegation from the Yugoslav Committee.

135. E. Beneš, *op. cit.*, Vol. II; L. Albertini, vol. *cit.*, *passim*.

136. *Agramer Tagblatt*, April 12, 1917.

137. The United States declared war on Germany (but not on Austria-Hungary, which had not violated the right of neutral powers to freedom of navigation) on April 6, 1917. The Vienna government was, however, obliged to break off diplomatic relations with Washington in order not to dissociate itself from its German ally. The American declaration of war on Austria-Hungary was delayed until December 7, 1917. On Wilson's international political ideas, cf. apart from the works of his biographers, from R. S. Baker to A. Link, Arno Mayer, *Political Origins of the New Diplomacy, 1917–18*, New Haven, 1959. Cf. also Lawrence W. Martin, 'Woodrow Wilson's Appeals to the People in Europe', *Political Science Quarterly*, December 1959, as well as Allan Nevins, *Henry White, Thirty Years of American Diplomacy*, New York, 1930.

138. General Landwehr, *op. cit.*, pp. 24 and 242. The meetings of the Joint Council of Austro-Hungarian Ministers on June 29 and subsequently were dominated by the extreme gravity of the situation. See the reports *cit.* of the meetings.

[389]

139. G. Gratz and R. Schüller, *op. cit.*, pp. 92 and 130.

140. *Ibid.*, pp. 113 and 161 ff.

141. Cf. Wolfgang Steglich, *Die Friedenspolitik der Mittelmächte 1917–1918*, Vol. I, Wiesbaden, 1964; R. A. Kann, *Die Sixtus-affäre und die geheimen Friedensverhandlungen Österreich-Ungarns im Ersten Weltkrieg*, Vienna, 1966.

142. M. Erzberger, *op. cit.*, p. 117. Czernin had asked Erzberger, in view of his Catholic connections, to enquire whether the Vatican might not be prepared to propose a general peace. Czernin's own *a posteriori* version, written after the end of the war, both of the part he played in the Sixtus affair and of how his memorandum came to Erzberger's knowledge, has now been found and published by Robert A. Kann, 'Josef Maria Baernreithers und Graf Ottokar Czernins fragmentarische Darstellung der Sixtus Affaire,' *Mitteilungen des Oesterreichischen Staatsarchivs*, Vol. XVI, Vienna, 1963. According to what Empress Zita recently told a British author, the memorandum of April 1917 had been drafted by her husband, who longed for peace; Czernin signed it only because the Emperor asked him to do so. Cf. Gordon Brook-Shepherd, *The Last Habsburg*, London, 1968, p. 78. Musulin, the Austro-Hungarian Minister in Berne, relates that, when he was sent to Switzerland in January 1917, Charles I received him and said to him, in the same terms that had been used by Benedict XV a few weeks earlier, that he desired an end of the slaughter and a quick peace without annexations, and asked him to try and find out who might be willing to act as mediator (Freiherr von Musulin, *op. cit.*, pp. 292 ff.) In Berne Musulin quickly discovered, and informed the Emperor, that without the cession of Alsace-Lorraine a general peace was impossible.

143. On Stürgkh's reactionary stubbornness, cf. J. Redlich, *Das Politische Tagebuch*, *op. cit.* Redlich considered the decisive factor to be Tisza's backing; Tisza was undoubtedly the stronger personality.

144. J. Redlich, *op. cit.*, Vol. II, p. 201. Czernin himself admitted that the Russian revolution necessitated a return to parliamentary constitutionalism in Austria (cf. Felix Höglinger, *Ministerpräsident Heinrich Graf Clam-Martinic*, Graz and Cologne, 1964). Cf. also A. Spitzmüller Harmersbach, *op. cit.*, p. 217, on how Czernin associated this decision with the need to secure the support of the Austrian Social Democrats at the Stockholm conference. Czernin at first hoped to be able to conclude a separate peace (together with Germany) with the Russian Provisional Government. This, however, presupposed a speedy declaration by the Petrograd Soviet against any continuation of the war on the Russian part. But the Soviet formula of peace without annexations, though it might possibly have been acceptable to Austria-Hungary, was unsatisfactory to Germany so long as she was not in a position (as she subsequently was at Brest-Litovsk) to impose annexations without having to call them by their right name. The German government in fact viewed the Stockholm conference with favour (and granted passports also to the Independent Socialists so that the majority Social Democratic delegation should not appear to be agents of the

government) because it hoped that it would increase the Entente peoples' desire for peace. The German calculations were, however, upset by the slogan of self-determination of the nations launched by the Russian revolution. Cf. the reports of the German diplomatists in *l'Allemagne, op. cit.*, Vol. II, pp. 197 ff. and 353 ff. On the conference itself, cf. the articles by Hildemarie Maynell in *International Review of Social History*, 1960, Nos. 1–2.

145. J. Redlich, *op. cit.*, Vol. II, p. 193.

146. The Christian Social Party, the strongest in Austria, whose intellectually most distinguished personalities, Lammasch and Mgr Seipel, were in favour of the federalization of the empire, was also determined, in spite of the views of the latter, to postpone the nationalities question until after victory had been won. (cf. Fritz Csoklich, 'Das Nationalitätenproblem in Oesterreich-Ungarn und die Christlich-sociale Partei', thesis for the faculty of philosophy in the University of Vienna, 1952). For Mgr Seipel's ideas, cf. J. Droz, *op. cit.*

147. F. Höglinger, *op. cit.*, p. 235. The Austrian Minister of the Interior Konrad Hohenlohe (the former governor of Trieste, who later became Prime Minister for a short time) told Berchtold in May 1916 that Austria-Hungary could survive only if reorganized, with the Polish and Yugoslav territories constituting a third and fourth kingdom, but that Tisza would certainly prevent this. Cf. H. Hantsch, *op. cit.*, p. 770.

148. *Ibid.*, and Arthur Polzer-Hoditz, *Kaiser Karl*, Vienna and Leipzig, 1929, *passim.*

149. *Bulletin Yougoslave*, No. 23, July 1917. Among the 516 deputies elected to the Austrian Lower Chamber in 1911 (some of whom died without others being elected in their place), there were twenty Slovenes (of whom seventeen were Clericals), eleven Croats from Istria and Dalmatia, and two Serbs. One Slovene Liberal deputy (Gregorin) had fled abroad and joined the Yugoslav Committee; another Slovene (Grafenauer) was in prison. Two Croat deputies from Dalmatia (the poet Tresić Pavičić and the Democrat J. Smodlaka) and one Serb had been interned. The Czechs had 108 deputies, twenty-six of them Social Democrats, forming a parliamentary group of their own. The strongest Czech party were the Agrarians, with thirty-seven seats. Two Czechs (Masaryk and Dürich) were abroad and three (Kramář, Rašin and Klofač) in prison. There were 229 German Austrian deputies, of whom seventy-six belonged to the Christian Social Party and forty-four were Social Democrats. The Italians had nineteen deputies, three of whom (Cesare Battisti, Giorio Pitacco and Vittorio Candussi) had taken refuge in Italy. There were twenty-nine Ruthenian deputies (including one Social Democrat), and the Romanians had five. Some deputies were registered as Independents, nationality unspecified. The balance of power was in the hands of the eighty Poles, only eight of whom were Social Democrats, while the others were generally pro-government, as were the Ruthenians, the Romanians and the clericals of all nationalities, not excluding the Italian (cf. Williams Alexander Jenks, *The Austrian Electoral Reform of 1907*, New York, 1950; Ernz Zellmayr,

'Das österreichische Parlament im Jahre 1918', thesis for the faculty of philosophy of the University of Vienna, 1951).

150. The Polish parliamentary union resolution of May 16, 1917 made support of the government conditional on an undertaking that Poland would be re-established in its entirety, with access to the sea (cf. the Vienna newspapers of May 18, 1917, as well as J. Redlich, *op. cit.*, Vol. II, p. 205; cf. also Edmund von Glaise-Horstenau, *Die Katastrophe. Die Zertrümmerung Oesterreich-Ungarns und das Werden der Nachfolgestaaten*, Vienna, 1929, p. 104.) The Polish Social Democratic Party of Galicia, through its leader I. Daszynski in the Reichsrat and its memorandum to the Stockholm conference, came out in favour of the reunification into an independent state of all three Polands, i.e., including that annexed by Germany. Cf. the *Arbeiter Zeitung* of June 16, 1917 and the volume *Comité Organizateur de la Conférence Socialiste Internationale de Stockholm*, Stockholm, 1918, p. 137. In May 1917, however, the Austro-Hungarian government had to agree to Poland's becoming a zone of influence of Germany alone. In July 1917 the Polish volunteers in Warsaw and elsewhere were put under the German High Command and were required to swear an oath of loyalty to the Central Powers, which led to protests, demonstrations, resignations, and to the arrest of Pilsudski and the internment of thousands of legionaries. Cf. W. Conze, *op. cit.*, pp. 291 ff. On the protracted negotiations between Germany and Austria-Hungary about the fate of Poland (as well as that of Romania, and all the other peace terms), cf. the documents in *l'Allemagne*, *op. cit.*, as well as W. Steglich, *op. cit.*, *passim*.

151. A. Polzer-Hoditz, *op. cit.*, pp. 400 ff.; F. Höglinger, *op. cit.*, p. 255. Czernin would have liked the Emperor to decree a solution of the problem of national autonomies in Bohemia, but in a way unfavourable to the Czechs, whom he regarded as unsatisfiable.

152. All the newspapers published long extracts, and the Social Democratic newspapers in Vienna, as well as in Prague, Trieste, and Budapest, published it in full.

153. Cf. the *Arbeiter Zeitung* of May 27, 1917, and following dates.

154. On the fraternization on the Russian front, which reached its peak at Easter 1917, cf. Carl Freiherr von Bardolff, *Soldat im alten Oesterreich*, Jena, 1938, pp. 254 ff.; Jenö Györkei and Antal Józsa, *Magya internacionalisták a nagy októberi orosz forradalomban*, Budapest, 1957, pp. 50 ff.

155. E. Beneš, *op. cit.*, Vol. I, p. 473.

156. E. Glaise, *op. cit.*, p. 102.

157. Cf. the text in the Austrian newspapers of May 31, 1917.

158. Cf. the Stockholm memoranda in *Comité organizateur, op. cit.*

159. Cf. the reply to the criticism of the Czech Social Democratic organ *Pravo lidu* in the *Arbeiter Zeitung* of June 5, 1917. The Czech Social Democratic delegation, which in its memorandum proposed the federal reorganization of Austria-Hungary, with Slovakia forming a unit with Bohemia and Moravia, was approached in Stockholm by two emissaries

of the National Council in exile. Cf. A.S.M.E.—50—Cecoslovakia 1916–19, the report of one of the delegates to Beneš. Cf. of course the latter's memoirs, *op. cit.*, Vol. I, pp. 504 ff. The Social Democratic deputies Nemec and Habrman decided on that occasion that Austria-Hungary had lost and that the interest of the Czech working class lay in joining the independence movement. On their return to Prague, with colleagues, such as Modraček, who had long sympathized with Masaryk, they began taking steps that led to the practical expulsion of Šmeral (who after the Russian revolution adopted an intransigent class position) from the party leadership. (Cf. the *Arbeiter Zeitung* of September 20, 1917 and following days.) The Czech Social Democratic parliamentary group (like the Polish) joined the 'union' of Czech national deputies in the Reichsrat. Cf. *Der Kampf*, 1917, No. 3.

160. Cf. the Vienna newspapers of May 31, 1917.

161. J. Redlich, *op. cit.*, Vol. II, p. 212. Czernin, believing the international situation to be favourable to Austria-Hungary, was in favour of a preventive war on Serbia in 1911–12. When the person to whom he confided this objected that it would be a gamble, he replied: 'War always is.' (J. M. Baernreither, *Die Südslavische Frage, op. cit.*, p. 176.) Charles I nevertheless appointed him to the Foreign Ministry because he knew that in 1915–16 his advice had been that war with Romania should be avoided by the granting of some concessions, which Burian and Tisza had refused. Cf. H. Hantsch, *op. cit.*, Vol. II, p. 794, and J. Redlich, *op. cit.*, *passim*. In pressing for timely concessions to the Romanians Czernin had, however, been in agreement with the German government. In 1917 Germany supported him against those in Austria-Hungary who desired his replacement, fearing that if he were replaced an Austrian separate peace would be facilitated. Cf. the report of Wedel, the German ambassador in Vienna, dated September 10, 1917, P.A.A.A., Oesterreich 92, No. 1.

162. F. Höglinger, *op. cit.*, pp. 273 ff. Charles I realized too late, in March 1918, and said so to Spitzmüller, the Finance Minister, that Austria-Hungary must become federalist and socialist (but waited another seven months before drawing the consequences). Cf. H. Hantsch, *op. cit.*, Vol. II, pp. 812 ff.

163. The amnesty resulted in the release of 1,441 prisoners and a reduction in the sentence on 111 others (R. Lorenz, *op. cit.*, p. 377). The Emperor decided on it after instructing his private secretary to investigate the principal political trials for high treason and receiving a report pointing to the lack of foundation for the sentences imposed (cf. A. Polzer-Hoditz, *op. cit.*, p. 425).

164. *Ibid.*, pp. 453 ff.; P. Lorenz, *op. cit.*, pp. 379 ff.; J. Redlich, *op. cit.*, Vol. II, pp. 213 ff.

165. Cf. Appendix II. A report to Sonnino of August 23 1917, from the Italian Minister in Berne, the Marquis Paulucci, whom the American Herron had informed of the visit of the German pacifist Professor Foerster, who had been received a few days before going to Switzerland by Charles I, confirms that the chief difficulty with which this peace move was faced was

the Austrian reluctance to make territorial concessions to Italy. 'Foerster', Paulucci wrote, 'seems to have gathered the impression that the Emperor Charles is animated by bitterly hostile feelings towards Italy and that the whole great federal design cherished by him could be realized only to our disadvantage'. Herron pointed out to Paulucci, however, 'that to avoid the harmful effects of this subtle propaganda tending to isolate us in the peace negotiations, nothing could be more useful than a plain demonstration of the justice and moderation of our national claims' and he said that they should reach 'full agreement with Serbia on the Adriatic question' (A.S.M.E. Svizzera 1917, Fasc. IV. 2309).

166. J. Redlich, *op. cit.*, Vol. II, p. 288. In his memoirs the Austro-Hungarian Foreign Minister, though confirming that he feared this, and had several times heard from Count Tisza threats of rebellion by Hungary, which refused to yield an inch of her territory or discuss the treatment of her nationalities with third parties, nevertheless admits that, even in the event of a general peace to which Germany agreed, he would have refused to yield Trieste, and *a fortiori* other parts of Istria, to Italy. At most he would have consented to granting her the Trentino and, perhaps, Gorizia. Cf. O. Czernin, *op. cit.*, pp. 35 ff. and 232 ff.

167. A. von Cramon, *Unser österreichisch-ungarischer Bundesgenosse im Weltkriege*, Berlin, 1920, p. 113; E. Glaise, *op. cit.*, p. 108. G. Thunig-Nittner, *op. cit.*

168. The massive St Stephen's crown should have been placed on the monarch's head by the Cardinal Primate of Hungary, aided by a champion, who was traditionally a prince of the blood. But Tisza held that, as the representative of political Hungary, he should carry out the task himself, and he had his way.

169. J. Kristóff, *op. cit.*, p. 476.

170. A. Polzer-Hoditz, *op. cit.*, pp. 417 ff.

171. *Ibid.*, p. 408. No doubt to avoid this, Francis Ferdinand had intended that his Hungarian coronation should not take place until at least a year after his accession to the throne.

172. M. Károlyi, *Egy egész világ, op. cit.*, p. 193. Czernin subsequently denied having ever considered making peace without Germany, but in that case he should not have dealt with an opponent of the German alliance such as Károlyi was now well known to be; still less should he have involved himself in the peace feelers carried out by Prince Sixtus without Germany's knowledge. On the other hand, in the summer of 1917, Károlyi told his colleague Batthyány, who criticized him for making too overtly pacifist speeches, that Czernin himself had suggested that he should make them, wanting to make use of them as a means of putting pressure on the Germans (cf. T. Batthyány, *Beszámolóm, op. cit.*, Vol. I, p. 155).

173. Cf. the Complete Works of I. Tisza, *op. cit.*, Vol. VI, p. 204.

174. *Népszava*, March 20, and *Magyarország*, March 22, 1917. When the dethronement of the Tsar was announced, Károlyi declared that the Russian revolution showed that countries that did not democratize themselves collapsed. Cf. *Magyarország*, March 17.

175. Hungary, with 40·96 per cent of the population of the Habsburg monarchy, provided 43·43 per cent of those called to the colours (cf. Gratz and R. Schüller, *op. cit.*, p. 153). Up to the end of the war, of the 3,800,000 Hungarians who were called up 661,000 were killed, 743,000 wounded or disabled, and 734,000 taken prisoner (cf. Ferenc Julier, *A. világháboru magyar szemmel*, Budapest, 1933, p. 297).

176. J. Redlich, *op. cit.*, p. 140. On May 10, 1917, Charles again asked Burian (cf. the latter's diary, *op. cit.*) to try to persuade Tisza that it was not 'possible to resist the powerful wave, not to see the danger approaching. Universal suffrage cannot be blocked for more than a couple of years'. Burian agreed with the Emperor, but failed to move Tisza, who believed Magyar supremacy in Hungary to be at stake.

177. I. Tisza, vol. *cit.*, p. 277.

178. I. Tisza, vol. *cit.*, p. 281. Wekerle, who assumed the Hungarian Prime Ministership in August 1917 and retained it until the eve of the revolution of October 31, 1918, had the reputation of having a great knowledge of administration and finance, and excelled in parliamentary debate. A rival of Tisza's in the past, he was no less opposed than he to a genuine democratization of Hungary.

179. *Ibid.*, p. 256.

180. *Magyarország*, March 24 and April 5, 1917. At the session of March 31 Károlyi succeeded in persuading the leaders of the other opposition parties to send a greeting to the Russian revolution. *Magyarország*, April 3, 1917.

181. *Magyarország*, April 13.

182. The newspaper quoted, though by no means socialist, in an article entitled 'the Red First of May' called on its readers not to work on May 1, 1917.

183. *Magyarország* and *Népszava* of May 3. Budapest, with its suburbs in 1919 had 1,100,000 inhabitants, of whom about 210,000 were industrial workers; of these 140,000 were employed in concerns having more than twenty employees. Five factories each employed more than 2,000 workers, and many others more than 1,000 (cf. Iván Berend and György Ránki, *Magyarország gyáripara 1900–1914*, Budapest, 1955, p. 76, footnote, and the work of the same authors on the formation of the city's industrial belt, Budapest, 1961). During the war the number of workers employed by the principal metal-working and chemical industries naturally increased because of the needs of armament production.

184. I. Tisza, vol. *cit.*, p. 278.

185. *Népszava*, May 25, 1917.

186. B. Gadanecz, *A forradolom vezérkarában*, Budapest, 1959, pp. 81 ff.

187. O. Czernin, *op. cit.*, p. 288. One of the Hungarian Social Democratic leaders had assured the Foreign Minister that he approved of his peace policy without reservations (cf. Jakab Weltner, *Milljók egy miatt*, Budapest, 1927, p. 283).

188. Cf. the Hungarian memorandum in the vol. *cit.*, of the *Comité*

[395]

organizateur and in *Népszava* of June 2, 1917. On the pre-war agreement between the French and German socialists, cf. *l'Humanité* March 1, 1913. On how it was brought about at the instigation of Jaurès and Haase, cf. B. W. Schaper, *Albert Thomas*, Assen, 1959, p. 88. At that time the Alsatians themselves were claiming no more than democratic federal autonomy within the German Reich. In 1917 the Social Democratic majority party was inclined to support such autonomy, on condition that it was accepted that Alsace belonged to Germany by historical right (cf. P. Scheidemann, *Der Zusammenbruch, op. cit.*, pp. 135 ff.). At the beginning of the war, however, the French Socialist Party simply demanded the return of Alsace-Lorraine to France. In Petrograd in April 1917 one of the French socialist delegates, Marcel Cachin, accepted the principle of self-determination proclaimed by the Soviet for Alsace-Lorraine. The French Socialist Party moved to the left and adopted this position some months later (cf. L. O. Frossard, *De Jaurès à Léon Blum. Souvenirs d'un militant*, Paris, 1943, pp. 69 ff.). The position adopted by the Hungarian Social Democrats, based on the principle, put forward in the Franco-German resolution of 1913, that all disputes between the two nations should be settled by arbitration, was closer to the Soviet than to the majority German socialist position. The German Independent Socialist delegation at Stockholm stood firmly by the Soviet formula of applying the principle of self-determination to Alsace-Lorraine (cf. Hugo Haase, *op. cit.*, pp. 142 ff.). The *Lavoratore* of Trieste took the same line on June 3, 1917. The exasperation roused in the German government by every hint of a plebiscite for Alsace-Lorraine can be seen by the reports reproduced in *l'Allemagne, op. cit.*, Vol. II, especially pp. 356–359.

189. Cf. this passage from the Hungarian Social Democratic statement—which at the time was deleted from the published text—in M. Buchinger, *Küzdelem a szocializmusért, op. cit.*, p. 241. Since the summer of 1916 the Budapest police, having heard that there had been talk at the international conference at Kienthal of an international general strike for peace, had forbidden *Népszava* to be sent to the fronts, and they sent for the Social Democratic leaders Garami and Buchinger to warn them against making any proposals of the kind. They denied that there was any substance in the police suspicions, and Garami, the more moderate of the two, who generally had a majority in the party leadership, said that he hoped and believed that the Central Powers would win the war (cf. H.H.St.A, Pol., Krieg 25–b–i–rot 952, Nos. 305–306, 312.) The internationalist position was adopted in Hungary by Z. Kunfi, Garami's colleague and rival in the editorship of *Népszava*, and in Austria—with greater resolution—by Friedrich Adler. The latter was given detailed information about the proceedings at the Zimmerwald conference by a Romanian socialist, Valeriu Marcu. Adler tried to go to Kienthal, but was stopped at Salzburg by the Austrian police, who made him return to Vienna. (I obtained this information from a letter written to me by I. Adler in May 1959. I am indebted to him and to Julius Braunthal, who were comrades and friends of his, for information about Kunfi.) At Zimmerwald and Kienthal Lenin

argued for a general strike, but for revolution and not for peace. Cf. the testimony of the French trade unionist Merrheim (whom Lenin spent a long time trying to persuade) in his preface to Max Hoschiller, *Le mirage du soviétisme*, Paris, 1921, pp. 8 ff. According to the Austro-Hungarian legation in Berne, there was also discussion of a general strike against the war at the congress of Italian socialists in Switzerland held at Zürich on November 15–16, 1916 (cf. H.H.St.A, *loc. cit.*, Nos. 338–4, 384–6). In May 1915 *Népszava* had praised the Italian Socialist Party for its campaign against intervention, pointing out that it had in mind the possibility of resorting to the weapon of the general strike. Karl Liebknecht himself took his cue from the Italian socialist anti-war campaign, which he called on the German socialists to imitate, claiming in a leaflet that 'the principal enemy is in our own country' (cf. W. Bartel, *op. cit.*, pp. 234 ff.). In Germany the Spartakists and the Independent Socialist left, who were very active in the strike against the trial and conviction of Liebknecht in June 1916, adopted this position. In Austria it was adopted only by very small groups of revolutionaries, who nevertheless succeeded in exercising an influence that exceeded their expectations in the general strike of January 1918. Though Kunfi did not approve of their policy, which he regarded as extremist, small group of revolutionaries in Budapest were in contact with him through E. Szabó, the theorist of syndicalism.

190. The Branting papers in the Arbetarrörelsens Arkiv in Stockholm. It appears from the *Magyarország* of June 2, 1917, that the important points in the Hungarian memorandum were drafted by Kunfi. On his international pacifism, and the limits of his revolutionary inclinations, cf. Zoltán Horváth, *Magyar századforduló*, Budapest, 1961 (German ed., *Zur Jahrhundertwende in Ungarn*, Budapest, 1966). Cf. also Otto Bauer's obituary of Kunfi, O. Bauer, *Eine Auswahl aus seinem Lebenswerk*, ed. Julius Braunthal, Vienna, 1961.

191. Cf. the reports by Fürstenberg, the counsellor of the Austro-Hungarian legation, to Czernin of May 30 and June 4, 1917, H.H.St.A, Pol. Archiv. Krieg 25 z-rot 958–9, Nos. 36 and 55. He also reported that Victor Adler had advised him not to take too dramatically the position adopted by his Hungarian comrades, which he considered to be a paper one only, and paper—he said—was just as patient in Stockholm as it was in Vienna and Budapest.

192. *Ibid.*, and *Népszava*, June 2, 1917.

193. On June 18, 1917 Sonnino forwarded to Imperiali a telegram from the Italian Minister in Stockholm in which the latter said: 'Branting told me that, while the Austrian socialists made a very bad impression on him, because they struck him as being no more than tools, not only of their government, but also of pan-Germanism, the Hungarians showed themselves to be of quite a different spirit . . . They are also said to have spoken vigorously in confidential conversations against German claims to supremacy over Austria-Hungary'. They insisted, however, on informing Branting that they considered Transylvania indispensable to Hungary, though they accepted the idea of federalization of the latter, as they did in

[397]

the case of Austria (A.S.M.E., Ambasciata Londra 1917, Fasc. III, 17, No. 3,743.).

194. M. Buchinger, *op. cit.*, p. 234.

195. *Népszava* on June 3, 1917, headlined the appeal: 'There will be no tranquillity until then.'

196. The Budapest newspapers estimated the number of strikers at 250,000. Many demonstrators sang a song the refrain of which contained the words: 'A rope for Tisza's neck'. Tisza was killed by rebellious soldiers on October 31, 1918, a few hours after the triumph of the revolution in Hungary.

197. M. Eszterházy, to the consternation of the aristocracy to which he belonged, agreed to work as an official under the Hungarian Soviet Republic in 1919. In 1917 the obvious candidate for the Prime Ministership was Count Andrássy, but the Emperor disliked the strong personality of the son of the celebrated Foreign Minister of 1871–79 and told Burian that he would even prefer Tisza to him. As Burian noted in his diary, on June 2, 1917, Andrássy asked for the right to dissolve parliament. The Emperor would have appointed Burian, who, however, declined. The British Foreign Office learnt from a person close to the Emperor that the German Foreign Minister was opposed to Károlyi's joining the Hungarian government. Cf. P.R.O., Austria-Hungary, Political 2862, information dated June 18, 1917.

198. J. Andrássy, *op. cit.*, pp. 257 ff. G. Gratz, *op. cit.*, Vol. II, p. 283. The author was Finance Minister in the Eszterházy government. Andrássy himself informed him of the pact with the Social Democratic leaders (cf. also the testimony of T. Batthyány, *op. cit.*, p. 147, who opposed the planned restriction of universal suffrage). Kunfi, who for the time being limited himself to criticizing (as in the *Arbeiter Zeitung* of August 25, 1917) the restrictions on Romanian schools which the new government, in which Count Apponyi was Education Minister, was unable to renounce, denounced the policy of compromise with a part of the old oligarchy which some of his comrades caused to prevail until the middle of 1918 only after the war and the revolution (cf. his sharp review of the memoirs of his colleague E. Garami, *Forrongó Magyarország*, Leipzig and Vienna, 1922, in the newspaper *Bécsi Magyar Ujság*, of August 6, 1922). The revolutionary syndicalist E. Szabó protested vigorously against the electoral pact agreed to by the Social Democrats in the radical newspaper *Világ*, March 24 1918 (cf. now Ervin Szabó, *Válogatott irásai*, Budapest, 1958, pp. 420 ff.).

199. Cf. the Budapest newspapers of June 29, 1917. The most popular left wing socialist agitator, E. Landler, admitted to a party colleague, P. Agoston, the law historian, that he had to restrain workers who wanted to campaign at all costs to bring about an end of the war. Cf. Agoston's diary at the Institute for the History of the Socialist Workers' party in Budapest.

200. *Magyarország*, July 12, 1917. Károlyi (who in the issue of July 3 had written that there were two Germanys, one militarist and the other pacifist) was hoping at the time that the German democratic parties'

attempt to make a policy of peace without annexations prevail in the Reichstag would succeed. The peace resolution passed by a majority in the Reichstag on July 19, 1917 (cf. C. Haussmann, *op. cit.*, and K. Epstein, *op. cit.*) was made inoperative by the German High Command and the Chancellors subservient to them. Károlyi quickly drew the consequences. While the Czech and Yugoslav *émigrés* denounced to the Entente the latent chauvinism of the Magyar independence movement, Károlyi's courageous struggle attracted the attention of their comrades at home. Thus Klofač declared in an interview republished in the *Agramer Tagblatt* of October 2, 1917, that the 'only far-seeing politician' in Hungary was Károlyi.

201. *Szakszervezeti mazgalom Magyarországon. 1914–1916*, Budapest, undated, *passim*. The great majority of the members were still concentrated in Budapest and its suburbs. The movement spread to the provinces in the second half of 1917. At the end of the year the number of trade unionists amounted to 215,000, and at the end of 1918, i.e. after the revolution, or 721,000.

202. *Ibid.*, p. 35.

203. *Szakszervezeti Értesitö*, 1917, No. 11. Cf. also in H.H.St.A, I, Generalia, IX/18, the report on the conference written by the Austro-Hungarian Minister in Berne, which noted the internationalist radicalism of the Hungarian resolution. During the conference the Czech trade-union delegates again clashed with the Austrians, who for years had disputed the latter's right to set up an independent trade-union federation since, according to the principles of social democratic trade unionism, each country should have only one such federation. As for the difference in attitude of the French and British trade-union leaders towards the Berne conference, it should be recalled that in France the Socialist Party had left the government, while in Britain only Arthur Henderson, who adhered to the Stockholm principles, had done so. The representative of the trade unions who stood for the moderate trend prevailing in them, remained in it.

204. Tisza had several times criticized Skerlecz, as for instance in August 1915 (cf. his Complete Works, Vol. IV, p. 128), for allowing himself to be excessively influenced by the Serbo-Croat coalition. In the *Agramer Tagblatt* of June 21, 1917, one of the leaders of the coalition, Dušan Popović, paid tribute to Skerlecz's liberalism on his leaving office. His successor Mihalović, however, could claim that as a high government official in 1907 he had resigned in protest against the Magyarization of the Croatian railways. This caused him to be elected to the Diet as a member of the Serbo-Croat coalition, into whose hands his appointment delivered the (actually not very great) powers at the Ban's disposal.

205. *Magyarország* of June 24, 1917, also supported this insistence on Hungarian supremacy, on recognition of which it made conditional the Magyar forty-eightist party's support for the democratization of Croatia.

206. Cf. the text in the *Bulletin Yougoslave*, No. 23, July 1917.

207. *Agramer Tagblatt*, July 13 and August 5, 1917. Cf. also Bogdan

Krizman, 'Stjepan Radić 1918', *Historijski Pregled,* 1959, No. 3. The German consul-general in Budapest, who followed Croatian affairs, immediately informed the Berlin government of this speech, which he considered very dangerous (cf. P.A. A.A., Osterreich 85, Kroatien-Slawonien, Vol. VI).

208. Cf. the vol. *cit. Comité organizateur,* as well as the report of the Austro-Hungarian Minister in Stockholm. H.H.St.A, I, Pol. Archiv, rot–Krieg 25–t. Cf. Roman Rosdolsky, 'Die Serbische Sozialdemokratie und die Stockholmer Konferenz,' *Archiv für Sozialgeschichte,* Vols. VI/VII.

209. *Ibid.* Cf. in A.S.M.E., Serbia, anni 1917–1919, Fasc. 18, posizione 15, 'Propaganda comitati nazionali yugoslavi,' a report dated January 28, 1918, from public security headquarters on the conversations that an Italian informer in Paris had with Dr Markić, who was now completely won over to the Yugoslav national movement.

210. Ivan Meštrović, 'The Yugoslav Committee in London and the Declaration of Corfu', in Anton F. Bonifacić and Clement S. Mihanović, *The Croatian Nation,* Chicago, 1955, p. 182 ff.

211. M. Paulova, *op. cit.,* p. 336. The first to realize that the Russian revolution would force Pašić to aim at a Yugoslavia rather than at a Greater Serbia was Supilo. Cf. his letter to Seton-Watson of May 26, 1917 (Seton-Watson papers), in which he also explains why he had resigned from the Yugoslav Committee during the previous year, when he decided that Trumbić was too weak in relation to Pašić and that nothing remained except to hope for an independent Croatia.

212. I. Meštrović, *op. cit.,* pp. 185 ff. Cf. also Meštrović's memoirs, *op. cit.,* pp. 71 ff.

213. *Ibid.* It seems that in the meantime the funds of the Yugoslav Committee had dried up, for one thing because after the United States' intervention American Croats subscribed directly to the American war loan, and that the resulting situation made Trumbić less intransigent. This suggestion was made by the Italian consul-general in Geneva in a report to Sonnino which the latter forwarded to the ambassador in Petrograd on March 31, 1917 (cf. A.S.M.E., Serbia, anni 1917–18 Fasc. 18. 181 posizione 15).

214. Smith Pavelič, *op. cit.,* p. 80.

215. This statement is made in Trumbić's obituary of Supilo in the *Bulletin Yougoslave,* No. 26, November 1917, and is confirmed by the letter from Supilo to Gina Lombroso of August 1, 1917. 'Without modesty,' he wrote, 'I can say that I have had the greatest triumph, the greatest moral and political satisfaction, that I ever dared to hope for in my life. All my demands on the Serbs have been met.' Cf. B. Radica, *op. cit.,* p. 398.

216. M. Paulova, *op. cit.,* pp. 341 ff. *Yougoslavie,* the organ of the Slovene federalists and revisionist socialists, which was published at Geneva, also vigorously criticized Trumbić.

217. Cf. the text in F. Šišać, *op. cit.,* and *Serbic,* August 5, 1917.

218. *Agramer Tagblatt,* August 6, 1917.

219. M. Paulova, *op. cit.*, pp. 350 ff. On Barac, cf. I. Meštrović, *Uspomene*, *op. cit.*, p. 98, and in particular B. Krizman's article on the contacts between the politicians in Austria-Hungary and their colleagues abroad in *Historijski Zbornik*, 1962, Nos. 1–4. It appears from these that Barac, who travelled between Croatia and Switzerland three times in 1917–18, was not the only one engaged in this liaison work; there were also other couriers.

220. Cf. the report of July 27, 1917 of the German consul-general in Prague to the ambassador in Vienna, P.A.A.A., Oesterreich 85, Vol. 6 A.

221. Korošec and Krek had gone to Zagreb and Sarajevo to co-ordinate their activity with that of the opposition parties in Croatia and Bosnia. Cf. *Agramer Tagblatt*, September 4, 1917.

222. *Hrvatska Država*, September 4, 1917.

223. *Ibid.*, September 29, 1917.

224. *Agramer Tagblatt*, September 25 and 26, 1917.

225. *Arbeiter Zeitung*, October 20, 1917.

226. P.A.A.A., Oesterreich 85—Vol. 6 A. The memorandum, unsigned, dated Berlin, December 21, 1917, lucidly surveys the Yugoslav movement abroad. It observes that in spite of the Corfu agreement, some of Pašić's Radicals did not want unification with Croatia and would have preferred the direct annexation of Bosnia-Hercegovina, Montenegro and Dalmatia. It goes on to deal with the position of the left-wing critics of the Trumbić–Pašić agreement. As for the Serbo-Croat coalition in the Zagreb Diet, it should be noted that its demand for the unification of Dalmatia and Bosnia with Croatia was opposed by the Budapest government, which wanted to annex these provinces—particularly Bosnia—to Hungary. The question was repeatedly considered by the Austro-Hungarian political and military leaders in 1918, but they never succeeded in arriving at a decision.

Notes (VI)

The Rome Congress

1. H.H.St.A, P.A. rot 583. Delegations-Akten 1917–18.

2. *Ibid.* This programme of Czernin's should be compared with what he wrote to the Foreign Minister Berchtold from Bucharest on March 11, 1914, when the Sarajevo tragedy was unforeseen: 'I have—and have had not since yesterday—the very lively feeling that if we want tranquillity at last in the Balkans we must liquidate present-day Serbia . . . Certainly no one in the monarchy wants "still more Serbs", but after a successful campaign we might be able to satisfy Bulgaria and Greece with Serbian territory—and at the same also indirectly Romania–Albania might be rounded off and Serbia reduced to a minimum. I believe that in politics a preventive war measure is not to be considered exclusively from the point of view of "digestibility".' As for Romania, guaranteed against further Bulgarian claims to the Dobruja, Czernin thought that to settle the question of her desire for union with Transylvania, she should be incorporated in Austro-Hungary, though with her own autonomy and reigning dynasty on the model of Bavaria and Saxony in the Reich. Cf. H.H.St.A., Nachlass Erzherzog Franz Ferdinand. II.B.–13. Cf. H. Hantsch, *op. cit.*, Vol. II, pp. 495 ff.

3. Cf. W. Steglich, *Die Friedenspolitik, op. cit.*, Vol. I, *passim*, and my review of it in *Rivista Storica Italiana*, LXXVII (1965), No. 1. But cf. above all G. Ritter, *op. cit.*, on Bethmann Hollweg as war-time Chancellor, which throws the best light on these problems. Cf. on pp. 465 and 670 the summary of the report by Wedel, the German ambassador in Vienna, who at the beginning of 1917 suggested to Czernin the annexation of a part of Moldavia or Wallachia in exchange for Austro-Hungarian renunciation of Russian Poland in Germany's favour. At that time Czernin seemed reluctant, but after the Russian revolution in March he asked Bethmann Hollweg for both Wallachia and western Moldavia. Ritter, without denying Czernin's acute intelligence, draws attention with good reason to his impressionability, nervousness and spirit of improvisation. In fact, less than a month after proposing these large-scale annexations he was painting the situation of Austria-Hungary in a disastrous light. His object was to induce Germany to agree to approaching France and Britain with a peace offer; if Germany consented to sacrifice a slice of Lorraine, he might be willing to sacrifice the Trentino. *Ibid.*, pp. 471 ff. The pessimistic terms he used were fully justified. The view of the Vienna professional diplomats was that he was a brilliant amateur. But in 1917 he took a

realistic view of the internal weakness of the Habsburg empire, even though he was mistaken about the remedy.

4. *Protokoll des Ministerrates für gemeinsame Angelegenheiten*, 22 März, 1917. Charles I, while making secret approaches to the Entente, agreed with his ministers that Belgrade and other Serbian territory should be annexed. See the explanation of this contradictory behaviour of the Emperor and Czernin in Friedrich Engel-Janosi, 'Ueber den Friedenswillen Kaiser Karls', *Festschrift für Otto von Habsburg, op. cit.* Czernin, having resigned himself to abandoning Poland, as well as Courland, Lithuania and other territories of imperial Russia to Germany, thought it essential, in order to induce her to make concessions to France in Lorraine, to restore the balance by compensations for Austria-Hungary in the Balkans. The documents published in *L'Allemagne et les problèmes de la paix, op. cit.*, Vol. II, confirm that at and after his conversation with the Reich Chancellor on March 16, 1917, Czernin acted in the way explained by Engel-Janosi, though with a nervousness and capriciousness that his German interlocutors noted and used for their own benefit. If he really believed that the Entente would sacrifice Poland, Serbia and Romania in return for the restoration of Belgium and part of Lorraine, it meant that after three years of war he had not yet realized that the French and British might perhaps persuade their allies to modify their claims to Austro-Hungarian territory, but not to sacrifice territory that they possessed before the war. He realized that Austria-Hungary was in urgent need of peace, but failed to appreciate that the Entente powers were in a position to go on fighting indefinitely.

5. H. H. St. A, P.A. rot 583. Delegations-Akten 1917–18. Czernin, whom Tisza criticized for making too many concessions to the Czechs, in fact wanted a settlement to be imposed on Bohemia that would exclude the territorial autonomy demanded by the Czech parties. Cf. Karl Werkmann, *Deutschland als Verbündeter. Kaiser Karls Kampf um den Frieden*, Berlin 1931, *passim*.

6. Cf. F. Höglinger, *op. cit.*, p. 213. In his negative attitude to the Slav nationalities Czernin was in fact being merely consistent. On December 13, 1913, he had written to Berchtold: 'We have never conducted a war with the sympathies of the whole monarchy behind us and we never shall; in practically every situation we shall have some of our peoples for us and others against us; if we are to pursue an active foreign policy, we are obliged more or less to ignore the moods of the peoples.' H. H. St. A, Nachlass Franz Ferdinand, II. B–13. In the opinion of Wedel, the German ambassador, however, it was 'inconceivable that the division of the Southern Slavs into five different groups pressing for unity should continue.' He therefore criticized the Magyars, who were willing to accept a certain amount of Yugoslav unification, but only within the framework of the Kingdom of Hungary, and the German Austrians, who refused to accept this, for their inability to reach agreement. Cf. his report of September 19, 1917, in P.A.A.A., Oesterreich 92 No. 1, Bd. 25–26. The aggravation of the dissension between Austrians and Hungarians, not only on this problem,

o   [403]

but also on the questions of food supply, common finances, and the independent Hungarian army demanded by the Budapest government itself since Count Apponyi's forty-eightists had entered it, runs like a thread through all Wedel's reports. The Berlin government, however, had put itself in the position of being unable to exercise pressure on its ally to reach reasonable compromises on these problems, because it had taken the unusual line—incidentally in direct contradiction to its insistence during the preceding months on concessions to Romania—of pointing out to Austria-Hungary (to dissuade it from the idea of demanding the unification of Russian Poland with Galicia and induce it to conclude a customs union with Germany when the war was over) that it interpreted the 1879 alliance as having been made by Bismarck with an Austria-Hungary in which the German Austrians and the Magyars would always predominate. Cf. Jagow's memorandum of November 13, 1915, *L'Allemagne et les problèmes de la paix*, *op. cit.*, pp. 211 ff. Behind the German concern about the Yugoslav problem in 1917–18 there was also the self-interested desire not to leave Romania (which she wanted to keep for herself) to Austria-Hungary and to persuade the latter to incorporate only Serbia and Montenegro. *Ibid.*, pp. 445 ff.

7. Cf. Appendix I.

8. H. H. St. A, Nachlass Mensdorff. Cf. also W. Steglich, *op. cit.*; W. K. Hancock, *Smuts. The Sanguine Years 1870–1919*, Cambridge, 1962; and of course D. Lloyd George, *War Memoirs*, *op. cit.*, Vol. V, pp. 2,461 ff. Mensdorff had been opposed to the policy that made war inevitable. Cf. the memoirs of his brother-in-law, A. Apponyi, *op. cit.*, Vol. II, p. 203. For the British version, cf. Appendix I.

9. *Berliner Monatshefte*, 1937 (1), pp. 401 ff.

10. Nachlass Mensdorff, *op. cit.* W. Steglich, *op. cit.*, *passim*, regards it as certain that Czernin would have been willing to sacrifice the Trentino in the event of a general peace. But here again he wavered. He began by informing the German Chancellor (on March 26, 1917, cf. *L'Allemagne*, *op. cit.*, Vol. II, p. 55) that Charles I intended to yield nothing to Italy (the Emperor, perhaps unknown to him, imprudently communicated this refusal to the Entente in his second letter to Prince Sixtus, whose mission was thus definitely condemned to failure). A few days later, when Germany gave him to understand that she could not guarantee Austria-Hungary the integrity of her pre-war frontier with Italy, Czernin changed his mind. On May 30, 1917, he again changed his mind and informed the Germans that he would not make territorial concessions to Italy. Cf. *L'Allemagne*, *op. cit.*, Vol. II, p. 379. Then he changed his mind yet again. In his letter to Tisza of November 17, 1917, he admitted the principle of a frontier rectification in favour of Italy. Cf. O. Czernin, *op. cit.*, pp. 296 ff. But at the beginning of 1918, his hopes of a German victory having revived, he again dismissed the idea, just at the time when Orlando was willing to negotiate through the Vatican.

11. Nachlass Mensdorff *cit*. Smuts, according to his own account, assured Mensdorff, who had drawn attention to the Entente reply to

[404]

President Wilson of January 10, 1917, that it had never been the British intention to dismember Austria-Hungary. If Britain asked territorial sacrifices of her, which he described as small, it was to put the Habsburg monarchy in a position 'to realize the greater destiny that may be reserved for it'. In his opinion, the addition of Poland—and possibly, through a federation, also of Romania—to Austria-Hungary might be considered by the Entente. Cf. Lloyd George, *loc. cit.*

12. W. K. Hancock, *op. cit.*, p. 446. Cf. Smuts' report in P.R.O., 2864. Cf. also Lord Hankey, *op. cit.*, Vol. I, p. 737. The Secretary of the War Cabinet persuaded Lord Cecil to drop the principle of the self-determination of the nationalities (which could have embarrassed the British government) from the draft of the War aims.

13. On the British left, cf. Austin van der Slice, *International Labour, Diplomacy and Peace, 1914–1919*, Philadelphia, 1941; Paul U. Kellogg and Arthur Gleason, *British Labour and the War*, New York, 1919; William P. Maddox, *Foreign Relations in British Labour Politics*, Cambridge 1934; Beatrice Webb, *Diaries*, London, 1952; Mary Agnes Hamilton, *Arthur Henderson. A Biography*, London, 1938; G. D. H. Cole, *A History of the British Labour Party from 1914*, London, 1948.

14. Cf. A. Nevins, *op. cit.*; A. J. Mayer, *op. cit.*; Lawrence W. Martin, *Peace without Victory*, New Haven, 1958. Among the leading members of the Union of Democratic Control were the Radical M.P.s: Buxton, Charles Trevelyan and Ponsonby, the Labour leaders Arthur Henderson, Ramsay MacDonald and Philip Snowden, the publicists Norman Angell and H. N. Brailsford, the economist J. A. Hobson, and others. W. H. Buckler, the counsellor of the American embassy who was in contact with them, was a step-brother of the diplomatist H. White, who had President Wilson's ear.

15. Harry Hanak, *Great Britain and Austria-Hungary during the First World War*, London, 1962. After the reopening of the Reichsrat and the Corfu agreement and just before Sonnino's visit to London, both the pacifist Radicals (Noel Buxton) and Wickham Steed's anti-Austrian friends (the Liberal M.P.s Whyte and Bryce) questioned the government on its policy towards Vienna. Balfour replied by expressing the hope that the nationalities of the Habsburg empire would be enabled to develop in their own way, but that he could not yet forsee what treatment would be meted out to 'a great and ancient monarchy like the Austrian'. Cf. the speech in *The Times*, August 2, 1917.

16. On June 28, 1917 Charles Trevelyan M.P. (the brother of the historian of Garibaldi) in a letter to Buckler put German imperialism on the same level as that of certain members of the Entente, not excluding Britain (in Mesopotamia), France, and above all Italy, 'with her imperialist demands to control the Adriatic together with the annexation of non-Italian populations'. Cf. A. Nevins, *op. cit.*, p. 345.

17. Cf. the text in the *Corriere della Sera*, August 11, 1917, and in *The Labour Party Memorandum on the Issues of the War*, London, September 1917. At Labour meetings the veteran Marxist H. M. Hyndman, who as a

war correspondent had followed Garibaldi to Bezzecca in 1866, was very favourable to Italy. In spite of this, he was, as a result of his friendship with Seton-Watson, a member of the Serbian Society. Cf. Rosalind Travers Hyndman, *The Last Years of H. M. Hyndman*, London, 1961.

18. W. P. Maddox, *op. cit.*, p. 150.

19. A. Mayer, *op. cit.*, p. 318. Harry Hanak, 'A Lost Cause: the English Radicals and the Habsburg Empire, 1914–1918', *Journal of Central European Affairs*, July 1963, points out that the Labour declaration followed in the footsteps of similar statements by the Union of Democratic Control. In any case, cf. the document *cit.* in the *War Aims of the British People, an Historic Manifesto*, the complete text of the official war aims memorandum adopted by the joint conference of the Labour Party and the parliamentary committee of the Trade Union Congress on December 28, 1917, London, 1918.

20. *Report of the Seventeenth Annual Conference of the Labour Party, Nottingham and London 1918*, London, 1918, p. 12.

21. *Ibid.*, pp. 94–95. Cf. in *The Intimate Papers of Colonel House, op. cit.*, Vol. III, p. 340, Balfour's telegram informing the Americans of the negotiations by which Lloyd George secured the support of the trade union leaders for a further mobilization of men from industry.

22. A. Mayer, *op. cit.*, p. 326.

23. D. Lloyd George, *op. cit.*, Vol. V, pp. 2,484 ff. Both Arthur Henderson and Lord Lansdowne declared their satisfaction with the Prime Minister's speech. Clemenceau telegraphed his approval. Cf. Lord Riddell, *op. cit.*, p. 305. The speech was reported at length in various Vienna newspapers of January 7, 1918. *Il Lavoratore* of Trieste commented on January 10 that 'not all that Lloyd George says is good, but not all is bad either'.

24. Lawrence E. Gelfand, *The Inquiry. American Preparations for Peace. 1917–1919*, New Haven, 1963, p. 135; House, *op. cit.*, Vol. III, pp. 318 ff.; George F. Kennan, *Soviet-American Relations. 1917–1920*, two vols. so far published, Princeton, 1957–58. The American military attaché in Petrograd was definitely in favour of trying to persuade the Soviet government not to sign a peace treaty with Germany.

25. A.S.M.E. Piscel regularly informed the Italian legation in Stockholm of his contacts with Huysmans and other representatives of international socialism. What he says is confirmed by the references in the Huysmans papers to the contacts with Vorovsky. Huysmans was opposed to calling an international conference, which the Entente socialists would not attend, fearing that in their absence the 'majority' Germans would prevail. The conversations that Scheidemann, who returned to Stockholm in the first half of December 1917, had had with Vorovsky and Huysmans had led to nothing, because he still supported the policy of the Berlin government. Cf. Philipp Scheidemann, *Memoiren eines Sozialdemokraten*, two vols., Dresden, 1929, ff. Cf. also Z. A. B. Zeman and W. B. Scharlau, *op. cit.*, p. 244. Only an agreement between the western socialists and the Bolsheviks could have counter-balanced the German Social Democrats. Axelrod had

said to Piscel on October 14, 1917, that the choice ultimately would be between granting passports to Stockholm by the Entente governments and Bolshevik acceptance of the German peace conditions. The Entente governments persisted in their refusal to grant passports, however.

26. Ray Stannard Baker, *Woodrow Wilson, Life and Letters*, eight vols., New York, 1927–39. On January 18 the Fourteen Points were printed in full by the Vienna newspapers. They were appreciated by the German democrats. Though they again rejected the French claim to Alsace-Lorraine, the Social Democrat David and the Catholic Erzberger said at the meeting of leaders of parliamentary groups in the Reichstag on January 28 that Wilson's message provided a basis for the discussion of peace between the belligerents. Cf. *Der Interfraktionelle Ausschus. 1917–18, op. cit.*, Vol. II, p. 128. Many members of the German Independent Socialist Party were pro-Soviet, but others were Wilsonians. On the latter, cf. Karl Kautsky, *Die Befreiung der Nationen*, fourth ed., Stuttgart, 1918, and *Die Wurzeln der Politik Wilsons*, Berlin, 1919. To the masses the difference between Wilson's peace proposals and those of the Soviet was not very clear. The Bolsheviks themselves distributed the Fourteen Points among German and Austrian troops on the Russian front. Cf. John W. Wheeler-Bennett, *The Forgotten Peace, Brest-Litovsk, March 18*, New York, 1939, p. 147. In Budapest the Social Democratic *Népszava* on January 10 explicitly approved the Fourteen Points, while Károlyi's *Magyarország* on January 11 maintained the untouchability of historical Hungary.

27. L. E. Gelfand, *op. cit.*, p. 142.

28. On Wilson's policy during this period, cf. Charles Seymour, *American Diplomacy during the World War*, Baltimore, 1934; V. S. Mamatey, *op. cit.* Cf. also Bogdan Krizman, 'Predsjednik Wilson i jadransko pitanje do primirja s Austro-Ugarskom', *Anali Jadranskog Instituta*, II, 1958. For confirmation that by his Point IX Wilson intended to repudiate the clauses of the Treaty of London that were inconsistent with it, cf. House, *loc. cit.*, p. 323. To the Italian ambassador who asked for an explanation, Wilson said that his points assumed the creation of a League of Nations based on collective security, which would result in Italy's having no more need for strategic frontiers on the eastern side of the Adriatic, and in any case the United States could not fight for these. Cf. *The Lansing Papers, 1914–1920*, two vols., Washington, 1939–40, Vol. II, p. 94.

29. R. E. Gelfand, *op. cit.*, p. 152. George Bárány, 'Wilsonian Central Europe: Lansing's contribution,' *The Historian*, 1966, n. 2. Robert Lansing, *Mémoires de guerre*, Paris, undated, p. 235. A year earlier, on February 10, 1917, Lansing had written to Wilson that it did not seem to him to be appropriate to talk of 'liberation' to the peoples of Austria-Hungary; Austria-Hungary should instead be encouraged to make peace by a guarantee of her preservation. Cf. *The Lansing Papers, op. cit.*, Vol. I, p. 596. At that time the United States was still neutral. But the Entente ambassadors were now the representatives of allied nations, and Lansing was aware of the criticisms that Vesnić, the head of the Serbian mission, who

had just arrived in the United States and was the only diplomat whom Wilson had consulted on Point X, had made, though in vain. Cf. C. Seymour, *op. cit.*, p. 287; V. S. Mamatey, *op. cit.*, pp. 185 ff.

30. *Ibid.* and C. Pergler, *op. cit.*; J. O'Grady, *op. cit.* Ex-President Theodore Roosevelt was vigorously supporting the Slav and Romanian claims to independence in public speeches. The Irish, however, were rather pro-Habsburg. Cf. A. Bernardy and V. Falorsi, *La questione adriatica vista d'oltre Atlantico. 1917–1919*, Bologna, 1923, p. 32.

31. T. N. Page, *op. cit.*; Hugh R. Wilson, *Diplomat between Wars*, New York, 1941.

32. Cf. the Vienna newspapers of December 28, 1917; W. Steglich, *op. cit.*, pp. 301 ff.; J. Wheler-Bennett, *op. cit.*, *passim*.

33. Cf. *La Nation tchèque*, March 1–15, 1918. Cf. also E. Beneš, *op. cit.*; J. Opocensky, *op. cit.* The censorship forbade publication of the resolution adopted in Prague, but it was the subject of debate in the Reichsrat and the Prime Minister himself intervened, so that the newspapers were able to mention it. Cf. E. Zellmayr, *op. cit.*

34. E. Strauss, *Die Entstehung*, *op. cit.*, p. 194; P. Molisch, *op. cit.*, pp. 130 ff. The Czech Social Democrats had twenty-six deputies in the Reichsrat, the National Socialists seventeen, and the Czech Agrarian Party thirty-eight.

35. Cf. the text in *La Serbie*, February 23, 1918, in the *Bulletin Yougoslave*, No. 30, and the *Corriere della Sera* and *Il Secolo* of February 27. Cf. also H. Michel *op. cit.* A Zagreb newspaper, the *Obzor*, published the document on February 3, but was immediately confiscated.

36. Millions of copies of *Die Fackel*, edited by Radek in Russia, were distributed in the German-Austrian lines. Cf. J. Wheeler-Bennett, *op. cit.*, p. 90. On the groups of Hungarian Communists in Russia, cf. *A magyar internacionalisták a nagy októberi szocialista forradalomban és polgárháboruban*, 2 vols., Budapest, 1967–68. On Austro-Hungarian soldiers' letters, cf. the documents collected in *Párttörténeti Közlemények*, 1958, No. 2.

37. Cf. the *Arbeiter Zeitung*, January 15, 1918. The Social Democratic newspaper had for several days been holding the German High Command responsible for the prolongation of the negotiations at Brest. It now contrasted the sham German adoption of the principle of self-determination in Russia with the fact that the Western labour movement was forcing Wilson and Lloyd George to modify their war aims.

38. The most vigorous personality among the Austrian Zimmerwaldians, who had foreseen the general strike (though they did not start it, for it broke out spontaneously), was Franz Koritschoner, a nephew of Hilferding's and a member of the extreme left wing of the Social Democrats, who in 1916 had gone to Kienthal (though he reached it after the conference was over), and in 1917 had organized a meeting of his sympathizers at Wiener-Neustadt. Cf. Leopold Hornik, 'Die Zimmerwalder Linke und die Linksradikalen in Oesterreich', *Weg und Ziel*, 1955, No. 9. (Koritschoner, who took refuge in the Soviet Union in the thirties,

was handed over to the Gestapo after the Hitler–Stalin pact of 1939 and died in a Nazi prison. Cf. the details given by Lucien Laurat in *Contributions à l'histoire du Comintern*, ed. Jacques Freymond, Geneva, 1965.) At the third conference of the Zimmerwald movement, held in Stockholm in September 1917, which was attended by two Austrian women socialists, Therese Schlesinger and another named Luzzatto, a manifesto was drafted calling for an international general strike. At the instigation of Haase, who did not want adventures, it was not made public, but Radek had it printed in a Finnish newspaper, from which it was copied by newspapers in other countries. (A general strike for 'power to the councils' in fact broke out in Finland on November 14, after the events in Petrograd.) Cf. *Die Zimmerwalder Bewegung. Protokolle und Korrespondentz*, ed. Horst Lademacher, 2 vols., The Hague, 1967; Olga Hess Gankin and H. H. Fischer, *The Bolsheviks and the World War. The Origins of the Third International*, Stanford, 1960; Angelica Balabanoff, 'Die Zimmerwalder Bewegung. 1914–1919', *Archiv für die Geschichte des Sozialismus und der Arbeiterbewegung*, Vol. XII; H. Meynell, *op. cit.* Therese Schlesinger, a sister of Gustav Eckstein, who was one of the most brilliant Austro-Marxist publicists, had for many years been one of the leading Social Democrats in Vienna. During the war she sided with Friedrich Adler, and at the party congress in October 1917 she and the philosopher Max Adler were among the few who advocated an all-out mass struggle for peace. Cf. *Protokoll der Verhandlungen des Parteitages der sozialdemokratischen Arbeiterpartei in Oesterreich. Abgehalten in Wien vom 19 bis 24 Oktober, 1917*, Vienna, 1918. During the events of January 1918 Therese Schlesinger was disciplined by the party leadership, in which Otto Bauer had become a left-wing representative.

39. *Protokolle, op. cit.*, pp. 285–286. As appears from the evidence quoted by Hartmut Lehmann, 'Czernins Friedenspolitik 1916–18', *Welt as Geschichte*, 1963, No. 1, and by W. Steglich, *op. cit.*, *passim*, Czernin was less straightforward to the Social Democratic leaders than they were to him. He gave them passports because of their willingness to defend his peace policy at Stockholm, but he did not want the conference to reach any decisions, as he regarded as *a priori* unacceptable any position on which the socialists of the various countries might have agreed. Thus by their refusal of passports the Entente governments without realizing it played into his hands.

40. On the Austrian labour movement during the war, cf. the documents in Rudolph Neck's valuable collection *Arbeiterschaft und Staat im Ersten Weltkrieg.* (A. Quellen). 1. *Der Staat (1. Vom Kriegsbeginn bis zum Prozess Friedrich Adlers. August 1914–Mai 1917)*, Vienna, 1964, and *Oesterreich im Jahre 1918. Berichte und Dokumente*, Vienna, 1968. On the strike of January 1918, cf. also O. Bauer, *Die österreichische Revolution*, Vienna, 1923.

41. The Social Democratic Party published a strike bulletin, *Mitteilungen an die Arbeiter*, on January 19. In Vienna 120,000 struck and—according to Socialist claims—700,000 in the whole empire. Cf. Josef Schiller,

'Neue Tatsachen über den Januarstreik 1918,' *Weg und Ziel*, 1960, No. 1. A contemporary Austrian police report evaluated the number of strikers at 550,000. In Hungary the number of strikers was estimated at 280,000, 150,000 of them in Budapest and suburbs.

42. L. Brügel, *Geschichte der österreichischen Sozialdemokratie, op. cit.*, Vol. V, pp. 335 ff.

43. *Arbeiter Zeitung*, January 17, 1918.

44. A general strike against the reduction in the bread ration broke out at Trieste on January 15 and also paralysed the tram service and the gas supply. The Trieste Social Democrats agreed to call off the strike, when the Governor promised to cancel the reduction, but it continued in the San Marco and San Rocco shipyards for another two days. When they heard about the strike movement taking place in the rest of Austria, the Trieste socialists decided on January 21 to resume the strike, but called it off when news arrived of the return to work in Vienna. Because of the coal shortage, gas production stopped at Trieste on January 26, and the exasperated workers began another strike, led by a 'workers' council' whose slogan was 'bread and work'. The strike lasted from January 28 to February 1. At Muggia, where the Trieste Social Democratic leaders were sharply criticized for not making the strike all-out, it continued for another day. At Pola the general strike began on January 22 and ended on the 28th. Cf. *Il Lavoratore*, January 15 to February 9, 1918. Cf. also Silvio Benco, *Gli ultimi anni della dominazione austriaca a Trieste*, three vols., Milan 1919. According to Benco, Vol. III, pp. 15 ff., at Trieste, where the workers shouted 'down with the war' and the students 'down with Austria', 'the masses were in a tumultuous frame of mind'.

45. Franz Brandl, *Kaiser, Politiker und Menschen. Erinnerungen eines Wiener Polizeipräsidenten*, Vienna, 1936, p. 44. Cf. also Julius Deutsch, *Aus Oesterreichs Revolution. Militärpolitische Erinnerungen*, Vienna, undated. The author, who was a reserve officer stationed in Vienna, during this period established the first Social Democratic groups in the army. In Budapest there were very few troops also. Cf. J. Szterényi, *op. cit.*, p. 80.

46. H. H. St. A, Nachlass Baernreither, File Y, Diary, Vol. XVIII, p. 122 ff.

47. F. Brandl, *op. cit.*, C. Bardolff, *op. cit.*, p. 295. General Alfred Krauss, *Die Ursachen unserer Niederlage*, Munich, 1920, p. 281. According to Graf Tomas von Erdödy's *Die Memoiren. Habsburgs Weg von Wilhelm zu Briand*, Vienna, 1931, the police and military authorities wanted to fire on the strikers, but the Emperor forbade them. In October 1918 he also refused to spill blood to crush the revolution.

48. Cf. the reports of the German ambassador in Vienna and the vice-consul general in Budapest, P.A.A.A. Oesterreich, 92 No. 1, Vols. 25–26, which show how dangerous the German observers considered the peace campaign conducted by Károlyi and some of the Hungarian Social Democratic leaders to be. Moreover, in Budapest, the small groups of extreme left-wing socialist or syndicalist revolutionaries, of whom the former controlled the clerical workers' trade union (including its technicians and engineers' section) and the latter some key positions among the shop

[410]

stewards in some big factories, played a prominent part in the agitation for a general strike. Pacifist students of the Galilei cultural club, who were in contact with the Zimmerwald movement through a girl student named Ilona Duczynska, who had called on Angelica Balabanov in Switzerland, had been taught how to carry out clandestine press work by a small group of Russian prisoners who were members of the Bolshevik or Social Revolutionary parties and were now working in Budapest factories. The leader of all these movements was Ervin Szabó; his right-hand man was the worker Mosolygó, who had come into contact with Italian revolutionary syndicalism at the Fiume torpedo works before the war.

49. S. Benco, *op. cit.*, Vol. III, p. 15, also believed that the announcement of a railway strike would have created a revolutionary situation, but the Austrian Social Democratic leaders did all in their power to prevent such an eventuality.

50. The strike was total, but it lasted for several days only in the mining district of Kladno. Cf. J. Opočensky, *op. cit.*, pp. 82 ff. The Reichsrat debate on these events made public the breach between the Czech and Austrian Social Democrats, each of whom charged the other with betraying the cause. Cf. the *Arbeiter Zeitung*, January 23, 1918.

51. Franz Borkenau, *The Communist International*, London, 1938. The German ambassador in Vienna reported on January 17 that 'the Czechs are still holding back, because they are not sure that the Socialists of Lower Austria will stand firm'. On January 21 he reported that the Czechs were still being cautious, knowing that if the mass struggle broke out in Bohemia its objective would be 'the collapse of the monarchy . . . They want to start the dangerous game only when they can be sure of success.' P.A.A.A., *loc. cit.*

52. *Protokoll der Verhandlungen, op. cit.* On Renner's ideas stated in his extensive writings, cf. J. Droz, *op. cit.* In *Il Lavoratore* of Trieste which on November 11, 1917, had greeted the formation of the Soviet government as a victory for the international revolution, Pittoni wrote on December 4 that in Austria the 'opponents of peace', in addition to the pan-Germans, also included 'the Czech and Southern Slav nationalists' who, while insisting 'that the right of self-determination of the Czech and Yugoslav peoples be an object of peace negotiations, do everything, even though unconsciously, to torpedo the latter'.

55. O. Bauer, *op. cit.*, p. 65. To his comrade J. Braunthal, Otto Bauer said that revolution was not possible as the Austro-Hungarian army was still disciplined and in the hands of its officers. Cf. Julius Braunthal, *Victor und Friedrich Adler*, Vienna, 1965, p. 254. On January 20, while the strike was still in progress, a meeting of the Social Democratic left wing gave its approval to Otto Bauer's platform of self-determination for all the peoples of Austria-Hungary, with the election of a constituent assembly for every compact ethnical territory and plebiscites for the mixed territories. Cf. the journal *Der Kampf*, April 1918. At Christmas 1917 O. Bauer had said to the secretary of the Hungarian Social Democratic Party, to his great surprise, that the break-up of the monarchy was inevitable, and that

German Austria would want to be incorporated into Germany. Cf. Buchinger Manó, *Tanuvallomás*, Budapest, 1936, p. 49. At the Christmas congress of the Slovene Social Democratic Party the supporters of an independent Yugoslav state were in a majority over the Austro-Marxists, represented by E. Tuma. Cf. the *Arbeiter Zeitung* of January 1, 1918, and Henrik Tuma, *Iz mojega življenja*, Ljubljana, 1937, pp. 363 ff. H. Mommsen, *op. cit.*, is illuminating on the influence that the Slovene Social Democrats had at the end of the nineteenth century on the development of the Austro-Marxist programme on the nationalities question.

54. J. Opočensky, *op. cit.*, p. 112; P. Molisch, *op. cit.*, p. 135. Hindenburg, referring to the Austrians who were opposed to annexationism, said at Brest to the German State Secretary: 'If they put up resistance, we shall simply enter Austria.' Cf. Richard Kühlmann, *Erinnerungen*, Heidelberg, 1948, pp. 516 ff. Kühlmann thought that in the event of an Austrian separate peace the threat might have been carried out. Czernin was convinced that it would be carried out, as he wrote to Tisza. Cf. O. Czernin, *op. cit.*, pp. 296 ff.

55. P. Molisch, *op. cit.*, p. 135.

56. J. Opočensky, *op. cit.*, p. 76.

57. The authority for this is the Austrian Social Democratic Party's own *communiqué*. Cf. *Mitteilungen an die Arbeiter*, No. 1.

58. *Ibid*. no. 2.

59. *Népszava*, January 22, 1918.

60. P.A.A.A., *loc. cit.*, Wedel to Hertling, January 22.

61. *Arbeiter Zeitung* and *Népszava*, January 22; Otto Bauer, *op. cit.*, pp. 65 ff.; Buchinger, *op. cit.*, p. 84. At the extraordinary congress of the Hungarian Social Democratic Party the leadership put through a resolution declaring that Freemasonry was incompatible with membership of the party. Some pacifist intellectuals who were Freemasons had been carrying out propaganda for continuation of the general strike. Kunfi, the deputy editor of *Népszava*, resigned from his Masonic lodge, but allowed the economist E. Varga to criticize the ending of the strike in his journal *Szocializmus*, 1918, pp. 417 ff. Another Social Democrat who was a Freemason whom the resolution was intended to embarrass was the journalist Diner-Dénes, Károlyi's adviser. A month later Diner-Dénes was arrested by the military authorities, but was released shortly afterwards. Cf. Wedel's reports of February 19 and March 14, 1918, in P.A.A.A. *loc. cit.* For some months the newspapers associated with Károlyi had in fact been calling for the ending, not only of the alliance with Germany, but also of the union between Hungary and Austria. Cf., e.g., *Magyarország* of November 29 and *Az Est* of December 6, 1917.

62. P.A.A.A., *loc. cit.*

63. Egmont Zechlin, 'Deutschland zwischen Kabinettskrieg und Wirtschaftskrieg', *Historische Zeitschrift*, October 1964, pp. 455 ff.

64. Bernard Stulli, 'Prilosi gradi o ustanku mornara u Boki Kotorskoj. 1–3 Februara 1918', *Arhivski Vjesnik* I (1958); cf. the proceedings at the sailor's trial, *ibid.*, IX (1967). Cf. also Richard G. Plaschka, *Cattaro-Prag*,

Graz and Cologne, 1963. Cf. my review of the latter volume in *Rivista Storica Italiana*, year LXXVII, 1964, No. 1. Three men succeeded in escaping to Italy by seaplane on February 3. Two were Poles and the third, Antonio Sesan, was a Croat from Dubrovnik. The Italian authorities interned him and delayed interrogating him. Cf. his account in *Gradja o stvaranju Yugoslavenske države* (1. I.–20. XII. 1918) eds. Dragoslav Janković and Bogdan Krizman, Belgrade, 1964, pp. 186 and 198 ff. He attributed the failure of the revolt to the counter-measures taken by naval headquarters at the Pola base.

65. J. Opočensky, *op. cit.*

66. Haase, the leader of the Independent Socialist Party, wrote this to a friend on January 20, saying that this was the German majority Social Democratic party's last chance of rehabilitating itself in the eyes of the Entente by a resolute struggle for peace. Cf. H. Haase, *op. cit.*, pp. 156 ff. Haase was persuaded of the possibility of a general strike in war-time by what he was told about events in Turin by a Soviet delegate on his way back from Italy. *Ibid.*, p. 151. The Budapest *Magyarország* on October 19, 1917 published an account of a conversation between its Lugano correspondent and an eye-witness of the Turin rising of August 1917.

67. *Die Auswirkungen der grossen sozialistischen Oktoberrevolution auf Deutschland. (Archivalische Forschungen zur Geschichte der deutschen Arbeiterbewegung, Bd. 4 I–IV)*, ed. Leo Stern, four vols., Berlin 1959, Vol. II, pp. 938 ff. Cf. now *Deutschland im ersten Weltkrieg*, ed. Fritz Klein, three vols., Berlin, 1968–69.

68. Walter Bartel, 'Der Januarstreik 1918 in Berlin', *Revolutionäre Ereignisse und Probleme in Deutschland während der Periode der grossen sozialistischen Oktober-Revolution, 1917–18*, ed. Albert Scheiner, Berlin, 1957, pp. 143 ff. At the proposal of Ledebour and A. Hoffmann, of whom the latter had been to Zimmerwald, the Independent Socialist Party leadership decided to declare a three-day strike for peace. At Munich the strike was led by Kurt Eisner, the future head of the Bavarian republic. Cf. his own account, in his prison diary, now published in *Beiträge zur Geschichte der deutschen Arbeiterbewegung*, 1967, No. 3. Cf. F. W. Foerster, *Mein Kampf gegen das militaristische und nationalistische Deutschland*, Stuttgart, 1920, p. 212; Allan Mitchell, *Revolution in Bavaria. 1918–1919. The Eisner Régime and the Soviet Republic*, Princeton, 1965, pp. 67 ff.

69. W. Bartel, *op. cit.*, *passim*.

70. Richard Müller, *Vom Kaiserreich zur Republik*, two vols., Vienna, 1924–25, Vol. I, pp. 98 ff. The author was the leader of the 'revolutionary' shop stewards among the Berlin turners. Shortly beforehand the Spartakist League, which consisted mostly of intellectuals who were followers of Rosa Luxemburg and Karl Liebknecht (both of whom were then in prison) had issued a leaflet calling for a mass strike to begin on January 28. Cf. the text which stated that the strike in Austria would be resumed, in Ernst Meyer, *Spartakus im Kriege*, Berlin, 1927, pp. 185 ff.

71. The Soviets of course issued strike appeals to the German proletariat.

But an author has also brought to light a leaflet addressed to the German workers and dropped by Entente aircraft, saying: 'Three days of mass strike and victory is yours.' Cf. Ernst Drahn and Susanne Leonhard, *Unterirdische Literatur im revolutionären Deutschland während des Weltkrieges*, Berlin, 1920, p. 181. The democratic electoral reform in Prussia desired by Bethmann-Hollweg and actually promised by William II had for some time been on the order of the day in the Diet which, however, again decided in July 1918 to emasculate it.

72. *Der Interfraktionelle Ausschuss, op. cit.,* p. 193; *Die Riechtagsraktion, op. cit.,* Vol. II, pp. 362 ff.

73. *W. Bartel, op. cit., passim.* News of the strike in Germany quickly reached President Wilson, confirming him in his view of the wisdom of banking on the German socialists. Cf. R. S. Baker, *op. cit.,* Vol. VIII, p. 513; House, *op. cit.,* Vol. III, p. 355; *Papers relating to the Foreign Relations of the United States, 1918,* Washington, 1933, Vol. I, Supplement 1, p. 45.

74. Thousands of militant workers were in fact called up.

75. *Der Interfraktionelle Ausschuss, op. cit.,* p. 242.

76. Protokoll des am 22 Jänner 1918 . . . abgehaltenen Kronrats, H.H.St.A.

77. *Ibid.*

78. *Ibid.* Cf. also O. Czernin, *op. cit., passim.* Cf. now W. Bihl, *Österreich-Ungarn und die Friedensschlüsse von Brest-Litovsk,* Vienna, 1970.

79. Cf. the Vienna newspapers of January 25. Not knowing what Czernin had in mind for the Ukraine, the Polish deputies again supported a vote of confidence in him. The news of the cession of Cholm led to violent protests by all Poles. There were strikes in Warsaw, Lvov, and Cracow. Many Polish legionaries hitherto loyal to Austria deserted. Cf. W. Conze, *op. cit.* When the Austrian government sought approval of military credits in the Reichsrat, the Poles, including those belonging to the traditionally pro-government parties, walked out. On the German governments during this period, cf. Karl Heinz Jansen, *Kriegszielpolitik der deutschen Bundesstaaten 1914–18,* Göttingen, 1963; also R. Kühlmann's memoirs, *op. cit.*; Friedrich Payer, *Von Bethmann-Hollweg bis Ebert,* Frankfurt, 1923; Victor Naumann, *Dokumente und Argumente,* Berlin, 1928.

80. Cf. Appendix II.

81. *Berliner Monatshefte,* 1937 (1) and 1938 (1). Cf. now Czernin's account in R. A. Kann, *op. cit.,* pp. 442 ff. According to F. W. Foerster, *op. cit.,* p. 240, Pichon, the French Foreign Minister, informed the Austrian Emperor through him that if he reorganized his empire on federal lines, giving satisfaction to the Slav nationalities, France would support the Habsburg dynasty. These soundings, however, were desired, not by Clemenceau, the Prime Minister, but by Poincaré, the President of the Republic. Cf. Raymond Poincaré, *Au service de la France,* Vol. IX, *L'Année trouble 1917,* Paris, 1932, p. 427.

82. *Berliner Monatshefte, op. cit.* Cf. now F. Engel-Janosi's account of

Charles I's peace efforts in the proceedings of the XIIth International Congress of Historical Sciences (Vienna, 1965) and his paper 'Die Friedensgespräche Graf Nikolaus Revertera mit Comte Abel Armand, 1914–18,' Vienna, 1965. According to what the distinguished Austrian historian found in Revertera's notes, Armand told the latter that the days of the Clemenceau Ministry were numbered and that Briand and Painlevé, who were believed to favour peace negotiations, might return to power. The possibility of the return to power of Painlevé, with whom he had been in contact through various intermediaries in 1917 (cf. *L'Allemagne, op. cit.*, Vol. II, especially, pp. 378 ff.), should have imposed extreme caution on Czernin in order not to compromise the latter in the eyes of French and British public opinion. Instead it was yet another factor in increasing the euphoria to which the impressionable Foreign Minister succumbed after the conclusion of peace at Brest-Litovsk.

83. Cf. now G. Ritter, *op. cit., passim.*

84. D. Lloyd George, *op. cit.*, Vol. V, p. 2,496. Cf. Appendix I on the Foreign Office documents now available at P.R.O.

85. H. H. St. A, Nachlass Mensdorff, 'Friedensgespräche Frühjahr 1918', Musulin's telegrams of February 17, ff.

86. *Ibid.*, Czernin to Musulin, from Bucharest, March 4.

87. *Ibid.*, Skrzynski's telegram of March 15.

88. *Ibid.*, Czernin's telegram of March 19. Czernin under-estimated the Italian claims, however. The German Foreign Minister learnt from a secret informer on March 19 and the following days that the Washington and London governments intended to secure from Vienna the cession to Italy of the Trentino and eastern Friuli. P.A.A.A., *Der Weltkrieg*, Vol. II, p. 71. Italy was in fact still asking for Trieste, but in return for it would have been willing at that time to give Austria colonial compensations in Africa and informed the Vatican to that effect. Czernin, not believing in an Italian recovery after Caporetto, failed to appreciate that this was Austria's last chance of negotiating.

89. On the position of the German Social Democratic majority, which was now opposed to the annexationism of the High Command but had not yet decided to break the 'sacred union', cf. *Der Interfraktionelle Ausschuss, op. cit.*; P. Scheidemann, *op. cit.*; also E. David's diary, *op. cit.* Scheidemann would personally have liked to vote against the Brest treaty (as the Independent Socialists did), but Ebert persuaded the party to abstain.

90. In the speech in question Czernin blamed the prolongation of the war on Entente annexationism and in particular on the propaganda of the 'wretched' Masaryk, adding threateningly that 'there are also Masaryks within the monarchy's borders'. Czernin was obviously worried by the information which (as appears from the Austrian and German records) was reaching him about the activities of the Czech *émigrés* in France and Italy. He believed these were being guided by Masaryk who, however, at the time was travelling from Russia to America by way of the Far East. In an attack on writers in the Entente press who had represented him as being in

conflict with the Berlin government, he disclosed, in an *excusation non petita*, that Clemenceau had enquired of him on what terms he would be ready to engage in peace negotiations, and he had replied that the obstacle to peace with France was the French claim to Alsace-Lorraine. (Cf. the Vienna newspapers of April 3, 1918.) According to Richard Fester, *Die politische Kämpe um den Frieden 1916–1918 und das Deutschtum*, Munich, 1938, p. 150, Czernin was so convinced of the success of the German offensive taking place in France (the first results of which were indeed encouraging) that he believed he would succeed in overthrowing Clemenceau. This was the excuse that he himself gave to Revertera, and his recent biographer (who, however, is a journalist and not a historian) Ladislaus Singer, *Ottokar Graf Czernin*, Graz and Vienna, 1965, p. 287, believes that he had been thinking about forcing the French to drop Clemenceau ever since Brest-Litovsk. But if he had considered the matter coolly, a man of Czernin's intelligence could not have failed to realize that a public attack on Clemenceau in Vienna would strengthen his position in France. Glaise-Horstenau, *op. cit.*, p. 206, takes the view, however, that the German government put pressure on Czernin to deny the rumours of Austro-Hungarian disloyalty to her ally. This assumption is confirmed by what Czernin himself said to Baernreither (cf. E. Kann, *op. cit.*, pp. 424 ff.) after the war. He admitted having made a mistake in mentioning Clemenceau, but said that he had to disown the advocates of an Austrian separate peace. What is certain is that, as we have emphasized, from the middle of 1917 onwards Czernin's personal position was supported by the Germans, while in Austria-Hungary he was losing ground to such an extent that there was talk of replacing him by Mensdorff or Andrássy, both of whom were regarded with disfavour in Berlin. Cf. Wedel's report, *cit.*, in P.A.A.A., Oesterreich 92, No. 1. The simplest explanation, however, is that given by Charles I's private secretary K. Werkmann, *op. cit.*, pp. 248 ff., in whose opinion the success of Czernin's previous speeches—he was a fertile and effective speaker—had gone to his head. A still more severe judgement is passed by H. Hantsch, *Oesterreichs Friedensbemü-hungen, 1916–18*, Brixlegg, undated. For Clemenceau's reply—to Poincaré's regret he published the letters that Charles I had entrusted to Prince Sixtus—cf. P. Cambon, *op. cit.*, Vol. III, pp. 239 ff. The French ambassador in London persuaded his brother Jules Cambon, the secretary-general of the French Foreign Ministry, to induce Clemenceau to repudiate Czernin in such a way as to render impossible British moves to secure a compromise peace, which he feared might be prejudicial to French ambitions. Cf. Général Mordacq, *Le Ministère Clemenceau. Journal d'un témoin*, four vols., Paris, 1930, Vol. I, pp. 272 ff.

91. Count Burian succeeded Czernin at the Foreign Ministry. His diary shows that since February 10, 1918, he had realized the necessity of choosing between a separate peace and 'the German adventure with its alarming prospects'. But on March 19 he had to admit that 'no one will now listen to the word "peace". Everything is based on the forthcoming offensive, as if everyone were entrusting himself without a tremor to that decision

of fate. The basic feeling is that *Ende ohne Schrecken* ['end without terror' —the words are in German in the Hungarian original] is better than *Schrecken ohne Ende* ['terror without end']'. On April 2 he too was momentarily impressed by what he considered Czernin's 'able' speech; only after Clemenceau's reply did he realize that Czernin had made a disastrous mistake. On April 8 he wrote: 'Now we are really tied to the fate of Germany, whether we want it or not . . . the vicious circle lies in the fact that the more Germany triumphs, the more difficult she makes peace by her policy.' That was the state of mind in which he entered office on April 16. He decided to attempt to secure a separate peace only at the end of the summer, when it was too late.

92. For this section I have relied on the Albertini papers and also those of Ugo Ojetti.

93. 'Not the least of the factors that impelled me towards the "renunciatory" policy was General Cadorna', Luigi Albertini wrote to Ugo Ojetti on November 12, 1920. 'On the visits I paid him at his headquarters he had occasion to tell me that he did not know the contents of the Treaty of London, that as Chief of the General Staff he had never asked for Dalmatia, and that he considered the possession of Dalmatia to be militarily useless and dangerous.' The Ojetti papers. According to what Albertini wrote to Emanuel on April 23, 1919, at the beginning of 1915 Sonnino himself did not want to ask for Dalmatia, but gave in to the arguments of the Italian navy. Then, with his well-known obstinacy, he made it a question of principle. In fact from the end of 1915 onwards he was at loggerheads with Cadorna; the Chief of the General Staff wanted to take part in strength in the principle operations in the Balkans, landing at Salonica and operating side by side with the remnants of the Serbian army (and later with the Anglo-French forces), while Sonnino wanted the useless Albanian expedition and had his way. Cf. Ugo Ojetti, *Lettere alla moglie, 1916–1916*, ed. and annotated by Fernanda Ojetti, Florence, 1964, pp. 138 ff. At the last meeting of the War Committee in which Bissolati took part at the end of 1918, when Diaz proposed giving up Dalmatia in exchange for Fiume, Sonnino and Admiral Thaon di Revel opposed the idea so vigorously that Orlando adjourned the meeting. Cf. L. Albertini, *Epistolario, op. cit.*, Albertini to Emanuel, April 8, 1919. Cf. also O. Malagodi, *op. cit.*, Vol. II, p. 464. The official report of the meeting not being available, we do not know whether it was pointed out to the navy that Yugoslavia, even if she were in possession of the whole of Dalmatia, could present no naval threat to Italy in the absence of the industrial and financial resources at the disposal of Austria-Hungary, and in particular the shipbuilding yards and torpedo works at Trieste, Pola and Fiume. Sonnino, strangely enough, realized better than the rest that after the end of Austria-Hungary (which for that reason he did not wish to see disappear completely) a new threat to Italy could come only from Germany, though he did not draw the conclusions from this that should have made him modify this policy. Cf. O. Malagodi, vol. *cit.*, p. 373.

94. After the armistice, when both Austria, now a minor state, and

Germany had been defeated and had become democratic nations, Albertini —to prevent the development of a revanchist spirit—favoured granting them the right to unite, and several times wrote to that effect in the *Corriere della Sera*. According to a letter of his to Emanuel dated January 24, 1919, he said so to Wilson in a conversation he had with the American President in Milan.

95. Cf. Salandra's confidences to O. Malagodi, vol. *cit.*, p. 381. For Admiral Thaon di Revel's position, cf. U. Ojetti, *op. cit.*, *passim*.

96. This was Albertini's opinion, expressed in his letter of August 8, 1917 (L. Albertini, *Epistolario, op. cit.*) to Salvemini who, however, since 1915 had taken the view, not shared at the time even by Bissolati, that Sonnino should be openly attacked. Cf. Salvemini's article on the subject in *Il Mondo*, February 9, 1952. His arguments were in any case carefully considered by the editor of the *Corriere della Sera*, who on September 9, 1917, in connection with the move for an Italo-Yugoslav agreement, wrote to Carlo Sforza, who from Corfu applauded the policy he had chosen: 'Perhaps it would have been better if I had done so sooner; but after the Corfu agreement it was necessary to take up a position without further delay.' In his *Vent'anni di vita politica, op. cit.*, Part II, Vol. II, Albertini reproached himself for not having had sufficient information in 1915 to raise the question of the inexpediency of demanding Dalmatia at that time.

97. Emanuel wrote to Albertini on January 21, 1918, that after the Russian revolution and the American intervention 'I believed I was best serving Italy's best interests by seeking closer relations with the Czechs and Yugoslavs, with Masaryk, Supilo and Trumbić. Perhaps the readier of the last two for an agreement with Italy was Supilo.'

98. A.S.M.E., Ambasciata Londra 1917. Propaganda yugo-slava, Fasc. II. Imperiali to Sonnino, May 24, 1917. This was certainly the moment when Supilo, who had resigned from the Yugoslav Committee, would have liked to return to independent political activity. To the deputy Giuseppe Bevione, whom he had met in Rome and who interviewed him in London in August, Supilo, though 'radiant' because of the Corfu agreement, said that 'all our actions should be directed to the attainment of a definite, unlimited and complete understanding with Italy', because 'there are only two powers in Europe who are directly interested in the break-up of the Habsburg monarchy, i.e. Italy and Serbia as the representative of the future Yugoslavia.' 'I believe', he said, 'that the Serbo-Croat-Slovene state, which has more need of Italian support than any other European power, must compensate for this collaboration with adequate concessions.' In reply to a question by Bevione, he excluded the possibility of the Yugoslavs' renouncing Dalmatia; he was evidently referring to Istria. Cf. the interview in the *Gazzetta del Popolo*, September 1, 1917. Cf. two letters from Bevione to Supilo in the records of the Yugoslav committee at Zagreb. In the first he thanks him for having agreed to meet him, and in the second for having arranged a conversation for him with Pašić, whom Bevione also interviewed. It appears from these letters that on this occasion Supilo also saw Gallenga-Stuart in London.

99. A.S.M.E., *loc. cit.*, Sforza's telegram of July 10, 1917.

100. *Ibid.*, Ambasciata Londra. Serbia, Fasc. IV. Sonnino to Imperiali September 11, 1917. On the Italian diplomatic attitude that emerges from these documents, cf. Angelo Tamborra, *L'idea di nazionalità e la guerra 1914–1918*, paper read to the XLIst Congress of the Institute for the History of the Italian Risorgimento, held at Trent, October 9–13, 1963, printed in the proceedings of the congress, Rome, 1965. Tamborra, however, takes a more favourable attitude of Sonnino than we do. Cf. in any case Carlo Sforza's memoirs, *Makers of Modern Europe*, London, 1930, pp. 152 and 295. Sforza accompanied Pašić to Rome and was disappointed at Sonnino's coolness. A year before Sforza too believed that Italian concessions to the Yugoslavs would be useless. (Cf. his report of October 21, 1916, from Corfu, in Sonnino papers.) He changed his mind, thanks to the attitude of Bissolati and Albertini. A desire that Italo-Serb conversations should take place had been expressed by Lord Robert Cecil during a recent visit to London by Sonnino and Pašić. Cf. *Il Secolo*, August 9, 1917.

101. L. Albertini, *op. cit.*, Part II, Vol. III, p. 235. Steed, in a letter to the *Corriere della Sera* in reply to an article by Andrea Torre that described him as a Yugoslavophile, though a friend of Italy, said that he supported the Yugoslav cause just because he was a real friend of the Italy that was fighting Austria-Hungary. In 1916, however, the *Corriere* still thought the time not yet ripe for an understanding with the Yugoslav Committee, which was claiming Trieste and Gorizia. But, 'because of its excessively violent language', it refused to print a letter from the Committee for an Italian Dalmatia attacking those who, like Salvemini, advocated such an understanding. Cf. the *Corriere*, October 7, 1916.

102. The *Corriere della Sera*, January 14, 1917. On March 7, 1917, it greeted the Russian revolution with a headline right across the page saying: 'Russian rising for liberty and for the war.'

103. *Delenda Austria* was the headline that the *Corriere della Sera*, on May 31, 1917, put on a message from Geneva on the significance of the Czech and Yugoslav statements in the Reichsrat. The message, and the editorial comment, contained a warning of the danger that the Habsburgs might regain the sympathies of the Yugoslavs by granting them a 'trialist' reorganization of the empire and take advantage of this to negotiate a compromise peace with the western powers at the Italian expense. That to Albertini the nationality principle was not just a tactical device to defeat the manoeuvres of the Habsburgs is shown by his campaign against blindly anti-Yugoslav Italian nationalism in 1919–20. The letters he wrote during the peace conference, when even Emanuel in Paris allowed himself to be influenced by Orlando's dispute with President Wilson, are admirable.

104. Cf. the *Corriere della Sera*, July 25–August 15, 1917. At first even Giovanni Amendola thought Albertini's stand for an independent Yugoslavia excessively audacious. Cf. the letters of August 8 and 11 in which the editor of the *Corriere* persuaded him to change his mind. For

the reactions to the Corfu agreement of the rest of the Italian press, cf. R. Vivarelli, *op. cit.*

105. Letter of G. A. Borgese of July 10, 1916.

106. That Paternò worked for Gallenga-Stuart's office is shown by his correspondence with Ojetti in the latter's papers and in those of Umberto Zanotti Bianco who, with Giuseppe Donati, was Ojetti's closest colleague in propaganda to the enemy in 1918. (Donati, the future editor of the Christian-Democrat and anti-fascist newspaper, *Popolo*, had been recommended to Ojetti by Salvemini. Cf. U. Ojetti, *op. cit.*, p. 515.) Emanuel also worked in London for Gallenga-Stuart's office, both in the propaganda to the enemy and in the press departments. Cf. L. Albertini, *op. cit.*, Part II, Vol. III, p. 256. Military attachés' reports and other political information that might be relevant to the conduct of the war went to the special office of the High Command.

107. Giovanni Amendola, G. A. Borgese, Ugo Ojetti and Andrea Torre, *Il Patto di Roma*, preface by Francesco Ruffini, Rome, Quaderni della 'Voce', 1919. The original of the Borgese–Paternò report, dated August 20, 1917, is in the Gallenga-Stuart papers at A.C.S., I, 39, Busta I. A. Tamborra, *op. cit.*, observes correctly that Borgese published the report under his own signature only in order not to involve Paternò, who was in the diplomatic service, in a controversy with the Foreign Ministry. For his activity cf. also G. A. Borgese, *Goliath. The March of Fascism*, New York, 1938.

108. As they soon realized, they also talked to some Yugoslavs suspected (and apparently with good reason) of being Austrian agents. Cf. Louis de Voinovitch, *Le Pacte de Rome*, Paris, 1920, p. 10.

109. In Switzerland Borgese and Paterno also saw the French historian L. Eisenmann, a specialist on Czech and Hungarian matters, and the Magyar journalists Vályi and Diner-Dénes. The latter was an old friend of Eisenmann's. Cf. his 'Fragments de souvenirs politiques', *Le Monde Slave*, 1936. Eisenmann remarked to Borgese that in Paris some believed that if Italian diplomacy 'wanted to prevent the union of the Croats and Serbs, it must desire a rapid peace with Austria, because only the preservation of Austria can prevent the formation of Yugoslavia'. Cf. G. Amendola, *op. cit.*

110. *Ibid.*

111. L. Albertini, *op. cit.*, Part II, Vol. II, *passim*. Borgese and Amendola regularly saw Orlando on behalf of their newspaper. When Caporetto put an end to the campaign against his domestic policy, Albertini saw him frequently too.

112. L. Albertini, *Epistolario, op. cit.* Ojetti himself noted on December 2, 1917, that both Ferdinando Martini and Badoglio spoke to him about their concern at the possibility that parliament might be inclined to a compromise peace. Cf. U. Ojetti, *op. cit.*, p. 432. That these fears were not entirely baseless is supported among other things by a report of the Austro-Hungarian ambassador to the Vatican, who some weeks after Caporetto had lively hopes of the formation of a Giolitti government that might be

[420]

willing to negotiate. Cf. also a telegram sent on November 14, 1917, by the Austro-Hungarian legation in Sweden to Czernin, informing him that it had learnt from the Dutch Minister that Marquis Carlotti, passing through Stockholm on the occasion of his transfer from Petrograd to Madrid, had told him that in the existing situation Austria-Hungary could secure peace with Italy *pour un beau geste*. H.H.St.A., P.A. rot, Krieg 25 s.t. Friedensverhandlungen. Lord Riddell, *op. cit.*, p. 291 states that on the same date Lloyd George was worried that Italy might be forced to extricate herself from the war.

113. House, *op. cit.*, Vol. II, pp. 276 ff.

114. *Ibid.*, p. 277.

115. *Ibid.*, p. 284.

116. H.H.St.A, *loc. cit.*

117. A.S.M.E. contains a great deal of information on the peace initiative of the Vatican, the Smuts mission, Wilson's peace feelers, and those attributed to Pašić. The secretary general to the Foreign Ministry, De Martino, proposed to Sonnino (cf. his report of August 14, 1917, in Sonnino papers S. 120. C. 32) to have an Italian diplomatic observer participating in the likely peace talks between the British, the French and the Austrians. In his opinion Italy would have been forced by the existing military situation to renounce some of its claims on Austrian territory. Sonnino, however, discarded this suggestion and refused any compromise. The correspondence between Nitti and Cardinal Gasparri, published in part by Alberto Monticone, *Nitti e la grande guerra (1914–1918)*, Milan, 1961, contains information about the Italian approach at the beginning of 1918. F. Engel-Janosi, *op. cit.*, Vol. II, pp. 337 ff., also discusses it on the basis of Vatican documents, and it is referred to by A. Pingaud, *op. cit.*, Vol. III, p. 352, who saw the Quai d'Orsay papers. Nitti made no concealment of the fact that he was in favour of a compromise peace, and said so to O. Malagodi, *op. cit.*, Vol. II, p. 269. Orlando, though he was the inspirer of all-out resistance to invasion, would not have been opposed to negotiations that secured at least Trento and Trieste for Italy, as he admitted to Malagodi, *ibid.*, pp. 252 and 350. In the Sonnino papers there is some information about the Vatican's claim (in September, 1917) that Austria would have been willing to grant some territorial concessions to Italy in exchange for some Italian colonies in Africa. It should be borne in mind that at the beginning of 1918 there were rumours in Paris and London as well as in Rome of another Austro-German offensive on the Piave. As for the anxieties that existed in the Italian capital about negotiations between Austria-Hungary and Serbia, these were reported by the German Minister in Berne, who had excellent informants about Italian affairs. Cf. his report of March 13, 1918, P.A.A.A. *Der Weltkrieg*. 2 Bd. 71. There is no evidence from any source that Pašić wanted such negotiations, even in a pessimistic mood after Caporetto and Brest-Litovsk. That he thought exclusively of Serbia, however, is shown by his reaction to Wilson's Fourteen Points. Though he criticized them for not looking forward to Yugoslav unity and the dismemberment of Austria-Hungary, he instructed

[421]

his Minister in Washington to ask only for American confirmation of the promise of Bosnia-Hercegovina that Serbia had been given by the Entente. Cf. the text in *Gradja, op. cit.*, pp. 44 ff. L. Mihailović, the Minister, however, being a resolute supporter of Yugoslav unity—he had met Supilo and Trumbić in Rome in 1914—made criticisms and informed the Yugoslav Committee of them, which led to his dismissal by Pašić some time afterwards. *Ibid.*, pp. 48 ff. Cf. also C. Jelavich, *op. cit.*, and I. J. Lederer, *op. cit.*, p. 38.

118. A. Monticone, *op. cit.*; F. Engel-Janosi, *op. cit.*, Vol. II, p. 337. Cardinal Gasparri's letters and his recollections of his contacts with Nitti and Orlando in Francesco Margiotta-Broglio, *Italia e Santa Sede dalla grande guerra alla conciliazione*, Bari, 1966, pp. 243–361. Nitti wrote again to the cardinal on March 30, 1918, suggesting that Austria in addition to leaving Italy with Valona, should cede to her the Trentino, Gorizia, Trieste and Curzolari, in exchange for Somalia and Benadir. Orlando informed him immediately afterwards, however, that he regarded negotiations as untimely in view of the German offensive in progress.

119. L. Albertini, *Epistolario, op. cit.*

120. H. W. Steed, *op. cit.*, pp. 459 ff.

121. Cf. the leading articles in *The Times* of October 27 and 29, 1917.

122. H. W. Steed, *op. cit.*, pp. 478 ff. L. Albertini, *op. cit.*, Part II, Vol. III, p. 253, wrongly dates it from January 14 and 18, 1918.

123. Emanuel to Albertini, January 21. I rely on this account, on a report sent to Albertini on February 10, and a report written by Trumbić, which is among the De Giulli papers at Zagreb, of which D. Sepić courteously provided me with a Croat translation. (I was unable to gain access to the French original.) On this, cf. also Trumbić's letter to Pašić of February 11, 1918, *Gradja, op. cit.*, pp. 96 ff. Emanuel said in a letter to Albertini of December 12, 1918: 'In view of Mola's position as military attaché and his consequent interest in ascertaining the possibility of Yugoslav co-operation for military purposes, I did not consider it necessary for him to have special instructions to take part in such conversations, which formed part of his normal duties.' Cf. in the Sonnino papers a memorandum of General Mola, defending his contacts with the Yugoslavs and asserting that he duly reported on them to the War Ministry.

124. Emanuel to Albertini, January 21.

125. *Ibid.*

126. *Ibid.*

127. Auguste Gauvain, 'L'Italie et les yougoslaves', *Revue de Paris*, June 1, 1919. 'Il retroscena del Patto di Roma', *La Vita Italiana*, July 15–August 18, 1919. (Cf. in the latter, pp. 120 ff., the first letters on the subject published in the *Giornale d'Italia* and elsewhere in December, 1918.) Attilio Tamaro, 'Il Patto di Roma', *Quaderni di 'Politica'*, No. 6, Rome, undated.

128. *La Vita Italiana, op. cit.*, pp. 120 ff.; A. Tamaro, *op. cit.*, pp. 14 ff. According to the Trieste nationalist deputy Giogio Pitacco, *La passione adriatica nei ricordi d'un irredento*, Bologna, 1929, pp. 137 and 167, both

Mola and Filippi were ardent supporters of the policy denounced by him as 'renunciatory', opposition to which caused him (in agreement with other Giulian and Dalmatian refugees who took the same line) to decline to take part in the Rome congress. The Sonnino papers do not disclose whether Orlando, to whom Emanuel submitted the report of the proceedings at the Italo-Yugoslav meetings, passed it on to Sonnino or not. But it is certain that Sonnino learned of the meetings, although not immediately. The Foreign Ministry official who followed Yugoslav affairs, C. Galli, *op. cit.*, pp. 295 ff., notes that he asked Sonnino in February 1918, whether Mola had acted under his instructions. The Minister did not reply, but did not show any great surprise. Senator Crespi, talking of what happened in Paris, where he and Orlando stopped on the way back from London, is even more explicit. 'Sonnino has arrived from Rome. Orlando has kept him informed by telegram of all the conversations in London, and his arrival shows his anxiety.' Cf. Silvio Crespi, *Alla difesa d'Italia in guerra e a Versailles.* (*Diario 1917–1919*), Milan 1937, p. 42. From the still unpublished notes of Imperiali it appears that the Italian ambassador in London reported to Sonnino on January 29 what he had learned about Mola's meetings with the Yugoslavs.

129. I have relied on the minutes of the proceedings enclosed with Emanuel's letter to Albertini of February 10, 1918. In his letter of December 12 Emanuel says that it was not Mola who spoke of the renunciation of Dalmatia.

130. Emanuel to Albertini, January 27, 1918. Cf. A.S.M.E., Gabinetto, Problema austriaco, a message from Imperiali dated January 12 forwarding a draft memorandum given him by Mola which Steed had drafted on propaganda to the Austro-Hungarian nationalities.

131. A.S.M.E., Cabinetto, T.G. Inghilterra. Sonnino to Imperiali, January 9, 1918. Cf. in A. Tamborra, *op. cit.*, Imperiali's telegrams to Sonnino of January 9 and 11. Sonnino similarly instructed his ambassador in Washington to express his dissatisfaction with the Fourteen Points. Cf. *The Lansing Papers, op. cit.*, Justus, *V. Macchi di Cellere all'ambasciata di Washington, Memorie e testimonianze*, Florence, 1920. A. Bernardy and V. Falorsi, *op cit.*

132. A.S.M.E. Gabinetto. Ambasciate d'italia a Londra, 1918. It should be recalled that Wilson's refusal to recognize secret treaties contributed to persuading Romania to make peace with the Central Powers. Cf. S. D. Spector, *op. cit.*, p. 49 ff.

133. A. Tamborra, *op. cit.*

134. *Ibid.*

135. Ibid. C. Sforza, *op. cit.*, p. 295, says that Sonnino used to say that he was like a peasant in the market-place who reduces his prices only at the last moment. The fact is that, as C. Galli, *op. cit.*, p. 365, observes, Sonnino, for all his undoubted culture, did not have 'much immediate political sensitivity'.

136. According to Aldo Valori, *La condotta politica della guerra,* the High Command, which in General Diaz, Cadorna's successor as Chief of the

General Staff, had at its head a man with a very supple mind, consented to the agreement with the Slav nationalities of Austria-Hungary because at that time it did not believe it could defeat the enemy in the field. At all events, A.C.S. Fondo Gallenga-Stuart, I. 39, contains a copy of a report (dated February 10, 1918) from Mola to the special office of the High Command on 'Austrophile trends in Britain'. In this the military attaché states that 'in view of the previous facts stated by me in another report', he had once more approached Steed with a view to persuading him to intensify the anti-Austrian campaign. As for the Yugoslavs, Mola states that they were not accurately stating the principles agreed on at the meetings he had attented. (We have not succeeded in tracing the previous report to which Mola refers.) As for General Alfieri, the War Minister, who had an acute political mind, in the opinion of a witness who was a loyal follower of his opponent (General Cadorna), Angelo Gatti, *Un italiano a Versailles* (*Dicembre 1917–Febbraio 1918*), Milan 1958, p. 237, Emanuel's letter of December 12, 1918, which we have already quoted, says that he was kept informed of the conversations in which the military attaché in London took part and had no thought—any more than did Orlando—of disowning him. Alfieri and Mola were in fact close friends; at the beginning of February 1918 Alfieri took Mola with him from London to the Paris meeting of the Allied Supreme Council which he wished him to attend. Cf. A. Gatti, *op. cit.*, p. 400, who, however, criticizes Mola for trying to draw Ministers' attention to himself. Alfieri was also on terms of close friendship both with Diaz, to whom Mola as head of a military mission was directly responsible, and with Nitti, who was certainly not an all-out supporter of the Treaty of London. Cf. A. Valori, *op. cit.*, p. 48. In Emanuel's opinion (letter of February 10, 1918), 'the Minister Alfieri, with whom Steed had a most interesting conversation, also fully shares the *Corriere* view'.

137. S. Crespi, *op. cit.*, p. 34. Orlando's journey had been preceded by some 'absolute priority' telegrams from him to the ambassadors in Paris and London. One of them, pressing for urgently needed coal supplies, was positively dramatic: 'The closing down of our military workshops is now no longer a question of days but of hours, and the effects would be disastrous, not only on our military effectiveness, but also because of the repercussions in the field of public order as a result of the great mass of workers who would be put out of work.' A.C.S. Fondo Orlando, undated, telegram, attributable to the end of 1917 or the beginning of 1918. Henceforward Orlando frequently sent telegrams directly to Italian ambassadors, informing Sonnino of their contents.

138. In regard to his anxiety, which was not without foundation, that Britain might easily have sacrificed Italian claims, Orlando, according to the information of the French ambassador, was reassured after his conversations with the Prime Minister. Cf. P. Cambon, *op. cit.*, Vol. III, pp. 212 ff. According to what Emanuel was told by Orlando himself, and reported to Albertini on January 27, Lloyd George did not conceal from his Italian colleague either the Smuts–Mensdorff conversations (which he explained as a manoeuvre intended to reinforce the pacifist trends in

Austria) or the fact that Vienna was not for the time being willing to make territorial concessions. In his conversations with the British Prime Minister, Orlando did not exclude in principle the possibility that Italy might agree to a compromise peace if her allies considered it essential, but saw no reason for Italy to modify her claims with a view to an eventuality that was not immediate. Cf. O. Malagodi, *op. cit.*, Vol. II, pp. 271 ff. But the conversations persuaded him to agree to Nitti's proposal that the Vatican should be asked to carry out peace feelers in Vienna. The Austrian refusal to make concessions to Italy at this point played into the Italian government's hands. Cf. now W. Steglich *ed. Der Friedensappell Papst Benedikt XV vom 1 August 1917 und die Mittelmächts*, Wiesbaden, 1971.

139. S. Crespi, *op. cit.*, p. 40. The note is dated January 27, but this must be a slip of the pen. The conversations took place on January 25 and 26.

140. *Ibid.*, p. 42.

141. Emanuel to Albertini, January 27. Cf. Orlando's account of his visit to London and his conversation with Trumbić, O. Malagodi, *loc. cit.* On this meeting, cf. also Trumbić's letters to Pašić and the Yugoslav Committee, *Gradja, op. cit.*, pp. 89 ff.

142. Emanuel, letter *cit.*

143. *Ibid.* In an interview in the Paris *Temps* of January 31, 1918, Orlando nevertheless held out his hand to the nations emerging from the ruins of Austria-Hungary.

144. Emanuel, letter *cit.*

145. Giolitti said to Malagodi that professors and lawyers when members of a government often made the mistake of trying to convince their colleagues or opponents by their dialectics, when what they should do was to make a decision on their own account and then impose it on them. Orlando was by profession a lawyer and a professor of law.

146. H. W. Steed, *op. cit.*, p. 490, and Emanuel to Albertini, February 19. Trumbić's translation into Serbo-Croat of Steed's letter is in the Yugoslav Committee's papers.

147. S. Crespi, *op. cit.*, p. 61. At this time Crespi believed Bissolati's position to be correct, as he thought that a revolt of the Slav nationalities of Austria-Hungary would spare many Italian lives. In August 1918 he still wrote (*ibid.*, pp. 147–148) that 'Orlando feels the necessities of the hour much more strongly, if only because he has much better contacts with the allies than those which the Hon. Sonnino has or has ever had', but that he did not dare replace his Foreign Minister, 'who to too many is still untouchable' and 'has the reputation (exaggerated in my opinion) of being a man of iron and great energy.' In other words, Orlando, though aware that he was living in a democratic age, at heart had a great deal of nationalist feeling, and he feared attacks by the nationalists, who used Sonnino as a shield. F. Martini's *Diario, op. cit.*, shows that in August 1918, Orlando wanted to replace Sonnino, but changed his mind when he realized that the Foreign Minister now had the support not only of the right, but also of the Giolittians who, though until recently they had opposed him, now

backed him because of their dislikes of the interventionism of the followers of Bissolati and Albertini.

148. A.S.M.E., Ambasciata Londra, 1918. Cf. Torre's telegrams to Orlando, *ibid.*, and in A.C.S.

149. L. Albertini, *Epistolario, op. cit.*

150. Borgese, writing to Albertini from Rome on February 1, 1918, informed him that Barrère was opposed to the congress's being held in the Italian capital. But cf. Camille Barrère, 'Souvenirs Diplomatiques', *Revue des deux mondes*, April 15, 1938, and above all F. Charlex-Roux, *Souvenirs Diplomatiques, op. cit.*, pp. 262 and 292 ff.

151. E. Beneš, *op. cit.*, Vol. II, p. 41, who, however, at this point, is not accurate about dates. On the formation of the Italian Socialist Union, cf. the *Anzione Socialista* of January 25, 1918. The greater part of the Serbian Social Democratic Party had remained internationalist and opposed to the war. Cf. *Srpski Socijalistički Pokret za Vreme Prvog Svetskog Rata*, ed. M. Todorović, Belgrade, 1958. The Yugoslav 'social patriots', however, had on their side the secretary of the Social Democratic organization set up among Serbs who had taken refuge in France, Aca Pavlović, who met the Italian delegates we have mentioned with some of his colleagues.

152. Cf. a note dated February 4, 1918, by Fournol, the secretary of the Comité parlementaire d'action à l'étranger, A.C.S., Fondo Gallenga-Stuart, B.–1. fasc. 1. Meanwhile Amendola also had urged Orlando to call the congress in Rome. Cf. the Albertini papers.

153. E. Beneš, *op. cit.*, Vol. II, p. 42. Cf. also the interview with Beneš in the *Corriere della Sera* of February 14, 1918.

154. L. Albertini, *op. cit.*, Part II, Vol. III, pp. 296 ff.

155. *Ibid.* Cf. also G. Amendola, *op. cit.*

156. Eighteen months later, in an open letter in reply to the *Giornale d'Italia*, which had accused him of having prejudiced Italian interests, Torre wrote: 'The Hon. Orlando, who had a conversation with Dr. Trumbić in London . . . then asked me to undertake the negotiations in which I took part . . . and put a substantial sum at the disposal of the committee . . . which the committee never used, because it preferred to raise the necessary funds privately among its friends.' Cf. the letter in the newspapers of June 26, 1919, in which Torre recalled having been praised by the Italian ambassador in Paris and, on his return to Rome, by the whole of the Italian committee. Albertini too could testify (cf. his letter to Emanuel of April 8, 1919 and others) that Orlando had told him many times in 1918 that he believed in the principle of self-determination of the nationalities. The funds the committee received from private sources were procured personally by Albertini, according to his letter to Salvemini of September 16, 1918.

157. Sir Campbell Stuart, *Secrets of Crewe House, the Story of a Famous Campaign*, London 1920, pp. 10 ff. The author was Northcliffe's deputy. On the corresponding American organization, cf. R. Mock and Cedric Larson, *Words that Won the War. The Story of the Committee on Public Information, 1917–1919*, Princeton, 1939.

158. Cf. the document, with Orlando's basically affirmative reply, sent 'urgently' on February 12 to Imperiali for Steed, A.C.S., Fondo Orlando. Cf. also H. W. Steed, *op. cit.*, and A. Tamborra, *op. cit.*

159. This was what Imperiali telegraphed to Orlando on February 13. A.C.S. *loc. cit.* Emanuel confirmed it in a letter to Albertini on February 19.

160. H. W. Steed, *op. cit.*, and Campbell Stuart, *op. cit.*, pp. 28 ff.

161. In his reply Northcliffe urged that the two alternatives could not be reconciled and again proposed that suggested to him by Steed.

162. O. Malagodi, *op. cit.*, Vol. II, p. 296.

163. Cf. the newspapers of February 13, 1918. In the debate that followed the deputy Bevione read out the text of the Treaty of London, which had been published by the Soviets. He defended the treaty but, in accordance with the Sonnino line, was opposed to any commitment to the destruction of Austria-Hungary. The Reformist deputy Ivanoe Bonomi followed the same line, thus differing from Bissolati. (*L'Azione socialista*, which was closer to the latter, criticized Bonomi's position in its issues of February 23 and March 2). The Radical deputy Agnelli criticized the government's dilatoriness in forming a Czechoslovak Legion in Italy. The socialist Claudio Treves applauded both President Wilson's Fourteen Points and the principle of self-determination of the nations proclaimed by the Bolsheviks and quoted 'the recent strikes in Germany and Austria' as examples of the struggle for a democratic peace. He also hoped for the success of the Anglo-Austrian negotiations which he said he had heard were taking place in Switzerland. In the subsequent debate in the Senate Francesco Ruffini argued the *Corriere* line, with the obvious approval of Orlando, who said that he wanted to 'remove the painful misunderstanding that had arisen between Italian aspirations and the feelings of the Southern Slavs'. Cf. the newspapers of March 5, 1918.

164. Imperiali's telegrams of February 13 and 14, 1918. A.C.S. Fondo Orlando.

165. A.C.S. Ministry of the Interior. Direzione Generale di P.S. Busta 48, serie A 5 G. Categ. A. Lett 5.

166. *Ibid.* A similar public security report from Paris on January 11 had stated that 'the majority French socialists . . . consider our national aspirations . . . as an imperialist movement to be pitilessly condemned' and that Socialist deputies were not hesitating to say these things at the Palais Bourbon. On that day a debate on war aims had in fact begun in the French Chamber, and the socialists had demanded a revision of these by the whole western alliance to bring them into harmony with Wilson's Fourteen Points. Pichon had replied that such a revision was impossible, allowing it to be inferred that it would be opposed by Italy. Cf. George Bernard Noble, *Policies and Opinions at Paris*, 1919, New York, 1935, p. 34.

167. A.S.M.E. T.G. Inghilterra, Gabinetto, Imperiali's telegram of February 7.

168. *L'Azione socialista*, January 25, 1918, and following issues. The Italian Socialist Union was joined by the reformist socialist party, the revolutionary interventionalist syndicalists and some independent socialists.

[427]

Its inspirer was Bissolati, who wanted also to bring in Mussolini, but he failed in this objective, because the editor of the *Popolo d'Italia* already had in mind ceasing to call himself a socialist, and was moving towards the nationalist position on the Dalmatian question.

169. I have taken this information from a long letter, dated November 23, 1960, which Edoardo Schott-Desico had the courtesy to write to me about these matters. Cf. also *La Voce Repubblicana* of May 4, 1960.

170. Thus in Schott-Desico's letter, *cit.* Schocchi had advocated an Italo-Slav understanding against the Habsburg monarchy ever since the Bosnian crisis of 1908. Cf. *Il Grido degli Oppressi* of September 5, 1918.

171. *Il Secolo*, January 15, and *Il Grido degli Oppressi*, June 20, 1918.

172. The Under-Secretary Gallenga-Stuart caused 3,000 lire to be paid to the delegates in London of the irredentist Social Democrats. Gallenga-Stuart to Imperiali, February 26. A.S.M.E. 1918. Ambasciata d'Italia a Londra, Miscellanea. Sonnino pointed out, however, that this delegation had no instructions from the Foreign Ministry. *Ibid.* Cf. the delegation's report to Bissolati and Gallenga-Stuart, A.C.S. Fondo Gallenga-Stuart I. 39, busta 1, Fasc. 5.

173. Cf. *Il Lavoro* of February 27 and 28, *Il Secolo* of March 8 and 15, *La Voce dei Popoli*, 1918, No. 2, and *Il Grido degli Oppressi* of June 20. Among the signatories were Lazzarini, Schott, Semich and Sestan for the D.S.I., Canepa, Arca, Mantica and Silvestri for the U.S.I., A. Pavlović and K. Novaković for the Serbian Social Democrats, F. Markić for the Bosnian Social Democrats, and the deputy Lupu for the Romanian Labour Party (which was not socialist). The Serbian signatories were disowned by their party leadership, which took a rigidly class line. Cf. the Paris *Populaire* of April 14, 1918.

174. Cf. the text in *L'Azione socialista* of February 16, the *Corriere della Sera* of February 18 and *Il Lavoro* of February 23.

175. *Ibid.*

176. Cf. *Il Secolo* of February 23, *L'Humanité* of February 25 and P. Kellogg and A. Gleason, *op. cit.*, p. 61. The representatives of the Italian Socialist Party at the conference (Modigliani and Schiavi) protested against the presence of the Italian Socialist Union delegation. The labour movement of each country should normally have been represented by its majority organization; thus in the case of Italy the Italian Socialist Party and the General Confederation of Labour. (Lodovico D'Aragona, the secretary to the C.G.L., in fact arrived in London on behalf of the latter on the closing day of the conference, and Serrati, the editor of *Avanti!* was later still.) The late Senator Alessandro Schiavi allowed me to see his notes (to be published in part in Vol. IV in the Turati-Kuliscioff correspondence edited by him). Cf. also the interview with Modigliani in *Avanti!* of March 11, 1918. The public security commissioner at the London consulate wrote a report on the Italian Socialist Party delegates. Cf. A.C.S. Ministero dell'Intermo. Dir. Gen. P.S.–busta 48 *cit.* They had the support of the pacifist leaders of the Independent Labour Party (MacDonald, Snowden, Lansbury) and of the French minority internationalists

(Longuet, Merrheim and Bourderon) and also met Errico Malatesta, Litvinov and Sylvia Pankhurst.

177. Cf. *Le Mémorandum des socialistes des Pays alliés*, adopté a la conférence de Londres, les 21, 22 et 23 février 1918, Paris, 1918. Cf. also P. Kellogg, A. Gleason, *op. cit.*, pp. 35 ff. The broad lines of the memorandum were to constitute the platform, not only of the parties of the Second International, but also of a substantial proportion of the non-socialist democratic left in Europe during the inter-war period.

178. *Ibid.*

179. *Ibid.* Cf. also the *Corriere della Sera* and *Il Lavoro* of February 25, *Il Lavoro* of May 23, *La Critica Sociale* of March 16–31 and April 1–15, 1918.

180. *Ibid.* The memorandum was sent and duly received, and was published by the Austro-Hungarian Social Democratic press. Cf. the reply, as well as that of the German and Bulgarian Social Democrats, in the *Labour Party Report of the Nineteenth Annual Conference, held in . . . Southport on June 25, 26 and 27, 1919*, London, 1919.

181. A. Schiavi's notes. Modigliani was violently attacked by the interventionist press, who accused him of having called for 'peace at any price'. Cf. his reply in *Avanti!*, April 10, 1918.

182. *Corriere della Sera* of February 25 and the *Azione socialista* of March 2, 1918. Cf. in these and in *Il Lavoro* of March 2 the interview with the deputy Canepa, who declared himself completely satisfied with the outcome of the London conference.

183. *L'Humanité*, February 27, and P. Kellogg and A. Gleason, *op. cit.*, pp. 63 ff.

184. *Il Lavoro*, May 23.

185. Cf. *The Times*, February 25, 1918.

186. A.S.M.E. T.G. Inghilterra. Gabinetto. Imperiali, February 27.

187. *Il Secolo*, February 5. Cf. the note drafted by Trumbić on the subject in *Gradja*, *op. cit.*, p. 79. The *Bulletin Yougoslave*, reproducing the letter in its No. 30 (March 10, 1918), took note of the change in Italian policy that was taking place and attributed it to the 'series of articles of remarkable depth and loftiness of spirit' in the 'great Milan newspaper, the *Corriere della Sera*'.

188. According to Borgese's report to Albertini on March 13, Torre conducted the negotiations with little flexibility. Cf. also H. W. Steed, *op. cit.*, pp. 490 ff.

189. Cf. the text in L. Albertini, *op. cit.*, Part II, Vol. III, pp. 268–269. The original of Torre's letter is in the records of the Yugoslav Committee. The Serbo-Croat translation is in *Gradja*, *op. cit.*, pp. 116 ff. On the discussions that preceded the agreement, the Albertini papers include two reports, that by Borgese referred to above and another by Emanuel, dated March 7, 1918. Trumbić's version is in Dragovan Šepić, *Yugoslavenski Odbor i Rimski Pakt*, Zagreb, 1966. Cf. now D. Šepić, *Italija Saveznici i Yugoslavensko pitanje, 1914–1918*, Zagreb, 1970.

190. L. Albertini, vol. *cit.*, p. 269. Torre, reporting the agreement to the

Italian ambassador in Paris, pointed out that in it 'there is no mention either of the Treaty of London or that of Corfu, nor is there any reference to any territorial demarcation'. A.S.M.E. Ambasciata Londra, 1918, Yugoslavi e Cecoslovacchi. Torre went on to praise Steed's intervention in favour of the Italian viewpoint; Imperiali telegraphed in the same sense to Sonnino on March 11. A.S.M.E., *loc. cit.*

191. Cf. various letters of Trumbić and his report to the Serbian government in *Gradja, op. cit.*, pp. 114 ff.

192. L. Albertini, vol. *cit.*, p. 268.

193. Cf. in the papers of the Yugoslav Committee a copy of Trumbić's letter to Torre, dated March 27, in which he informs him of the approval given by the committee. Cf. in A.S.M.E., *loc. cit.*, Sforza's telegram of March 26 from Corfu in which he reports that Pašić told him 'that the Torre-Trumbitch agreement was submitted for the approval both of the Serbian and the Italian governments and that he found it satisfactory and expedient'. Pašić, like Trumbić, was, however, mistaken in believing that the agreement was to be submitted to the Italian government; Sonnino would never have agreed to it. Actually Trumbić had some doubts, and before travelling to Rome asked that Orlando should publicly endorse the agreement signed by Torre. Seton-Watson, who was already in Rome, telegraphed to Trumbić at the beginning of April advising him not to insist on an official statement of this kind. Cf. the telegram in Seton-Watson's papers.

194. Cf., in the papers of the Yugoslav Committee, Torre's telegram to Trumbić (from Rome, March 21) informing him that 'the Italian committee for agreement between the peoples subject to Austria-Hungary has approved the London exchange of letters'.

195. Amendola wrote to Albertini on March 12 that 'Orlando and Bissolati, besides the two ambassadors, have declared themselves to be satisfied with what Torre has done; Orlando has renewed the commitment that the Rome congress *will be held*.'

196. For the history of this committee, cf. Pietro Silva's article in *La Voce dei Popoli*, 1918, No. 2, pp. 110 ff., as well as *Il Secolo* of March 10. Cf. also a circular dated February 9, 1918, signed by the chief editor of *Il Secolo*, Mario Borsa, appealing for people to join the committee. Various documents and letters concerning his participation in the Rome congress are in the Salvemini papers. Thus a letter to his wife of April 16, 1918 shows that the nationalists wanted to exclude him from the congress but failed to do so, because the well-known economist and radical deputy, Professor De Viti De Marco vigorously took his part.

197. G. Amendola, *op. cit.*, and the newspapers of the time. For the Romanian participation, cf. the contribution of A. Otetea, D. Berindei, E. Campus, N. Fotino and C. Muresan to *Oesterreich-Ungarn in der Welt-politik, op. cit.* For the Romanian Legion formed in Italy on October 15, 1918, cf. A. Tamborra, *op. cit.*, p. 218.

198. The resolutions adopted were published in nearly all the languages of the Austrian empire. The German versions are in *Konferenz der von*

Oesterreich-Ungarn unterdrückten Nationalitäten, Zürich, 1918. On how they came to be drafted by the congress, cf. F. Martini, *op. cit.,* pp. 1,145–1,146.

199. Cf. *Il Secolo* and the other newspapers of April 11, 1918.

200. *Ibid.,* April 12.

201. H. W. Steed, *op. cit.,* pp. 506 ff.

202. Letter of April 8, Salvemini papers. On the differences that also existed among the Italian nationalists, cf. R. Vivarelli, *op. cit.*

203. Salvemini papers. Letters of April 9 and 10. The Austro-Hungarian Minister in Berne in his report of April 24 on the Rome congress expressed a not dissimilar view of the Polish hesitation about making a definite break with Austria. Cf. H.H.St.A, I. Generalia, IX. 7.

204. Two accounts of these meetings are in existence; the first and more detailed is by Pietro Silva, in the Salvemini papers (used by A. Tamborra, *op. cit.*); the other, marked 'private and confidential', is in the Pontremoli papers in possession of Signor Eucardio Momigliano. This, according to his letter to Silva of April 13, 1918 (Salvemini papers) must have been written by Salvemini himself. There are copies of them in the Sonnino papers. The Foreign Minister must have felt that these reports, by his opponents, proved him right. It may be useful at this point to mention what Salvemini, whose chief concern, as is evident from these reports, was to make sure of Istria for Italy, thought on the question of Fiume. On December 15, 1920, he wrote to a Yugoslav journalist who had praised him that he must warn him that he had asked for Istria as far as Monte Maggiore but not beyond, while in the case of Fiume up to the peace conference he had 'maintained that it should be re-established in its autonomy guaranteed by Italy . . . After April 1919, I realized that an autonomous Fiume would be a hive of disorder and continual incidents and I became convinced that Bissolati was right in calling for its annexation.' Salvemini papers.

205. Ernest Denis, 'Du Congrès de Rome au Congrès de Paris', *La Nation tchèque,* October 15–November 1, 1918.

206. A.S.M.E., 1918. Ambasciata di Londra, Yugo-Slavi e Ceco-Slovacchi, Sonnino to Imperiali, who received the message on April 16. In his previously quoted directives of January 31 Sonnino had used the opposite argument. Then he declined to negotiate with the Yugoslavs, but did not exclude the possibility of doing so with the Entente powers. Shifting from one argument to another may, of course, be useful in the course of a diplomatic skirmish. What Sonnino did not take into account was the weight that President Wilson, who had not recognized the Treaty of London, would have at the peace conference. As for Sir Rennel Rodd's message cf. the text in Sonnino papers, S. 110. C. 8 D.

207. Cf. the statement, made on June 3, 1918, in L. Albertini, vol. *cit.,* p. 350. Orlando himself acknowledged that through Sonnino's fault the formula adopted was too 'cool'; cf. his letter to the Italian ambassador in Paris in A. Tamborra, *op. cit.,* p. 235. As stated by Bissolati in a letter to A. Thomas (of June 30, 1918, in Sonnino papers) the fact that the Croat soldiers of Austria-Hungary fought very vigorously on the Italian Front, strengthened Sonnino's hostility to the Yugoslav idea.

[431]

208. Cf. P.R.O., Political. Austria-Hungary 3135 (1918), containing the correspondence, the internal memoranda, drafts and other documents concerning the recognition of the Czechoslovak National Council.

209. *Papers, op. cit.*, 1918, Vol. I, Supplement I, pp. 795 ff., and T. N. Page, *op. cit.*, pp. 344 ff. According to the American ambassador, the Rome congress achieved much more than had originally been thought possible.

210. *Papers, op. cit.*, pp. 804 ff.

211. *Lansing Papers, op. cit.*, Vol. II, pp. 126 ff. On May 9, 1918 the head of the Near East section of the State Department, Professor A. H. Putney, who was in contact with the Czech *émigrés* and was aware of the decisions of the Rome congress, submitted a memorandum to Lansing in which he argued that the independence movement of the Slavs of Austria-Hungary should be used to neutralize the effect of the treaty of Brest-Litovsk. Cf. C. Pergler, *op. cit.*, p. 88. Cf. also Dragan R. Zivojinovic, 'The emergence of American policy in the Adriatic: December, 1917– April 1919', *East European Quarterly*, 1967, n. 3.

212. *Papers*, vol. *cit.*, pp. 803 ff.; R. S. Baker, *op. cit.*, Vol. VIII, pp. 136 ff.

213. *Ibid.*, p. 155.

214. *Ibid.*, p. 177.

215. R. Lansing, *Mémoires, op. cit.*, p. 241.

216. G. Kennan, *op. cit.*, Vol. II, pp. 99 ff. Cf. also Leonid I. Strakhovsky, *American Opinion about Russia, 1917–1920*, Toronto, 1961, p. 60.

217. According to G. Thunig-Nittner, *op. cit.*, about 35,000 Czechs had already enlisted by then into the legion. Cf. also J. Bradley, 'The Czechoslovak Revolt against the Bolsheviks,' *Soviet Studies*, October 1963; G. Kennan, vol. *cit.*, pp. 152 ff.

218. *Ibid.*

219. C. Pergler, *op. cit.*, pp. 47 ff.; R. S. Baker, *op. cit.*, Vol. VIII, p. 205. D. Perman, *The Shaping of the Czechoslovak State. Diplomatic History of the Boundaries of Czechoslovakia, 1914–1920. (Studien zur Geschichte Osteuropas VII)*. Leiden, 1962, pp. 339. Wilson and Masaryk had had an old friend in common in the person of the wealthy industrialist Crane, whose son was Lansing's private secretary. Cf. T. G. Masaryk, *op. cit.*; P. Selver, *op. cit.*, p. 196.

220. R. Lansing, *op. cit.*, pp. 242–243.

221. *Ibid.*; R. S. Baker, *op. cit.*, Vol. VIII, p. 232. The contacts made by Károlyi with the American Legation in Berne in November 1917, worked in favour of the Hungarian independence movement (cf. Appendix II) and influenced the Hungarian-born members of the staff of the American Committee for Propaganda to Enemy Countries. Cf. R. Mock and C. Larson, *op. cit.*, pp. 220 ff.; V. S. Mamatey, *op. cit.*, p. 269.

222. C. Pergler, *op. cit.*, p. 93. This statement was also drafted by Professor Putney. The Italian ambassador was told at the State Department that Lansing's statement was due to the Rome congress and to Masaryk's insistence. Cf. his report, of May 29, 1918, in Sonnino papers.

223. R. S. Baker, *op. cit.*, Vol. VIII, p. 378. Pergler was appointed diplomatic representative in Washington of the Czechoslovak National

Council. On Masaryk's activity in the United States, cf. now Vlastimil Vavra, 'T. G. Masaryk und Wilson's Administration im Weltkrieg', *Conférence Internationale du 50. anniversaire, op. cit.*

224. D. Perman, *op. cit.*, p. 37. The Czech Legion recruited in France—its strength was, of course, limited, because few Austro-Hungarian prisoners were taken in France—was sent to the front line at the same time. French recognition was, however, officially announced only on September 28.

225. H. W. Steed, *op. cit.*, p. 520.

226. R. S. Baker, *op. cit.*, Vol. VIII, pp. 485 ff.

227. The State Department reply was published in Vienna on October 21, 1918. The Austro-Hungarian Note accepting the American terms was dated October 28, but was signed on the previous evening. Cf. Jean Opočensky, *La fin de l'Autriche et la genèse de l'Etat tchéchoslovaque*, Paris, 1928.

228. Ministero della Guerra. Comando del Capo di Stato Maggiore. Ufficio Storico. Lieutenant-Colonel Giulio Cesare Gotti Porcinari, *Coi legionari cecoslovacchi al fronte italiano e in Slovacchia (1918–1919)*, Rome, 1933. Cesare Pettorelli Lalatta, I.T.O., *Informazioni Truppe Operanti.* 'Note di un capo del servizion informazioni armata'. 1915–1918, 2nd edition, Milan, 1934. Emo Egoli, *I legionari cecoslovacchi in Italia (1915–1918)*, Rome, 1968.

229. U. Ojetti, *op. cit.*, p. 498. A letter from Albertini to Ojetti shows that at that date Sonnino was still opposed to the formation of a Czech legion. Ojetti papers. In the following weeks he evidently resigned himself to what Orlando was doing.

230. Vlastimil Kybal, *Le origini diplomatiche dello Stato cecoslavacco*, with preface by V. E. Orlando, Prague, 1929, p. 169. Cf. of course E. Beneš, *op. cit.*, Vol. II, pp. 51 ff.

231. V. Kybal, *op. cit.*, p. 26. The Italian official recognition (October 3) was thus, according to Orlando, only a formality. The Italian government granted the Czechoslovak National Council a loan to meet the expenses of the legion, while the French government gave it a direct subsidy from secret funds. *Ibid.*, p. 138. This also emphasized the greater autonomy of the legion in Italy.

232. G. C. Gotti Porcinari, *op. cit., passim.*

233. Cf. the announcement, signed by Alfieri sent by the War Ministry on February 25, 1918, to the Prime Minister and Foreign Minister, A.S.M.E., Serbia, anni 1917–19. Fasc. 18. Sforza had previously submitted a request made by Pasić to this effect.

234. G. Amendola, *op. cit.*, pp. 119 ff.; C. Pettorelli Lalatta, *op. cit.*, pp. 228 ff. Of the pro-Yugoslav statements of September 8, 1918, cf. the vols *cit.* of L. Albertini and O. Malagodi; also R. Colapietra, *op. cit.* The statement was preceded in August by the 'controversy' between the *Corriere della Sera* and the *Giornale d'Italia* on Foreign Ministry policy. It was rendered inoperative by Sonnino's remaining at the Foreign Ministry. On the 'controversy' itself, which was desired by Amendola and also by

[433]

Ojetti, cf. the correspondence between them and with Albertini in the Ojetti and Albertini papers, as well as the works referred to above. As is correctly observed by R. Vivarelli, *op. cit.*, the *Corriere's* campaign did not achieve its purpose of getting rid of Sonnino, because the greater part of the press, including the pro-Giolitti press, took his part. The Giolittians, and the socialists, should have had more sympathy with the international democracy advocated by Bissolati, Albertini and Amendola, but still deeply resented their anti-neutralist campaign of the previous three years and, if anything, preferred Orlando. Incidentally, in 1917, when the Giolittians, hoping in a compromise peace, had tried to secure Sonnino's removal from the government, he had had the support of the *Corriere* and of Bissolati, who did not want the decision to go on fighting the war until total victory to be attacked in the person of the Foreign Minister. Cf. also the paper by Vittorio de Caprariis, 'Partiti politici e opinione pubblica durante la grande guerra' presented at the XLI congress of the Institute for the History of the Italian Risorgimento, in the Proceedings of the Congress, Rome, 1965.

235. The Austrian official history of the war states: 'An extraordinarily dangerous weapon, used to perfection, threatened the morale of the Austro-Hungarian army at the front from the time of the Rome congress.' Cf. *Oesterreich-Ungarns letzter Krieg, 1914–1918*, seven vols., Vienna, 1930–1938, Vol. VII, p. 19. Cf. also Musolin's reports from Berne on the Rome congress and its consequences, H.H.St.A, I. Generalia, IX, 7. The Vienna government asked Berlin to reply by organizing a congress of Egyptian, Irish and Indian seekers of national independence, but the Berlin government refused. *Ibid.* The German government placed its last hopes on the possibility of Italy's preventing the Entente from recognizing Yugoslav independence. Cf. the report of the German ambassador in Vienna of September 30, 1918, P.A.A.A., Oesterreich 85, Bd. 6. The ambassador now realized that the Habsburg monarchy could have taken advantage of this only if it had duly created a third kingdom of Yugoslavia to take its place alongside Austria and Hungary (as we know it was too late for this, apart from the fact that the Hungarian government blocked it to the end).

236. Cf. in the Ojetti papers the letters of February 23 and March 5 in which Albertini informed him that he had obtained from Orlando his appointment to head this new office. Cf. *Relazione sui lavori della Commissione Centrale di Propaganda sul nemico. 1 maggio–30 giugno 1918. Seconda Relazione sui lavori della Commissione Centrale di Propaganda sul nemico 1 novembre 1918.* Both are signed by Ugo Ojetti, the first as captain, the second as major. For purposes of Yugoslav propaganda, Trumbić went to the front several times, and was also received by the King of Italy and by General Diaz.

237. *Seconda Relazione, op. cit.* Cf. in P.A.A.A., Oesterreich 85, Bd. 6 Kroatien u. Slawonien, a report on the dropping of leaflets by Italian aircraft on June 24 at Zagreb and Ljubljana. The leaflets, which bore Trumbić's signature, announced the Italo-Yugoslav agreement reached at the Rome

[434]

congress and called on the troops to desert. Cf. now Márton Farkas, *Katonai összeomlás és forradalom 1918-ban*, Budapest, 1969, p. 96.

238. *Relazione, op. cit.*, p. 5. One of the most distinguished Hungarian Social Democratic intellectuals, Professor P. Agoston, who was serving as an officer on the Piave, noted the daily droppings of Italian leaflets in his diary, *op. cit.* on May 10 and the next few days. Those in German and Hungarian said that Italy was not fighting the peoples of Austria-Hungary, but only the militarism by which they were oppressed; those in Slav or Latin languages were incitements to national revolt.

239. C. Pettorelli Lalatta, *op. cit.*, p. 236; E. V. Voška and W. Irwin, *op. cit.*, p. 243. In October, 1918, when the Italian General Staff was still hesitating about launching the offensive, it was not for nothing that Orlando wrote to Bissolati: 'Certainly Italy is saved at this moment by its policy towards the nationalites.' Cf. Fernando Manzotti, *Il Socialismo riformista e la guerra '15–'18*. Extract of *Nuova Antologia*, 1963, p. 34.

240. U. Ojetti, *op. cit.*, pp. 540 and 554; Campbell Stuart, *op. cit.*, p. 44. Cf. also P.A.A.A., *loc. cit.* The number of Serbo-Croat prisoners mounted steadily. On the various Italian army fronts it increased between June 13 and June 20 from 786 to 9,433; between June 20 and June 30 from 1,409 to 6,761; from July 1 to July 15 from 3,199 to 5,648. Cf. A.C.S., Fondo Bissolati, busta 3, Fasc. 12.

241. For the mutinies begun on October 23 and 24 by Magyar, Serbo-Croat and Czech regiments and followed a day later by Slovak, Romanian and Ruthenians, cf. *Oesterreich-Ungarns lezter Krieg*, vol. *cit.*; Hugo Kerchnawe, *Der Zusammenbruch der oesterreich-ungarischen Wehrmacht im Herbst 1918*, Munich, 1921; Zoltan Szende, *Die Ungarn im Zusammenbruch. 1918. Feldherr, Hinterland*, Oldenburg, 1931; F. Julier, *op. cit.* This was the final stage of a process that had been going on for a long time. According to Hungarian military figures, in the first quarter of 1918 the number of deserters in Hungary and Croatia-Slovenia exceeded 200,000, and subsequently increased until reaching a figure of about 800,000. Most were men recalled to service of the more than 1,000,000 who had been released from Russian prisoner-of-war camps. Cf. the account of Ludwig Jedlicka, 'Der Untergang der Monarchie in Oesterreich-Ungarn', in *Weltwende 1917. Monarchie, Weltrevolution, Demokratie* edited by Hellmuth Rössler for the Ranke Gesellschaft, Göttingen, 1965, p. 214. Cf. also M. Farkas, *op. cit.*

242. On the revolutionary movements cf. E. I. Rubinstein, *Krušenije Austro-Vengerskoj Monarhii*, Moscow, 1963. Cf. also Henryk Batowski, *Rozpad Austro-Wegier 1914–1918*, Cracow, 1965.

243. Cf. *La Serbie*, March 9, 1918. One Budapest newspaper, *Magyarország*, reported the *Corriere della Sera* campaign on February 22.

244. Cf. *Il Lavoratore* of Trieste of February 27. The *Bulletin Yougo-slave*, No. 31, copied the news from the Ljubljana *Slovenski Narod* of the same date. *La Voce dei Popoli*, 1918, No. 1, copied from the Trieste *Edinost* of February 2 the news of a meeting of Italian, Slovene and Croat

[435]

trade unionists in Istria. Cf. also Igino Giordani, *La verità storica e una campagna di denigrazioni*, Trento, 1925, p. 19.

245. Cf. the text, with the names of those present, in *Gradja, op. cit.*, pp. 113–114. Cf. also A. Smith Pavelić, *op. cit.*, pp. 138 ff. The meeting, which began in a hotel, was interrupted by the police, who clashed violently with a big crowd that applauded the participants. The meeting was then resumed in Dr Pavelić's house. One of those who took part was the priest Professor Barać, who had gone to Switzerland in the summer of 1917 to meet Trumbić and was to repeat the journey in August 1918. *Ibid.*, p. 142. The presence of the Croat Social Democrats was partly due to the publication in the Zagreb newspapers (cf. the *Agramer Tagblatt* of February 24) of the memorandum of the inter-allied socialist conference in London.

246. Cf. the report of the meeting in *Arhivski Vjesnik*, II, 1959, pp. 281 ff. The view that Yugoslav feeling was now stronger in Croatia than the desire for any kind of 'trialism' has been succinctly but convincingly argued by Henryk Batowski, 'Die drei Trialismen', *Oesterreichische Osthefte*, 1965, No. 4, who notes that the situation was similar in Poland, where the possibility of an Austro-Polish solution had lost all its appeal.

247. At the Crown Council of May 30, 1918, at which Sarkotić and Mihalović, the Ban of Croatia, were present, Burian attributed the fact to the success of Entente propaganda. The Austro-Hungarian authorities in fact discovered that various appeals signed by Trumbić were circulating clandestinely in Croatia and Dalmatia. Cf. *Arhivski Vjesnik*, 1958 I, pp. 78 and 91 ff.

248. P.A.A.A. Oesterreich 85, Bd. 6, report of March 21, 1918. According to the German ambassador in Vienna, if the whole of Croatia, whose troops had fought enthusiastically during the early war years, had grown rebellious by the spring of 1918, it was the result of the short-sighted 'divide and rule' policy of the Austrian and Hungarian governments. *Ibid.*, report of July 11, 1918. At this point the ambassador considered it certain that the Serbo-Croat coalition at Zagreb was playing a double game. One of the delegates of the Yugoslav Committee to the Ojetti committee expressed a not dissimilar view in a letter to Salvemini of July 6, 1918, and defended the coalition for that reason. Cf. the Salvemini papers.

249. Cf. *Agramer Tagblatt*, April 11 and 16, 1918. The Vienna *Arbeiter Zeitung* announced the news more briefly on April 12.

250. *Arbeiter Zeitung*, April 14; *Agramer Tagblatt*, April 16. 'Seventy years ago', the Croat Pavelić said, in 1848 'the sons of our people met at Prague to save the monarchy. Today we have gathered to save ourselves.'

251. Walter Tschuppik, *Die tschechische Revolution*, Vienna, 1920, p. 48.

252. *Agramer Tagblatt*, May 2, 1918. Cf. the full text, *Gradja, op. cit.*, pp. 181 ff.

253. M. Gosiorovsky, *op. cit.*, p. 75.

254. The German ambassador in Vienna took a very grave view of the Polish participation. Cf. his report of May 17, 1918, in P.A.A.A., *loc. cit.* For the rest, he observed, reasonably enough, that the shortages prevailing

in Bohemia contributed to the mass success of the demonstration. Among the various accounts, cf. those in the *Arbeiter Zeitung*, May 21, the *Corriere della Sera*, May 20 and 21, *La Voce dei Popoli*, 1918, No. 4, *La Nation tchèque*, June 15. Some accounts, but not all, mention the presence of De Gasperi at Conci's side.

255. Cf. the text in Manlio Udina, *L'estinzione dell'Impero austro-ungarico nel Diritto Internazionale*, second edition, Trieste, 1933, pp. 45–46.

256. Letter of June 15, 1918. L. Albertini papers.

257. Enrico Tamanini, *Il Sen. Enrico Conci e la sua vita politica (24 giugno 1866–25 marzo 1960)*. *Memoria*, Trent, undated; I. Giordani, *op. cit.*, p. 20. Cf. also *Il Lavoratore* of July 17 and the *Arbeiter Zeitung* of July 18, 1918. The file on Mgr Endrici, the Bishop of Trent, preserved in Allgemeines Verwaltungs-Archiv, Vienna, Ministerium des Innern, Präsidiale, 22 in gen. Irredenta, 1915–1916, and 1917–1918, states (Prot. 7,065 ex 1916) that the military authorities removed him from Trent and restricted his liberty of movement because on August 18, 1915, he had declined to issue a 'patriotic' pastoral letter as the Austro-Hungarian command asked him to do; he had not done any propaganda for war loans or for victory, and had protected irredentist 'traitors'. General Conrad, noting (Prot. 22,683 ex 1917) that Mgr Endrici 'notwithstanding his puni-tive removal from the South Tyrol, obstinately maintains his anti-patriotic activity', in 1917 asked that he be removed from his see. Cf. Hans Kramer, 'Fürstbischof Dr Cölestin Endrici von Trient während des ersten Weltkrieges', *Mitteilungen des österreichischen Staatsarchivs*, 1956. Cf. also O. Regele, *op. cit.*, p. 431. C. Führ, *op. cit.*, p. 83.

258. Cf. *Il Lavoratore* of May 23, 1918, which defended Conci, arguing that the Italians of the Trentino could regard their national problem differently from their compatriots in Trieste. The struggle against Austria of Italian irredentists in Venezia Giulia, whether nationalist or democratic, and the story of the irredentist volunteers who made their way to Italy during the war and enlisted in the Italian army, form a chapter by them-selves which we leave aside in the present work. In any case, cf. *Il movimento nazionale a Trieste op. cit.* F. Benco, *op. cit.*, and G. Pitacco, *op. cit.*, on the subject, as well as Galiano Fogar, *Gabriele Foschiatti*, Udine, 1966.

259. *Il Lavoratore*, May 28, 1918.

260. *A Magyar munkásmozgalom történetének*, *op. cit.*, Vol. V, pp. 198 ff. *Oesterreich-Ungarns letzter Krieg*, *op. cit.*, Vol. VII, pp. 98 ff.

261. Burian diary, June 8, 1918. He added that, if the offensive succeeded, Austria-Hungary would herself be able to propose peace. 'In the event of the opposite, things will start with us. In the autumn the peoples will make peace.'

262. *Oesterreich-Ungarns letzter Krieg*, Vol. VII, pp. 241 ff. Cf. also A. Cramon, *op. cit.*, p. 165; L. Jedlicka, *op. cit.*, pp. 67 ff. A press *communiqué* of the Austro-Hungarian High Command, announcing the defeat on the Piave, put the blame on Czech and Yugoslav deserters who had given the plan for the offensive to the Italians. 'For some time', the

communiqué continued, 'the Italian army command has been trying to introduce treasonable activities into our lines. In the prisoner of war camps in Italy Slav soldiers are worked on with bribes and promises, in a manner forbidden by international law, to induce them to enlist in the Czech Legion.' The *communiqué* admitted that Italian propaganda had infiltrated into the Austro-Hungarian lines, inciting the Slavs to desertion. Cf. the text in the Vienna newspapers of July 28, 1918.

263. Cf. *Népszava* of June 20 and 28, 1918. Cf. also Andras Fehér, 'A magyarországi munkásság 1918 juniusi sztrájkharcjáról', *Párttörténeti Közlemények*, 1958, No. 1. Cf. also, in P.A.A.A. Oesterreich 92 n. 1 Bd. 25/26, the reports of the German consul-general in Budapest, who had been stating since the end of April that some Hungarian socialists were determined to call a political general strike at the first opportunity and were trying to reach agreement to that end with their Vienna comrades. For his part, the German ambassador to Austria-Hungary (as he wrote to the Reich Chancellor on April 19, 1918) tried to distribute among the Magyars E. Denis's book on the Slovaks and other publications from which it appeared that the Entente were planning the dismemberment of historical Hungary. *Ibid.* The majority in the Hungarian Lower House in fact passed an electoral reform bill that continued to deprive the bulk of the non-Magyar nationalities of the suffrage.

264. Cf. the *Arbeiter Zeitung* of June 2, 1918.

265. *Arbeiter Zeitung*, June 23 and 25. When it learnt about these strikes, 'the workers' council of Trieste, urgently summoned . . . on the evening of June 25' . . . expressed 'its active and fraternal solidarity with the proletariat of Vienna and Budapest for the energetic action carried out for the defence of its daily bread and for the attainment of peace' and proposed 'co-ordinated action by all the workers' councils in Austria'. The Triestine resolution (for which cf. *Il Lavoratore* of June 26) came late in the day, however.

266. Helmut Rumpler, *Max Hussarek. Nationalitäten und Nationalitätenpolitik in Oesterreich im Sommer des Jahres 1918*, Graz, 1965. Id. *Das Völkermanifest Kaiser Karls vom 16. Oktober 1918*, Munich, 1966.

267. *Il Lavoratore*, May 29, 1918, and following issues.

268. *Il Lavoratore*, June 6, 18 and 27, 1918. The debate went on for several weeks, speakers for the most part favouring Pittoni's argument. The spokesmen of pro-Bolshevik extremism also spoke in favour of it out of class intransigence towards the 'bourgeois' parties; the Trieste Socialist Party adopted it by a big majority, cf. *Il Lavoratore*, August 5, 1918. Nevertheless in the vital days of the beginning of November 1918 the Trieste Socialist Party, with the consent of Pittoni (who refused to make a common front with the pro-Bolsheviks), took a line closer to that which had been proposed by Puecher and accepted annexation to Italy. On subsequent developments cf. Dennison J. Rusinow, *Italy's Austrian heritage*, [*1919–1946*, Oxford, 1966.].

Notes—Appendix I

1. *L'Allemagne et les problèmes de la paix pendant la première guerre mondiale.* II. *De la guerre sous-marine à outrance à la révolution soviétique.* (*1 février 1917–7 novembre, 1917*), ed. André Scherer et Jacques Grunewald, Paris, 1966.

2. Cf. the original text in Prince Sixte de Bourbon, *L'offre de paix séparée de l'Autriche* (*5 décembre, 1916–12 octobre, 1917*), London, 1921. Cf. also G. de Manteyer, *Austria's Peace Offer, 1916–1917*, London, 1921. Cf. also Philippe Amiguet, *La vie du Prince Sixte de Bourbon; Lettres*, Paris, 1934; François Charles-Roux, *La paix des Empires centraux*, Paris, 1947. Cf. now R. A. Kann, *op. cit.*

3. *L'Allemagne, op. cit.*, p. 199. In his account of the Sixtus affair, dictated to Baernreither probably in 1920 (cf. R. A. Kann, *op. cit.*, p. 434) Czernin stated that he informed Bethmann-Hollweg immediately of the Entente proposals. In reality he informed him of them after the Austrian Emperor's brother-in-law's second visit, i.e. six weeks after the first.

4. *L'Allemagne, op. cit., passim.* Cf. W. Steglich, *Die Friedens-politik der Mittelmächte, op. vit.*

5. *L'Allemagne, op. cit.*, p. 199. The document was published in 1922, but here, inserted among all the other German documents, it assumes a more definite significance. It should be added, however, that Italy was informed of Prince Sixtus's mission belatedly.

6. *Ibid.*

7. *Ibid.*

8. *Ibid.*, pp. 204–206. The document (which was also published in the immediate post-war period) asserted the Bulgarian claims to Serbian and Romanian territory and said that negotiation for an economic and customs union between Germany and Austria (notoriously desired by the Germans) would continue.

9. *Ibid.*, p. 205.

10. 'Proceedings in regard to a separate peace with Austria', memorandum dated May 14, 1918, by P. M. A. Hankey, P.R.O. 1918—Political, Austria-Hungary, 3134. The memorandum should have been in three parts, but only two up to June 1917 are to be found there. Gordon Brook-Shepherd, *op. cit.*, p. 92, has seen the memorandum in the Beaverbrook Library. Cf. now H. Hanak, 'Government, Foreign Office and Austria-Hungary, 1917–1918', *Slavonic and East European Review*, January 1969.

11. *Ibid.*

12. *Ibid.* We mention the matter here only because of its connection with feelers for a separate peace.

[439]

13. W. Steglich, *op. cit.*, p. 148.

14. Friedrich Engel-Janosi, *Die Friedensaktion der Frau Hofrat Szeps-Zuckerkandl im Frühjahr 1917*, Vienna, 1966. Cf. the same author's *Die Friedensgespräche Graf Nikolaus Reverteras mit Comte Abel Armand, 1917–1918*, Vienna, 1965.

15. *L'Allemagne, op. cit.*, pp. 291 ff.; W. Steglich, *op. cit.*, pp. 146 ff.

16. *L'Allemagne, op. cit.*, pp. 296 ff.

17. *Ibid.*

18. *Ibid.*, pp. 339 ff. The Germans were naturally very well aware, not only that the Russian Poles would prefer being transferred to Austria rather than to Germany, but also that in the Vienna Reichsrat the Polish deputies from Galicia were opposed to the Kingdom of Poland, which was established by the Central Powers in November 1916, remaining under German domination.

19. *Ibid., passim.* Michaelis informed Czernin in writing on August 17 of the terms imposed by Ludendorff, including those concerning Belgium. *Ibid.*, pp. 347 ff.

20. *Ibid.*, pp. 378 ff.

21. *Ibid.*, p. 460. Cf. Armand's report, accompanied by the French documents concerning his mission to Switzerland in *l'Opinion*, July 10–31, 1920, and also W. Steglich, *op. cit., passim.* It was the head of the Deuxieme Bureau who informed Painlevé, the War Minister, that an army officer, Count Armand, had been sent to Switzerland to meet the Austrian diplomatist Count Revertera, to whom he was distantly and indirectly related. Painlevé mentioned the matter to Ribot, who was opposed to the step, which he expected to fail because of the Austrian reluctance to make concessions to Italy. Nevertheless, at Painlevé's insistence, Ribot at the beginning of August informed Lloyd George, who gave his approval, with the result that Armand met Revertera. In his opinion the conversations were abortive because of the Austrian refusal to negotiate the cession of Trieste, but the idea of a meeting between Czernin and a member of the French government was put forward on this occasion. The initiative for Armand's second mission, in February 1918, according to his own account, also came from Revertera. It was authorized by Clemenceau who was now Prime Minister, and his instructions were *écouter, ne rien dire.* This time Armand had the impression that the Austrian position had stiffened as a result of Caporetto and Brest-Litovsk. Cf. *l'Opinion*, of July 24 and 31, 1920.

22. *L'Allemagne*, pp. 375 ff.

23. *Ibid.*, p. 379.

24. *Ibid.*, p. 383.

25. *Ibid.*, p. 384.

26. *Ibid.*, p. 493. Painlevé remained Prime Minister until November 13, 1917. He was succeeded by Clemenceau, in whose Cabinet he was not included.

27. *Ibid.*, p. 520.

28. *Ibid.*, pp. 533 ff.

29. W. Steglich, *op. cit.*, pp. 224 ff. and 249 ff.

30. P.R.O. Austria-Hungary. 2864.

31. *L'Allemagne, op. cit.*, pp. 65 ff. Cf. also Eleonore Jenicek, 'Albert Graf Mensdorff-Pouilly-Dietrichstein', thesis for the faculty of philosophy of Vienna University, 1965.

32. P.R.O. Austria-Hungary. 2864.

33. *Ibid.*

34. *Ibid.*

35. *Ibid.*

36. *Ibid.*

37. *Ibid.* The genuineness of the British intention to preserve Austria at that time is also shown by the comment of Sir Charles Hardinge, Permanent Under-Secretary in the Foreign Office, on a request submitted to him by Beneš at the end of October 1917. Beneš wanted a declaration assuring the Czechs that it was not the Entente intention to keep Austria-Hungary unchanged. Hardinge expressed sympathy with the principle of self-government for minor nationalities, but said that 'the geographical position of Bohemia is an almost insurmountable stumbling-block'. Cf. also J. R. M. Butler, *Lord Lothian (Philip Kerr), 1882–1940*, London, 1960.

38. P.R.O. Austria-Hungary. 2864. Telegrams of December 23 and 24, 1917.

39. *Ibid.* P.R.O. Austria-Hungary. 2864, telegrams of December 23 and 24, 1917.

40. E. Jenicek, *op. cit.*, pp. 177 ff.; memorandum from Mensdorff to Czernin. Smuts urged on Mensdorff that at least the Trentino should be yielded, but the latter's instructions made it impossible for him to give any undertaking in the matter. *Ibid.*, pp. 239 ff. In retrospect, in September 1918, Mensdorff bitterly regretted in his diary that no notice had been taken of Smuts's suggestion of a federal reorganization of Austria (which Charles I, not uninfluenced by him, was proposing to carry out now, when it was too late) and that the last favourable opportunity of making peace between the Habsburg monarchy and the Entente had been thrown away. *Ibid.*, p. 205. On January 9, 1919, he concluded retrospectively in his diary: 'With us the chief blame attaches to the German Austrian politicians and the Hungarian statesmen who were in the grip of incomprehensible illusions and megalomania. In the face of this madness and deep-rooted arrogance no emperor and no statesman could have imposed the negotiation of a reasonable peace settlement or overcome the implacable resistance of the proud and ignorant German military.' *Ibid.*, pp. 209–210.

41. P.R.O. Austria-Hungary. 3133. Telegram of Sir Horace Rumbold, January 13, 1918.

42. *Ibid.* Telegram of March 2.

43. Balfour's telegram and note of March 6.

44. *Ibid.* Telegram of March 12.

45. *Ibid.* Sir Horace Rumbold's telegram of March 25.

46. *Ibid.*

47. *Ibid.* Telegram of March 27.

48. D. Lloyd George, *op. cit.*, Vol. V, pp. 2502 ff.

Notes—Appendix II

1. Heinrich Benedikt, *Dir Friedensaktion der Meinlgruppe 1917–18. Die Bemühungen um einen Verständigungsfrieden nach Dokumenten, Aktenstücken und Briefen*, Graz and Cologne, 1962, p. 308. Benedikt's observation obviously refers to the latest life of the last Emperor of Austria, Reinhold Lorenz, *Kaiser Karl und der Untergang der Donaumonarchie*, Graz, 1959, the tendency of which is to condemn all moves for a separate peace.

2. Magda Lammasch, Hans Sperl (and others), *Heinrich Lammasch. Seine Aufzeichnungen, sein Wirken and seine Politik*, Vienna, 1922. A German account of the Herron–Lammasch conversations is included in the report of the parliamentary inquiry *Die Ursachen des deutschen Zusammenbruchs im Jahre 1918*, twelve vols., Berlin, 1925–29, Vol. II, p. 147. Cf. also Benno Mayer, 'Lammasch als Politiker', thesis for the faculty of philosophy of Vienna University, 1941.

3. Stephen Osusky, 'The Secret Peace Negotiations between Vienna and Washington', *Slavonic Review*, March 1926; Conrad Haussmann, *Journal d'un député au Reichstag*, Paris, 1928; Mitchell Pirie Briggs, *George D. Herron and the European Settlement*, Stanford, 1932: Ralph Haswell Lutz, *Documents on the German Revolution. Fall of the German Empire 1914–1918*, two vols., Stanford, 1932, Vol. I, pp. 49 ff.; *Papers relating to the Foreign Relations of the United States. 1917*, Vol. I, Supplement 2, Washington 1932, and *1918*, Vol. I, Supplement I, Washington, 1933. Cf. also *The Lansing Papers, op. cit.* and Ray Stannard Baker, *Woodrow Wilson, op. cit.*, which confirm that President Wilson attached great importance to Herron's reports. Cf. also Hugh R. Wilson, *Diplomat between Wars*, New York, 1941; *The War Memoirs of William Graves Sharp, American Ambassador to France. 1914–1918*, London, 1931; F. W. Foerster, *Mein Kampf gegen das militaristische und nationalistische Deutschland*, Stuttgart, 1920, and *Erlebte Weltgeschichte 1869–1953. Memoiren*, Nuremburg, 1953; Victor Naumann, *Dokumente und Argumente*, Berlin, 1928.

4. I am obliged to Mrs Arline Paul, head of the reference department of the Hoover Institution, Stanford, N.J., who in 1961 provided me with photocopies of the Herron papers.

5. H. Benedikt, *op. cit.*, pp. 14–20.

6. Cfr. Károlyi Mihály, *Egy egész világ ellen, op. cit.*; and the same author's *Faith without illusion, op. cit.* Charles I said to Károlyi when he received him in audience on March 22: 'I am determined to end the war in the course of 1917.'

7. H. Benedikt, *op. cit.*, pp. 89 ff.

8. For the federal plan of 1871, cf. Karl Friedrich Hugelmann, *Das Nationalitätenrecht des alten Oesterreich*, two vols., Vienna, undated; Eduard Wertheimer, *Graf Julius Andrássy, sein Leben und seine Zeit*, three vols., Stuttgart, 1910–13.

9. On Lammasch's proposals to Francis Ferdinand, which Czernin opposed, cf. *M. Lammasch, op. cit.*, pp. 84 ff., and Robert A. Kann, 'Count Ottokar Czernin and Archduke Francis Ferdinand', *Journal of Central European Affairs*, July 1956.

10. A. Polzer-Hoditz, *op. cit.* Felix Höglinger, *Ministerpräsident Heinrich Graf Clam-Martinic*, Graz and Cologne, 1967.

11. Redlich and Meinl (particularly the former) were on terms of friendship with a friend of Károlyi's, Jószef Diner-Dénes who, as the Budapest correspondent of the Social Democratic *Arbeiterzeitung* of Vienna and as a cultured, able and open-minded individual had the *entrée* to the most varied circles in Vienna, including highly placed ones. Diner-Dénes put Károlyi in contact with the leaders of the Hungarian Slovak National Party. Károlyi's papers confirm, however, that, because of the nationalism of even the left wing of the Magyar independence movement, their contact with the Slovaks, and with the Romanians of Transylvania, took shape only at the beginning of the autumn of 1918, when it was too late.

12. Letter of November 29, 1919.

13. Robert Danneberg, one of the young Austrian Social Democratic leaders who then belonged to the left wing, wrote to Karl Kautsky on April 13, 1917 that 'here the most romantic rumours about peace have been current for several days, on the whole they are believed. The desire for peace is extraordinarily great in all circles. But nowhere is there to be seen any trace of a political will'. Kautsky papers (D. VII, 306), at the International Institute of Social History, Amsterdam.

14. H. Benedikt, *op. cit.*, pp. 95–111.

15. *Ibid.*, p. 114.

16. *Das politische Tagebuch J. Redlichs, op. cit.*, Vol. II, pp. 216–218.

17. R. Lorenz, *op. cit.*, p. 383.

18. F. W. Foerster, *Memoiren, op. cit.*, pp. 209 and 237.

19. H. Benedikt, *op. cit.*, pp. 127–129. B. Mayer, *op. cit.*, pp. 35 ff., reproduces a letter from Lammasch to Polzer-Hoditz of July 29, 1917, and summarizes another (unpublished) letter of the following day from which it appears that Lammasch declined the appointment among other things because his speech of June 28 in the Upper House on the necessity of a peace of conciliation, based on the right to national self-determination kept within reasonable limits, had not found favour on either side.

20. *Das politische Tagebuch, op. cit.*, Vol. II, pp. 230 ff.

21. H. Benedikt, *op. cit.*, pp. 133 and 196. On Lord Lansdowne's activities, cf. Kent Forster, *The Failures of Peace. The Search for a Negotiated Peace during the First World War*, Washington, 1941. Balfour, the British Foreign Secretary, wrote to Lord Lansdowne on November 16, 1917,

assuring him that he favoured neither the dismemberment of Germany nor of Austria-Hungary. Cf. Blanche E. C. Dugadale, *Arthur James Balfour*, two vols., London, 1936, Vol. II, pp. 147 ff. Cf. also Rodney O. Davis, 'Lloyd George, Leader or Led in British War Aims', *Essays in Honour of Eber Malcolm Carroll*, Durham, 1959.

22. Friedrich Engel-Janosi, *Oesterreich und der Vatikan, op. cit.*

23. Letter to Lammasch of August 28, 1917, reproduced in H. Benedikt, *op. cit.*, p. 151. Though Lammasch, according to Herron, was convinced of the supreme importance of reaching an agreement with Italy, the utmost he was willing to concede in February 1918 was a plebiscite in the Trentino and the turning of Trieste into an international free port. Cf. M. Lammasch, *op. cit.*, p. 191.

24. P.R.O. Austria-Hungary. 2862. Report of the British consul-general at Zürich. A.D.M.A.E. Direction Affaires Politiques—guerre 1914. Autriche-Hongrie. Report from Zürich of August 29, 1917. Cf. also *l'Opinion* of January 24, 1920.

25. For his life, cf. M. P. Briggs, *op. cit.*, James Dombrowski, *The early days of Christian Socialism in America*, New York, 1936. Cf. also a biographical sketch by the Hungarian revolutionary syndicalist Oedön Pór who became a friend of his when living in the United States (between 1903 and 1905) and saw a great deal of him in Italy, where both went to live. Pór intended it to be printed as a preface to the Hungarian translation, edited by himself, of a pamphlet of Herron's (entitled in the original *From Revolution to Revolution*) on the Paris Commune. It was, however, published in Budapest in 1905 with a historico-political introduction by Ervin Szabó, the well-known theorist of Hungarian revolutionary syndicalism. Cf. the biographical sketch in Pór's letter to Szabó (dated New York, July 13, 1904, published in *Acta Historica*, 1963, Vol. IX, Nos. 1–2, pp. 190–191). Pór there describes Herron as a man of exceptional gifts who 'influences both the spirit and the intellect'. Herron subsequently several times sent funds through Pór to the Hungarian socialist student movement. Later Pór began to have doubts about Herron. On January 17, 1907, he described him in a letter to E. Szabó from Florence as 'one of the most complicated of men . . . he likes lying like an elementary schoolboy . . . but when he is in action he dares express the strongest truths. Double personality'. Cf. Pór's letters in *Párttörténeti Közlemenyek*, 1965-No. 2. Herron's Hungarian contacts (his fine villa at Fiesole was restored with the co-operation of the great Hungarian sculptor M. Vedres) are referred to by Alexander Bernhard, 'Der Amerikaner Herron', *Pester Lloyd*, August 6, 1922.

26. *Die Zimmerwalder Bewegung, op. cit.*, Vol. II. R. Rolland was aware of these pro-Zimmerwaldian payments, and noted their inconsistency with Herron's interventionism. Cf. Romain Rolland, *Diario degli anni di guerra. 1914–1919*, Milan and Florence, Vol. I, p. 766. The sum of 100 Swiss francs may seem small nowadays, but it was the monthly subscription that a mass party such as the Italian Socialist Party paid to the International Socialist Commission of which it was *magna pars*. We may

note that Herron was introduced to Grimm by the Italian socialist Edmondo Peluso, who was an *émigré* in Switzerland. Cf. in *Die Zimmerwalder Bewegung, op. cit.*, Vol. II. Peluso's letters of May 15 and July 1, 1916; the latter mentions Herron's offer to make a monthly payment of the above-mentioned amount.

27. *Die Zimmerwalder Bewegung, op. cit.*, Vol. II.

28. *Ibid.*

29. *Journal de Genève*, June 28, 1916. Incidentally, the conference of the Union des Nationalités was a fiasco. Peluso himself describes it as such in his letter to Grimm of July 1, 1916, referred to above, and adds that Herron was very disappointed. On the Union des Nationalités, cf. now Marc Ferro, 'La politique des nationalités du gouvernement provisoire', *Cahiers du monde russe et soviétique*, 1961, No. 2.

30. *Journal de Genève*, December 31, 1916. The same ideas reappear in G. D. Herron's pamphlet *La minaccia della pace germanica*, Florence 1917. For a sharp criticism of Herron's missionary warmongering, see R. Rolland, *op. cit.*, Vol. II.

31. F. W. Foerster, *op. cit.*, p. 195.

32. New York, 1917. Of this work President Wilson wrote to a friend on October 1, 1917, that he had read it 'with the deepest appreciation of Mr Herron's insight into all the elements of a complicated situation and into my own motives and purposes'. Cf. the letter in R. S. Baker, *op. cit.*, Vol. VII, p. 228. Cf. also H. Benedikt, *op. cit.*, pp. 145–146.

33. M. P. Briggs, *op. cit., passim.*

34. The correspondence with the two Italian diplomatists is in the Herron papers (Vol. VI, Italy), and runs from December 19, 1916, to the end of the war. Herron shows himself in his letters to have been a warm friend of Italy, even during the Versailles conference. In opposition to the American delegation and in disagreement with President Wilson, he emphasized the vital part in winning the war played by the Italian intervention and the consequent allied obligation to meet Italian demands. Cf. also George D. Herron, *Der Pariser Frieden und die Jugend Europas*, Berlin, 1920, which is an attack on the imperialist aspects of the peace treaties as the precursors of new wars, granting extenuating circumstances only to Italy, to the underlying Mazzinian spirit of which he appeals, and in spite of all disappointments, to President Wilson. At the end of 1920 Herron went to Italy on a study trip, and was received by the King and by Count Sforza. He was favourably impressed by the policy of Giolitti's last government. Cf. his notes, *loc. cit.*, on his conversations in Italy, and his book, G. D. Herron, *The Revival of Italy*, London, 1922.

35. Paulucci had the reputation of being a man of great perspicacity and ability. According to the foreign editor of the *Journal de Genève*, who was appointed Swiss Minister in Italy in 1918, he drew the attention of his superiors in 1917 to the transfer of German troops to the south and foresaw that they would be used in a big offensive on the Italian front. Cf. Georges Wagnière, *Dix-huit ans à Rome. Guerre mondiale et fascisme. 1918–1936*, Geneva, undated (but published in 1944), p. 29.

36. Herron papers, *loc. cit.*, Doc. III.
37. H. Benedikt, *op. cit.*, p. 157.
38. *Papers, op. cit.*, Supplement 2 pp. 225 ff.
39. H. Benedikt, *op. cit.*, p. 148.
40. Prince Sixte, *L'Offre de paix séparée de l'Autriche, op. cit.*, pp. 166 ff.
41. R. A. Kann, *Die Sixtus-Affäre*, Vienna, 1966.
42. *L'Allemagne, op. cit.*, Vol. II, pp. 55 and 61–65.
43. H.H.St.A, Politisches Archiv–Krieg–25t.–rot–u. 146. The recipient of the preceding telegram informed Czernin that in the middle of the month the former German Chancellor Prince Bülow was going to meet Italian personalities at Lucerne. According to the Germans, cf. *L'Allemagne, op. cit.*, p. 61, the Italian approach was made by one Carbone. A Captain Carbone was a member of the Italian military mission to Vienna in 1919.
44. H.H.St.A, Pol. Ar ch.–Krieg 25–s.t.
45. *Ibid.*, 25–S. 148.
46. *Ibid.*, 118, 128.
47. *Ibid.*, 124.
48. *Ibid.*, 118.
49. Cf. the text in the Vienna newspapers of January 25, 1918. We quote from the *Arbeiterzeitung.* Cf. in the issue of January 26 the reply of the spokesman of the Social Democratic parliamentary group, W. Ellenbogen, who deplored the 'victor's tone' used by Czernin in relation to the Italians and wanted 'negotiations with Italy to be conducted in a conciliatory spirit'.
50. *Comando Supremo dell'Esercito. Servizio Informazioni. Segreto. Pubblicazione n. 3. (Serie verde). Propaganda palese ed approcci clandestini per la pace nella primavera del 1917–30 giugno, 1917*, Rome 1919 (reprinted) cf. p. 16.
51. *Ibid., Pubblicazione n. 4 (Serie verde), luglio 1917–novembre 1918*, Rome 1918, cf. pp. 20 ff.
52. *Ibid.*, pp. 23–24. Diner-Dénes, however, according to his own account, met G. A. Borgese and Marquis F. Gentili-Farinola of Florence, in Switzerland. The latter was believed to be a supporter of Giolitti's. Cf. *Fragments, op. cit.*, pp. 107–115.
53. *Pubblicazione n. 4. op. cit.*, p. 36. The pamphlet to which the Italian informant refers is G. D. Herron, *La minaccia, op. cit.*
54. *Papers, op. cit.*, 1917, Vol. I. Supplement 2.
55. M. P. Briggs, *op. cit.*, p. 28.
56. H. Benedikt, *op. cit.*, p. 146. Cf. in *Papers, op. cit.*, vol. *cit.*, p. 286, the telegram of November 1, 1917, from the American ambassador in Rome to Lansing, the Secretary of State, urging a declaration of war on Austria-Hungary at Sonnino's request, because of the moral effect that this would have in Italy. The Italian ambassador in Washington, who made the representations to the same effect, wrote to the Italian Foreign Ministry: 'The failure of the United States to declare war on Austria is, among other things, the result of Wilson's stubborn personal illusion that Vienna might detach itself or be detached from Berlin.' Cf. Justus,

V. *Macchi di Cellere all' ambasciata di Washington. Memorie e testimonianze*, Florence, 1920, p. 65.

57. M. P. Briggs, *op. cit.*, p. 29.

58. *Papers, op. cit.*, vol. *cit.*, pp. 332–334.

59. R. S. Baker, *op. cit.*, p. 390.

60. H. Benedikt, *op. cit.*, p. 164.

61. M. Károlyi, *op. cit.*, J. Diner-Dénes, *op. cit.* Cf. also Oskar Jászi, *Magyariens Schuld—Ungarns Sühne*, Munich 1923, with introduction by Eduard Bernstein, who also took part in the pacifist congress in Berne. The English edition, O. Jászi, *Revolution and Counter-Revolution in Hungary*, London, 1927, has an introduction by R. W. Seton-Watson.

62. Letter of September 17, 1917, in the Károlyi papers.

63. Cf. Musulin's reports, Nos. 146 and 148 of November 26, 1917, No. 143 of November 27, No. 133 of December 3 and No. 126 of December 12 in H.H.St.A, I. Personalien II. 445.—Graf Michael Károlyi. Károlyi also wanted a conversation with Sir Horace Rumbold, the British Minister in Berne. The latter telegraphed to the Foreign Office and received permission to meet him, but in the meantime Károlyi had returned to Budapest. P.R.O., Austria-Hungary, 2864, 3138. However, the British agent Edwards met Jászi and Károlyi, and his report was telegraphed to London.

64. Cf. Hugh Wilson's report, *Papers, op. cit.*, pp. 322–325, and his *Diplomat Between Wars, op. cit.* On the Hungarians in the United States cf. the chapter by G. Bárány in J. O'Grady, *op. cit.* Cf. also M. Károlyi, *Egy egész villág, op. cit.*, p. 259. As we have seen, a general strike in fact broke out in Austria-Hungary in January 1918 as a result of the food shortage, the repercussions of the statements made by the Soviet delegates at the Brest-Litovsk conference, and the activities of some small groups of Zimmerwaldian revolutionary socialists, whose clandestine agitation in the industrial belt of Vienna and Budapest met with unexpected response. In Budapest Károlyi was in contact with the militant workers who were the *de facto* strike leaders. This brought him into conflict with some of the Social Democratic leaders who, following the example of their more authoritative Vienna counterparts, after a few days ended the strike movement which the workers still wanted to continue. Cf. Irén Nevelö, 'Néhány adat az 1918 januári tömegsztrájk történetéhez', *Párttörténeti közlemények*, 1958, No. 2.; Márta Tömöry, 'Duczynska Ilona feljegyzései az 1918-as januári sztrájk elözményeiröl', *Története Szemle*, 1958, Nos. 1–2; the same author's *Uj vizeken járok. A Galilei kör története*, Budapest 1960. It should be noted that the Hungarian militant Zimmerwaldians were followers of E. Szabó, who was the intellectual leader of the anti-militarist movement in Hungary during the war; Herron succeeded in resuming contact with him through a doctor cousin of his who went to Geneva from Budapest. This is stated in Herron's report of April 19, 1918 (Herron papers, Austria I, Document XXV), in which he states that some of his information on social movements in Austria-Hungary came to him from 'Ervin Szabó, head of the big Budapest public library, one of the ablest and best known

[447]

Hungarian writers on social and economic questions', and a long-standing friend of his. The conclusion of this report of Herron's is that the total collapse of Austria-Hungary, either as the result of a proletarian revolution of the Bolshevik type or of national revolutions by the Czechs and Southern Slavs, was now inevitable. That his contacts with the revolutionaries were considered useful by the American administration is evident from R. Mock and Cedric Larson, *Words that Won the War, op. cit.*, p. 262.

65. H. Benedikt, *op. cit.*, p. 147.

66. *Ibid.*, p. 111.

67. Cf. Meinl's memorandum on his mission, H. Benedikt, *op. cit.*, pp. 195 ff. Cf. also C. Haussmann, *op. cit.*, pp. 198 ff.

68. S. Osuský, *op. cit.*, p. 666, was the first to reveal that Wilson's speech of February 11, 1918, was due to information supplied by Herron. This is confirmed in *Papers, op. cit.*, Vol. I, Supplement 1, which reproduce on p. 82 the telegram from the American Legation in Berne suggesting an appeal to Austria-Hungary in the terms that Wilson in fact used. R. S. Baker, *op. cit.*, Vol. VII, p. 547, refers to Lansing's telegram of February 15 assuring Lammasch of United States' economic aid to Austria if she dissociated herself from Germany. George Bárány, 'A Note on the Genesis of Wilson's Point Ten', *Journal of Central European Affairs*, July 1963, suggests that the information that Lansing received on January 3, 1918, about Meinl's mission may have favourably influenced the drafting of the Fourteen Points in relation to Austria.

69. H. Benedikt, *op. cit.*, pp. 231 ff.

70. *Ibid.*, p. 208.

71. Czernin, in a conversation with Baernreither on April 12, 1918, explained the speech in which he challenged Clemenceau by his desire to put an end to the campaign of 'Lammasch, Foerster, Meinl and the rest of them' for a separate peace. Cf. R. A. Kann, J. M. Baernreither, *op. cit.* A pacifist speech made by Lammasch in the Upper House (Herrenhaus) a few weeks previously had in fact been received with violent interruptions and hostile murmurs.

72. Otto Bauer, in his letters to Kautsky, written after his return from Russia, where he was a prisoner of war, in particular those of September 28 and December 17, 1917, and January 4, 1918 (cf. the Kautsky papers, *cit.*, D. II. 500–502–503), in substance defended the line taken by Lenin and Trotsky (though with reservations about their illusions on the omnipotence of the guillotine) and deplored Kautsky's rejection of it *en bloc*, thus making more difficult the adoption of a revolutionary policy in Austria and Germany. Nevertheless, as appears from a letter of Danneberg to Kautsky of April 15, 1918 (*loc. cit.*, D. VII.–319), though 'a very great radicalization of the working class' had taken place in Vienna, Otto Bauer thought it best not to put a left-wing group in opposition to the Austrian Social Democratic Party leadership, but to continue to work inside the party. This in fact led to his peaceable assumption of the party leadership a few months later, but by this time the possibility of revolution in

Austria-Hungary had passed from the Vienna socialists into the hands of the various Slav nationalities.

73. P.R.O., Austria-Hungary. 3136.

74. H. Benedikt, *op. cit.*, p. 227.

75. For Herron's authorization to go to Vienna in case of need, cf. S. Osuský, *op. cit.*, p. 667.

76. R. Lorenz, *op. cit.*, p. 446, dates Charles I's message February 17, while H. Benedikt, *op. cit.*, p. 241, dates it February 19. The former is correct, as the documents used by R. S. Baker, *op. cit.*, Vol. VII, p. 551, show that President Wilson received the British interception of the Austrian Emperor's telegram on February 18.

77. H. Benedikt, *op. cit.*, p. 241.

78. *Ibid.*, p. 242. Cf. also *The Intimate Papers of Colonel House*, four vols., London, 1926, Vol. III, p. 375.

79. R. Lorenz, *op. cit.*, p. 466.

80. *Ibid.*, pp. 447–448.

81. Herron papers, Austria I. Document XXV.

82. Herron who, as appears from his correspondence, saw some of the Yugoslav delegates to the Rome congress of the nations subject to Austria-Hungary (April 8–10, 1918) both before and afterwards, was referring to the agreement which was approved there. The ideas contained in his letter of April 19 are repeated in the report to the State Department made by the United States Minister in Berne on May 16, 1918, which concludes that the agreement reached with the Italians by the Czechs and Yugoslavs and their increased hostility to Austria-Hungary, pointed to the advisability of dropping direct efforts to detach Vienna from Berlin and relying instead on the revolt of the oppressed nationalities. Cf. *Papers, op. cit.*, 1918, Vol. I, Supplement 1, p. 804.

83. Cf. Herron's letters to Hugh Wilson of February 28 and March 1, 1918, Herron papers, *loc. cit.*, Documents XIII and XIV. Incidentally it is very probable that Štefanik, who maintained contacts with the Italian government and General Diaz's general staff, was kept informed by Osuský, who at the time was a close collaborator with Herron, but was devoted to the cause of Czechoslovak independence, of the contacts between the United States and Austria, at any rate to the extent of enabling him to foresee the danger of a sacrifice of the Czech cause. Štefanik saw clearly that it was in the interests of Italy to support the Czechs since the possibility of an Austro-American agreement was equally alarming to her.

84. Herron papers, *loc. cit.*, Document XXIX.

85. That Herron's reports reached Wilson and Lansing is confirmed by R. S. Baker, *op. cit.*, Vol. VII, p. 282, footnote, and indirectly also by Robert Lansing, *Mémoires de Guerre, op. cit.*, pp. 230 ff. *The Lansing Papers, op. cit.*, Vol. II, p. 138, contains a telegram from Wilson to Herron dated January 17, 1918 telling him that his previous proposals (about the League of Nations) had greatly impressed him.

86. *Papers, op. cit.*, vol. cit., and *Lansing Papers, op. cit., passim.* As is also shown by Herron's letter of May 3, 1918, the Americans were especially

gratified by the agreement they believed had genuinely been reached between the Italians and the Yugoslavs, with the consequent Italian renunciation of Dalmatia. In their eyes this would have compensated for the disappearance of Austria-Hungary and the resulting void in eastern central Europe. So Herron told Paulucci, who reported this conversation to Sonnino, on May 23, 1918.

87. Allan Mitchell, *Revolution in Bavaria, op. cit.*, p. 130.

88. Helmut Rumpler, *Das Völkermanifest Kaiser Karls vom 16. Oktober, 1918*, Munich 1966.

89. Cf. in the *Prager Tageblatt* of August 24, 1924, the testimony of the last Austrian governor of Bohemia, Count Coudenhove, who was ordered by Lammasch to avoid bloodshed at all costs.

Notes—Appendix III

1. I am indebted to M. Maurice Degros, Conservateur en chef des Archives Diplomatiques du Ministère des Affaires Etrangères (henceforward referred to as A.D.M.A.E.) and to Dr Georges Dethan, chief librarian of the above, for the great courtesy with which they facilitated my researches.

2. A.D.M.A.E. Guerre 1914. Autriche-Hongrie. 8. Les Yougoslaves. On Barrère, cf. (though it is not exhaustive for this period) Enrico Serra, *Camille Barrère e l'intesa italo-francese*, Milan, 1950.

3. Cf. Robert de Billy, 'Charles Loiseau', *Revue d'Histoire Diplomatique*, 1946.

4. Cf. what Loiseau himself wrote about this in 'Ma mission supres du Vatican (1914–1918)', *ibid.*, 1960.

5. Cf. these reports, beginning with that of July 10, 1916, A.D.M.A.E., *loc. cit.* Barrère, forwarding a report of Loiseau's to the Prime Minister and Foreign Minister on March 30, 1917, described it as a *remarquable étude*. The revolution had of course already broken out in Russia, and this gave a new topicality to the problems of the Slavs.

6. *Ibid.*, report of April 19, 1916.

7. Reports of Robert de Billy, French chargé d'affaires in Rome, July 24 and August 5, 1917.

8. Barrère was at the meeting at St Jean de la Maurienne (April 1917) at which Ribot, the French Prime Minister, mentioned to Sonnino the Austrian peace feelers. Barrère did not conceal his opposition to such contacts, which the Italian government could not approve. Cf. E. Serra, *op. cit.*, p. 339. Sonnino and Orlando talked to Barrère about Lloyd George's subsequent attempts to resume conversations with Austria-Hungary, and he wrote to Paris expressing his opposition to such exchanges, because of their incompatibility with Italian claims. Cf. his reports of December 7 and 8, 1917, A.D.M.A.E. Guerre 1914–1918. Italie. Dossier XXVI.

9. Cf. the reports of February 6, April 30, October 21, 23 and 26 and November 10, 1917, *loc. cit.* Dossiers XXII–XXII–XXV. When Nitti became Italian Prime Minister in June 1919 he gave the Foreign Ministry to Tittoni, but that does not in any way prove the existence during the war of the pacifist plot in which Barrère stubbornly believed without ever succeeding in producing any evidence for it.

10. A.D.M.A.E. Guerre. 1914. Autriche-Hongrie. 8. Les Yougoslaves.

11. Reports of January 20, April 29, November 12 and 18, December 7 and 16, 1917 and March 20, 1918 in A.D.M.A.E., Italie. Dossiers XXV, XXVI, XXVIII. Sir Rennel Rodd, the British ambassador in Rome, shared

Barrère's opinion. On September 25, 1918, when the war was virtually won, he wrote to the Foreign Office that, while Nitti did not create an impression of firmness, 'Sonnino is identified by the country with an uncompromising spirit, sustaining to the end the war policy for which he is primarily responsible.' P.R.O. Political. Austria-Hungary 3137. In fact at that moment Nitti, like Diaz, the Chief of the General Staff, was hesitant about the advisability of a big Italian military offensive, which was advocated by Orlando and by Sonnino.

12. Reports of November 27, 1917. A.D.M.A.E. Italie. Dossier XXVI.

13. Reports of December 29, 1917, January 3 and 28, 1918, *loc. cit.* Dossiers XXVI–XXVII.

14. *Ibid*. Pichon to Barrère, December 5, 1917.

15. E. Serra, *op. cit.*, p. 347. It was not by chance that in 1922–23, at the end of his career, Barrère sympathized with Mussolini's government, without foreseeing that it would soon become anti-French.

16. A.C.S. Nitti papers. *Diario diun soggiorno a Parigi dal 15 al 24 maggio 1919.* We have been unable to identify the author of this diary. For Italian policy during this period, cf. Roberto Vivarelli, *Il dopoguerra in Italia e l'avvento del fascismo (1918–1922)*, Vol. I, *Dalla fine della guerra all'impresa di Fiume*, Naples, 1967.

17. A.D.M.A.E. Italie. Dossier XXVII. The British envoy to the Vatican also reported on April 13, 1918, that Cardinal Gasparri was pointing out that, while Austria was a barrier to the southward expansion of Germany, its possible successor states, e.g. the projected Yugoslavia, would be too weak to form such a barrier. P.R.O. Austria-Hungary. 2134. It should be added that one reason why the Catholics preferred Giolitti to Albertini and Bissolati was that he was less anti-clerical then they. (Bissolati was distinctly anti-clerical. Albertini had always been the severest critic of Giolitti's domestic and foreign policy).

18. A.D.M.A.E. Guerre 1914–1918. Autriche-Hongrie. Mouvement national tchèque.

19. *Ibid*. Barrère's report of October 14, 1917.

20. *Ibid*. 8. Les Yougoslaves. Sous-dossier—Série A.—Carton 313. Congrès des nationalités à Rome (Mars-avril 1918). On the day after Caporetto, the Italian Minister to Romania, having heard that Masaryk, who was in Russia, had made contact with Romanian politician-*émigrés* from Transylvania, with a view to organizing a congress of nationalities subject to Austria-Hungary at Odessa, did all in his power to dissuade the Romanian Government. *Ibid*. 8. Les Yougoslaves. French Minister's telegram from Jassy, November 14, 1917.

21. A.D.M.A.E. Italie, Dossier XXVIII. Reports of March 7 and April 4, 1918.

22. A.D.M.A.E. Congrès des nationalités, *loc. cit.* Report of March 26, 1918.

23. *Ibid*. Telegram from Paris of April 8, 1918.

24. *Ibid*. F. Charles-Roux's reports of April 13, 1918. The Poles, with the exception of Zamorski, the former deputy for Tarnopol, who had fled

from Austria, also struck the head of the French press office in Rome as being Austrophile. Cf. his report of April 10, *loc. cit.*

25. *Ibid.* Telegram of April 10. In the report that the Poles submitted to Pichon (*ibid.*, April 17) after their return to Rome, they said that they, the Romanians and the Serbs had advised prudence, while the Italians, Czechs, Croats and Wickham Steed had maintained the importance of passing uncompromising resolutions.

26. Report of April 17.

27. Telegram of May 28.

28. Albertini was quick to see, and wrote on June 28, 1918, to Emanuel, the London correspondent of his newspaper (cf. L. Albertini, *Epistolario, op. cit.*) that the British and French had not put much pressure on Orlando and Sonnino to recognize Czechoslovakia. Two days later Bissolati expressed the same view when he wrote to his brother-in-law Luigi Campolonghi (I am grateful to Signora Lidia Campolonghi for having allowed me to see her father's papers), that the British and French statesmen were taking advantage of Sonnino's opposition to keep a balance between the *Austria delenda* slogan and the trend of opinion favourable to the preservation of Austria-Hungary.

29 P.R.O. Political. Rome Embassy. 1093. Procès verbaux of the three meetings of the seventh session of the Supreme War Council, held at Versailles, July 2–4, 1918. The difficulties over the oath arose from the fact that the Serbian government wished the legionaries to swear loyalty to the King of Serbia, while the Yugoslav Committee wanted them to swear to Yugoslavia, whose right to existence was not yet admitted by Sonnino. Pašić's formula naturally suited Sonnino better. Trumbić wrote bitterly in a memorandum to Balfour on October 7, 1918: 'The position in which Mr Pashitch would hold the Yugoslavs of Austria-Hungary is one of subjection and humiliation. This people would be an *object* of liberation, not a *subject* of right and liberty.' P.R.O. Austria-Hungary, 3137.

30. In the bitter debate of September 1918 on the Yugoslav movement both Bissolati and Sonnino offered to resign, but Orlando persuaded both to accept a compromise. Cf. Campolonghi's papers; also R. Colapietra, *Leonida Bissolati, op. cit.*; O. Malagodi, *Conversazioni della guerra, op. cit.*

31. Ivo J. Lederer, *Yugoslavia at the Paris Peace Conference, op. cit.*

32. Cf. the letters exchanged on June 12, 1918. A.C.S., Carte Orlando. Busta 2.

33. Report of September 25, 1918. P.R.O. Austria-Hungary. 3137.

34. *Corriere della Sera*, September 6, 1918.

35. Ugo Ojetti, *Lettere alla moglie, 1915–1919*, Florence, 1964, p. 669. For the statement by the Grand Master of the Italian Freemasons and his closest colleagues in favour of Sonnino's foreign policy, cf. *Il Secolo* of December 12, 1918, and Maria Rygier, *La franc-maçonnerie italienne devant la guerre et le fascisme*, Paris, 1929.

36. Bissolati to L. Campolonghi, November 25, 1919.

37. Report of January 13, 1919. P.R.O. Political. Italy 1919–1920. 3804.

However, on December 10, 1918, Sir Rennel Rodd thought it advisable for Bissolati and Albertini not to renew their criticisms of Sonnino. *Ibid.*

38. A.D.M.A.E. Report of December 29, 1918.

39. *Ibid.* Zara is, of course, in Dalmatia, but at that time, in contrast to the rest of the province which was 97 per cent Yugoslav, its population was predominantly Italian.

40. Orlando, however, had no intention of risking the popularity he had gained by leading Italy to victory, which he had done with undeniable skill. Also he admitted in a private conversation that, as the representative of the fourth generation of a family of lawyers, his blood boiled at Bissolati's willingness to renounce something without the assurance of a *quid pro quo*.

41. P.R.O., *loc. cit.* Report of December 29.

42. *Ibid.* Report of January 18, 1919. Nitti resigned because Sonnino, knowing that he would not fight for all the annexations stipulated by the London Treaty, did not want to include him in the delegation to the Paris Peace Conference. Cf. Sonnino papers, S. 117. Nitti's ultimate intention was to form a government with the Socialist Party and the new Catholic popular party. This was one reason why he did not wish to tie himself to Bissolati, who was not liked either by most of the Socialists or by the Catholics. P.R.O. *loc. cit.* Report of January 25. The Vatican clearly preferred Nitti to Sonnino. Cf. Giuseppe Spataro, *I democratici cristiani della dittatura alla repubblica*, Milan, 1968, p. 372.

43. Cf. the peace conference documents and the vast literature on the subject; in particular O. Malagodi, *op. cit.*; V. E. Orlando, *Memorie*, Milan, 1960; René Albrecht-Carrie, *Italy at the Paris Peace Conference*, New York, 1938; Paolo Alatri, *Nitti, D'Annunzio e la questione adriatica (1919–1920)*, Milan, 1959. Arno J. Mayer, *Politics and Diplomacy of Peacemaking, Containment and Counterrevolution at Versailles. 1918–1919*, New York, 1967. The clash between Wilson and Orlando produced nationalism even in those who had previously been immune to it, e.g. in Emanuel, the correspondent of the *Corriere della Sera*, who was sent to Paris to cover the conference. There he became the spokesman of the Orlando thesis, in spite of the repeated remonstrances of Luigi Albertini, his editor, who continued to advocate a policy very different from Sonnino's.

44. For the Wilson–Bissolati conversation, cf. A. J. Mayer, *op. cit.*, p. 213.

45. The text of the speech is in Leonida Bissolati, *La politica estera dell'Italia dal 1897 al 1920*, Milan, 1923. For the demonstration at the Scala, cf. the newspapers of January 12, 1919, and the vivid accounts by Bianca Ceva, *Storia di una passione*, Milan, 1948, and of G. A. Borgese, *Goliath. The March of Fascism, op. cit.*

Index

(A-H. is used as an abbreviation for Austria-Hungary)

Borgese, Professor G. A., 173, 221, 224, 231, 232, 238, 280
Borkenau, Franz, 214
Boroević, Field-Marshal, 197
Borsa, Mario, 237
Boselli, Paolo, 173, 235
Bosnia-Hercegovina, annexation, 5, 7, 31–2; nationalism in, 5; Francis Ferdinand's plans for, 11; rail development obstructed by Budapest, 30; annexation reinforces Serbo-Croat solidity, 32; annexation supported by F. Kossuth, 33; student violence, 36, 41; sympathy with Austria's enemies, 75; Serbian rebellion against war, 76; Tisza's view of future, 78; to be given to Serbia under Russian war aims, 83, 108; Serbian claim to, 84; Salvemini's view of future, 96
Bossi, Professor Luigi Maria, 136, 137–8
Brancaccio, Col. Nicola, 172
Branting, Hjalmar, 190
Brătianu, Jon, 97, 127, 164
Braun, Otto, 217
Brest-Litovsk, peace conference, 181, 201, 207, 209, 211, 218, 262, 265, 266, 282
Briand, Aristide, 122, 158, 161, 162, 168
Briey basin, 147
Briggs, Mitchell Pirie, 267
Britain, sympathies with A-H., 89, 158–9; informed of Italian conditions for intervention, 110; accepts Italian demands, 111; and Italian fear of strong Yugoslavia, 153; and future of Bohemia and Hungary, 173; and Serbian claims, 196; and separate peace with A-H., 203; favourable to preservation of A-H., 204–5; war aims, 204, 206; trade unions and the war, 204, 205; growth of peace movement, 204–5; emissaries seek negotiation with Czernin, 220; Labour Party, 234, 236; continued sounding of Vienna, 233, 262, 263–6; represented at Rome congress, 239; readiness to recognize independence of subject nationalities, 241; recognizes Czech National Council, 244
Brosch, Major Alexander, 13, 37, 38, 45
Brünn (Brno), 212
Brusilov, General Alexej, 161
Buchanan, George William, 83, 105
Bucharest, capture of, 133; Treaty of, 163–5
Buchinger, M., 74
Buchlau, 32
Budapest, 24; industry, 27; growth of Social Democratic trade unions, 42;

workers' resistance to Tisza, 42; unrest, 187; demand for universal suffrage, 188–9; strikes and mass protests against the war, 191, 212; demonstrations against Germany, 217; workers' council set up, 250–1
Budisavljević, S., 16
Bukovina, 59, 75, 76, 80–1, 96, 97, 123, 164, 165, 174, 204
Bulgaria, 45, 83, 108, 109, 122, 139, 146, 195, 200
Bülow, Prince Bernhard von, 57, 58, 61, 70, 71, 72, 103
Burian, Count Stephan von, 31–2, 53–4, 67; Berchtold's view of, 59; and Tisza, 59; appointed Foreign Minister, 59; accepts necessity of ceding Trent, 61, 62; rejects concessions to Romanians in Transylvania, 63; and concessions to Italy, 66, 70, 126; favours end to war in 1916, 146; acknowledges failure of Empire to reform, 255

Čabrinović, Nedeljko, 5
'Cadets', the. See Constitutional Democratic Party
Cadorna, General, 56, 57, 157, 173, 222, 259
Caillaux, Joseph, 124, 144, 170, 288
Calboli, Paulucci de'. See Paulucci de' Calboli
Cambon, Jules, 168
Cambon, Paul, 162, 169
Campolonghi, Luigi, 86, 173
Canepa, Giuseppe, 235
Caporetto, Italian defeat at, 174, 183, 197, 201, 203, 263, 278, 289; effect of, 224–5, 227, 231
Carinthia, 114
Carlotti, Marquis, 111, 135, 172
Carol, King of Romania, 14
Carso Region, 157
Catholic Popular Party (Hungary), 25, 118, 129
Catholic Popular Party (Slovene), 174
Cattaro. See Kotor.
Cavour, Count Camillo Benso, 136, 223, 276
Cecil, Lord Robert, 115, 170, 204
Central Committee for Propaganda to the Enemy, 245–6
Central Organization for Lasting Peace, 280
Central Powers, areas occupied at end of 1916, 144; conclude peace with Ukraine, 219; peace with Russia, 225; war aims, 258–9; and Bolshevik revolution, 262;

Croatia, Croats—*continued*
all Southern Slavs, 195; fears of Serbian supremacy, 196; scepticism over Corfu Agreement, 197; company surrenders on Piave, 246; increased press freedom, 246; explosive situation, 247; 'green cadres', 247; Fiume promised to, 290, 295

Croat Peasant Party, 23

Croat Progressive Party, 23, 112

Croat Right Party, 16, 17, 21, 23, 34, 41, 45, 112, 114, 194, 197, 246, 247

Croat Social Democratic Party, 23, 247, 248

Cromer, Lord, 171

Csernova, massacre at, 30, 118

Curzolari (Korcula) islands, 65, 70

Cuvaj, Eduard, 41, 47

Czech Agrarian Party, 117, 174

Czech Committee Abroad, calls for Czechs and Slovaks to form single nation, 121–2; becomes National Committee of Czech Countries, 122

Czech Legion, in Russia, 181–2, 185; in Siberia, 243

Czech National Theatre, 248

Czechoslovakia, absorbs Ruthenians, 95; independence advocated, 100, 209, 235; Masaryk's aim to establish, 116; map of future state printed in *La Nation tchèque*, 119; Russian attitude to establishment of independent state, 167; Slovaks Social Democrats support, 191; Lansing calls for establishment of independence, 209; consequences of denying German self-determination, 210, 252; establishment dependent on defeat of A-H., 215; delegation at Rome congress, 239; U.S. won over to cause of independence, 242, 243; National Council recognized as *de facto* government by U.S., 244; recognition of independence, 293

Czechoslovak Legion, recruited in Italy, 245, 291; valorous conduct on Piave, 245; in France, 245, 291

Czechoslovak National Council, 167–8, 172, 235, 242; recognition by Entente, 244–5

Czech National Socialist Party, 3, 7, 8, 117, 214–15; renamed Czech Socialist Party, 210

Czech Progressive Party, 7, 117, 182

Czech Realist Party, 120

Czechs, victory of, xii; provinces of A-H., xii, 4; hopes based on Tsarist Russia, 5–6; German opposition to official use of Czech language, 8; attitude to the war, 75; desertions during war, 76, 93, 94, 185, 246; death sentences on, 76; in, Russia, 81, 116, 166; prisoners volunteer to serve with Russian armies, 82; request to set up legion in Russia, 82, 167; few in favour of independence in 1914, 83; independence movement, 99, 115; committee formed in Paris, 118; convention in U.S., 121; National Committees formed in France and Italy, 166; Steed's and Seton-Watson's exertions on behalf of, 169; Entente in favour of self-determination, 169; Berthelot's support for cause, 169; and Italo-Yugoslav conflict, 171–2; politicians' tactical loyalty to Habsburgs, 174; Austrian opposition to concessions to, 178; and union with Slovaks, 183; demand self-determination at meeting with Czernin, 201; Lloyd George and, 207; Reichsrat deputies proclaim right to self-determination, 209; Austrian Social Democrats reluctance to accept claims, 214; U.S. won over to cause of independence, 242

Czech Social Democratic Party, 3, 117, 174, 178, 182, 210, 213–14

Czech Socialist Party, 210

Czernin, Count, 52, 74; agrees to German control of Russian Poland, 179, 180–1; and Kreuznach agreement, 181, 258; opposed to national autonomies, 181, 185; Redlich's description, 183; character and policies, 183–4; resignation, 184, 221; programme of November, 1917, 199–200; realizes programme of annexations illusory, 200; admits Austria unable to continue war, 200–1; acts as if victory won after Caporetto, 201; and Meinl's contacts with Herron, 202; sends Mensdorff to meet Smuts, 202–3; adroitness in 1918 January strike crisis, 215; seeks authorization to conclude peace with Bolsheviks, 218; plan for peace with Ukraine, 218–19; approval of most of Fourteen Points, 219; and peace talks with Lloyd George, 220, 265; suggests yielding part of Lorraine, 220, 257–8; successes reawaken belief in German invincibility, 221; and Italy, 226, 277–8; and Clemenceau affair, 242; approaches to Entente through Prince Sixtus, 257–8; favours 'legitimate' separate peace, 258, 260; contacts with Painlevé, 259–60, 261, 262; regards French peace proposals as 'bad joke', 261–2; signs post-war agreement with

Czernin, Count—*continued*
Germany, 262; and Polish question, 263; rejects British peace feelers, 263; willingness to meet Lloyd George in Switzerland, 265; his terms for further peace conversations, 265; intervenes to prevent Redlich's appointment as premier, 272; and Italian peace feelers, 277–8; breaks off contacts with Entente, 282

Dakar, 147
Dalmatia, 16, 110; nationalism in, 5; Francis Ferdinand's plan for, 11; under Austrian administration, 21, 30; Aehrenthal's plan for, 31; students' strike, 41; and reunification with Croatia, 47; promised by Entente to Italy, 64; Italian claim to, 64, 88, 103, 108, 172, 222, 287; restoration to St Stephen's Crown desired by Tisza, 78; Russia and, 83, 153; Serbian claim to, 84, 108, 196; disclaimed by Salvemini, 96; Ferrero argues Italy should disclaim, 102; Galli's doubts on Italian claim, 102; Yugoslav Committee claims, 114; dispute between Italy and Yugoslavia over, 115, 294; Treaty of London and, 154; Albertini proposes Italian renunciation, 222; Sonnino insists on assignment of part to Italy, 222; Trumbić's insistence on Yugoslav claim to, 222; Orlando and, 294, 295
Dalmatian Democratic Party, 21
Dalmatian 'Right' Party, 21
Danilevsky, J., 6
D'Annunzio, Gabriele, 245, 290
Dardanelles, 108, 110, 122
Daszynski, I., 77
D'Avarna, Duke. *See* Avarna
Davidović, Ljuba, 196
Deák, Ferenc, 22
De Ambris, Alceste, 235
De Broukère, Louis, 236
De Filippi, Major, 227
De Gasperi, Alcide, 246, 249–50
Delcassé, Théophile, 89, 90, 92, 105, 108, 113
De Martino, Giacomo, 64–5, 172
Denis, Prof. E., 94, 95, 118–19, 121, 168, 172, 240
De Viti, Antonio De Marco, 157
Diaz, General, 222
Di Cesaso, Colonna Giovanni Antonio, 157
Diner-Dénes, József, 280
Dmowski, Roman, 77, 79, 160

Dobrudja, 164
Drummond, E., 140
Dürich, Josip, 120, 121, 167

Ebert, Friedrich, 145, 217
Economy, of A-H., xi, 4, 177
Eisenmann, Prof. Louis, 119, 121, 168, 172, 280
Emancipazione. See L'Emancipazione
Emanuel, Guglielmo, 221, 222, 225, 227, 228, 230
Endrici, Mgr Celestino, 249
Engel-Janosi, Prof. Friedrich, 273
Entente, and dismemberment of A-H., 142, 143, 206; peace terms, 148–9; war aims, 159, 202–3, 275; reply to Wilson on war aims, 162–4, 169, 173–4, 206, 223, 226; war aims drafted by Lord Cecil and Berthelot, 170; Sonnino associates himself with war aims, 171; A-H. nationalities protest against war aims, 173–4; and Hungary, 191; desire for capitulation of Central Powers after German offensive, 204; and secret treaties, 208, 267; Prince Sixtus's negotiations with, 221; peace feelers with Vienna, 257–66; aim to divide A-H. and Germany, 258; unwilling to sacrifice Italian claims, 273
Eötvös, Jósef, 22
Erzberger, Matthias, 61, 103
Eszterházy, Prince Maurice, 192, 193

Facta, Luigi, 61, 62
Faidutti, Mgr, 174
Falbo, Italo, 157
Fasciotti, Baron, 97, 109
Federalism, 78, 180; nationalism and, xii; Šmeral's idea of, 3–4; Kramář aims at, 7, 9; Francis Ferdinand and, 10, 11, 182; urged by Hodža and Maniu, 15; Tisza's hostility towards, 44; abandoned by Masaryk and Beneš, 169; Stanek's call for, 182; opposition of German Austrian parties, 182; Reichsrat deputies call for, 182–3; Czernin's opposition to, 183; western powers advise Emperor to carry out reform, 183; Hungarian opposition, 224; Hussarek government's reform proposals, 252; proclaimed in Imperial Manifesto, 285
Fejérváry, General Géza, 21, 23, 25–6
Ferrero, Gina Lombroso, 16, 85, 101; correspondence with Supilo, 18, 19, 20, 21, 152–3
Ferrero, Guglielmo, 16, 102, 157
Ferri, Enrico, 153

Fiume (Rijeka), 16, 17, 21–2, 127; Giolitti advises full autonomy for, 67, 68; Italian interest and claims, 70, 139, 154, 221; free port proposal, 92; Salvemini on future of, 101; Yugoslav Committee claims, 114; Sonnino and, 123; fate reserved till peace signed, 139; Serbian claim to, 139; Yugoslavs see as Free City, 224; irredentists call for annexation to Italy 235; Orlando's view, 290; D'Annunzio's adventure, 290; Fiume National Council, 294

Florence, 103

Foch, Marshal Ferdinand, 289

Foerster, F. W., 268, 275, 285

Forgách, Count, 35, 59, 67, 72

Foscari, Piero, 156, 157

Fournol, Étienne, 118

Fourteen Points, 246, 265, 282; repercussions, 208; and Habsburg monarchy, 208, 209, 219; Czernin replies to, 278

Fradeletto, Antonio, 85, 152

France, Delcassé states war aims, 89; sympathies with A-H., 89, 168, 173; Slovak colony, 118; Russian support for annexation of Saar, 163; allows Czech National Council to carry out propaganda, 167, 168; desire to detach Austria from Germany, 168; hostility to Magyars, 168; attitude at London talks, Dec., 1906, 170; and United States, 203; internationalists gain ground, 205; peace terms proposed to Revertera, 219–20; represented at Rome congress, 239; proposals to Czernin for peace negotiations, 261–2; government in favour of Sonnino remaining in office, 289

Franchise, effects of reform, 12–13; Croat call for extension, 22; in Hungary, 22; extension proposed by Kristóffy, 24, 26–7; extended in Austria, 24–5; Hungarian national coalition opposed to extension, 36; Andrássy's proposals to manipulate, 36; extension desired by Francis Joseph, 37–8; extension opposed by Tisza, 39–40; Romanian demand for extension, 44; Polzer-Hoditz urges extension, 186; sham extension in Hungary, 193. See also Universal suffrage

Francis Ferdinand, Archduke, 27, 37; and federalism, xii; innovations expected of, 9; plan for administrative autonomy of Slavs, 9–11; and Serbia, 10, 15; and Magyars, 10, 11; personalities in his orbit, 13–14; assassination, 15, 36, 48; in favour of peace, 15; aims to reconcile Habsburgs with Romanovs, 15, 43, 45; Burian's fears about his policy, 31–2; Aehrenthal and, 32; and Kristóffy, 38; opposes invasion of Serbia, 43; and Tisza, 44; and ethnic autonomy within A-H., 44, 45, 184; attempts to keep A-H. out of war, 45; reform programme for Hungary, 253

Francis Joseph I, Emperor, 35, 40; and the 1867 Settlement, 2; grants universal suffrage in Austria, 3, 12, 24; German and Hungarian opposition to Prague coronation, 10; and Count Khuen-Héderváry, 18; rejects demand for military use of Magyar, 18, 20; refuses to entrust government to Hungarian national coalition, 20; appoints Fejérváry as head of government, 20–1; approves Kristóffy's electoral reform plans, 25, 38; and Hungarian national coalition, 25–7; and annexation of Bosnia-Hercegovina, 31, 32; desire for agreement with Serbo-Croat coalition and Romanians, 43; reliance on Tisza, 43; refusal to cede Trentino, 58

Frank, Dr Josip, 13, 21, 23, 28, 30, 40, 41

Franklin, Martin, 125–7

Franklin-Bouillon, (Fr. politician), 231, 232

Franta, (Czech politician), 116

Frassati, Alfredo, 67, 68–9, 70

Frederick, Archduke, 76

French Socialist Party, 232, 234

Friedjung, Prof. H., 33–4

Friedjung trial, 16, 85

Friuli, Austrian, 67, 68, 70

Fusinato, Guido, 55

Gačinović, Vladimir, 5

Galicia, 62, 96, 180, 260, 261, 281; and Austria's enemies, 75; Poles' rights in, 76; Polish opposition to War, 76–7; national committee of Polish parties formed, 77; Ukrainian Socialists, 80; and reunification with Congress Poland, 80, 83, 160; Ruthenians in, 80–1; Russian defeat, 122; Ruthenians demand reunification, 179

Gallenga-Stuart, Romeo, 224, 228, 232

Galli, Carlo, 101, 102

Gallipoli, 122

Garami, E., 24

Gasparri, Cardinal, 148, 149, 170, 176

Gauvain, A., 228
Gazzari, Julije, 227
Germans, nationalism after defeat, xii; dominant position in A-H., 1, 9, 11–12; opposition to Czech language in Bohemia and Moravia, 8; Masaryk sees inclusion in Czech state, 95; in Sudetenland, 214; compact masses in successor states, 255
Germany, in favour of promising concessions to Italy, 54, 65–6; promise to obtain free hand for A-H. in Balkans, 62, 63; government urges concessions to Italy, 67; Salvemini on, 101; aim of economic union with A-H., 131; advance into Romania, 133; Bissolati's view of, 143; High Command not in favour of compromise peace, 144–5, 146–7; compromise with Petrograd favoured by heads of steel industry, 145; Social Democrats propose negotiated peace, 145; proclamation of new Polish kingdom, 145; intention to keep Poland in post-war settlement, 179; support for Czernin, 184; responsibility for the War, 189; and reform of Habsburg empire, 203; Wilson and militant Socialists, 208; repercussions of Fourteen Points, 208; Social Democrats applaud Soviet seizure of power, 211; mass meetings call for peace, 211; repercussions of mass struggle for peace, 215–18; arrests of strikers' leaders, 218; war aims set out by Hertling, 219; harsh terms imposed on Soviet Russia, 220, 243; defeat on Western Front, 252; and soundings for separate peace, 257–66; aim to annex Courland and Lithuania, 258; and Russian Poland, 258, 260–1; Czernin signs post-war alliance with, 262; recognizes independent Ukraine, 262; Social Democratic support for the War, 274–5
Ghisleri, Arcangelo, 238, 239
Giers, Mikhail Nikolaevič, 108
Giolitti, Giovanni, 170, 289; neutralism, 25, 55, 60, 68, 149, 225, 289; discloses that Vienna had asked for support against Serbia, 56; support for Italian government in negotiations with Vienna, 61–2; conflict with Salandra, 62; and final offer from A-H., 66; advises acceptance by Italy of Trentino and part of Friuli, 67, 68–9; efforts to persuade Vienna to accept his proposals, 69, 70; ready to accept Bülow's concessions, 71; refusal to return to power, 71

Giornale d'Italia (Rome), 67, 68
Giuriati, Giovanni, 228
Goremykin, (Russian premier), 79
Gorizia, 65, 70, 71, 84, 96, 114, 144, 149, 171, 224
Gorlice, 55, 82
Gradisca, 65
Granello, Prof. Luigi, 238
Grátz, Gusztáv, xi
Graziani, Gen. Andrea, 244
Greece, 87, 158
Gregorin, G., 112, 227
Grey, Sir Edward, 92, 106, 110, 114, 123, 139, 141, 142
Grimm, Robert, 274, 275
Grippo, Pasquale, 71
Gršković, Father N., 112
Gurko, General, 161, 162, 163, 167

Habrman, Gustav, 247
Haguenin, Prof., 263
Hanák, Péter, xi
Hankey, Sir Maurice, 259
Hantsch, Hugo, 49
Haumant, Émile, 119
Haussmann, Konrad, 267, 281
Hej Slovene!, 94
Henderson, Arthur, 204, 205, 207, 234, 235, 237
Herron, George Davis, 202, 219, 242, 267–8, 273–5, 279, 280, 281–2, 283, 284, 285
Hertling, Georg von, 218, 219
Hindenburg, Field-Marshal Paul von, 145, 146–7, 218, 258
Hinković, H., 85, 104, 108, 113, 174, 196
Hlas, 117–18
Hlaváček, František, 235
Hlinka, A., 30, 118
Hodža, Milan, 13, 14, 15, 29, 37, 38, 45, 118, 186
Hoffman, Gen. Adolf, 211
Hohenlohe, Prince, 66
Holló, B., 134–5
Holló, L., 135
Holy Synod, 153
Hoover Institution on War, Revolution and Peace, 268
House, Col., 225
Hoyos, Count, 57
Hrvatska Država (Zagreb), 246
Hrvoj, D., 112
Hungarian Social Democratic Party, campaign for universal suffrage, 2–3, 166; basis in trade unions, 24, 42; organizes strike of 1905, 24; in favour of customs autonomy, 28, 29; calls for

[463]

Masaryk, Thomas G.—*continued*
desertions, 16; denounces Zagreb trial (1909), 33; part in demolishing charges against Supilo, 34; view of Czech national struggle, 93, 116, 117; message to Tsarist government, 93–4; meets Seton-Watson, 94–5; and future of Bohemia, 95; contacts with Croatian exiles, 115–16; in exile, 116; identification of Slovaks with Czechs, 117; visits Paris and London, 119; lives in London, 121; president of Czech Committee Abroad, 122; abandons idea of federalism within Habsburg empire, 169; in Petrograd, 181; received by Wilson, 243
Max of Baden, Prince, 216
Mazzini, Giuseppe, 1, 2, 4, 20, 100, 150, 223, 276
Medakovic, Bogdan, 16, 46–7
Meinl, Julius, 185, 202, 267–9, 271–2, 273, 279, 280, 281–2, 284
Mensdorff-Pouilly, Count, 202, 203, 226, 263, 264, 281
Mérey, Count, 51–2, 264
Messagero, 156
Meštrović, Ivan, 85, 99, 103, 113, 115, 195, 196, 239, 286
Michaelis, Georg, 260, 261
Mihajlović, Ljuba, 85
Mihalović, A., 194
Miljukov, P. N., 111, 157–8, 160, 162, 164, 176, 195
Miller, W., 114
Mitteleuropa, German plan for, 131
Modigliani, G. E., 236, 237
Mola, Gen. Armando, 227, 228
Montenegro, 50, 53, 63, 114, 179
Moravia, 3, 4, 8, 95
Morgari, Oddino, 98
Morning Post, 114, 295
Mosca, Prof. Gaetano, 152–3
Moscow, 81
Moysset, Prof., 118
Muir, Ramsay, 99
Mussolini, B., 98, 238
Musulin, Baron, 31, 280

Namier, Lewis, 169
Narodni Listy (Prague), 176
Nathan, Ernesto, 153
National Committee of the Czech Countries, 122
National Council of Czechoslovak Countries, 244
National Democratic Party (Polish), 77, 78, 160

Nationalist Party (Italian), 228
Nationality principle, 1; Bissolati's views, 148, 150; A-H. and, 150; Entente powers and, 154, 159
Nationalities, Czernin restricts right of self-determination, 209; Fourteen Points and, 208; Lansing calls for establishment of independent states, 209; Rome congress of (1918), 231, 232, 238–40
National Party (Slovak), 118
National Work, Hungarian Party of, 39
Neo-Slav movement, 6
Neue Freie Presse (Vienna), 34
Nicholas II, Tsar, 81, 105, 161, 163
Nicholas of Montenegro, 16
Nicolson, Sir Arthur, 92
Nikolai, Grand Duke, 79, 81, 111
Niš, 104, 107, 108
Nitti, Francesco Saverio, 226, 287
Northcliffe, Lord, 232, 233
Novi List (Fiume), 16, 17, 19

Obrenović dynasty, 18
Ojetti, Ugo, 173, 221, 244, 245
Opočensky, Jan, 1
Orlando, V. E., 173, 221; adopts Borgese's programme, 224; conditions for settlement with A-H., 226; policy after Vatican soundings, 227; meeting with Lloyd George, 229–30; meets Trumbić in London, 230; agrees to Italo-Yugoslav agreement, 230; unwilling to replace Sonnino, 231; backs Rome congress, 232–3, 239; sympathy with aspirations of nationalities, 233; and British and French socialists, 234; recognizes autonomous Czech army, 244–5; conversations with Trumbić, 246; two-pronged policy, 264; alarm at possible separate peace with Austria, 284; and Sonnino, 289–90; realizes inconsistency of Italian demands, 290
Orsini, Felice, 5
Orthodox Church, 76
Österreichische Politische Gesellschaft, 268, 269, 272, 276
Osusky, S., 239, 267
Otlet, Prof. Paul, 275
Ottoman empire, 31

Pacelli, Mgr, 273
Pacifism, 117, 149, 289
Paderewski, Ignace, 160
Page, T. N., 239
Paget, Ralph, 142
Painlevé, Paul, 259–60, 261, 262

Paléologue, Maurice Georges, 83, 105, 161, 162, 169
Pallavacino, Capt., 227
Pancsova, 75
Pan-Germanism, 12, 14, 19, 111, 121, 204, 286
Pan-Slavism, 6
Pares, Sir Bernard, 94
Paris, 225, 232
Party of Independence and 1848 (Hungarian), and dynastic union, 2; demand for use of Magyar, 18, 20; and Croats, 18, 19–20; aims, 19–20; in 'national coalition', 20, 26; successes in 1905 and 1906 elections, 20, 26; agrees to renew customs union, 29; repressive measures against Southern Slavs, 33; divided on Andrássy's franchise manipulation, 36; split, 37, 39, 132–3; approach to Italian government, 123–4, 130; intransigence towards Rumania, 127; tied to alliance with Germany, 132; efforts to resume contacts with Sonnino, 134; soundings for separate peace, 135–6
Paternò, Gaetano, 224
Pašić, Nikola, seeks *modus vivendi* with Vienna, 6, 46; sets out war aims, 84; and an independent Yugoslavia, 84, 104, 113, 157; opposes excessive concessions to Italy, 84, 122; claim to represent all Serbs, 103; sends Serbian delegation to Italy, 103; opposes concessions to Bulgaria, 108, 109, 122; demands Croatia-Slavonia, Slovenia and western Banat, 139; resentment against Supilo, 141; opposes Grey's self-determination idea, 141; demand that southern Dalmatia and southern Hungary be assigned to Serbia, 195–6; proposes agreement with Trumbić and Meštrović, 196; meeting with Sonnino, 223; evasive reply to Sonnino's approach, 229
Paulucci de' Calboli, Marquis, 135, 275, 284
Pavelić, Dr Ante, 41, 112, 194–5, 247
Peace Conference (1919), 245, 255, 289, 290, 293, 294, 295
Peano, Camillo, 55
Peasant Party (Croatian), 23
Pécs, 250
Pejačević, T., 18
Petrograd, 81, 189, 190
Piave, River, 245, 246, 250
Pichon, Stephen, 289, 292, 293
Pilsen, 272

Pilsudski, Marshal, 77, 160
Pirolini, Giovanni Battista, 157
Piscel, Antonio, 207
Pittoni, Valentino, 216, 234, 253–4
Pittsburgh, 243
Poincaré, Raymond, 1, 124, 163, 257, 260
Pokrovsky, N. N., 162
Pola (Pula), 4, 114, 148, 212
Poland, Russian, 76, 78, 79, 145, 146, 258, 260–1; Tisza's veto on autonomous kingdom under Habsburgs, 78; Sazonov supports reunification, 81; independence advocated by Seton-Watson, 100; proclamation of independence urged by Dmowski, 160; Entente plans for future, 159, 162–3, 206; German proclamation of kingdom, 160, 161; Kreuznach agreement on future of, 179, 180, 181; Austrian Poles call for reunification, 179; Andrássy in favour of incorporation in A-H., 180; independence favoured by Batthyány and Károlyi, 180; treatment under German occupation, 180; Czernin's idea of personal union with Austria, 180–1; proposed German annexation agreed by Austria, 200, 258, 260–1; Lloyd George calls for independence, 206; to be reunited under Fourteen Points, 208, 243; German aim to dominate, 258; French proposal for future, 261; and Cholm award, 262
Poles, 3; liberties under Habsburg monarchy, 76; lack of enthusiasm for cause of Central Powers, 77; volunteers fight against Tsarism, 77; Russian manifesto promises autonomy to, 79–80; delegation at Rome nationalities congress, 239, 240; support Prague independence demands, 248
Polish Legion, established in France, 163
Polish National Council, 291
Polish Peasant People's Party, 78
Polzer-Hoditz, Count, 181, 185, 186, 270–1, 280
Popovici, A., 13, 44
Popular Progressive Party (Croat), 23
Population, of A-H., xi, 4
Posen (Poznan), 77, 79, 83
Potočnjak, F., 112, 113
Prague, revolutionary trends, 7; pro-war demonstrations, 75; Labour Academy, 117; workers' council under Social Democratic leadership, 181; bloodless revolution, 244; leaders' oath of independence, 247; mass meetings and

[467]

Russia—*continued*

86; support for Serbian outlet on Adriatic, 87; urges Italian intervention, 88; efforts to draw Italy and Romania into Entente camp, 90, 110; promises Transylvania to Romania, 91; offer to release ethnic Italian prisoners-of-war, 103; and Yugoslav claims, 104; and possibility of A-H. defeat, 105; and separate peace with A-H., 106; urges Pašić to grant concessions to Bulgaria, 108; agrees to Italian claim to Dalmatian coast, 111; and Serbo-Croat unification, 113, 153; Slovak immigrants, 118; failure of 1916 offensive, 144; Tsarist attitude to Dmowski's proposals, 160–1; and Polish autonomy plan, 162, 163; Austro-German peace offer rejected, 162, 163; Czech societies in, 166; Czech Legion founded, 167; and possibility of Czechoslovak state, 167; policy of Provisional government, 176, 200; effects of revolution, 176–7, 187; German terms at Brest-Litovsk, 207; Wilson's view of leaders, 207; readiness to continue war, 207. *See also* Soviet Russia

Russian Polish Socialist Party, 77
Russo-Japanese war, 18–19
Ruthenians, 6, 76, 77, 80, 95, 164, 218
Rybař, O., 101, 112, 120

St Petersburg, Slav congress, 6
St Wenceslas's Crown, 81
Salandra, Antonio, 57, 137, 222, 288; conflict with Giolitti, 56, 60, 62; proclaims *sacro egoismo*, 64; negotiations with both blocs simultaneously, 64; rejects Russian offer of release of prisoners-of-war, 103
Salonica, 6
Salvemini, Gaetano, 16, 119, 157, 221, 223; views on fate of A-H., 95–6; and Italian intervention, 96, 97; opposition to annexationist aims, 97, 102, 222; influenced by Battisti, 99; favours destruction of A-H., 100–1; his papers, 154; warning to Yugoslavs, 171; at Rome congress, 239–40
Salviati, A., 89, 92
Šamal, Premysl, 120
San Giuliano, Marquis di, 49–50, 52, 55–6, 64, 87, 97, 123
Sarajevo, 5, 7, 253
Sarkotić, Lt.-Gen., 247
Sazonov, S. D., 6, 9, 79, 89, 90; favours administrative autonomy for Poland,

79, 161; favours liberation of Bohemia, 81; agrees to Czech volunteer force, 81; manifesto to peoples of A-H., 81–2; support for Czech cause, 82, 83, 95; war aims, 83; opposed to treating with Magyar emissaries, 91; anti-Germanism, 94; favours dismemberment of A-H., 105; enthusiasm for Yugoslav unity, 109; and Italian claims, 110; dismissed, 161

Scarpa, Gino, 172
Scheck, A., 76
Scheidemann, Phillip, 217
Scheiner, Josef, 6, 116, 120
Schiavi, Alexandro, 237
Schilling, Baron, 111
Schocchi, Angelo, 234
Schönburg, Prince, 58, 66
Schott-Desico, Edoardo, 234
Schüller, Richard, xi
Scialoja, Senator, 232
Sebenico (Šibenik), 43, 111, 123, 150
Second International, the, 207, 236
Seidler, Ernst, 185, 213, 215, 272
Seipel, Mgr, 185
Self-determination, considered by Grey for A-H. nationalities, 141, 142; enters calculations of Entente powers, 142; Czernin uses as tool at Brest-Litovsk, 201. *See also* Nationality principle.
Serbia, xii; A-H. declaration of war on, 1; Black Hand and, 5; economic relations with A-H., 6; Austrian threats, 7, 33; Kramář advises rapprochement with, 7; and annexation of Bosnia-Hercegovina, 31, 34; prestige of government increased by Supilo trial, 36; triumph in Balkan wars, 43; Conrad advocates invasion of, 43; and access to Adriatic, 46, 87, 110, 208; Austrian ultimatum, 50, 51; annexation opposed by Tisza and Burian, 63; Russian war aims and, 83; war aims, 84; Russian view of future, 90; Salvemini sides with, 95–6; Pašić's ambitions for, 108; alarm at Italian claims to Dalmatia, 110; protest to Russia over Italian claims, 111; protest to Entente against promises to Italy, 113; crushed, 122; asked to cede part of Macedonia by allies, 139; offered Srem and Bačka, 139; future under Russo-Italian compromise, 153; future under Kreuznach agreement, 179, 180; Hungarian social democrats and, 189; monarchy loses support, 195; Britain and claims of, 196, 205; plan for inclusion in A-H. customs union, 200; Wilson favours access to

[469]

Sonnino, Baron Sidney—*continued*
state, 141; insists on respect for Treaty
of London, 149–50; fears dissolution of
A.-H., 150; contradictory policy, 150;
opposition to Yugoslav agitators, 153;
opposes idea of Czech Legion, 172, 173;
and German socialists, 208; fear of
pan-Slav empire, 222; unwillingness to
negotiate with Yugoslavs, 222–3, 229,
231, 289; replaced, 224–5; opposed to
Lloyd George's proposals, 225, 228;
his obstinacy, 226; approach to Pašić,
229; against nationalities conference in
Rome, 232, 240–1, 242; negative reply
to U.S. proposals to co-operate with
independence movements, 242; coolness towards Italo-Yugoslav reconciliation, 288; Italian intervention due
to, 288; reluctance to join Orlando's
government, 289
Sosnovice, 61
Southern Slavs, 33, 247; problem of, xii;
nationalism, 5; future state conceived
by Supilo, 16–17; reconciliation between
ethnic groups, 18; reform and revolutionary groups, 41; attitude of France
and Russia, 86; Salviati's memorandum
on, 92; democratic outlook, 96, 99; reunification envisaged by Seton-Watson,
100; Sonnino and, 102. *See also* Slavs
and Yugoslavs
South Tyrol, 64, 85, 148
Soviet Russia, 220, 225. *See also* Russia
Spalajković, Miroslav, 34, 35, 109
Spalato (Split), 21, 43, 84, 110, 111
Spinčić, V., 112, 247
Srem, 139
Šrobar, V., 117, 118, 248
Starčević, Ante, 41
Stanek, František, 174, 182, 216, 247
Steed, H. Wickham, memoirs, 1; sympathies with Supilo, 19, 85, 92, 106;
criticism of Italian annexationist ambitions, 88; support for Yugoslavs, 88,
89, 113, 232, 233; and Masaryk, 93–4,
95; in favour of break-up of A.-H., 150,
158; helps found Serbian Society of Gt
Britain, 171; friendship with Albertini,
223; arranges Italo-Yugoslav meetings
in London, 227–8; persuades Orlando
to receive Trumbić, 230; advises
Sonnino to reach agreement with
Yugoslavs, 231; and Rome nationalities meeting, 233; and inter-allied
socialist war aims, 237; indiscretions, 264
Štefanik, Milan, 122, 167, 168, 169, 171–2,
239, 244, 287

Steinacker, E., 14
Štepanek, A., 117
Stepniak (Russian revolutionary), 5
Stockholm, international socialist con-
ferences, 178, 181, 182, 189, 190–1, 195,
207–8
Stodola, C., 13
Stojanović, N., 84, 103, 108, 224, 284
Strbrný, Georg, 210
Štur, Ludovit, 6
Stürgkh, Count, 43, 53, 58, 62, 63, 98, 120,
123; assassination, 177, 181
Stürmer, Boris, 161, 162
Styria, 114
Südekum, Albert, 145
Sudetenland, 116, 150, 214, 252
Suffrage, universal. *See* Universal suffrage
Supilo, Frano, his importance recognized,
7; escapes arrest in 1914, 15–16; work
for dismemberment of A.-H., 16; early
political life, 16, 17; Voinovich's
description, 16–17; aim of independent
Yugoslavia, 16–17, 84; advocate of
Serbo-Croat understanding, 16–18; anti-
clericalism, 18, 19; seeks Slav-Latin
alliance, 19; correspondence with Gina
Lombroso, 18–19, 20, 101; campaign
among Croats, 21; at Ragusa meeting
(1905), 21; leads obstruction to railway
regulations, 30; accused by Friedjung,
34; sues *Neue Freie Presse*, 34; political
isolation, 40; conflict with Zagreb colleagues, 46–7; wartime exile in Venice,
85; meetings with Izvolsky, 89, 90, 92;
opposition to cession of Dalmatia and
Istria to Italy, 90; meets Delcassé, 90;
Asquith's view of, 90; memorandum on
Yugoslav state, 92; in London, 92–3,
106–7, 122; wins esteem of British
diplomats, 93; on future of Adriatic,
101, 222; confers with Serbs in Florence,
103; launches idea of Yugoslav legion,
104–5; reiterates arguments for Yugoslav unity with Grey, 106–7, 114, 141;
Petrograd visit, 107, 109, 111; and
Pašić, 108–9, 140–1, 157; protests
against Entente agreement to Italian
claims, 111, 114; and Masaryk, 122;
restates Yugoslav terms of settlement,
139; Yugoslav Committee rejects his
proposals, 151; returns to Italy, 151,
287; contacts in Italy, 152–3, 157;
meeting with Bissolati, 153–4; charges
against, 154–6; denounced by nationalists, 154, 171; resigns from Yugoslav
Committee, 157; meeting with Miljukov, 157; advocates Italo-Yugoslav

[471]

Wilson, Woodrow—*continued*
make peace, 209; rejects Hertling's war aims statement, 219; calls for renunciation of secret treaties, 222; receives Masaryk, 243; promises independence to Czechs, Yugoslavs and Poles, 243–4; opposed to dismemberment of A-H., 265; authorizes Herron to meet Austrian emissaries, 267; and Herron, 276, 279; asks Charles I to state concrete proposals, 283

Witte, Sergei Juljević, 87

Xavier, Prince, 177, 257

Yanuskievich, General, 79, 91
'Young Czechs', 8
'Young Turks', 31, 32
Yugoslav Committee, 224, 284; formed in Paris, 113; Delcassé criticizes claims of, 113–14; its excessive demands, 114–15; headquarters established in London, 115; rejects Supilo's position, 151; Supilo resigns from, 157; delegation to Corfu, 196; exchanges with Italians in London, 227–8; protests at Lloyd George speech, 229; approval of Torre–Trumbić agreement, 238
Yugoslavia, Supilo's vision of, 16, 92; Steed's support for idea, 88; Izvolsky in favour of creation, 90; establishment recommended by Salvemini, 92; advocated by Trevelyan, 99; advocated by Seton-Watson, 100; Pašić against premature use of term, 103; role of Orthodox and Catholics in, 109; Serbian supremacy in, 114; Sonnino opposed to idea of, 123, 242, 289; fear of Italy leads to militarism, 140; as envisaged by Steed and Seton-Watson, 171; Miljukov's statement in favour of, 176; support for idea at Stockholm socialist conference, 195; Croat Social Democrats call for establishment, 195; agreement between Pašić and Slav exiles to establish, 196; Lansing calls for independent state, 209; Italian Socialist Union calls for establishment, 235; Italian fears of, 242; U.S. support for, 242–3; Sonnino opposed to recognition, 245

Yugoslavs, and Italian claims, 92, 93, 102, 106, 223; idea of legion of volunteers launched, 104–5; Entente and, 105; Supilo's memorandum to Grey on unity of, 106–7; Sazonov and unification of, 109; Supilo's proposals to Pašić, 109; Grey asks Italy to consider desiderata of leaders, 110; Trumbić authorized to form independence committee, 112; committee set up in U.S., 112–13; volunteers fight on Salonica front, 164; Italian hostility to claims, 171; claims on Trieste and Gorizia, 171; claims criticized by Eisenmann, 172; call for independence by Korošec, 211; delegation to Rome congress, 239, 240; Wilson promises independence to, 243; Italian declaration in favour of, 245; Italy and national movement of, 245, 286–97; Loiseau's sympathies with, 286; claim to territory assigned to Italy, 287. *See also* Southern Slavs.

Zagreb, 7, 16, 22, 33, 41, 75, 244, 245, 246–7, 248, 285
Zamorski, Jan, 239
Zanella, Riccardo, 235
Zanotti-Bianco, Umberto, 157, 173
Zara (Zadar), 22, 23, 101, 111, 221, 224, 235
Zichy, Count Aladar, 25, 126, 129, 130
Zimmerwald movement, 212, 236, 274
Zita, Empress of Austria, 257
Zuckerkandl, Prof. Emil, 260, 262
Zuppelli, General, 244